e first and only analytics tool of its kind, Connect Insight™ is a series of visual
ta displays—each framed by an intuitive question—to provide at-a-glance
formation regarding how your class is doing.

> **Make It Intuitive.**
You receive instant, at-a-glance
view of student performance
matched with student activity.

> **Make It Dynamic.**
Connect Insight™ puts real-time
analytics in your hands so you can
take action early and keep struggling
students from falling behind.

> **Make It Mobile.**
Connect Insight™ travels from office to
classroom, available on demand wherever
and whenever it's needed.

WE THE PEOPLE

WE THE PEOPLE

AN INTRODUCTION TO AMERICAN GOVERNMENT

ELEVENTH EDITION

THOMAS E. PATTERSON

Bradlee Professor of Government and the Press
John F. Kennedy School of Government
Harvard University

WE THE PEOPLE: AN INTRODUCTION TO AMERICAN GOVERNMENT, ELEVENTH EDITION

Published by McGraw-Hill Education, 2 Penn Plaza, New York, NY 10121. Copyright © 2015 by McGraw-Hill Education. All rights reserved. Printed in the United States of America. Previous edition © 2013, 2011, and 2009. No part of this publication may be reproduced or distributed in any form or by any means, or stored in a database or retrieval system, without the prior written consent of McGraw-Hill Education, including, but not limited to, in any network or other electronic storage or transmission, or broadcast for distance learning.

Some ancillaries, including electronic and print components, may not be available to customers outside the United States.

This book is printed on acid-free paper.

1 2 3 4 5 6 7 8 9 0 DOC/DOC 1 0 9 8 7 6 5 4

ISBN 978-0-07-802479-5
MHID 0-07-802479-X

Senior Vice President, Products & Markets: Kurt L. Strand
Vice President, General Manager, Products & Markets: Michael Ryan
Vice President, Content Design & Delivery: Kimberly Meriwether David
Managing Director: Gina Boedecker
Brand Manager: Laura Wilk
Director, Product Development: Meghan Campbell
Marketing Manager: April Cole
Lead Product Developer: Dawn Groundwater
Senior Product Developer: Cara Labell

Director, Content Design & Delivery: Terri Schiesl
Program Manager: Marianne Musni
Content Project Managers: Susan Trentacosti, Emily Kline, Karen Jozefowicz
Buyer: Michael McCormick
Design: Tara McDermott
Content Licensing Specialists: Shawntel Schmitt, DeAnna Dausener
Cover Illustration: McCutcheon Design
Compositor: Aptara®, Inc.
Typeface: 10.5/13 Janson Text LT Std
Printer: R. R. Donnelley

All credits appearing on page or at the end of the book are considered to be an extension of the copyright page.

Library of Congress Cataloging-in-Publication Data

Patterson, Thomas E.
  We the people / Thomas E. Patterson, Bradlee Professor of Government and the Press John F. Kennedy School of Government, Harvard University.—Eleventh edition.
      pages cm
  ISBN 978-0-07-802479-5 (alk. paper)
1. United States—Politics and government. I. Title.
  JK276.P38 2015
  320.473–dc23   2014029916

The Internet addresses listed in the text were accurate at the time of publication. The inclusion of a website does not indicate an endorsement by the authors or McGraw-Hill Education, and McGraw-Hill Education does not guarantee the accuracy of the information presented at these sites.

www.mhhe.com

To My Children.
Alex and Leigh

Thomas E. Patterson is Bradlee Professor of Government and the Press in the John F. Kennedy School of Government at Harvard University. He was previously Distinguished Professor of Political Science in the Maxwell School of Citizenship at Syracuse University. Raised in a small Minnesota town near the Iowa and South Dakota borders, he attended South Dakota State University as an undergraduate and served in the U.S. Army Special Forces in Vietnam before enrolling at the University of Minnesota, where he received his Ph.D. in 1971.

Since then, he has regularly taught the introductory American government course. In 2013 he was chosen as teacher of the year and adviser of the year by students at Harvard University's Kennedy School of Government, the first time a member of its faculty has received both awards simultaneously.

He has authored numerous books and articles, which focus mainly on elections, the media, and citizenship. His most recent book, *Informing the News*, which was described as "superb" and "mesmerizing" in one review, examines the public misinformation resulting from the emergence of partisan outlets and the decline in citizens' attention to news. An earlier book, *The Vanishing Voter* (2002), describes and explains the long-term decline in Americans' electoral participation. His book *Out of Order* (1994) received national attention when President Clinton advised every politician and journalist to read it. In 2002 *Out of Order* received the American Political Science Association's Graber Award for the best book of the past decade in political communication. Another of Patterson's books, *The Mass Media Election* (1980), received a Choice award as Outstanding Academic Title, 1980–1981. Patterson's first book, *The Unseeing Eye* (1976), was selected by the American Association for Public Opinion Research as one of the fifty most influential books of the past half century in the field of public opinion.

His research has been funded by major grants from the National Science Foundation, the Markle Foundation, the Smith-Richardson Foundation, the Ford Foundation, the Knight Foundation, the Carnegie Corporation, and the Pew Charitable Trusts.

CONTENTS

CHAPTER THREE

FEDERALISM: FORGING A NATION

CHAPTER FOUR

CIVIL LIBERTIES:
PROTECTING INDIVIDUAL RIGHTS   100

CHAPTER FIVE

EQUAL RIGHTS: STRUGGLING TOWARD FAIRNESS

CHAPTER SIX

PUBLIC OPINION AND POLITICAL SOCIALIZATION: SHAPING THE PEOPLE'S VOICE

CHAPTER SEVEN

POLITICAL PARTICIPATION:
ACTIVATING THE POPULAR WILL

CHAPTER EIGHT

POLITICAL PARTIES, CANDIDATES, AND CAMPAIGNS: DEFINING THE VOTER'S CHOICE

CHAPTER NINE

INTEREST GROUPS: ORGANIZING FOR INFLUENCE

CHAPTER TEN

THE NEWS MEDIA:
COMMUNICATING POLITICAL IMAGES

CHAPTER ELEVEN

CONGRESS: BALANCING NATIONAL GOALS AND LOCAL INTERESTS

CHAPTER TWELVE

THE PRESIDENCY: LEADING THE NATION

CHAPTER THIRTEEN

THE FEDERAL BUREAUCRACY: ADMINISTERING THE GOVERNMENT

CHAPTER FOURTEEN

THE FEDERAL JUDICIAL SYSTEM: APPLYING THE LAW 441

CHAPTER FIFTEEN

ECONOMIC AND ENVIRONMENTAL POLICY: CONTRIBUTING TO PROSPERITY 475

CHAPTER SIXTEEN

WELFARE AND EDUCATION POLICY: PROVIDING FOR PERSONAL SECURITY AND NEED   510

CHAPTER SEVENTEEN

FOREIGN POLICY:
PROTECTING THE AMERICAN WAY

A LETTER FROM THE AUTHOR

Anyone who writes an introductory program on American government faces the challenge of explaining a wide range of subjects. One way is to pile fact upon fact and list upon list. It's a common approach to textbook writing but it turns politics into a pretty dry subject. Politics doesn't have to be dry, and it certainly doesn't have to be dull. Politics has all the elements of drama, and the added feature of affecting the everyday lives of real people.

My goal has been to make this program the most readable one available. Rather than piling fact upon fact, the program relies on narrative. A narrative program weaves together theory, information, and examples in order to bring out key facts and ideas. The response to this approach has been gratifying. As the previous edition was being prepared, I received the following note from a longtime instructor:

> I read this book in about three days, cover to cover. . . . I have never seen a better basic government/politics textbook. I think reading standard textbooks is "boring" (to use a favorite student word), but this one overcomes that. Dr. Patterson has managed to do something that I heretofore thought could not be done.

When writing, I regularly reminded myself that the readers were citizens as well as students. For this reason, the program highlights "political thinking," by which I mean critical thinking in the context of both the study of politics and the exercise of citizenship. Each chapter has a set of boxes that ask you to "think politically." It is a skill that can be developed and help you to become a more responsible citizen, whether in casting a vote, forming an opinion about a public policy, or contributing to a political cause.

Strengthening your capacity for critical thinking is also a central goal of this program. If the only result of reading this program was to increase your understanding of American government, I would judge it a pedagogical failure. Political science programs like those in other social science and humanities disciplines, should help students to hone their skill in critical thinking—the ability to assess and apply information through reflection and reasoning. The program's "Political Thinking" boxes are designed for this purpose. So, too, is the "Critical Thinking Zone" at the end of each chapter. This feature asks you to make use of each chapter's information through the application of the three skills—conceptualizing, analyzing, and synthesizing—that are at the core of critical thinking.

Finally, I have attempted in this program to present American government through the analytical lens of political science but in a way that captures the vivid world of real-life politics. Only a tiny fraction of students in the introductory course are taking it because they intend to pursue an academic career in political science. Most students take it because they are required to do so or because they have an interest in politics. I have sought to write a book that will deepen political interest in the second type of student and kindle it in the first type.

We the People has been in use in college classrooms for more than two decades. During this time, the program has been adopted at more than a thousand colleges and universities. I am extremely grateful to all who have used it. I am particularly indebted to the many instructors and students who have sent me recommendations for making it better. Ashley Wilson, a student at Fullerton College, was among the students who offered a suggestion for this edition. The University of Northern Colorado's Steve Mazurana and his students provided detailed feedback that broadly informed this edition's revisions. If you have ideas you would like to share, please contact me at the John F. Kennedy School, Harvard University, Cambridge, MA 02138, or by e-mail: thomas_patterson@harvard.edu.

Thomas E. Patterson

BETTER DATA, SMARTER REVISION, IMPROVED RESULTS

■ connect American Government

We the People is available to instructors and students in traditional print format as well as online within McGraw-Hill Connect® American Government, an integrated assignment and assessment platform. Connect American Government's online tools make managing assignments easier for instructors—and make learning and studying more compelling and efficient for students.

- **LearnSmart™** This powerful learning system helps students assess their knowledge of course content through a series of adaptive questions, intelligently pinpointing concepts the student does not understand and mapping out a personalized study plan for success. Fueled by LearnSmart, SmartBook is the first and only adaptive reading experience currently available. SmartBook creates a personalized reading experience by highlighting the most impactful concepts a student needs to learn at that moment in time.

- **Real Data from Real Students** Collected anonymously from LearnSmart, McGraw-Hill authors can now pinpoint the areas where students struggle the most and revise the content based on that feedback.

- **Real-time Reports** These printable, exportable reports show how well each student (or section) is performing on each course segment. Instructors can use this feature to spot problem areas before they crop up on an exam.

Chapter 11: Congress: Balancing National Goals and Local Interests 373

THE MAJOR FUNCTIONS OF CONGRESS

Function	Basis and activity
Lawmaking	Through its constitutional grant to enact law, Congress makes the laws authorizing federal programs and appropriating the funds necessary to carry them out.
Representation	Through its elected constitutional officers—U.S. senators and representatives—Congress represents the interests of constituents and the nation in its deliberations and its lawmaking.
Oversight	Through its constitutional responsibility to see that the executive branch carries out the laws faithfully and spends appropriations properly, Congress oversees and sometimes investigates executive action.

The Lawmaking Function of Congress

Under the Constitution, Congress is granted the **lawmaking function:** the authority to make the laws necessary to carry out the powers granted to the national government. The constitutional powers of Congress are substantial; they include the power to tax, to spend, to regulate commerce, and to declare war. However, whether Congress takes the lead in the making of laws usually depends on the type of policy at issue.

Broad Issues: Fragmentation as a Limit on Congress's Role

Congress is structured in a way that can make agreement on large issues difficult to obtain. Congress is not one house but two, each with its own authority and constituency base. Neither the House nor the Senate can enact legislation without the other's approval, and the two chambers are hardly identical. California and North Dakota have exactly the same representation in the Senate, but in the House, which is apportioned by population, California has fifty-three seats compared to North Dakota's one.

Congress also includes a lot of lawmakers: 100 members of the Senate and 435 members of the House. They come from different constituencies and represent different and sometimes opposing interests, which leads to disagreements. Nearly every member of Congress, for example, supports the principle of global free trade. Yet when it comes to specific trade provisions, members often disagree. Foreign competition means different things to manufacturers who produce automobiles, computer chips, or

- **Assignable and Assessable Activities** Instructors can easily deliver assignments and tests online, and students can practice skills that fulfill learning objectives at their own pace and on their own schedule.

Practice • **Government in Action** Government in Action is an award-winning education game in which students play the role of a congressperson, from running for election to passing legislation. Government in Action weaves in every aspect of your American government course as students compete for political capital, approval, and awareness. Students play to learn and campaign to win to develop a fundamental understanding of American democracy.

LEARN TO THINK POLITICALLY, AND THINK CRITICALLY

Political thinking enables us, as citizens, to gather and weigh evidence, to apply foundational principles to current events, and to consider historical context when evaluating contemporary issues. In short, it allows us to make informed judgments. This program aims to help you learn how to think about politics by introducing you to the perspectives and tools of political science.

This program will not tell you *what* to think politically. Instead, it will help you learn *how* to think politically by providing you with analytical tools that can sharpen and deepen your understanding of American politics:

- Reliable information about how the U.S. political system operates
- Systematic generalizations about major tendencies in American politics
- Terms and concepts that precisely describe key aspects of politics

CRITICAL THINKING

In addition to the twenty-seven new Political Thinking boxes that have been added throughout the text, each chapter in *We the People* now includes an end-of-chapter **Critical Thinking Zone** that is designed to sharpen your ability to think critically.

NEW! CRITICAL THINKING ZONE

At the end of each chapter, there's a **Critical Thinking Zone** that asks you, in the context of American politics, to apply each of the basic skills involved in critical thinking: conceptualizing, synthesizing, and analyzing.

This feature is designed not only to test whether you have mastered major

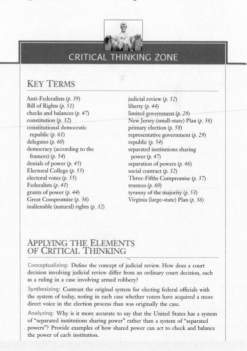

CRITICAL THINKING ZONE

KEY TERMS

Anti-Federalists (p. 39)
Bill of Rights (p. 51)
checks and balances (p. 47)
constitution (p. 32)
constitutional democratic republic (p. 61)
delegates (p. 60)
democracy (according to the framers) (p. 54)
denials of power (p. 45)
Electoral College (p. 55)
electoral votes (p. 55)
Federalists (p. 41)
grants of power (p. 44)
Great Compromise (p. 36)
inalienable (natural) rights (p. 32)

judicial review (p. 52)
liberty (p. 44)
limited government (p. 29)
New Jersey (small-state) Plan (p. 36)
primary election (p. 58)
representative government (p. 29)
republic (p. 54)
separated institutions sharing power (p. 47)
separation of powers (p. 46)
social contract (p. 32)
Three-Fifths Compromise (p. 37)
trustees (p. 60)
tyranny of the majority (p. 53)
Virginia (large-state) Plan (p. 36)

APPLYING THE ELEMENTS OF CRITICAL THINKING

Conceptualizing: Define the concept of judicial review. How does a court decision involving judicial review differ from an ordinary court decision, such as a ruling in a case involving armed robbery?

Synthesizing: Contrast the original system for electing federal officials with the system of today, noting in each case whether voters have acquired a more direct voice in the election process than was originally the case.

Analyzing: Why is it more accurate to say that the United States has a system of "separated institutions sharing power" rather than a system of "separated powers"? Provide examples of how shared power can act to check and balance the power of each institution.

points in the chapter but to help you develop the capacity for critical thinking, a skill with lifelong benefits regardless of your chosen career.

CONTENT CHANGES

This revision of *We the People* includes the many remarkable political developments of the past two years, ranging from the 2014 midterm elections to the gridlock in Washington to the rising foreign policy challenges in Eastern Europe, Asia, and the Middle East. Nearly every chapter also has significant updates based on the most recent scholarly research on American politics.

Each chapter has a new feature: a chapter-ending **Critical Thinking Zone**. In addition to providing students with an assessment of their understanding of the chapter's major points, each **Critical Thinking Zone** aims to strengthen students' critical thinking ability. Accordingly, the feature's questions are organized around each of the basic skills involved in critical thinking: conceptualizing, synthesizing, and analyzing. In the chapter on political parties, for example, the conceptualizing component asks students to explain the difference between proportional representation and the single-member district system and then explain why proportional representation is more likely to foster a multiparty system.

This edition's revisions were guided, for the first time, by data gathered through McGraw-Hill's **LearnSmart** system. This system, which collects information as students work online through the program's content, identifies the subjects that students have mastered and those they are struggling to master. **LearnSmart's** "Heat Map" measures such things as the length of time the typical student spends on a study question and how frequently students answer it incorrectly. Question topics where students were having difficulty were targeted for revision, which could include, for instance, a fuller explanation of a concept or the use of a clarifying example. No part of an introductory program should defy the understanding of a student who seeks to master it, and the "Heat Map" contributes to that end.

The program's other revisions were guided by recent scholarship and developments in American politics. I have listed below the chapters that have been most substantially revised. The list significantly understates the extent of the changes. Virtually every chapter has important modifications from the previous edition.

Chapter 4: Civil Liberties: Protecting Individual Rights Additions include the NSA's secret surveillance program, and the controversy surrounding it, as well as several recent Supreme Court rulings, including its landmark 2014 decision extending search-and-seizure protection to cell phones and other digital devices.

Chapter 5: Equal Rights: Struggling toward Fairness Updates include the changing legal and social environment of same-sex marriage, as well as a number of recent Supreme Court rulings, including its key 2014 decision upholding the Michigan electorate's ban on affirmative action in admissions to the state's public colleges and universities.

Chapter 10: The News Media: Communicating Political Images Additions include expanded discussion of the growing political role of the "new media"—partisan and Internet-based outlets.

Chapter 11: Congress: Balancing National Goals and Local Interests Updates include the 2014 midterm elections and how they affect the partisan balance in Congress, as well as a fuller examination of the causes and consequences of party polarization within Congress and its effect on legislative action.

Chapter 12: The Presidency: Leading the Nation Additions include the Obama administration's efforts to expand executive authority in the face of congressional deadlock, as well as an early look at the 2016 presidential election.

Chapter 14: The Federal Judicial System: Applying the Law Revisions include a close look at the conservative–liberal divide on the Supreme Court, and the ideological positioning of the Court relative to earlier Courts.

Chapter 16: Welfare and Education Policy: Providing for Personal Security and Need Updates include the rocky implementation of the 2010 Patient Protection and Affordable Care Act, as well as the growing strength of the Charter School movement.

Chapter 17: Foreign Policy: Protecting the American Way Revisions include the many important foreign policy developments of the past two years, including the Afghan troop withdrawal, the surge in Islamic militancy in the Middle East, the turmoil in Ukraine, and China's increasingly aggressive foreign policy in East and Southeast Asia.

TEACHING AND LEARNING WITH *WE THE PEOPLE*

Available in Connect, the instructor's manual includes the following for each chapter: learning objectives, focus points and main points, a chapter summary, a list of major concepts, and suggestions for complementary lecture topics. The test bank consists of approximately fifty multiple-choice questions and five suggested essay topics per chapter, with page references given alongside the answers. PowerPoints are also available to instructors.

ACKNOWLEDGMENTS

Nearly two decades ago, when planning the first edition of *We the People*, my editor and I concluded that it would be enormously helpful if a way could be found to bring into each chapter the judgment of those political scientists who teach the introductory course year in and year out. Thus, in addition to soliciting general reviews from a select number of expert scholars, we sent each chapter to a dozen or so faculty members at U.S. colleges and universities of all types—public and private, large and small, two-year and four-year. These political scientists, 213 in all, had well over a thousand years of combined experience in teaching the introductory course, and they provided countless good ideas.

Since then, several hundred other political scientists have reviewed subsequent editions. These many reviewers will go unnamed here, but my debt to all of them remains undiminished by time. For the eleventh edition, I have benefited yet again from the thoughtful advice of conscientious reviewers. Their sound advice has helped shape nearly every page of the book. These scholars are:

Steve Anthony, *Georgia State University*
Craig Cunningham, *Kishwaukee College*
Reynaldo S. Flores, *Richland College*
Daniel Franklin, *Georgia State University*
Michael Hoover, *Seminole State College*
Richard Kiefer, *Waubonsee Community College*
Joon S. Kil, *Irvine Valley College*
Beth Rosenson, *University of Florida*
Anjali Sahay, *Gannon University*
Scot Schraufnagel, *Northern Illinois University*

I also want to thank those at McGraw-Hill who contributed to the eleventh edition. At McGraw-Hill, I'd like to thank Laura Wilk, Dawn Groundwater, Iris Kim, and Susan Trentacosti, as well as freelance development editor Bruce Cantley. At Harvard, I had the painstaking and cheerful support of Kristina Mastropasqua. I owe her a deep thanks.

Thomas Patterson

1
CHAPTER

POLITICAL THINKING AND POLITICAL CULTURE: BECOMING A RESPONSIBLE CITIZEN

66 The worth of the state, in the long run, is the worth of the individuals composing it. **99**

JOHN STUART MILL[1]

As U.S. troops moved into position along the Iraq border, pollsters were busy asking Americans what they thought about the prospect of war with Iraq. A narrow majority expressed support for an attack on Iraq without United Nations approval if President George W. Bush deemed it necessary. But Americans' level of support for war varied with their knowledge of the enemy.

Contrary to fact, about half of the American public believed that Iraq was aligned with al Qaeda, the terrorist group that had attacked the United States on September 11, 2001. Some of these Americans mistakenly thought that Iraq helped plan the attacks; others erroneously believed that Iraq was equipping al Qaeda.[2] Some Americans even claimed that Iraqi pilots were flying the passenger jets that slammed into the World Trade Center towers and the Pentagon on that tragic September day.[3]

Compared with Americans who knew that Iraqi leader Saddam Hussein and al Qaeda were avowed enemies, those who falsely believed they were allies were more than twice as likely to support an American attack on Iraq.[4] Some of these individuals undoubtedly had other reasons for backing the invasion. Hussein was a tyrant who had brutalized his own people and thwarted United Nations resolutions calling for inspection of his weapons systems. But their belief that Iraq was in league with al Qaeda terrorists was pure fiction and hardly a reasonable basis for supporting an invasion.

The journalist Walter Lippmann worried that most citizens are unprepared to play the role democracy assigns them. They live in the real world but think in an imagined one. "While men are willing to admit that there are two sides to a question," Lippmann noted, "they do not believe that there are two sides to what they regard as fact."[5] In a self-governing society, citizens are expected to act on behalf of themselves and others. But how can they govern themselves if they are out of touch with reality?

Lippmann's concern has been confirmed by dozens of scholarly studies. Political scientists Bruce Ackerman and James Fishkin put it bluntly: "If six decades of modern public opinion research establish anything, it is that the general public's political ignorance is appalling by any standard."[6] *Newsweek* recently gave one thousand Americans who were already citizens the test that immigrants must pass as a condition of citizenship. Four of every ten who took the test failed it.[7] In a survey conducted shortly after Americans went to the polls in the 2010 midterm election, respondents were asked multiple-choice factual questions about eleven issues, ranging from health care to the Afghanistan War, that had been raised during the campaign. The question on Afghanistan, for example, asked whether troop levels had increased, decreased, or stayed the same during the two years that Barack Obama had been president. On every issue, a third or more of the respondents picked a wrong answer and, on most issues, half or more did so.[8]

A lack of information obviously does not keep citizens from voting, nor are uninformed citizens lacking in opinions. Some of them speak out more often and more loudly than people who are informed. But their sense of the world is wildly at odds with the reality of it. They are like the ancient mariners who, thinking the world was flat, stayed close to shore, fearing they might sail off the edge.

LEARNING TO THINK POLITICALLY

This text aims to help students, as citizens, learn how to think about politics. Political thinking is not the mere act of voicing an opinion. **Political thinking** is critical thinking focused on deciding what can reasonably be believed and then using this information to make political judgments. It enables citizens to act responsibly, whether in casting a vote, forming an opinion on a political issue, or contributing to a political cause. It is not defined by the conclusions that a person reaches. Individuals differ in their values and interests and can reasonably have opposing opinions. Political thinking is defined instead by the process through which conclusions are reached. It involves the critical evaluation of information in the process of forming a judgment about the issue at hand. Opinions not reached in this way are likely to be incomplete at best, perhaps even wildly off base. "Ignorance of the [facts]," Mark Bauerlein notes, "is a fair gauge of deeper deficiencies."[9]

Responsible citizenship was what English philosopher John Stuart Mill had in mind when he said that democracy is the best form of government. Any form of government, Mill asserted, should be judged on its ability to promote the individual "as a progressive being."[10] It was on this basis that Mill rejected authoritarianism and embraced democracy. Authoritarian governments suppress individuality, forcing people to think and act in prescribed ways or risk punishment. Democracy liberates the individual. Although democracy provides the *opportunity* for personal development,

A lack of information about the candidates does not keep some citizens from voting or from having strong opinions on political issues.

the individual bears responsibility for using this opportunity. In this sense, democracy is double edged. By liberating individuals, democracy frees them to make choices. They can develop the habit of political thinking, or they can devise cockeyed visions of reality. There is nothing to stop them from thinking the world is flat rather than round.

Obstacles to Political Thinking

The major barrier to political thinking is the unwillingness of citizens to make the effort. Political thinking requires close attention to politics, a responsibility that many people refuse to accept. They are, as James David Barber said, "dangerously unready when the time comes for choice."[11]

Others pay close attention, but they do so in counterproductive ways. A paradox of modern communication is that, although political information is more widely available than ever before, it is also less trustworthy than ever before. Two decades ago, the "knowledge gap" was defined largely by the amount of attention that people paid to the news. Citizens who followed the news closely were much better informed on average than those who did not.[12] That's less true today because of where people get their information. Many Americans now get most of their news from cable television, talk shows, or Internet blogs.[13] Most of these outlets—whether on the left or right—have dropped all but the pretense of accuracy. They rarely tell flat-out lies, but they routinely slant information to fit their purpose while burying contradictory facts. Once in a while, they expose a truth that mainstream news outlets have missed or were too timid to tackle. For the most part, however, they are in the business of concocting versions of reality that will lure an audience and promote a cause. "The talk show culture," media analyst Ellen Hume notes, "is a blur of rumor, fact, propaganda, and infotainment."[14] A recent University of Maryland study concluded that "false or misleading information is widespread in [today's] information environment."[15]

Political leaders also "spin" their messages. Although this has always been true, the scale of the effort today is unlike anything that has gone before.[16] The White House press office, for example, was once run by a single individual. It is now a communication machine that reaches deep into the federal agencies and involves scores of operatives, each of whom is intent on putting a presidential slant on the day's news.[17] In the period before the Iraq war, the Bush administration, through its hold on the intelligence agencies, tightly controlled the messages coming from the U.S. government. Iraq and al Qaeda were lumped together as targets of

Stephen Colbert (in cape) and Jon Stewart are part of the "new media" but, unlike many of the others, do not pretend that all of the information they provide is reliable. Says Stewart, "It's style over substance."

the war on terror, leading some Americans—most of them Republicans—to conclude that Iraq and al Qaeda were indistinguishable. During the recent economic downturn, the Obama administration put a favorable slant on the impact of its economic stimulus program, leading some Americans—most of them Democrats—to conclude that the administration had saved or created many more jobs than it actually had.

Research suggests that faulty perceptions are becoming more prevalent, and that changes in communication are largely to blame.[18] During the buildup to the Iraq invasion, for example, the worst-informed Americans were those that obtained their news from cable television shows. Their misinformation level exceeded even that of citizens who paid infrequent attention to news.

The audience appeal of the "new news" is understandable.[19] Many people prefer messages that conform to what they already believe. It is not surprising that liberal bloggers and talk show hosts have an audience made up mostly of liberals, whereas conservative bloggers and talk show hosts have a largely conservative audience. Studies indicate that misinformation spreads easily when those in touch with the like-minded are not also in contact with other information sources.[20] Rather than expanding people's thinking, such exposure tends to narrow and distort it.[21]

Citizens cannot know whether their ideas are sound until they have heard alternative views and weighed them against their own. The test of an opinion is not whether it sounds good by itself but whether it makes sense when held up against opposing views. "He who knows only his one side of the case knows little of that," Mill wrote. "His reasons may be good, and no one may have been able to refute them. But if he is equally unable to refute the reasons of the opposite side, if he does not so much as know what they are, he has no ground for preferring either opinion."[22]

Beyond its contribution to sound opinions, political knowledge fosters an interest in politics. The more citizens know about politics, the more likely they are to want to play an active part in it. For more than fifty years, the Intercollegiate Studies Association (ISA) has surveyed college students to determine their political information and participation levels. The ISA has found that the best predicator of students' later participation in the nation's civic and political life is not whether they finished college but whether they have a solid understanding of public affairs. "Greater civic knowledge," the ISA says, is "positively correlated with all . . . facets of active engagement . . . [everything from] the private functions of writing a letter to the editor and contacting a public official . . . [to] the more public role of a campaign worker or attendee at a political meeting or rally."[23]

What Political Science Can Contribute to Political Thinking

This text will not try to tell you *what* to think politically. There is no correct way of thinking when it comes to the "what" of politics. People differ in their political values and interests and, thus, also differ in their political opinions.

Instead, this text will help you learn *how* to think politically by providing you with analytical tools that can sharpen your understanding of American politics. The tools are derived from **political science**—the systematic study of government and politics. Political science has developed largely through the work of scholars, but political practitioners and writers have also contributed. One of America's foremost political scientists was the chief architect of the U.S. Constitution and later a president. Even today, James Madison's essays on constitutional design (two of which can be found in this book's appendixes) are masterpieces of political science.

As a discipline, political science is descriptive and analytical—that is, it attempts to depict and explain politics. This effort takes place through various frameworks, including rational choice theory, institutional analysis, historical reasoning, behavioral studies, legal reasoning, and cultural analysis.

Political science offers a set of analytical tools that can increase one's ability to think politically:

- Reliable information about how the U.S. political system operates
- Systematic generalizations about major tendencies in American politics
- Terms and concepts that precisely describe key aspects of politics

These tools will broaden your understanding of American politics and help you to think critically about it.

Like any skill, political thinking needs to be developed through practice. For this reason, each of the text's chapters includes boxes that ask you to think politically. Some political thinking boxes deal with perennial questions, such as the president's war powers and the proper relation between the nation and the states. Still other boxes ask you to think politically by comparing how politics in the United States and in your state differs from that of other nations and states. Finally, some boxes deal with current controversies, including the rising level of party polarization in America. These boxes particularly reflect John Stuart Mill's test of a sound opinion—whether you can refute opposing views as effectively as you can defend your own.

POLITICAL CULTURE: AMERICANS' ENDURING BELIEFS

An understanding of U.S. politics properly begins with an assessment of the nation's political culture. Every country has its **political culture**—the widely shared and deep-seated beliefs of its people about politics.[24] These beliefs derive from the country's traditions and help to define the relationship of citizens to their government and to each other.

Although every country has a distinctive political culture, the United States, as the British writer James Bryce observed, is a special case.[25] Americans' beliefs are the foundation of their national identity. Other people take their identity from the common ancestry that led them gradually to gather under one flag. Thus, long before there was a France, Germany, or Japan, there were French, German, and Japanese people, each a kinship group united through ancestry. Even today, it is kinship that links them. There is no way to become fully Japanese except to be born of Japanese parents. Not so for Americans. They are a multitude of people from different lands—England, Germany, Ireland, Africa, Italy, Poland, Mexico, and China, to name just a few. Americans are linked not by a shared ancestry but by allegiance to a common set of ideals. The French writer Alexis de Tocqueville was among the first to recognize how thoroughly certain beliefs were embedded in the American mind. "Habits of the heart" was how he described them.

America's core ideals are rooted in the European heritage of the first white settlers. They arrived during the Enlightenment period, when people were awakening to the idea of individual choice, a possibility that was much larger in the New World than in the Old World. Ultimately, the colonists overturned the European way of governing. The American Revolution was the first successful large-scale rebellion in human history driven largely by the desire to create a radically different form of society.[26] In the words of the Declaration of Independence:

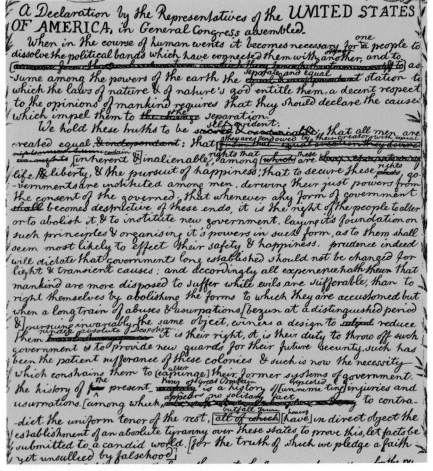

This is a portion of Thomas Jefferson's handwritten draft of the Declaration of Independence, a formal expression of America's governing ideals.

We hold these truths to be self-evident, that all men are created equal; that they are endowed by their Creator with certain unalienable rights; that among these, are life, liberty, and the pursuit of happiness. That, to secure these rights, governments are instituted among men, deriving their just powers from the consent of the governed; that, whenever any form of government becomes destructive of these ends, it is the right of the people to alter or to abolish it, and to institute a new government, laying its foundation on such principles, and organizing its powers in such form, as to them shall seem most likely to effect their safety and happiness.

A decade later, in the drafting of the Constitution of the United States, many of these ideas were put into writing: leaders would be required to govern within a set of rules designed to protect people's rights and interests.

Core Values: Liberty, Individualism, Equality, and Self-Government

An understanding of America's cultural ideals begins with recognition that the individual is paramount. Government is secondary. Its role is to serve the people, as opposed to a system where people are required to serve it. No clearer statement of this principle exists than the Declaration of Independence's reference to "unalienable rights"—freedoms that belong to each and every citizen and that cannot lawfully be taken away by government.

Liberty, individualism, equality, and self-government are widely regarded as America's core political ideals. **Liberty** is the principle that individuals should be free to act and think as they choose, provided they do not infringe unreasonably on the freedom and well-being of others. The United States, as political scientist Louis Hartz said, was "born free."[27] Political liberty was nearly a birthright for early Americans. They did not have to accept the European system of absolute government when greater personal liberty was as close as the next area of unsettled land. Religious sentiments also entered into the thinking of the early Americans. Many of them had fled Europe to escape religious persecution and came to look upon religious freedom as part of a broader set of rights, including freedom of speech. Unsurprisingly, these early Americans were determined, when forming their own government, to protect their liberty. The Declaration of Independence rings with the proclamation that people are entitled to "life, liberty, and the pursuit of happiness." The preamble to the Constitution declares that the U.S. government was founded to secure "the Blessings of Liberty to ourselves and our Posterity."

Early Americans also enjoyed unprecedented economic opportunities. Unlike Europe, America had no hereditary nobility that owned virtually all the land. The New World's great distance from Europe and its vast

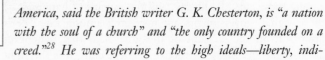

How Important Has Religion Been?

America, said the British writer G. K. Chesterton, is "a nation with the soul of a church" and "the only country founded on a creed."[28] He was referring to the high ideals—liberty, individualism, equality, and self-government—that defined the Declaration of Independence. Chesterton could have extended the argument to include the Constitution. The first colonists formed religious communities governed by written covenant, a model for the written Constitution drafted and ratified by Americans more than a century later. Can you think of ways today that religious beliefs affect American politics?

stretches of open territory gave ordinary people the chance to own property, provided they were willing to work hard enough to make it a success. Out of this experience grew a sense of self-reliance and a culture of "rugged individualism." **Individualism** is a commitment to personal initiative and self-sufficiency. Observers from Tocqueville onward have seen fit to note that liberty in America, as in no other country, is tied to a desire for economic independence. Americans' chief aim, wrote Tocqueville, "is to remain their own masters."[29]

A third American political ideal is **equality**—the notion that all individuals are equal in their moral worth and thereby entitled to equal treatment under the law. Europe's rigid system of aristocratic privilege was unenforceable in frontier America. It was this natural sense of personal equality that Thomas Jefferson expressed so forcefully in the Declaration of Independence: "We hold these truths to be self-evident, that all men are created equal." However, equality has always been America's most perplexing ideal. Even Jefferson professed not to know its exact meaning. A slave owner, Jefferson distinguished between free citizens, who were entitled to equal rights, and slaves, who were not. After slavery was abolished, Americans continued to argue over the meaning of equality, and the debate continues today. Does equality require that wealth and opportunity be widely shared? Or does it merely require that artificial barriers to advancement be removed? Despite differing opinions about such questions, an insistence on equality is a distinctive feature of the American experience. Americans, said Bryce, reject "the very notion" that some people might be "better" than others merely because of birth or position.[31]

America's fourth great political ideal is **self-government**—the principle that the people are the ultimate source of governing authority and

HOW THE U.S. DIFFERS

POLITICAL THINKING THROUGH COMPARISONS

Individualism and Tax Policy

The United States was labeled "the country of individualism par excellence" by William Watts and Lloyd Free in their book *State of the Nation.*[30] They were referring to the emphasis that Americans place on economic self-reliance. In European democracies, such views are moderated by a greater acceptance of policies that aim to help the economically disadvantaged, such as government-provided health care for all citizens. The differences between Americans and Europeans reflect their differing political cultures. Colonial America was an open country ruled by a foreign power, and its revolution was fought largely over the issue of personal liberty. In the European revolutions, economic and social inequality was also at issue, because wealth was held by hereditary aristocracies. Europeans' desire to create an economically more equal society was gradually translated into a willingness to use government as a means of redistributing wealth.

These cultural differences affect tax rates, as the figure here indicates. As measured by the total amount of individual taxes relative to a country's

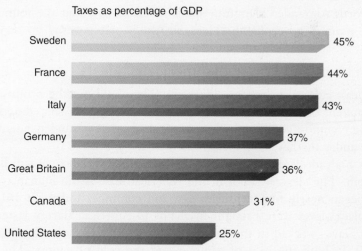

Taxes as percentage of GDP

Sweden	45%
France	44%
Italy	43%
Germany	37%
Great Britain	36%
Canada	31%
United States	25%

Source: Organization for Economic Cooperation and Development, 2014.

Continued

gross domestic product (GDP), the tax rate is relatively high in Canada and Europe, reflecting the greater extent to which these governments seek through taxes to fund programs designed to help the less affluent meet their basic needs in areas such as food, housing, and health care.

Q: Government spending includes programs other than economic assistance for the less-well-off. In which policy area do you think the United States spends significantly more than do European democracies?

A: Military spending by the United States easily exceeds that of European nations. The United States spends roughly 5 percent of its annual GDP on defense, which is about twice that of the average European country.

should have a voice in their governing. Americans' belief in self-government formed in colonial America. The Old World was an ocean away, and European governments had no option but to give the American colonies a substantial degree of self-determination. Out of this experience came the vision of a self-governing nation that led tens of thousands of ordinary farmers, merchants, and tradesmen to risk their lives during the American Revolution. "Governments," the Declaration of Independence proclaims, "deriv[e] their just powers from the consent of the governed." The Constitution of the United States opens with the words "We the People." Etched in a corridor of the Capitol in Washington, D.C., are the words Alexander Hamilton spoke when asked about the foundation of the nation's government: "Here, sir, the people govern."

The Limits and Power of Americans' Ideals

America's cultural beliefs are idealistic. They hold out the promise of a government of high purpose, in which power is widely shared and used for the common good, and where individuals are free, independent, and equal under the law.

Yet high ideals do not come with a guarantee that people will live up to them. The clearest proof in the American case is the human tragedy that began nearly four centuries ago and continues today. In 1619 the first black slaves were brought in chains to America. Slavery lasted 250 years. Slaves worked in the fields from dawn to dark (from "can see, 'til can't"), in both the heat of summer and the cold of winter. The Civil War brought an end to slavery but not to racial oppression. Slavery was followed by the Jim Crow era of legal segregation: black people in the

During the Jim Crow era of racial segregation in the South, black citizens were prohibited from using the same public facilities as whites. Included in the ban were schools, transportation facilities, and parks.

South were forbidden by law to use the same schools, hospitals, restaurants, and restrooms as white people. Those who spoke out against this system were subjected to beatings, firebombings, rapes, and murder—hundreds of African Americans were lynched in the early 1900s by white vigilantes. Today, African Americans have equal rights under the law, but in fact they are far from equal. Compared with white children, black children are twice as likely to live in poverty and to die in infancy.[32] There have always been two Americas, one for whites and one for blacks.

Despite the lofty claim that "all men are created equal," equality has never been an American birthright. In 1882, Congress suspended Chinese immigration on the assumption that the Chinese were an inferior people. Calvin Coolidge in 1923 asked Congress for a permanent ban on Chinese immigration, saying that people "who do not want to be partakers of the American spirit ought not to settle in America."[33] Not to be outdone, California enacted legislation prohibiting individuals of Japanese descent from purchasing property in the state. Not until 1965 was discrimination against the Chinese, Japanese, and other Asians eliminated from U.S. immigration laws.

America's callous treatment of some groups is not among the stories that the American people like to tell about themselves. A University of Virginia survey found that American adults are far more likely to want children to be taught about the nation's achievements than its shortcomings. For example, more than four out of five of those surveyed said children should be taught that "with hard work and perseverance anyone can succeed in

America," while less than three in five said the same about teaching children of the nation's "cruel mistreatment of blacks and American Indians." Selective memory can be found among all peoples, but the tendency to recast history is perhaps exaggerated in the American case because Americans' beliefs are so idealistic. How could a nation that claims to uphold the principle of equality have barred the Chinese, enslaved the blacks, declared wives to be the "property" of their husbands,[34] and stolen Indian lands?

Although America's ideals obviously do not determine exactly what people will do, they are far from empty promises. If racial, gender, ethnic, and other forms of intolerance constitute the nation's sorriest chapter, the centuries-old struggle of Americans to build a more equal society is among its finest. Few nations have battled so relentlessly against the insidious discrimination that stems from superficial human differences such as the color of one's skin. The abolition and suffrage movements of the 1800s and the more recent civil rights movements of black Americans, women, Hispanics, and gays testify to Americans' persistent effort to build a more equal society. In 1848, at the first-ever national convention on women's rights, the delegates issued the Declaration of Sentiments, which read in part: "We hold these truths to be self-evident: that all men and women are created equal." At the height of the Civil War, which was one of the bloodiest conflicts to date in the whole of world history, Abraham Lincoln emancipated the slaves, saying "I never, in my life, felt more certain that I was doing right."[35] A century later, speaking at the Lincoln Memorial at the peak of the black civil rights movement, Martin Luther King Jr. said: " 'We hold these truths to be self-evident, that all men are created equal.' "[36]

Americans' determination to build a more equal society can also be seen in its public education system. In the early 1800s, the United States pioneered the idea of a free public education for children—this at a time when education in Europe was reserved for children of the wealthy. Even today, the United States spends more heavily on public education than do European countries. Compared with Great Britain or France, for example, the United States spends about 30 percent more per pupil annually on its primary and secondary schools. The United States also has the world's most elaborate system of higher education, which now includes more than three thousand two-year and four-year institutions. Although some of America's youth do not have a realistic chance of attending college, the nation's college system is a relatively open one. Roughly a fourth of America's adult citizens have a college degree, which ranks second only to Canada worldwide. Even the American states with the lowest proportion of college graduates have a higher percentage of residents with a bachelor's degree than does the typical European country (see "How the 50 States Differ").

HOW THE 50 STATES DIFFER

POLITICAL THINKING THROUGH COMPARISONS

A College Education

Reflecting their cultural beliefs of individualism and equality, Americans have developed the world's largest college system. Every state has at least eight colleges within its boundaries. No European democracy has as many colleges as either California or New York— each of which has more than three hundred institutions of higher education. Among American adults aged twenty-five years or older, roughly one in four is a college graduate. Even the low-ranking states have a higher percentage of college graduates than do most European countries.

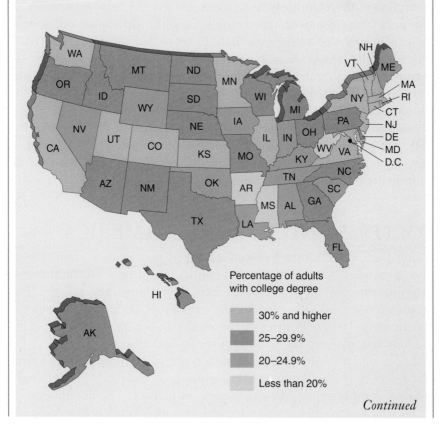

Percentage of adults with college degree

- 30% and higher
- 25–29.9%
- 20–24.9%
- Less than 20%

Continued

Q: Why do the northeastern and western coastal states have a higher percentage of adults with college degrees?

A: The northeastern and western coastal states are wealthier and more urbanized than most states. Accordingly, young people in these states can better afford the costs of college and are more likely to pursue careers that require a college degree.

The principles of liberty and self-government have also shaped American society. No country holds as many elections or has as many publicly elected officials as does the United States, which is also nearly the only country to have instituted primary elections in order to give voters the power to choose party nominees. And few people have pursued their individual rights—ranging from free-expression rights to fair-trial protections—as relentlessly as Americans have. Every generation of Americans has embraced the nation's founding principles and sought ways to update and strengthen them. The writer Theodore H. White aptly described America as a nation doggedly "in search of itself"—a country striving to realize its founding principles." Said White: "Americans are a nation born of an idea; not the place, but the idea, created the United States Government."[37]

America's distinctive cultural beliefs are only one of the elements that affect the nation's politics, as subsequent chapters will show. The rest of this chapter introduces concepts and distinctions that are basic to an informed understanding of politics.

POLITICS AND POWER IN AMERICA

Political scientist Harold Lasswell described politics as a conflict over "who gets what, when, and how."[38] Politics would be a simple matter if everyone thought alike and could have everything they pleased. But people do not think alike, and society's resources are limited. Conflict is the inevitable result. **Politics** is the means by which society settles its conflicts and allocates the resulting benefits and costs.

Those who prevail in political conflicts are said to have **power,** a term that refers to the ability of persons, groups, or institutions to influence political developments.[39] Power is basic to politics. The distribution of power in a society affects who wins and who loses when policy decisions

table 1-1	GOVERNING SYSTEMS AND POLITICAL POWER
System	**Description and Implications**
Democratic	A system of majority rule through elections; empowers majorities (majoritarianism), groups (pluralism), and officials (authority)
Constitutional	A system based on rule of law, including legal protections for individuals; empowers individuals by enabling them to claim their rights in court (legal action)
Free market	An economic system that centers on the transactions between private parties; empowers business firms (corporate power) and the wealthy (elitism)

are made. Those with enough power can raise or cut taxes, permit or prohibit abortions, protect or take away private property, impose or relax trade barriers, and make war or declare peace. With so much at stake, it is not surprising that Americans, like people elsewhere, seek political power.

French philosopher Michel Foucault called politics "war by other means,"[40] a phrase that literally describes politics in some countries. An **authoritarian government** is one that openly represses its political opponents, mostly through intimidation and prohibitions on free expression but sometimes by brutalizing or imprisoning opposition leaders. Such regimes are backed by the country's police and armed forces, forego free and fair elections, and exert tight control over the media. The authoritarian regime in China, for example, blocks Facebook, Twitter, YouTube, and other outlets—including those within the country—that convey messages contrary to what the Chinese government wants its people to hear.[41]

The United States operates by a different standard. It has "rules" designed to keep government in check. These rules—democracy, constitutionalism, and a free market—determine which side will prevail when conflict occurs, as well as what is off limits to the winning side (see Table 1-1).

A Democratic System

The word *democracy* comes from the Greek words *demos*, meaning "the people," and *kratis*, meaning "to rule." In simple terms, **democracy** is a

The clearest expression of majoritarianism (the principle of majority rule) in the American case occurs during elections, when voters decide who will represent them in public office. Here, voters stand in a long line waiting to cast their ballots at a polling place in Fort Mill, South Carolina.

form of government in which the people govern, either directly or through elected representatives. A democracy is thus different from an *oligarchy* (in which control rests with a small group, such as top-ranking military officers or a few wealthy families) and from an *autocracy* (in which control rests with a single individual, such as a king or dictator).

In practice, democracy has come to mean majority rule through the free and open election of representatives. More direct forms of democracy exist, such as town meetings in which citizens vote directly on issues affecting them, but the impracticality of such an arrangement in a large society has made majority rule through elections the operative form of democratic government, including that of the United States (see Chapter 2).

When political leaders respond to the policy desires of the majority, the result is **majoritarianism**.[42] In the American case, majoritarianism occurs primarily through the competition between the Republican and Democratic parties. When the economy went into a tailspin in 2008, it helped the Democrats win control of the presidency and both houses of Congress. The Democrat-controlled Congress in 2009 enacted a

$787 billion economic stimulus bill, responding to majority demand for economic assistance. Unemployment was rising, and a CNN poll showed that 54 percent of Americans backed the legislation. A year later, with the economy still reeling, a CNN poll showed that 56 percent of Americans viewed the stimulus bill as a mistake. With majority opinion now having turned against the spending bill, Republicans had a powerful campaign issue that helped them take control of the House of Representatives in the 2010 midterm elections.

Although competition between the political parties has intensified in the past few decades (see "Party Polarization"), majoritarianism has its limits. The public as a whole takes an interest in only a few of the hundreds of policy decisions that officials make each year (see Chapter 6). Even if they wanted to, party leaders would have difficulty getting the majority to pay attention to most issues. Accordingly, most policies are formulated in response to the groups that have an immediate interest in the issue. Farmers, for example, have more influence over agricultural price supports than do other groups, even though farm subsidies have far-reaching effects, including the price that shoppers pay for food. Some political scientists, like Yale's Robert Dahl, argue that democracies more often operate as pluralistic (multi-interest) systems than as majoritarian systems.[43] **Pluralism** holds that, on most issues, the preference of the special interest largely determines what government does (see Chapter 9).

A democratic system also bestows another form of power. Although officials are empowered by the majority, they also exercise power in their own right as a result of the positions they hold. When President Obama decided in 2009 to increase troop levels in Afghanistan, he did so despite polls that showed most Americans would have preferred a reduction in U.S. forces there.[44] In making the decision, Obama was exercising his constitutional authority as commander-in-chief of the armed forces. Such grants are a special kind of power. **Authority** is the recognized right of officials to exercise power. Members of Congress, judges, and bureaucrats, as well as the president, routinely make authoritative decisions, only some of which are a response to power asserted by the majority or special interests.

A Constitutional System

In a democracy, the votes of the majority prevail over those of the minority. If this principle were unlimited, the majority could treat the minority in any manner of its choosing, including depriving it of its liberty and property. As fanciful as this prospect might seem, it preoccupied the

P A R T Y
POLARIZATION

Political Thinking in Conflict

Conflict between the Political Parties Has Risen Sharply in Recent Years.

Conflict between America's two major parties—the Republicans and the Democrats—has intensified in the past few decades. Partisan divisions have surfaced on nearly every major issue, and the fights have been bitter and prolonged, so much so that the term **party polarization** is used to characterize today's party politics. Subsequent chapters will examine the roots and manifestations of this polarization, but two things should be noted at the outset: the situation is much different than it was a few decades ago but is not very different from what it was during most of the nation's history.

A high level of bipartisanship—cooperation between the parties—marked the period from the end of World War II in 1945 until the late 1960s, particularly in the area of foreign affairs. Leaders and voters of both parties were in agreement on the need to contain Soviet communism and to spread U.S. influence in the world. In addition, Republican leaders had largely abandoned their effort to turn back the New Deal policies of President Franklin Roosevelt, which had given the federal government a larger role in economic security (for example, the social security program) and economic regulation (for example, oversight of the stock market). During much of their earlier history, however, America's major political parties had fought intensely and, in the case of the Civil War, took the fight to the battlefield. In fact, periods of bipartisanship are the exception rather than the rule. President George Washington's first years in office, the so-called Era of Good Feeling in the early 1800s, and the World War I and World War II periods are among the few times Americans have put partisan differences largely aside.

Q. Do you see any contradiction in the fact that Americans share a common set of ideals and yet often find themselves on opposite sides when it comes to party politics?

writers of the U.S. Constitution. The history of democracies was filled with examples of majority tyranny, and the nation's early experience was no exception. In 1786, debtors had gained control of Rhode Island's legislature and made paper money a legal means of paying debts, even though

Authority is a particular form of power that refers to the recognized right of officials to make policy decisions. In the case of the United States, the president, who has authority over a range of policy areas, is the most visible of these officials.

contracts called for payment in gold. Creditors were then hunted down and held captive in public places so that debtors could come and pay them in full with worthless paper money. A Boston newspaper wrote that Rhode Island ought to be renamed Rogue Island.

To guard against oppressive majorities, the writers of the Constitution devised an elaborate system of checks and balances, dividing authority among the legislative, executive, and judicial branches so that each branch could check the power of the others (see Chapter 2). The Bill of Rights was added to the Constitution a few years later as a further check on the majority. For example, Congress was prohibited from enacting laws that abridge freedom of speech, press, or religion. These limits reflect the principle of **constitutionalism**—the idea that there are lawful restrictions on government's power. Officials are obliged to act within the limits of the law, which include the protection of individual rights.

The Bill of Rights in combination with an independent judiciary and a firm attachment to private property have made **legal action**—the use of the courts as a means of asserting rights and interests—a channel through which ordinary citizens exercise power. Americans have an expansive view of their rights and turn more readily to the courts to make their claims than do people elsewhere (see Chapters 4 and 5).[45] A handwritten note by a penniless convict, for example, triggered the U.S. Supreme Court's landmark *Gideon v. Wainwright* ruling.[46] Clarence Gideon had

---

POLITICAL THINKING | **Just Like Kansas City?**

In 1940 Senator Kenneth Wherry of Nebraska soberly exclaimed: "With God's help, we will lift Shanghai up and up, ever up, until it is just like Kansas City." (At the time, Shanghai was brutally occupied by Japanese forces, which, a year later, would attack the United States at Pearl Harbor.) Like many Americans before and since, Wherry assumed that the American system of government could be transplanted almost anywhere in the world. The United States has recently established governments in Afghanistan and Iraq based on democratic principles, such as free elections. Do you think true democracy can take root in countries with a tradition of authoritarian rule or where the population is deeply divided along religious, ethnic, or tribal lines?

---

been made to stand trial in Florida without the aid of a lawyer for breaking into a pool hall. When he appealed his conviction, the Supreme Court concluded that his Sixth Amendment right to counsel had been violated. The ruling established a new policy: if the accused is too poor to hire a lawyer, the government must provide one.

The significance of legal action in the United States can be seen from the size of its legal profession.[47] On a per-capita basis, there are roughly twice as many lawyers in the United States as in Britain, Italy, and Germany, and five times as many as in France (see Figure 1-1). The United States, as political scientist James Q. Wilson noted, is "not more litigious because we have more lawyers; we have more lawyers because we are so litigious."[48]

A Free-Market System

Politics is not confined to the halls of government. Many of society's costs and benefits are allocated through the private sector, although economic systems differ in the degree of government intervention. Under *communism*, which characterized the former Soviet Union and is practiced most fully today in North Korea, the government owns most or all major industries and also takes responsibility for overall management of the economy, including production quotas, supply points, and pricing. Under *socialism*, as it is practiced today in Sweden and other countries, government does not attempt to manage the overall economy, but owns a number of major industries and guarantees every individual a minimal standard

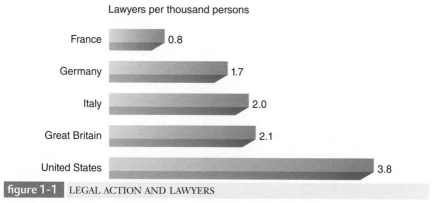

Lawyers per thousand persons

France 0.8

Germany 1.7

Italy 2.0

Great Britain 2.1

United States 3.8

figure 1-1   LEGAL ACTION AND LAWYERS

Reflecting the country's emphasis on legal action as a means of pursuing individual rights and interests, the United States has more lawyers than do other Western democracies. *Source:* Compiled by the author from multiple sources, 2014.

of living. In contrast, a **free-market system** operates mainly on private transactions. Firms are largely free to make their own production, distribution, and pricing decisions, and individuals depend largely on themselves for economic security.

The U.S. economy is chiefly a free-market system, although government intervenes through regulatory, taxing, and spending policies. The nation's economy is similar in this respect to that of most European democracies, but is nonetheless distinctive in the extent to which private transactions determine the allocation of economic costs and benefits. The tax rate, as we saw earlier in the chapter, is lower in the United States than in European countries because they make greater use of taxation to redistribute income to the less advantaged in the form of economic assistance, such as government-provided health care for all.

Enormous concentrations of wealth and power exist in the U.S. private sector, primarily in the hands of large corporations like Google, Ford, and Bank of America. **Corporate power** operates in part through the influence that firms have with government officials. Roughly two-thirds of all lobbyists in the nation's capital represent business firms, which also contribute heavily to political candidates. Corporate power can also be seen in the workplace, where U.S. firms have greater control over wages and working conditions than do firms in other Western democracies. The annual income of a minimum-wage worker, for instance, is roughly $15,000 in the United States, compared with roughly $18,000 in France and $22,000 in Great Britain.[49]

As C. Wright Mills and other theorists have noted, corporate elites must be taken into account in assessing how power in America is distributed and used. The influence of the nation's major corporations goes beyond the workplace. Through advertising and public relations efforts, they have sought to build public support for the private enterprise system.

Wealth is also the foundation of **elitism,** which refers to the power exercised by well-positioned and highly influential individuals.[50] Sociologist C. Wright Mills concluded that corporate elites, operating behind the scenes, have more control over economic policy than do "the politicians in the visible government."[51] Some scholars dispute Mills's claim, while others contend that some elites are motivated to serve society's interests as well as their own.[52] Few scholars, however, dispute the claim that corporate elites have more political power in America than they do in most Western democracies.

Who Governs?

This text's perspective is that a full explanation of American politics requires an accounting of all these forms of power—as exercised by the majority, interest groups, elites, corporations, individuals through legal action, and those in positions of governing authority. In fact, a defining characteristic of American politics is the widespread sharing of power. Few nations have as many competing interests and institutions as does the United States.

THE TEXT'S ORGANIZATION

American politics operates within a constitutional system that defines how power is to be obtained and exercised. This system is the focus of the next few chapters, which examine how, in theory and practice, the Constitution defines the institutions of governments and the rights of individuals. The discussion then shifts to the political role of citizens and of the intermediaries that enable citizens to act together and connect them to government. These subjects are explored in chapters on public opinion, political participation, political parties, interest groups, and the news media. The functioning of governing officials is then addressed in chapters on the nation's elective institutions—the Congress and the presidency—and its appointive institutions—the federal bureaucracy and the federal courts. These chapters describe how these institutions are structured but aim chiefly to explain how their actions are affected by internal and external factors, as well as by the constitutional system in which they operate.

Throughout the text, but particularly in the concluding chapters, attention is given to **public policies,** which are the decisions of government to pursue particular courses of action. No aspect of a nation's politics is more revealing of how it is governed than are its policies—everything from how it chooses to educate its children to how it chooses to use its military power.

Underlying the text's discussion of American politics and policy is the recognition of how difficult it is to govern effectively and how important it is to try. It cannot be said too often that the issue of governing is the most difficult issue facing a democratic society. It also cannot be said too often that governing is a quest rather than a resolved issue. Political scientist E. E. Schattschneider said it clearly: "In the course of centuries, there has come a great deal of agreement about what democracy is, but nobody has a monopoly on it and the last word has not been spoken."[53]

SUMMARY

Political thinking is the careful gathering and sifting of information in the process of forming knowledgeable views of political developments. Political thinking is a key to responsible citizenship, but many citizens avoid it by virtue of paying scant attention to politics. The tools of political science can contribute to effective political thinking.

The United States is a nation that was formed on a set of ideals. Liberty, individualism, equality, and self-government are foremost among these ideals. These ideals became Americans' common bond and today are the basis of their political culture. Although imperfect in practice, these ideals have guided what generations of Americans have tried to achieve politically.

Politics is the process by which it is determined whose values will prevail in society. The basis of politics is conflict over scarce resources and competing values. Those who have power win out in this conflict and are able to control governing authority and policy choices. In the United States, no one faction controls all power and policy. Majorities govern on some issues, while other issues are dominated by groups, elites, corporations, individuals through legal action, or officials who hold public office.

Politics in the United States plays out through rules of the game that include democracy, constitutionalism, and free markets. Democracy is rule by the people, which in practice refers to a representative system of government in which the people rule through their elected officials. Constitutionalism refers to rules that limit the rightful power of government over citizens. A free-market system assigns private parties the dominant role in determining how economic costs and benefits are allocated.

CRITICAL THINKING ZONE

KEY TERMS

authoritarian government (*p. 17*)
authority (*p. 19*)
constitutionalism (*p. 21*)
corporate power (*p. 23*)
democracy (*p. 17*)
elitism (*p. 24*)
equality (*p. 10*)
free-market system (*p. 23*)
individualism (*p. 10*)
legal action (*p. 21*)
liberty (*p. 9*)

majoritarianism (*p. 18*)
party (partisan) polarization (*p. 20*)
pluralism (*p. 19*)
political culture (*p. 7*)
political science (*p. 6*)
political thinking (*p. 2*)
politics (*p. 16*)
power (*p. 16*)
public policies (*p. 25*)
self-government (*p. 10*)

APPLYING THE ELEMENTS OF CRITICAL THINKING

Conceptualizing: Distinguish between political power (generally) and authority (as a special kind of political power).

Synthesizing: Contrast the American political culture with that of most Western democracies. What in the American experience has led its people to derive their national identity from a set of shared political ideals?

Analyzing: Explain the types of power that result from each of America's major systems of governing—democracy, constitutionalism, and a free market.

EXTRA CREDIT

A Book Worth Reading: Gordon S. Wood, *The Idea of America: Reflections on the Birth of the United States.* New York: Penguin Press, 2011. A perceptive book by a Pulitzer Prize–winning historian, it explores the ideals, such as liberty and equality, that were the driving force behind the American Revolution.

A Website Worth Visiting: www.realclearpolitics.com Real Clear Politics is a politically balanced website packed with information and opinions about current issues of American politics.

PARTICIPATE!

Political thinking is a key to responsible citizenship. As a prelude to preparing yourself for effective political thinking, reflect on your current habits. From what sources do you get most of your political information? Are they reliable sources (that is, do they place a premium on accuracy)? How frequently do you encounter opposing arguments or opinions? How carefully do you listen to them? When forming political opinions, do you tend to reflect upon your choices or do you tend to make snap judgments?

2
CHAPTER

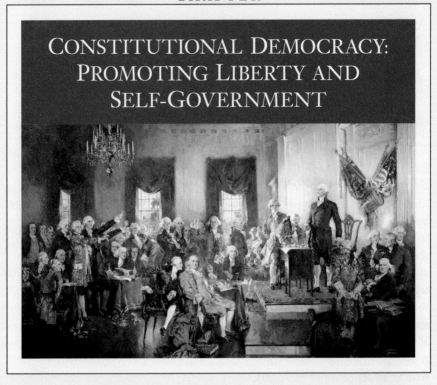

CONSTITUTIONAL DEMOCRACY: PROMOTING LIBERTY AND SELF-GOVERNMENT

66 Why has government been instituted at all? Because the passions of man will not conform to the dictates of reason and justice, without constraint. 99

ALEXANDER HAMILTON[1]

Late on the night of November 6, 2012, Barack Obama stepped to the podium to accept his reelection as president of the United States. Earlier that day, more than 100 million Americans had cast their ballots, choosing Obama over his Republican challenger, Mitt Romney. In his victory speech, Obama spoke of renewing the American dream. He called upon Americans to move forward in common purpose and to put aside the differences that were dividing them. He pledged to use his second term to strengthen the nation's values and to restore Americans' confidence in their government. "America's never been about what can be done for us," said President Obama. "It's about what can be done by us together through the hard . . . but necessary work of self-government."

The ideas that guided Obama's speech would have been familiar to any generation of Americans. The same ideas have been invoked when Americans have gone to war, declared peace, celebrated national holidays, launched major policy initiatives, and asserted new rights.[2] The ideas expressed in Obama's speech were the same ones that shaped the speeches of George Washington and Abraham Lincoln, Susan B. Anthony and Franklin D. Roosevelt, Martin Luther King Jr., and Ronald Reagan.

The ideas were there at the nation's beginning, when Thomas Jefferson put them into words in the Declaration of Independence. They had been nurtured by the colonial experience in the New World, which offered the settlers a degree of liberty, equality, and self-government unimaginable in Europe. When the Revolutionary War settled the issue of American independence in the colonists' favor, they faced the question of how to turn their ideals into a system of government. The Constitution of the United States became the instrument for that effort. The framers of the Constitution sought to create a **limited government**—one that is subject to strict legal limits on the uses of power, so that it would not threaten the people's liberty. They also sought to establish a system of **representative government**—one in which the people would govern through the selection of their representatives.

The challenge facing the framers was that, although limited government and representative government can be reinforcing, they can also conflict. Representative government requires that the majority through its elected representatives has the power to rule. However, limited government requires that majority rule stop at the point where it infringes on the legitimate rights and interests of the minority. This consideration led the framers to forge a constitution that provides for majority rule but has built-in restrictions on the power of the majority and its elected representatives.

This chapter describes how the principles of representative government and limited government are embodied in the Constitution and explains the tension between them. It also indicates how these principles have been modified in practice in the course of American history. The main points presented in this chapter are:

- *America during the colonial period developed traditions of limited government and representative government.* These traditions were rooted in governing practices, political theory, and cultural values.

- *The Constitution provides for limited government mainly by defining lawful powers and by dividing those powers among competing institutions.* The Constitution, with its Bill of Rights, also prohibits government from infringing on individual rights. Judicial review is an additional safeguard.

- *The Constitution in its original form provided for representative government mainly through indirect methods of electing representatives.* The framers' theory of representative government was based on the notion that political power must be separated from immediate popular influences if sound policies are to result.

- *The idea of popular government—in which the majority's desires have a more direct and immediate impact on governing officials—has gained strength since the nation's beginning.* Originally, the House of Representatives was the only institution subject to direct vote of the people. This mechanism has been extended to other institutions and, through primary elections, even to the nomination of candidates for public office.

BEFORE THE CONSTITUTION: THE COLONIAL AND REVOLUTIONARY EXPERIENCES

Early Americans' admiration for limited government stemmed from their British heritage. Unlike other European governments of the time, Britain did not have an absolute monarchy. Parliament was an independent body with lawmaking power and local representation. Many of the colonial charters conferred upon Americans "the rights of Englishmen," which included, for example, the right to trial by jury.

The colonies also had experience in self-government. Each colony had an elected representative assembly, which was subject to British oversight but nevertheless had important legislative powers. Moreover, most colonists were Protestants, and many of them belonged to sects that had self-governing congregations.

The American Revolution was partly a rebellion against Britain's failure to uphold the colonies' established traditions. After the French and Indian War (1754–1763), during which colonists fought alongside British soldiers to drive the French out of the western territories, the British government for the first time imposed heavy taxes on the colonies. The war with France, which was also waged in Europe, had created a budget crisis in Britain. Taxing the colonies was a way to reduce the debt, so Parliament levied a stamp tax on colonial newspapers and business documents. The colonists were not represented in Parliament, and they objected. "No taxation without representation" was their rallying cry.

Although Parliament backed down and repealed the Stamp Act, it then passed the Townshend Act, which imposed taxes on all glass, paper, tea, and lead sold in the colonies. The colonists again objected, and Parliament again backed down, except for the tax on tea, which Britain retained to

At daybreak of April 19, 1775, colonial militiamen fought for the first time against British troops. The battle on the village green of Lexington, Massachusetts, marked the start of the Revolutionary War.

show that it was still in charge of colonial affairs. The tea tax sparked an act of defiance that became known as the Boston Tea Party. In December 1773, under the cover of darkness, a small band of patriots disguised as Native Americans boarded an English ship in Boston Harbor and dumped its cargo of tea overboard. When the British demanded that the city pay for the tea, and Boston refused, the British navy blockaded its port.

In 1774, the colonists met in Philadelphia at the First Continental Congress to formulate their demands on Britain. They asked for their own councils for the imposition of taxes, an end to the British military occupation, and a guarantee of trial by local juries. (British authorities had resorted to shipping "troublemakers" to London for trial.) King George III rejected their demands, and British troops and Massachusetts minutemen clashed at Lexington and Concord on April 19, 1775. Eight colonists died on the Lexington green in what became known as "the shot heard 'round the world." The American Revolution had begun.

The Declaration of Independence

Although grievances against Britain were the immediate cause of the American Revolution, ideas about the proper form of government also fueled the rebellion.[3] Building on the writings of Thomas Hobbes,[4] John Locke claimed that government is founded on a **social contract.** Locke asserted that people living in a state of nature enjoy certain **inalienable rights** (or **natural rights**), including those of life, liberty, and property, which are threatened by individuals who steal, kill, and otherwise act without regard for others. To protect against such individuals, people agree among themselves to form a government (the social contract). They submit to the government's authority in return for the protection it can provide, but, in doing so, they retain their natural rights, which the government is obliged to respect. If it fails to do so, Locke contended, people can rightfully rebel against it.[5]

Thomas Jefferson declared that Locke "was one of the three greatest men that ever lived, without exception." Jefferson paraphrased Locke's ideas in passages of the Declaration of Independence, including those asserting that "all men are created equal," that they are entitled to "life, liberty, and the pursuit of happiness," that governments derive "their just powers from the consent of the governed," and that "it is the right of the people to alter or abolish" a tyrannical government. The Declaration was a call to revolution rather than a framework for a new form of government, but the ideas it contained—liberty, equality, individual rights, self-government, lawful powers—became the basis, eleven years later, for the Constitution of the United States. (The Declaration of Independence and the Constitution are reprinted in their entirety in this book's appendixes.)

The Articles of Confederation

A **constitution** is the fundamental law that defines how a government will legitimately operate—the method for choosing its leaders, the institutions through which these leaders will work, the procedures they must follow in making policy, and the powers they can lawfully exercise. The U.S. Constitution is exactly such a law; it is the highest law of the land. Its provisions define how power is to be acquired and how it can be used.

The first government of the United States, however, was based not on the Constitution but on the Articles of Confederation. The Articles, which were adopted during the Revolutionary War, created a very weak national government that was subordinate to the states. Under the Articles, each state retained its full "sovereignty, freedom, and independence." The colonies had always been governed separately, and their people considered themselves Virginians, New Yorkers, Pennsylvanians, and so on, as much as they thought of themselves as Americans. Moreover, they were wary of a powerful central government. The American Revolution was sparked by grievances against the arbitrary policies of King George III, and Americans were in no mood to replace him with a strong national authority of their own making.

Under the Articles of Confederation, the national government had no judiciary and no independent executive. All authority was vested in the Congress, but it was largely a creature of the states. Each of the thirteen states had one vote in Congress, and each state appointed its congressional representatives and paid their salary. Legislation could be enacted only if nine of the thirteen state delegations agreed to it. The rule for constitutional amendments was even more imposing. The Articles of Confederation could be amended only if each state agreed.

The Articles prohibited Congress from levying taxes, so it had to ask the states for money. It was slow to arrive, if it arrived at all. During one period, Congress requested $12 million from the states but received only $3 million. By 1786, the national government was so desperate for funds that it sold the navy's ships and reduced the army to fewer than a thousand soldiers—this at a time when Britain had an army in Canada and Spain had one in Florida. Congress was also prohibited from interfering with the states' trade policies, so it was powerless to forge a national economy. Free to do what they wanted, states enacted policies designed to protect their manufacturers from competitors in nearby states. Connecticut, for example, placed a higher tariff on goods built in neighboring Massachusetts than it did on the same goods built in England.

The American states had stayed together out of necessity during the Revolutionary War. They would have lost to the British if each state had tried to fend for itself. Once the war ended, however, the states felt free to go their separate ways. Several states sent representatives to Europe to negotiate their own trade agreements. New Hampshire, with its eighteen-mile coastline, established a separate navy. In a melancholy letter to Thomas Jefferson, George Washington wondered whether the United States deserved to be called "a nation."

A Nation Dissolving

In late 1785 at his Mount Vernon home, Washington met with leaders of Virginia and Maryland to secure an agreement between the two states on commercial use of the Potomac River. During the meeting, they decided on the desirability of a commerce policy binding on all the states, which would require an amendment to the Articles of Confederation.

Drafting the Declaration of Independence, a painting by J. L. Ferris. Benjamin Franklin, John Adams (seated, center), and Thomas Jefferson (standing) drafted the historic document. Jefferson was the principal author; he inserted the inspirational words about liberty, equality, and self-government. The initial draft included criticism of slavery but it was removed out of fear that it would lead southern states to reject the call for independence.

A revolt in western Massachusetts added urgency to the situation. A ragtag army of two thousand farmers armed with pitchforks marched on county courthouses to prevent foreclosures on their land. Many of the farmers were veterans of the Revolutionary War; their leader, Daniel Shays, had been a captain in the American army. They had been given assurances during the Revolution that their land, which sat unploughed because they were away at war, would not be confiscated for unpaid debts and taxes. They were also promised the back pay owed to them for their military service. (Congress had run out of money during the Revolution.) Instead, they received no back pay, and heavy new taxes were levied on their farms. Many farmers faced not only losing their property but being sent to prison for unpaid debts.

Shays' Rebellion frightened wealthy interests, who called on the governor of Massachusetts to put down the revolt. He in turn asked Congress for help, but it had no army to send. Although Shays' Rebellion was quashed by a private militia hired and funded by wealthy merchants, the rebellion exposed the weaknesses of the national government, which led Virginia and Maryland to invite the other eleven states to join them at Annapolis to work out amendments to the Articles of Confederation. Only five states sent delegates to the Annapolis Convention, which meant no change could be made in the Articles. However, James Madison and Alexander Hamilton convinced the delegates to adopt a resolution calling for a convention "to render the Constitution of the Federal government adequate to the exigencies of Union." Congress concurred and scheduled a constitutional convention of all the states in Philadelphia. Congress placed a restriction on the delegates: they were to meet for "the sole and express purpose of revising the Articles of Confederation."

POLITICAL THINKING	How Powerful Should Government Be?

The American political tradition includes a suspicion of government power, expressed in the adage "That government is best which governs least." Government sometimes tries to do too much. But can government also do too little? What is the lesson of the government under the Articles of Confederation? Is the issue of government's power a question, not of how much or how little power, but whether its power is equal to its responsibilities?

NEGOTIATING TOWARD A CONSTITUTION

The delegates to the Philadelphia constitutional convention ignored the instructions of Congress, instead drafting a constitution for an entirely new form of government. Prominent delegates (among them George Washington, Benjamin Franklin, and James Madison) were determined from the outset to establish an American nation built on a stronger central government.

The Great Compromise: A Two-Chamber Congress

Debate at the constitutional convention of 1787 began over a plan put forward by the Virginia delegation, which was dominated by strong nationalists. The **Virginia Plan** (also called the **large-state plan**) included separate judicial and executive branches as well as a two-chamber Congress that would have supreme authority in all areas "in which the separate states are incompetent," particularly defense and interstate trade. Members of the lower chamber would be chosen by the voters, while members of the upper chamber would be selected by members of the lower chamber from lists of nominees provided by their respective state legislatures. In both chambers, the heavily populated states would have a greater number of representatives than would the lightly populated ones. Small states such as Delaware and Rhode Island would be allowed only one representative in the lower chamber, while large states such as Massachusetts and Virginia would have more than a dozen.

The Virginia Plan was sharply attacked by delegates from the smaller states. They rallied around a counterproposal made by New Jersey's William Paterson. The **New Jersey Plan** (also called the **small-state plan**) called for a stronger national government than that provided for by the Articles of Confederation. It would have the power to tax and to regulate commerce among the states. In most other respects, however, the Articles would remain in effect. Congress would have a single chamber in which each state, large or small, would have a single vote.

The debate over the two plans dragged on for weeks before the delegates reached what is now known as the **Great Compromise.** It provided for a bicameral (two-chamber) Congress. One chamber, the House of Representatives, would be apportioned on the basis of population. States with larger populations would have more House members than states with smaller populations, although each state would have at least one representative. The other chamber, the Senate, would be apportioned on the basis of an equal number of senators (two) for each state. This compromise was critical. The small states would not have agreed to join a union in which their vote was always weaker than that of large states, a fact reflected in Article V of the Constitution: "No state, without its consent, shall be deprived of its equal suffrage in the Senate."

The Three-Fifths Compromise: Issues of Slavery and Trade

Differences between the interests of northern states and southern states forced a second major compromise, this time over the issues of slavery and trade. The South's delegates were concerned that northern representatives in Congress would tax or even bar the importation of slaves. A decade earlier, at the insistence of southern states, a statement critical of slavery had been deleted from Jefferson's initial draft of the Declaration of Independence, and southern delegates to the Philadelphia convention were determined to block any attempts to end slavery through a new constitution.

The southern delegates were also concerned that the North, which included more states and had a larger population, would use its numerical majority in the House and Senate to enact tax policies injurious to the South. Most of the nation's manufacturing was based in the North, and if Congress sought to protect it by placing a heavy tax (tariff) on manufactured products imported from Europe, the higher cost of these imports would be borne by the South, which was more dependent on them. If Congress also imposed a heavy tariff on the export of agricultural goods, which would make them more expensive and therefore less attractive to foreign buyers, the South would again bear most of the tax burden because it provided most of the agricultural goods shipped abroad, such as cotton and tobacco.

After extended debate, a compromise was reached. Congress would have the authority to tax imports but would be prohibited from taxing exports. Congress also would be prohibited until 1808 from passing laws to end the slave trade. However, the most controversial trade-off was the so-called **Three-Fifths Compromise.** For purposes of apportionment of taxes and seats in the U.S. House of Representatives, each slave was to count as less than a full person. Northern delegates had argued against the counting of slaves because they did not have legal rights. Southern delegates wanted to count them as full persons for purposes of apportioning House seats (which would have the effect of increasing the number of southern representatives) and to count them as nonpersons for purposes of apportioning taxes (which would have the effect of decreasing the amount of federal taxes levied on the southern states). The delegates finally settled on a compromise that included both taxation and apportionment but counted each slave as three-fifths of a person, which was the ratio necessary to give the southern states nearly half of the seats in the House of Representatives. If slaves had not been counted at all, the southern states would have had only about a third of the House seats. If they had been counted as full persons, southern states would have had a majority of House members, even though slaves would have had no say in their selection.

These compromises have led critics to claim that the framers of the Constitution had no objections to slavery. In fact, most of the delegates were deeply troubled by it, recognizing the stark inconsistency between the practice of slavery and the nation's professed commitment to liberty and equality. "It is inconsistent with the principles of the Revolution," Maryland's Luther Martin stated. George Mason, a Virginian and a slaveholder, said: "[Slaveholders] bring the judgment of heaven on a country."[6] Benjamin Franklin and Alexander Hamilton were among the delegates who were involved in antislavery organizations.

Yet the southern states' dependence on slavery was a reality that had to be confronted if there was to be a union of the states. The northern states had few slaves, whereas the southern economies were based on slavery (see Figure 2-1). John Rutledge of South Carolina asked during the convention debate whether the North regarded southerners as "fools." Southern delegates insisted that their states would form a separate union rather than join one that banned slavery.

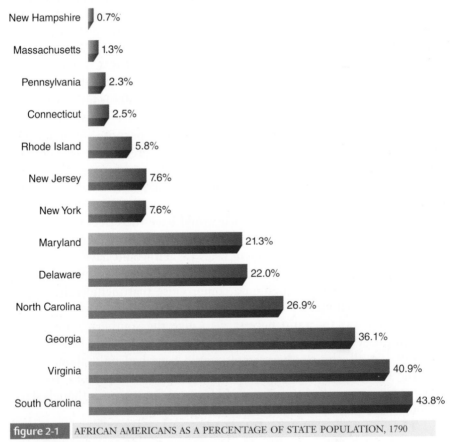

New Hampshire	0.7%
Massachusetts	1.3%
Pennsylvania	2.3%
Connecticut	2.5%
Rhode Island	5.8%
New Jersey	7.6%
New York	7.6%
Maryland	21.3%
Delaware	22.0%
North Carolina	26.9%
Georgia	36.1%
Virginia	40.9%
South Carolina	43.8%

figure 2-1 AFRICAN AMERICANS AS A PERCENTAGE OF STATE POPULATION, 1790

At the time of the writing of the Constitution, African Americans (most of whom were slaves) were concentrated in the southern states. *Source:* U.S. Census Bureau.

A Strategy for Ratification

The compromises over slavery and the structure of the Congress took up most of the four months that the convention was in session. Some of the other issues were the subject of remarkably little debate. Decisions on the structure of the federal judiciary and bureaucracy, for example, were largely delegated to Congress.

The last issue that had to be decided was a process for ratifying the proposed constitution. The delegates realized that all their work would amount to nothing if the states could not be persuaded to adopt the new constitution. They also recognized that ratification would be difficult; many state leaders would oppose giving strong powers to the national government. Moreover, Congress had not authorized a complete restructuring of the federal government. In fact, in authorizing the Philadelphia convention, Congress had stated that any proposed change in the Articles of Confederation would have to be "agreed to in Congress" and then "confirmed by [all] the states."

In a bold move, the delegates ignored Congress's instructions and established their own ratification process. The document was to be submitted to the states, where it would become law if approved by at least nine states in special ratifying conventions of popularly elected delegates. It was a masterful strategy. There was little hope that all thirteen state legislatures would approve the Constitution, but nine states through conventions might be persuaded to ratify it. Indeed, North Carolina and Rhode Island were steadfastly opposed to the new union and did not ratify the Constitution until the other eleven states had ratified it and begun the process of establishing the new government.

The Ratification Debate

The debate over ratification was historic. The **Anti-Federalists** (as opponents of the Constitution were labeled) raised arguments that still echo in American politics. They claimed that the national government would be too powerful and would threaten self-government in the separate states and the liberty of the people. Many Americans had an innate distrust of centralized power and worried that the people's liberty could be eclipsed as easily by a distant American government as it had been by the British king.

The fact that the Constitution contained no bill of rights heightened this concern. Did its absence indicate that the central government would be free to define for itself what the people's rights would be? Patrick Henry expressed outrage at the omission, saying: "The necessity of a Bill of Rights appears to be greater in this government than ever it was in any government before." The proposed constitution, Henry noted, would require the states to surrender to Congress the powers of taxation, spending, and the military "without a Bill of Rights, without check, limitation, or control." The consequences in his mind were dire: "our republic will be lost, and tyranny must and will arise."

Looking ahead, the Anti-Federalists saw a central government controlled by political elites. The Anti-Federalists admired state governments for having legislatures in which the members were not greatly different in wealth from the voters who elected them. New York's Melancton Smith, a powerful public speaker, argued that such representatives are "more competent" than "those of a superior class" whose concerns were far removed from the realities of most people's lives. The election districts in the new Congress would be so large that ordinary people would not have much contact with their representatives, or they with the people they represented. "I am convinced," Smith said, that members of Congress will become "the natural aristocracy of the country. . . . The government will fall into the hands of the few and the great. This will be a government of repression."

The presidency was another source of contention. The office of chief executive did not exist under the Articles of Confederation, and some worried that it would degenerate into an American monarchy. The fact

"Join, or Die" is one of America's most famous political cartoons. Created in 1754 by Benjamin Franklin, it became a symbol of freedom two decades later at the onset of the Revolutionary War. It was resurrected again during the debate over ratification of the Constitution.

that the president would be chosen by electors appointed by the states (the Electoral College) lessened but did not eliminate this concern.

Even the motives of the men who wrote the Constitution came under attack. They were men of wealth and education who had acted in response to debtors' riots. Would the Constitution become a tool by which the wealthy ruled over those with little or no money? And who would bear the burden of additional taxation? For Americans struggling to pay local and state taxes, the thought of also paying national taxes was not appealing.

The Anti-Federalists acknowledged the need for more economic cooperation between the states and for a stronger common defense, but they opposed the creation of a strong national government as the mechanism, arguing that a revision of the Articles of Confederation could accomplish these goals without the risk of establishing an overly powerful central government. (The Anti-Federalist argument is discussed further in Chapter 3.)

The **Federalists** (as the Constitution's supporters called themselves) responded with a persuasive case of their own. Their strongest arguments were set forth by James Madison and Alexander Hamilton, who along with John Jay wrote a series of essays (*The Federalist Papers*) that were published in a New York City newspaper under the pen name Publius. Madison and Hamilton argued that the government of the Constitution would correct the defects of the Articles; it would have the power necessary to forge a secure and prosperous union. At the same time, because of restrictions on its powers, the new government would endanger neither the states nor personal liberty. In *Federalist* Nos. 47, 48, 49, 50, and 51, for example, Madison explained how the separation of national institutions was designed both to empower and to restrict the federal government. (The Federalist argument is discussed further in Chapter 3.)

Whether the ratification debate changed many minds is unclear. Historical evidence suggests, however, that a majority of ordinary Americans opposed the Constitution's ratification. But their voice in the state ratifying conventions was smaller than that of wealthier interests, which in the main supported the change. The proratification forces were also bolstered by the assumption that George Washington, the country's most trusted and popular leader, would become the first president. In the view of historians, this assumption, and the fact that Washington had presided over the Philadelphia convention, tipped the balance in favor of ratification.

Delaware was the first state to ratify the Constitution, and Connecticut, Georgia, and New Jersey soon followed, an indication that the Great Compromise had satisfied some of the small states. In the early summer of 1788, New Hampshire became the ninth state to ratify. The Constitution was law. But neither Virginia nor New York had ratified it, and a stable union without these two large states was almost unthinkable. As large in area as many European countries, they conceivably could have survived as independent nations. In fact, they nearly did choose their own paths. In both states, the Constitution passed only after Federalists said they would support amending it to include a bill of rights.

The Framers' Goals

The Englishman James Bryce ranked America's Constitution as its greatest contribution to the practice of government. The Constitution offered the world a new model of government in which a written document defining the government's lawful powers was a higher authority than the dictates of any political leader or institution.

The Constitution embodied the framers' vision of a proper government for the American people (see Table 2-1). One of the framers' goals was the creation of a national government strong enough to meet the nation's needs, particularly in the areas of defense and commerce. Another goal was to preserve the states as governing entities. Accordingly, the framers established a system of government (federalism) in which power is divided between the national government and the states. Federalism is discussed at length in Chapter 3, which also explains how the Constitution laid the foundation for a strong national government.

The framers' other two goals will be the focus of the rest of this chapter. These goals were: first, to establish a national government that was restricted in its lawful uses of power (limited government) and second, to

table 2-1	MAJOR GOALS OF THE FRAMERS OF THE CONSTITUTION

1. To establish a government strong enough to meet the nation's needs—an objective sought through substantial grants of power to the federal government in areas such as defense and commerce (see Chapter 3)

2. To establish a government that would not threaten the existence of the separate states—an objective sought through federalism (see Chapter 3) and through a Congress connected to the states through elections

3. To establish a government that would not threaten liberty—an objective sought through an elaborate system of checks and balances

4. To establish a government based on popular consent—an objective sought through provisions for the direct and indirect election of public officials

P A R T Y	Political Thinking in Conflict
POLARIZATION	

The Fight over Ratification of the Constitution

The intense partisanship that is so much a part of today's politics also marked the debate over ratification of the Constitution. Angry exchanges marked the debate between those arguing for a stronger national government and those wanting the continuation of a state-centered union. Historians have concluded that Americans were split nearly fifty-fifty on the issue. Although the pro-Constitution side handily prevailed in most states, the balloting in the New York and Virginia conventions was so close that it took the promise of a Bill of Rights to secure the votes for ratification. North Carolina and Rhode Island (the latter had refused even to send delegates to the Philadelphia Convention) initially rejected the Constitution, ratifying it only after it became clear that the other states would form a union without them. Here is the breakdown of the ratifying vote in each state:

State	Date of Ratification	Vote Totals
Delaware	December 12, 1787	46 for, 23 against
Pennsylvania	December 17, 1787	30 for, 0 against
New Jersey	December 18, 1787	38 for, 0 against
Georgia	January 2, 1788	26 for, 0 against
Connecticut	January 9, 1788	128 for, 40 against
Massachusetts	February 6, 1788	187 for, 168 against
Maryland	April 28, 1788	63 for, 11 against
South Carolina	May 23, 1788	149 for, 73 against
New Hampshire	June 21, 1788	57 for, 47 against
Virginia	June 25, 1788	89 for, 79 against
New York	July 26, 1788	30 for, 27 against
North Carolina	November 21, 1789	194 for, 77 against
Rhode Island	May 29, 1790	34 for, 32 against

Q. If historians are correct in concluding that Americans were evenly split over ratification of the Constitution, why might the pro-Constitution side have prevailed in so many states and so easily in some states?

A. State and local governments were in charge of selecting the delegates to the state ratifying conventions. For the most part, they choose prominent individuals to serve as delegates, with the result that merchants,

Continued

city dwellers, large landholders, and leading public officials were over-represented at the conventions. These groups were more supportive of the Constitution than were the underrepresented groups, which included small farmers, craftsmen, and storeowners.

create a national government that gave the people a voice in their governance (representative government).

PROTECTING LIBERTY: LIMITED GOVERNMENT

The framers of the Constitution sought a national government that could act decisively but not one that would act irresponsibly. History had taught them to mistrust unrestricted majority rule. In times of stress or danger, popular majorities had often acted recklessly, trampling on the liberty of others. In fact, **liberty**—the principle that individuals should be free to act and think as they choose, provided they do not infringe unreasonably on the freedom and well-being of others—was the governing ideal that the framers sought most to uphold. Americans enjoyed an unparalleled level of personal freedom as a result of their open society, and the framers were determined that it not be sacrificed to either European-style monarchy or mob-driven democracy.

The threat to liberty was inherent in government because of its coercive power. Government's unique characteristic is that it alone can legally arrest, imprison, or even kill people who violate its directives. Force is not the only basis by which government maintains order, but without it, lawless individuals would prey on innocent people. The dilemma is that government itself can use force to intimidate or brutalize its opponents. "It is a melancholy reflection," James Madison wrote to Thomas Jefferson shortly after the Constitution's ratification, "that liberty should be equally exposed to danger whether the government has too much or too little power."[7]

Grants and Denials of Power

The framers chose to limit the national government in part by confining its scope to constitutional **grants of power** (see Table 2-2). Congress's lawmaking powers are specifically listed in Article I, Section 8 of the Constitution. Seventeen in number, these listed powers include, for example, the powers to tax, establish an army and navy, declare war, regulate

table 2-2	CONSTITUTIONAL PROVISIONS FOR LIMITED GOVERNMENT
Mechanism	**Purpose**
Grants of power	Powers granted to the national government; accordingly, powers not granted it are denied it unless they are necessary and proper to the carrying out of the granted powers.
Separated institutions	The division of the national government's power among three power-sharing branches, each of which is to act as a check on the powers of the other two.
Federalism	The division of political authority between the national government and the states, enabling the people to appeal to one authority if their rights and interests are not respected by the other authority.
Denials of power	Powers expressly denied to the national and state governments by the Constitution.
Bill of Rights	The first ten amendments to the Constitution, which specify rights of citizens that the national government must respect.
Judicial review	The power of the courts to declare governmental action null and void when it is found to violate the Constitution.
Elections	The power of the voters to remove officials from office.

commerce among the states, create a national currency, and borrow money. Powers *not* granted to the government by the Constitution are in theory denied to it. In a period when other governments had unrestricted powers, this limitation was remarkable.

The framers also used **denials of power** as a means to limit government, prohibiting certain practices that European rulers had routinely used to oppress political opponents. The French king, for example, could imprison a subject indefinitely without charge. The U.S. Constitution prohibits such action: citizens have the right to be brought before a court under a writ of habeas corpus for a judgment as to the legality of their confinement. The Constitution also forbids Congress and the states from passing ex post facto laws, under which citizens can be prosecuted for acts that were legal at the time they were committed.

Although not strictly a further denial of power, the framers made the Constitution difficult to amend, thereby making it hard for those in office to increase their power by changing the rules. An amendment could be proposed only by a two-thirds majority in both chambers of Congress or by a national constitutional convention called by two-thirds of the state legislatures. A proposed amendment would then become law only if ratified by three-fourths of state legislatures or state conventions. (Over the course of the nation's history, all amendments have been proposed by Congress and only one amendment—the Twenty-First, which repealed the prohibition on alcohol—was ratified by state conventions. The others were ratified by state legislatures.)

Using Power to Offset Power

Although the framers believed that grants and denials of power could act as controls on government, they had no illusion that written words alone would suffice. As a consequence, they sought to limit government by dividing its powers among separate branches.[8]

Decades earlier, the French theorist Montesquieu had argued that the power of government could be controlled by dividing it among separate branches rather than investing it entirely in a single individual or institution. His concept of a **separation of powers** was widely admired in America, and when the states drafted new constitutions after the start of the Revolutionary War, they built their governments around the ideal. Pennsylvania was an exception, and its experience only seemed to prove the necessity of separated powers. Unrestrained by an independent judiciary or executive, Pennsylvania's all-powerful legislature ignored basic rights and freedoms: Quakers were disenfranchised for their religious beliefs, conscientious objectors to the Revolutionary War were prosecuted, and the right of trial by jury was eliminated.

In *Federalist* No. 10, Madison asked why governments often act according to the interests of overbearing majorities rather than according to principles of justice. He attributed the problem to "the mischiefs of faction." People, he argued, are divided into opposing religious, geographical, ethnic, economic, and other factions. These divisions are natural and desirable in that free people have a right to their personal opinions and interests. Yet if a faction gains full power, it will seek to use government to advance itself at the expense of all others. (*Federalist* No. 10 is widely regarded as the finest political essay ever written by an American. It is reprinted in this book's appendixes.)

Out of this concern came the framers' special contribution to the doctrine of the separation of powers. They did not believe that it would be enough, as Montesquieu had proposed, to divide the government's authority strictly along institutional lines, granting all legislative power to the legislature, all judicial power to the courts, and all executive power to the presidency. This total separation would make it too easy for a single faction to exploit a particular type of political power. A faction that controlled the legislature, for example, could enact laws ruinous to other interests. A safer system would be one in which each branch had the capacity to check the power of the others. This system would require separate but overlapping powers. Because no one faction could easily gain control over all institutions, factions would have to work together, a process that would result in compromise and moderation.[9]

Separated Institutions Sharing Power: Checks and Balances

Political scientist Richard Neustadt devised the term **separated institutions sharing power** to describe the framers' governing system.[10] The separate branches are interlocked in such a way that an elaborate system of **checks and balances** is created (see Figure 2-2). No institution can act decisively without the support or acquiescence of the other institutions. Legislative, executive, and judicial powers in the American system are divided in such a way that they overlap: each of the three branches of government checks the others' powers and balances those powers with powers of its own.

As natural as this system now might seem to Americans, most democracies are of the parliamentary type, with executive and legislative power combined in a single institution rather than vested in separate ones. In a parliamentary system, the majority in the legislature selects the prime minister, who then serves as both the legislative leader and the chief executive (see "How the U.S. Differs" on p. 49).

Shared Legislative Powers   Under the Constitution, Congress has legislative authority, but that power is partly shared with the other branches and thus is checked by them. The president can veto acts of Congress, recommend legislation, and call special sessions of Congress. The president also has the power to execute—and thereby interpret—the laws Congress makes.

The Supreme Court has the power to interpret acts of Congress that are disputed in legal cases. The Court also has the power of judicial review: it can declare laws of Congress void when it finds that they are not in accord with the Constitution.

Within Congress, there is a further check on legislative power: for legislation to be passed, a majority in each chamber of Congress is required. Thus, the Senate and the House of Representatives can block each other from acting.

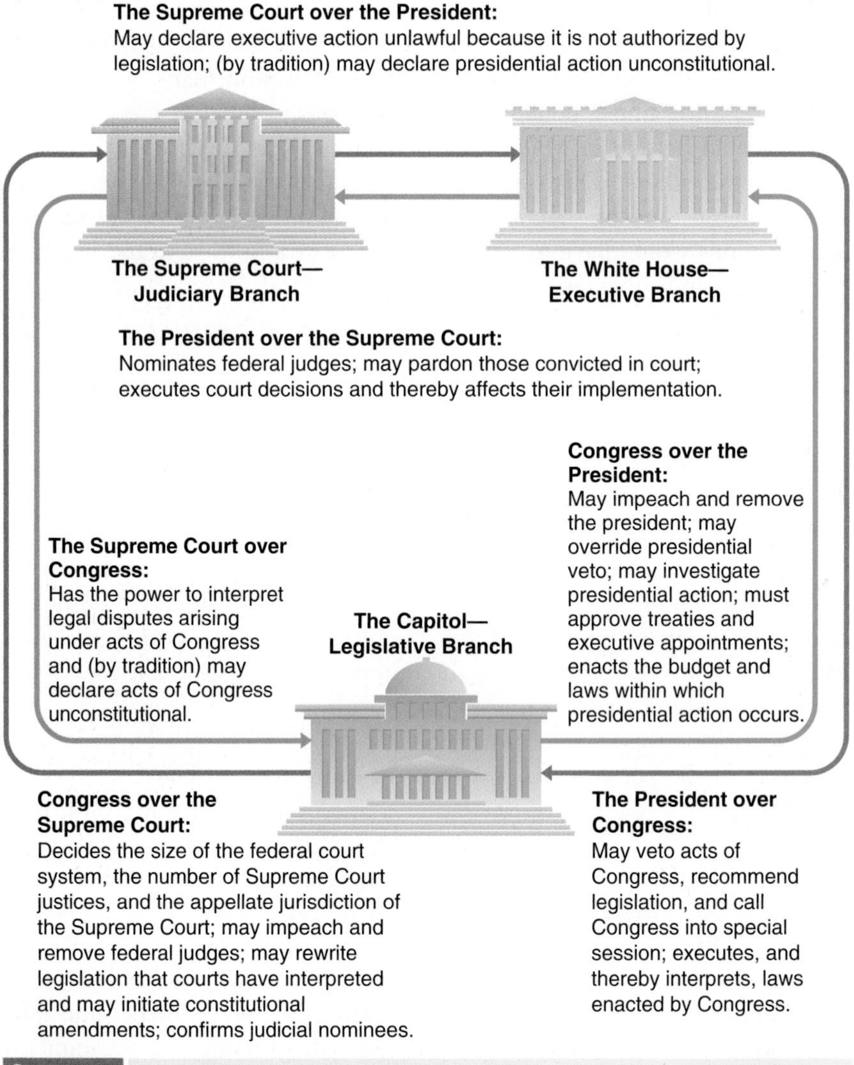

The Supreme Court over the President:
May declare executive action unlawful because it is not authorized by legislation; (by tradition) may declare presidential action unconstitutional.

The Supreme Court— Judiciary Branch

The White House— Executive Branch

The President over the Supreme Court:
Nominates federal judges; may pardon those convicted in court; executes court decisions and thereby affects their implementation.

Congress over the President:
May impeach and remove the president; may override presidential veto; may investigate presidential action; must approve treaties and executive appointments; enacts the budget and laws within which presidential action occurs.

The Supreme Court over Congress:
Has the power to interpret legal disputes arising under acts of Congress and (by tradition) may declare acts of Congress unconstitutional.

The Capitol— Legislative Branch

Congress over the Supreme Court:
Decides the size of the federal court system, the number of Supreme Court justices, and the appellate jurisdiction of the Supreme Court; may impeach and remove federal judges; may rewrite legislation that courts have interpreted and may initiate constitutional amendments; confirms judicial nominees.

The President over Congress:
May veto acts of Congress, recommend legislation, and call Congress into special session; executes, and thereby interprets, laws enacted by Congress.

figure 2-2 THE SYSTEM OF CHECKS AND BALANCES

This elaborate system of divided spheres of authority was provided by the U.S. Constitution as a means of controlling the power of government. The separation of powers among the branches of the national government, federalism, and the different methods of selecting national officers are all part of this system.

Shared Executive Powers Executive power is vested in the president but is constrained by legislative and judicial checks. The president's power to make treaties and appoint high-ranking officials, for example, is subject to Senate approval. Congress also has the power to impeach and remove the president from office. In practical terms, Congress's greatest checks on executive action are its lawmaking and appropriations powers. The executive branch cannot act without laws that authorize its activities or without the money that pays for these activities.

HOW THE U.S. DIFFERS
POLITICAL THINKING THROUGH COMPARISONS

Checks and Balances

All democracies place constitutional limits on the power of government. Democracies differ, however, in the extent to which political power is restrained through constitutional mechanisms. The United States is an extreme case in that its government rests on an elaborate system of constitutional checks and balances. The system employs a separation of powers among the executive, legislative, and judicial branches. These constitutional restrictions on power are not part of the governing structure of all democracies. Most democracies have parliamentary systems, which invest both executive and legislative leadership in the office of prime minister. Britain is an example of this type of system. Parliament under the leadership of the prime minister is the supreme authority in Britain. Its laws are not subject to override by Britain's high court, which has no power to review the constitutionality of parliamentary acts.

Q: The framers of the Constitution saw checks and balances as a means of fostering political moderation. Is there a relationship between the number of checks and balances Western democracies have and their tendency toward political moderation?

A: There is no clear relationship. Great Britain, for example, is often cited as an example of political moderation although it lacks an elaborate system of checks and balances. By contrast, Mexico, which has such a system, is often held up as an example of political extremes. This fragmentary evidence does not mean that checks and balances are ineffective in controlling power, but the evidence does suggest that other factors, such as a country's political traditions, must also be taken into account in any full explanation of political moderation.

The judiciary's major check on the presidency is its power to declare an action unlawful because it is not authorized by the laws that the executive claims to be implementing.

Shared Judicial Powers   Judicial power rests with the Supreme Court and with lower federal courts, which are subject to checks by the other branches of the federal government. Congress is empowered to establish the size of the federal court system, to restrict the Supreme Court's appellate jurisdiction in some circumstances, and to impeach and remove federal judges from office. More important, Congress can rewrite legislation that the courts have misinterpreted and can initiate amendments when it disagrees with court rulings on constitutional issues.

The president has the power to appoint federal judges with the consent of the Senate and to pardon persons convicted in the courts. The president also is responsible for executing court decisions, a function that provides opportunities to influence the way rulings are carried out.

The Bill of Rights

Although the delegates to the Philadelphia convention discussed the possibility of placing a list of individual rights (such as freedom of speech and the right to a fair trial) in the Constitution, they ultimately decided that such a list was unnecessary because of the doctrine of expressed powers: government could not lawfully engage in actions, such as the suppression of speech, that were not authorized by the Constitution. Moreover, the delegates argued that a bill of rights was undesirable because government might feel free to disregard any right that was inadvertently left off the list or that might emerge in the future.

These arguments did not persuade leading Americans who believed that no possible safeguard of liberty should be omitted. Of particular concern was the fact that the Constitution, unlike the Articles of Confederation, granted the federal government direct authority over individual citizens and yet did not contain a list of their rights. "A bill of rights," Jefferson argued, "is what the people are entitled to against every government on earth, general or particular, and what no just government should refuse or rest on inference." Jefferson had included a bill of rights in the constitution he wrote for Virginia at the outbreak of the Revolutionary War, and all but four states had followed Virginia's example.

Ultimately, the demand for a bill of rights led to its addition to the Constitution. Madison himself introduced a series of amendments during the First Congress, ten of which were soon ratified by the states. These amendments, traditionally called the **Bill of Rights,** include rights such as freedom of speech and religion and due process protections (such as the right to a jury trial) for persons accused of crimes. (These rights, termed *civil liberties*, are discussed in Chapter 4.)

The Bill of Rights is a precise expression of the concept of limited government. In consenting to be governed, the people agree to accept the authority of government in certain areas but not in others; the people's constitutional rights cannot lawfully be denied by government officials.

Judicial Review

The writers of the Constitution both empowered and limited government. But who was to decide whether officials were operating within the limits of their constitutionally authorized powers? The framers did not specifically entrust this power to a particular branch of government, although they did grant the Supreme Court the authority to decide on "all cases arising under this Constitution." Moreover, at the ratifying conventions of at least eight of the thirteen states, it was claimed that the judiciary would have the power to nullify actions that violated the Constitution.[11]

Nevertheless, because the Constitution did not explicitly grant the judiciary this authority, the principle had to be established in practice. The opportunity arose with an incident that occurred after the election of 1800, in which John Adams lost his bid for a second presidential term after a bitter campaign against Jefferson. Between November 1800, when Jefferson was elected, and March 1801, when he was inaugurated, the Federalist-controlled Congress created fifty-nine additional lower-court judgeships, enabling Adams to appoint loyal Federalists to the positions before he left office. However, Adams's term expired before his secretary of state could deliver the judicial commissions to all the appointees. Without this authorization, an appointee could not take office. Knowing this, Jefferson told his secretary of state, James Madison, not to deliver the commissions. William Marbury was one of those who did not receive his commission, and he asked the Supreme Court to issue a writ of mandamus (a court order directing an official to perform a specific act) that would force Madison to deliver it.

Marbury v. Madison (1803) became the foundation for judicial review by the federal courts. Chief Justice John Marshall wrote the *Marbury* opinion, which declared that Marbury had a legal right to his commission. The opinion also said, however, that the Supreme Court could not issue him a writ of mandamus because it lacked the constitutional authority to do so. Congress had passed legislation in 1789 that gave the Court this power, but Marshall noted that the Constitution prohibits Congress from expanding the Supreme Court's authority except through a constitutional amendment. That being the case, Marshall argued, the legislation that provided the authorization was constitutionally invalid.[12] In striking down this act of Congress on constitutional grounds, the Court asserted its power of **judicial review**—that is, the power of the judiciary to decide whether a government official or institution has acted within the limits of the Constitution and, if not, to declare its action null and void. (Note that not every court case involves judicial review. It refers only to judgments of whether government officials or institutions have acted within the boundaries of their constitutional power.)

Marshall's decision was ingenious because it asserted the power of judicial review without creating the possibility of its rejection by either the executive or the legislative branch. In declaring that Marbury had a right to his commission, the Court in effect said that President Jefferson had failed in his constitutional duty to execute the laws faithfully. However, because it did not order Jefferson to deliver the commission, he was deprived of the opportunity to disregard the Court's ruling. At the same time, the Court reprimanded Congress for passing legislation that exceeded its constitutional authority. But Congress also had no way to retaliate. It could not force the Court to accept the power to issue writs of mandamus if the Court itself refused to issue them.

POLITICAL THINKING

Too Much Fragmentation?

The use of power to offset power is a basic principle of American government. Is this principle as appropriate today as it was two centuries ago when fear of abuse of power was widespread? Consider the deadlock that has resulted during many recent policy debates in Washington. Disputes within Congress and between Congress and the presidency have often brought the policy process to a standstill. Is the separation of powers an obstacle to the kind of energetic government that modern society requires?

PROVIDING FOR REPRESENTATIVE GOVERNMENT

"We the People" is the opening phrase of the Constitution. It expresses the idea that in the United States the people will have the power to govern themselves. In a sense, there is no contradiction between this idea and the Constitution's provisions for limited government, because individual *liberty* is an essential element of *representative government*. If people cannot express themselves freely, they cannot be truly self-governing. In another sense, however, the contradiction is clear: restrictions on the power of the majority are a denial of its right to govern society as it sees fit.

The framers believed that the people deserved and required a voice in their government, but they worried that the people would become inflamed by a passionate issue or fiery demagogue and act rashly. To the framers, the great risk of popular government was **tyranny of the majority:** the people acting as an irrational mob that tramples on the rights of the minority. The history of unfettered democracies was not encouraging, leading James Madison to say in *Federalist* No. 10 that they "have ever been spectacles of turbulence and contention; have ever been found incompatible with personal security or the rights of property; and have in general been as short in their lives as they have been violent in their deaths."

Democracy versus Republic

No form of representative government could eliminate the possibility of majority tyranny, but the framers believed that the risk would be greatly diminished by creating a republican government as opposed to a

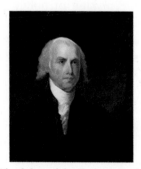

James Madison has been called "the father of the Constitution." Madison himself rejected that label, but he was the framer who saw most clearly how the new government should be structured. Through his *Federalist* essays, Madison was also instrumental in securing ratification of the Constitution. Madison would go on to serve as the nation's fourth president.

democratic government.[13] Today, the terms *democracy*, *republic*, and *representative government* are often used interchangeably to refer to a system of government in which political power rests with the people through their ability to choose representatives in free and fair elections. To the writers of the Constitution, however, a democracy and a republic were different forms of government.

By the term **democracy**, the framers meant a government in which the power of the majority is unlimited, whether exercised directly (as in the case of town meetings open to all citizens) or through a representative body. The majority's will is absolute. Should it decide to act tyrannically—to run roughshod over the minority—there is nothing in the law to stop it. By the term **republic**, the framers meant a government that consists of carefully designed institutions that are responsive to the majority but not captive to it. It is representative democracy in a true sense, but the people's representatives decide policy through institutions that are structured in ways that foster deliberation, slow the decision process, and operate within constraints that protect individual rights. A republic is designed, not to prevent the people from having a say in their governing, but to filter popular sentiment in ways that reduce the likelihood of hasty, ill-conceived, and reckless policies. To the framers, the Constitution's separation of powers and other limits on power were features of the republican form of government, as opposed to the democratic form, which places no limits on the majority.[14]

Limited Popular Rule

The Constitution provided that all power would be exercised through representative institutions. There was no provision for any form of direct popular participation in the making of policy decisions. In view of the fact that the United States was much too large to be governed directly by the people in popular assemblies, a representative system was a necessity. However, the framers went beyond this point, creating a system of representation that placed most federal officials a step removed from the people they represented (see Table 2-3).

The House of Representatives was the only institution that would be based on direct popular election—its members would be elected to serve for two years by a vote of the people. Frequent and direct election of House members was intended to make government responsive to the concerns of popular majorities.

U.S. senators would be appointed by the legislatures of the states they represented. Because state legislators were popularly elected, the people

table 2-3	ORIGINAL METHODS OF CHOOSING NATIONAL LEADERS	
Office	**Method of Selection**	**Term of Service**
President	Electoral College	4 years
U.S. senator	State legislature	6 years (one-third of senators' terms expire every 2 years)
U.S. representative	Popular election	2 years
Federal judge	Nominated by president, approved by Senate	Indefinite (subject to "good behavior")

would be choosing their senators indirectly. Every two years, a third of the senators would be appointed to six-year terms. The Senate, by virtue of the less frequent and indirect election of its members, was expected to be less responsive to popular pressure and thereby serve as a check on the House.

Presidential selection was an issue of considerable debate at the Philadelphia convention. Direct election of the president was twice proposed and twice rejected because it would link executive power directly to popular majorities. The framers finally chose to have the president selected by the votes of electors (the so-called **Electoral College**). Each state would have the same number of **electoral votes** as it had members in Congress and could select its electors by a method of its choosing. The president would serve four years and be eligible for reelection.

The framers decided that federal judges and justices would be appointed rather than elected. They would be nominated by the president and confirmed through approval by the Senate. Once confirmed, they would "hold their offices during good behavior." In effect, they would be allowed to hold office for life unless they committed a crime. The judiciary was an unelected institution that would uphold the rule of law and serve as a check on the elected branches of government.[15]

These differing methods of selecting national officeholders would not prevent a determined majority from achieving unchecked power, but control could not be attained quickly. Unlike the House of Representatives, institutions such as the Senate, presidency, and judiciary would not yield to an impassioned majority in a single election. The delay would reduce the chance that government would degenerate into mob rule driven by momentary passions.

Altering the Constitution: More Power to the People

The framers' conception of representative government was at odds with what the average American in 1787 would have expected.[16] Self-government was an ideal that had led tens of thousands of ordinary farmers, merchants, and tradesmen to risk their lives in the American Revolution. The ensuing state constitutions had put the ideal into practice. Every state but South Carolina held annual legislative elections, and several states also chose their governors through direct annual election.

Not long after ratification of the Constitution, Americans began to challenge the Constitution's restrictions on majority rule (see Table 2-4).

Jeffersonian Democracy: A Revolution of the Spirit   Thomas Jefferson was among the prominent Americans who questioned the Constitution's limited provisions for self-government. In a letter to Madison, he objected to its system of representation, voicing the Anti-Federalist's fear that federal officials would lose touch with the people and discount their interests. His concern intensified when John Adams became president after Washington's retirement. Under Adams, the national government increasingly favored the nation's wealthy interests. Adams publicly indicated that the Constitution was designed for a governing elite and hinted that he might use force to suppress dissent.[17] Jefferson asked whether Adams, with the aid of a strong army, intended to deprive ordinary people of their rights. Jefferson challenged Adams in the next presidential election and, upon defeating him, hailed his victory as the "Revolution of 1800."

table 2-4	MEASURES TAKEN TO MAKE GOVERNMENT MORE RESPONSIVE TO POPULAR MAJORITIES
Earlier Situation	**Subsequent Development**
Separation of powers, as a means of dividing authority and blunting passionate majorities	Political parties, as a means of uniting authorities and linking them with popular majorities
Indirect election of all national officials except House members, as a means of buffering officials from popular influence	Direct election of U.S. senators and popular voting for president (linked to electoral votes), as a means of increasing popular control of officials
Nomination of candidates for public office through political party organizations	Primary elections, as a direct means of selecting party nominees

Although Jefferson was a champion of the common people, he had no clear vision of how a popular government might work in practice. He saw Congress, not the presidency, as the institution better suited to representing majority opinion.[18] He also had no illusions about the ability of a largely uneducated population to play a substantial governing role and feared the consequences of encouraging the masses to rise against the rich. Jeffersonian democracy was mostly a revolution of the spirit. Jefferson taught Americans to look on national government institutions as belonging to all, not just to the privileged few.[19]

Jacksonian Democracy: Linking the People and the Presidency   Not until the election of Andrew Jackson in 1828 did the nation have a powerful president who was willing and able to involve the public more fully in government. Jackson carried out the constitutional revolution that Jeffersonian democracy had foreshadowed.

Jackson recognized that the president was the only official who could legitimately claim to represent the people as a whole. Unlike the president, members of Congress were elected from separate states and districts rather than from the entire country. Yet the president's claim to popular leadership was weakened by the fact that the president was chosen by electors rather than by the voters. To connect the presidency more closely to the people, Jackson urged the states to award their electoral votes to the candidate who wins the state's popular vote. Soon thereafter, nearly all states adopted this method. This arrangement, still in effect, places the selection of the president in the voters' hands in most elections. The candidate who gets the most popular votes nationally is also likely to finish first in enough states to win a majority of the electoral votes. Since Jackson's time, only three candidates—Rutherford B. Hayes in 1876, Benjamin Harrison in 1888, and George W. Bush in 2000—have won the presidency after losing the popular vote. (The Electoral College is discussed further in Chapter 12.)

The Progressives: Senate and Primary Elections   The Progressive Era of the early 1900s brought another wave of democratic reforms. The Progressives sought to weaken the influence of large corporations and political party bosses by placing power more directly in the hands of the people.[20] They succeeded in changing the way some state and local governments operate. Progressive reforms at state and local levels include the initiative and the referendum, which enable citizens to vote directly on legislative issues (see "How the 50 States Differ" on p. 59). Another Progressive reform is the recall election, which enables citizens through petition to force an officeholder to submit to reelection before the regular expiration

"SAY, UNCLE, WE'VE CUT LOOSE FROM THE OLD PARTIES, AND DECIDED TO
COME TOGETHER AND FORM A NEW PARTY. CAN YOU SUGGEST A NAME?"

The Progressive Movement of the early 1900s succeeded in loosening the tight grip of Democratic and Republican leaders and machines on the nation's politics. Among the Progressive Movement's reforms is the primary election, which allows voters to directly pick the party nominees for public office.

of his or her term. (In 2003, a recall election enabled actor Arnold Schwarzenegger to become California's governor.)

The Progressives also instigated two changes in federal elections. One was the **primary election,** which gives rank-and-file voters the power to select party nominees. In the early 1900s, nearly all states adopted the primary election as a means of choosing nominees for at least some federal and state offices. Prior to this change, nominees were selected by party leaders. The second change was the direct election of U.S. senators, who before the ratification of the Seventeenth Amendment in 1913 were chosen by state legislatures and were widely perceived as agents of big business (the Senate was nicknamed the "Millionaires' Club"). Senators who stood to lose their seats in a direct popular vote had blocked earlier attempts to change the Constitution. However, as a result of several developments, including revelations that a number of senators owed their seats to corporate bribes, the Senate was finally persuaded to support the amendment.

The Progressive Era even spawned attacks on the framers. A prominent criticism was laid out in historian Charles S. Beard's *An Economic*

HOW THE 50 STATES DIFFER

POLITICAL THINKING THROUGH COMPARISONS

Direct Democracy: The Initiative and Popular Referendum

In some states, by gathering enough signatures on a petition, citizens can directly enact or defeat legislation through their votes in an election. This action can occur through either an initiative (in which citizens place a legislative proposal of their own choosing on the ballot) or a popular referendum (in which citizens place an act of the state legislature on the ballot, which the voters can then accept or reject). A popular referendum is different from a legislative referendum, in which the state legislature itself places a proposal on the ballot for the voters to accept or reject. All states have a form of the legislative referendum, but only some states, as indicated in the accompanying map, have the initiative and the popular referendum.

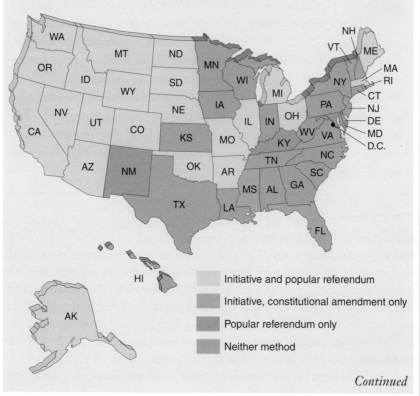

Initiative and popular referendum

Initiative, constitutional amendment only

Popular referendum only

Neither method

Continued

Q: Why are the northeastern and southern states less likely than states in other regions to have the initiative and popular referendum?

A: The initiative and popular referendum were introduced in the early 1900s by the Progressives, who sought to weaken the power of political bosses and give voters a larger voice in their governance. In the Northeast, party machines had enough strength in state legislatures to block their enactment. In the South, these devices were blocked by the white establishment, which feared that blacks and poor whites might use them to gain power.

POLITICAL THINKING

Trustees or Delegates?

The proper role of elected representatives has long been a source of debate. In his Letter to the Sheriffs of Bristol *in 1777, English theorist Edmund Burke argued that representatives should act as the public's **trustees**. He claimed that representatives are obliged to serve the interests of those who elect them but should use their own judgment in determining what is best for their constituents. In contrast, leaders of the Progressive Movement held that officeholders should behave as **delegates** who act in accordance with the expressed desires of the people they represent. They argued that the people themselves are the best judge of their interests. Which position is closer to your own? Can you think of an issue on which you would take the opposite position?*

Interpretation of the Constitution.[21] Arguing that the Constitution grew out of wealthy Americans' fears of the debtor rebellions, Beard claimed that the Constitution's elaborate systems of power and representation were devices for keeping power in the hands of the rich. As evidence, Beard cited the Constitution's protections of property and referred to Madison's notes on the Philadelphia convention, which showed that property concerns were high on the framers' agenda. Beard further noted that not one of the delegates was a workingman or farmer. Most of the framers had large landholdings and controlled substantial interests, or were major credit holders.

Beard's thesis was challenged by other historians, and he later acknowledged that he had not taken the framers' full array of motives into account. Their conception of separation of powers, for example, was a governing principle that had earlier been incorporated into state constitutions. Nevertheless, Beard held onto his claim that the Constitution was designed to protect the interests of the wealthy rather than to promote self-government.

Beard's claim has some validity, but to say that the framers were foes of democracy is inaccurate. Although they did not have great trust in popular rule, they were determined to balance the need to create a system of self-government with the need to create a system of limited government. Convinced that unchecked majority rule was likely to devolve into tyranny, the framers devised institutions that were responsive to majority opinion without being captive to it.

CONSTITUTIONAL DEMOCRACY TODAY

The type of government created in the United States in 1787 could accurately be called a **constitutional democratic republic.** It is constitutional in its requirement that power gained through elections be exercised in accordance with law and with due respect for individual rights; democratic in its provisions for majority influence through elections; and a republic in its mix of deliberative institutions, each of which moderates the power of the others.[22]

By some standards, the American system of today is a model of *representative government.*[23] The United States schedules the election of its larger legislative chamber (the House of Representatives) and its chief executive more frequently than does any other democracy. In addition, it is the only major democracy to rely extensively on primary elections rather than party organizations for the selection of party nominees. The principle of direct popular election to office, which the writers of the Constitution regarded as a method to be used sparingly, has been extended further in the United States than anywhere else.

By other standards, however, the U.S. system is less democratic than some. Popular majorities must work against the barriers to power devised by the framers—divided branches, staggered terms of office, and separate constituencies. In fact, the link between an electoral majority and a governing majority is less direct in the American system than in nearly all other democratic systems. In the European parliamentary democracies, for example, legislative and executive power is not divided, is not subject to close check by the judiciary, and is acquired through the winning of a legislative majority in a single national election. The framers' vision was a different one, dominated by a concern with liberty and therefore with controls on political power. It was a response to the experiences they brought with them to Philadelphia in the summer of 1787.

SUMMARY

The Constitution of the United States is a reflection of the colonial and revolutionary experiences of the early Americans. Freedom from abusive government was a reason for the colonies' revolt against British rule, but the English tradition also provided ideas about government, power, and freedom that were expressed in the Constitution and, earlier, in the Declaration of Independence.

The Constitution was designed in part to provide for a limited government in which political power would be confined to proper uses. The framers wanted to ensure that the government they were creating would not itself be a threat to freedom. To this end, they confined the national government to expressly granted powers and also denied it certain specific powers. Other prohibitions on government were later added to the Constitution in the form of stated guarantees of individual liberties in the Bill of Rights. The most significant constitutional provision for limited government, however, was a separation of powers among the three branches. The powers given to each branch enable it to act as a check on the exercise of power by the other two, an arrangement that during the nation's history has in fact served as a barrier to abuses of power.

The Constitution, however, made no mention of how the powers and limits of government were to be judged in practice. In its historic ruling in *Marbury v. Madison*, the Supreme Court assumed the authority to review the constitutionality of legislative and executive actions and to declare them unconstitutional and thus invalid.

The framers of the Constitution, respecting the idea of self-government but distrusting popular majorities, devised a system of government that they felt would temper popular opinion and slow its momentum so that the public's "true interest" (which includes a regard for the rights and interests of the minority) would guide public policy. Different methods were advanced for selecting the president, the members of the House and the Senate, and federal judges as a means of insulating political power against momentary majorities.

Since the adoption of the Constitution, the public gradually has assumed more direct control of its representatives, particularly through measures that affect the way officeholders are chosen. Presidential popular voting (linked to the Electoral College), direct election of senators, and primary elections are among the devices aimed at strengthening the majority's influence. These developments are rooted in the idea, deeply held by ordinary Americans, that the people must have substantial direct influence over their representatives if government is to serve their interests.

CRITICAL THINKING ZONE

KEY TERMS

Anti-Federalists (*p. 39*)
Bill of Rights (*p. 51*)
checks and balances (*p. 47*)
constitution (*p. 32*)
constitutional democratic
  republic (*p. 61*)
delegates (*p. 60*)
democracy (according to the
  framers) (*p. 54*)
denials of power (*p. 45*)
Electoral College (*p. 55*)
electoral votes (*p. 55*)
Federalists (*p. 41*)
grants of power (*p. 44*)
Great Compromise (*p. 36*)
inalienable (natural) rights (*p. 32*)

judicial review (*p. 52*)
liberty (*p. 44*)
limited government (*p. 29*)
New Jersey (small-state) Plan (*p. 36*)
primary election (*p. 58*)
representative government (*p. 29*)
republic (*p. 54*)
separated institutions sharing
  power (*p. 47*)
separation of powers (*p. 46*)
social contract (*p. 32*)
Three-Fifths Compromise (*p. 37*)
trustees (*p. 60*)
tyranny of the majority (*p. 53*)
Virginia (large-state) Plan (*p. 36*)

APPLYING THE ELEMENTS OF CRITICAL THINKING

Conceptualizing: Define the concept of judicial review. How does a court decision involving judicial review differ from an ordinary court decision, such as a ruling in a case involving armed robbery?

Synthesizing: Contrast the original system for electing federal officials with the system of today, noting in each case whether voters have acquired a more direct voice in the election process than was originally the case.

Analyzing: Why is it more accurate to say that the United States has a system of "separated institutions sharing power" rather than a system of "separated powers"? Provide examples of how shared power can act to check and balance the power of each institution.

EXTRA CREDIT

A Book Worth Reading: Joseph J. Ellis, *Founding Brothers: The Revolutionary Generation.* New York: Vintage, 2002. A Pulitzer Prize–winning book by a preeminent historian, it explores the political aspirations and beliefs of America's founding leaders, including Washington, Hamilton, Jefferson, and Madison.

A Website Worth Visiting: **www.archives.gov** The National Archive is the repository of America's important documents. Its site includes, for example, an in-depth history of the writing of the Declaration of Independence.

PARTICIPATE!

The classroom provides an everyday opportunity to develop a skill that is basic to effective citizenship—the ability to speak clearly and persuasively. To the Greek philosopher Aristotle, rhetoric was the defining skill of citizenship. Aristotle did not define rhetoric as it is often used today, as a derisive term for speech that is long on wind and short on reason. Rather, he saw rhetoric as a tool in the search for truth, a form of persuasion that flourishes when people exchange ideas. The college classroom is a good place to develop rhetorical skills. Speak up in the classroom when you have a point to make and can support it. Rhetorical skills are honed only through practice, and few settings offer more opportunities for practice than the classroom.

3
CHAPTER

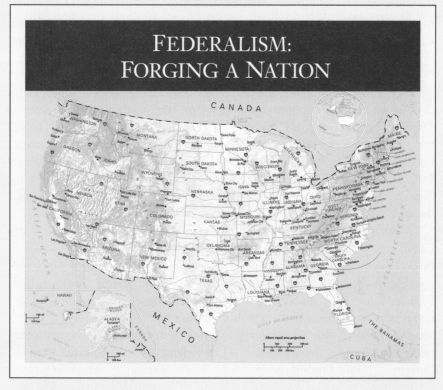

FEDERALISM:
FORGING A NATION

"The question of the relation of the states to the federal government is the cardinal question of our Constitutional system. It cannot be settled by the opinion of one generation, because it is a question of growth, and each successive stage of our political and economic development gives it a new aspect, makes it a new question."

WOODROW WILSON[1]

It was one of the most anxiously awaited Supreme Court decisions in years. At issue was the constitutionality of provisions of the 2010 health care reform act that required individuals to purchase health insurance or face a tax penalty. Enacted by the Democratic-controlled Congress at the urging of President Barack Obama, the legislation had been opposed from the start by Republicans. Every Senate and House Republican voted against the bill, and Republican state attorneys general quickly filed suit to have the bill declared unconstitutional on grounds that it usurped the authority of the states to decide whether their residents will be required to have health insurance. Democrats saw the issue differently, claiming that Congress has the lawful power to require individuals to have personal health insurance or face a penalty.

Challenges to the law in federal district courts produced mixed verdicts, with some judges upholding the law and others striking it down. In late 2011, the Supreme Court announced that it would take up the issue by hearing a case in which the state of Florida was challenging the law on grounds that it was an improper exercise of federal authority. Joining Florida's challenge were twenty-five other states: Alabama, Alaska, Arizona, Colorado, Georgia, Idaho, Indiana, Iowa, Kansas, Louisiana, Maine, Michigan, Mississippi, Nebraska, Nevada, North Dakota, Ohio, Pennsylvania, South Carolina, South Dakota, Texas, Utah, Washington, Wisconsin, and Wyoming.

In June of 2012, the Supreme Court issued its ruling, upholding the health care act in a 5-4 decision based on the power of Congress to levy taxes. Writing for the majority, Chief Justice John Roberts said: "It is reasonable to construe what Congress has done as increasing taxes on those who have a certain amount of income, but choose to go without health insurance. Such legislation is within Congress's power to tax." Roberts went on to say: "The federal government does not have the power to order people to buy health insurance. . . . The federal government does have the power to impose a tax on those without health insurance." The four justices in the minority issued a vigorous dissent: "Whether federal spending legislation crosses the line from enticement to coercion is often difficult to determine. . . . In this case, however, there can be no doubt."[2]

The controversy surrounding the health care reform act is one of thousands of disagreements over the course of American history that have hinged on whether national or state authority should prevail. Americans possess what amounts to dual citizenship: they are citizens both of the United States and of the state where they reside. The American political system is a *federal system*, in which constitutional authority is divided between a national government and state governments. Each government is assumed to derive its powers directly from the people and therefore to have sovereignty (final authority) over the policy responsibilities assigned to it. The federal system consists of states and nation, separate yet indivisible.[3]

The relationship between the states and the nation was the most pressing issue when the Constitution was written and has been a divisive issue ever since. In one case, the Civil War, it nearly caused the dissolution of the United States. Throughout the nation's history, federalism has been a source of contention between the Republican and Democratic parties, although they have shifted sides when it served their political goals. This chapter examines federalism—its creation through the Constitution, its evolution during the nation's history, and its current status. The main points presented in the chapter are:

- *The power of government must be equal to its responsibilities.* The Constitution was needed because the nation's preceding system (under the Articles of Confederation) was too weak to accomplish its expected goals, particularly those of a strong defense and an integrated economy.
- *Federalism—the Constitution's division of governing authority between two levels, nation and states—was the result of political bargaining.* Federalism was not a theoretical principle, but rather a compromise made necessary in 1787 by the prior existence of the states.
- *Federalism is not a fixed principle for allocating power between the national and state governments, but rather a principle that has changed over time in response to political needs and partisan ideology.* Federalism has passed through several distinct stages in the course of the nation's history.
- *Contemporary federalism tilts toward national authority, reflecting the increased interdependence of American society.*

FEDERALISM: NATIONAL AND STATE SOVEREIGNTY

At the time of the writing of the Constitution, some of America's top leaders were dead set against the creation of a stronger national government. When rumors began to circulate that the Philadelphia convention was devising just such a government, Virginia's Patrick Henry said that he "smelt a rat." His fears were confirmed when he obtained a copy of the draft constitution. "Who authorized them," he asked, "to speak the language of 'We, the People,' instead of 'We, the States'?"

The question of "people versus states" was precipitated by the failure of the Articles of Confederation. It had created a union of the states, and they alone had authority over the people (see Chapter 2). The national government could not tax or conscript citizens, nor could it regulate their economic activities. Its directives applied only to the states, and they often ignored them. Georgia and North Carolina, for example, contributed no money at all to the national treasury between 1781 and 1786, and the federal government had no way to force them to pay. The only feasible solution to this problem was to give the federal government direct authority over the people. If individuals are ordered to pay taxes, most of them will do so rather than accept the alternative—imprisonment or confiscation of their property.

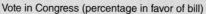

| P A R T Y | Political Thinking in Conflict |
| POLARIZATION | |

The Federal Government's Role in Health Care

The United States is nearly alone among Western democracies in not having government-provided health care for all citizens. The U.S. system is instead a combination of federal programs and private insurance, most of it provided through employers. For decades, Democrats have sought to expand the government's role while Republicans have fought the expansion. In 2010, the Democrat-controlled Congress passed the Patient Protection and Affordable Care Act, commonly known as the health care reform act, which is the most significant expansion of government-directed health insurance since Medicare and Medicaid were enacted in the 1960s. The 2010 legislation was tied up for months in Congress, with Republican and Democratic lawmakers on opposite sides of the issue. They argued over everything from the cost of the program to its effect on the quality of coverage, as well as whether it violated states' rights. The partisan division spilled over to the public. Self-identified Republicans and Democrats were far apart in their opinions on the issue.

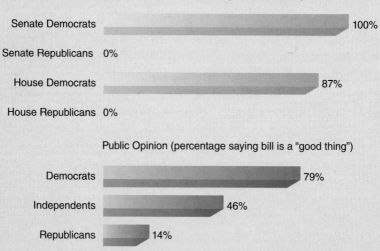

Q. Partisan debate over the health care bill focused on both its substance (greater government involvement in order to expand the number of insured Americans) and its constitutionality (whether the federal government was acting within its lawful authority). Which of these issues—the substantive one or the constitutional one—do you think was more important in the response of Democratic and Republican lawmakers to the issue? Which do you personally regard as the more significant aspect of the issue?

"GIVE ME LIBERTY, OR GIVE ME DEATH !"

PATRICK HENRY delivering his great speech on the Rights of the Colonies, before the Virginia Assembly

Patrick Henry was a leading figure in the American Revolution ("Give me liberty or give me death!"). He later opposed ratification of the Constitution on grounds that the national government should be a union of states and not also a union of people.

At the same time, the writers of the Constitution wanted to preserve the states. The states had their own constitutions and a governing history extending back to the colonial era. Although their residents thought of themselves as Americans, many of them identified more strongly with their states. When Virginia's George Mason said that he would never agree to a constitution that abolished the states, he was speaking for nearly all the delegates.

These two realities—the need to preserve the states and the need for a national government with direct authority over the people—led the framers to invent an entirely new system of government. Before this point in history, **sovereignty** (supreme and final governing authority) had been regarded as indivisible. By definition, a government cannot be sovereign if it can be overruled by another government. Nevertheless, the framers divided sovereignty between the national government and the states, a system now know as **federalism.** Each level—the national government and the state governments—directly governs the residents within its assigned territory. Each level has authority that is not subject to the other's approval. And each level is constitutionally protected. The national government cannot abolish a state, and the states cannot abolish the national government.

In 1787, other nations in the world were governed by a **unitary system,** in which sovereignty is vested solely in the national government. Local or regional governments in a unitary system do not have sovereignty. They have authority only to the degree that it is granted by the national government, which can also withdraw any such grant. (This situation applies to America's local governments. They are not sovereign, but instead derive their authority from their respective state governments, which can, though it occurs rarely, even choose to abolish a local unit of government.)

Federalism is also different from a **confederacy,** which was the type of government that existed under the Articles of Confederation. In a confederacy, the states alone are sovereign. They decide the authority, even the continuing existence, of the central government. Confederacies have been rare in human history, but the government of the Articles was not the first. The ancient Greek city-states and medieval Europe's Hanseatic League were of this type. (Despite its name, the Confederate States of America—the South's Civil War government—had a federal constitution rather than a confederate one. Sovereignty was divided between the central and state governments.)

The federal system established in 1787 divides the responsibilities of government between the nation and the states (see Figure 3-1). The system gives states the power to address local issues in ways of their choosing; they have primary responsibility, for example, for public education and police protection. The national government, on the

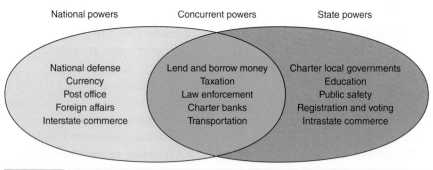

National powers	Concurrent powers	State powers
National defense Currency Post office Foreign affairs Interstate commerce	Lend and borrow money Taxation Law enforcement Charter banks Transportation	Charter local governments Education Public safety Registration and voting Intrastate commerce

figure 3-1   FEDERALISM AS A GOVERNING SYSTEM: EXAMPLES OF NATIONAL, STATE, AND CONCURRENT POWERS

The American federal system divides sovereignty between a national government and the state governments. Each is constitutionally protected in its existence and authority, although their powers overlap somewhat even in areas granted to one level (for example, the federal government has a role in education policy).

HOW THE U.S. DIFFERS

POLITICAL THINKING THROUGH COMPARISONS

Differences in Federal Systems

Federalism involves the division of sovereignty between a national government and subnational (state) governments. It was invented in the United States in 1787 to maintain the preexisting American states while establishing an effective central government. Since then two dozen countries (for example, Canada, Mexico, and Germany) have established a *federal* government, but most countries (for example, Great Britain, France, and Japan) continue to have a *unitary* government, in which sovereignty is vested solely in the national government.

Even federal systems differ in how they distribute power between their national and state governments. In Germany's federal system, for example, the states have limited lawmaking powers but exercise broad authority in implementing national laws. By comparison, the U.S. federal system grants substantial lawmaking powers to the states except in specified areas such as national defense and currency. The U.S. and Canadian federal systems also differ in how they allocate power; for example, the national government has greater authority over commerce in the United States than it does in Canada.

In federal systems, the national legislature has two chambers—one apportioned by population (as in the case of the U.S. House of Representatives) and the other by geographical area (as in the case of the U.S. Senate). The U.S. Senate is a pure federal institution in the sense that each state has the same number of senators. In some federal systems, such as Canada's, the states are not equally represented even in the legislative chamber apportioned on the basis of geography rather than population.

Q: Federal systems typically have a two-chamber legislature. Unitary systems, on the other hand, typically have a single legislative chamber. Why?

A: In a unitary system, there is no constitutional need for a second legislative chamber based on geographical subdivisions (states), as is the case with a federal system.

other hand, is responsible for matters of national scope, such as military defense and the currency. The national and state governments also have some concurrent powers (that is, powers exercised over the same policy areas). Each of them has, for example, the power to raise taxes and borrow money.

The Argument for Federalism

The strongest argument for federalism in 1787 was that it would correct the defects in the Articles. Two of the defects were particularly troublesome: the national government had neither the power to tax nor the power to regulate commerce among the states. Without money from taxes, the national government lacked the financial means to maintain an army strong enough to prevent encroachment by European powers or to maintain a navy strong enough to protect America's merchant ships from harassment and attack by foreign navies and pirates. And without the ability to regulate commerce, the national government could neither promote the general economy nor prevent trade wars between the states. New York and New Jersey were among the states that imposed taxes on goods shipped into their state from other states.

Although it is sometimes claimed that "the government which governs least is the government that governs best," the Articles proved otherwise. The problems with the too-weak national government were severe: public disorder, economic chaos, and an inadequate defense. Although the problems were widely recognized, many Americans in 1787 feared that a strong central government would eventually swallow up the states. An outspoken Anti-Federalist (as opponents of the Constitution were called) proclaimed: "[The states] will eventually . . . have power over little else than yoking hogs or determining the width of cart wheels."[4]

The challenge of providing a response fell to James Madison and Alexander Hamilton. During the ratification debate, they argued in a series of essays (the so-called *Federalist Papers*) that a federal system would protect liberty and moderate the power of government.

Protecting Liberty   Although theorists such as John Locke and Montesquieu had not proposed a division of power between national and local authorities as a means of protecting liberty, the framers argued that federalism was a part of the system of checks and balances.[5] Alexander Hamilton wrote in *Federalist* No. 28 that the American people could shift their loyalties back and forth between the national and state governments in order to keep each under control. "If [the people's] rights are invaded by either," Hamilton wrote, "they can make use of the other as the instrument of redress." In *Federalist* No. 46, Madison echoed that argument: "The people ought not surely to be precluded from giving most of their confidence where they may discover it to be the most due."

Moderating the Power of Government   To the Anti-Federalists, the sacrifice of the states' power to the nation was unwise. They argued that a distant national government could never serve the people's interests as well as the states could. Liberty *and* self-government, the Anti-Federalists argued, were enhanced by state-centered government. To support their case, they turned to the French theorist Montesquieu, who had claimed that a small republic is more likely than a large one to serve people's interests. When government encompasses a smaller area, he argued, its leaders are in closer touch with the people.

In *Federalist* No. 10, James Madison took issue with this claim. He argued that whether a government serves the common good is a function not of its size but of the range of interests that share political power. The problem with a small republic, Madison claimed, is that it can have a dominant faction—whether it be landholders, financiers, an impoverished majority, or some other group—that is strong enough to control government and use it for selfish purposes. A large republic is less likely to have an all-powerful faction. If financiers are strong in one area of a large republic, they are likely to be weaker elsewhere. The same will be true of farmers, merchants, laborers, and other groups. A large republic, Madison argued, would make it difficult for a single group to gain full control, which would force groups to share in the exercise of power. In making this claim, Madison was arguing not for central authority but for limited government, which he believed would result if power were shared widely. "Extend the sphere," said Madison, "and you take in a greater variety of parties and interests; you make it less probable that a majority of the whole will have a common motive to invade the rights of other citizens."

The Powers of the Nation and the States

The U.S. Constitution addresses the lawful authority of the national government, which is provided through *enumerated and implied powers.* Authority that is not granted to the national government is left—or "reserved"—to the states. Thus, the states have *reserved powers.*

Enumerated Powers and the Supremacy Clause   Article I of the Constitution grants to Congress seventeen **enumerated (expressed) powers.** The framers expected these powers to establish a government strong enough to forge a union that was secure in its defense and stable in its economy.

THE

FEDERALIST:

A COLLECTION OF

E S S A Y S,

WRITTEN IN FAVOUR OF THE

NEW CONSTITUTION,

AS AGREED-UPON BY THE

FEDERAL CONVENTION,

SEPTEMBER 17, 1787.

IN TWO VOLUMES.
VOL. I.

NEW-YORK:
PRINTED AND SOLD BY JOHN TIEBOUT,
No. 358 PEARL-STREET.

1799.

America's most noted essays were written to urge ratification of the Constitution. Penned mostly by James Madison and Alexander Hamilton, but written anonymously under the pen name Publius, they appeared in serial in two New York City papers. A year later, they were published together as *The Federalist*. More than a century elapsed before they came to be called *The Federalist Papers*, which is the common reference today.

Congress's powers, for example, to regulate commerce among the states, to create a national currency, and to borrow money would provide a foundation for a sound national economy. Its power to tax, combined with its authority to establish an army and navy and to declare war, would enable it to provide for the common defense.

In addition, the Constitution prohibits the states from actions that would encroach on national powers. Article I, Section 10, prohibits the states from making treaties with other nations, raising armies, waging war, printing money, or entering into commercial agreements with other states without the approval of Congress.

The writers of the Constitution recognized that the lawful exercise of national authority would at times conflict with the laws of the states. In such instances, national law was intended to prevail. Article VI of the Constitution grants this dominance in the so-called **supremacy clause,** which provides that "the laws of the United States . . . shall be the supreme law of the land."

Implied Powers: The Necessary and Proper Clause   The writers of the Constitution recognized that government, if it was to be effective, had to be capable of adjusting to change. A weaknesses of the Articles was that the national government was prohibited from exercising powers not expressly granted it, which limited its ability to meet the country's changing needs after the end of the Revolutionary War. To avoid this problem with the new government, the framers included in Article I of the Constitution the **"necessary and proper" clause** or, as it later came to be known, the **elastic clause.** It gives Congress the power "to make all laws which shall be necessary and proper for carrying into execution the foregoing [enumerated] powers." This clause gives the national government **implied powers:** powers that are not listed in the Constitution but are related to the exercise of the powers that are listed.

Reserved Powers: The States' Authority   The supremacy and "necessary and proper" clauses were worrisome to the Anti-Federalists. The two clauses stoked their fear of an overly powerful national government because they provided a constitutional basis for expanding federal authority. Such concerns led them to demand a constitutional amendment that would protect

---

POLITICAL THINKING

More National Power?

Section 8 of Article I of the Constitution (which can be seen in this book's appendixes) lists the powers of the federal government. Since the Constitution was written, changes in transportation, technology, and the economy have linked Americans more closely together. Recognizing this fact, would you assign additional powers to the national government if you were rewriting the Constitution today? What's the basis for your thinking?

states' rights and interests. Ratified in 1791 as the Tenth Amendment to the Constitution, it reads: "The powers not delegated to the United States by the Constitution, nor prohibited by it to the States, are reserved to the States." The states' powers under the U.S. Constitution are thus called **reserved powers.**

FEDERALISM IN HISTORICAL PERSPECTIVE

Since ratification of the Constitution over two centuries ago, no aspect of it has provoked more frequent or bitter conflict than federalism. By establishing two levels of sovereign authority, the Constitution created two centers of power and ambition, each of which was sure to claim disputed areas as belonging to it. Ambiguities in the Constitution have also contributed to conflict between the nation and the states. For example, the document does not specify the dividing line between *inter*state commerce (which the national government is empowered to regulate) and *intra*state commerce (which is reserved for regulation by the states).

Not surprisingly, federalism has been a contentious system, its development determined less by constitutional language than by the strength of the contending interests and the country's changing needs. Federalism can be viewed as having progressed through three historical eras, each of which has involved a different relationship between the nation and the states. At the same time, each era has ended with a national government that was stronger than at the start of the era. Over the long term, the United States has undergone a process of **nationalization**—an increase in national authority.

An Indestructible Union (1789–1865)

The issue during the first era—which lasted from the time the Constitution went into effect (1789) until the end of the Civil War (1865)—was the Union's survival. Given America's state-centered history before the Constitution, it was inevitable that the states would dispute national policies that threatened their interests.

The Nationalist View: McCulloch v. Maryland   An early dispute over federalism arose when President George Washington's secretary of the treasury, Alexander Hamilton, proposed that Congress establish a national bank. Hamilton and his supporters claimed that because the federal government had constitutional authority to regulate currency, it had the "implied power" to establish a national bank. Thomas Jefferson, Washington's secretary of state, opposed the bank on the grounds that its activities would enrich the wealthy at the expense of ordinary people. Jefferson claimed the bank was unlawful because the Constitution did not expressly authorize it. Jefferson said: "I consider the foundation of the Constitution as laid on this ground that 'all powers not delegated to the United States by the Constitution, nor prohibited by it to the states, are preserved to the states or to the people.' . . . To take a single step beyond the boundaries thus drawn . . . is to take possession of a boundless field of power, no longer susceptible of any definition."

Jefferson's argument failed to sway Congress. In 1791, it established the First Bank of the United States, granting it a twenty-year charter. Although Congress did not renew the bank's charter when it expired in 1811, Congress decided in 1816 to establish the Second Bank of the United States. State and local banks did not want competition from a national bank and sought help from their state legislatures. Several states, including Maryland, levied taxes on the national bank's operations within their borders, hoping to drive it out of existence by making it unprofitable. James McCulloch, who was in charge of the Maryland branch of the national bank, refused to pay the Maryland tax and the resulting dispute was heard by the Supreme Court.

Of the framers, Alexander Hamilton had the clearest vision of what was needed to create a strong national government and economy. As secretary of the treasury under President Washington, Hamilton persuaded Congress to establish the First Bank of the United States, which contributed to the growth of the nation's commercial sector. The First Bank's headquarters, located in Philadelphia, is still standing.

The chief justice of the Supreme Court, John Marshall, was a fervent nationalist, and in *McCulloch v. Maryland* (1819) the Court ruled decisively in favor of national authority. It was reasonable to infer, Marshall concluded, that a government with powers to tax, borrow money, and regulate commerce could establish a bank in order to exercise those powers effectively. Marshall's argument was a clear statement of *implied powers*—the idea that through the "necessary and proper" clause, the national government's powers extend beyond a narrow reading of its enumerated powers.

Marshall's ruling also addressed the meaning of the Constitution's supremacy clause. The state of Maryland had argued that, even if the national government had the authority to establish a bank, a state had the authority to tax it. The Supreme Court rejected Maryland's position, concluding that valid national law overrides conflicting state law. Because the national government had the power to create the bank, it also could protect the bank from state actions, such as taxation, that might destroy it.[6]

The *McCulloch* decision served as precedent for later rulings in support of national power. In *Gibbons v. Ogden* (1824), for example, the Marshall-led Court rejected a New York law granting one of its residents a monopoly on a ferry that operated between New York and New Jersey, concluding that New York had encroached on Congress's power to regulate commerce among the states. The Court asserted that Congress's commerce power was not limited to trade between the states, but to all aspects of that trade, including the transportation of goods. The power over commerce, the Court said, "is vested in Congress as absolutely as it would be in a single government."[7]

Marshall's opinions asserted that legitimate uses of national power took precedence over state authority and that the "necessary and proper" clause and the commerce clause were broad grants of power to the national government. As a nationalist, Marshall provided a legal basis for expanding federal power in ways that fostered the development of the United States as a nation rather than as a collection of states. As Justice Oliver Wendell Holmes Jr. noted a century later, the Union could not have survived if each state had been allowed to decide for itself which national laws it would obey.[8]

The States' Rights View: The Dred Scott *Decision*   Although John Marshall's rulings strengthened national authority, the issue of slavery posed a growing threat to the Union's survival. Westward expansion and immigration into the northern states were tilting power in Congress toward the free states, which increasingly signaled their determination to outlaw slavery at some future time. Fearing the possibility, southern leaders did what

others have done throughout American history: they developed a constitutional interpretation fitted to their political purpose. John C. Calhoun
declared that the United States was founded upon a "compact" between
the states. The national government, he said, was "a government of states
. . . not a government of individuals."[9] This line of reasoning led Calhoun
to his famed "doctrine of nullification," which declared that a state has
the constitutional right to nullify a national law.

In 1832, South Carolina invoked the doctrine, declaring "null and
void" a national tariff law that favored northern interests. President
Andrew Jackson called South Carolina's action "incompatible with the
existence of the Union," a position that gained strength when Congress
gave Jackson the authority to take military action against South Carolina.
The state backed down after Congress agreed to changes in the tariff act.
The dispute foreshadowed the Civil War, a confrontation of far greater
consequence. Although war would not break out for another three decades,
the dispute over states' rights was intensifying.

The Supreme Court's infamous *Dred Scott* decision (1857), written by
Chief Justice Roger Taney, an ardent states'-rights advocate, inflamed the
dispute. Dred Scott, a slave who had lived in the North for four years,

The American Civil War was one of the bloodiest conflicts the world had yet known. Ten
percent of fighting-age males died in the four-year war, and uncounted others were wounded.
The death toll—618,000 (360,000 from the North, 258,000 from the South)—exceeded that of
the American war dead in World War I, World War II, the Korean War, and the Vietnam War
combined. This death toll was in a nation with a population only one-tenth the size it is today.
Shown here, in one of the earliest war photos ever taken, are the bodies of soldiers killed at the
battle of Antietam.

applied for his freedom when his master died, citing a federal law—the Missouri Compromise of 1820—that made slavery illegal in a free state or territory. The Supreme Court ruled against Scott, claiming that slaves were not citizens and therefore had no right to have their case heard in federal court. The Court also invalidated the Missouri Compromise by holding that slaves were property, not people. Accordingly, since the Constitution prohibited Congress from interfering with owners' property rights, Congress lacked the power to outlaw slavery in any state.[10]

The Taney Court's decision provoked outrage in the North and contributed to a sectional split in the nation's majority party, the Democrats. In 1860, the Democratic Party's northern and southern wings nominated separate candidates for the presidency, which split the Democratic vote, enabling the Republican candidate, Abraham Lincoln, to win the presidency with only 40 percent of the popular vote. Lincoln had campaigned on a platform that called, not for an immediate end to slavery, but for its gradual abolition through payments to slaveholders. Nevertheless, southern states saw Lincoln's election as a threat to their way of life. By the time Lincoln took office, seven southern states, led by South Carolina, had left the Union. Four more states followed. In justifying his decision to wage war on the South, Lincoln said, "The Union is older than the states." In 1865, the superior strength of the Union army settled by force the question of whether national authority is binding on the states.

Dual Federalism and Laissez-Faire Capitalism (1865–1937)

Although the North's victory in the Civil War preserved the Union, new challenges to federalism were surfacing. Constitutional doctrine held that certain policy areas, such as interstate commerce and defense, belonged exclusively to the national government, whereas other policy areas, such as public health and intrastate commerce, belonged exclusively to the states. This doctrine, known as **dual federalism,** was based on the idea that a precise separation of national and state authority was both possible and desirable. "The power which one possesses," said the Supreme Court, "the other does not."[11]

American society, however, was in the midst of changes that raised questions about the suitability of dual federalism as a governing concept. The Industrial Revolution had given rise to large business firms, which were using their economic power to dominate markets and exploit workers. Government was the logical counterforce to this economic power. Which level of government—state or national—would regulate business?

There was also the issue of the former slaves. The white South had lost the war but was hardly of a mind to share power with the newly freed slaves. Would the federal government be allowed to intervene in state affairs to ensure the fair treatment of African Americans?

Dual federalism became a barrier to an effective response to these issues. From the 1860s through the 1930s, the Supreme Court held firm to the idea that there was a sharp dividing line between national and state authority and that neither level of government would be allowed to substantially regulate the economy. The era of dual federalism was characterized by state supremacy in racial policy and business supremacy in commerce policy.

The Fourteenth Amendment and State Discretion   Ratified after the Civil War, the Fourteenth Amendment was intended to protect the newly freed slaves from discriminatory action by state governments. A state was prohibited from depriving "any person of life, liberty, or property without due process of law," from denying "any person within its jurisdiction the equal protection of the laws," and from abridging "the privileges or immunities of citizens of the United States."

Supreme Court rulings in subsequent decades, however, undermined the Fourteenth Amendment's promise of liberty and equality for all. In 1873, for example, the Court held that the Fourteenth Amendment did not substantially limit the power of the states to determine the rights to which their residents were entitled.[12] Then, in *Plessy v. Ferguson* (1896), the Court issued its infamous "separate but equal" ruling. A black man, Homer Adolph Plessy, had been convicted of violating a Louisiana law that required white and black citizens to ride in separate railroad cars. The Supreme Court upheld his conviction, concluding that state governments could force blacks to use separate facilities as long as the facilities were "equal" in quality to those reserved for use by whites. "If one race be inferior to the other socially," the Court concluded, "the Constitution of the United States cannot put them on the same plane." The lone dissenting justice in the case, John Marshall Harlan, had harsh words for his colleagues: "Our Constitution is color-blind and neither knows nor tolerates classes among citizens. . . . The thin disguise of 'equal' accommodations . . . will not mislead anyone nor atone for the wrong this day done."[13]

With its *Plessy* decision, the Supreme Court endorsed government-based racial segregation in the South. Black children were forced into separate public schools that had few teachers. Public hospitals for blacks had few doctors and almost no medical supplies. The *Plessy* ruling had become a justification for the separate and *unequal* treatment of black Americans.[14]

Judicial Protection of Business   After the Civil War, the Supreme Court also gave nearly free rein to business. A majority of the Court's justices favored laissez-faire capitalism (which holds that business should be "allowed to act" without interference) and interpreted the Constitution in ways that restricted government's attempts to regulate business activity. In 1886, for example, the Court decided that corporations were "persons" within the meaning of the Fourteenth Amendment, and thereby were protected from substantial regulation by the states.[15] In other words, a constitutional amendment that had been enacted to protect newly freed slaves from being treated as second-class persons was ignored for that purpose but used instead to protect fictitious persons—business corporations.

The Court also weakened the national government's regulatory power by narrowly interpreting its commerce power. The Constitution's **commerce clause** says that Congress shall have the power "to regulate commerce" among the states. However, the clause does not spell out the economic activities included in the grant of power. When the federal government invoked the Sherman Antitrust Act (1890) in an attempt to break up the monopoly on the manufacture of sugar (a single company controlled 98 percent of it), the Supreme Court blocked the action, claiming that interstate commerce covered only the "transportation" of goods, not their "manufacture."[16] Manufacturing was deemed part of intrastate commerce and thus, according to the dual federalism doctrine, subject to state regulation only. However, because the Court had previously ruled

---

| POLITICAL THINKING | Protector of Rights, Nation or States? |

During the debate over ratification of the Constitution, Americans argued over whether individual liberty and equality would be better protected by the states or by the nation. The Anti-Federalists argued that a small republic was closer to the people and therefore would do more to uphold individual rights. Arguing for the Federalist side, James Madison countered by saying that a large republic was preferable because its wide diversity of interests would prevent a dominant group from taking control and using government's power to suppress weaker groups. Historically, which level of government do you think has been the more protective of liberty and equality? What historical issues or examples would you use to support your argument? Can you think of contemporary issues or examples that would suggest one level of government or the other is more protective today of liberty and equality?

that the states' regulatory powers were limited by the Fourteenth Amendment, the states were largely prohibited from regulating manufacturing.

Although some business regulation was subsequently allowed, the Court remained an obstacle to efforts to curb business practices. An example is the case of *Hammer v. Dagenhart* (1918), which arose from a 1916 federal law that prohibited the interstate shipment of goods produced by child labor. The law had public support in that factory owners were exploiting children, working them for long hours at low pay. Nevertheless, the Court invalidated the law, ruling that the Tenth Amendment gave the states, and not the federal government, the power to regulate factory practices.[17] However, in an earlier case, *Lochner v. New York* (1905), the Court had blocked states from regulating labor practices, concluding that such action violated factory owners' property rights.[18]

In effect, the Court had negated the principle of self-government. Neither the people's representatives in Congress nor those in the state legislatures were allowed to regulate business. America's corporations, with the Supreme Court as their protector, were in control.[19]

National Authority Prevails   The Democratic Party with its working-class base attacked the Court's position, and its candidates increasingly called for greater regulation of business and more rights for labor. Progressive Republicans like Theodore Roosevelt also fought against uncontrolled business power, but the Republican Party as a whole was ideologically committed to unregulated markets and to a small role for the federal government. Accordingly, when the Great Depression began in 1929, Republican president Herbert Hoover refused to use federal authority to put people back to work. Adhering to his party's free-market philosophy, Hoover argued that the economy would quickly rebound on its own and that government intervention would only delay the recovery.

In the 1932 election, voters elected as president the Democratic candidate, Franklin D. Roosevelt, who recognized that the economy had become a national one. More than 10 million workers (compared to 1 million in 1860) were employed by industry, whose products were marketed throughout the nation. Urban workers typically were dependent on landlords for their housing, on farmers and grocers for their food, and on corporations for their jobs. Farmers were more independent, but they too were increasingly a part of a larger economic network. Farmers' income depended on market prices and shipping and equipment costs.[20] Economic interdependence meant that, when the depression hit in 1929, its effects could not be contained. At the depths of the Great Depression, one-fourth of the nation's workforce was jobless.

Between 1865 and 1937, the Supreme Court's rulings severely restricted national power. Narrowly interpreting Congress's regulatory power under the commerce clause, the Court allowed business monopolies to act largely as they pleased in establishing prices, wages, and working conditions.

The states had responsibility for helping the poor, but they were nearly penniless because of declining tax revenues and the high demand for welfare assistance. Franklin Roosevelt's New Deal programs were designed to ease the hardship. The 1933 National Industry Recovery Act (NIRA), for example, established a federal jobs program and enabled major industries to coordinate their production decisions. Economic conservatives opposed such programs, accusing Roosevelt of leading the country into socialism. They found an ally in the Supreme Court. In *Schecter Poultry Corp. v. United States* (1935), just as it had done in previous New Deal cases, the Supreme Court in a 5-4 ruling declared the NIRA to be unconstitutional.[21]

Frustrated by the Court's rulings, Roosevelt in 1937 sought to exploit the fact that the Constitution gives Congress the power to determine the number of Supreme Court justices. Although the number had stayed at nine justices for seven decades, there was no constitutional barrier to increasing the number, which, in fact, had been altered several times in the nation's early years. Roosevelt asked Congress to pass legislation that would allow a president to nominate a new justice whenever a seated member passed the age of seventy and a half. Since some of the justices had already reached that age, the legislation would enable Roosevelt to appoint enough new justices to swing the Court to his side. Congress hesitated to do so, but the attempt ended with the "switch in time that saved nine."

For reasons that have never been fully clear, Justice Owen Roberts switched sides on New Deal cases, giving the president a 5-4 majority on the Court.

Within months, the Court upheld the 1935 National Labor Relations Act, which gave employees the right to organize and bargain collectively.[22] In passing the legislation, Congress claimed that disputes between labor and management disrupted the nation's economy and therefore could be regulated through the commerce clause. In upholding the act, the Supreme Court endorsed Congress's reasoning.[23] In a subsequent ruling, the Court declared that Congress's commerce power is "as broad as the needs of the nation."[24] Congress would be allowed to regulate *all* aspects of commerce. During this same period, the Court also loosened its restrictions on Congress's power to tax and spend.[25]

The Supreme Court had finally acknowledged the obvious: that an industrial economy is not confined by state boundaries and must be subject to national regulation. It was a principle that business also increasingly accepted. The nation's banking industry, for example, was saved from almost complete collapse in the 1930s by the creation of a federal regulatory agency, the Federal Deposit Insurance Corporation (FDIC). By insuring depositors' savings against loss, the FDIC stopped the panic withdrawals that had already ruined thousands of the nation's banks.

Subsequent Supreme Court decisions altered the constitutional doctrine of federalism in other policy areas, including civil rights. In *Brown v. Board of Education* (1954), for example, the Supreme Court held that states could not force black children to attend public schools separate from those for white children.[26] Equal citizenship—the notion that Americans should have the same constitutional rights regardless of the state in which they live—was becoming national policy (see Chapters 4 and 5).

CONTEMPORARY FEDERALISM (SINCE 1937)

Since the 1930s, the relation of the nation to the states has changed so fully that dual federalism is no longer an accurate description of the American system. An understanding of today's federalism requires the recognition of two countervailing developments. The larger trend is a long-term *expansion* of national authority that began in the 1930s and continues to this day. The national government now operates in many policy areas that were once almost exclusively within the control of states and localities. The national government does not dominate in these policy areas, but it does play a significant role.

Many of the federal initiatives trace to the 1960s as part of President Lyndon Johnson's Great Society program. A Democrat in the mold of Franklin Roosevelt, Johnson believed that federal power should be used to assist the economically disadvantaged. However, unlike Roosevelt's New Deal, which dealt mostly with the economy, Johnson's Great Society dealt mostly with social welfare issues, which have an indirect constitutional basis. The Constitution does not grant Congress the power to regulate "social welfare." However, Congress may tax and spend for that purpose, which was the basis of the Great Society. Johnson's presidency was marked by dozens of new federal assistance grants to states for programs in health care, public housing, nutrition, public assistance, urban development, education, and other policy areas traditionally reserved to states and localities. Johnson's initiatives were both creative and coercive: creative in the large number of new federal programs and coercive in the restrictions placed on states and localities as a condition of their receipt of federal funds.

A smaller and more recent development is the attempt to "pass down" authority from the national level to the state and local levels in selected areas. Known as *devolution*, this development peaked in the 1990s. Although it has since receded, devolution remains a component of contemporary federalism, as is discussed later in the chapter.

Interdependency and Intergovernmental Relations

Interdependency is a reason national authority has increased substantially. Modern systems of transportation, commerce, and communication transcend local and state boundaries. These systems are national—and even international—in scope, which means that problems affecting Americans living in one part of the country will affect Americans living elsewhere. This situation has required Washington to assume a larger policy role. National problems usually require national solutions.

Interdependency has also encouraged national, state, and local policymakers to work together to solve policy problems. This collaborative effort has been described as **cooperative federalism**.[27] The difference between the older dual federalism and cooperative federalism has been likened to the difference between a layer cake, whose levels are separate and a marble cake, whose levels flow together.[28]

Cooperative federalism is based on shared policy responsibilities rather than sharply divided ones. An example is the Medicaid program, which was created in 1965 as part of President Johnson's Great Society initiative and provides health care for the poor. The Medicaid program is jointly funded by the national and state governments, operates within eligibility standards set by the national government, and gives states some latitude in determining

President Barack Obama and New Jersey governor Chris Christie meet in the aftermath of the Hurricane Sandy disaster that devastated parts of the East Coast in 2012. Federal, state, and local officials worked together in the relief effort. *Cooperative federalism* is a term used to describe such joint efforts.

recipient eligibility and benefits. The Medicaid program is not an isolated example. Literally hundreds of policy programs today are run jointly by the national and state governments. In many cases, local governments are also involved. These programs have the following characteristics:

- Jointly funded by the national and state governments (and sometimes by local governments)
- Jointly administered, with the states and localities providing most of the direct service to recipients and a national agency providing general administration
- Jointly determined, with both the state and national governments (and sometimes the local governments) having a say in eligibility and benefit levels and with federal regulations, such as those prohibiting discrimination, imposing a degree of uniformity on state and local efforts

Cooperative federalism should not be interpreted to mean that the states are powerless and dependent.[29] States have retained most of their traditional authority in areas such as education, health, public safety, and roadways. Nevertheless, the federal government's involvement in policy areas traditionally reserved for the states has increased its policy influence and diminished state-to-state policy differences.

Government Revenues and Intergovernmental Relations

The interdependency of American society—the fact that developments in one area affect what happens elsewhere—is one of three major reasons the federal government's policy role has expanded greatly since the early twentieth century. A second reason is that Americans expect government help. Whenever an area of the country is hit by a natural disaster, for example, its residents seek relief from Washington. Moreover, whenever a federal program, such as student loans or farm supports, has been established, its recipients will fight to keep it. As a consequence, federal programs rarely end while new ones get added each year. A third reason is the federal government's superior taxing capacity. States and localities are in a competitive situation with regard to taxation. A state with high corporate and personal income taxes will lose firms and people to states with lower taxes. On the other hand, firms and people are less likely to move to another country in search of lower taxes. The result is that the federal government raises as much in tax revenue as do all fifty states and the thousands of local governments combined (see Figure 3-2).

Fiscal Federalism   The federal government's revenue-raising advantage has made money a basis for relations between the national government and the states and localities. **Fiscal federalism** refers to the expenditure of federal funds on programs run in part through state and local governments.[30] The federal government provides some or all of the money through **grants-in-aid** (cash payments) to states and localities, which then administer the programs. The pattern of federal assistance to states and localities is shown in

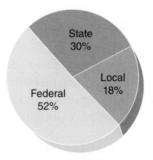

| figure 3-2 | FEDERAL, STATE, AND LOCAL SHARES OF GOVERNMENT TAX REVENUE |

The federal government raises as much tax revenues as do all state and local governments combined. *Source:* U.S. Department of Commerce, 2014.

Figure 3-3. Federal grants-in-aid have increased dramatically since the mid-1950s. Roughly one in every five dollars spent by local and state governments in recent decades has been raised not by them, but by the federal government in Washington (see "How the 50 States Differ").

Cash grants to states and localities increase Washington's policy influence. State and local governments can reject a grant-in-aid, but if they accept it they must spend it in the way specified by Congress. Also, because most grants require states to contribute matching funds, the federal programs in effect determine how states will allocate some of their own tax dollars.

Nevertheless, federal grants-in-aid also serve the policy interests of state and local officials. Although they often complain that federal grants contain too many restrictions and infringe too much on their authority, most of them are eager to have the money because it permits them to

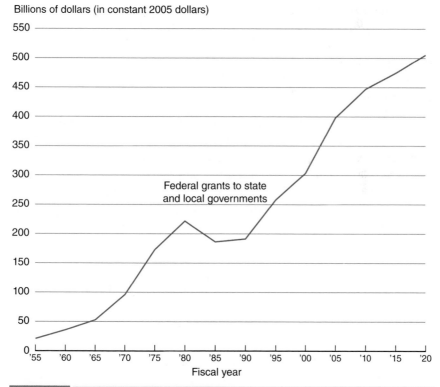

figure 3-3   FEDERAL GRANTS TO STATE AND LOCAL GOVERNMENTS

Federal aid to states and localities has increased dramatically since the 1950s.
Source: Office of Management and Budget (OMB), FY2015. Figures are based on constant (2005) dollars to control for effects of inflation. Figure for each year is the average per year for previous five years. Figure for 2020 is based on OMB estimates.

HOW THE 50 STATES DIFFER
POLITICAL THINKING THROUGH COMPARISONS

Federal Grants-in-Aid to the States

Federal assistance accounts for a significant share of state revenue, but the variation is considerable. New Mexico (with a third of its total revenue coming from federal grants-in-aid) is at one extreme. Nevada (a seventh of its revenue) is at the other.

Q: Why do states in the South, where anti-Washington sentiment is relatively high, get more of their revenue from the federal government than do most other states?

A: Many federal grant programs are designed to assist low-income people, and poverty is more widespread in the South. Moreover, southern states traditionally have provided fewer government services, and federal grants accordingly constitute a larger proportion of their budgets.

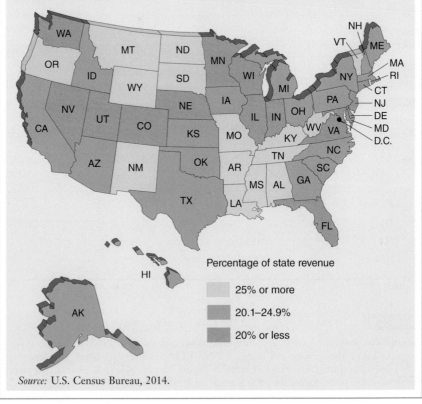

Percentage of state revenue

- 25% or more
- 20.1–24.9%
- 20% or less

Source: U.S. Census Bureau, 2014.

offer services they could not otherwise afford. During the congressional debate in 2009 over a bill that would stimulate the nation's ailing economy, the majority of state governors, Republican and Democratic alike, urged passage of the bill. It contained more than $100 billion to help states cover their widening budget and program deficits. Said one observer: "For governors, it's free money—they get the benefits and they don't have to pay the costs of raising the revenues."[31]

Categorical and Block Grants   State and local governments receive two major types of assistance—categorical grants and block grants—which differ in the degree to which Washington restricts their use. **Categorical grants,** the more restrictive type, can be used only for a designated activity. An example is funds directed for use in school lunch programs. These funds cannot be diverted to other school purposes, such as the purchase of textbooks or the hiring of teachers. **Block grants** are less restrictive. The federal government specifies the general area in which the funds must be used, but state and local officials select the specific projects. A block grant targeted for the education area, for example, might give state and local officials the authority to decide whether to use the money for school construction, computer equipment, teacher training, or some other education-related activity.

State and local officials prefer federal money that comes with fewer strings attached and thus favor block grants. In contrast, members of Congress have typically preferred categorical grants, because it gives them more control over how the money is spent. Most grants are of the categorical type, but block grants have increased in frequency since the 1980s as a result of a movement known as devolution.

Devolution

Devolution embodies the idea that American federalism can be strengthened by a partial shift in power from the federal government to the state and local governments.[32] Devolution rests on a belief—held more strongly by Republicans than Democrats—that federal authority has intruded too far into areas belonging to state and local governments.

The expansion of the federal government's domestic policy role from the 1930s onward was largely initiated by Democratic lawmakers, with strong backing from the public. The New Deal and Great Society programs had broad public support at the outset. After the 1960s, however, public support for federal domestic spending declined. Some of the programs, particularly those providing welfare benefits to the poor, were widely seen as too costly, too bureaucratic, and too lax—there was a widespread perception that many welfare recipients were getting benefits they neither needed nor deserved. Republican leaders increasingly questioned the effectiveness of the programs, a position that meshed with the party's ideology of lower taxes and local control.

Upon taking office in 1981, Republican president Ronald Reagan proposed a "new federalism" that would give more control to states and localities. In issuing an executive order to initiate the change, Reagan said: "Federalism is rooted in the knowledge that our political liberties are best assured by limiting the size and scope of national government." Reagan advocated the use of block grants as opposed to categorical grants and prohibited federal agencies from submitting to Congress legislative proposals that would "regulate the states in ways that would interfere" with their "traditional governmental functions."

The Republican Revolution   When the Republican Party scored a decisive victory in the 1994 congressional elections, Speaker of the House Newt Gingrich declared that "1960s-style federalism is dead." Republican lawmakers proposed to cut some federal programs, but, even more, they sought to devolve power to the state and local levels. The GOP-controlled Congress grouped a number of categorical grants into block grants in order to give states more control over how the federal money would be spent. Congressional Republicans also passed legislation to reduce *unfunded mandates*—federal programs that require action by states or localities but provide no or insufficient funds to pay for it. The Clean Air Act of 1963, for example, required states to comply with national air quality standards but did not provide them the funds necessary to implement their plans.

The most significant change occurred in 1996, when Congress enacted the sweeping Welfare Reform Act. Opinion polls at the time indicated that a majority of Americans felt that government was spending too much on welfare and that too many welfare recipients were abusing the system. The Welfare Reform Act tightened spending and eligibility. The legislation's key element, the Temporary Assistance for Needy Families (TANF) block grant, ended the decades-old federal program that granted cash assistance to poor families with children. TANF restricts a family's eligibility for federal assistance to five years and gives states wide latitude in setting benefit levels. TANF also places states in charge of developing training programs that have the goal of moving people off of welfare and into jobs. (TANF and other aspects of the 1996 welfare reform legislation are discussed further in later chapters.)

This familiar sign illustrates the power of fiscal federalism. Less than four decades ago, persons younger than twenty-one could legally buy alcohol in half the states. The policy changed when Congress enacted legislation requiring states to set the drinking age at twenty-one in order to receive federal highway funds. Although the states complained, the financial stakes were too high for them to maintain their lower age limits.

The Supreme Court's Contribution to Devolution   After ruling in the 1930s that the federal government had broad commerce, taxing, and spending powers, the Supreme Court said that the states should rely on the political process rather than the courts for protection against unwarranted federal encroachment. Reasoning that members of Congress are elected from states and districts within states, the Court said that the states should look to these elected officials for protection from national actions that "unduly burden the states."[33]

The Court's position began to change with the appointment of more conservative justices to the Court by Reagan and his Republican successor, George H. W. Bush. In the view of these justices, Congress had overstepped its constitutional authority in some areas.[34] In *United States v. Lopez* (1995), the Court cited the Tenth Amendment in striking down a federal law that prohibited the possession of guns within one thousand feet of a school. Congress had invoked the commerce power in passing the bill, but the Republican-dominated Supreme

POLITICAL THINKING	More State Power?

Devolution is the idea that federalism would be strengthened by shifting some of the power from the federal government to the state governments. Can you think of a policy area that would work better if state authorities had greater control over it? What's the basis for your thinking?

Court ruled that the ban had "nothing to do with commerce, or any sort of economic activity."[35] It was the first time since the New Deal that the Court had set limits on Congress's power under the Constitution's commerce clause.

The Court has also used the Eleventh Amendment to limit Congress's authority over state governments. The Eleventh Amendment—sometimes called the "sovereign immunity amendment"—protects a state from being sued in federal court by a private citizen, unless the state agrees to the suit. The amendment has limits; it does not protect a state from suit in federal court when the state is alleged to have violated a right guaranteed by the U.S. Constitution, such as the right of the accused to have legal counsel. But the Supreme Court recently has used the Eleventh Amendment to restrict the scope of a few federal laws. In *Kimel v. Board of Regents* (2000), for example, the Supreme Court held that age discrimination, unlike racial and sexual discrimination, is not among the rights guaranteed under the Constitution and that states are not bound by federal law in deciding the age policies that apply to their own employees.[36] (It should be noted that this ruling applies only to *state* government *employees*. Other employees in a state are protected by federal age discrimination laws.)

Nationalization, the More Powerful Force   Despite having some success, proponents of devolution were unable to substantially alter, much less reverse, the long-term shift of power toward the federal government. In fact, the devolution movement slowed dramatically after passage of the 1996 Welfare Reform Act. One of Republican president George W. Bush's first domestic policy initiatives after taking office in 2001 was the No Child Left Behind Act (NCLB), which thrust federal authority more deeply than ever into local and state education policy. Bush argued that the United States needed a *national* education standard in order to meet the challenge of the global economy. NCLB requires the states to test their public school students annually as a condition of receiving federal education aid. A commission of the National Conference of State Legislatures questioned whether Congress had the constitutional authority to compel states to administer standardized tests under threat of losing their federal assistance.

The terrorist attacks of September 11, 2001, also led to an expansion of federal authority, including the creation in 2002 of the Department of Homeland Security. It is a cabinet-level federal agency with policing and emergency responsibilities traditionally belonging to states and localities.

Of recent developments, however, nothing is more indicative of the long-term trend toward federal authority than is the Patient Protection and Affordable Care Act, which was passed by Congress in 2010 and implemented

In the 1990s, some policy responsibilities were shifted from the federal government to the states, a process called *devolution*. This trend stalled after 2000 for several reasons, including the terrorist attacks of September 11, 2001, which required a national response. Part of that response was a larger role for the federal government in the area of public safety. Shown here is a scene familiar to air travelers. The screening of airline passengers is the responsibility of federal officers rather than state or local police.

at the individual level in 2014. Among other things, the act requires Americans to have health insurance or pay a federal tax penalty; requires business firms of a certain size to provide their employees with health insurance or pay a penalty; and requires insurance companies to provide insurance to individuals with preexisting medical conditions. Although the federal government assumed a role in health insurance policy in the 1960s with the enactment of Medicare and Medicaid, the states have traditionally had the authority to regulate health insurance. They were in charge of everything from which insurance companies could operate in the state to the rates they could charge. Today, however, the particulars of health insurance policy are governed by federal law as well as by state law.

The fact is, American federalism is today a vastly different system than what it was before the 1930s. The demands of contemporary life—an economy that is complex and integrated, a public that is insistent on its rights and accustomed to government services, a global environment that is filled with challenges and opportunities—have combined to give the federal government a bigger role in federal-state relations. The change can be seen even in the structure of the federal government. Five cabinet departments—Health and Human Services, Housing and Urban Development, Transportation, Education, and Homeland Security—were created after the 1930s to administer federal programs in policy areas traditionally reserved to the states.

THE PUBLIC'S INFLUENCE: SETTING THE BOUNDARIES OF FEDERAL-STATE POWER

Public opinion has had a decisive influence on the ebb and flow of federal power during the past century. As Americans' attitudes toward the federal government and the states changed, the balance of power between these two levels of government also shifted. Every major change in federalism has been driven by a major shift in public support toward one level of government or the other.

During the Great Depression, when it was clear that the states would be unable to help, Americans turned to Washington for relief. For people without jobs, the fine points of the Constitution were of little consequence. President Roosevelt's New Deal programs, which offered both jobs and income security, were a radical departure from the past, but quickly gained public favor. A 1936 Gallup poll indicated, for example, that 61 percent of Americans supported Roosevelt's social security program, whereas only 27 percent opposed it.[37] The second great wave of federal social programs—Lyndon Johnson's Great Society—was also driven by public demands. Income and education levels had risen dramatically after the Second World War, and Americans wanted more and better services from government.[38] When the states were slow to respond, Americans pressured federal officials to act. The Medicare and Medicaid programs, which provide health care for the elderly and the poor, respectively, are examples of the Johnson administration's response. A 1965 Gallup poll indicated that two-thirds of Americans approved of federal involvement in the provision of medical care, despite the fact that health was traditionally the states' responsibility.

Public opinion was also behind the rollback of federal authority in the 1990s. Polls showed that a majority of Americans had come to believe that the federal government had become too large and intrusive. Americans' dissatisfaction with federal programs and spending provided the springboard for the Republican takeover of Congress in the 1994 midterm election, which led to policies aimed at devolving power to the states, including the widely popular 1996 Welfare Reform Act.[39]

The public's role in determining the boundaries between federal and state power would come as no surprise to the framers of the Constitution. For them, federalism was a pragmatic issue, one to be decided by the nation's needs rather than by inflexible rules. Alexander Hamilton suggested that Americans would shift their loyalties between the nation and the states according to whichever level seemed more likely to serve their immediate needs. James Madison said much the same thing in predicting that Americans would look to whichever level of government was more responsive to their interests. Indeed, each succeeding generation of Americans has seen fit to devise a balance of federal and state power suited to its needs.

SUMMARY

A foremost characteristic of the American political system is its division of authority between a national government and state governments. The first U.S. government, established by the Articles of Confederation, was essentially a union of the states.

In establishing the basis for a stronger national government, the U.S. Constitution also made provision for safeguarding state interests. The result was the creation of a federal system in which sovereignty was vested in both national and state governments. The Constitution enumerates the general powers of the national government and grants it implied powers through the "necessary and proper" clause. Other powers are reserved to the states by the Tenth Amendment.

From 1789 to 1865, the nation's survival was at issue. The states found it convenient at times to argue that their sovereignty took precedence over national authority. In the end, it took the Civil War to cement the idea that the United

States was a union of people, not of states. From 1865 to 1937, federalism reflected the doctrine that certain policy areas were the exclusive responsibility of the national government, whereas responsibility in other policy areas belonged exclusively to the states. This constitutional position validated the laissez-faire doctrine that big business was largely beyond governmental control. It also allowed the states to discriminate against African Americans in their public policies. Federalism in a form recognizable today began to emerge in the 1930s.

In the areas of commerce, taxation, spending, civil rights, and civil liberties, among others, the federal government now plays an important role, one that is the inevitable consequence of the increasing complexity of American society and the interdependence of its people. National, state, and local officials now work closely together to solve the nation's problems, a situation known as cooperative federalism. Grants-in-aid from Washington to the states and localities have been the chief instrument of national influence. States and localities have received billions in federal assistance; in accepting federal money, they also have accepted both federal restrictions on its use and the national policy priorities that underlie the granting of the money.

Throughout the nation's history, the public through its demands on government has influenced the boundaries between federal and state power. The expansions of federal authority in the 1930s and the 1960s, for example, were driven by Americans' increased need for government assistance, whereas the devolutionary trend of the 1990s was sparked by Americans' sense that a rollback in federal power was desirable.

CRITICAL THINKING ZONE

KEY TERMS

block grants (*p. 91*)
categorical grants (*p. 91*)
commerce clause (*p. 82*)
confederacy (*p. 70*)
cooperative federalism (*p. 86*)
devolution (*p. 91*)
dual federalism (*p. 80*)
enumerated (expressed)
  powers (*p. 73*)
federalism (*p. 69*)

fiscal federalism (*p. 88*)
grants-in-aid (*p. 88*)
implied powers (*p. 75*)
nationalization (*p. 76*)
"necessary and proper" (elastic)
  clause (*p. 75*)
reserved powers (*p. 76*)
sovereignty (*p. 69*)
supremacy clause (*p. 75*)
unitary system (*p. 70*)

APPLYING THE ELEMENTS OF CRITICAL THINKING

Conceptualizing: Distinguish between a federal system, a unitary system, and a confederacy. What circumstances led the framers of the Constitution to create a federal system?

Synthesizing: Contrast dual federalism and cooperative federalism. Is the distinction between a layer cake and a marble cake useful in explaining the difference between dual federalism and cooperative federalism?

Analyzing: How have the federal government's superior taxing policy and the interdependency of the American states and people contributed over time to a larger policy role for the national government? What role have federal grants-in-aid played in the expansion of federal authority?

EXTRA CREDIT

A Book Worth Reading: Samuel H. Beer, *To Make a Nation: The Rediscovery of American Federalism.* Cambridge, MA: Belknap Press of Harvard University Press, 1993. Written by a distinguished political scientist who served as president of the American Political Science Association, this insightful book explores the nature of American federalism, arguing that it was intended to create a union of the American people rather than a compact between the states.

A Website Worth Visiting: **http://avalon.law.yale.edu/subject_menus/fed.asp**. A Yale Law School site that includes a documentary record of the *Federalist Papers*, the Annapolis convention, the Articles of Confederation, the Madison debates, and the U.S. Constitution.

PARTICIPATE!

The U.S. federal system of government offers an array of channels for political participation. Vital governing decisions are made at the national, state, and local levels, all of which provide opportunities for citizens to make a difference and also to build skills—such as public speaking and working with others—that will prove valuable in other areas of life. You have a participatory arena close at hand: your college campus. Most colleges and universities support a variety of activities in which students can engage. Student government is one such opportunity; another is the student newspaper. Most colleges and universities offer a wide range of groups and sponsored programs, from debate clubs to fraternal organizations. If you are not now active in campus groups, consider joining one. If you join—or if you already belong to—such a group, take full advantage of the participatory opportunities it provides.

CIVIL LIBERTIES: PROTECTING INDIVIDUAL RIGHTS

0101010010110100101101001011010101000101010000101010100011101001 0010101010100101101010100001010101010010110101010000101010101001 101010010110100101101001011 01010100001010101000111010010 0101010101001011010101 011010101010000101010101001 01010001011010010110101 010101110101000101010100011101001 0101001011010010110101 010101000101010101 101010100001010101010000101010100011101001 1010101010010110101010101010101000101010101 0101010100001010101010 10100101101001011010 01011 WE'RE 0010101010101010100011101001 0101010100101110110 WATCHING 010101010000101010101010 0100101101001011011010100YOU1011010101010101000111010010 1010101001011010110100001010101110101010000101010101010 1001011010010110101010101001010100010101010100011101001 0101010010110101010101010101010 0101010100001010101010 00101101001011010010110101101010101010101010001110100 01010100101101010100001010101010010110100001010101 01011010010110100101101010101000101010000101010001110100 10101001011010101000010101010100101110101 0101010101 10110100101101001011010101010001010100001010 010111010 0101001011010101000010101010100101101010101010101 101001011010010110101010000101010101010001011010101 010 101001011010010110101010000101010101010001010101 010 10100101101010100001010101010010110101010000101010 010101010000101010101010010110101010000101010100011101

Without a warrant from a judge, the police and FBI had secretly attached a GPS tracking device to Antoine Jones's car and knew exactly where it was at any time of the day or night. For a month, they monitored the car's every turn. They subsequently arrested Jones on charges of conspiracy to sell drugs. The evidence obtained through the tracking device helped prosecutors to convict him, and he was sentenced to life in prison.

Jones appealed his conviction and won a temporary victory when a federal appellate court—noting that individuals are protected by the Fourth

Amendment from "unreasonable searches and seizures"—concluded that the officers should have sought a warrant from a judge, who would have decided whether they had sufficient cause to justify a search of Jones's possessions, much less the placing of a tracking device on his car.

In a unanimous 9-0 vote, the Supreme Court in *United States v. Jones* (2012) upheld the lower-court's ruling. The Court rejected the government's argument that attaching a small device to a car's undercarriage was too trivial an act to constitute an "unreasonable search." The government had also claimed that anyone driving a car on public streets can expect to be monitored, even continuously in some circumstances—after all, police had legally been "tailing" suspects for decades. The Court rejected those arguments, though the justices disagreed on exactly why the Constitution prohibits what the officers had done. Five justices said that the Fourth Amendment's protection of "persons, houses, papers, and effects" reasonably extends to private property such as an automobile. For them, the fact that the officers had placed a tracking device on the suspect's property without a warrant invalidated the evidence. Four justices went further, saying that the officers' actions intruded not only on the suspect's property rights but also on his "reasonable expectation of privacy." At its core, they said, the Fourth Amendment "protects people, not places."[2]

As the case illustrates, issues of individual rights have become increasingly complex. The framers of the Constitution could not possibly have envisioned a time when technology would have enabled authorities to electronically track people's locations. The framers understood that authorities would sometimes be tempted to snoop on people, which is why they wrote the Fourth Amendment. At the same time, the amendment protects Americans not from *all* searches but from *unreasonable* searches. The public would be unsafe if law officials could never track a suspect. Yet citizens would forfeit their privacy if police could track at will anyone they choose. The challenge for a civil society is to establish a level of police authority that meets the demands of public safety without infringing unduly on personal freedom. The balance point, however, is always subject to dispute. In this particular case, the Supreme Court sided with the accused. In other cases, it has sided with law enforcement officials.

This chapter examines issues of **civil liberties**—specific individual rights, such as the right to a fair trial, that are constitutionally protected against infringement by government. Although the term *civil liberties* is sometimes used synonymously with the term *civil rights*, they can be distinguished. Civil rights (which will be examined in Chapter 5) are a question of whether members of differing groups—racial, sexual, religious, and the like—are treated equally by government and, in some cases, by private parties. On the other hand, civil liberties refer to individual rights, such as freedom of speech and the press. They are the subject of this chapter, which focuses on these points:

- *Freedom of expression is the most basic of democratic rights, but like all rights, it is not unlimited.*
- *"Due process of law" refers to legal protections (primarily procedural safeguards) designed to ensure that individual rights are respected by government.*
- *Over the course of the nation's history, Americans' civil liberties have been expanded in law and more fully protected by the courts.* Of special significance has been the Supreme Court's use of the Fourteenth Amendment to protect individual rights from action by state and local governments.
- *Individual rights are constantly being weighed against the demands of majorities and the collective needs of society.* All political institutions are involved in this process, as is public opinion, but the judiciary plays a central role and is the institution that is typically most protective of civil liberties.

THE BILL OF RIGHTS, THE FOURTEENTH AMENDMENT, AND SELECTIVE INCORPORATION

As was explained in Chapter 2, the Constitution's failure to enumerate individual freedoms led to demands for the **Bill of Rights**. Ratified in 1791, these first ten amendments to the Constitution list a set of rights that the federal government is obliged to protect. Among them are freedoms of speech, press, assembly, and religion (First Amendment); the right to bear arms (Second Amendment); protection against unreasonable search and seizure (Fourth Amendment); protection against self-incrimination and double jeopardy (Fifth Amendment); right to a jury trial, to an attorney, and to confront witnesses (Sixth Amendment); and protection against cruel and unusual punishment (Eighth Amendment).

At the time the Bill of Rights was adopted, it applied only to action by the federal government and not also to action by the states, a position that the Supreme Court affirmed a few decades later.[3] Today, however, most of the rights contained in the Bill of Rights are also protected from action by the state governments, a development that owes to adoption of the Fourteenth Amendment in the aftermath of the Civil War.

Americans' civil liberties include protection against unreasonable search and seizure, which is intended to make individuals secure in their persons and their homes. Police cannot lawfully intrude without evidence suggesting an individual is involved in criminal activity. Even then, police may have to obtain a search warrant, which requires them to convince a judge that their evidence is solid and not based on speculation or a dislike of the suspect.

Soon after the war, several southern states enacted laws denying newly freed slaves their rights, including the rights to own property and to travel freely. Congress responded by proposing a constitutional amendment designed to protect their rights. The former Confederate states with the exception of Tennessee refused to ratify it. Congress then passed the Reconstruction Act, which placed the southern states under military rule until they did so. In 1868, the Fourteenth Amendment was ratified. It includes a **due process clause** that says "No State shall . . . deprive any person of life, liberty, or property, without due process of law."

Initially the Supreme Court largely ignored the due process clause, allowing states to decide for themselves what rights their residents would have. In 1925, however, the Court changed course by invoking the Fourteenth Amendment in a case involving state government. Although the Court upheld New York's law making it illegal to advocate the violent overthrow of the U.S. government, it ruled in *Gitlow v. New York* that states do not have complete power over what their residents can legally say. The Court said: "For present purposes we may and do assume that freedom of speech and of the press—which are protected by the First Amendment from abridgement by Congress—are among the fundamental personal rights and 'liberties' protected by the due process clause of the Fourteenth Amendment from impairment by the states."[4]

The ruling marked a fundamental shift in constitutional doctrine. In essence, the Court had concluded that a right protected by the Bill of Rights from action by the federal government was now also protected from action by individual states. Shortly thereafter, the Court in a series of cases applied the new principle to other First Amendment rights. The Court invalidated state laws restricting expression in the areas of speech (*Fiske v. Kansas*), press (*Near v. Minnesota*), religion (*Hamilton v. Regents, University of California*), and assembly and petition (*DeJonge v. Oregon*).[5] The *Near* decision is the best known of these rulings. Jay Near was the publisher of a Minneapolis weekly newspaper that regularly made defamatory statements about blacks, Jews, Catholics, and labor union leaders. His paper was closed down on the basis of a Minnesota law banning "malicious, scandalous, or defamatory" publications. Near appealed the shutdown on the grounds that it infringed on freedom of the press, and the Supreme Court ruled in his favor, saying that the Minnesota law was "the essence of censorship."[6]

Three decades later, the Supreme Court extended the principle to include the rights of the criminally accused. The breakthrough case was *Mapp v. Ohio* (1961). Police had forcibly entered the home of Dollree Mapp, saying they had a tip she was harboring a fugitive. They found no one but handcuffed her anyway and began rummaging through her possessions, where they found obscene photographs. Mapp was convicted of violating an Ohio law that prohibited the possession of such material. The Supreme Court overturned her conviction, ruling that police had acted unconstitutionally, citing the Fourth Amendment prohibition on unreasonable searches and seizures. The Court concluded that evidence acquired through an unconstitutional search cannot be used to obtain a conviction in state courts.[7]

During the 1960s, the Court also ruled that defendants in state criminal proceedings must be provided a lawyer in felony cases if they cannot afford to hire one,[8] cannot be compelled to testify against themselves,[9] have the right to remain silent and to have legal counsel at the time of arrest,[10] have the right to confront witnesses who testify against them,[11] must be granted a speedy trial,[12] have the right to a jury trial in criminal proceedings,[13] and cannot be subjected to double jeopardy.[14]

In these various rulings, the Court was applying what came to be called the doctrine of **selective incorporation**—the use of the Fourteenth Amendment to apply selected provisions of the Bill of Rights to the

HOW THE U.S. DIFFERS

POLITICAL THINKING THROUGH COMPARISONS

Civil Liberties

Individual rights are a cornerstone of the American governing system and receive strong protection from the courts. The government's ability to restrict free expression is limited, and the individual's right to a fair trial is protected by significant due process guarantees, such as the right to legal counsel. According to Freedom House, an independent organization that tracks civil liberties, the United States ranks among the "most free" nations for its protection of civil liberties. Many countries rank lower as a result of, for example, their mistreatment of political opponents. In determining its civil liberties rankings, Freedom House evaluates countries for their policies in four areas: freedom of expression, associational and organizational rights, rule of law, and personal autonomy and individual rights.

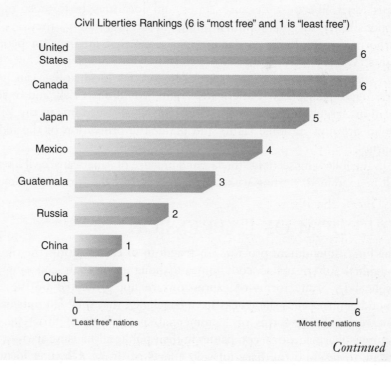

Civil Liberties Rankings (6 is "most free" and 1 is "least free")

- United States: 6
- Canada: 6
- Japan: 5
- Mexico: 4
- Guatemala: 3
- Russia: 2
- China: 1
- Cuba: 1

0 "Least free" nations — 6 "Most free" nations

Continued

The accompanying chart shows how the United States compares with selected other countries on the Freedom House index.

Q: What do the "least free" countries on the chart have in common?

A: The "least free" countries in the chart are characterized by one-party rule.

states. In its *Gitlow* ruling, for example, the Court selectively incorporated the First Amendment protections of free speech and press into the Fourteenth Amendment, thereby protecting them from infringement by states and localities. (The incorporation process is called selective because the Supreme Court has chosen to protect some Bill of Rights guarantees from state action but not others. Even today, for example, the Seventh Amendment right to a jury trial in civil cases is not binding on the states.)

Selective incorporation through the Fourteenth Amendment's due process clause has been of utmost importance in the protection of Americans' civil liberties. Because states and localities bear most of the responsibility for maintaining public order and safety, they are the authorities most likely to engage in actions that infringe on people's rights. If they were allowed to determine for themselves what these rights mean in practice—for example, how far local police can go in interrogating suspects—Americans' rights would be at risk, and in some locations largely ignored. As it stands, nearly all freedoms in the Bill of Rights are now national rights and under the protection of the federal courts.

In the following sections, the law and practice of Americans' civil liberties will be examined, starting with rights protected by the First Amendment.

FREEDOM OF EXPRESSION

The First Amendment provides for **freedom of expression**—the right of individual Americans to communicate thoughts of their choosing (see Table 4-1). Some forms of expression are not protected by the First Amendment because the courts have concluded that they fall outside the civic realm. Some forms of "commercial speech" are of this type. For example, pharmaceutical companies in their public advertising are required by law to disclose the harmful side effects of drugs. Obscene forms of

table 4-1	BILL OF RIGHTS: A SELECTED LIST OF FIRST AMENDMENT PROTECTIONS

First Amendment

Speech: You are free to say almost anything except that which is obscene, slanders another person, or has a high probability of inciting others to take imminent lawless action.

Press: You are free to write or publish almost anything except that which is obscene, libels another person, seriously endangers military action or national security, or has a high probability of inciting others to take imminent lawless action.

Assembly: You are free to assemble, although government may regulate the time and place for reasons of public convenience and safety, provided such regulations are applied evenhandedly to all groups.

Religion: You are protected from having the religious beliefs of others imposed on you, and you are free to believe what you like.

sexual expression—child pornography as an example—also do not have First Amendment protection.*

The First Amendment had an inauspicious beginning. Although the amendment prohibits Congress from abridging freedom of expression, Congress ignored the restriction in passing the Sedition Act of 1798, which made it a crime to print harshly critical newspaper stories about the president or other national officials. Thomas Jefferson called the Sedition Act an "alarming infraction" of the Constitution and, upon replacing John Adams as president in 1801, pardoned those who had been convicted under it. However, the Sedition Act was not ruled upon by the Supreme Court, which left open the question of whether Congress had the power to regulate free expression and, if so, how far its power extended.

Today, free expression is vigorously protected by the courts. Like other rights, it is not absolute in practice. Free expression does not entitle individuals to say whatever they want to whomever they want. Free expression can be denied, for example, if it endangers national security, wrongly damages the reputation of others, or deprives others of their basic rights. Nevertheless, in nearly every circumstance Americans can freely express their political views without fear of government interference or retribution.

---

*Although the Supreme Court has categorically excluded child pornography from First Amendment protection, it has struggled otherwise to develop a legal test for determining whether sexual material is obscene. It has said that such material must be of a "particularly offensive type" and must be perceived as such by a "reasonable person," but in practice the Court has had trouble applying that standard, or any other, in determining the sexually explicit material that adults are not allowed to produce, see, or possess.

Free Speech

Until the twentieth century, free expression was rarely at issue in the United States. However, as the country began to get enmeshed in world affairs and face threats from abroad, the government started to place restrictions on expression that it believed was a danger to national security. A first restriction was the 1917 Espionage Act, which prohibited forms of dissent that could have harmed the nation's effort in World War I.

The legislation became the object of the first-ever Supreme Court free-expression decision. In *Schenck v. United States* (1919), the Supreme Court sustained the conviction of defendants who had distributed leaflets urging draft-age men to refuse induction into the military service. Writing for a unanimous Court, Justice Oliver Wendell Holmes upheld the constitutionality of the Espionage Act, saying that Congress had the authority to restrict expression that posed "a clear and present danger" to the nation's security. In a famous passage, Holmes argued that not even the First Amendment would permit a person to falsely yell "Fire!" in a crowded theater and create a panic that could kill or injure innocent people.[15]

Although the *Schenck* decision upheld a law that limited free expression, it also established a constitutional standard—the **clear-and-present-danger test**—for determining when government could legally do so. To meet the test, the government has to clearly demonstrate that spoken or written expression presents a clear and present danger before it can prohibit the expression. (The use of a "test" to judge the limits of government's authority is a common practice of the Supreme Court.)

In the early 1950s, the Court applied the clear-and-present-danger test in upholding the convictions of eleven members of the U.S. Communist Party who had been prosecuted under a federal law (the Smith Act of 1940) that made it illegal to advocate the forceful overthrow of the U.S. government.[16] The Court concluded that "the gravity of the 'evil' . . . justifies such invasion of free speech as necessary to avoid the danger."

By the late 1950s, fear of internal communist subversion was subsiding, and the Supreme Court changed its position.[17] Ever since, it has held that national security must be truly endangered before government can lawfully prohibit citizens from speaking out. Because the spoken word does not pose that kind of threat, Americans are free to say what's on their minds when it comes to politics. Over the past six decades, which includes the Vietnam and Iraq wars, not a single individual has been convicted solely for criticizing the government's war policies. (Some dissenters have been found guilty on other grounds, such as inciting a riot or assaulting a police officer.)

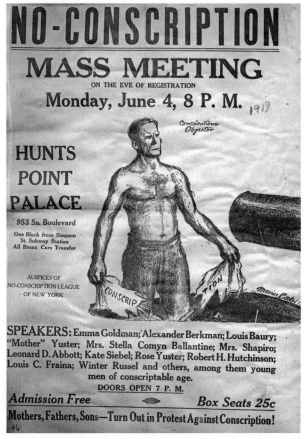

The 1917 Espionage Act made it a crime to distribute antiwar leaflets that could harm the nation's efforts in World War I. The Supreme Court upheld the law but used it as the basis for establishing a constitutional test—the clear-and-present-danger test—for judging how far the government can lawfully go in restricting free expression.

In addition to curbing the federal government's attempts to limit free speech, the Supreme Court has moved to protect speech from actions by the states. A defining case in this respect is *Brandenburg v. Ohio* (1969). In a speech at a Ku Klux Klan rally, Clarence Brandenburg said that "revenge" might have to be taken if the national government "continues to suppress the white Caucasian race." He was convicted under an Ohio law, but the Supreme Court overturned the conviction, saying a state cannot prohibit speech that advocates the unlawful use of force unless it meets a two-part test: first, the speech must be "directed at inciting or producing imminent lawless action" and, second, it must be "likely to produce such action."[18] This test—the likelihood of

imminent lawless action—is an imposing barrier to any government attempt to restrict speech. It is extremely rare for words alone to lead others to engage in rioting or other forms of lawless action.

The imminent lawless action test effectively gives Americans the freedom to voice nearly any political opinion they desire, including "hate speech." In a unanimous 1992 opinion, the Court struck down a St. Paul, Minnesota, ordinance making it a crime to engage in speech likely to arouse "anger or alarm" on the basis of "race, color, creed, religion or gender." The Court said that the First Amendment prohibits government from "silencing speech on the basis of its content."[19] (This protection of hate *speech* does not, however, extend to hate *crimes*, such as assault, motivated by racial or other prejudice. A Wisconsin law that provided for increased sentences for hate crimes was challenged as a violation of the First Amendment. In a unanimous 1993 opinion, the Court said that the law was aimed, not at free speech, but at "conduct unprotected by the First Amendment.")[20]

Few cases illustrate more clearly the extent to which Americans are free to speak their minds than does *Snyder v. Phelps* (2011). Pastor Fred Phelps of the Westboro Baptist Church (WBC) led a protest demonstration at the funeral of Matthew Snyder, a U.S. Marine killed in Iraq. Like their protests at other military funerals, WBC's protest at Snyder's funeral service was directed at what WBC claims is America's tolerance of gays and lesbians. Displaying signs such as "Fag troops" and "Thank God for dead soldiers," the protestors were otherwise orderly, holding down their voices and staying three blocks away from the memorial service. Snyder's father sued WBC for "emotional distress" and was awarded $5 million in a federal jury trial. In an 8-1 decision, the Supreme Court overturned the award, concluding that the WBC's protest, although "hurtful," was protected by the First Amendment."[21]

The priority of free speech is also evident in another recent unanimous Supreme Court decision, *McCullen v. Coakley* (2014), in which the Court invalidated a Massachusetts law that prohibited anti-abortion advocates from protesting within thirty-five feet of an abortion clinic. The Court concluded that the ban infringed on protesters' free-speech rights and that states have other laws to punish protestors who go beyond their free-speech rights to assault clinic patients or employees.[22]

The Supreme Court's protection of **symbolic speech** (action, not words) has been nearly as substantial as its protection of verbal speech. In 1989, for example, the Court ruled that the symbolic burning of the American flag is a lawful form of expression. The ruling came in the case of Gregory Lee Johnson, who had set fire to a flag outside the hall in

Members of the Westboro Baptist Church picket the funeral of an American killed in the Middle East. Despite the horrific nature of their signs and slogans, which they have displayed at numerous military funerals, the Supreme Court has ruled that their actions are protected by the First Amendment.

Dallas where the 1984 Republican National Convention was being held. The Supreme Court rejected the state of Texas's argument that flag burning is, in every instance, an imminent danger to public safety. "If there is a bedrock principle underlying the First Amendment," the Court ruled in the *Johnson* case, "it is that the Government may not prohibit the expression of an idea simply because society finds the idea itself offensive or disagreeable."[23]

In general, the Supreme Court has held that government regulation of the *content* of a message is unconstitutional. In the flag-burning case, for

---

POLITICAL THINKING

Should Flag Burning Be a Crime?

Flag burning as a form of political protest has been an issue ever since the Supreme Court in 1989 held that it is a form of expression protected by the First Amendment. Since then, Congress has tried unsuccessfully to initiate a constitutional amendment that would make it a crime to burn the American flag as a form of protest. Would you support such an amendment? Or do you believe that the First Amendment's guarantee of free expression takes priority?

example, Texas was regulating the content of the message—contempt for the flag and the principles it represents. Texas could not have been regulating the act itself, for the Texas government's own method of disposing of worn-out flags is to burn them.

Free Assembly

In a key case involving freedom of assembly, the U.S. Supreme Court in 1977 upheld a lower-court ruling against local ordinances of Skokie, Illinois, that had been invoked to prevent a parade there by the American Nazi Party.[24] Skokie had a large Jewish population, including survivors of Nazi Germany's concentration camps. The Supreme Court held that the right of free assembly takes precedence over the mere *possibility* that the exercise of that right might have undesirable consequences. Before government can lawfully prevent a speech or rally, it must demonstrate that the event will likely cause harm and also must demonstrate that it lacks an alternative way (such as assigning police officers to control the crowd) to prevent the harm from happening.

The Supreme Court has recognized that freedoms of speech and assembly may conflict with the routines of daily life. Accordingly, individuals do not have the right to hold a public rally at a busy intersection during rush hour, nor do they have the right to immediate access to a public auditorium or the right to turn up the volume on loudspeakers to the point where they can be heard miles away. The Court allows public officials to regulate the time, place, and conditions of public assembly, provided the regulations are reasonable and are applied fairly to all groups, whatever their issue.[25]

Press Freedom and Libel Law

Freedom of the press also receives strong judicial protection. In *New York Times Co. v. United States* (1971), the Court ruled that the *Times*'s publication of the "Pentagon Papers" (secret government documents revealing that officials had deceived the public about aspects of the Vietnam War) could not be blocked by the government, which claimed that publication would harm the war effort. The documents had been obtained illegally by antiwar activists, who then gave them to the *Times*. The Court ruled that "any system of prior restraints" on the press is unconstitutional unless the government can provide a compelling argument for the restriction.[26]

The unacceptability of **prior restraint**—government prohibition of speech or publication before it occurs—is basic to the current doctrine of free expression. The Supreme Court has said that attempts by government to prevent expression carries "a 'heavy presumption' against its constitutionality."[27] News organizations are legally responsible after the fact for what they report (for example, they can be sued by an individual whose reputation is wrongly damaged by their words), but government ordinarily cannot prevent a news organization from reporting what it wants. One exception is wartime reporting; in some circumstances, the government can censor news reports that contain information that might compromise a military operation or risk the lives of American troops.

The constitutional right of free expression is not a legal license to avoid responsibility for the consequences of what is said or written. If false information harmful to a person's reputation is published (**libel**) or spoken (**slander**), the injured party can sue for damages. Nevertheless, slander and libel laws in the United States are based on the assumption that society has an interest in encouraging news organizations and citizens to express themselves freely. Accordingly, public officials can be criticized nearly at will without fear that the writer or speaker will have to pay them damages for slander or libel. (The courts are less protective of the writer or speaker when allegations are made about a private citizen. What is said about private individuals is considered to be less basic to the democratic process than what is said about public officials.)

The Supreme Court has held that factually accurate statements, no matter how damaging they might be to a public official's career or reputation, are a protected form of expression.[28] Even false statements enjoy considerable legal protection. In *New York Times Co. v. Sullivan* (1964), the Supreme Court overruled an Alabama state court that had found the *New York Times* guilty of libel for publishing an advertisement that claimed Alabama officials had mistreated student civil rights activists. Although only some of the allegations were true, the Supreme Court backed the *Times*, saying that libel of a public official requires proof of actual malice, which was defined as a knowing or reckless disregard for the truth.[29] It is very difficult to prove that a news outlet recklessly or deliberately published a false accusation. In fact, no federal official has won a libel judgment against a news organization in the five decades since the *Sullivan* ruling.

FREEDOM OF RELIGION

Free religious expression is the forerunner of free political expression, at least within the English tradition of limited government. England's Glorious, or Bloodless, Revolution of 1689 resulted in the Act of Toleration, which gave members of Protestant sects the right to worship freely and publicly. The First Amendment reflects this tradition; it protects religious freedom, as well as political expression.

In regard to religion, the First Amendment reads: "Congress shall make no law respecting an establishment of religion, or prohibiting the free exercise thereof." It will be noted that this statement contains two clauses, one referring to the "establishment of religion" (the establishment clause) and one referring to the "free exercise" of religion (the free-exercise clause). Each clause has been the subject of Supreme Court rulings.

The Establishment Clause

The **establishment clause** has been interpreted by the courts to mean that government may not favor one religion over another or support religion over no religion. (This position contrasts with that of a country such as England, where Anglicanism is the official, or "established," state religion, though no religion is prohibited.)

To this end, the Court has largely prohibited religious teachings and observances in public schools. A leading case was *Engel v. Vitale* (1962), which held that the establishment clause prohibits the reciting of prayers in public schools.[30] A year later, the Court struck down Bible readings in public schools.[31] Efforts to bring religion into the schools in less direct ways have also been invalidated. For example, an Alabama law attempted to circumvent the prayer ruling by permitting public schools to set aside one minute each day for silent prayer or meditation. In 1985, the Court declared the law unconstitutional, ruling that "government must pursue a course of complete neutrality toward religion."[32]

Because children are impressionable, the Supreme Court has sought to keep religious messages out of public schools, but has been less strict about other venues. Congress and state legislatures, for example, open their sessions with a prayer, which the Court accepts as long-standing traditions. The Court reaffirmed that rule in 2014, upholding a New York town's practice of opening its town board meetings with a prayer. The Court said such prayer is permissible as long as it does not discriminate against minority religions and does not require those at the meeting to join in the prayer.[33]

The Court also takes tradition into account in determining whether religious displays on public property are permissable. Because of the prominence of religion in American life, many public buildings display religious symbols. For instance, a statue of Moses holding the Ten

Commandments stands in the rotunda of the Library of Congress build-ing, which opened in 1897. Legal challenges to such displays have rarely succeeded.[34] In contrast, the Supreme Court in 2005 ordered the removal of displays of the Ten Commandments on the walls of two Kentucky courthouses. The displays were recent and had initially hung alone on the courtroom walls. Only after county officials were sued did they place a few historical displays alongside the religious ones. The Supreme Court concluded that the officials had religious purposes in mind when they erected the displays and had to remove them.[35]

Although the Court can be said to have applied the *wall of separation doctrine* (a strict separation of church and state) in these rulings, it has also relied upon what is called the *accommodation doctrine*. This doctrine allows government to aid religious activity if no preference is shown toward a particular religion and if the assistance is of a nonreligious nature. In applying the doctrine, the Court at times has used a test articulated in *Lemon v. Kurtzman* (1971), a case involving state funding of the salaries of religious school instructors who teach secular subjects, such as math and English. In its ruling, the Court articulated a three-point test that has come to be known as the **Lemon test.** Government policy must meet all three conditions for it to be lawful: first, the policy must have a non-religious purpose; second, its principal or primary effect must be one that neither advances nor inhibits religion; finally, the policy must not foster "an excessive government entanglement with religion."[36]

In the *Lemon* case, the Court held that state funding of the salaries of religious school teachers failed the test. The Court concluded that such

The First Amendment's protection of free expression includes religious freedom, which has led the courts to hold that government cannot in most instances promote or interfere with religious practices.

payments involve "excessive government entanglement with religion" because an instructor, even though teaching a subject such as math or science, could use the classroom as an opportunity to engage in religious teaching. In contrast, the Court in another case allowed states to pay for math, science, and other secular textbooks used in church-affiliated schools, concluding that the textbooks had little if any religious content in them.[37]

The Supreme Court's most significant departure from its wall-of-separation doctrine came in a 2002 decision (*Zelman v. Simmons-Harris*), which upheld an Ohio law that allows students in Cleveland's failing public schools to receive a tax-supported voucher to attend a private or religious school. Even though 90 percent of the vouchers were being used to attend religious schools, the Court's majority concluded that the program did not violate the establishment clause because students had a choice between secular and religious education. Four members of the Court voted against the ruling. Justice John Paul Stevens said the ruling went beyond accommodation and had in effect removed a "brick from the wall that was once designed to separate religion from government."[38]

The Free-Exercise Clause

The First and Fourteenth Amendments also prohibit government interference with the free exercise of religion. The **free-exercise clause** has been interpreted to mean that Americans are free to hold any religious belief of their choosing. Americans are not always free, however, to act on their belief. The Supreme Court has allowed government interference when the exercise of religious belief conflicts with otherwise valid law. An example is court-ordered medical care for children with life-threatening illnesses whose parents have denied them treatment on religious grounds.

In a potentially far-reaching free-exercise decision (*Burwell v. Hobby Lobby Stores*), the Supreme Court in 2014 held that "closely held" companies (those with only a few owners) are not required, if the owners object on religious grounds, to include contraceptives in their employees' health insurance coverage. The case stemmed from the 2010 health care reform act, which requires companies that provide employee health insurance to include contraceptives. The Court's majority said the requirement violates the owners' free-exercise rights if the use of contraceptives contradicts their religious beliefs. In a strongly worded dissent, Justice Ruth Bader Ginsburg criticized the majority's opinion as a radical rewriting of

POLITICAL THINKING	Establishment or Free Exercise?

The Supreme Court ruled in 1987 that creationism (the biblical account of how the world was created) cannot be taught in public school science courses. The Court held that creationism is a religious doctrine rather than a scientific theory and that teaching it as an alternative to evolutionary theory is a violation of the First Amendment's establishment clause. Opponents of the ruling claim that it violates the First Amendment's free-exercise clause because some students are forced to study a version of creation—the theory of evolution—that conflicts with their religious beliefs. How would you have ruled in this case? What argument would you make to support your position?

corporation rights, saying it opened the door for business firms to challenge numerous other laws on religious grounds.[39]

In some instances, the free exercise of religion clashes with the prohibition on the establishment of religion, and the Supreme Court is forced to choose between them. In 1987, for example, the Court overturned a Louisiana law that required creationism (the Bible's account of how God created the world in seven days) to be taught along with the theory of evolution in public school science courses. The Court concluded that creationism is a religious doctrine, not a scientific theory, and that its inclusion in public school curricula violates the establishment clause by promoting a religious belief.[40] To some, this ruling constituted a violation of the free-exercise clause because it forces students who believe in creationism to study a version of creation—evolution—that conflicts with their religious beliefs.

THE RIGHT TO BEAR ARMS

The Second Amendment to the Constitution says: "A well regulated Militia, being necessary to the security of a free State, the right of the people to keep and bear Arms shall not be infringed." The amendment is widely understood to prevent the federal government from abolishing state militias (such as National Guard units), but there has been disagreement over whether the amendment also gives individuals the right to possess weapons outside their use in military service.

Remarkably, more than two centuries passed before the Supreme Court squarely addressed the issue of how the Second Amendment is to be interpreted. The decision came in *District of Columbia v. Heller* (2008). In its ruling, the Court said that "the Second Amendment protects an individual right to possess a firearm unconnected with service in a militia, and to use that arm for traditionally lawful purposes, such as self-defense within the home." The ruling struck down a District of Columbia law that had banned the possession of handguns but not rifles or shotguns within the district's boundaries. Writing for the 5-4 majority, Justice Antonin Scalia said that the justices were "aware of the problem of handgun violence in this country." But Scalia concluded: "The enshrinement of constitutional rights necessarily takes certain policy choices off the table. These include the absolute prohibition of handguns held and used for self-defense in the home."[41] In a sharply worded dissent, Justice John Paul Stevens said the majority had devised a ruling that fit its partisan agenda rather than what the framers intended. Stevens declared: "When each word in the text is given full effect, the Amendment is most naturally read to secure to the people a right to use and possess arms in conjunction with service in a well-regulated militia. So far as it appears, no more than that was contemplated by its drafters or is encompassed within its terms."

The District of Columbia is federal territory, so the *Heller* decision was binding only on the federal government. However, in a 2010 decision, *McDonald v. Chicago*, the Supreme Court through selective incorporation applied the same standard to state and local governments in striking down a Chicago ordinance that banned handgun possession.[42] In its *Heller* and *McDonald* decisions, the Court did not rule out all gun restrictions, such as a ban on gun ownership by former felons. However, the Court did not list all of the allowable restrictions, leaving the issue to be decided in future cases.

THE RIGHT OF PRIVACY

Until the 1960s, Americans' constitutional rights were confined largely to those listed in the Bill of Rights. This situation prevailed despite the Ninth Amendment, which reads, "The enumeration of the Constitution, of certain rights, shall not be construed to deny or disparage others retained by the people." In 1965, however, the Supreme Court added to the list of individual rights, declaring that Americans have "a right of privacy." This judgment derived from the case of *Griswold v. Connecticut*, which challenged a state law prohibiting the use of condoms and other birth control devices, even by married couples. The Supreme Court struck down the law, concluding that a state has no business dictating a married couple's method of birth control. Rather than invoking the Ninth Amendment, the Court's majority reasoned that the freedoms in the Bill of Rights imply an underlying **right of privacy.** The Court held that individuals have a "zone of [personal] privacy" that government cannot lawfully invade.[43]

Although the right of privacy has not been applied broadly by the Supreme Court, it has been invoked in two major areas—a woman's right to choose an abortion and consensual relations among same-sex adults.

Abortion

The right of privacy was the basis for the Supreme Court's ruling in *Roe v. Wade* (1973), which gave women full freedom to choose abortion during the first three months of pregnancy. In overturning a Texas law banning abortion except to save the life of the mother, the Court said that the right of privacy is "broad enough to encompass a woman's decision whether or not to terminate her pregnancy."[44]

The *Roe* decision was met with praise by some Americans and condemnation by others, provoking a still-continuing debate. Americans are sharply divided over the abortion issue and have been throughout the nearly four decades since *Roe* (see the "Party Polarization" box).

Gay rights proponents won a civil liberties lawsuit when the Supreme Court in 2003 overturned a state ban on sexual relations among consenting adults of the same sex.

P A R T Y
POLARIZATION

Political Thinking in Conflict

Pro-Life vs. Pro-Choice

Although party polarization in the United States has risen dramatically since the 1980s, some issues predate this development and have contributed to it. Abortion is such an issue. It has divided Americans from the day that the Supreme Court said in *Roe v. Wade* (1973) that a woman has a constitutional right to choose abortion. At first, Republicans and Democrats differed only slightly in how they saw the issue but the gap has widened to the point where they are far apart. Some Republican voters and Republican-aligned groups (such as the Christian Coalition of America) regard opposition to abortion as a "litmus test" for political candidates and judicial nominees. They refuse to support anyone who upholds a woman's right to choose. Some Democratic voters and Democrat-aligned groups (such as Emily's List) apply the opposite test in determining whom they will support. Since *Roe*, every Republican national party platform has expressed opposition to abortion. In the same period, every Democratic national party platform has had a pro-choice plank. The partisan divide can also be seen in where self-identified Democratic and Republican voters stand on the issue, as the following graph shows.

Percentage agreeing that *Roe v. Wade* should be:

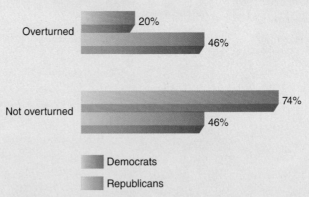

Overturned — 20% / 46%

Not overturned — 74% / 46%

■ Democrats
■ Republicans

Source: Pew Research Center for the People and the Press, 2013.

Q: Do you think there is a "middle ground" that could bring Republicans and Democrats together on the abortion issue? Or is the moral and political divide over the issue so great that no compromise is possible?

After the *Roe* ruling, anti-abortion activists sought a constitutional amendment that would ban abortion, but failed in that effort, prompting them to pursue alternatives. They persuaded the Missouri legislature to pass a law that prohibited abortions from being performed in the state's publicly funded medical facilities, a policy that the Supreme Court upheld in *Webster v. Reproductive Health Services* (1989).[45] Then in *Planned Parenthood v. Casey* (1992), the Court upheld a Pennsylvania law that requires a minor to have parental or judicial consent before obtaining an abortion. Any such restriction, the Court said, is constitutional as long as it does not impose an "undue burden" on the woman.[46]

In *Gonzales v. Carhart* (2007), the Supreme Court for the first time upheld a ban on the use of a particular type of abortion. At issue was the federal Partial-Birth Abortion Ban Act, passed by Congress in 2003. The law provides for a fine and prison term for physicians who perform an abortion when the mother is giving birth even if her life or health is in danger. Writing for the 5-4 majority, Justice Anthony Kennedy said that the federal act did not place an "undue burden" on women. In her dissenting opinion, Justice Ruth Bader Ginsburg, the lone woman on the Court, called the decision "alarming," arguing that it put women's lives and health at risk.[47]

Consensual Sexual Relations among Same-Sex Adults

Although the Supreme Court's 1965 *Griswold* ruling on contraceptive use was widely said to have taken "government out of people's bedrooms," an exception remained. Every state prohibited sexual relations between consenting adults of the same sex. Over the next two decades, many states eliminated this prohibition and others stopped enforcing it. Nevertheless, in a 1986 Georgia case, *Bowers v. Hardwick*, the Supreme Court held that the right of privacy did not extend to consensual sexual relations among adults of the same sex.[48]

In 2003, the Court reversed itself and in the process struck down the sodomy laws of the thirteen states that still had them. In *Lawrence v. Texas*, the Court in a 6-3 vote concluded that Texas's sodomy law violated "the right of privacy" implied by the grant of liberty in the Fourteenth Amendment's due process clause. The Court said: "The petitioners are entitled to respect for their private lives. The State cannot demean their existence or control their destiny by making their private sexual conduct a crime."[49] The decision was hailed by gay and lesbian rights groups but condemned by some religious groups, who said it opened the door to same-sex marriage (see Chapter 5).

RIGHTS OF PERSONS ACCUSED OF CRIMES

Due process refers to legal protections that have been established to preserve the rights of individuals. The most significant of these protections is **procedural due process;** the term refers primarily to procedures that authorities must follow before a person can lawfully be punished for an offense. No system of justice is foolproof. Even in the most careful systems, innocent people have been wrongly accused, convicted, and punished with imprisonment or death. But the scrupulous application of procedural safeguards, such as a defendant's right to legal counsel, greatly increases the likelihood of a fair trial. "The history of liberty has largely been the history of the observance of procedural guarantees," said Justice Felix Frankfurter in *McNabb v. United States* (1943).[50]

The U.S. Constitution offers procedural safeguards designed to protect a person from wrongful arrest, conviction, and punishment. The Fifth and Fourteenth Amendments provide generally that no person can be deprived of life, liberty, or property without due process of law. Specific procedural protections for the accused are listed in the Fourth, Fifth, Sixth, and Eighth Amendments.[51] (See Table 4-2.)

Suspicion Phase: Unreasonable Search and Seizure

In 1766, Parliamentary leader William Pitt forcefully expressed a principle of English common law: "The poorest man may, in his cottage, bid defiance to all the forces of the Crown. It may be frail; its roof may shake; the wind may blow through it; the rain may enter; but the King of England may not enter; all his force dares not cross the threshold."[52] In the period immediately preceding the American Revolution, few things provoked more anger among the colonists than Britain's disregard for the sanctity of the home. British soldiers regularly forced their way into colonists' houses, looking for documents or other evidence of anti-British activity.

The Fourth Amendment was included in the Bill of Rights to prohibit such actions by the U.S. government. The Fourth Amendment reads: "The right of the people to be secure in their persons, houses, papers, and effects, against unreasonable searches and seizures, shall not be violated, and no Warrants shall issue, but upon probable cause, supported by Oath or affirmation, and particularly describing the place to be searched, and the persons or things to be seized."

The Fourth Amendment protects individuals against arbitrary police action. Although a person caught in the act of a crime can be arrested

table 4-2	BILL OF RIGHTS: A SELECTED LIST OF DUE PROCESS PROTECTIONS
Fourth Amendment	**Sixth Amendment**

Fourth Amendment

Search and seizure: You are protected from unreasonable searches and seizures, although you forfeit that right if you knowingly waive it.

Arrest: You are protected from arrest unless authorities have probable cause to believe that you have committed a crime.

Fifth Amendment

Self-incrimination: You are protected against self-incrimination, which means that you have the right to remain silent and to be protected against coercion by law enforcement officials.

Double jeopardy: You cannot be tried twice for the same crime if the first trial results in a verdict of innocence.

Due process: You cannot be deprived of life, liberty, or property without proper legal proceedings.

Sixth Amendment

Counsel: You have a right to be represented by an attorney and can demand to speak first with an attorney before responding to questions from law enforcement officials.

Prompt and reasonable proceedings: You have a right to be arraigned promptly, to be informed of the charges, to confront witnesses, and to have a speedy and open trial by an impartial jury.

Eighth Amendment

Bail: You are protected against excessive bail or fines.

Cruel and unusual punishment: You are protected from cruel and unusual punishment, although this provision does not protect you from the death penalty or from a long prison term for a minor offense.

(seized) and searched for weapons and incriminating evidence, the police ordinarily cannot search an individual merely on the basis of suspicion. In such instances they have to convince a judge that they have "probable cause" (sufficient evidence) to believe that a suspect is engaged in criminal activity. If the judge concludes that the evidence is strong enough, the police will be granted a search warrant. The Court has also held that police must have a search warrant to investigate a suspect using modern technology, such as a listening or thermal-imaging device.[53]

In a unanimous 2014 decision, the Supreme Court delivered what many legal experts consider a landmark ruling. At issue were two cases, one from California and the other from Massachusetts, in which police without a warrant searched a suspect's cell phone after an arrest. In each case, they found information implicating the suspect. In *Riley v. California* and *United States v. Wurie*, the Court noted that, although police upon making an arrest can normally search a suspect and seize relevant physical items (such as weapons or drugs), cell phones and similar electronic devices are different in kind in that they contain large amounts of personal information. To equate such devices to physical objects, the Court argued, "is like saying a ride on horseback is materially indistinguishable from a flight to the moon. Both are ways of getting from point A to point B, but little else justifies lumping them together." The Court said that police normally cannot tear apart a suspect's home without a search warrant and concluded that the search of a cell phone similarly requires a warrant, except in extreme circumstances where police reasonably believe the phone contains information that could prevent a serious imminent crime, such as a terrorist attack. The Court noted that "a cell phone search would typically expose to the government far more than the most exhaustive search of a house." The Court acknowledged that its ruling would make the work of police more difficult but concluded that the protection of Americans' constitutional rights took precedence. "We cannot deny that our decision today will have an impact on the ability of law enforcement to combat crime," said the Court. "Privacy comes at a cost."[54]

However, protection against unreasonable search and seizure does not prohibit police from requiring a photo and fingerprints of a suspect or even, as the Supreme Court ruled in 2013, of taking a cheek swab of the suspect's DNA. Although such information is then entered into a national database, even if the suspect is found innocent, the Court argued that such information results from "a legitimate booking procedure that is reasonable under the Fourth Amendment."[55]

The Supreme Court allows warrantless searches in some circumstances. For example, the Court has generally given school administrators wide latitude to search students for drugs, weapons, and other dangerous items, on the grounds that they bear responsibility for the safety of other students.[56] The Court has also held, for example, that police roadblocks to check drivers for signs of intoxication are legal as long as the action is systematic and not arbitrary (for example, stopping only young drivers would be unconstitutional, whereas stopping all drivers is acceptable). The Court justified this decision by saying that roadblocks serve an important highway safety objective.[57] However, the Court does not allow police roadblocks to check for drugs. In *Indianapolis v. Edmund* (2001), the Court held that narcotics roadblocks serve a general law enforcement purpose rather than one specific to highway safety and therefore violate the Fourth Amendment's requirement that police have suspicion of wrongdoing before they can search an individual's auto.[58]

KANSAS CITY, MISSOURI POLICE DEPARTMENT
ADULT MIRANDA WARNING
1. You have the right to remain silent.
2. Anything you say can and will be used against you in a court of law.
3. You have the right to talk to a lawyer and have him present with you while you are being questioned.
4. If you cannot afford to hire a lawyer, one will be appointed to represent you before any questioning, if you wish.
5. You can decide at any time to exercise these rights and not answer any questions or make any statements.

Few Supreme Court decisions have had a more direct impact than the Miranda ruling, which requires police to read suspects their rights before they can be interrogated. The Miranda warnings include the Fifth Amendment right to remain silent and the Sixth Amendment right to have an attorney.

Arrest Phase: Protection against Self-Incrimination

The Fifth Amendment says, in part, that an individual cannot "be compelled in any criminal case to be a witness against himself." This provision is designed to protect individuals from the age-old practice of coerced confession. Trickery, torture, and the threat of an extra-long prison sentence can lead people to confess to acts they did not commit.

At the time of arrest, police cannot legally begin their interrogation until the suspect has been warned that his or her words can be used as evidence. This warning requirement emerged from *Miranda v. Arizona* (1966), which centered on Ernesto Miranda's confession to kidnapping and rape during police questioning. The Supreme Court overturned his conviction on the grounds that police had not informed him of his right to remain silent and to have legal assistance. The Court reasoned that suspects have a right to know their rights. The Court's ruling led to the formulation of the "Miranda warning" that police are now required to read to suspects: "You have the right to remain silent. . . . Anything you say can and will be used against you in a court of law. . . . You have the right to an attorney." (Miranda was subsequently retried and convicted on the basis of evidence other than his confession.)

The Miranda warning has served to protect suspects, usually those who are poor and uneducated, who are unaware of their rights at the time of arrest. In a 2000 case, *Dickerson v. United States*, the Supreme Court reaffirmed the *Miranda* decision, saying that it was an established "constitutional rule" that Congress could not abolish by ordinary legislation.[59] The Court further strengthened the Miranda precedent in *Missouri v. Siebert* (2004). This ruling came in response to a police strategy of questioning suspects before informing them of their Miranda rights and then questioning them a second time often with the use of a tape or video recorder. In such instances, suspects who admitted wrongdoing in the first round of questioning often did so also in the second round. The Court concluded that the police strategy was intended "to undermine the Miranda warnings" and was a violation of suspects' rights.[60]

On the other hand, as a result of a 2010 Supreme Court decision, police can question suspects who are informed of their rights and then fail to ask for an attorney or fail to say they want to remain silent.[61] The decision was a reversal of the Court's earlier position, which held that suspects must "knowingly and intelligently waive" their rights before they can be questioned.

Trial Phase: The Right to a Fair Trial

The right to a fair trial is basic to any reasonable notion of justice. If the trial process is arbitrary or biased against the defendant, justice is denied. It is sometimes said the American justice system is based on the principle that it is better to let one hundred guilty parties go free than to convict one innocent person. The system does not actually work that way. Once a person has been arrested and charged with a crime, prosecutors are determined to get a conviction. Defendants in such instances have fair-trial guarantees that are designed to protect them from wrongful conviction.

Legal Counsel and Impartial Jury   Under the Fifth Amendment, suspects charged with a *federal* crime cannot be tried unless indicted by a grand jury. The grand jury hears the prosecution's evidence and decides whether it is strong enough to allow the government to try the suspect. (This protection has not been incorporated into the Fourteenth Amendment. As a result, states are not required to use grand juries, although roughly half of them do so. In the rest of the states, the prosecutor usually decides whether to proceed with a trial.)

The Sixth Amendment provides a right to legal counsel before and during trial. But what if a person cannot afford a lawyer? For most of the nation's history, poor people had no choice but to serve as their own attorneys. In *Johnson v. Zerbst* (1938), the Supreme Court held that criminal defendants in federal cases must be provided a lawyer at government expense if they cannot afford one.[62] The Court extended this requirement to include state cases with its ruling in *Gideon v. Wainwright* (1963). This case centered on Clarence Gideon, who had been convicted in a Florida court of breaking into a pool hall. He had asked for a lawyer, but the trial judge denied the request, forcing Gideon to act as his own attorney. He appealed his conviction, and the Supreme Court overturned it on grounds that he did not have adequate legal counsel.[63]

Criminal defendants also have the right to a speedy trial and to confront witnesses against them. At the federal level and sometimes at the state level, they have a right to jury trial, which is to be heard by an "impartial jury." The Court has ruled that a jury's impartiality can be compromised if the prosecution stacks a jury by race or ethnicity.[64] There was a period in the South when blacks accused of crimes against whites were tried by all-white juries, which invariably returned a guilty verdict. The jury's makeup can be an issue for other reasons as well. In *Witherspoon v. Illinois* (1968), for example, the Supreme Court invalidated Illinois's policy of allowing the prosecution to challenge an unlimited number of potential jurors in capital cases. The prosecution used the challenges to remove from the jury anyone who showed any hesitancy about sentencing the defendant to death if found guilty. To allow that practice, the Court ruled, is to virtually guarantee "a verdict of death." "Whatever else might be said of capital punishment," the Court said, "it is at least clear that its imposition by a hanging jury cannot be squared with the Constitution."[65]

The Exclusionary Rule   An issue in some trials is the admissibility of evidence obtained in violation of the defendant's rights. The **exclusionary rule** bars the use of such evidence in some circumstances. The rule was formulated on a limited basis in a 1914 Supreme Court decision and was devised to deter police from violating people's rights. If police know that illegally obtained evidence will be inadmissible in court, they presumably will be less inclined to obtain it. As the Court wrote in *Weeks v. United States* (1914): "The tendency of those who execute the criminal laws of the country to obtain convictions by means of unlawful searches and enforced confessions . . . should find no sanction in the judgment of the courts."[66]

In the 1960s, the liberal-dominated Supreme Court expanded the exclusionary rule to the point where almost any illegally obtained evidence was inadmissible in federal or state court. Opponents accused the Court of "coddling criminals," and the appointment of more conservative justices to the Court led to the watering down of the rule.

The change has taken the form of exceptions to the exclusionary rule. One such exception emerged from *United States v. Leon* (1984), where the

Court ruled that evidence discovered under a faulty warrant was admissible because the police had acted in "good faith."[67] The **good faith exception** holds that otherwise excludable evidence can be admitted in trial if police believed they were following proper procedures.

A second instance in which tainted evidence can be admitted is the **inevitable discovery exception.** It was developed in the case of *Nix v. Williams* (1984). An eyewitness account had led police to believe that Williams had kidnapped a young girl. Police obtained a warrant and arrested him. While being transported by police, despite verbal assurances to his lawyer that he would not be questioned en route, Williams was interrogated and told police where the girl's body could be found. When Williams appealed his conviction, the Court acknowledged that his rights had been violated but concluded that police had other evidence that would have led them to the girl's body. "Exclusion of physical evidence that would have inevitably been discovered adds nothing to either the integrity or fairness of a criminal trial," the Court said.[68]

A third instance is the **plain view exception.** In a key 1996 case, *Whren v. United States*, the Court upheld the conviction of a man stopped for a minor traffic infraction who had drugs sitting in plain view in the front seat of his car.[69] The ruling reaffirmed an earlier decision upholding the admissibility of evidence found in plain sight even when the evidence relates to an infraction other than the one for which the individual was stopped.[70]

As some observers see it, the Court has weakened the exclusionary rule almost to the point where it applies only to extreme forms of police misconduct. Some Court's rulings would support that contention. On the

---

POLITICAL
THINKING

What Constitutes "Unreasonable Search and Seizure"?

Now that you've had the opportunity to read about the fair-trial guarantees provided by the U.S. Constitution, think back to the chapter's opening example—the case of Antoine Jones. Police and FBI officers, acting without a warrant and using a GPS device, tracked his car 24 hours a day for nearly a month. The information they gathered contributed to his arrest and conviction on drug charges. If you had been on the Supreme Court, how would you have voted in this case? Would you have allowed the evidence to be used? What arguments would you have made to support your position?

other hand, the Court's recent rulings on cell phones and tracking devices indicate it is unwilling to give police broad latitude in the use of modern technology, recognizing that it can easily be applied in ways that abridge constitutional rights.

Sentencing Phase: Cruel and Unusual Punishment

Most issues of criminal justice involve *procedural* due process. However, adherence to proper procedures does not necessarily produce reasonable outcomes. The Eighth Amendment was designed to address this issue. It prohibits "cruel and unusual punishment" of those convicted of crime. The Supreme Court has applied several tests in determining whether punishment is cruel and unusual, including whether it is "disproportionate to the offence," violates "fundamental standards of good conscience and fairness," and is "unnecessarily cruel."

However, the Supreme Court has typically let Congress and the state legislatures determine the appropriate penalties for crime. For example, the Court upheld a conviction under California's "three strikes and you're out" law that sent a twice previously convicted felon to prison for life without parole for shoplifting videotapes worth $100.[71]

On the other hand, the Supreme Court has recently employed the Eighth Amendment to narrow the use of the death penalty. The Court recently outlawed the death penalty for those who are mentally disabled on grounds that it constitutes "cruel and unusual punishment."[72] The Court tightened that restriction in a 2014 ruling (*Hall v. Florida*) that invalidated Florida's use of an IQ score of 69 or lower as the strict cutoff for determining mental disability in capital murder cases. Noting that IQ tests have an inherent margin of error, the Court said that states must take additional evidence into account in gauging mental incapacity.[73] The Court also recently invoked the Eighth Amendment to ban the death penalty in cases involving juveniles and for crimes other than murder.[74] In 2010, the Supreme Court broadened the ban on extreme punishment of juveniles to include life without parole in nonhomicide cases. The ruling grew out of a Florida case in which a teenager, who had previously been convicted of robbery, was sentenced to life without parole for participating in a home invasion.[75]

Appeal: One Chance, Usually

The Constitution does not guarantee an appeal after conviction, but the federal government and all states permit at least one appeal. The Supreme

HOW THE 50 STATES DIFFER

POLITICAL THINKING THROUGH COMPARISONS

Incarceration Rates

The U.S. Constitution imposes some uniform requirements on state justice systems. All states are required, for example, to provide legal counsel to defendants who cannot afford to hire an attorney. Otherwise, the states are free to go their own way, with the result that the state justice systems differ markedly in some areas. Some states, for example, prohibit the death penalty, while other states apply it liberally. Roughly a third of all executions in the past quarter century have taken place in Texas alone. States also differ substantially in the size of their prison populations. Louisiana has the highest incarceration rate, with

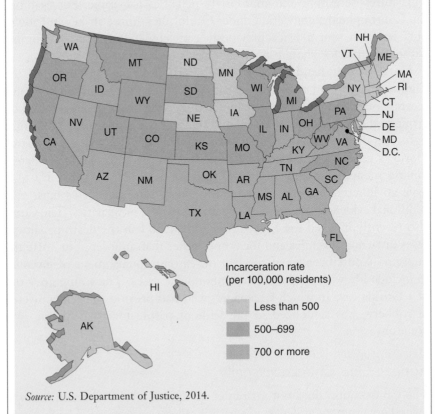

Incarceration rate
(per 100,000 residents)

Less than 500

500–699

700 or more

Source: U.S. Department of Justice, 2014.

865 inmates for every 100,000 residents. Mississippi, Texas, Oklahoma, and Alabama are the other states in the top five. Maine has the lowest incarceration rate—159 inmates per 100,000 residents. On a per-capita basis, Louisiana imprisons more than five times as many of its residents as does Maine. The four other states in the lowest five in terms of prison population are Minnesota, North Dakota, Rhode Island, and Utah.

Q: What do many of the states with low incarceration rates have in common?

A: Most of these states are relatively affluent and rank high on indicators of educational attainment, which are correlated with lower crime rates. Most of these states also have relatively small minority-group populations. Studies have found that the poor and minority-group defendants are more likely than affluent and white defendants to be convicted and, when convicted, to receive a lengthier sentence.

Court has ruled that the appeal process cannot discriminate against poor defendants. At a minimum, government must provide indigent convicts with the legal resources to file a first appeal.

Prisoners who believe their constitutional rights have been violated by state officials can appeal their conviction to a federal court. With a few exceptions, the Supreme Court has held that prisoners have the right to have their appeal heard in federal court unless they had "deliberately bypassed" the opportunity to first make their appeal in state courts.[76]

The main restriction on appeals is a federal law that bars in most instances a second federal appeal by a state prison inmate.[77] Upheld by the Supreme Court in *Felker v. Turpin* (1996), this law is designed to prevent frivolous and multiple federal court appeals. State prisoners had used appeals to contest even small issues, and some inmates—particularly those on death row—had filed appeal after appeal. An effect was the clogging of the federal courts and a delay in hearing other cases. The Supreme Court has ruled that, except in unusual cases,[78] it is fair to ask inmates to first pursue their options in state courts and then to confine themselves to a single federal appeal.

Crime, Punishment, and Police Practices

Although the exclusionary rule and the appeals process have been weakened, there has not been a return to the lower procedural standards that prevailed prior to the 1960s. Most of the key precedents established in that decade remain in effect, including the most important one of all: the principle that procedural protections guaranteed to the accused by the Bill of Rights must be observed by the states as well as by the federal government.

Supreme Court rulings have changed police practices. Most police departments, for example, require their officers to read suspects the Miranda warning before questioning them. Nevertheless, constitutional rights are applied unevenly. An example is the use of *racial profiling*, which is the targeting of individuals from particular groups, such as blacks, Hispanics, and Muslims. Research indicates that such individuals are more likely than other Americans to be arbitrarily stopped, searched, and detained by police on everything from traffic infractions to suspicion of criminal activity. An important early study found, for example, that 80 percent of the motorists stopped and searched by Maryland State Police on Interstate 95 were minorities and only 20 percent were white, despite the fact that white motorists constituted 75 percent of all drivers and were just as likely as minority motorists to violate the traffic laws.[79] Such findings prompted federal, state, and local law enforcement agencies to create training programs aimed at reducing the practice. Although racial profiling continues to be a problem, recent studies indicate its frequency is declining.[80]

Sentencing policies are also an issue. Being "tough on crime" is popular with some voters, and most state legislatures during the past two decades have enacted stiffer penalties for crime while also limiting the ability of judges to reduce sentences, even for nonviolent crime when the perpetrator has no prior criminal record. As a result, the number of federal and state prisoners has more than doubled since 1990. In fact, on a per-capita basis, the United States has the largest prison population in the world (see Figure 4-1). Cuba and Russia are the only countries that are even close to the United States in terms of the percentage of its citizens who are behind bars.

As the human and financial costs of keeping so many people in prison have risen, debate over America's criminal justice system has intensified. The incarceration of nonviolent drug offenders is one such issue. U.S. drug policy is at odds with those of other Western countries, which rely more heavily on treatment programs than on prisons in dealing with drug offenders.

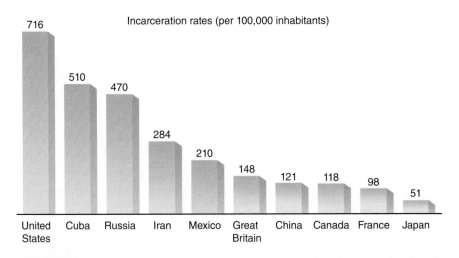

Incarceration rates (per 100,000 inhabitants)

716 — United States
510 — Cuba
470 — Russia
284 — Iran
210 — Mexico
148 — Great Britain
121 — China
118 — Canada
98 — France
51 — Japan

figure 4-1   INCARCERATION RATES, BY COUNTRY

The United States is the world leader in terms of the number of people it places behind bars. More than half of the people in U.S. prisons were convicted of nonviolent offenses, such as drug use or property theft. *Source:* International Centre for Prison Studies, 2014.

RIGHTS AND THE WAR ON TERRORISM

In time of war, the courts have upheld government policies that would not be permitted in peacetime. After the Japanese attack on Pearl Harbor in 1941, for example, President Franklin D. Roosevelt ordered the forced relocation of tens of thousands of Japanese Americans living on the West Coast to detention camps in Arizona, Utah, and other inland locations. Congress endorsed the policy, and the Supreme Court upheld it in *Korematsu v. United States* (1944).[81] Another Supreme Court ruling during World War II denied a U.S. citizen arrested as a Nazi collaborator a court trial after the government decided to try him before a military tribunal.[82] After the terrorist attacks of September 11, 2001, the Bush administration invoked precedents such as these in declaring that customary legal protections would not be afforded to individuals it deemed to have engaged in terrorist activity.

Detention of Enemy Combatants

The Bush administration soon announced its policy for handling captured "enemy combatants"—individuals judged to be engaged in, or in support of, hostile military actions against U.S. military forces. Some of these prisoners were sent to a detention facility created at the U.S. naval base at Guantanamo Bay on the tip of Cuba. Others were imprisoned in Afghanistan, Iraq, and elsewhere. Requests by lawyers and international agencies like the Red Cross to see the detainees were denied or strictly limited. Some prisoners were subject to abusive treatment, although the practice was denied by U.S. officials until photographic and other evidence surfaced.

In 2004, the Supreme Court issued its first ruling on these practices, holding that the Guantanamo Bay detainees have the right to challenge their detention in court. The Court reasoned that the naval base, though in Cuba, is on land leased to the United States and therefore under the jurisdiction of U.S. courts.[83] In a second 2004 case (*Hamdi v. Rumsfeld*), the Court ruled that one of the Guantanamo Bay detainees, who was a U.S. citizen by virtue of having been born in the United States though he was raised in Saudi Arabia, had the right to be heard in U.S. courts. The Court said: "As critical as the government's interest may be in detaining those who actually pose an immediate threat to the national security of the United States during ongoing international conflict, history and common sense teach us that an unchecked system of detention carries the potential to become a means of oppression and abuse of others who do not present that sort of threat."[84]

Two years later, the Supreme Court issued its sharpest rebuke of the Bush administration's detention policies. In a ruling nearly unprecedented in its challenge to a president's wartime authority, the Court held that the detainees were protected both by the U.S. Uniform Code of Military Justice and by the Geneva Conventions. At issue was the Bush administration's use of secret military tribunals to try detainees. In *Hamdan v. Rumsfeld* (2006), the Court ruled that the tribunals were unlawful because they did not provide even minimal protections of detainees' rights, including the right to see the evidence against them. The Court said that the detainees were entitled to be tried by a "regularly constituted court affording all the judicial guarantees which are recognized as indispensable by civilized peoples."[85]

Surveillance of Suspected Terrorists

After the September 11 terrorist attacks, Congress passed the USA Patriot Act, which lowered the standard for judicial approval of wiretapping when terrorist activity was at issue. The law also allowed information from intelligence surveillance to be shared with criminal investigators when evidence was found of criminal activity unrelated to terrorism. Previously, such information could be shared only when obtained by the stricter standards that apply to criminal investigations. The new law also gave government increased authority to examine medical, financial, and student records and allowed the government in some situations to secretly search homes and offices (so-called "sneak and peek" searches).

The Bush administration promised to act with restraint in its exercise of the new powers, and congressional oversight committees were generally satisfied with its actions until *The New York Times* revealed in late 2005 that President Bush without judicial approval had secretly authorized the National Security Agency (NSA) to wiretap international phone calls and e-mail messages originating in the United States. Such wiretaps are expressly prohibited by the Foreign Intelligence Surveillance Act (FISA) of 1978. Bush rejected allegations that he had broken the law, saying that he had acted legally under his wartime powers as commander-in-chief and under authority implicitly granted him by the Patriot Act.

When Barack Obama became president, observers expected him to disclose the scope of the NSA's warrantless surveillance activities. Instead the Obama administration declared that release of the information "would cause exceptionally grave harm to national security." In 2013 Edward Snowden, an NSA contractor, leaked documents to the press that showed that the NSA surveillance program was far more extensive than the government had previously indicated. The NSA had gathered data on nearly every call made by Americans and had eavesdropped on the calls of some foreign leaders, including German chancellor Angela Merkel. Republican Rand Paul of Kentucky and Democrat Ron Wyden of Oregon were among the members of Congress calling for a halt to the program. Political pressure forced Obama to alter the program, including storing the data with communication companies rather than with the NSA in order to make it harder for NSA employees to misuse the data. At the same time, the Obama administration insisted that the domestic surveillance program was lawful in that it involved collecting phone call records rather than actually monitoring Americans' conversations. The records were used to detect patterns in phone traffic that might suggest terrorist activity, at which point a warrant had to be obtained from a federal judge before officials were allowed to monitor specific conversations. Lower-court rulings on the constitutionality of the program have been inconsistent, raising the possibility that the Supreme Court might take up the issue in the near future.

Seen by some as a traitor and by others as a hero, Edward Snowden was an NSA contractor with access to classified documents about the NSA's surveillance activities, which he disclosed to the press. The release of the documents led to changes in the NSA's program but also forced Snowden to seek asylum outside the country. He was charged by the U.S. government with the crime of revealing classified information.

THE COURTS AND A FREE SOCIETY

The United States was founded on the idea that individuals have an innate right to liberty—to speak their minds, to worship freely, to be secure in their homes and persons, to be assured of a fair trial. Americans embrace these freedoms in the abstract. In particular situations, however, many Americans think otherwise. A 2010 CNN survey found, for example, that more than two in five Americans think that individuals arrested by police on suspicion of terrorism should not be read their Miranda rights.

The judiciary is not isolated from the public mood. Judges inevitably must balance society's need for security and public order against the rights of the individual. Nevertheless, relative to elected officials, police officers, or the general public, judges are more protective of individual rights. How far the courts will go in protecting a person's rights depends on the facts of the case, the existing status of the law, prevailing social needs, and the personal views of the judges (see Chapter 14). Nevertheless, most judges and justices regard the protection of individual rights as their constitutional duty, which is the way the framers saw it. The Bill of Rights was created to transform the abstract idea that individuals have a right to life, liberty, and happiness into a set of specified constitutional rights, thereby bringing them under the protection of courts of law.[86]

SUMMARY

The Bill of Rights was added to the Constitution shortly after its ratification. These amendments guarantee certain political, procedural, and property rights against infringement by the national government.

The guarantees embodied in the Bill of Rights originally applied only to the national government. Under the principle of selective incorporation of these guarantees into the Fourteenth Amendment, the courts extended them to state governments, though the process was slow and uneven. In the 1920s and 1930s, First Amendment guarantees of freedom of expression were given protection from infringement by the states. The states continued to have wide discretion in criminal proceedings until the early 1960s, when most of the fair-trial rights in the Bill of Rights were given federal protection.

Freedom of expression is the most basic of democratic rights. People are not free unless they can freely express their views. Nevertheless, free expression may conflict with the nation's security needs during times of war and insurrection. The courts at times have allowed government to limit expression substantially for purposes of national security. In recent decades, however, the courts have protected a wide range of free expression in the areas of speech, press, and religion. They have also established a right of privacy, which in some areas, such as abortion, remains a source of controversy and judicial action.

Due process of law refers to legal protections that have been established to preserve individual rights. The most significant form of these protections consists of procedures designed to ensure that an individual's rights are upheld (for example, the right of an accused person to have an attorney present during police interrogation). A major controversy in this area is the breadth of the exclusionary rule, which bars the use in trials of illegally obtained evidence.

The war on terrorism that began after the attacks on September 11, 2001, has raised new issues of civil liberties, including the detention of enemy combatants, the use of harsh interrogation techniques, and warrantless surveillance. The Supreme Court has not ruled on all such issues but has generally held that the president's war-making power does not include the authority to disregard provisions of statutory law, treaties (the Geneva Conventions), and the Constitution.

Civil liberties are not absolute but must be judged in the context of other considerations (such as national security or public safety) and against one another when different rights conflict. The judicial branch of government, particularly the Supreme Court, has taken on much of the responsibility for protecting and interpreting individual rights. The Court's positions have changed with time and conditions, but the Court is usually more protective of civil liberties than are elected officials or popular majorities.

CRITICAL THINKING ZONE

KEY TERMS

Bill of Rights (*p. 102*)
civil liberties (*p. 101*)
clear-and-present-danger test (*p. 108*)
due process clause (of the Fourteenth
  Amendment) (*p. 103*)
establishment clause (*p. 114*)
exclusionary rule (*p. 127*)
freedom of expression (*p. 106*)
free-exercise clause (*p. 116*)
good faith exception (*p. 128*)
imminent lawless action test (*p. 110*)

inevitable discovery exception
  (*p. 128*)
Lemon test (*p. 115*)
libel (*p. 113*)
plain view exception (*p. 128*)
prior restraint (*p. 112*)
procedural due process (*p. 122*)
right of privacy (*p. 119*)
selective incorporation (*p. 104*)
slander (*p. 113*)
symbolic speech (*p. 110*)

APPLYING THE ELEMENTS OF CRITICAL THINKING

Conceptualizing: Distinguish between the establishment clause and the free-exercise clause of the First Amendment. To which one does the *Lemon* test apply, and what are the components of that test?

Synthesizing: Assume that an individual has been arrested and is eventually brought to trial. Identify the procedural due process rights that the individual has at each step in the legal process. How might the exclusionary rule affect the outcome?

Analyzing: What is the process of selective incorporation, and why is it important to the rights Americans have today?

EXTRA CREDIT

A Book Worth Reading: Anthony Lewis, *Gideon's Trumpet: How One Man, a Poor Prisoner, Took His Case to the Supreme Court—and Changed the Law of the United States.* New York: Vintage, 1964. Written by a two-time Pulitzer Prize winner, this best-selling book recounts the story of how James Earl Gideon got the Supreme Court to accept his case, which led to a constitutional ruling requiring government to provide the poor with legal counsel.

A Website Worth Visiting: **www.fepproject.org** The Free Expression Policy Project aggregates news and information on a wide variety of contemporary First Amendment–related issues.

PARTICIPATE!

Although their right of free expression is protected by law, Americans often choose not to exercise this right for fear of social pressure or official reprisal. Yet constitutional rights tend to wither when people fail to exercise them. The failure of citizens to speak their minds, Alexis de Tocqueville said, reduces them "to being nothing more than a herd of timid and industrious animals of which government is the shepherd." Think of an issue that you care about but that is unpopular on your campus or in your community. Consider writing a letter expressing your opinion to the editor of your college or local newspaper. (Practical advice: Keep the letter short and to the point; write a lead sentence that will get readers' attention; provide a convincing and courteous argument for your position; and be sure to sign the letter and provide a return address so that the editor can contact you if there are questions.)

5
CHAPTER

EQUAL RIGHTS: STRUGGLING TOWARD FAIRNESS

❝ The assertion that 'all men are created equal' was of no practical use in effecting our separation from Great Britain, and it was placed in the Declaration not for that, but for future use. **❞**

ABRAHAM LINCOLN[1]

The producers of ABC television's *Primetime Live* put hidden cameras on two young men, equally well dressed and groomed, and then sent them on different routes to do the same things—search for an apartment, shop for a car, look at albums in a record store. The cameras recorded people's reactions to the two men. One was more often greeted with smiles and quick service, while the other was more often greeted with suspicious looks and was sometimes made to wait. Why the difference? The explanation was straightforward: the young man who was routinely well received was white; the young man who was sometimes treated poorly was black.

The Urban Institute conducted a more substantial experiment. It included pairs of specially trained white and black male college students who were comparable in key aspects—education, work experience, speech patterns, physical builds—except for their race. The students responded individually to nearly five hundred classified job advertisements in Chicago and Washington, D.C. The black applicants got fewer interviews and received fewer job offers than did the white applicants. An Urban Institute spokesperson said, "The level of reverse discrimination [favoring blacks over whites] that we found was limited, was certainly far lower than many might have been led to fear, and was swamped by the extent of discrimination against black job applicants."[2]

The two studies suggest why some Americans still struggle for equality. Although Americans in theory have equal rights, they are not now equal, nor have they ever been. African Americans, women, Hispanic Americans, individuals with disabilities, Jews, Native Americans, Catholics, Mormons, Asian Americans, gays and lesbians, and members of other minority groups have been victims of discrimination in fact and in law. The nation's creed—"all men are created equal"—has encouraged disadvantaged groups to demand equal treatment, but there is considerable disagreement over how far government should go in helping them attain it. Should government's responsibility extend only to efforts aimed at ensuring Americans are treated equally under the law? Or should its responsibility extend also to efforts aimed at reducing Americans' unequal access to opportunities, such as employment and college admission?

This chapter focuses on **equal rights**, or **civil rights**—terms that refer to the right of every person to equal protection under the laws and equal access to society's opportunities and public facilities. As Chapter 4 explained, civil liberties refer to specific *individual* rights, such as freedom of speech, that are protected from infringement by government. Equal rights, or civil rights, are a question of whether individual members of differing *groups*, such as racial, gender, and ethnic groups, are treated equally by government and, in some instances, by private parties.

Although the law refers to the rights of individuals first and to those of groups in a secondary and derivative way, this chapter concentrates on groups because the history of civil rights has been largely one of group claims to equality. The catchphrase of nearly every group's claim to a more equal standing in American society has been "equality under the law." When secure in their legal rights, people are positioned to pursue equality in other arenas, such as the economic sector. This chapter examines the major laws relating to equality and the conditions that led to their adoption. The chapter concludes with a brief look at some of the continuing challenges facing America's historically disadvantaged groups. The chapter emphasizes these points:

- *Americans have attained substantial equality under the law.* In purely legal terms, although not always in practice, they have equal protection under the laws, equal access to accommodations and housing, and an equal right to vote.

- *Legal equality for all Americans has not resulted in de facto equality.* African Americans, women, Hispanic Americans, and other traditionally disadvantaged groups have a disproportionately small share of America's opportunities and benefits. However, the issue of what, if anything, government should do to deal with this problem is a major source of contention.

- *Disadvantaged groups have had to struggle for equal rights.* African Americans, women, Native Americans, Hispanic Americans, Asian Americans, and a number of other groups have had to fight for their rights in order to achieve a fuller measure of equality.

EQUALITY THROUGH LAW

Equality has always been the least developed of America's founding concepts. Not even Thomas Jefferson, who wrote the words, believed that a precise meaning could be given to the claim of the Declaration of Independence that "all men are created equal."[3] Nevertheless, the promise contained in that phrase has placed history on the side of those seeking greater equality. Every civil rights movement, from suffrage for males without property in the 1830s to gay rights today, has derived moral strength from the nation's pledge of equality for all.

Nevertheless, America's history reveals that disadvantaged groups have never achieved greater equality without a struggle.[4] The policies that protect these groups today are the result of sustained political action that forced entrenched interests to relinquish or share their privileged status.

POLITICAL THINKING | **What Does Equality Mean?**

From the nation's beginning, Americans have debated the meaning of equality. Although the term is enshrined in the Declaration of Independence—"all men are created equal"—it has been the source of endless dispute. How would you define equality? Do you see it purely as a question of equal treatment under the law, or do you think equality should extend to other things, such as access to jobs, health care, and college admission?

The Fourteenth Amendment: Equal Protection

The Fourteenth Amendment, which was ratified in 1868 after the Civil War, declares in part that no state shall "deny to any person within its jurisdiction the equal protection of the laws." The **equal-protection clause** was designed to require states to treat their residents equally, but the Supreme Court at first refused to interpret it that way. As discussed in Chapter 3, the Court in *Plessy v. Ferguson* (1896) ruled that "separate" public facilities for black citizens did not violate the Constitution as long as the facilities were "equal."[5] The *Plessy* decision became a justification for the separate and *unequal* treatment of African Americans. Black children were forced, for example, to attend separate schools that rarely had libraries or enough teachers.

These practices were challenged through legal action, but not until the late 1930s did the Supreme Court begin to respond. In a first ruling, the Court held that blacks must be allowed to use public facilities reserved for whites in cases where they did not have separate facilities. When Oklahoma, which had no law school for blacks, was ordered to admit Ada Sipuel as a law student in 1949, it created a separate law school for her—she sat alone

Two police dogs attack a black civil rights activist (center left) during the 1963 Birmingham demonstrations. Such images of hatred and violence shook many white Americans out of the complacency about the plight of African Americans.

in a roped-off corridor of the state capitol building. The white students, meanwhile, continued to meet at the University of Oklahoma's law school in Norman, twenty miles away. The Supreme Court then ordered the law school to admit her to regular classes. The law school did so but roped off her seat from the rest of the class and stenciled the word *colored* on it. In her memoir, Sipuel wrote that, although law school administrators were unreceptive, a number of law students reached out to her, including those who shared their notes from classes she missed while studying alone at the capitol building.[6]

Segregation in the Schools   Substantial judicial intervention on behalf of African Americans finally occurred in 1954 with *Brown v. Board of Education of Topeka*. The case began when Linda Carol Brown, a black child in Topeka, Kansas, was denied admission to an all-white elementary school that she passed every day on her way to her all-black school, which was twelve blocks farther away. In a unanimous decision, the Court invoked the Fourteenth Amendment's equal-protection clause, declaring that racial segregation of public schools "generates [among black children] a feeling of inferiority as to their status in the community that may affect their hearts and minds in a way unlikely ever to be undone. . . . Separate educational facilities are inherently unequal."[7]

A 1954 Gallup poll indicated that a sizable majority of southern whites opposed the *Brown* decision, and billboards were erected along southern roadways that called for the impeachment of Chief Justice Earl Warren. In the so-called Southern Manifesto, southern congressmen urged their state governments to "resist forced integration by any lawful means." Rioting broke out in 1957 when Arkansas's governor called out the state's National Guard to prevent black students from entering Little Rock's high school. They achieved entry only after President Dwight D. Eisenhower used his power as commander in chief to place the Arkansas National Guard under federal control.

Although the *Brown* decision banned forced segregation in the public schools, it did not require states to take active steps to integrate their schools. Most children attended neighborhood schools, and because most residential neighborhoods were racially segregated, so too were the schools. Even as late as fifteen years after *Brown*, 95 percent of black children were attending schools that were mostly or entirely black.

In 1971, the Supreme Court endorsed the busing of children as a remedy for segregated schools. The Court held in *Swann v. Charlotte-Mecklenburg County Board of Education* (1971) that the busing of children out of their neighborhoods for the purpose of achieving racially integrated schools was constitutionally permissible in cases where previous acts of racial discrimination contributed to school segregation.[8] Few Court decisions have provoked the outcry that followed *Swann*. Angry demonstrations lasting weeks took place in Charlotte. When busing was ordered in Detroit and Boston, the protests turned violent as white demonstrators burned buses and beat black residents. Unlike *Brown*, which affected mainly the South, *Swann* also applied to northern communities where blacks and whites lived separately because of discriminatory real estate practices.

Racial busing had mixed results. Studies found that busing improved school children's racial attitudes and improved minority children's performance on standardized tests without diminishing the performance of white classmates.[9] On the other hand, the policy forced many children to spend long hours each day riding buses to and from school. Busing also contributed to white flight to the suburbs, which were protected by a 1974 Supreme Court decision that prohibited busing across school districts except where district boundaries had been deliberately drawn to keep the races apart.[10] The declining number of white students in city schools made it harder, even with the use of busing, to create racially balanced classrooms.

In the 1990s, the Supreme Court ordered cutbacks in busing, saying that it was meant to be a temporary solution.[11] Then, in 2007, the Supreme Court essentially declared an end to forced busing. At issue were voluntary (as opposed to court-ordered) busing programs in Seattle and Louisville that took race, neighborhood, and student preference into account in assigning students to particular schools. The large majority of students were placed in their school of choice, but some were forced to go elsewhere, which led to lawsuits on their behalf. In a 5-4 decision, the Supreme Court ruled they had been denied equal protection under the Fourteenth Amendment. Writing for the majority, Chief Justice John Roberts said, "Before *Brown*, schoolchildren were told where they could and could not go to school based on the color of their skin. The school districts in [Seattle and Louisville] have not carried the heavy burden of demonstrating that we should allow this once again—even for very different reasons." In the dissenting opinion, Justice Stephen Breyer said, "It is a cruel distortion of history to compare Topeka, Kansas in the 1950s to Louisville and Seattle in the modern day."[12]

As a result of the end of racial busing and white flight to private and suburban schools, America's schools have become less racially diverse. Compared with 40 percent at the peak of the busing era, only 30 percent of Hispanic and black children now attend a school that is predominately white. In fact, America's schools are now more ethnically and racially segregated than they were when busing began.[13]

Judicial Tests of Equal Protection The Fourteenth Amendment's equal-protection clause does not require government to treat all groups or classes of people equally in all circumstances. The judiciary allows inequalities that are "reasonably" related to a legitimate government interest. In applying this **reasonable-basis test,** the courts require government only to show that a particular law is reasonable. For example, twenty-one-year-olds can legally drink alcohol but twenty-year-olds cannot. The courts have held that the goal of reducing fatalities from alcohol-related accidents involving young drivers is a valid reason for imposing an age limit on the purchase and consumption of alcohol.

The reasonable-basis test does not apply to racial or ethnic classifications (see Table 5-1). Any law that treats people differently because of race or ethnicity is subject to the **strict-scrutiny test,** which presumes that the law is unconstitutional unless government can provide a compelling basis for it. The Supreme Court's position is that race and national origin are **suspect classifications**—in other words, laws that classify people differently on the basis of their race or ethnicity are assumed to have discrimination as their purpose.

Although the notion of suspect classifications was implicit in earlier cases, including *Brown,* the Court did not use those words until *Loving v. Virginia* (1967). The state of Virginia had a law that prohibited white residents from marrying a person of a different race. When Richard Loving, a white man, and Mildred Jeter, a woman of African American and Native American descent, went to Washington, D.C., to get married and then returned home to Virginia, police invaded their home and arrested them. The state of Virginia claimed that its ban on interracial marriage

table 5-1	LEVELS OF COURT REVIEW FOR LAWS THAT TREAT AMERICANS DIFFERENTLY	
Test	**Application**	**Standard Used**
Strict scrutiny	Race, ethnicity	Suspect category—assumed unconstitutional in the absence of an overwhelming justification
Intermediate scrutiny	Gender	Almost suspect category—assumed unconstitutional unless the law serves a clearly compelling and justified purpose
Reasonable basis	Other categories (such as age and income)	Not suspect category—assumed constitutional unless no sound rationale for the law can be provided

did not violate the equal-protection clause because the penalty for the offense—a prison sentence of one to five years—was the same for both the white and the nonwhite spouse. The Supreme Court ruled otherwise, saying the Virginia law was "subversive of the principle of equality at the heart of the Fourteenth Amendment." The Court concluded that the law was based solely on "invidious racial discrimination" and that any such "classification" was unconstitutional.[14]

When women began to assert their rights more forcefully in the 1970s, some observers thought the Supreme Court would expand the scope of strict scrutiny to include gender. Instead, the Court held that men and women can be treated differently if the policy in question is "substantially related" to the achievement of "important governmental objectives."[15] The Court thus placed gender classifications in an intermediate (or almost suspect) category. Gender classifications were to be scrutinized more closely than some others (for example, income or age) but were constitutionally valid if government could clearly show why men and women should be treated differently. In *Rostker v. Goldberg* (1980), the Court upheld such a classification, ruling that the male-only draft registration law served the important objective of excluding women from *involuntary* combat duty.[16]

Since then, however, the Supreme Court has struck down nearly every gender-based law it has reviewed. A leading case is *United States v. Virginia* (1996), in which the Court invalidated the male-only admissions policy of Virginia Military Institute (VMI), a 157-year-old state-supported college. In its ruling, the Court said that Virginia had failed to provide an "exceedingly persuasive" argument for its policy.[17]

The Civil Rights Act of 1964

The Fourteenth Amendment prohibits discrimination by government but not by private parties. As a result, for a long period in American history, private employers could freely discriminate in their hiring practices, and owners of restaurants, hotels, theaters, and other public accommodations could legally bar black people from entering. That changed with passage of the 1964 Civil Rights Act. Based on Congress's power to regulate commerce, the legislation entitles all persons to equal access to public accommodations. The legislation also bars discrimination on the basis of race, color, religion, sex, or national origin in the hiring, promotion, and wages of employees of medium-size and large firms. A few forms of job discrimination are still lawful under the Civil Rights Act. For example, a church-related school can take religion into account in hiring teachers.

The Black Civil Rights Movement   The impetus behind the 1964 Civil Rights Act was the black civil rights movement. Without it, the legislation would have come later, and possibly have been less sweeping.

During World War II, African American soldiers fought against Nazi racism only to return to an America where racial discrimination was legal and oppressive.[18] The stark contradiction led to demands for change, which intensified after an incident in Montgomery, Alabama, on December 1, 1955. Upon leaving work that day, Rosa Parks boarded a bus for home, taking her seat as required by law in the section reserved for blacks. When all the seats for white passengers were occupied, the bus driver ordered Parks to give her seat to a white passenger. She refused, whereupon she was arrested. The incident provoked outrage in Montgomery's black community, which organized a boycott of the city's bus system. A young pastor at a local Baptist church, Dr. Martin Luther King Jr., led the boycott, which spread to other cities. The black civil rights movement was under way and would persist for more than a decade. A peak moment occurred in 1963 with the March on Washington for Jobs and Freedom, which attracted 250,000 marchers, one of the largest gatherings in the Capital's history. In a riveting speech to the massive crowd, King expressed his dream of a better America, one where people are judged by the quality of their personal character rather than by their race or ethnicity.[19]

The momentum of the March on Washington carried over into Congress, where major civil rights legislation was languishing in House committee. Although opponents employed every possible legislative maneuver

Civil rights movements dominated the decades of the 1950s and 1960s and produced a remarkable set of leaders. Among them were Martin Luther King Jr., who was the pivotal figure in the black civil rights movement; Caesar Chavez, who led the farmworker strikes that benefited migrant laborers, the large majority of whom were Hispanic; and Betty Friedan, who founded the National Organization for Women (NOW) and wrote *The Feminine Mystique* (1963), which helped spark the women's rights movement.

in an effort to block it, it finally cleared the House the following February. Senate maneuvering and debate—including a fifty-five-day filibuster—took another four months. Finally, in early July, President Lyndon Johnson signed into law the Civil Rights Act of 1964.

Resistance to the Civil Rights Act was widespread. Many restaurants, hotels, and other establishments refused to serve black customers. An Atlanta restaurant owner, Lester Maddox, responded to the legislation by standing outside his restaurant brandishing a handgun, threatening to shoot any African American who entered. Maddox was elected governor of Georgia three years later, but lawsuits against Maddox and other defiant proprietors slowly ended resistance to the new law, with the effect that overt forms of discrimination in the area of public accommodations gradually ceased. Even today, some restaurants and hotels may provide better service to white customers, but outright refusal to serve African Americans or other minority-group members is rare. Any such refusal violates federal law and can be proven in many instances. Discrimination in job decisions is harder to prove, and the Civil Rights Act has been less effective in stopping it, as is discussed in a later section.

The Movement for Women's Rights   The black civil rights movement inspired other disadvantaged groups to demand their rights. Women were the most vocal and successful of these groups.

The United States carried over from English common law a political disregard for women, forbidding them to vote, hold public office, or serve on juries.[20] Upon marriage, a woman essentially lost her identity as an individual and could not own and dispose of property without her husband's consent. Even a wife's body was not fully hers. A wife's adultery was declared by the Supreme Court in 1904 to be a violation of the husband's property rights.[21]

The first large and well-organized attempt to promote women's rights came in 1848 in Seneca Falls, New York. Lucretia Mott and Elizabeth Cady Stanton had been barred from the main floor of an antislavery convention and decided to organize a women's rights convention. Thereafter, the struggle for women's rights became closely aligned with the abolitionist movement. However, when Congress wrote the Fifteenth Amendment after the Civil War, women were not included in its provisions despite promises to the contrary. The Fifteenth Amendment declared only that the right to vote could not be abridged on account of race or color. Not until passage of the Nineteenth Amendment in 1920 did women acquire the right to vote.

The Nineteenth Amendment's ratification encouraged women's leaders in 1923 to propose a constitutional amendment granting equal rights

| PARTY POLARIZATION | Political Thinking in Conflict |

The Politics of Civil Rights

Before the 1960s, neither political party stepped forward to take up the issue of civil rights out of fear of the long-term electoral consequences. The Democratic Party finally took the lead in enacting the 1964 Civil Rights Act and 1965 Voting Rights Act. Backed by large Democratic majorities in the House and Senate, President Lyndon Johnson pressed for passage of the legislation but said Democrats were "signing away the South" for a generation or more. It was more than a prophecy. Enough white southern Democrats switched sides to quickly turn the South into a Republican stronghold in presidential elections and later into a Republican stronghold in congressional elections as well. The civil rights issue has broadly affected partisan alignments. The groups that have benefited most directly from civil rights policies—particularly African Americans and Hispanics—are far more Democratic than those that have not—white males particularly. The accompanying figures show some of the differences. Independents have been excluded from the calculations; the percentages are based only on survey respondents who said they identified with either the Republican or the Democratic Party.

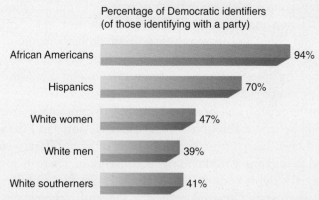

Percentage of Democratic identifiers (of those identifying with a party)

- African Americans 94%
- Hispanics 70%
- White women 47%
- White men 39%
- White southerners 41%

Source: Pew Research Center for the People & the Press, July 22, 2011.

Q. Factors such as race and ethnicity are only part of the explanation for the partisan differences among the groups shown in the graph. What other factors do you think need to be taken into account in a fuller explanation?

A. Several factors need to be taken into account, but income is the main one. Disadvantaged groups have substantially lower incomes on average than do advantaged groups. The Republican and Democratic parties have differed in their income and tax policies and therefore in their appeal to different income groups (see Chapter 8).

to women. Congress rejected the proposal but fifty years later approved the Equal Rights Amendment (ERA) and submitted it to the states for ratification. The ERA failed by three states to receive the required three-fourths majority.[22] Women did succeed in other efforts, however. Among the congressional measures were the Equal Pay Act of 1963, which prohibits sex discrimination in salary and wages by some categories of employers; Title IX of the Education Amendment of 1972, which prohibits sex discrimination in education; and the Equal Credit Act of 1974, which prohibits sex discrimination in the granting of financial credit. Women are also protected by Title VII of the Civil Rights Act of 1964, which bans gender discrimination in employment, a topic that is discussed in a later section.

Hispanic Americans and the Farmworkers' Strikes   Inspired by the black civil rights movement, Hispanic farm laborers in California, most of whom were migrant workers, went on strike over labor rights in the late 1960s. Migrants were working long hours for low pay, were living in shacks without electricity or plumbing, and were unwelcome in many local schools and hospitals. Farm owners at first refused to bargain with the workers, but a well-organized national boycott of California grapes and lettuce forced the state to pass a law giving migrant workers the right to bargain collectively. The strikes were led by Cesar Chavez, who had grown up in a Mexican American migrant family. Chavez's tactics were copied with less success in other states, including Texas.[23]

The Hispanic civil rights movement lacked the scope of the black civil rights movement but brought about some policy changes, including a congressional act that requires states to provide bilingual ballots in local areas with large numbers of non-English-speaking minorities.

Native Americans and Their Long-Delayed Rights   When white settlers first arrived, an estimated five to ten million Native American lived in what is now the United States. By 1900, they numbered only about a quarter of a million. In the whole of recorded history, no people had suffered such a huge population decline in such a short period. Smallpox and other diseases brought by white settlers took the heaviest toll, but wars and massacres also contributed. As part of a policy of westward expansion, settlers and U.S. troops mercilessly drove the eastern Indians from their ancestral lands to the Great Plains and then seized most of the territory there as well. Until Congress changed the policy in 1924, Native Americans by law were denied citizenship, which meant they lacked even the power to vote.

At first, Native Americans were not part of the 1960s civil rights movement. That changed in 1972 when Native American leaders organized the "Trail of Broken Treaties," a caravan that journeyed from California to Washington, D.C., to protest federal policy. Upon arriving in Washington, they occupied the Bureau of Indian Affairs, renaming it the Native American Embassy. The occupation ended when the government agreed to establish

During the 1960s civil rights era, Native Americans voiced long-standing grievances. Their first major protest was held at the abandoned federal prison on Alcatraz Island in San Francisco Bay. For nineteen months beginning in late 1969, Native Americans from tribes across the country occupied the prison. From there, the protest spread to other locations, including Washington, D.C., and Wounded Knee, South Dakota.

a committee to investigate their grievances. The next year, armed Native Americans took control of the village of Wounded Knee on a Sioux reservation in South Dakota; over the next two months they exchanged sporadic gunfire with U.S. marshals that left two Native Americans dead and one marshal paralyzed. Eight decades earlier at Wounded Knee, U.S. cavalry had shot to death three hundred disarmed Sioux men, women, and children.

In 1974, Congress passed legislation that granted Native Americans living on reservations greater control over federal programs affecting them. Six years earlier, Congress had enacted the Indian Bill of Rights, which gives Native Americans on reservations constitutional guarantees similar to those held by other Americans.

Asian Americans and Immigration   Chinese and Japanese laborers were brought to the western states during the late 1800s to work in mines and to build railroads. When the need for this labor declined, Congress in 1892 suspended Asian immigration on grounds that Asians were an inferior people. Over the next seven decades, laws and informal arrangements blocked residents of most Asian countries, including China and Japan, from coming to the United States. In 1965, as part of its broader civil rights agenda, Congress lifted restrictions on Asian immigration. Strict limits on Hispanic immigration were also lifted at this time, and since then, most immigrants have come from Latin America and Asia (see Figure 5-1).

Asian Americans were not politically active to any great extent during the 1960s, but their rights were expanded by the 1964 Civil Rights Act and other policies adopted in response to action by other minority groups.

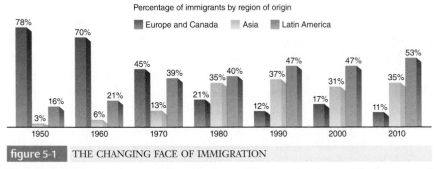

Percentage of immigrants by region of origin

■ Europe and Canada   ▦ Asia   ■ Latin America

figure 5-1   THE CHANGING FACE OF IMMIGRATION

Until 1965, immigration laws were biased in favor of European immigrants. The laws enacted in 1965 increased the proportion of immigrants from Asia and Latin America. Percentages are totals for each decade; for example, the 2010 figures are for the 2001–2010 period. *Source:* U.S. Immigration and Naturalization Service, 2014.

POLITICAL THINKING | **Should Private Discrimination Be Allowed?**

The Fifth and Fourteenth Amendments prohibit discrimination by government, but not by private organizations. The courts have ruled that social clubs and other private organizations are often within their rights in discriminating against individuals because of color, gender, national origin, creed, and other characteristics. How far would you go in eliminating discrimination by private organizations?

However, in *Lau v. Nichols* (1974), a case initiated by a Chinese American family, the Supreme Court ruled unanimously that placing public school children for whom English is a second language in regular classrooms without special assistance violates the Civil Rights Act because it denies them the opportunity to obtain a proper education.[24] The Court did not mandate bilingual instruction, but the *Lau* decision prompted many schools to offer it. Since then, some states have restricted its use. For example, California's Proposition 227, enacted in 1998, requires most children for whom English is a second language to take courses taught in English after a single year in school.

The Voting Rights Act of 1965

Free elections are the bedrock of American democracy, but the right to vote has only recently become a reality for many Americans, particularly African Americans. Although the 1870 Fifteenth Amendment granted blacks the right to vote, southern whites invented an array of devices, from whites-only primaries to rigged literacy tests, to keep blacks from registering and voting. In the mid-1940s, for example, there were only 2,500 registered black voters in the entire state of Mississippi, even though its black population numbered half a million.[25]

Racial barriers to voting began to crumble in the mid-1940s when the Supreme Court declared that whites-only primary elections were unconstitutional.[26] Two decades later, the Twenty-fourth Amendment outlawed the poll tax, which was a fee that an individual had to pay in order to register to vote. However, the major policy change was passage of the Voting Rights Act of 1965, which prohibits discrimination in voting and registration. The legislation empowers federal agents to register voters and, as interpreted by the courts, forbids the use of literacy tests as a registration requirement. The Voting Rights Act had an immediate impact on black participation. In the ensuing presidential election, black turnout in the South increased by twenty percentage points.

Congress has regularly renewed the Voting Rights Act, most recently in 2006. It has been used to stop state officials from taking action intended to suppress or dilute the vote of a minority group. In 2006, for example, the Supreme Court cited the Voting Rights Act in ordering the state of Texas to redraw the boundaries of a congressional district that had been drawn in a way intended to make Hispanics a minority of voters within the district. The Court said: "The troubling blend of politics and race—and the resulting vote dilution of a group that was beginning to [overcome] prior electoral discrimination—cannot be sustained."[27]

In a 2013 decision (*Shelby County v. Holder*) that surprised some observers, the Supreme Court in a 5-4 ruling invalidated the provision (Section 4) of the Voting Rights Act that included the formula for determining which states and counties were subject to federal oversight. The formula included such factors as whether an area had an unusually low rate of voter registration or had a history of devising tests or requirements aimed at restricting minority participation. Designated states and counties were required by the preclearance provision (Section 5) of the Voting Rights Act to receive permission from federal officials before they made changes—such as redrawing electoral districts or altering registration requirements—that might adversely affect a minority group. In its *Shelby County* decision, the Court's majority held that the formula for identifying the states and counties subject to federal oversight was based on "obsolete statistics" and could not be applied unless Congress updates it to reflect today's situation. Writing for the Court's majority, Chief Justice Roberts said: "Our country has changed, and while any racial discrimination in voting is too much, Congress must ensure that the legislation it passes to remedy that problem speaks to current conditions." Roberts said that the formula for singling out particular states and counties once "made sense," but "nearly 50 years later, things have changed dramatically." In a dissenting opinion, Justice Ruth Bader Ginsburg said that the Court's majority was overlooking the fact that, even though many of the earlier devices (such as literacy tests) for suppressing the minority vote are no longer employed, more subtle devices (such as voter ID requirements) are still being used.[28] (Although the *Shelby County* decision did not strike down Section 5, it is inapplicable unless Congress revises Section 4 to identify the states and counties subject to preclearance. As things stand, all states and localities are now free to alter electoral rules in ways of their choosing, though their decisions are subject to after-the-fact challenges in state and federal courts. The practical effect of the *Shelby County* ruling is to eliminate the requirement that some states and counties receive federal permission *before* they can make a change in their voting process.)

The Civil Rights Act of 1968

In 1968, Congress passed civil rights legislation designed to prohibit discrimination in housing. A building owner cannot refuse to sell or rent housing because of a person's race, religion, ethnicity, or sex. An exception is allowed for owners of small multifamily dwellings who reside on the premises.

Despite legal prohibitions on discrimination, housing in America remains highly segregated. Only a third of African Americans live in a neighborhood that is mostly white. One reason is that the annual income of most black families is substantially below that of most white families. Another reason is banking practices. At one time, banks contributed to housing segregation by *redlining*—refusing to grant mortgage loans in

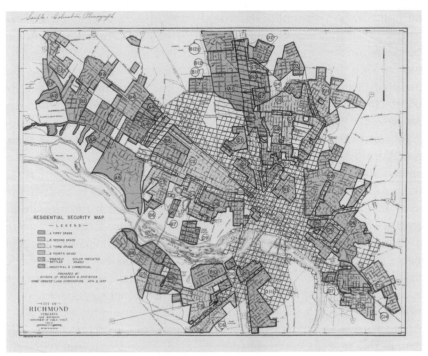

Until prohibited by the 1968 Civil Rights Act, redlining was a common banking practice in many cities. It involved the blanket denial of mortgages in certain neighborhoods, usually those with large black populations. The effect was to drive down housing prices, which contributed to white flight from these neighborhoods, resulting in increasingly segregated cities with blacks concentrated in certain neighborhoods and whites in others.

certain neighborhoods, typically those with large black populations. Since buyers could not get a mortgage, homeowners had to lower the price of their houses to sell them. As home values plummeted, white families increasingly left these neighborhoods, which had the effect of increasing the percentage of black families. The 1968 Civil Rights Act prohibits redlining, but many of the segregated neighborhoods it helped to create still exist. Moreover, minority status continues to be a factor in the lending practices of some banks. Studies indicate that Hispanics and African Americans have more difficulty obtaining mortgages than do white applicants of comparable income levels.[29]

Affirmative Action

Changes in the law seldom have large or immediate effects on how people behave. For example, although the 1964 Civil Rights Act prohibited discrimination in employment on the basis of race, color, religion, sex, or national origin, disadvantaged group members did not suddenly obtain jobs for which they were qualified. Many employers continued to prefer white male employees. Other employers adhered to established employment procedures that kept women and minorities at a disadvantage. Membership in many union locals, for example, was handed down from father to son. Moreover, the Civil Rights Act did not require employers to prove that their employment practices were not discriminatory. Instead, the burden of proof was on the woman or minority-group member who was denied a job. It was costly and usually difficult for an individual to prove in court that gender or race was the reason for not being hired or promoted. Moreover, a victory in court applied only to the individual in question; it did not help other women and minorities faced with job discrimination.

Affirmative-action programs were devised as a remedy for such problems. **Affirmative action** refers to deliberate efforts to provide full and equal opportunities in employment, education, and other areas for members of traditionally disadvantaged groups. Affirmative action applies only to organizations—such as universities, agencies, and construction firms—that receive federal funding or contracts. These organizations are required to establish programs designed to ensure that all applicants are treated fairly. They also bear a burden of proof. If an organization grants a disproportionate share of opportunities to white males, it must show that the pattern is the result of necessity (such as the nature of the job or the locally available labor pool) and not the result of systematic discrimination.

Although most equality-oriented policies have been established through congressional or judicial action, affirmative action is an exception. It was established by presidential action. The term *affirmative action* first appeared in an executive order issued in 1961 by President John F. Kennedy, who directed federal contractors to "take affirmative action to ensure that applicants are employed . . . without regard to their race, creed, color, or national origin." In 1967, President Lyndon Johnson extended affirmative action to include women and summarized the policy's goal: "We seek . . . not just equality as a right and a theory, but equality as a fact and a result." *Equality of result* was a new concept. Other major civil rights policies had sought to eliminate **de jure discrimination,** which is discrimination based on law, as in the case of the state laws requiring black and white children to attend separate schools during the pre-*Brown* period. Affirmative-action policy sought to alleviate **de facto discrimination**— the condition whereby historically disadvantaged groups have fewer opportunities and benefits because of prejudice and economic circumstances, such as their inability to pay for a college education.

Few issues have sparked more controversy than has affirmative action, and even today the public has a mixed response to it. Most Americans support programs designed to ensure that historically disadvantaged groups receive equal treatment, but oppose programs that would give them preferential treatment. Preference programs are deeply divisive. Whereas roughly 60 percent of African Americans and 50 percent of Hispanics support them, only about 20 percent of whites do so.[30]

Policies that pit individuals against each other typically end up in the Supreme Court, and affirmative action is no exception. In *University of California Regents v. Bakke* (1978), the Court issued its first affirmative-action ruling. A white male, Alan Bakke, had been rejected by a medical school that admitted minority applicants with significantly lower test scores. The Court ruled that the medical school, because it had reserved a fixed number ("a quota") of admissions for minority applicants, had violated Bakke's right to equal protection. However, the Court did not strike down affirmative-action admissions per se, saying instead that race could be among the factors taken into account by schools in their effort to create a diverse student body.[31]

The scope of affirmative action has narrowed considerably since the *Bakke* decision. Subsequent appointees to the Supreme Court have taken the policy in a conservative direction. In *Adarand v. Pena* (1995), for example, the Court overturned an earlier ruling that had upheld a federal policy that "set aside" a certain percentage of federally funded construction projects for minority-owned firms.[32] In its *Adarand* decision, the Court said that "past discrimination in a particular industry cannot justify" granting an advantage to minority-owned construction firms that have not been the direct victims of this discrimination.[33] Another example is *Ricci v. DeStefano*, in which the Supreme Court held that an organization, after establishing an equal opportunity program, has to abide by it even if minorities are adversely affected. At issue was a promotion test that the city of New Haven administered to firefighters. None of the city's black firefighters scored high enough to be considered for promotion and, after an exhaustive assessment of the exam's contents, the city concluded it had been biased and rescinded the results. The white firefighters who passed the exam then sued, and the Supreme Court ruled in their favor, concluding that New Haven had violated the 1964 Civil Rights Act's prohibition on discrimination by employers.[34]

Opponents of affirmative action have argued that the Supreme Court should end the policy entirely. They thought the Court might do so when it reviewed two University of Michigan admission policies in 2003. By a 6-3 vote in *Gratz v. Bollinger*, the Court did strike down Michigan's undergraduate admission policy, which had a point system that granted 20 points (out of 150 possible points) to minority applicants. The Court said the policy was unconstitutional because it assigned a specific weight to race.[35] However, by a 5-4 vote in *Grutter v. Bollinger*, the Court upheld

In 2006, by a 58-42 percent margin, Michigan voters passed Proposal 2, which prohibits preferential treatment on the basis of race, gender, and ethnicity in public education, public employment, and government contracting. Opponents took the issue to court, arguing that the ballot initiative violated the Fourteenth Amendment's equal-protection clause. In a 2014 case involving admissions to Michigan's public universities and colleges, the Supreme Court by a 6-2 majority upheld the results of the ballot initiative.

Michigan's law school admission policy, which took race (along with other factors such as work experience and extracurricular activities) into account in admission decisions. The Court concluded that Michigan's program was being applied sensibly and that it fostered Michigan's "compelling interest in obtaining the educational benefits that flow from a diverse student body."[36] In 2013 the Supreme Court reaffirmed its diversity position in a case involving the University of Texas, while simultaneously making it harder for colleges to take race into consideration in admission decisions. The Court said that colleges bear the burden of proof in showing that race has not been given undue weight in who gets admitted—in other words, if a college's admission policy is challenged in court, it is the college that must prove its case for the policy to be upheld.[37]

Although the Supreme Court has upheld a limited form of affirmative action in college admissions, it issued a decision in 2014 that could effectively ban affirmative action in many states. At issue was a 2006 referendum passed by Michigan voters that bars publicly funded colleges in the state from granting "preferential treatment to any individual or group on the basis of race, sex, color, ethnicity or national origin." By a 6-2 vote, the Supreme Court in *Schuette v. Coalition to Defend Affirmative Action* upheld the results of the Michigan referendum. The Court wrote that "[t]here is no authority in the Constitution of the United States or in this Court's precedents for the Judiciary to set aside Michigan laws that commit this policy determination to the voters."[38] Other states are expected to follow Michigan's lead, placing in voters' hands the issue of affirmative action. With the exception of a 2008 Colorado referendum, affirmative-action opponents have prevailed in every statewide vote held to date.

THE CONTINUING STRUGGLE FOR EQUALITY

Although progress has been made toward a more equal America, civil rights problems involve deeply rooted conditions, habits, and prejudices. As a consequence, America's traditionally disadvantaged groups are still substantially unequal in their daily lives. The following discussion describes some, though hardly all, of the problems these groups confront.

African Americans

Martin Luther King Jr.'s dream of an equal society for black Americans remains elusive.[39] Poverty is a persistent problem in the black community, affecting everyone from the very old to the very young. The median net worth of households headed by retired black people is less than $20,000, compared with roughly $200,000 for retired white people. Among adults of employment age, the jobless rate of African Americans is twice that of white Americans. As for black children, roughly 40 percent live below the government-defined poverty line, compared with about 10 percent of white children. The mortality rate of black infants is two-and-a-half times higher than that of white babies.[40]

Even the legal rights of African Americans do not, in practice, match the promise of the civil rights movement. Studies have found that African Americans accused of crime are more likely than white Americans to be convicted, and they are more likely to receive stiffer sentences for comparable offenses. The U.S. Department of Justice found, for example, that among persons convicted of drug felonies in state courts, half of black defendants received prison sentences, compared with a third of white defendants.[41] Crime rates are also substantially higher in the black community, a situation attributable in part to higher unemployment and lower education rates. An effect is that Africans Americans make up more than a third of all prison inmates, even though they account for only one-eighth of the U.S. population. Based on current incarceration rates, roughly one in four black males will spend time in prison, which is higher than the number projected to finish college. By comparison, Hispanic males have about a one in six chance of going to prison, and non-Hispanic white males have a one in twenty-three chance.[42]

A distinguishing characteristic of the black community, and a source of controversy within it, is the status of the family. Compared with other children, many fewer black children grow up in a household with both parents (see Figure 5-2). More than half of black children grow up in a single-parent family, and 8 percent grow up in a home where neither parent is present. The African American entertainer Bill Cosby was widely criticized within the black community when he suggested that many of its problems trace to the unwillingness of many black fathers to meet their family responsibilities. Nearly everyone within the black community agrees, however, that black children are harmed by the disintegration of the black family—the proportion of black children living with a single parent or no parent has nearly doubled since the 1960s. Those who grow up in a single-parent household are substantially more likely to have inadequate nutrition, not finish high school, not attend college, end up in prison, and be unemployed.

One area in which African Americans have made substantial progress since the 1960s is elective office. Although the percentage of black elected officials is still far below the proportion of African Americans in the population, it has risen sharply in recent decades.[43] There are now roughly

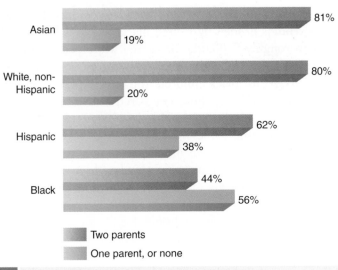

figure 5-2   FAMILY STRUCTURE, BY RACE AND ETHNICITY

Most American children live in two-parent households. The exception is black children, who are more likely to be raised in a single-parent family. *Source:* U.S. Census Bureau, 2014.

five hundred black mayors and forty-five black members of Congress. Barack Obama's election to the presidency in 2008 marked the first time an African American was chosen to fill the nation's highest office.

Women

Women, too, have made substantial gains in the area of appointive and elective offices. In 1981, President Ronald Reagan appointed the first woman to serve on the Supreme Court, Sandra Day O'Connor. When the Democratic Party in 1984 chose Geraldine Ferraro as its vice presidential nominee, she became the first woman to run on the national ticket of a major political party. Sarah Palin became the second when she ran as the 2008 Republican vice presidential nominee. Hillary Clinton nearly won the 2008 Democratic presidential nomination, which would have been the first time that a woman headed a major party's national ticket. After the 2008 election, President Obama chose Clinton to head the State Department. Each of the last three presidents has appointed a woman as secretary of state—Madeleine Albright and Condoleezza Rice are the other two women to serve in that position, which is regarded as the top cabinet post. Nevertheless, women are still a long way from attaining political parity.[44] Women hold only one in six congressional seats and one in five statewide and city council offices (see "How the U.S. Differs").

HOW THE U.S. DIFFERS

POLITICAL THINKING THROUGH COMPARISON

Women's Representation in National Legislatures

For a long period in world history, women were largely barred from holding positions of political power. The situation has changed dramatically in recent decades, and women now hold more seats in national legislatures than at any time in history. Yet in only a few countries have they even approached parity with men. The Scandinavian countries (of which Sweden is an example) rank highest in terms of the percentage of female lawmakers. Other northern European countries have lower levels, but their levels are higher than that of the United States, as the figure below indicates.

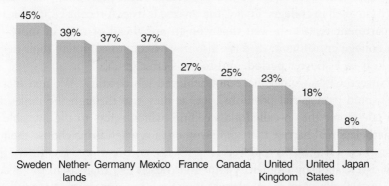

Percentage of legislative seats held by women

Sweden 45% · Netherlands 39% · Germany 37% · Mexico 37% · France 27% · Canada 25% · United Kingdom 23% · United States 18% · Japan 8%

Source: Inter-Parliamentary Union, Women in National Parliaments (2014). Based on number of women in the single or lower legislative chamber. In the case of the United States, that chamber is the U.S. House of Representatives. Reprinted with permission, www.ipu.org.

Q: Why does the United States have fewer women in its national legislature than do European democracies?

A: Public opinion in the United States does not differ greatly from that in Europe on the issue of women in public office. An explanation for why Europe has more women legislators is its reliance on proportional representation. In this system, the parties get seats in proportion

Continued

to the votes they receive in the election, which allows them to arrange for women candidates to occupy a set number of the seats. In the U.S. electoral system, by comparison, only the candidate who attracts the most votes in a district is elected, which makes it relatively difficult for a party to control the demographic makeup of its officeholders. (Chapter 8 provides a fuller explanation of the difference between proportional representation and single-member districts as methods of election.)

In recent decades, increasing numbers of women have entered the job market. They are six times more likely today than a half century ago to work outside the home and have made inroads in male-dominated occupations. Women now compose, for example, nearly half of graduating lawyers and physicians. The change in women's work status is also reflected in general education statistics. A few decades ago, more men than women were enrolled in college. Today, the reverse is true. A recent U.S. Education Department report showed that women are ahead of men in more than just college enrollment; they are also more likely to complete their degree, to do it in a shorter period, and to get better grades.[45]

Nevertheless, women have not achieved job equality. Women increasingly hold managerial positions, but, as they rise through the ranks, they can encounter the so-called glass ceiling, which refers to the invisible but nonetheless real barrier that some women face when firms choose their top executives. Of the five hundred largest U.S. corporations, less than 5 percent are headed by women. Women also earn less than men: the average pay for full-time female employees is about 80 percent of that for full-time male employees. One reason is that women are more likely than men to interrupt their careers to raise a family. Another reason is that many of the jobs traditionally held by women, such as office assistant, pay less than many of the jobs traditionally held by men, such as truck driver. Women's groups have had only limited success in persuading courts and employers to institute *comparable worth policies* that would give women and men equal pay for jobs that require a similar level of training and education.[46]

Women gained a major victory in the workplace in 1993 when Congress passed the Family and Medical Leave Act. It provides for up to twelve weeks of unpaid leave for employees to care for a new baby or a seriously ill family member. Upon return from leave, the employee ordinarily must be given the original or an equivalent job position with equivalent pay and benefits. These provisions apply to men as well as women, but women were the instigating force behind the legislation and are the primary beneficiaries in that they usually bear most of the responsibility for newborn or sick family members.

Most single-parent families are headed by women, and about one in three of these families live below the poverty line, which is five times the level of two-parent families (see Figure 5-3). The situation has been described as "the feminization of poverty." Especially vulnerable are single-parent families headed by women who work in a nonprofessional field. Women without a college education or special skills often cannot find jobs that pay significantly more than the child-care expenses they incur if they work outside the home. Adding to their burden is the fact that some of them receive no or only token child-support payments from the father.

Native Americans

Full-blooded Native Americans, including Alaska Natives, currently number more than two million, about half of whom live on or close to reservations set aside for them by the federal government. State governments have no direct authority over federal reservations, and the federal government's authority is defined by the terms of its treaty with the particular tribe. U.S. policy toward the reservations has varied over time, but the current policy is aimed at fostering self-government and economic self-sufficiency.[47] Preservation of Native American culture is another policy goal.[48] For example, children in schools run by the Bureau of Indian Affairs can now be taught in their native language. At an earlier time, English was required. Nevertheless, tribal languages have declined

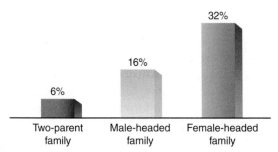

figure 5-3   PERCENTAGE OF FAMILIES LIVING IN POVERTY, BY FAMILY COMPOSITION

Poverty is five times higher among female-headed households than among two-parent households. *Source:* U.S. Census Bureau, 2012.

sharply in use. Of the larger tribes, the Navajo and Pueblo are the only ones in which a majority of the people still speak their native language at home. Ninety percent or more of the Cherokee, Chippewa, Creek, Iroquois, and Lumbee speak only English.

Native Americans have filed suit to reclaim ancestral lands. In 2006, for example, land that had once belonged to the Seneca tribe in New York was returned to it after property owners agreed to vacate their property in return for cash settlements from New York State. However, such settlements are infrequent and have involved only small parcels of land.

In recent years, some tribes have erected gaming casinos on reservation land. The world's largest casino, Foxwoods, is operated by the Mashantuket Pequots in Connecticut. Casinos have brought economic opportunities to the Native Americans living on or near the reservations where they are located. The employment level of these Native Americans has increased by a fourth and their income has increased substantially.[49] However, the casinos have also brought controversy—traditionalists argue that the casinos are creating a gaming culture that, whatever its economic benefits, is eroding tribal traditions. Political scientist W. Dale Mason notes that the gaming issue has also created conflict with state governments. The tribes claim the legal right to conduct their own affairs while the states claim the power to regulate gambling within their borders. "What remains to be seen," Mason writes, "is whether the historic tribal-state conflict can be alleviated and replaced by a new era of trust and cooperation."[50]

Although casino gambling has raised Native Americans' average income level, it is still far below the national average. Native Americans are a disadvantaged group by other indicators as well. For example, they are less than half as likely as other Americans to have completed college, and their infant mortality rate far exceeds the national average.[51]

Hispanic Americans

Hispanic Americans—that is, people of Spanish-speaking background—are one of the nation's oldest ethnic groups. Hispanics helped colonize California, Texas, Florida, New Mexico, and Arizona before those areas were annexed by the United States. Most Hispanics, however, are immigrants or the children or grandchildren of immigrants.

Hispanics are the fastest-growing minority in the United States and recently surpassed African Americans as the nation's largest racial or ethnic minority group. More than 50 million Hispanics live in the United States—twice the number of two decades ago. They have emigrated to the United States primarily from Mexico and the Caribbean islands, mainly Cuba and Puerto Rico. About half of all Hispanics in the United States were born in Mexico or claim a Mexican ancestry. Hispanics are concentrated in their states of entry. Florida, New York, and New Jersey have large numbers of Caribbean Hispanics, whereas California, Texas, Arizona, and New Mexico have many Mexican immigrants. Hispanics, mostly of Mexican descent, constitute more than half of the population of Los Angeles.

A significant number of Hispanics—ten million or more by some estimates—are in the United States illegally. Their presence became a headline issue in 2010 when the state of Arizona enacted legislation that called for police to check for evidence of legal status whenever in the course of duty they stopped a person for another reason. If the person was an illegal alien, he or she would be detained, charged with a state crime, and turned over to federal authorities for deportation. In response, Hispanics organized protest rallies in communities throughout Arizona and elsewhere, claiming that the law was a thinly disguised assault on the Latino community. Most Americans, however, supported the Arizona law. A Pew Research Center poll found that Americans, by a margin of two to one, believed local police should be required to ascertain the citizenship of individuals they encounter in the course of duty. In 2012, the Supreme Court invalidated part of the Arizona law, concluding that states cannot interfere with the federal government's constitutional authority to determine immigration policy (see Chapter 3).

On the other hand, Americans have divided opinions on the question of the long-term answer to illegal immigration. Polls indicate that most Americans favor a path to citizenship for illegal aliens who have been in the country for a relatively long period if they meet certain conditions, including holding a job, paying back taxes, and having no criminal record. However, most Americans also believe that border security should be tightened greatly, that new illegal entrants should be deported immediately, and that employers who hire undocumented aliens should face stiff penalties.

Hispanics' average annual income is substantially below the national average, but the consequences are buffered somewhat by the fact that the family is the foundation of the Hispanic culture. As compared with black Americans, Hispanics are nearly twice as likely to live in a two-parent family, often a two-income family. As a result, fewer Hispanic families live below the poverty line. Health researchers have concluded that family structure also helps to account for the fact that Hispanics are healthier and have a longer life expectancy than would be expected based on their education and income levels.

HOW THE 50 STATES DIFFER

POLITICAL THINKING THROUGH COMPARISONS

Hispanic Population in the States

Since the 1960s, Hispanics have constituted the largest percentage of new immigrants. There are now roughly 50 million Hispanics in the United States, which is twice that of two decades ago. During this period, Hispanics surpassed blacks as America's largest minority group. They now account for roughly one in six Americans. As their numbers have risen, Hispanics have acquired political influence. More than four thousand Hispanics now hold public office in the United States. Nevertheless, Hispanics' political influence varies considerably from one state to the next, depending largely on their proportion of the state population. The map shows the percentage of each state's population that is Hispanic.

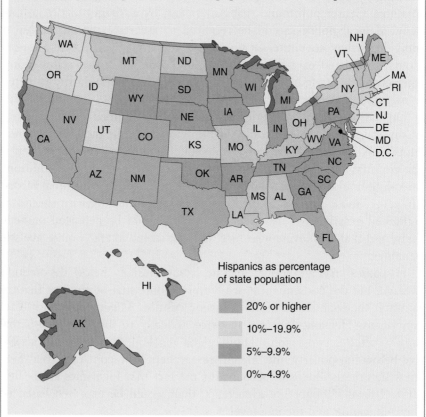

Hispanics as percentage
of state population

■ 20% or higher

■ 10%–19.9%

■ 5%–9.9%

■ 0%–4.9%

> **Q:** What accounts for differences between the states in the percentage of Hispanic population?
>
> **A:** The Hispanic population is concentrated in states on or near the border with Mexico, as in the case of California and Texas, or in states that are major ports of entry into the United States, as in the case of Florida and New York. Most Hispanics that hold public office have been elected in states with large Hispanic populations, particularly California, New Mexico, Texas, and Florida.

More than four thousand Hispanic Americans hold public office. Hispanics have been elected to statewide office in several states, including New Mexico and Arizona, and nearly three-dozen Hispanic Americans currently serve in the House of Representatives. In 2009, Sonia Sotomayor was appointed to serve on the U.S. Supreme Court, becoming the first Hispanic to do so. The political influence of Hispanic Americans continues to increase. At present, only about half of all Hispanics are registered to vote, limiting the group's political power. Nevertheless, the sheer size of the Hispanic population in states such as Texas and California will make the group a potent political force in the years to come (see Chapter 8).

Asian Americans

Asian Americans now number about twelve million, or roughly 4 percent of the total U.S. population. Most Asian Americans live on the West Coast, particularly in California. China, Japan, Korea, India, Vietnam, and the Philippines are the ancestral homes of most Asian Americans.

Asian Americans are an upwardly mobile group.[52] Most Asian cultures emphasize family-based self-reliance, which, in the American context, includes an emphasis on educational achievement. For example, Asians make up a disproportionate share of the students at California's leading public universities, which base admission primarily on high school grades and standardized test scores. Asian Americans have the highest percentage of two-parent families of any racial group, which, in combination with educational attainment, has led to their emergence in the past two decades as the group with the highest median family income. The median Asian American family's income exceeds $60,000, which is about $10,000 more than that of the median non-Hispanic white family and almost double that of the median black or Hispanic family.

Nevertheless, Asian Americans are still underrepresented in certain areas of the workplace. According to U.S. government figures, Asian Americans account for about 5 percent of professionals and technicians, which is slightly more than their percentage of the population. Yet they have not attained a proportionate share of top business positions; they hold less than 2 percent of managerial jobs.

Asian Americans are also underrepresented politically, even by comparison with Hispanics and blacks.[53] Only a dozen Asian Americans currently serve in the Congress. Not until 1996 was an Asian American elected governor of a state other than Hawaii, and not until 2000 did an Asian American hold a presidential cabinet position. A prominent Asian American politician today is Bobby Jindal, who became a leading figure in Republican politics upon winning Louisiana's 2007 race for governor. In 2011 he was reelected to a second term by a landslide.

Gays and Lesbians

The Civil Rights Act of 1964 classified women and minorities as legally protected groups, which has made it easier for them to pursue their claims in federal court. Other disadvantaged groups do not have the same high level of legal protection, but they have increasingly resorted to judicial action, none more so than gays and lesbians.[54] They gained a major legal victory when, in *Lawrence v. Texas* (2003), the Supreme Court invalidated state laws that prohibited sexual relations between consenting adults of the same sex (see Chapter 4).[55]

Gays and lesbians can now also serve openly in the armed services. Earlier, they had to adhere to the military's "don't ask, don't tell" (or, "don't harass, don't pursue") policy. As long as they did not by word or action reveal their sexual preference, they could enlist and stay in the service. In turn, other service members were prohibited from trying to entrap them. Nevertheless, roughly a thousand gays and lesbians were dismissed from service each year because of their sexual orientation.[56]

In 2000, Vermont became the first state to legalize the civil union of same-sex couples, thereby granting them the same rights in Vermont as opposite-sex couples had. Four years later, by order of the state's high court, Massachusetts became the first state to give same-sex couples the right to marry. Other states followed Massachusetts's lead and, in 2014, the Supreme Court refused to review lower-court decisions that had negated bans on same-sex marriage in several states. As a result, same-sex marriage is now legal in more than thirty states with additional lower-court challenges likely to increase that number in the near future.

POLITICAL THINKING	Should Same-Sex Marriage Be Legal?

Americans are divided in their opinions about same-sex marriage. Some believe it should be legalized, whereas others believe that marriage should be restricted to opposite-sex couples. What's your opinion? What's the basis for it? If you support same-sex marriage, do you think each state should decide for itself whether to permit it or do you think the Supreme Court should require it of all states? Why?

Although same-sex marriage is likely to remain a source of controversy, one issue surrounding it was settled when the Supreme Court in 2013 ruled that lawfully married same-sex couples are entitled to the same federal benefits (such as the opportunity to file a joint federal income tax return) as are available to opposite-sex married couples. At issue was a provision of the 1996 Defense of Marriage Act (DOMA) that denied them such benefits by declaring that marriage was "a legal union of one man and one woman as husband and wife." The Court struck down the provision as a violation of the Constitution's right to equal protection.[57]

The American public has become increasingly accepting of gay and lesbian relationships. Two decades ago, less than one in four Americans expressed support for same-sex marriage. Today more than half do so. The support level is particularly high among younger adults—more than two-thirds of them say same-sex couples should be allowed to marry. Within all age groups, however, the support level has risen substantially since the 1990s (see Figure 5-4). Among Americans over 65 years of age, for example, three in every seven are now in favor of same-sex marriage, compared with only one in every seven two decades ago.

Other Disadvantaged Groups

The Age Discrimination Act of 1975 and the Age Discrimination in Employment Act of 1967 prohibit discrimination against older workers in hiring for jobs in which age is not a critical factor in job performance. More recently, mandatory retirement ages for most jobs have been eliminated by law. Nevertheless, age discrimination is not among the forms of discrimination prohibited by the U.S. Constitution, and the courts have given government and employers some leeway in establishing age-based policies.[58] Forced retirement for reasons of age is permissible, for example, if justified by the nature of a particular job or the performance of a

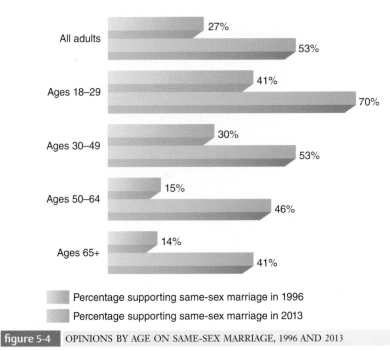

All adults
27%
53%

Ages 18–29
41%
70%

Ages 30–49
30%
53%

Ages 50–64
15%
46%

Ages 65+
14%
41%

Percentage supporting same-sex marriage in 1996
Percentage supporting same-sex marriage in 2013

figure 5-4   OPINIONS BY AGE ON SAME-SEX MARRIAGE, 1996 AND 2013

A majority of Americans now say they support same-sex marriage, though opinions vary considerably by age group. *Source:* Gallup poll, 2013.

particular employee. Commercial airline pilots, for instance, are required by law to retire at sixty-five years of age and must pass a rigorous physical examination to continue flying after they reach the age of sixty.

People with disabilities are also not protected by the Constitution from discrimination, but they are protected through statutes. In 1990, for example, Congress passed the Americans with Disabilities Act, which grants employment and other protections to this group. Government entities are required, for instance, to take reasonable steps, such as installing access ramps, to make public buildings and services available to those with disabilities.[59] Earlier, through the Education for All Handicapped Children Act of 1975, Congress required that schools provide all children, however severe their disability, with a free and appropriate education. Before the legislation, four million children with disabilities were getting either no education or an inappropriate one (as in the case of a blind child who is not taught braille).

Other groups could be described in this section. The United States has, for example, a long history of religious discrimination, targeted at various times and places against Catholics, Jews, Mormons, Muslims, various Protestant sects, and others. Numerous ethnic groups, including the Irish, the Italians, and the Poles, have likewise faced severe discrimination. Space precludes the discussion of the various forms of discrimination in America, but the point of any such discussion would be the same: equality has been America's most elusive ideal.

DISCRIMINATION: SUPERFICIAL DIFFERENCES, DEEP DIVISIONS

In 1944, Swedish sociologist Gunnar Myrdal gained fame for his book *An American Dilemma*, whose title referred to deep-rooted racism in a country that idealized equality.[60] Equality is a difficult idea in practice because it requires people to shed preconceived notions about how other people think, behave, and feel. People have difficulty looking beyond superficial differences—whether those differences relate to skin color, national origin, religious preference, gender, age, disability, or lifestyle.[61] Myrdal called discrimination "America's curse." He could have broadened the generalization. Discrimination is civilization's curse, as is clear from the thousands of ethnic, national, and religious conflicts that have marred human history. But America carries a special responsibility because of its high ideals. In the words of Abraham Lincoln, the United States is a nation "dedicated to the proposition that all men are created equal."

SUMMARY

During the past half century, the United States has undergone a revolution in the legal status of its traditionally disadvantaged groups, including African Americans, women, Native Americans, Hispanic Americans, and Asian Americans. Such groups are now provided equal protection under the law in areas such as education, employment, and voting. Discrimination by race, sex, and ethnicity has not been eliminated from American life, but it is no longer substantially backed by the force of law. This advance was achieved against strong resistance from established interests, which only begrudgingly and slowly responded to demands for equality in law.

Traditionally disadvantaged Americans have achieved fuller equality primarily as a result of their struggle for greater rights. The Supreme Court has been an instrument of change for disadvantaged groups. Its ruling in *Brown v. Board of Education* (1954), in which racial segregation in public schools was declared a violation of the Fourteenth Amendment's equal-protection clause, was a major breakthrough in equal rights. Through its affirmative action and other rulings, such as those providing equal access to the vote, the Court has also mandated the active promotion of social, political, and economic equality. However, because civil rights policy involves large issues concerned with social values and the distribution of society's opportunities and benefits, questions of civil rights are inherently contentious. For this reason, legislatures and executives have been deeply involved in such issues. The history of civil rights includes landmark legislation, such as the 1964 Civil Rights Act and 1965 Voting Rights Act.

In more recent decades, civil rights issues have receded from the prominence they enjoyed during the 1960s. The scope of affirmative-action programs has narrowed, and the use of forced busing to achieve racial integration in America's public schools has been nearly eliminated. At the same time, new issues have emerged, including the question of whether same-sex couples will have the same rights as opposite-sex couples.

The legal gains of disadvantaged groups over the past half century have not been matched by material gains. Although progress in areas such as education, income, and health care has been made, it has been slow. Tradition, prejudice, and the sheer difficulty of social, economic, and political progress stand as formidable obstacles to achieving a more equal America.

CRITICAL THINKING ZONE

KEY TERMS

affirmative action (p. 157)
civil rights (p. 141)
de facto discrimination (p. 158)
de jure discrimination (p. 158)
equal-protection clause (p. 143)

equal rights (p. 141)
reasonable-basis test (p. 146)
strict-scrutiny test (p. 146)
suspect classifications (p. 146)

APPLYING THE ELEMENTS OF CRITICAL THINKING

Conceptualizing: Distinguish between de jure discrimination and de facto discrimination. Why is the latter form of discrimination more difficult to overcome?

Synthesizing: Using material in this chapter and the previous one, contrast the Fourteenth Amendment's due process clause with its equal-protection clause. What level of government in America's federal system is governed by the two clauses?

Analyzing: What role have political movements played in securing the legal rights of disadvantaged groups?

EXTRA CREDIT

A Book Worth Reading: Taylor Branch, *Parting the Waters*. New York: Simon & Schuster, 1989. Winner of the National Book Critics Circle Award and the Pulitzer Prize for History, this book examines the black civil rights movement during the years from 1954 (when the *Brown* ruling was issued) through 1963 (when the March on Washington occurred).

A Website Worth Visiting: **www.cawp.rutgers.edu** The Center for American Woman and Politics at Rutgers University tracks women's political participation. Its website has state-by-state information on the subject.

PARTICIPATE!

Think of a disadvantaged group that you would like to assist. It could be one of the federal government's designated groups (such as Native Americans), one of the other groups mentioned in the chapter (such as people with disabilities), or some other group (such as individuals who are homeless). Contact a college, community, national, or international organization that seeks to help this group, and volunteer your assistance. (The Internet provides the names of thousands of organizations, such as Habitat for Humanity, that are involved in helping those who are disadvantaged.)

PUBLIC OPINION AND POLITICAL SOCIALIZATION: SHAPING THE PEOPLE'S VOICE

> "Towering over Presidents and [Congress] . . . public opinion stands out, in the United States, as the great source of power, the master of servants who tremble before it."
>
> JAMES BRYCE[1]

As President Barack Obama and House Speaker John Boehner weighed their options on how best to address immigration reform in advance of the 2014 midterm elections, polls indicated that Americans were divided in their opinions. Although a majority favored creating a path to citizenship for the undocumented immigrants already here, they were divided over the qualifying conditions. Some wanted to impose a waiting period and require payment of back taxes. Others favored a speedier process. Then there were those who opposed a path to citizenship under any conditions, as well as those who thought immigration reform should reward high-skill workers rather than those with little in the way of education. Polls showed that Americans were also split between those who believed immigration reform was a top priority and those who felt it would be better to put it off for a few years.

For Obama and Boehner, the issue had more urgency. Each year of his presidency, Obama had promised to pursue immigration reform, only to find reasons to delay. With his presidency now midway through the final term, his Hispanic supporters were getting impatient. Boehner's concern was a different one. His political party had lost the Hispanic vote by two-to-one in recent congressional elections—a trend that threatened the Republican Party's long-term viability. Although immigration reform would help Republicans' efforts to woo the Hispanic vote, Boehner was mindful of the fact that many within his party were dead set against a path to citizenship for those who had entered the country illegally.

Immigration reform is a telling example of the influence of public opinion on government. Although it rarely forces public officials to take a particular stand, public opinion is something that officials must take into account when deciding major policy issues. Public opinion affects officials' ability to lead, as well as the likelihood that their political party will achieve its policy and electoral goals. At the same time, public opinion is an imprecise guide to action. On nearly every issue of importance, the public is divided in its views.

This chapter discusses public opinion and its influence on U.S. politics. In this text, **public opinion** is viewed as the politically relevant opinions held by ordinary citizens that they express openly. Their expression could be verbal, as when a citizen voices an opinion to a neighbor or responds to a question asked over the phone in an opinion poll. But the expression

---

POLITICAL THINKING	Path to Citizenship, Yes or No?

Public opinion polls indicate that Americans are divided in their opinions on whether immigrants who have entered the country illegally should be given a chance to become citizens ("a path to citizenship"). What's your opinion on the issue? On what do you base your opinion?

need not be verbal. It can also take the form, for example, of participating in a protest demonstration or casting a vote in an election. The key point is that people's private thoughts become public opinion when they are revealed to others.

A major theme of the chapter is that public opinion is a powerful yet inexact force.[2] The policies of the U.S. government cannot be understood apart from public opinion; at the same time, public opinion is not a precise determinant of public policies. The main points made in this chapter are:

- *Public opinion consists of those views held by ordinary citizens that are openly expressed.* Public officials have various means of gauging public opinion but increasingly use public opinion polls for this purpose.
- *The process by which individuals acquire their political opinions is called political socialization.* This process begins during childhood, when, through family and school, people acquire many of their basic political values and beliefs. Socialization continues into adulthood, during which time the news media, peers, and political leaders are important influences.
- *Americans' political opinions are shaped by several frames of reference, including partisanship, ideology, and group attachments.*
- *Public opinion has an important influence on government but ordinarily does not determine exactly what officials will do.*

POLITICAL SOCIALIZATION: THE ORIGINS OF AMERICANS' OPINIONS

People's opinions form in response to events, issues, and problems that catch their attention or are enduring enough to retain their interest. But opinions also reflect people's interests and values. Developments invariably provoke different responses, depending on people's prior beliefs. A particularly striking example is the differing opinions of Republicans and Democrats toward U.S. military intervention in Kosovo in 1999 and in Iraq in 2003. Democrats were more supportive of the first war, whereas Republicans were more supportive of the second war. Although differences in the nature and purpose of these wars might partially explain this split, partisanship clearly does. The first of these conflicts was initiated by a Democratic president, Bill Clinton. The second was begun by a Republican president, George W. Bush.

Partisanship is a learned response. People are not born as Democrats or as Republicans, but instead they acquire these attachments. This learning is called **political socialization.** Just as a language, a religion, or an athletic skill is acquired through a learning process, so too are people's political orientations. Opinions originate in the attitudes and information that people have acquired. When Mitt Romney pledged during the 2012 presidential campaign to increase the defense budget by $100 billion a year, most Americans had an opinion on the issue. Their views owed mainly to long-standing attitudes about military spending.

Broadly speaking, the process of political socialization has two distinguishing characteristics. First, although socialization continues throughout life, most people's political outlooks are influenced by childhood learning. Basic ideas about which political party is better, for example, are often formed uncritically in childhood, in much the same way that belief in the superiority of a particular religion—typically, the religion of one's parents—is acquired. A second characteristic of political socialization is that its effect is cumulative. Early learning affects later learning because people's beliefs affect how new information is interpreted. Prior attitudes serve as a psychological screen through which new information is filtered, as in the case of the contrasting responses of Republicans and Democrats to the wars in Kosovo and Iraq.

The political socialization process takes place through **agents of socialization.** They can be divided between primary and secondary agents. *Primary agents* interact closely and regularly with the individual, usually early in life, as in the case of the family. *Secondary agents* have a less intimate connection with the individual and are usually more important later in life, as in the case of work associates. It is helpful to consider briefly how various primary and secondary agents affect political learning.

Primary Socializing Agents: Family, School, and Church

The family is a powerful primary agent because it has a near-monopoly on the attention of the young child, who places great trust in what a parent says. By the time children reach adulthood, many of the beliefs and values that will stay with them throughout life are firmly in place. Indeed, as sociologist Herbert Hyman concluded from his research: "Foremost among agencies of socialization into politics is the family."[3] Many adults are Republicans or Democrats today almost solely because their parents backed that party. They can give all sorts of reasons for preferring their party to the other, but the reasons came later in life. The family also contributes to basic orientations that, while not directly political, have political significance. American children, for example, often have a voice in family decisions, contributing to a sense of social equality.[4]

The school, like the family, affects children's basic political beliefs. Teachers at the elementary level praise the country's political institutions and extol the exploits of national heroes such as George Washington, Abraham Lincoln, and Martin Luther King.[5] Although teachers in the middle and high school grades present a more nuanced version of American history, they tend to emphasize the nation's great moments—for example, its decisive role in the two world wars. U.S. schools are more instrumental in building support for the nation and its cultural beliefs than are the schools in most other democracies. The Pledge of Allegiance, which is recited daily in many U.S. schools, has no equivalent in Europe. Schools there do not open the day by asking students to take a pledge of national loyalty.

Religious organizations are a powerful socializing agent for some children. Although many American children do not experience religion or do so only fleetingly, others attend church regularly. Scholars have not studied the influence of religion on childhood political socialization as closely as they have studied the influence of families or schools.[6] Nevertheless, religion can have a formative influence on children's attitudes, including beliefs about society's obligations to the poor and the unborn.

Grade school is a primary agent of political socialization, serving to introduce students to American ideals, customs, and historical heroes.

Secondary Socializing Agents: Peers, Media, Leaders, and Events

With age, additional socializing agents come into play. An individual's peers—friends, neighbors, coworkers, and the like—become sources of opinion. Research indicates that many individuals are unwilling to deviate too far politically from what their peers think. In *The Spiral of Silence*, Elisabeth Noelle-Neumann shows that individuals tend to withhold opinions that are at odds with those of the people around them. If nearly everyone in a group favors legalizing same-sex marriage, for example, a person who believes otherwise is likely to remain silent. As a result, the group's dominant opinion will appear to be more widely held than it actually is, which can persuade those with lightly held opinions to adopt the group opinion as their own.[7]

The mass media are also a powerful socializing agent. Politics for the average citizen is a secondhand affair, observed mainly through the media rather than directly. In the words of journalist Walter Lippmann, "the pictures in our heads of the world outside" owe substantially to how that world is portrayed for us by the media.[8] For example, heavy exposure to crime on television, whether through news or entertainment, can lead people to believe that society itself is more dangerous than it actually is.[9] The example illustrates the media's *agenda-setting effect*—the ability of the media to influence what is on people's minds. (This media effect and others are discussed more fully in Chapter 10.)

Individuals in positions of authority are also sources of opinion.[10] In the American case, no authority figure has more influence on public opinion than does the president. After the terrorist attacks of September 11, 2001, for example, many Americans were confused about who the enemy was and how America should respond. Their opinions became firmer a few days later when President George W. Bush in a nationally televised speech identified al Qaeda members as the perpetrators and declared that America would attack Afghanistan if it continued to provide them sanctuary. Polls indicated that nine of every ten Americans supported Bush's stance on Afghanistan. On the other hand, political leaders' ability to influence public opinion depends on their standing. After President Bush led America into a costly war in Iraq on the erroneous claim that it had weapons of mass destruction, his political support weakened, as did his ability to persuade Americans that the war in Iraq was worth fighting.

Finally, no accounting of the political socialization process would be complete without considering the impact of major events. The Great Depression, World War II, the Vietnam War, and the 2001 terrorist

HOW THE U.S. DIFFERS
POLITICAL THINKING THROUGH COMPARISONS

National Pride

Americans are justifiably proud of their nation. It is the oldest continuous democracy in the world, an economic powerhouse, and a diverse yet harmonious society. What Americans may not recognize, because it is so much a part of everyday life in America, is the degree to which they are bombarded with messages and symbols of their nation's greatness. Political socialization in the United States is not the rigid program of indoctrination that some societies impose on their people. Nevertheless, Americans receive a thorough political education. Their country's values are impressed on them by every medium of communication: newspapers, daily conversations, television, movies, books, magazines, and so on.

The words and symbols that regularly tell Americans of their country's greatness are important to its unity. In the absence of a

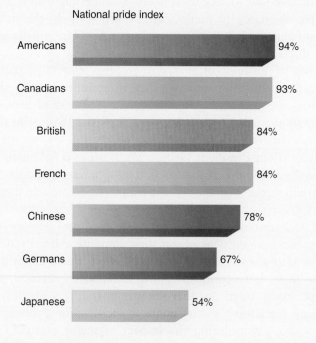

National pride index

Americans	94%
Canadians	93%
British	84%
French	84%
Chinese	78%
Germans	67%
Japanese	54%

common ancestral heritage to bind them, Americans need other methods to instill and reinforce the idea that they are one people. America's political ideals have this effect, as do everyday reminders such as the flying of the flag on homes and private buildings, a practice that is almost uniquely American. (Elsewhere, flags are typically displayed only on public buildings.)

One indicator of Americans' political socialization is the pride they express in their nationality. Americans rank high on this indicator, as shown by the accompanying chart, which is based on polls conducted by the World Values Survey. The percentages are the proportion of respondents in each country who said they were "very proud" or "proud" of their nationality.

attacks are examples of events that had a lasting influence on Americans' opinions. America's costly and inconclusive war in Vietnam, for example, changed how many citizens thought about military force. Opinion polls in the war's aftermath revealed a sharp decline in public support for military intervention and spending. As with other such events, the Vietnam War affected the views of adults of all ages, but particularly those of a young age. Major developments make a greater impression on younger citizens because their political beliefs are usually less fully developed.

FRAMES OF REFERENCE: HOW AMERICANS THINK POLITICALLY

Through the socialization process, citizens acquire frames of reference (or schemas) that serve as reference points by which they evaluate issues and developments. These frames of reference are important for two reasons. First, they provide an indication of how people think politically. Second, they are a basis for common cause. The opinions of millions of Americans would mean almost nothing if everyone's opinions were different from those of all others. If enough people share the same frame of reference, however, they have strength in numbers and have a chance of exerting political influence.

The subject of how Americans think politically fills entire books. Outlined here are three of the major frames of reference through which

Americans evaluate political developments: partisanship, ideological leanings, and group attachments.

Party Identification

Partisanship is a major frame of political reference for many Americans. **Party identification** refers to a person's sense of loyalty to a political party. Party identification is not formal membership in a party but rather an emotional attachment to it—the feeling that "I am a Democrat" or "I am a Republican." Scholars and pollsters typically have measured party identification with a question of the following type: "Generally speaking, do you think of yourself as a Republican, a Democrat, an Independent, or what?" About two-thirds of adults call themselves either Democrats or Republicans (see Figure 6-1). Of the one-third who prefer the label "Independent," most say they lean toward one party or the other and usually vote for that party's candidates. In short, most self-described independents have a partisan tendency.

Early studies of party identification concluded that it was highly stable and seldom changed over the course of adult life.[11] Subsequent studies have shown that party loyalty is more fluid than originally believed; it can be influenced by the issues and candidates of the moment.[12] Nevertheless,

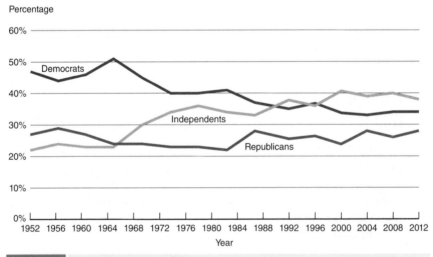

figure 6-1 PARTY IDENTIFICATION

When asked, most Americans say they identify with the Republican or Democratic Party. Of those who describe themselves as independents, most say they "lean" toward a party, and they tend overwhelmingly to support that party's candidates in elections.
Source: American National Election Studies.

many adults remain lifelong Republicans or Democrats even if their personal lives change in ways that might reasonably lead them to identify with the other party. Historically, major shifts in the party attachments of large numbers of Americans have occurred only in the context of a momentous upheaval. Even then, the shift has usually been concentrated among younger adults because their partisanship tends to be less firmly rooted. During the Great Depression, for example, Franklin Roosevelt's New Deal prompted many younger Republicans, but relatively few older ones, to change their loyalty to the Democratic Party.

Once acquired, partisanship affects what people "see." *Selective perception* is the process whereby people selectively choose from incoming information those aspects that support what they already believe. Studies of presidential debates have found, for example, that Republicans and Democrats are watching the same candidates but "seeing" different ones. When their party's candidate is speaking, they tend to see sincerity and strength. When the other party's candidate is speaking, they tend to see evasiveness and weakness.[13]

In the everyday world of politics, no source of opinion divides Americans more clearly than does their partisanship. On nearly every major issue, Republicans and Democrats have contrasting opinions. As budget cuts were being deliberated in Congress in 2011, for example, a Pew Research Center poll asked Americans about their preferences. Republicans and Democrats had differing opinions, with Republicans favoring cuts in domestic programs and Democrats favoring cuts in military spending (see Figure 6-2).

For most people, partisanship is not blind faith in their party. Although Republican and Democratic identifiers vote predominately for their party's candidates, their votes in most cases have roots in party traditions and policies. The Democratic Party, for example, has promoted the nation's social welfare and workers' rights policies, whereas the Republican Party has spearheaded the nation's pro-business and tax reduction policies. The fact that most union workers are Democrats and most people in business are Republicans is hardly a coincidence.[14] (Partisanship is examined in additional detail at various points later in this book, particularly in Chapters 7, 8, 11, and 12.)

Political Ideology

Karl Marx's collaborator, Friedrich Engels, said that he saw no real chance of communism taking root in the United States. Writing in 1893, Engels said America's workers lacked sufficient class consciousness, being concerned

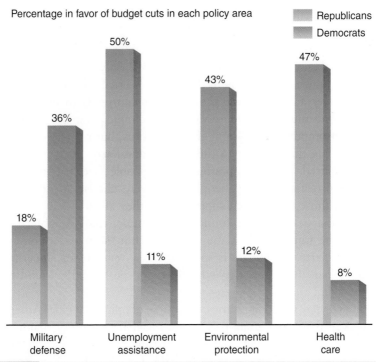

figure 6-2   PARTISANSHIP AND OPINIONS ON FEDERAL BUDGET CUTS

Opinions on which areas of the federal budget should be cut are an example of the differing policy preferences of Republicans and Democrats. *Source:* Pew Research Center for the People and the Press, 2011.

instead about getting ahead on their own.[15] In broader historical terms, Americans did not embrace any of the large twentieth-century ideologies—communism, fascism, or socialism—that captured the imagination of many Europeans. Historian Daniel Boorstin argued that Americans are pragmatists at heart, driven less by allegiance to ideology than by a desire to find workable solutions to problems.[16]

Of course, political ideology does not have to take extreme forms, as it did in the case of Soviet communism and German fascism. In simplified form, an **ideology** can be defined as a general belief about the role and purpose of government.* Some Americans believe, for instance, that

---

*Some scholars define ideology in a stricter way, arguing that it can be said to exist only when an individual has a consistent pattern of opinions across a broad range of specific issues. By this definition, most Americans don't have an ideology. This conception is analytically useful in some situations, but it blunts the discussion of general belief tendencies in the public as a whole, which is the purpose here.

HOW THE 50 STATES DIFFER

POLITICAL THINKING THROUGH COMPARISONS

Party Loyalties in the States

The strength of the major parties varies substantially among the states. One indicator of party dominance is the degree to which the party identification of state residents favors one party or the other. In opinion polls, party identification is measured by a question of the following type: "Generally speaking, do you think of yourself as a Republican, a Democrat, an Independent, or what?" The Gallup Organization has aggregated the results of its daily tracking polls to estimate the state-by-state distribution of Republican and Democratic identifiers. Nationwide, more Americans identify with the Democratic Party than the Republican Party, but the variation across the states is considerable.

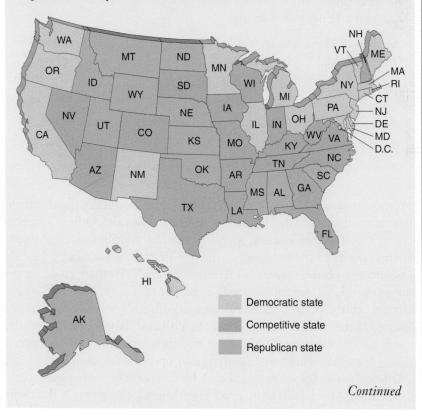

Democratic state

Competitive state

Republican state

Continued

For the accompanying map, the fifty states (plus the District of Columbia) have been divided into three groups, using the categorization method employed by Gallup. States are considered Democratic or Republican if one party's identifiers exceed those of the other party by more than five percentage points. Competitive states are those where the difference is less than five percentage points. By this indicator, Republican strength is concentrated in the Plains and the Rocky Mountains, whereas Democratic strength is concentrated in the coastal states and the northern Midwest. According to the Gallup indicator, Hawaii, Maryland, Rhode Island, New York, Massachusetts, and Connecticut (in that order) are the six most heavily Democratic states, whereas Utah, Wyoming, Idaho, North Dakota, Nebraska, and Kansas (in that order) are the most heavily Republican states. It might be noted that several southern states are categorized as competitive by the Gallup indicator, even though Republicans dominate most elections in the region, largely because of their higher rate of turnout and party-line voting.

Q: Why is there a heavy concentration of Republicans in the Great Plains and the Rocky Mountains?

A: The Great Plains and Rocky Mountain areas have traditionally been Republican, a reflection in part of the rugged individualism that defined their early settlement and contributed to a preference for small government.

government should use its power to help the economically disadvantaged. Such individuals can be labeled **economic liberals.** Other Americans believe that the government should leave the distribution of economic benefits largely to the workings of the free market. They can be described as **economic conservatives.** Americans differ also in their views on government's role in regard to social and cultural issues, such as same-sex marriage and abortion. **Cultural (social) liberals** would leave lifestyle choices to the individual. In contrast, **cultural (social) conservatives** would use government to promote traditional values—for example, by passing laws that would limit marriage to opposite-sex couples.

Although it is sometimes said that liberals believe in big government while conservatives believe in small government, this claim is inaccurate, as the foregoing discussion would indicate. Conservatives prefer a smaller role for government on economic issues but want to use the power of government to uphold cultural traditions. The reverse is true of liberals. Each group wants government to be active or inactive, depending on which approach serves its policy goals.

There is no logical reason, of course, why an economic liberal also has to be a cultural liberal. Although most economic liberals are also cultural liberals, some are not. The term **populist** (although some analysts prefer the term *communitarian*) is used to describe an individual who is an economic liberal and a cultural conservative. Similarly, some economic conservatives are cultural liberals. They believe government should refrain from undue intervention in the economic marketplace *and* in people's private lives. The term **libertarian** is used to characterize someone with this set of beliefs.

Group Orientations

Many Americans see politics through the lens of a group affinity. Their identity or self-interest is tied to the group, and they respond accordingly when a policy issue arises that affects it. Issues surrounding social security,

POLITICAL THINKING	What Is Your Ideology?

The Gallup poll measures Americans' ideology by posing two sets of alternatives: (1) Some people think the government should make greater use of its taxing and spending power to help the less-well-off while other people think government should do less in this realm, leaving economic benefits to be distributed largely through the marketplace. (2) Some people think the government should make greater use of its power to promote traditional values in our society while other people think government should do less in this realm, leaving decisions about lifestyle to each individual. According to Gallup, a conservative *thinks government should do less in the economic realm but do more to promote traditional values; a* liberal *thinks government should do more to help the less-well-off but do less in promoting traditional values; a* libertarian *would like government to do less in both areas; and a* populist *would like government to do more in both realms. Do you ever use one of these labels to describe yourself? Is it the same one that would be assigned to you by the Gallup method? If not, how would you explain the difference?*

for example, usually evoke a stronger response from senior citizens than from younger adults. Later chapters examine group tendencies more fully, but it is useful here to describe briefly a few groupings—religion, economic class, region, race and ethnicity, gender, and age.

Religion   Religious beliefs have long been a source of solidarity among group members and a source of conflict with outsiders. As Catholics and Jews came to America in large numbers in the nineteenth and early twentieth centuries, they encountered intense hostility from some Protestants. Today, Catholics, Protestants, and Jews hold similar opinions on many policy issues. Nevertheless, important religious differences remain, although the alignment shifts as the issue shifts.[17] Fundamentalist Protestants and Roman Catholics are more likely than mainline Protestants and Jews to oppose legalized abortion, a split that partly reflects differing religious beliefs about whether human life begins at conception or later in the development of the fetus. Religious beliefs also affect opinions on poverty programs. Support for such programs is higher among Catholics and Jews than among Protestants. An obligation to help the poor is a central theme of Catholic and Jewish teachings, whereas self-reliance is a central theme in the teachings of some Protestant denominations.

The most powerful religious force in today's politics is the so-called religious right, which consists mostly of white evangelical Protestants (see "Party Polarization"). Their opinions on issues such as gay rights, abortion, and school prayer differ significantly from those of the population as a whole. A recent Pew Research Center survey, for example, found that white evangelical Protestants were less than half as likely as other Americans to approve of gay marriage.

Economic Class   Economic class has less influence on political opinion in the United States than in Europe, but income and education levels do affect Americans' opinions on some issues. Welfare assistance programs and business regulation, for example, have more support among lower-income Americans, whereas higher-income Americans are more supportive of tax cuts.

An obstacle to class-based politics in the United States is that people with similar incomes but differing occupations do not share the same outlook. Support for collective bargaining, for example, is higher among factory workers than among small farmers, white-collar workers, and workers in the skilled crafts, even though the average income of each of these groups is similar. The interplay of class and opinion is examined more closely in Chapter 9, which discusses interest groups.

P A R T Y
POLARIZATION

Political Thinking in Conflict

Religion and Politics

Between the 1930s Great Depression and the early 1970s, religion was a small part of American politics, except in 1960 when John F. Kennedy became the first Catholic to win the presidency. In the 1972 presidential election, however, a gap opened in the voting pattern of those who went to church frequently and those who did not. Ever since, religious values have been a part of the so-called culture war that has been waged between the Republican and Democratic parties over issues such as abortion, school prayer, same-sex marriage, and stem-cell research. The Republican Party has made major gains among white fundamentalist Christians, who now regularly cast about 75 percent of their votes for GOP presidential and congressional candidates. Catholics were once reliable Democratic voters but are now split, with tradition-oriented Catholics voting mostly Republican and modern-oriented Catholics voting mostly Democratic. The level of formal religious commitment also matters in how Americans vote. According to a Pew research poll, for example, roughly 60 percent of those who went to church at least once a week voted Republican in the 2012 presidential race compared with roughly 40 percent of those who seldom or never went to church. Americans of the Jewish faith have been less affected politically by the increased salience of religion in politics. They vote heavily Democratic and have done so for decades.

Q. What's your sense of the heightened salience of religion in American politics? Overall, how large a role do you think a particular religion's beliefs should play in elections and in determining national policy?

Region   For a period in U.S. history, region was the defining dimension in American politics. The North and South were divided over the issues of race and states' rights. Racial progress has diminished the regional divide, as has the relocation to the South of millions of Americans from the Northeast and Midwest. The newcomers are generally less conservative than natives to the region. Nevertheless, regional differences continue to exist on some issues, including social welfare and civil rights. The differences are large enough that when analysts talk about "red states" (Republican bastions) and "blue states" (Democratic bastions), they are generally referring to regions. The red states are clustered in the South, Great Plains, and Rocky Mountains, whereas the blue states are found mostly in the Northeast, the northern Midwest, and the West Coast.

Race and Ethnicity As was discussed in Chapters 4 and 5, race and ethnicity affect opinions on civil rights and civil liberties issues. Blacks and Hispanics, for example, are generally more supportive of affirmative action and less trusting of police and the judicial system than are non-Hispanic whites. Blacks and Hispanics also tend to differ from non-Hispanic whites on economic assistance programs, although this difference mostly reflects differences in their income and education levels.

Gender Men and women tend to think alike on many issues, including abortion rights, but tend to disagree on others.[18] Polls have found, for example, a consistent difference of about ten percentage points between women and men on support for affirmative action. The difference is even larger on some social welfare issues, such as poverty and education assistance. Women tend to have more liberal opinions on these issues, reflecting in part their greater economic vulnerability and their greater role in child care. A recent *Washington Post*/ABC News poll found, for example, that women were 20 percent more likely than men to favor increased spending for public education. Women and men also differ on national security policies, with men more likely than women to support the use of military force. Support for the Iraq and Afghanistan wars, for example, was consistently higher among men than women.

Generations and Age As a generation comes of age, it encounters a different political environment than its predecessors, with the result that its political views will differ somewhat from those of earlier generations. Those Americans who came of age during World War II, for example, acquired a sense of civic duty unmatched by the preceding generation or by any generation since. On the other hand, those who came of age during the Vietnam War era were more mistrustful of government than the generation before them or the one that followed. Today's young adults are no exception to the pattern. Their political views are to some extent a reflection of their generation's experiences. Unlike senior citizens, for example, a substantial majority of today's young adults believe that gays and lesbians should have the right to marry.[19]

Crosscutting Groups Although group loyalties have an impact on people's opinions, this influence is diminished when identification with one group

Religion is a powerful socializing force in American life. Churches, synagogues, mosques, and temples are places where Americans acquire values and beliefs that can affect their opinions about politics. Pictured here is the interior of the Lakewood Church in Houston, Texas. It is the largest of America's "megachurches"—those that hold thousands of worshipers.

is offset by identification with other groups. In a pluralistic society such as the United States, groups tend to be "crosscutting"—that is, each group includes individuals who also belong to other groups, where they can encounter different opinions. Exposure to such opinions fosters political moderation. By comparison, in societies such as Northern Ireland, where group loyalties are reinforcing rather than crosscutting, opinions are intensified by personal interactions. Catholics and Protestants in Northern Ireland live largely apart from each other, differing not only in their religious beliefs but also in their income levels, residential neighborhoods, ethnic backgrounds, and loyalties to the government. The result has been widespread mistrust between Northern Ireland's Catholics and Protestants and a willingness on the part of some on each side to resort to violence.

In the past few decades in the United States, the overlap between groups has diminished. Although the situation is still far different than in a place like Northern Ireland, Americans today interact less with those of a different background. Residential neighborhoods, for example, are now less diverse. Workplaces are also less diverse today than in the past. Many office workers and professionals, for example, spend their workday interacting almost entirely with others of the same occupation. Even Americans' "virtual" interaction has narrowed. Through the 1980s, Americans were exposed through television to a version of news that included Republican and Democratic arguments in roughly equal amount. Today, many Americans get their news from a cable outlet or Internet site that plays up one side of the partisan debate while dismissing the other (see Chapter 10).

"Information cocoons" is how legal scholar Cass Sunstein describes Americans' preference for like-minded associates and information sources.[20] The tendency contributes to the party polarization that is now a defining characteristic of American politics. Partisan differences are sharper and harder to bridge when citizens have a poor understanding of the opinions of people not like themselves (see "Party Polarization" boxes throughout the book).

THE MEASUREMENT OF PUBLIC OPINION

In a democracy, the central issue of public opinion is its impact on the governing process. Does government heed public opinion? Before addressing this question, it is helpful to discuss how political leaders find out about public opinion. Woodrow Wilson once said that he had spent much of his adult life in government and yet had never seen a "government." What Wilson was saying, in effect, was that government is a system of relationships. A government is not tangible in the way that a building is. So it is with public opinion. No one has ever seen a "public opinion," and thus it cannot be measured directly. It must be assessed indirectly.

Election returns are a traditional method for assessing public opinion. Politicians routinely draw conclusions about what citizens are thinking by studying how they voted. Letters to the editor in newspapers and the size of crowds at mass demonstrations are among the other means of judging public opinion. All these indicators are useful guides for policymakers. Each of them, however, is a limited guide to what is on people's minds.

Election returns indicate how many votes each candidate received but do not indicate why voters acted as they did. As for letter writers and demonstrators, research indicates that their opinions are more intense and usually more extreme than those of most citizens.[21]

Public Opinion Polls

Today, opinion polls or surveys are the primary method for estimating public sentiment.[22] In a **public opinion poll,** a relatively few individuals—the **sample**—are interviewed in order to estimate the opinions of a whole **population,** such as the residents of a city or country.

How is it possible to measure the thinking of a large population on the basis of a relatively small sample of that population? How can interviews with, say, one thousand Americans provide a reliable estimate of what millions of them are thinking? The answer is found in the laws of probability. Consider the hypothetical example of a huge jar filled with a million marbles, half of them red and half of them blue. If a blindfolded person reaches into the jar, the probability of selecting a marble of a given color is fifty-fifty. And if one thousand marbles are chosen in this random way, it is likely that about half of them will be red and about half will be blue. Opinion sampling works in the same way. If respondents are chosen at random from a population, their opinions will approximate those of the population as a whole.

Random selection is the key to scientific polling, which is theoretically based on *probability sampling*—a sample in which each individual in the population has a known probability of being chosen at random for inclusion. The key is random selection. Individuals do not step forward to be interviewed; they are selected at random to be part of the sample. A scientific poll is thereby different from an Internet survey that invites visitors to a site to participate. Any such survey is biased because it includes only individuals who use the Internet, who happen for one reason or another to visit the particular site, and who decide to complete the survey. A scientific poll is also different from the "people-in-the-street" interviews that news reporters sometimes conduct. Although a reporter may say that the opinions of those interviewed represent the views of the local population, this claim is clearly faulty. Interviews conducted on a downtown street at the noon hour, for example, will include a disproportionate number of business employees on their lunch breaks. Stay-at-home mothers, teachers, and factory workers are among the many groups that would be underrepresented in such a sample.

The science of polling is such that the size of the sample, as opposed to the size of the population, is the key to accurate estimates. Although it might be assumed that a much larger sample would be required to poll accurately the people of the United States as opposed to, say, the residents of Georgia or San Antonio, the sample requirements are nearly the same. Consider again the example of a huge jar filled with marbles, half of them red and half of them blue. If one thousand marbles were randomly selected, about half would be red and about half would be blue, regardless of whether the jar held one million, ten million, or one hundred million marbles. On the other hand, the size of the sample—the number of marbles selected—would matter. If only ten marbles were drawn, it might happen that five would be of each color but, then again, it would not be unusual for six or seven of them to be of the same color. In fact, the odds are about one in twenty that eight or more would be of the same color. However, if one thousand marbles were drawn, it would be highly improbable for six hundred of the marbles, much less seven or eight hundred of them, to be of the same color. The odds of drawing even six hundred of the same color are about one in one hundred thousand.

The accuracy of a poll is expressed in terms of **sampling error**—the degree to which the sample estimates might differ from what the population actually thinks. The larger the sample, the smaller the sampling error, which is usually expressed as a plus-or-minus percentage. For

President Harry Truman holds up the early edition of the *Chicago Tribune* with the headline "Dewey Defeats Truman." The *Tribune* was responding to analysts' predictions that Dewey would win the 1948 election. A Gallup poll a few weeks before the election had shown Dewey with a seemingly insurmountable lead. The Gallup Organization decided that it did not need to do another poll closer to the election, a mistake that it has not since repeated.

example, a properly drawn sample of one thousand individuals has a sampling error of roughly plus or minus 3 percent. Thus, if 55 percent of a sample of one thousand respondents say they intend to vote for the Republican presidential candidate, there is a high probability that between 52 percent and 58 percent (55 percent plus or minus 3 percent) of all voters actually plan to vote Republican. It should be noted that if the poll had found the candidates separated by one percentage point, it would be mathematically incorrect to claim that one of them is "leading." The one-point difference is smaller than the poll's three-point sampling error.

The impressive record of the Gallup poll in predicting the outcome of presidential elections indicates that the theoretical accuracy of polls can be matched in practice. The Gallup Organization has polled voters in every presidential election since 1936 (nineteen elections in all) and has erred badly only once: it stopped polling several weeks before the 1948 election and missed a late voter shift that carried Harry Truman to victory.

Problems with Polls

Although pollsters assume that their samples are drawn from a particular population, such as all citizens of adult age, pollsters rarely have a list of all individuals in the population from which to sample. An expedient alternative is a sample based on telephone numbers. Pollsters use computers to randomly pick telephone numbers (including now also cell-phone numbers), which are dialed by interviewers to reach households. Within each of these households, a respondent is then randomly selected. Because the computer is as likely to pick one telephone number as any other, a sample selected in this way is assumed to be representative of the whole population. Nevertheless, some Americans do not have phones, and many of those who are called will not be home or refuse to participate. Such factors reduce the accuracy of telephone polling. Indeed, pollsters are concerned about the future of telephone polling. The refusal rate has increased sharply in recent decades.

The accuracy of polling is also diminished when respondents are asked about unfamiliar issues. Although respondents may answer the question anyway in order not to appear uninformed, their responses cannot be regarded as valid. Scholars label such responses "non-opinions." Less often, respondents will have an opinion but choose not to reveal it. On sensitive topics, interviewees will sometimes give what they regard as the socially correct response. For example, although turnout in presidential elections rarely exceeds 60 percent, 75 percent or more of respondents in post-election polls will claim to have voted. Some of them are not being truthful, but they are unwilling to tell the interviewer that they neglected to vote. Respondents are also not always truthful when it comes to expressing opinions that relate to race, gender, or ethnicity.

Question wording can also affect poll results. Consider the issue of the death penalty. Do Americans favor or oppose its use? As it turns out, the answer depends to some extent on how the issue is worded. Respondents in some Gallup polls have been asked the question: "Are you in favor of the death penalty for a person convicted of murder?" Respondents in other Gallup polls have been asked a different version: "If you could choose between the following two approaches, which do you think is the better penalty for murder—the death penalty or life imprisonment, with absolutely no possibility of parole?" The two versions produce different results. When asked the first question, Americans by roughly two-to-one say they favor the death penalty. When asked the second question, Americans are evenly divided on whether the death sentence is the proper penalty.[23]

Despite such problems, the poll or survey is the most relied-upon method of measuring public opinion. More than one hundred organizations are in the business of conducting public opinion polls. Some, like the Gallup Organization, conduct polls that are released to the news media by syndication. Most large news organizations also have their own polls—an example is the CBS News/*New York Times* poll. Other polling firms specialize in conducting surveys for candidates and officeholders.

THE INFLUENCE OF PUBLIC OPINION ON POLICY

As yet unaddressed in the discussion is a central question about public opinion: what is its impact on the policies of government? The question does not have a firm or simple answer, either in theory or in practice.

Writers have long disagreed about the impact that public opinion *should* have on government. Some have contended that the opinions citizens hold, except the most fleeting or malignant, deserve to be taken into account by officials, who otherwise would promote policies that are out of line with the public's interests. This tradition was expressed by George Gallup, a pioneer in the field of polling: "The task of the leader is to decide how best to achieve the goals set by the people." Other writers have argued that public opinion is too whimsical to be a basis for sound policies. "Effective government," journalist Walter Lippmann wrote, "cannot be conducted by legislators and officials who, when a question is presented, ask themselves first and last not what is the truth and which is the right and necessary course, but 'What does the Gallup Poll say?'"

There is also disagreement over the impact public opinion actually has on government. It is not a simple matter to pinpoint the influence of public opinion on particular public policies, and analysts do not entirely agree on what the evidence indicates. Nevertheless, most studies have concluded that public opinion has a significant influence on policymakers, though it varies across situations and issues.

Limits on the Public's Influence

Even if officials were intent on governing by public opinion, they would face obstacles, including inconsistencies in citizens' policy preferences. In polls, for example, Americans say they want a balanced federal budget. Yet only a minority say they would support deep cuts in costly programs like social security and defense even if the budget could not be balanced without them. Nor are most citizens willing to balance the budget through a large tax increase. In the entire history of polling, there has never been a national survey in which a majority of respondents said their taxes should be raised significantly. In a 2011 Gallup poll, for example, 50 percent of respondents claimed that taxes were too high, and only 5 percent said taxes were too low.[24]

Many citizens also lack an understanding of issues, even vitally important ones. In the buildup to the U.S. invasion of Iraq in 2003, for example, polls revealed that more than half of adult Americans wrongly believed that Iraq had close ties to the al Qaeda terrorist network. Moreover, despite widespread opposition to the American invasion in most other countries, one in four Americans believed that world opinion supported the invasion. Americans who held these mistaken views were more likely than other Americans to support sending U.S. troops into Iraq.[25]

Only a minority of citizens can truly be said to be politically well informed. Even a college education is no guarantee that a citizen will have more than a passing familiarity with public affairs. The Intercollegiate Studies Institute surveyed fourteen thousand college students in 2007, giving them a multiple-choice exam to test their "civic literacy." The average college student received a grade of F, answering barely half of the questions correctly. Only 46 percent of college seniors, for example, could identify the phrase "We hold these truths to be self-evident, that all men are created equal" as being part of the Declaration of Independence.[26] An earlier survey of Ivy League students found that one-third

To become an American citizen, immigrants must pass a citizenship test that asks basic questions about the U.S. political system. Ironically, when the test is given to a cross section of Americans who are already citizens, many of them fail it. Citizens' lack of information serves to limit the impact of public opinion on policy.

could not identify the British prime minister, half could not name both U.S. senators from their state, and three-fourths could not identify Abraham Lincoln as the author of the phrase "a government of the people, by the people, and for the people."[27]

Of course, citizens do not have to be fully informed to have a reasonable opinion about some issues.[28] Knowing only that the economy is performing poorly, a citizen could reasonably believe that government should take action to fix it. The fact that the citizen is unaware of the government's economic policy options would not render his or her opinion irrelevant. As one research team noted: "It is true that individual Americans have a weak grasp on the essentials of economics and economic policy, and it is also true that Americans, in the aggregate, are highly sensitive to real economic performance."[29]

On the other hand, there are issues where information is nearly a prerequisite to a sound opinion. The health care reform legislation that Congress debated in 2009–2010, for example, had cost and coverage provisions that affected people in different ways. Yet many Americans had no awareness of these provisions or were misinformed about them. A Gallup poll found, for instance, that nearly a third of the public mistakenly believed that the legislation included government committees (the so-called death panels) that would decide which elderly patients would receive life-saving treatment and which would not. Those who held this erroneous belief were more likely than other citizens to oppose the legislation. Many of these individuals might have opposed it anyway for other reasons, but mistaken beliefs are not the basis for sound opinions.

Public Opinion and the Boundaries of Action

Such considerations led political scientist V. O. Key to conclude that the role of public opinion is to place boundaries on the actions of political leaders.[30] The public is seldom attentive enough or informed enough to dictate exactly what officials will do. However, politicians must operate within the boundaries of what the public deems reasonable and acceptable.

Certain policy actions are outside these boundaries. Opinions on some issues are so settled that officials have little chance of success if they try to work against them. During his second presidential term, for example, George W. Bush attempted to privatize aspects of social security, only to back down in the face of determined opposition from senior citizens. The founder of social security, Franklin D. Roosevelt, understood that public opinion would preserve the program. "No damn politician," he reportedly said, "can ever scrap my social security program." Roosevelt recognized that, by having

POLITICAL THINKING	Can Citizens Meet the Demands of Democracy?

Nearly a century ago, two of America's leading thinkers—the journalist Walter Lippmann and the philosopher John Dewey—debated whether citizens could play the role democracy asks of them. Lippmann and Dewey were in agreement that citizens' ability to think sensibly about public affairs was undermined by the numbing distractions of the entertainment media and the propaganda efforts of powerful officials and special interests. But Lippmann and Dewey differed sharply on the public's potential. Lippmann concluded that citizens lacked the necessary level of involvement and understanding to be given a large voice in their own governing. Dewey felt that advances in education and communication would position citizens to make sound judgments on public issues. Which argument do you find more persuasive? What's the basis for your conclusion?

social security benefits funded by payroll taxes, workers would feel they had rightfully earned their retirement benefits and would fight to keep them.

The greater the level of the public's involvement in an issue, the more likely officials will respond to public sentiment. In a study spanning four decades, Benjamin Page and Robert Shapiro found that changes in public opinion were usually followed by a shift of public policy in the same direction, particularly on issues of concern to large numbers of citizens.[31] Political scientist John Kingdon reached a similar conclusion, saying that when public opinion is intense and unmistakable as to a preferred course of action, politicians nearly always follow it.[32]

Nevertheless, even on issues that substantially engage the public, leaders usually have a degree of discretion. As political scientists Jeff Manza and Fay Lomax Cook noted from their study of public opinion: "Politicians and policy entrepreneurs often have substantial room to maneuver."[33] When the economy goes into a tailspin, for example, Americans expect officials to take action. However, Republican leaders typically respond with measures such as tax cuts and interest-rate adjustments, whereas Democratic leaders tend to rely on measures such as increased unemployment benefits and spending-level adjustments. Each approach can boost the economy, but they differ in their impact. The Republican approach helps mainly business

Public opinion can affect government policy, as in 2014 when, following the beheading of two Americans by Islamic State militants, polls showed public support for military action. President Obama responded with air strikes and other measures.

interests and upper-income citizens whereas the Democratic approach helps mainly labor interests and lower-income citizens.

Officials also have latitude when the public is divided in its opinions. When significant numbers of citizens are aligned on opposite sides of an issue, officials cannot easily satisfy both sides. However, this situation often is not politically difficult because the split falls largely along party lines. The 2009–2010 health care reform issue was of this type, enabling most members of Congress to take positions aligned with the views of most of their party's voters. A February 2010 Gallup poll, for example, found that Republican identifiers by more than three-to-one opposed comprehensive health care reform whereas Democratic identifiers by more than three-to-one favored it.

On issues that do not attract widespread public attention, leaders ordinarily have wide room to maneuver. On most policy issues, "the public"—if one means by that the whole citizenry—has no discernible opinion. Agricultural conservation programs, for example, are of keen interest to some farmers, hunters, and environmentalists but of little or no concern to most people. The pattern is so common that opinion analysts have described America as a nation of *many* publics.[34] The "public" for agricultural policy is a different one than, say, the "public" for financial regulation policy. Not surprising, in deciding such issues, political leaders are usually more responsive to the smaller number who are keenly interested in the issue than they are to the larger number who haven't given it any thought or don't feel intensely about it.[35]

Leaders and Public Opinion

The fact that public opinion and public policy coincide at points does not necessarily mean that officials are choosing policies on the basis of what citizens would prefer. Officials often go to great lengths to win public support for their policies.[36]

If leaders succeed in persuading the public to accept their point of view, policy and opinion will coincide but they will do so because leaders have been able to influence public opinion. A case in point is the period leading up to the U.S. invasion of Iraq in 2003. Although Americans had been hearing about Iraqi leader Saddam Hussein for years and had concluded that he was a tyrant and a threat, they were unsure whether an attack on Iraq made sense. Polls indicate that some Americans preferred to give United Nations inspectors ample time to investigate Iraq's weapons program before an invasion decision was made. Other Americans expressed support for an invasion only if the United States had the backing of its

European allies. Still others thought that, if a war was launched, it should be conducted entirely through the air. However, over the course of a roughly six-month period, the Bush administration pressed the case for war, which gradually increased public support for it.[37] When the war began, polls showed that President Bush's decision to use ground and air forces against Iraq had the backing of 70 percent of Americans.

Such examples have led some analysts to claim that major policies more fully reflect the preferences of leaders than those of citizens.[38] The linguist Noam Chomsky, for example, claims that public opinion is largely the product of elite manipulation or, as he calls it, "manufactured consent."[39] Nevertheless, systematic studies have found that policy on high-profile issues usually changes in the direction of public opinion, rather than the reverse. Until the beheading of two Americans by Islamic State militants in 2014, President Obama had hesitated to launch attacks on the radical Islamists who had seized territory in Syria and Iraq. Polls showed that Americans were opposed to getting drawn into another conflict in the Middle East. The beheadings changed the public's attitude, and Obama immediately took steps to put military pressure on the Islamic State, including airstrikes and sending advisors to help Kurdish and Iraqi forces counter the threat. Such examples are commonplace. On the basis of their study of more than 350 policy-opinion relationships, Page and Shapiro concluded, "When Americans' policy preferences shift, it is likely that congruent changes in policy will follow."[40] In their more recent but similarly extensive study of the opinion-policy linkage, Robert Erikson, Michael MacKuen, and James Stimson found the same pattern, concluding that "public opinion influences policy."[41]

SUMMARY

The process by which individuals acquire their political opinions is called political socialization. During childhood, the family, schools, and church are important sources of basic political attitudes, such as beliefs about the parties and the nature of the U.S. political and economic systems. Many of the basic orientations that Americans acquire during childhood remain with them in adulthood, but socialization is a continuing process. Adults' opinions are affected mostly by peers, the news media, and political leaders. Events themselves also have a significant short-term influence on opinions.

The frames of reference that guide Americans' opinions include political ideology, although most citizens do not have a strong and consistent ideological attachment. In addition, individuals develop opinions as a result of group orientations—notably, religion, economic class, region, race and ethnicity, gender, and age. Partisanship is a major source of political opinions; Republicans and Democrats differ in their voting behavior and views on many policy issues.

Public opinion can be defined as those opinions held by ordinary citizens that they openly express. Public officials have many ways of assessing public opinion, such as the outcomes of elections, but they have increasingly come to rely on public opinion polls. There are many possible sources of error in polls, and surveys sometimes present a misleading portrayal of the public's views. However, a properly conducted poll can be an accurate indication of what the public is thinking.

Public opinion has a significant influence on government but seldom determines exactly what government will do in a particular instance. Public opinion serves to constrain the policy choices of officials but also is subject to their efforts to mold and channel what the public is thinking. Evidence indicates that officials are particularly attentive to public opinion on highly visible and controversial issues of public policy.

CRITICAL THINKING ZONE

KEY TERMS

agents of socialization (*p. 179*)
cultural (social) conservatives (*p. 188*)
cultural (social) liberals (*p. 188*)
economic conservatives (*p. 188*)
economic liberals (*p. 188*)
ideology (*p. 186*)
libertarians (*p. 189*)
party identification (*p. 184*)

political socialization (*p. 179*)
population (*p. 195*)
populists (*p. 189*)
public opinion (*p. 177*)
public opinion poll (*p. 195*)
sample (*p. 195*)
sampling error (*p. 196*)

APPLYING THE ELEMENTS OF CRITICAL THINKING

Conceptualizing: *Population*, *sample*, and *sampling error* are terms associated with public opinion polling. Explain each term and how it relates to the others.

Synthesizing: Contrast the views of conservatives and liberals on how far government should go to help the economically disadvantaged, and then contrast their views on how far government should go to promote traditional social (cultural) values. Note that each group wants government to be active or inactive, depending on which approach serves its policy goals.

Analyzing: What factors limit the influence of public opinion on the policy choices of public officials?

EXTRA CREDIT

A Book Worth Reading: Walter Lippmann, *Public Opinion* (New York: Free Press, 1997). Written by the twentieth-century's preeminent journalist and originally published in 1922, this book predates polling research and yet offers timeless insights on the nature of public opinion. (The book is available free on Google Books.)

A Website Worth Visiting: **www.people-press.org** The Pew Research Center for the People and the Press is an independent, nonprofit institute. Its website includes recent and past poll results, including cross-national comparisons.

PARTICIPATE!

Studies have regularly found that Americans, in relative and in absolute terms, are substantially uninformed about the issues affecting their state, their nation, and the world. As a result, Americans' opinions about policy issues and problems are not as informed as they could and should be. Citizenship entails responsibilities, one of which is to stay informed about problems and developments that affect the community, the state, and the nation. As an informed citizen, you will be better able to make judgments about policy issues, to choose wisely when voting during elections, and to recognize situations that call for greater personal involvement. Fortunately, you have access to one of the most substantial news systems in the world. News about public affairs is virtually at your fingertips—through your computer, on television, and in the newspaper. Spending only a small amount of time each day following the news will help you to be a more effective and involved citizen.

7
CHAPTER

"We are concerned in public affairs, but immersed in our private ones."

WALTER LIPPMANN[1]

The stakes in the 2014 midterm congressional elections could not have been much higher. Partisan wrangling between Republicans and Democrats had dominated nearly every legislative issue, and public confidence in Congress was near an all-time low. Polls showed that the election was close enough that either party could conceivably gain control of the House and Senate. Yet, in the November election, most eligible voters did not bother to go to the polls, even though both parties waged intensive get-out-the-vote campaigns.

Voting is a form of **political participation**—involvement in activities intended to influence public policy and leadership. Political participation involves other activities in addition to voting, such as joining political groups, writing to elected officials, demonstrating for political causes, and giving money to political candidates. Such activities contribute to a properly functioning democratic society. The concept of self-government is based on the idea that citizens have a right and a duty to participate in public affairs. Democracies differ, however, in their levels of political participation. The United States is an unusual case. Compared with other Western democracies, it has relatively low levels of voter participation. Yet it has relatively high levels of citizen participation in political and civic organizations. This chapter describes and explains this participation paradox. The chapter's main points are below:

- *Voter turnout in U.S. elections is low in comparison with that of other Western democracies.* The reasons include U.S. election laws, particularly those pertaining to registration requirements and the scheduling of elections.

- *Most citizens do not participate actively in politics in ways other than voting.* Only a minority of Americans can be classified as political activists. Nevertheless, Americans are more likely than citizens of other democracies to contribute time and money to political and community organizations.

- *Most Americans make a distinction between their personal lives and public life.* This outlook reduces their incentive to participate and contributes to a pattern of participation dominated by citizens of higher income and education.

VOTER PARTICIPATION

At the nation's founding, **suffrage**—the right to vote—was limited to property-owning males. Benjamin Franklin ridiculed the restriction. Observing that a man whose only item of property was a jackass would lose his right to vote if the jackass died, Franklin asked, "Now tell me, which was the voter, the man or the jackass?" Fifty years elapsed before the property restriction was lifted in all the states.

African Americans appeared to have gained suffrage after the Civil War with passage of the Fifteenth Amendment, which says that the right to vote cannot be abridged "on account of race, color, or previous condition of servitude." Nevertheless, African Americans were disenfranchised throughout the South by intimidation and electoral trickery, including rigged literacy tests as a precondition of being allowed to register to vote. The tests contained questions so difficult that often the examiner had to look up the answers. If that was not enough of an obstacle, the names of those who took the test were sometimes published in the local newspaper so that employers, the local police, and even the KKK would know the identity of the "troublemakers." It is no surprise that some counties in the South had almost no black registrants. Not until the 1960s did Congress and the courts sweep away the last legal barriers to equal suffrage for African Americans (see Chapter 5).

Women did not secure the vote until 1920, with the ratification of the Nineteenth Amendment. Decades earlier, Susan B. Anthony had tried to vote in her hometown of Rochester, New York, claiming that as a U.S. citizen she had a right to vote. She was arrested for "illegal voting" and told that her proper place was in the home. By 1920, men had run out of excuses for denying the vote to women. As Senator Wendell Phillips observed, "One

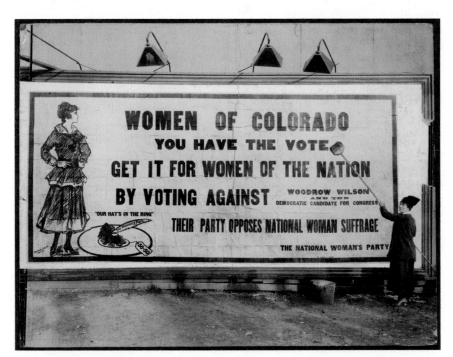

After a hard-fought, decades-long campaign, American women finally won the right to vote in 1920.

of two things is true: either woman is like man—and if she is, then a ballot based on brains belongs to her as well as to him. Or she is different, and then man does not know how to vote for her as she herself does."[2]

The nation's youngest adults are the most recent beneficiaries of a suffrage amendment. Ratified during the Vietnam War—a time when the military draft was in full swing and the minimum voting age in nearly every state was twenty-one years—the Twenty-sixth Amendment lowered the voting age to eighteen years. "If you're old enough to die, you're old enough to vote" was the rallying cry of its proponents.

Factors in Voter Turnout: The United States in Comparative Perspective

Today, nearly any American adult—rich or poor, man or woman, black or white—who is determined to vote can legally and actually do so. Nearly all Americans embrace the symbolism of the vote, saying that they have a duty to vote in elections. Nevertheless, many Americans shirk their duty. Millions choose not to vote regularly, a tendency that sets Americans apart from citizens of most other Western democracies. In the past two decades, **voter turnout**—the proportion of adult citizens who actually vote in a given election—has averaged roughly 60 percent in presidential elections (see Figure 7-1). In other words, about three in five eligible citizens have gone to the polls in recent presidential elections while two in five have stayed away.

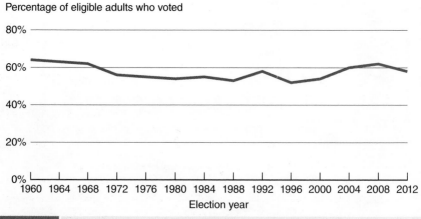

Percentage of eligible adults who voted

figure 7-1   VOTER TURNOUT IN PRESIDENTIAL ELECTIONS, 1960–2012

During the three decades after 1960, turnout steadily declined. In the three most recent presidential elections, turnout has been high relative to the two preceding elections—1996 and 2000. *Source:* U.S. Census Bureau. Figures are based on percentage of vote-eligible adults who voted.

Although turnout in presidential elections is not particularly high, it is significantly higher than the turnout in the midterm congressional elections that take place between presidential elections. Midterm turnout has not reached 50 percent since 1920 and has hovered around 40 percent in recent decades. Turnout in local elections is lower still. In many places, only about 20 percent of eligible citizens—a mere one in five—bother to vote.

Voter participation is lower in the United States than in most other democracies (see "How the U.S. Differs"). For example, turnout in recent national elections has averaged more than 90 percent in Belgium and more than 75 percent in Germany and Denmark.[3] America's lower turnout is partly the result of its more demanding registration requirements and the greater frequency of its elections.

Registration Requirements   Before Americans are allowed to vote, they must be registered—that is, their names must appear on an official list of eligible voters. **Registration** began around 1900 as a way of preventing voters from casting more than one ballot on Election Day. Multiple balloting had become a tactic of big-city party machines—"vote early and often" was their mantra. Although registration reduced illegal voting, it also placed a burden on honest citizens. Because they were required to register beforehand, citizens who forgot or otherwise failed to do so were unable to vote. Turnout in U.S. elections declined steadily after registration began.

Although other democracies also require registration, most of them place the responsibility on government. When someone moves to a new address, for example, the postal service will notify registration officials of the change. The United States—in keeping with its individualistic culture—is one of the few democracies in which registration is the individual's responsibility. Moreover, registration is largely controlled by the state governments. Although the 1993 Motor Voter Act requires them to allow people to register when they apply for a driver's license or public assistance,[4] some states make little effort otherwise to inform citizens about registration times and locations.[5] Scholars estimate that turnout would be roughly ten percentage points higher in the United States if it had European-style registration.[6]

States with more convenient registration laws have higher turnout than other states. A few states, including Idaho, Maine, and Minnesota, allow people to register at their polling places on Election Day. Their turnout rates are more than ten percentage points above the national average. States with the most restrictive registration laws—for example, those that require residents to register at least two or three weeks before Election Day—have turnout rates well below the national average. Several of these states are in the South, which, even today, has the lowest turnout rate of any region (see "How the 50 States Differ").

HOW THE U.S. DIFFERS

POLITICAL THINKING THROUGH COMPARISONS

Voter Turnout

The United States ranks near the bottom among the world's democracies in the percentage of eligible citizens who participate in national elections. One reason for the low voter turnout is that individual Americans are responsible for registering to vote, whereas in most other democracies voters are registered automatically by government officials. In addition, unlike some other democracies, the United States does not promote voting by holding elections on the weekend or by imposing penalties, such as fines, on those who do not participate.

Country	Approximate Voter Turnout (%)	Automatic Registration?	Election on Holiday or Weekend?
Belgium	90	Yes	Yes
Italy	80	Yes	Yes
Germany	75	Yes	Yes
France	70	No	Yes
Great Britain	70	Yes	No
Canada	65	Yes	No
United States	55	No	No

Source: Developed from multiple sources. Turnout percentages are a rough average of national elections during the past two decades.

Q: How might American election campaigns differ if voter turnout were as high in the United States as in most European democracies?

A: If turnout in U.S. elections were in the 80-percent to 90-percent range, lower-income voters would make up a much larger share of the electorate, and candidates would have to pay more attention to their policy concerns. As it stands, most candidates aim their appeals at middle-income voters. Such voters constitute a substantially larger share of the electorate in the United States than in Europe.

elections more often than other nations. No other democracy has elections for the lower chamber of its national legislature (the equivalent of the U.S. House of Representatives) as often as every two years, and no democracy schedules elections for chief executive more frequently than every four years.[9] In addition, most local elections in the United States are held in odd-numbered years, unlike the even-year schedule of federal elections and most state elections. Finally, the United States uses primary elections to select the party nominees. In other democracies, party leaders pick them.

At an earlier time, most statewide elections coincided with the presidential election, when turnout is highest. This scheduling usually worked to the advantage of the party that won the presidential race—its candidates got a boost from the strong showing of its presidential nominee. In an effort to eliminate "presidential coattails," states began in the 1930s to hold their gubernatorial elections in nonpresidential years. Over three-fourths of the states have adopted this schedule, and two states—Virginia and New Jersey—elect their governors in odd-numbered years, insulating them even further from the turnout effects of federal elections.

Americans are asked to vote two to three times as often as Europeans, which increases the likelihood that they will not participate every time.[10] Moreover, elections in the United States have traditionally been scheduled on Tuesday, forcing most adults to find time before or after work to get to the polls. Many European nations hold their elections on Sunday or make Election Day a national holiday, making it easier for working people to vote.

POLITICAL THINKING

What Should the Right to Vote Mean in Practice?

Although adult Americans see themselves as having the right to vote, voting does not have the same constitutional status as, say, the right to free expression and the right to a fair trial. With those rights, government is obliged to take steps (for example, by providing legal counsel to poor defendants) to ensure that a right is upheld in practice. Voting is different. State governments have been granted wide leeway in controlling access to the ballot—for example, in determining registration periods, polling place hours, and identification requirements. Some states have instituted policies aimed at making voting harder rather than easier. Do you favor the existing approach to voting rights, or do you think government should be obligated to take positive steps to ensure that every citizen who wants to vote is able to do so? Why?

Why Some Americans Vote and Others Do Not

Even though turnout is lower in the United States than in other major Western democracies, some Americans vote regularly while others seldom or never vote. Among the explanations for these individual differences are education and income, age, and civic attitudes.

Education and Income   College-educated and upper-income Americans have above-average voting rates. They have the financial resources and communication skills that encourage participation and make it personally rewarding. Nevertheless, the United States is unusual in the degree to which education and income are related to voter participation. Europeans with less education and income vote at only slightly lower rates than other citizens. By comparison, Americans with a college degree or high income are substantially more likely to vote in a presidential election than are those who did not finish high school or have a low income.

Why the great difference between the United States and Europe? For one thing, Europeans with less income and education are encouraged to participate by the presence of class-based organizations and appeals—

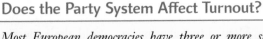

POLITICAL THINKING	Does the Party System Affect Turnout?

Most European democracies have three or more significant political parties that are shaped around class and social divisions, and sometimes along religious and ethnic divisions as well. Labor and socialist parties abound in Europe, as do middle-class, environmental, and right-wing parties. Accordingly, European voters have a broad range of choices, which some analysts cite as a reason why voter turnout in Europe is higher than in the United States, where voters basically have only two choices, the Republican and Democratic parties. Moreover, most European democracies have proportional representation systems, In such a system, parties get legislative seats according to their percentage of the total vote. The United States has a plurality system where representatives are chosen by legislative district, with the winner in each district getting the seat. Some district races are so lopsided that the outcome is a forgone conclusion, thereby reducing the incentive for voters to go to the polls. By comparison, every vote in a proportional representation system counts in the sense that it contributes to the party's percentage of the vote. What significance do you attach to these differences in the European and American party systems? Would you be more inclined to vote if you had more choices? What type of alternative party—religious, environmental, labor, or whatever—might be particularly attractive to you?

socialist or labor parties, politically oriented trade unions, and class-based political ideologies. The United States has never had a major socialist or labor party. Although the Democratic Party represents the working class and the poor to a degree, it is chiefly responsive to middle-class voters, who hold the balance of power in U.S. elections.[11] In addition, Americans with less income and education are the people most adversely affected by the country's registration system. Many of them do not own cars or homes and are thus less likely to be registered in advance of an election. They are also less familiar with registration locations and requirements.[12] Indeed, Americans in the bottom fifth in terms of income are a third less likely to be registered to vote than those in the top fifth (see Figure 7-2).

Age   Young adults are substantially less likely than middle-aged and older citizens to vote. Even senior citizens, despite the infirmities of old age, have a far higher turnout rate than do voters under the age of thirty. The difference is greater in local and state elections than in presidential elections. Only a small percentage of young adults vote regularly in local elections. Younger adults are less likely to live in the same residence from one election to the next and are more likely to have to reregister in order to establish their eligibility to vote.

Civic Attitudes   **Apathy**—a lack of interest in politics—typifies some citizens. They rarely if ever vote. Just as some people would not attend

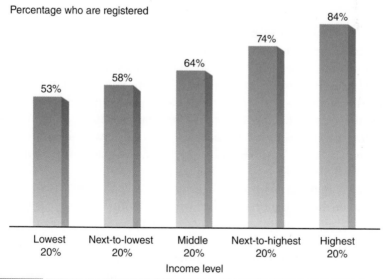

Percentage who are registered

				84%
			74%	
		64%		
	58%			
53%				
Lowest 20%	Next-to-lowest 20%	Middle 20%	Next-to-highest 20%	Highest 20%

Income level

figure 7-2   VOTER REGISTRATION AND INCOME LEVEL

Americans of lower income are much less likely to vote than those of higher income.
Source: U.S. Census Bureau, 2014.

the Super Bowl even if it was free and being played across the street, some Americans care so little about politics that they would not bother to vote even if a ballot were delivered to their door. Still other Americans refrain from voting because of **alienation**—a feeling of powerlessness rooted in the belief that government pays no attention to their interests. Many of these citizens regard voting as a waste of time, convinced that government won't respond to their concerns even if they do vote.

On the other hand, some Americans have a keen sense of **civic duty**—a belief that they ought to participate in public affairs. Citizens who hold this belief tend to vote more regularly. Civic duty and apathy are attitudes that are usually acquired from one's parents. When parents vote regularly and take an active interest in politics, their children usually grow up thinking they have a duty to participate. When parents never vote and show no interest in public affairs, their children are likely to be politically apathetic. Alienation can be traced to childhood socialization but often has adult roots. For example, when the Democratic Party took the lead on civil rights issues in the 1960s, some working-class white Democrats felt left out, believing that gains for African Americans would come at their expense. Some of these Democrats switched parties, but others simply stopped voting. Voter turnout among working-class whites dropped sharply in 1968 and in 1972—two presidential elections in which civil rights issues were paramount.[13]

Political Interest and Party Identification   Finally, the likelihood that citizens will vote varies with their interest in politics. As would be expected, citizens with a strong or moderate interest in politics are much more likely to vote than those with little or no interest. What makes this fact noteworthy is that political interest is in large part a consequence of partisanship. Although "independents" are sometimes idealized in high school civics classes, they have much lower voting rates than citizens who identify with a political party. In recent presidential elections, party identifiers have turned out at a rate in excess of 75 percent, compared with a mere 50 percent for independents.

A reason that party loyalists are more likely to vote than independents is that they are more familiar with the policy differences between the parties and therefore more likely to be aware of the election's consequences. Moreover, party loyalty is like people's other loyalties—it deepens their involvement. Although party loyalists have but one vote to cast, it is a way of expressing their commitment (see "Party Polarization").

P A R T Y **Political Thinking in Conflict**

POLARIZATION

The Role of Voter Turnout

Strong Republicans tend to be substantially more conservative than independents or weak Republican identifiers, while strong Democrats tend to be substantially more liberal than independents or weak Democratic identifiers. In addition, strong partisans are substantially more likely to vote than independents or weak identifiers. As a result (see graph below) the voting public is more polarized in its political positions than is the public as a whole.

This situation prods candidates to take more extreme positions in order to secure the votes of those on their side of the partisan divide. If candidates had to pitch their appeals to the full public, they might be inclined to take more moderate positions. This possibility is what led William Galston of the University of Maryland and the Brookings Institution to propose mandatory voting. Galston notes that some democracies, including Australia and Italy, require citizens to vote or pay a fine. These countries have exceptionally high turnout levels. "Our low turnout rate," Galston says, "pushes American politics toward increased polarization."*

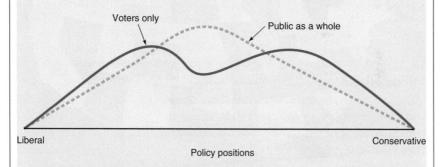

Q: Would you favor a law requiring Americans to vote or pay a fine if they fail to do so? If the United States had such a policy do you think, as William Galston does, that it would significantly reduce the level of party polarization?

*William A. Galston, "Telling Americans to Vote, or Else," *New York Times*, November 5, 2011, p. SR9.

CONVENTIONAL FORMS OF PARTICIPATION OTHER THAN VOTING

No form of political participation is as widespread as voting. Nevertheless, voting is a limited form of participation. Citizens have the opportunity to vote only at a particular time and only for the choices listed on the ballot. Fuller opportunities for participation exist, including contributing time and money to political and civic causes.

Campaign and Lobbying Activities

Compared with voting, working for a candidate is more time-consuming. Not surprisingly, only a small percentage of citizens engage in such activities. Nevertheless, the number is substantially higher in the United States than in Europe (see Figure 7-3). One reason Americans are more active in campaigns, even though they vote less, is that the United States is a federal system with campaigns for national, state, and local offices. A citizen who wants to participate can easily find an opportunity at one level of office or another. Most of the European governments are unitary in form (see Chapter 3), which means that there are fewer elective offices and thus fewer campaigns. (Election campaigns are discussed further in Chapter 8.)

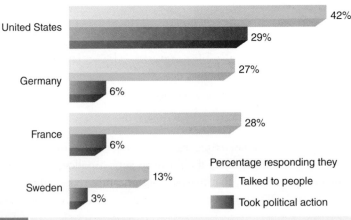

figure 7-3   CAMPAIGN ACTIVITY

Although Americans are less likely to vote in elections than citizens elsewhere, they are more likely to engage in other campaign activities, such as trying to influence the vote choice of others. *Source:* From Russell J. Dalton, "The Myth of the Disengaged American," *CSES Report* (October 25, 2005). Reprinted with permission.

Americans are also more likely than citizens elsewhere to support the activities of political groups. This support usually takes the form of a monetary contribution but also includes more active forms, such as contacting lawmakers or attending public rallies. Among the hundreds of groups that depend on citizen contributions are Greenpeace, Common Cause, AARP (formerly known as the American Association of Retired Persons), the Christian Coalition of America, and the National Conservative Political Action Committee. (Lobbying groups are discussed further in Chapter 9.)

Virtual Participation

The introduction of the World Wide Web in the 1990s opened up an entirely new venue for political participation—the Internet. Through e-mails, blogs, chat rooms, social networks, and the like, the Internet has created participation possibilities previously unimaginable. Although this participation is "virtual" rather than face-to-face, much of it involves contact with friends, acquaintances, and activists through Facebook, Twitter, e-mail, and other social media. Internet participation peaks during presidential campaigns and now easily outstrips conventional participation. Internet fundraising also is flourishing. In 2012, more than five million Americans contributed online to a candidate, usually in an amount of $100 or less.[14]

A number of groups have built extensive online organizations. MoveOn .org, for example, has a network of more than three million "online activists" that it mobilizes in support of liberal causes. During the 2014 midterm elections, for example, MoveOn commissioned polls in more than two dozen Republican-held congressional districts in an effort to identify those where the Democrats could win. It then urged its followers to donate money to these districts' Democratic candidates. (The Internet is discussed further in Chapter 10.)

Community Activities

Political participation extends beyond campaigns and elections to involvement in the community. Citizens can join community groups, work to accomplish community goals, and let officials know their opinions on community matters. These forms of participation offer citizens a substantial degree of control over the timing and extent of their participation. The chief obstacle to participation is not opportunities, which are abundant, but the motivation to join in. Most people choose not to get involved, particularly when it comes to time-consuming activities.

HOW THE 50 STATES DIFFER

POLITICAL THINKING THROUGH COMPARISONS

Volunteer Activity

Volunteer work in the community is an American tradition and occurs through a variety of groups. At the top of the list are church groups, followed by education groups such as parent-teacher associations. Many Americans also get involved in their communities through social service, health, and civic groups. The volunteer rate varies considerably by state, however, as indicated by a recent study by the Corporation for National and Community Service, the government corporation that manages federally funded service programs such as AmeriCorps. Utah has the highest volunteer rate; 44 percent of its residents sixteen years of age or older are engaged yearly in community volunteer work of one type or

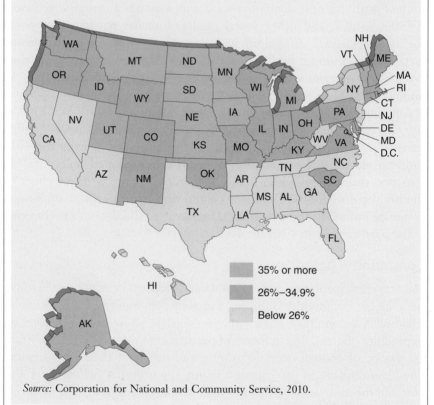

Source: Corporation for National and Community Service, 2010.

another. Nebraska (39 percent), Minnesota and Alaska (each at 38 percent), and Iowa (37 percent) are the other states in the top five.

Q: Why does the Upper Midwest region (which includes Iowa, Minnesota, Nebraska, and the Dakotas) have the highest volunteer rate?

A: Political scientist Daniel Elazar found that states in the Upper Midwest have a strong community orientation, reflecting the values of the Scandinavians and others who settled in the region. In addition to their more active community life, states in the regions spend more heavily on community-centered policies, such as the public schools, than do most other states. Utah's high participation rate stems from a different tradition. A majority of its population is Mormon, a religious faith that emphasizes the individual's community responsibilities.

Nevertheless, many Americans are involved in community affairs through local organizations such as parent-teacher associations, neighborhood groups, business clubs, and church-affiliated groups. The actual number of such participants is difficult to estimate, but they number in the tens of millions, reflecting in part a tradition of local participation that dates to colonial times. Moreover, compared with cities and towns in Europe, those in the United States have greater authority over local policies, giving their residents a motive to participate actively. Because of increased mobility and other factors, Americans may be less tied to their local communities than in the past and therefore less involved in community activity. Nevertheless, Americans are more than twice as likely as Europeans to work together in groups on issues of local concern.[15]

In a widely discussed book titled *Bowling Alone*, Harvard's Robert Putnam claims that America has been undergoing a long-term decline in its **social capital** (the sum of the face-to-face civic interactions among citizens in a society).[16] Putnam attributes the decline largely to television and other activities that draw people away from involvement in civic and political groups. Some scholars dispute Putnam's claim, but it appears to hold for older citizens. On the other hand, young adults have become more involved in their communities in recent decades, partly because of high school and college internship and volunteer programs.[17] According to a University of Maryland study, volunteering among young people has increased by roughly 20 percent since 1990.[18]

UNCONVENTIONAL ACTIVISM: SOCIAL MOVEMENTS AND PROTEST POLITICS

During the predemocratic era, people resorted to protest as a way of expressing displeasure with their rulers. Tax and food riots were the typical forms of protest. When democratic governments came into existence, citizens had a regular and less disruptive way to express themselves—through their votes. Voting is double-edged, however. Although the vote gives citizens control over government, *the vote also gives government control over citizens.*[19] Because they have been elected by the voters, public officials can claim to be constitutionally empowered even if they pursue policies that are opposed by a majority of the people or that contradict what they promised to do if elected.

Social movements, or **political movements** as they are sometimes called, are a way for citizens disenchanted with government policy to actively express their opposition.[20] These efforts are channeled through conventional forms of participation, such as political lobbying, but citizens sometimes take to the streets in protest against government. No protest movement in modern time had a larger or more lasting effect

Tea Party protestors stage a rally at the Capitol against federal spending and taxes.

than the black civil rights movement. Beginning in the 1950s with boycotts of businesses that gave African Americans second-class treatment, the movement grew to include mass demonstrations and marches. It succeeded on a level beyond what even its leaders might have imagined. The landmark 1964 Civil Rights Act and 1965 Voting Rights Act were a direct result of the pressure the movement placed on lawmakers (see Chapter 5).

Political protests have taken on new forms in recent years. Protest was traditionally a desperate act that began when a group had lost hope of succeeding by conventional methods. Today, however, protest is usually a planned event—a means of getting attention.[21] These tactical protests often involve a great deal of planning, including, in some instances, the busing of thousands of people to Washington for a rally staged for television. Civil rights, environmental, and pro-choice and anti-abortion groups are among the many groups that have recently staged such protests.

The Tea Party and Occupy Wall Street Protest Movements

The past few years have witnessed two of the best organized and most sustained protest movements in decades—the Tea Party and Occupy Wall Street movements. They each started from anger at established interests but otherwise have little in common.

The Tea Party came to the public's attention on April 15, 2009—the date that federal income taxes were due. The timing was not a coincidence, nor was the movement's name. Like the participants in the legendary Boston Tea Party, those that took to the streets in hundreds of cities and towns on that April day were expressing their opposition to high taxes. In Washington, D.C., the protesters hurled tea bags over the White House fence.

Backed by wealthy conservative donors, the Tea Party quickly became a major force in American politics. Although it was aligned from the start with factions of the Republican Party, its initial target was Republican lawmakers who had supported the bailout of banks in the aftermath of the 2008 financial crisis. Tea Party activists successfully challenged establishment GOP candidates in the 2010 primaries, prevailing in several states, including Utah, Alaska, Delaware, and South Carolina. Their platform, which was labeled a "Contract from America," called for sharp reductions in federal spending: "Our moral, political, and economic liberties are inherent, not granted by our government. It is essential to the practice of these liberties that we be free from restriction over our peaceful political expression and free from excessive control over our economic choices."

The Tea Party played a key role in the Republican takeover of the House of Representatives in the 2010 elections, and its influence carried into Congress. Tea Party–backed Republicans in Congress took a hard line on fiscal issues, demanding large cuts in federal spending and opposing any increase in taxes. Their unwillingness to compromise contributed to a congressional deadlock in 2011 that nearly put the U.S. government into default on its debt for the first time in history and to a congressional stalemate in 2013 that resulted in a temporary shutdown of some federal agencies and programs. In each case, the public was turned off by the legislative turmoil, and opinion polls indicated a decline in the Tea Party's public support.[22]

The Occupy Wall Street movement also saw its public support decline, but for a different reason—Americans' unease with movements that pit protesters against the police. When the Occupy Wall Street (OWS) movement emerged in 2011, it began small—a single encampment in New York City's Zuccotti Park, adjacent to Wall Street. Within a few weeks, however, it had spread to dozens of other American cities, and even some

Occupy Wall Street protesters rallying against policies that favor the wealthy. The building in the background is home to the New York Stock Exchange.

abroad. Like the Tea Party, OWS was angry at the government's bailout of the financial industry and its failure to hold the bankers accountable for their role in the country's financial crisis. Unlike the Tea Party, however, OWS's target was private wealth. It aimed to curb the political influence of large donors and to rescind the Bush-era tax policies that benefited the wealthiest 1 percent of Americans. "We are the 99%" soon became the movement's slogan.

OWS succeeded in directing public attention toward the widening gap between rich and poor in America and, for a time, support for OWS and its message was on the rise.[23] Its momentum slowed and then reversed when local officials began to disband OWS encampments, citing safety and health concerns. In some locations the protesters clashed with police. As the headlines shifted from the issue of wealth to the issue of public order, OWS's public support weakened.[24]

Although the Tea Party and Occupy Wall Street movements served to mobilize hundreds of thousands of Americans, their futures are uncertain. Tea Party followers are competing with more traditional Republicans for control of the Republican Party, and it is unclear whether they will win out in the long run. Occupy Wall Street's uncertain future has a different basis. The movement resisted ties with the Democratic Party, which meant that much of its momentum was lost when its encampments were disbanded. OWS is attempting to redefine itself as a more conventional movement but has not yet had much success. Whatever their futures, the Tea Party and Occupy Wall Street movements represent the largest wave of political protest since the civil rights and antiwar movements of the 1960s. In this sense, their political legacy is assured.

POLITICAL THINKING

Tea Party versus Occupy Wall Street: Which Had the Better Strategy?

The Tea Party and Occupy Wall Street employed different political strategies. The Tea Party chose to direct much of its effort at a political party, seeking to influence the Republican Party's platform and selection of candidates. Occupy Wall Street chose to operate largely outside the party system, seeking to put grassroots pressure on media, corporate, and political leaders. Which tactic do you think was more effective and why?

The Public's Response to Protest Activity

Protest politics has a long history in America. Indeed, the United States was founded on a protest movement that sparked a revolution against Britain. Despite this tradition, protest activity is less common today in the United States than in many Western democracies. Spain, France, Germany, Sweden, and Mexico are among the countries that have higher rates of protest participation.

Public support for protest activity is also relatively low in the United States. The Vietnam War protests, which in some cases were accompanied by the burning of the American flag, had only marginal public support. When unarmed student protesters at Kent State University and Jackson State University were shot to death in May 1970 by members of the National Guard, most American polls faulted the students. In a *Newsweek* poll, 58 percent of respondents blamed the Kent State killings on the student demonstrators, while only 11 percent said the guardsmen were at fault. The public was more accepting of the Iraq war protest in 2003. Three in every five Americans said they saw the protests as "a sign of a healthy democracy." Still, almost two in five poll respondents said that "opponents of the war should not hold antiwar demonstrations" and half of them said that antiwar demonstrations should be outlawed.

In short, although most Americans recognize that protest is part of America's tradition of free expression, they do not embrace it in the way they do voting or community work. In this sense, protest is seen as something to be accepted but not necessarily to be admired.

PARTICIPATION AND THE POTENTIAL FOR INFLUENCE

Most Americans are not highly active in politics. One reason is the emphasis that the American culture places on individualism. Most Americans under most conditions expect to solve their problems on their own rather than through political action. "In the United States, the country of individualism *par excellence*," William Watts and Lloyd Free write, "there is a sharp distinction in people's minds between their own personal lives and national life."[25]

Paradoxically, given their greater need for government help, lower-income Americans are the least likely to vote or to otherwise engage in collective action. They lack the financial resources and communication skills that encourage participation in politics and make it personally rewarding.[26] As a consequence, their political influence is relatively limited. In *Unequal Democracy*, political scientist Larry Bartels demonstrates that elected officials are substantially less responsive to the concerns of their less affluent constituents than to those who are wealthier.[27] In other words, the pattern of economic political influence in the United States parallels the distribution of economic influence. Those who have the least power in the marketplace also have the least power in the political arena. However, the issue of individual participation is only one piece of the larger puzzle of how power in America is distributed. Subsequent chapters will furnish additional pieces.

SUMMARY

Political participation is involvement in activities designed to influence public policy and leadership. A main issue of democratic government is the question of who participates in politics and how fully they participate.

Voting is the most widespread form of active political participation among Americans. Yet voter turnout is significantly lower in the United States than in other democratic nations. The requirement that Americans must personally register in order to become eligible to vote is one reason for lower turnout among Americans; other democracies place the burden of registration on government officials rather than on the individual citizens. The fact that the United States holds frequent elections also discourages some citizens from voting regularly.

Only a minority of citizens engage in the more demanding forms of political activity, such as work on community affairs or on behalf of a candidate during a political campaign. Nevertheless, the proportion of Americans who engage in these more demanding forms of activity exceeds the proportion of Europeans who do so. Most political activists are individuals of higher income and education; they have the skills and material resources to participate effectively and tend to take a greater interest in politics. More than in any other Western democracy, political participation in the United States is related to economic status.

Social movements are broad efforts to achieve change by citizens who feel that government is not properly responsive to their interests. These efforts sometimes take place outside established channels; demonstrations, picket lines, and marches are common means of protest. Despite America's tradition of free expression, protest activities do not have a high level of public support.

Overall, Americans are only moderately involved in politics. Although they are concerned with political affairs, they are mostly immersed in their private pursuits, a reflection in part of a cultural belief in individualism. The lower level of participation among low-income citizens has particular significance in that it works to reduce their influence on public policy and leadership.

CRITICAL THINKING ZONE

KEY TERMS

alienation (*p. 218*)
apathy (*p. 217*)
civic duty (*p. 218*)
political participation (*p. 208*)
registration (*p. 211*)

social capital (*p. 223*)
social (political) movements
  (*p. 224*)
suffrage (*p. 208*)
voter turnout (*p. 210*)

APPLYING THE ELEMENTS OF CRITICAL THINKING

Conceptualizing: How do alienation, apathy, and civic duty differ?

Synthesizing: Compare voting rates in the United States with those in Europe. Why are they lower in the United States? Then compare community participation rates in the United States with those in Europe. Why are they higher in the United States?

Analyzing: Why does economic status—differences in Americans' education and income levels—make such a large difference in their level of political participation? Why does it make a larger difference in the United States than in Europe?

EXTRA CREDIT

A Book Worth Reading: Larry Bartels, *Unequal Democracy: The Political Economy of the New Gilded Age.* Princeton, NJ: Princeton University Press, 2008. An award-winning study by a top political scientist of why politicians are more responsive to upper- and middle-income citizens than to lower-income citizens.

A Website Worth Visiting: **www.votesmart.org.** Project Vote Smart is a nonpartisan, nonprofit organization. Its website includes helpful information for voters on the backgrounds and policy positions of Republican and Democratic candidates for office.

PARTICIPATE!

If you are not currently registered to vote, consider registering. You can obtain a registration form from the election board or clerk in your community of residence. Several websites contain state-by-state registration information. One such site is https://electionimpact3.votenet.com/declareyourself/voterreg2_ret/. If you are already registered, consider participating in a registration or voting drive on your campus. Although students typically register and vote at relatively low rates, they will often participate if encouraged by other students to do so.

8
CHAPTER

POLITICAL PARTIES, CANDIDATES, AND CAMPAIGNS: DEFINING THE VOTER'S CHOICE

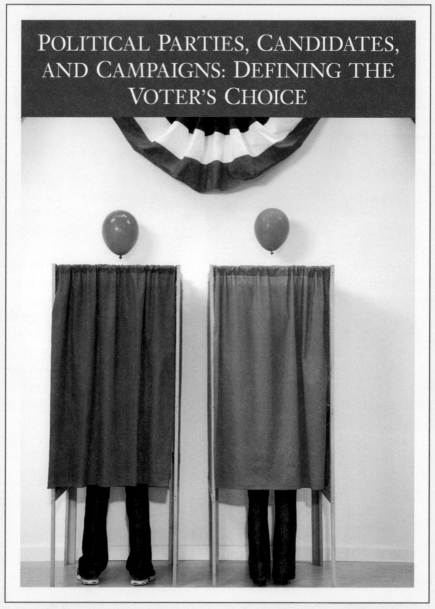

66 Political parties created democracy and . . . modern democracy is unthinkable save in terms of the parties. 99

E. E. SCHATTSCHNEIDER[1]

Six hundred miles and a week apart, they faced off, each offering its own plan for a better America.

The Republicans met first, in Tampa, Florida. Their platform included the promise to cut government spending, lower taxes, limit abortions, expand school choice, stimulate the business sector, expand offshore drilling, and strengthen the armed forces. The Republicans picked former Massachusetts governor Mitt Romney as their presidential nominee, the first Mormon ever chosen for the position. Their vice presidential nominee was Paul Ryan, U.S. Representative from Wisconsin and a leading voice within the Republican Party on government spending issues. The Democrats met in North Carolina's largest city, Charlotte. They renominated Barack Obama as their presidential candidate and Joe Biden as their vice presidential candidate. Their 2012 platform included pledges to draw down U.S. forces in the Middle East, protect social security and Medicare, raise taxes on the wealthy, expand educational opportunities, promote clean energy, and create job programs.

The political parties, as their 2012 presidential nominees and platforms illustrate, are in the business of offering voters a choice. A **political party** is an ongoing coalition of interests joined together in an effort to get its candidates for public office elected under a common label.[2] By offering a choice between policies and leaders, parties give voters a chance to influence the direction of government. "It is the competition of [parties] that provides the people with an opportunity to make a choice," political scientist E. E. Schattschneider wrote. "Without this opportunity popular sovereignty amounts to nothing."[3]

This chapter examines political parties and the candidates who run under their banners. U.S. campaigns are **party centered** in the sense that the Republican and Democratic parties compete across the country election after election. Yet campaigns are also **candidate centered** in the sense that individual candidates devise their own strategies, choose their own issues, and form their own campaign organizations. The following points are emphasized in this chapter:

- *Political competition in the United States has centered on two parties, a pattern that is explained by the nature of America's electoral system, political institutions, and political culture.* Minor parties exist in the United States but have been unable to compete successfully for governing power.

- *To win an electoral majority, candidates of the two major parties must appeal to a diverse set of interests.* This necessity has typically led them to advocate moderate and somewhat overlapping policies, although this tendency has weakened in recent years.

- *U.S. party organizations are decentralized and fragmented.* The national organization is a loose collection of state organizations, which in turn

Republican Party presidential nominee Mitt Romney is surrounded by party faithful during the 2012 presidential campaign.

are loose associations of local organizations. This feature of U.S. parties can be traced to federalism and the nation's diversity, which have made it difficult for the parties to act as instruments of national power.

- *The ability of America's party organizations to control nominations and election to office is weak, which strengthens the candidates' role.*
- *Candidate-centered campaigns are based on money and media and utilize the skills of professional consultants.*

PARTY COMPETITION AND MAJORITY RULE: THE HISTORY OF U.S. PARTIES

Through their numbers, citizens can exert influence, but it cannot be realized unless they act together. Parties give them that capacity. Parties are **linkage institutions;** they serve to connect citizens with government. When Americans go to the polls, they have a choice between candidates representing the Republican and Democratic parties. This **party competition** narrows voters' options to two and in the process enables people with different backgrounds and opinions to act in unison. In casting a majority of its votes for one party, the electorate chooses that party's candidates, philosophy, and policies over those of the opposing party.

The history of democratic government is inseparable from the history of parties. When the people of eastern Europe gained their freedom from the Soviet Union in the early 1990s, one of their first steps toward democracy was the formation of political parties. When the United States was founded over two centuries ago, the formation of parties was also a first step toward building its democracy. The reason is simple: it is the competition among parties that gives popular majorities a choice over how they will be governed.[4] If there were no mechanism like the party to enable citizens to act as one, they would be powerless—each too weak to influence government.

The First Parties

Many of America's early leaders mistrusted parties. George Washington in his farewell address warned the nation of the "baneful effects" of parties, and James Madison likened parties to special interests. However, Madison's misgivings about parties slowly gave way to grudging admiration. He came to realize that parties were the best way for like-minded leaders and citizens to work together to accomplish their common goals.

America's first parties originated in the rivalry between Alexander Hamilton and Thomas Jefferson, who opposed Hamilton's attempts to strengthen the federal government through national commerce. To advance his goal, Hamilton organized his followers into the Federalist Party, taking the name from the faction that had spearheaded the ratification of the Constitution (see Figure 8-1). Jefferson responded by creating the Democratic-Republican Party. The name harkened to the spirit behind the Declaration of Independence and reflected the party's strength

---

POLITICAL THINKING	**Is There Any Substitute for Political Parties?**

When the United States established its democracy, political parties soon followed. Was this mere coincidence? If so, then why have political parties emerged whenever a democracy has been established? Can you think of an alternative means, such as interest groups or the mass media, by which citizens can act as effectively together as they can through a political party? What are the advantages and disadvantages of parties as compared with the alternatives?

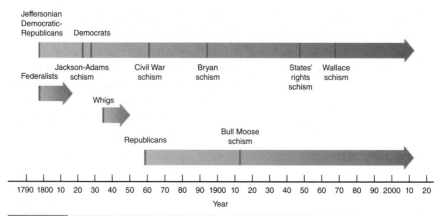

figure 8-1 A GRAPHIC HISTORY OF AMERICA'S MAJOR PARTIES

The U.S. party system has been remarkable for its continuity. Competition between two major parties has been a persistent feature of the system.

among small farmers and states' rights advocates. The Federalists' preoccupation with commercial and moneyed interests fueled Jefferson's claim that they were bent on establishing a government of the rich and wellborn. After Jefferson in the election of 1800 defeated John Adams, who had succeeded Washington as president, the Federalists never again controlled the White House or Congress.

During the so-called Era of Good Feeling, when James Monroe ran unopposed in 1820 for a second presidential term, it appeared as if the political system might operate without competing parties. Yet by the end of Monroe's second term, policy differences had split the Democratic-Republicans. The dominant faction, under the leadership of Andrew Jackson, embraced Jefferson's commitment to the common people and adopted the label "Democrats." Thus, the party of Jefferson is the forerunner of today's Democratic Party rather than of today's Republican Party.

Andrew Jackson and Grassroots Parties

Jackson's goal was to wrest political power from the established elite—the previous presidents had all come from old-line Virginia and Massachusetts families. Jackson saw a reorganized Democratic Party as the vehicle for change. Whereas Jefferson's party had operated largely at the leadership level, Jackson sought a **grassroots party.** As such, it was organized chiefly at the local level and was open to all citizens, The efforts of the local party organizations, along with the extension of voting rights to citizens without property, contributed to a nearly fourfold rise in election turnout during the 1830s.[5] Writing at the peak of Jacksonian democracy, Alexis de Tocqueville claimed that "The People reign in the American political world as the Deity does in the universe."[6]

During this period, a new opposition party—the Whig Party—emerged to challenge the Democrats. The Whigs were united less by a governing philosophy than by their opposition for one reason or another to Jackson and his followers. Competition between the Whigs and the Democrats was relatively short-lived, however. During the 1850s, the slavery issue began to tear both parties apart. The Whig Party disintegrated, and a northern-based new party, calling itself Republican, emerged as the Democrats' main challenger. In the 1860 presidential election, the Democratic Party's northern faction nominated Stephen A. Douglas, who held that the question of whether slavery would be allowed in a new state was for its voters to decide, while the southern faction nominated

Although largely forgotten, the Whig Party was once a major force in American politics. Four Whigs served as president—William Henry Harrison, John Tyler, Zachary Taylor, and Millard Fillmore. The party came into being in the early 1830s and lasted into the 1850s before being supplanted by the newly formed Republican Party.

John C. Breckinridge, who called for legalized slavery in all states. The Democratic vote split sharply along regional lines between these two candidates—with the result that the Republican nominee, Abraham Lincoln, who had called for the gradual elimination of slavery, was able to win the presidency with only 40 percent of the popular vote. Lincoln's election prompted the southern states to secede from the Union.

The Civil War was the first and only time in the nation's history that the party system failed to peacefully settle Americans' political differences. The issue of slavery was simply too explosive to be settled through electoral competition.[7]

Republicans versus Democrats: Realignments and the Enduring Party System

After the Civil War, the nation settled into the pattern of competition between the Republican and Democratic parties that has lasted through today. The durability of the two parties is due not to their ideological consistency but to their willingness to adapt during periods of crisis. By abandoning at these crucial times their old ways of doing things, the Republican and Democratic parties have reorganized themselves—with new bases of support, new policies, and new public philosophies.

These periods of extraordinary party change are known as **party realignments.** A realignment typically involves three basic elements:

1. The emergence of unusually powerful and divisive issues
2. An election contest or contests in which the voters shift their partisan support
3. An enduring change in the parties' policies and coalitions

Realignments are rare. They do not occur simply because one party takes control of government from the other in a single election. Realignments result in deep and lasting changes in the party system that affect subsequent elections as well. By this standard, there have been four realignments since the 1850s.

The first was a result of the nation's Civil War and worked to the advantage of the Republicans. Called the "Union Party" by many, the Republicans dominated elections in the larger and more populous North, while the Democrats acquired a stronghold in what became known as "the Solid South." During the next three decades, the Republicans held the presidency except for Grover Cleveland's two terms in office and had a majority in Congress for all but four years.

The 1896 election also resulted in realignment. Three years earlier, a banking crisis had caused a severe depression. The Democrat Cleveland was president when the crash happened, and people blamed him and his party. In the aftermath, the Republicans made additional gains in the Northeast and Midwest, solidifying their position as the nation's dominant party. During the four decades between the 1890s realignment and the next one in the 1930s, the Republicans held the presidency except for Woodrow Wilson's two terms and had a majority in Congress for all but six years.

The Great Depression of the 1930s triggered a third realignment. The Republican Herbert Hoover was president when the stock market crashed in 1929, and many Americans blamed Hoover, his party, and its business allies for the economic catastrophe that followed. The Democrats became the country's majority party. Their political and policy agenda called for an expanded role for the national government. Franklin D. Roosevelt's presidency included unprecedented policy initiatives in the areas of business regulation and social welfare (see Chapter 3). Roosevelt's election in 1932 began a thirty-six-year period of Democratic presidencies that was interrupted only by Dwight D. Eisenhower's two terms in the 1950s. In this period, the Democrats also dominated Congress, losing control only in 1947–1948 and 1953–1954.

These realignments had a lasting effect on subsequent elections because they shaped voters' long-term party loyalties (see Chapter 6). Young voters in particular embraced the newly ascendant party, giving it a solid base of support for years to come. First-time voters in the 1930s, for example, came to identify with the Democratic Party by a two-to-one margin and stayed with it, enabling it to dominate national politics for the next three decades.[8]

The Nature and Origins of Today's Party Alignment

A party realignment gradually loses strength as the issues that gave rise to it decline in importance. By the late 1960s, with the Democratic Party divided over the Vietnam War and civil rights, it was apparent that the era of New Deal politics was ending.[9]

The change was most dramatic in the South. The region had been solidly Democratic at all levels since the Civil War, but the Democratic Party's leadership on civil rights alienated white conservatives. In the 1964 presidential election, five southern states voted Republican, an indicator of what was to come. The South gradually became the most heavily Republican region in the country. Republicans routinely win the large majority of the region's presidential electoral votes and hold most of its top elected offices. More slowly and less completely, the northeastern states have become increasingly Democratic. The shift has been partly attributable to the declining influence of the Republican Party's moderate wing, which was concentrated in the region. As southern conservatives came to dominate Republican politics, the party's stands on social issues such as abortion and affirmative action shifted to the right, cutting into the party's following in the Northeast.[10]

The net result of these and other regional changes has been a remaking of the party landscape. Rather than occurring abruptly in response to a disruptive issue, as was the case in the 1860s, 1890s, and 1930s realignments, the change took place gradually and is the product of several issues rather than an overriding one. Nevertheless, the result has been much the same. The parties' coalitions and platforms have changed markedly. In effect, America's parties have realigned without going through the sudden shock of a single realigning election.

Democratic President Lyndon Johnson signs into law the 1964 Civil Rights Act, which gave black Americans equal access to restaurants, hotels, and other public accommodations. In much of the South, these accommodations had previously had a "whites' only" policy. In signing the bill, Johnson said to an aide, "We [the Democratic Party] have lost the South for a generation." The prediction was accurate. Within a few elections, the South had changed from being a heavily Democratic region to a heavily Republican one, changing the nature of the U.S. party system.

The GOP (short for "Grand Old Party" and another name for the Republican Party) has gained the most from the change. In the decades following the 1930s Great Depression, the GOP was decidedly the weaker party. Since 1968, however, Republicans have held the presidency more often than the Democrats, and have controlled one or both houses of Congress more than a third of the time. However, the Republican Party has not duplicated the success that the advantaged party had in the realignments of the 1860s, 1890s, and 1930s, partly because of missteps by two of its presidents. After winning the presidency in 1968 and 1972, Republican Richard Nixon became embroiled in the Watergate affair and was forced to resign, the first and only president to do so. The Republicans lost a huge number of congressional seats in the 1974 midterm election and did not recover the lost ground until the 1980s. After the 2000 election, the GOP for the first time in a half century held the presidency and both houses of Congress. However, President George W. Bush's decision to invade Iraq in 2003 proved increasingly unpopular, contributing to his party's loss of the House and Senate in the 2006 midterm elections and its loss of the presidency in the 2008 election.

Analysts differ in their judgment on where the party system is heading in the long run. The two parties are now closely matched in terms of voters' party loyalties but that could change in the coming years (see Figure 8-2). Some observers foresee a period of Republican resurgence if the GOP is able to refocus the public's attention on the issues, such as taxes and smaller government, that worked for it before the Iraq war derailed its momentum.[11] Other observers foresee a period of Democratic dominance if the Democratic Party continues to receive strong support from Hispanics and young adults.[12] They are the major emerging voting blocs and, if they continue to cast the large majority of their votes for Democratic candidates, the GOP will struggle to keep up.

Parties and the Vote

The power of party is at no time clearer than when, election after election, Republican and Democratic candidates reap the vote of their party's identifiers. In the 2012 presidential election, both Barack Obama and Mitt Romney had the support of roughly 90 percent of their party's identifiers. It is relatively rare—in congressional races as well as in the presidential race—for a party nominee to get less than 80 percent of the partisan vote.

Even "independent" voters are less independent than might be assumed. When Americans are asked in polls if they are a Republican, a Democrat,

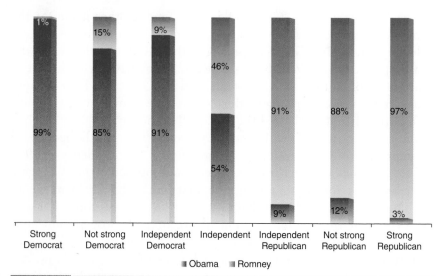

1%	15%	9%				
			46%	91%	88%	97%
99%	85%	91%	54%			
				9%	12%	3%
Strong Democrat	Not strong Democrat	Independent Democrat	Independent	Independent Republican	Not strong Republican	Strong Republican

■ Obama   ■ Romney

figure 8-2   VOTING IN THE 2012 PRESIDENTIAL ELECTION BY STRENGTH OF PARTY IDENTIFICATION

Most adult Americans identify with a political party. Of the more than one-third of adults who describe themselves as independents, most say they "lean" toward one of the two major parties and tend to vote for that party's candidates. In fact, they vote more strongly for their preferred party than those who say they identify with it but "not strongly."
Source: American National Election Study.

or an independent, more than a third say they are independents. However, in the follow-up question that asks if they lean toward the Republican or Democratic Party, about two in three independents say they lean toward one of the parties. Most of these independents vote in the direction they lean. In fact, they are more likely to support their party's candidates than are voters who call themselves Republicans or Democrats but say they do not identify strongly with their preferred party (see Figure 8-2). In other words, most self-described independents are independents in name only. Fewer than 15 percent of all voters are "true" independents in the sense that party loyalty plays little to no part in the votes they cast.

The power of partisanship can be seen in the tendency of most voters to cast a *straight ticket*—meaning that they uniformly support their party's candidates. Most voters who cast a ballot for the Republican or Democratic presidential candidate also vote for that party's congressional candidate. Less than 20 percent of today's voters cast a *split-ticket*, voting for one party's presidential candidate and for the other party's congressional candidate (see "Party Polarization").

P A R T Y	**Political Thinking in Conflict**
POLARIZATION	

Voting a Straight Ticket

The 1970s were marked by what political scientists called dealignment—a movement of voters away from partisan commitments. One indicator was the prevalence of split-ticket voting. More than a fourth of voters supported one party's candidate for president and the other party's candidate for Congress. Many voters also divided their vote when it came to state offices, such as governor and state legislator. In recent elections, however, straight-ticket voting (supporting candidates of the same party at all levels of office) has reasserted itself. As the gap in the policy positions of Democratic and Republican candidates has widened, and as candidates within each party have become more alike in their positions, voters have faced a clearer choice during elections. Moreover, the gap in the policy opinions of Democratic and Republican party identifiers has widened. The net effect of these changes has been to increase the likelihood that Democratic and Republican voters will look less favorably on the policy positions of the other party's candidates and thus less likely to vote for them. As can be seen in the figure below, the percentage of voters who split their ticket has declined substantially in recent decades.

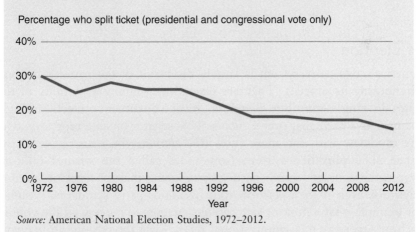

Percentage who split ticket (presidential and congressional vote only)

Source: American National Election Studies, 1972–2012.

Q: How might the decline in split-ticket voting have contributed to the increased level of polarization in Congress?

Continued

A: Moderate congressional candidates benefit from split-ticket voting. Compared with candidates who take more extreme positions, their issue positions are more likely to appeal to the other party's voters. However, as the gap in the partisan attitudes of voters has widened, even the other party's moderate candidates hold less appeal with the result that fewer of them get elected. Many analysts believe that the declining number of congressional moderates is a major reason why Republican and Democratic lawmakers have found it harder to reach compromise positions on legislative issues.

ELECTORAL AND PARTY SYSTEMS

Throughout nearly all of its history, the United States has had a **two-party system:** Federalists versus Jeffersonian Democratic-Republicans, Whigs versus Democrats, Republicans versus Democrats. A two-party system, however, is the exception rather than the rule (see "How the U.S. Differs"). Most democracies have a **multiparty system,** in which three or more parties have the capacity to gain control of government, separately or in coalition. Why the difference? Why are there three or more major parties in most democracies but only two major parties in the United States?

The Plurality (Single-Member-District) System of Election

America's two-party system is largely the result of the nation's method of choosing its officials. They are elected by winning a plurality of the votes in **single-member districts.** Each constituency elects a single member to a particular office, such as U.S. senator or state representative; the candidate with the most votes (*the plurality*) in a district wins the office. The **plurality system** (sometimes called the **winner-take-all system**) discourages minor parties by reducing their chances of winning anything, even if they perform well by minor-party standards. Assume, for example, that a minor party receives exactly 20 percent of the vote in each of America's 435 congressional races. Even though one in five voters nationwide backed the minor party, it would not win any seats in Congress because none of its candidates would have placed first in any of the 435 single-member-district races. The winning candidate in each race would be the major-party candidate with the larger share of the remaining 80 percent of the vote.

By comparison, most European democracies use some form of a **proportional representation system,** in which seats in the legislature are allocated according to a party's share of the popular vote. This type of electoral system enables smaller parties to compete for power. In Germany's 2013 election, for example, the Green Party received 8 percent of the national vote and thereby won several dozen seats in the German parliament. If the Greens had been competing under American electoral rules, they would not have won any seats.

Politics and Coalitions in the Two-Party System

The overriding goal of a major American party is to gain power by getting its candidates elected to office. Because there are only two major parties, however, the Republicans or Democrats can win consistently only by attracting majority support. In Europe's multiparty systems, a party can hope for a share of power if it has the firm backing of a minority faction. In the United States, if either party confines its support to too narrow a slice of voters, it can forfeit its chance of victory.

Seeking the Center, without Losing the Support of the Party Faithful   A two-party system usually requires the major parties to avoid positions that will carry them too far from the political center. The **median voter theorem** holds that, if there are two parties, the parties can maximize their vote only if they position themselves at the location of the median voter—the voter whose preferences are exactly in the middle.[13]

POLITICAL THINKING	Which Is Better—Proportional or Plurality?

Politics is conducted by predetermined rules. Although such rules are often viewed as neutral, they can affect who wins and loses. An example is electoral systems. The United States has a single-member district system in which the winner is the candidate who gets the most votes in the district in which the election is conducted. By comparison, most European democracies have a proportional representation system in which legislative seats are distributed to each party in proportion to its share of the total popular vote. The European rule makes it possible for smaller parties to win legislative seats. In contrast, the American rule favors larger parties because one of their candidates is almost certain to get the most votes in each legislative district. Which rule do you think is the better one? Why?

HOW THE U.S. DIFFERS

POLITICAL THINKING THROUGH COMPARISONS

Party and Electoral Systems

Since 1860, electoral competition in the United States has centered on the Republican and Democratic parties. By comparison, most democracies have a multiparty system, in which three or more parties receive substantial support from voters.

Whether a country has a two-party or a multiparty system depends on several factors, but particularly its electoral system. The United States has a single-member, plurality district system in which only the top vote getter in a district is elected. This system is biased against smaller parties; even if they have some support in a great many races, they win nothing unless one of their candidates places first in an electoral district. By comparison, proportional representation systems enable smaller parties to compete; each party acquires legislative seats in proportion to its share of the total vote. Nearly every democracy with proportional representation, which includes most European countries, has at least three competitive parties, usually more than that number.

Q: Like the United States, Canada and Great Britain have the single-member district system of election. Yet, unlike the United States, they have more than two parties. Why?

A: Canada's third parties have stemmed from regional differences and resentments. French-speaking Quebec has a strong regional party, and from time to time, strong regional parties have appeared in the western provinces. Britain's strongest third party (currently the Liberal Democrats) has been able to survive because the British House of Commons is much larger than the U.S. House of Representatives (659 seats versus 435 seats) and the population of Britain is much smaller than that of the United States. As a result, British election districts have only about a tenth as many voters as U.S. House districts. Britain's Liberal Democrats have enough concentrated strength in some of these districts to win the seat.

Although hypothetical, the median voter theorem helps explain the risk a party faces if it moves too far from the center, leaving it open to the other party. In 1964, the Republican nominee, Barry Goldwater, proposed the elimination of mandatory social security and suggested he might be open to the use of small nuclear weapons in the Vietnam conflict— extreme positions that cost him many votes. Eight years later, the Democratic nominee, George McGovern, took positions on Vietnam and income security that alarmed many voters; like Goldwater, he was buried in one of the biggest landslides in presidential history.

The balance of power in American elections sometimes rests with the moderate voters in the center rather than with those who hold more extreme positions. Democratic lawmakers, for example, overplayed their hand after winning control of the presidency and Congress in 2008. Although the moderate voters who had fueled the Democratic Party's victory expected it to pursue policies that would restore the nation's economy, they didn't anticipate that it would go on a spending spree. In the 2010 congressional elections, moderate voters swung sharply toward the Republicans, contributing to its landslide victory.

However, bold policies do not always lead to electoral defeat. When Ronald Reagan won the presidency in 1980, for example, the voters were thoroughly discouraged with the nation's direction and wanted a new approach. Reagan moved the policy agenda to the right, opposed at each step by liberal Democrats. In this case, the moderates shifted toward Reagan's position. The lesson of such periods is that, although the parties risk crushing defeat by straying too far from the center during normal times, they may do so with some success during turbulent times.

The rising level of party polarization over the past two decades has altered the parties' electoral strategies somewhat. When the bulk of the electorate was clustered in the middle of the political spectrum, the parties usually converged on the center, knowing that defeat could result from straying too far from it. But as the voters themselves have moved away from the center, the parties have also had to worry about keeping their regular voters happy. If these voters think the party nominee is too moderate, they might choose not to vote. Mitt Romney took this possibility into account when running for president in 2012. Although Romney did not ignore moderate voters, he pitched his campaign toward conservatives and then organized a massive effort to get them to the polls on Election Day.

Party Coalitions   The groups and interests that support a party are collectively referred to as the **party coalition.** The Republican and Democratic coalitions are relatively broad. Each includes a substantial proportion of voters of nearly every ethnic, religious, regional, and economic grouping. Only a few groups are tightly aligned with a party. African Americans are the clearest example; more than 80 percent of them regularly vote Democratic.

Nevertheless, the Republican and Democratic coalitions are hardly identical (see Figure 8-3).[14] The party coalitions have been built largely around conflict over the federal government's role in solving social and economic problems. The Democratic Party has consistently favored a greater level of government involvement than has the GOP. Virtually every major assistance program for the poor, the elderly, and low-wage workers since the 1930s has been initiated by the Democrats. Accordingly, the Democratic coalition draws support disproportionately from society's underdogs—blacks, union members, the poor, city dwellers, Hispanics, Jews, and other "minorities."[15] The Democratic Party also draws more support from women than men, although the **gender gap** is characteristic of white voters only. Whereas the Democratic vote is equally strong among minority-group women and men, it is usually 5 to 10 percentage points higher among white women than among white men. On a number

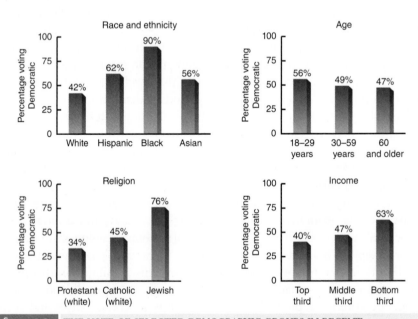

figure 8-3   THE VOTE OF SELECTED DEMOGRAPHIC GROUPS IN RECENT PRESIDENTIAL ELECTIONS

Although the Democratic and Republican coalitions overlap substantially, there are important differences, as illustrated by the Democratic Party's percentage of the two-party vote among some major demographic groups in recent elections. *Source:* Compiled by author from American National Election Studies and other surveys.

of policy issues, including education and social welfare, white women hold opinions that are more liberal on average than those held by white men.[16]

The Republican coalition consists mainly of white middle-class Americans. The GOP has historically been the party of tax cuts and business incentives. It has also been more supportive of traditional values, as reflected, for example, in its opposition to same-sex marriage. Not surprisingly, the GOP is strongest in the regions where traditional values are strongest, such as in the South and Great Plains. The Republican Party has made major inroads in recent decades among white fundamentalist Christians, who are attracted by its positions on abortion, school prayer, same-sex marriage, stem cell research, and other social issues.[17] In recent presidential elections, they have cast roughly three-fourths of their vote for the Republican nominee.

A key to the future of both parties is the Hispanic vote. With the exception of Cuban Americans, who are concentrated in southern Florida, Hispanics lean heavily Democratic. Hispanics who call themselves Democrats outnumber those who call themselves Republicans by more than two to one. However, compared with African Americans, Hispanics are a less cohesive voting bloc. Whereas blacks of all income levels are solidly Democratic, lower-income Hispanics vote Democratic at substantially higher rates than do upper-income Hispanics. Polls show Hispanics to be relatively liberal on economic issues and relatively conservative on social issues, providing both parties a basis for appealing for their support.[18]

In the recent elections, however, Hispanics have sided heavily with the Democratic Party, seeing it as more closely aligned with their interests (see Figure 8-4). This perception has been heightened by recent Republican efforts to identify and deport illegal immigrants, most of whom are Hispanic. In late 2005, for example, the Republican majority in the House of Representatives passed a bill that would have authorized the mass deportation of illegal immigrants and imposed heavy penalties on employers that hire illegal immigrants. Seeing the bill as targeted at their community, Hispanics responded with huge protest rallies—ones reminiscent of the 1960s civil rights movement. The rally in Los Angeles drew an estimated half-million marchers, reputedly the largest such gathering in the city's history. In the subsequent 2006 congressional election, two-thirds of Hispanics voted Democratic—a 10 percent increase from the 2004 level.

Minor (Third) Parties

Although the U.S. electoral system discourages the formation of third parties (or, as they are more properly called, minor parties), the nation has always had them—more than a thousand over its history.[19] Most minor

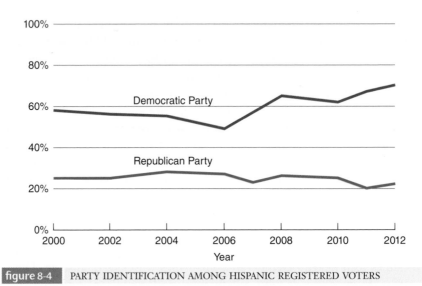

| figure 8-4 | PARTY IDENTIFICATION AMONG HISPANIC REGISTERED VOTERS |

By a wide and increasing margin, Hispanic voters have identified with the Democratic Party rather than the Republican Party. *Source:* Created from 2000–2012 surveys of the Pew Hispanic Center, a project of the Pew Research Center.

parties have been short-lived, and only a few have had a lasting impact. Only one minor party, the Republican Party, has achieved majority status.

Minor parties in the United States have formed largely to promote policies that their followers believe are not being represented adequately by either of the two major parties. A major party is always somewhat captive to its past, which is the source of many of its ideas and most of its followers. When conditions change, major parties can be slow to respond, and a minor party can try to capitalize on neglected issues. Whatever success it achieves, however, is usually temporary. If a minor party gains a following, one or both major parties typically awaken to its issue, at which time the minor party begins to lose support. Nevertheless, the minor party will have served the purpose of making the major parties more responsive to the public's concerns.

Minor parties were at their peak in the nineteenth century, when the party system was still in flux.[20] Many of these parties were *single-issue parties* formed around a lone issue of overriding interest to their followers. Examples are the Free Soil Party, which fought the extension of slavery into new territories, and the Greenback Party, which sought a currency system based on paper money rather than gold and silver. The role that single-issue parties played in the nineteenth century is now played by single-issue interest groups (see Chapter 9).

The most important minor parties of the twentieth century were *factional parties* that resulted from a split within one of the major parties. Although the Republican and Democratic parties are usually successful at managing internal conflict, it has sometimes led the dissidents to break away and form their own party. The most electorally successful of these factional parties was the Bull Moose Party in 1912.[21] Four years earlier, Theodore Roosevelt had declined to seek another presidential term, but he became disenchanted with the conservative policies of his handpicked successor, William Howard Taft, and challenged him for the 1912 Republican nomination. After losing out in the nominating race, Roosevelt proceeded to form the progressive Bull Moose Party (a reference to Roosevelt's claim that he was "as strong as a bull moose"). Roosevelt won 27 percent

Although the United States has long had a two-party system, numerous minor parties have surfaced. A few of them have been influential, including the Free Soil Party, which emerged before the Civil War with a platform that called for the abolition of slavery in new states and territories. Shown here is a Free Soil Party poster from the 1848 election. The party's presidential nominee was Martin Van Buren, who had been president from 1837 to 1841 as a member of the Democratic Party.

of the presidential vote to Taft's 25 percent, which enabled the Democratic nominee, Woodrow Wilson, to win the 1912 presidential election with 42 percent of the vote. The States' Rights Party in 1948 and George Wallace's American Independent Party in 1968 are other examples of strong factional parties. They were formed by white southern Democrats angered by northern Democrats' support of black civil rights.

Other minor parties have been characterized by their ideological commitment to a broad and noncentrist ideological position, such as redistribution of economic resources. The strongest ideological party was the Populists, whose 1892 presidential nominee, James B. Weaver, won 9 percent of the national vote and carried six western states on a radical platform that included a call for government takeover of the railroads.[22] The strongest of today's *ideological parties* is the Green Party. A liberal party that emphasizes environmental and related issues, the Green Party won 3 percent of the presidential vote in 2000.

Some minor parties have been virtually "antiparties" in the sense that they arose out of a belief that partisan politics is a corrupting influence. The strongest of these *reform parties* was the Progressive Party, which in the early 1900s successfully pressured a number of states and localities into adopting primary elections, recall elections, nonpartisan elections, initiatives, and popular referendums (see Chapter 2). A more recent reform party was titled just that—the Reform Party. Created by Texas businessman Ross Perot after he garnered an astonishing 19 percent of the vote in 1992 as an independent presidential candidate (second only to Roosevelt's 27 percent in 1912), the Reform Party virtually disappeared after a bruising internal fight over its 2000 presidential nomination.

PARTY ORGANIZATIONS

The Democratic and Republican parties have organizational units at the national, state, and local levels. These **party organizations** concentrate on the contesting of elections.

Primary Elections and the Weakening of Party Organizations

A century ago, party organizations enjoyed nearly complete control of elections. Although today's party organizations perform all the activities in which parties formerly engaged—candidate recruitment, fundraising, policy development, canvassing—they do not control these activities as fully as they once did. For the most part, the candidates now have the lead role.[23] They do so in large part because of the use of primary elections as the means of choosing party nominees.

Nomination refers to the selection of the individual who will run as the party's candidate in the general election. Until the early twentieth century, the party organizations picked the nominees, who, if elected, were expected to share with it the spoils of office—government jobs and contracts. The party built its organization by giving the jobs to loyalists and by granting contracts to donors. Bribes and kickbacks were part of the process in some locations. New York City's legendary Boss Tweed once charged the city twenty times what a building had actually cost, amassing a personal fortune before winding up in prison. Reform-minded Progressives invented primary elections as a way to deprive party bosses of their power over nominations (see Chapter 2).

A **primary election** (or **direct primary**) gives control of nominations to the voters (see Chapters 2 and 12). The candidate who gets the most votes in a party's primary gets its nomination for the general election. In some states, the nominees are chosen in *closed primaries*, in which participation is limited to voters registered or declared at the polls as members of the party whose primary is being held. Voters of the other party are not allowed to "cross over" to vote in the primary. The logic of a closed primary is that a party's voters should have the power to choose its general election candidate without interference from voters who might not have its best interests in mind. In contrast, some states use *open primaries*, which allow independents and sometimes voters of the other party to vote in the party's primary (although they cannot vote simultaneously in both parties' primaries). The logic of the open primary is that it gives all voters a say in the choices they will have in the general election. California, Louisiana, Nebraska, and Washington conduct *top-two primaries*. Candidates are listed on the same ballot without regard to party; the top two finishers become the general election candidates.

Primaries hinder the building of strong party organizations. If there were no primaries, candidates would have to seek nomination through the party organization, and they could be denied renomination if they were disloyal to the party's policy goals. Because of primaries, however, candidates can seek office on their own and create a personal following that places them beyond the party organization's direct control.

In Europe, where there are no primary elections, the parties are stronger. They control their nominations, and their candidates are expected to support the national platform. A candidate or officeholder who fails to do so is likely to be denied renomination in the next election.

HOW THE 50 STATES DIFFER

POLITICAL THINKING THROUGH COMPARISONS

Primary Elections

Primary elections were introduced in the United States in the early 1900s as a way of reducing the power of party organizations. Although some states resisted their use, primaries have gradually come to be employed in all states for at least some elections. However, the states differ in the type of primary they use. Nearly a fourth of them have *open primaries*, which allow any registered voter to vote in the primary (though not in the primary of both parties simultaneously). Another fourth have *closed primaries*, which are limited to voters registered as members of the party holding the primary. Other states have *partially open primaries* that allow

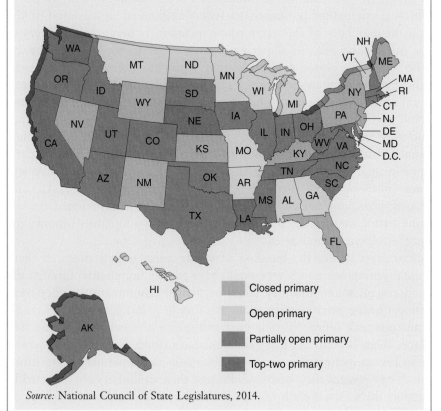

Closed primary
Open primary
Partially open primary
Top-two primary

Source: National Council of State Legislatures, 2014.

independents but not registered voters of the other party to participate or that allow the parties to choose the type of primary they will conduct. In recent Alaska elections, for example, Democrats have held open primaries while Republicans have operated closed primaries. Finally, four states—California, Louisiana, Nebraska, and Washington—employ *top-two primaries* in which candidates of both parties are on the same ballot and the top-two finishers compete in the general election.

Q: The relatively new top-two primary was recently adopted in California and Washington and is under consideration in other states. What do you think are the chief arguments for and against this type of primary?

A: Proponents argue that top-two primaries give independent voters a larger say in the selection of nominees and may result is the selection of more moderate nominees. Opponents say that this type of primary hurts the state's weaker party and narrows voters' choice in the general election when two candidates of the same party are the nominees.

The Structure and Role of Party Organizations

Although party organizations have lost influence, parties are in no danger of extinction. Candidates and activists need an organization through which to work, and the party meets that need. Moreover, certain activities, such as get-out-the-vote efforts on Election Day, affect all of a party's candidates and are done more efficiently through the party organization. Indeed, parties have staged a comeback of sorts.[24] National and state party organizations now assist candidates with fundraising, polling, research, and media production, all essential ingredients of a successful modern campaign.

U.S. parties are organized at the national, state, and local levels, but there is no chain of command that connects them. The national party organization cannot tell the state organizations what to do and, in turn, the state organizations cannot tell the local organizations what to do. The Texas state Democratic Party, for example, does not take orders from the national Democratic Party and does not give orders to the state's local Democratic parties, whether in a large city like Dallas or Houston or in a smaller one like McAllen or Amarillo. Each party organization is largely free to act as it wants. Nevertheless, party organizations at all levels have a shared stake in their party's success and thus have an incentive to work together to get the party's candidates elected to office and to build up a loyal base of support among the voters.[25]

Local Party Organizations   Of the roughly five hundred thousand elective offices in the United States, fewer than five hundred are contested statewide and only two—the presidency and vice presidency—are contested nationally. The rest are local offices; not surprisingly, at least 95 percent of party activists work within local organizations. Local parties vary greatly in their activities. Only a few of them, including the Democratic organizations in Philadelphia and Chicago, bear even a faint resemblance to the fabled old-time party machines that were able to deliver the vote on Election Day. In many urban areas, and in most suburbs and towns, the party organizations today do not have enough activists to do organizing work outside the campaign period, at which time—to the extent their resources allow—they conduct registration drives, hand out leaflets, and help get out the vote. Local parties concentrate on elections that coincide

"SO, CAN I PUT YOU DOWN AS UNDECIDED?"

Door-to-door canvassing for votes is a time-honored though not always welcomed component of political party activity during elections. *Source:* Brian Fray/www.CartoonStock.com.

with local boundaries, such as races for mayor, city council, state legislature, and county offices. Local parties take part in congressional, statewide, and presidential contests, but in these cases, their role is typically secondary to that of the candidates' personal campaign organizations, which are discussed later in the chapter.

State Party Organizations   At the state level, each party is headed by a central committee made up of members of local party organizations and local and state officeholders. State central committees do not meet regularly and provide only general policy guidance for the state organizations. Day-to-day operations are directed by a chairperson, who is a full-time, paid employee of the state party. The state party organizations engage in activities, such as fundraising and voter registration, that can improve their candidates' chances of success. State party organizations concentrate on statewide races, including those for governor and U.S. senator, and also focus on races for the state legislature. They play a smaller role in campaigns for national or local offices, and in most states, they do not endorse candidates in their statewide primaries.

National Party Organizations   The national Republican and Democratic party organizations, which are located in Washington, D.C., are structured much like those at the state level: they have a national committee and a national party chairperson. Neither the Democratic National Committee (DNC) nor the Republican National Committee (RNC) has great power. The RNC (with more than 150 members) and the DNC (with more than 300 members) are too large and meet too infrequently to actually run the national organization. Their power is largely confined to setting organizational policy, such as determining the site of the party's presidential nominating convention and deciding the rules governing the selection of convention delegates. They have no power to pick nominees or to dictate candidates' policy positions. The national party's day-to-day operations are directed by a national chair chosen by the national committee, although the committee defers to the president's choice when the party controls the White House.

The RNC and DNC, among other things, run training programs for candidates and their staffs, raise money, seek media coverage of party positions and activities, conduct issue and group research, and send field representatives to help state and local parties with their operations. In some cases, the national parties also try to recruit potentially strong candidates to run in House and Senate races.

The national parties' major role in campaigns is raising money. Although the RNC and the DNC spend most of the money they raise to fund their

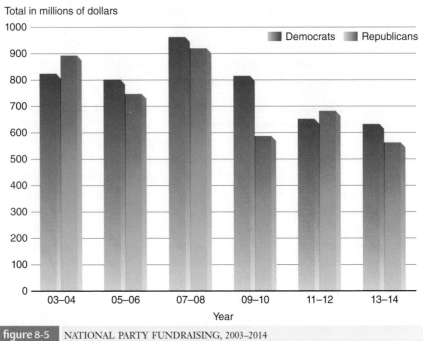

Total in millions of dollars

figure 8-5   NATIONAL PARTY FUNDRAISING, 2003–2014

The national Democratic and Republican parties raise huge sums of money to spend on campaigns during each two-year election cycle.
Source: Center for Responsive Politics, 2014. The figures include fundraising by the DNC and RNC, as well as the parties' Senate-based organizations (DSCC and NRSC) and House-based organizations (DCCC and NRCC). The 2013–2014 figures are author's projections from unofficial reports.

own operations, they give some of it to the party's House and Senate candidates, who also get funding from campaign committees that the parties have formed in the House and Senate. In any case, the amount of money that a party committee can give a candidate is limited by law—$5,000 for House candidates and $42,600 for Senate candidates. However, the total amount of money raised and spent by national party organizations is staggering (see Figure 8-5). It was roughly $1.3 billion for the 2012 election.

THE CANDIDATE-CENTERED CAMPAIGN

As previously noted, today's campaigns are largely controlled by the candidates, particularly in congressional, statewide, and presidential races. Each candidate has a personal organization, created especially for the campaign and disbanded once it is over. The candidates are engaged in what political consultant Joe Napolitan labeled "the election game."[26] The game begins with money—lots of it.

Campaign Funds: The Money Chase

Campaigns for high office are expensive, and the costs keep rising. In 1980, about $250 million was spent by Senate and House candidates in the general election. The figure had jumped to $425 million by 1990. In 2012, the figure exceeded $2 billion—eight times the 1980 level.[27] As could be expected, incumbents have a distinct advantage in fundraising. They have contributor lists from past campaigns and the policy influence that donors seek. House and Senate incumbents outspend their challengers by more than two to one.

Because of the high cost of campaigns, candidates spend much of their time raising funds, which come primarily from individual contributors, interest groups (through PACs, discussed in Chapter 9), and political parties. The **money chase** is relentless.[28] A U.S. senator must raise nearly $20,000 a week on average throughout the entire six-year term in order to raise the minimum $5 million it takes to run a competitive Senate campaign in even a small state. A Senate campaign in a larger state can easily cost far more than that amount. In the 2014 Kentucky Senate race, incumbent Mitch McConnell and his Democratic challenger, Alison Lundergan Grimes, combined to spend more than $50 million. House campaigns are less costly, but expenditures of $1 million or more are now commonplace. As for presidential elections, the numbers are astronomical. In 2012, Barack Obama spent more than $600 million on his campaign while Mitt Romney spent more than $400 million.

The money that candidates raise from political parties, individuals, and interest groups is subject to legal limits (for example, $2,500 from an individual contributor and $5,000 from a group per election). These contributions are termed **hard money**—the money is given directly to the candidate and can be spent as he or she chooses.

Candidates are also the beneficiaries (and sometimes the casualties) of spending by super PACs, which are organizations that can raise and spend money freely on campaigns as long as they do not coordinate their efforts with those of the candidate they support. In 2012, super PACs spent more than $600 million on the presidential and congressional races. (Super PACs are discussed at greater length in Chapter 9.)

Organization and Strategy: Political Consultants

The key operatives in today's campaigns—congressional as well as presidential—are highly paid *political consultants*: campaign strategists, pollsters, media producers, and fundraising and get-out-the-vote specialists. They include campaign strategists who help the candidate to plot and execute a game plan. Over the years, some of these strategists, including James Carville and Roger Ailes, developed legendary reputations. Fundraising specialists are also part of the new politics. They are adept at tapping donors and interest groups that regularly contribute to election campaigns. The consultant ranks also include experts on polling and focus groups (the latter are small groups of voters brought together to discuss at length their thoughts on the candidates and issues). Polls and focus groups are used to identify issues and messages that will resonate with voters.[29] Media consultants are another staple of the modern campaign. They are adept at producing televised political advertising, generating news coverage, and developing Internet-based strategies.

Campaign consultants are skilled at **packaging** a candidate—highlighting those aspects of the candidate's policy positions and personality that are thought most attractive to voters. Packaging is not new to politics. Andrew Jackson's self-portrayal in the nineteenth century as "the champion of the people" is an image that any modern candidate could appreciate. What is new is the need to fit the image to the requirements of a world of sound bites, thirty-second ads, televised debates, and Internet messages, and to do it in a persuasive way. In the old days, it was sometimes enough for candidates to drive home the point that they were a Republican or a Democrat, playing on the tendency of voters to choose a candidate on that basis. Party appeals are still critical, but today's voters also expect to hear about a candidate's personal life and policy proposals.

Over the course of a campaign, voters usually hear more about the candidates' weaknesses than about their strengths.[30] Of course, negative campaigning is as old as American politics. Thomas Jefferson, Andrew Jackson, and Abraham Lincoln were the target of vicious attacks. Lincolnwas portrayed as "a hick" and "a baboon" for his gangly look and backwoods roots. But today's version of attack politics is unprecedented in its reach and scale. Negative television ads were once the exception, but they have increased to the point where they now constitute the largest share of political ads.[31] Many of the ads are "badly misleading," according to Fact Check.org, which monitors ads and assesses their accuracy.[32]

Voter Contacts: Pitched Battle

Today's elections for high office have no historical parallel in their length and penetration. Candidates start their active campaigning much earlier—often two years in advance of Election Day—than they did in times past. The modern campaign is relentless. Voters are bombarded with messages that arrive by air, by land, and by Web.

Air Wars   The main battleground of the modern campaign is the mass media, particularly television. Television emerged in the 1960s as the major medium of campaign politics and has remained so ever since.

Candidates spend heavily on televised political advertising, which enables them to communicate directly—and on their own terms—with voters. *Air wars* is the term that political scientist Darrell West applies to candidates' use of televised ads.[33] Candidates increasingly play off each other's ads, seeking to gain the strategic advantage. Modern production techniques enable well-funded candidates to get new ads on the air within a few hours' time, which allows them to rebut attacks and exploit fast-breaking developments, a tactic known as *rapid response*. The production and airing of televised political ads accounts for roughly half of all campaign spending, and an even larger proportion in the case of presidential campaigns (see Figure 8-6). Indeed, televised ads are the main reason for the high cost of U.S. campaigns. In most democracies, televised campaigning takes place through parties, which receive free air time to make their pitch. Many democracies, including France and Great Britain, prohibit the purchase of televised advertising time by candidates.

Candidates also use the press to get their message across, although the amount of news coverage they get varies widely by location and office. Many House candidates are almost completely ignored by local news media. The New York City media market, for example, includes more than a score of

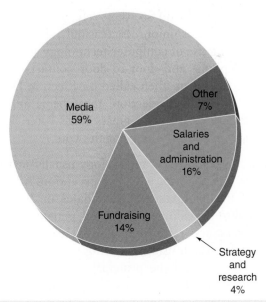

| figure 8-6 | PRESIDENTIAL CAMPAIGN SPENDING, 2012 |

Media expenditures, mostly for televised advertising, account for the largest share of what presidential candidates spend. *Source:* Center for Responsive Politics, 2014. Figure based on combined spending of Obama and Romney campaigns.

House districts in New York, New Jersey, Pennsylvania, and Connecticut, and candidates in these districts get little or no coverage from the New York media. They also get little exposure through televised ads because it is too expensive to buy ads in a metropolitan area where the congressional district is only a small fraction of the audience. Such candidates campaign the old-fashioned way, through leafleting, door-to-door canvassing, and the like. In contrast, presidential candidates get daily coverage from both national and local media. Between these extremes are Senate races, which always get some news coverage and, if hotly contested, may get close coverage.

Debates are also part of the media campaign. Although many House candidates find it impossible to convince local television stations to carry debates, they are routine occurrences in Senate and presidential races. Debates can be risky encounters, because they give viewers a chance to compare the candidates directly. A weak or bumbling performance can hurt a candidate. Yet debates can also present a golden opportunity for a candidate who needs a boost. The 2012 presidential debates are a case in point. Before the first debate, Romney was slipping in the polls. His strong performance in that debate, and Obama's weak performance, combined to dramatically tighten the presidential race.

Ground Wars   On Election Day, candidates concentrate on getting their supporters to the polls. To do so, they rely on the parties and other organizations, such as labor unions. Increasingly, they also conduct their own operation, making use of computer technology and information collected through telephone and door-to-door contacts to create lists of potential supporters, who are then called on Election Day and urged to vote. In the 2012 presidential election, the Obama and Romney campaigns spent millions of dollars to amass huge voter lists, which were used to raise funds as well as to get out the vote.

Web Wars   New communication technology usually makes its way into campaign politics, and the Internet is no exception. All the presidential and nearly all of the congressional candidates in 2012 had elaborate websites dedicated to providing information, generating public support, attracting volunteers, and raising money. Barack Obama's website was the most successful at fundraising, bringing in more than $100 million.

Although television is still the principal medium of election politics, some analysts believe that the Internet will eventually overtake it. Internet messaging is less expensive than television advertising. Because it is a targeted medium, the Internet could become the channel through which candidates reach identifiable voting groups. However, the Internet also has some disadvantages relative to television, especially in the greater control that individual users have over the message. With television, when a brief political ad appears during a favorite program, many viewers will sit through it. An unsolicited message on the Internet is more easily ignored or deleted. In general, the Internet has shown itself to be the better medium for fundraising and mobilizing supporters while television has proven to be the better medium for building name recognition and reaching less-interested voters.

In Retrospect: The Consequences of the Last War   A strong campaign effort can be the difference between winning and losing.[34] In the end, however, nothing so tips the balance in close races as voters' satisfaction with the party that holds power as a result of the previous election. Although some voters are swayed by what candidates promise to do if elected (a form of voting known as *prospective voting*), a greater number respond to past performance (*retrospective voting*). National economic conditions are particularly important in voters' judgments about whether to support the party in power. A weak economy, in conjunction with an unpopular war in Iraq, contributed heavily to the GOP's loss of Congress in 2006 and its loss of the presidency in 2008. When Americans think the country is headed in the wrong direction, the in-party has nearly always lost support in the next election. When times are good, the in-party has less to fear. The 2012 presidential election was a departure from the usual pattern. Although voters were less than pleased with President Obama's handling of the economy, they narrowly elected him to a second term, partly because they doubted that Romney could do any better.

PARTIES, CANDIDATES, AND THE PUBLIC'S INFLUENCE

Candidate-centered campaigns have some distinct advantages. First, they can infuse new blood into electoral politics. Candidate recruitment is typically a slow process in party-centered systems. Would-be officeholders pay their dues by working in the party and, in the process, tend to adopt the outlook of those already there. By comparison, a candidate-centered system is more open and provides opportunities for newcomers to gain office quickly. Barack Obama is a case in point. He had run unsuccessfully for the U.S. House of Representatives in 2000 before winning the 2004 U.S. Senate race in Illinois. Barely two years later, Obama announced his candidacy for president of the United States, winning his party's 2008 nomination against the more experienced U.S. senator Hillary Clinton and then beating the even more experienced U.S. senator

POLITICAL THINKING	Does It Make More Sense to "Vote the Person"?

It is sometimes said that it is better to "vote the person, not the party." Is that good advice, or bad? In voting for a president, Americans are choosing more than the person who will sit behind the desk in the Oval Office. They are also selecting scores of other top executives, including the secretary of state and the attorney general. The president also picks federal judges and justices. Presidents typically appoint members of their party to these positions. The election of a senator or a representative also has broad implications. No single member of Congress has control over legislation. On vote after vote in Congress, most Republicans are aligned on one side while most Democrats are aligned on the other side. In light of these considerations, do you think it makes more sense to "vote the person" or more sense to "vote the party"?

John McCain in the general election. Obama's quick rise from political obscurity to the highest office in the country would be almost unthinkable in a party-centered democracy. Nor is he the only example. In 1976, Jimmy Carter went from being an obscure one-term governor of Georgia to winning the presidency two years later.

Candidate-centered campaigns also encourage national officeholders to be responsive to local interests. In building personal followings among their state or district constituents, members of Congress respond to local needs. Nearly every significant domestic program enacted by Congress is adjusted to accommodate the interests of states and localities that otherwise would be hurt by the policy. Where strong national parties exist, national interests take precedence over local concerns. In both France and Britain, for example, the pleas of legislators from underdeveloped regions have often gone unheeded by their party's majority.

In other respects, candidate-centered campaigns have distinct disadvantages. They provide abundant opportunities for powerful interest groups to shower money on the candidates. The role of campaign money, and the influence it buys, has long been an issue in American politics and has achieved new heights as a result of the Supreme Court's *Citizens United* decision (see Chapters 1 and 9). In no other Western democracy does money play as large a role as does in American elections.

Candidate-centered campaigns also weaken accountability by making it easier for officeholders to deny personal responsibility for government's actions. If national policy goes awry, an incumbent can always say that he or she represents only one vote out of many and that the real problem resides with "others" in Congress. The problem of accountability is apparent from surveys that have asked Americans about their confidence in Congress. Many citizens have a low opinion of Congress as a whole but say they have confidence in their local representative in Congress. This paradoxical attitude is so prevalent that the large majority of incumbents are reelected time and again (see Chapter 11). Party-centered campaigns are different in this respect. When problems surface, voters tend to hold the majority party responsible and vote large numbers of its members out of office.

In short, candidate-centered campaigns strengthen the relationship between the voters and their individual representatives while reducing institutional accountability. Whether this arrangement serves the public's interest is debatable. Nevertheless, candidate-centered campaigns are here to stay. (Congressional and presidential campaigns are discussed further in Chapters 11 and 12, respectively.)

SUMMARY

Political parties serve to link the public with its elected leaders. In the United States, this linkage is provided by the two-party system; only the Republican and Democratic parties have any chance of winning control of government. The fact that the United States has only two major parties is explained by several factors: an electoral system—characterized by single-member districts—that makes it difficult for third parties to compete for power; each party's willingness to accept differing political views; and a political culture that stresses compromise and negotiation rather than ideological rigidity.

Because the United States has only two major parties, each of which seeks to gain majority support, their candidates typically avoid controversial or extreme political positions. Sometimes, Democratic and Republican candidates do offer sharply contrasting policy alternatives, particularly during times of crisis. Ordinarily, however, Republican and Democratic candidates pursue moderate and somewhat overlapping policies. Each party can count on its party loyalists, but U.S. elections can hinge on swing voters, who respond to the issues of the moment either prospectively, basing their vote on what the candidates promise to do if elected, or retrospectively, basing their vote on their satisfaction or dissatisfaction with what the party in power has already done.

America's parties are decentralized, fragmented organizations. The national party organization does not control the policies and activities of the state organizations, and these in turn do not control the local organizations. Traditionally, the local organizations have controlled most of the party's workforce because most elections are contested at the local level. Local parties, however, vary markedly in their vitality. Whatever their level, America's party organizations are relatively weak. They lack control over nominations and elections. Candidates can bypass the party organization and win nomination through primary elections. Individual candidates also control most of the organizational structure and money necessary to win elections. The state and national party organizations have recently expanded their capacity to provide candidates with modern campaign services. Nevertheless, party organizations at all levels have few ways of controlling the candidates who run under their banners. They assist candidates with campaign technology, workers, and funds, but they cannot compel candidates to be loyal to organizational goals.

American political campaigns, particularly those for higher office, are candidate centered. Most candidates are self-starters who become adept at "the election game." They spend much of their time raising campaign funds, and they build their personal organizations around campaign consultants: pollsters, media producers, fundraisers, and election consultants. Strategy and image making are key components of the modern campaign, as is televised political advertising, which accounts for half or more of all spending in presidential and congressional races.

The advantages of candidate-centered politics include a responsiveness to new leadership and local concerns. Yet this form of politics can result in campaigns that are personality driven, depend on powerful interest groups, and blur responsibility for what government has done.

CRITICAL THINKING ZONE

KEY TERMS

candidate-centered campaigns (*p. 233*)
gender gap (*p. 248*)
grassroots party (*p. 236*)
hard money (*p. 259*)
linkage institution (*p. 234*)
median voter theorem (*p. 245*)
money chase (*p. 259*)
multiparty system (*p. 244*)
nomination (*p. 253*)
packaging (of a candidate) (*p. 260*)
party-centered campaigns (*p. 233*)
party coalition (*p. 247*)

party competition (*p. 234*)
party organizations (*p. 252*)
party realignment (*p. 238*)
plurality (winner-take-all) system (*p. 244*)
political party (*p. 233*)
primary election (direct primary) (*p. 253*)
proportional representation system (*p. 245*)
single-member districts (*p. 244*)
two-party system (*p. 244*)

APPLYING THE ELEMENTS OF CRITICAL THINKING

Conceptualizing: Explain the difference between proportional representation and single-member districts as methods of electing candidates to office. Why is the first method more likely than the second to foster a multiparty system?

Synthesizing: Contrast the pattern of earlier political party realignments (such as the realignment brought about by the Great Depression) with the pattern of the most recent party realignment.

Analyzing: Why are elections conducted so differently in the United States than in European democracies? Why are American campaigns more expensive and more candidate centered?

EXTRA CREDIT

A Book Worth Reading: Mark Halperin and John Heilemann, *Double Down: Game Change 2012*. New York: Penguin Press, 2013. This best-selling book takes the reader inside the 2012 Republican and Democratic presidential campaigns. The authors also wrote *Game Change*, an account of the 2008 presidential campaign that became an Emmy Award–winning movie.

A Website Worth Visiting: **www.gop.org** or **www.democrats.org** These are the websites of the Republican Party and the Democratic Party, respectively. Each site has information on the party's issue positions, as well as information on how to become a party volunteer.

PARTICIPATE!

Consider becoming a campaign or political party volunteer. The opportunities are numerous. Parties and candidates at every level from the national on down seek volunteers to assist in organizing, canvassing, fundraising, and other activities. As a college student, you have communication and knowledge skills that would be valuable to a campaign or party organization. You might be pleasantly surprised by the tasks you are assigned.

9
CHAPTER

INTEREST GROUPS: ORGANIZING FOR INFLUENCE

"The flaw in the pluralist heaven is that the heavenly chorus sings with a strong upper-class bias.**"**

E. E. SCHATTSCHNEIDER[1]

The 2014 farm bill had barely reached the Senate before the farm lobbies began to attack it. The House version of the bill, which had passed by a vote of 217 to 210, changed the formula by which farmers would receive government subsidies. Instead of being calculated based on a farm's full acreage, subsidies would be based on the number of acres planted—a smaller number. Moreover, the House bill had different formulas for different commodities, and soon the corn and soybean producers were fighting with the sugar and cotton producers over their share of the subsidies.

The agricultural lobbies' effort to shape the 2014 farm bill suggests why interest groups are both necessary and unloved. Farmers have legitimate interests that are affected by public policy. It is perfectly appropriate for them to lobby on policy issues. The same can be said of banks, consumers, minorities, college students—indeed, of virtually every interest in society. In fact, the *pluralist* theory of American politics (see Chapter 1) holds that society's interests are represented most effectively through group action.

Yet groups can wield too much power, getting their way at an unreasonable cost to the rest of society. When Congress addressed the farm issue in 2014, it was determined to cut the costs of agricultural programs as part of a broader effort to reduce government spending. Farm lobbies were equally determined to protect their government benefits. Did the resulting legislation strike a reasonable balance between the legitimate interests of farmers and the legitimate interests of taxpayers?

Opinions differ on the answer to this question, but there is no doubt that groups have considerable influence over public policy. Indeed, group influence has increased significantly in recent decades. The situation raises a perennial issue, one that James Madison addressed in his famous essay *Federalist* No. 10. Madison warned against "the dangers of faction," by which he meant a polity where factions (groups) become so powerful that they trample on the legitimate interests of other groups and society as a whole. Madison acknowledged that society has an obligation to protect the right of groups to organize and petition government but also said that society suffers if groups become overly powerful.

An **interest group**—also called a "faction," "pressure group," "special interest," or "organized interest"—can be defined as any organization that actively seeks to influence public policy.[2] Interest groups are similar to political parties in some respects but differ from them in important ways.[3] Like parties, groups are a linkage mechanism: they serve to connect citizens with government. However, political parties address a broad range of issues so as to appeal to diverse blocs of voters. Above all, parties are in the business of trying to win elections. Groups, on the other hand, concentrate on policies directly affecting their interests. A group may involve itself in elections, but its major purpose is to influence the policies that affect it.

This chapter examines the degree to which various interests in American society are represented by organized groups, the process by which interest groups exert influence, and the costs and benefits of group politics. The main points made in the chapter are:

* *Although nearly all interests in American society are organized to some degree, those associated with economic activity, particularly business activity,*

are by far the most thoroughly organized. Their advantage rests on their superior financial resources and on the private goods (such as wages and jobs) they provide to those in the organization.

- *Groups that do not have economic activity as their primary function often have organizational difficulties.* These groups pursue public or collective goods (such as a safer environment) that are available even to individuals who are not group members, so individuals may free ride, choosing not to pay the costs of membership.

- *Lobbying and electioneering are the traditional means by which groups communicate with and influence political leaders.* Recent developments, including grassroots lobbying and political action committees, have heightened interest groups' influence.

- *The interest-group system overrepresents business interests and fosters policies that serve a group's interest more than the society's broader interests.* Thus, although groups are an essential part of the policy process, they also distort that process.

THE INTEREST-GROUP SYSTEM

In the 1830s, the Frenchman Alexis de Tocqueville wrote that the "principle of association" was nowhere more evident than in America.[4] His description still holds. Americans are more likely than citizens of other nations to join organized groups (see "How the U.S. Differs"). However, not all of these organizations are interest groups. Book clubs, softball teams, social clubs, and most church groups are examples of groups that are not in the interest-group category because they do not seek to influence the policy process. Even so, no other nation has as many organized interest groups as does the United States. The country's tradition of free association makes it natural for Americans to join together for political purposes, and their diverse interests give them reason to pursue policy influence through group action.

The nation's political structure also contributes to group action. Because of federalism and the separation of powers, groups have multiple points of entry through which to influence policy. The structure of the American system even contributes to a type of lobbying that is sometimes overlooked. While the vast majority of organized interests represent private interests, some represent governments. Most states and major cities have at least one Washington lobbyist. Intergovernmental lobbying also occurs through groups such as the Council of State Governments, the National Governors Association, the National Association of Counties, the National League of Cities, and the U.S. Conference of Mayors. These organizations sometimes

HOW THE U.S. DIFFERS

POLITICAL THINKING THROUGH COMPARISONS

Groups: "A Nation of Joiners"

"A nation of joiners" is how the Frenchman Alexis de Tocqueville described the United States during his visit to this country in the 1830s. Tocqueville suggested that Europeans would find it hard to comprehend. "The political activity that pervades the United States," said Tocqueville, "must be seen to be understood." Even today, Americans are more fully involved in groups than are Europeans, as the accompanying figures from the World Values Survey indicate. Among the reasons are the nation's tradition of free association and the prominence of religion and public education. Much of the nation's group life revolves around its churches and its schools.

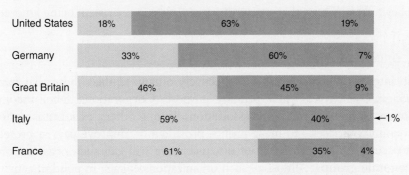

	No group	1–3 groups	4 or more groups
United States	18%	63%	19%
Germany	33%	60%	7%
Great Britain	46%	45%	9%
Italy	59%	40%	←1%
France	61%	35%	4%

Percentage belonging to: ▢ No group ▢ 1–3 groups ▢ 4 or more groups
Source: World Values Survey Association, 2012.

Q: How does the structure of the U.S. government contribute to the proliferation of interest groups in America?

A: Because of federalism and the separation of powers, the American system offers numerous points at which groups can try to influence public policy. If unsuccessful with legislators, groups can turn to executives or to the courts. If thwarted at the national level, groups can turn to state and local governments. By comparison, the governments of most democratic nations are not organized in ways that facilitate group access and influence. Great Britain's unitary government, for example, concentrates power at the national level.

play a major role in national policy debates. For example, as Congress was preparing in 2011 to renew the antiterrorism legislation that had gone into effect in 2001, the National Governors Association and the U.S. Conference of Mayors lobbied to ensure that the changes reflected their concerns. Even foreign governments lobby in Washington. Arms sales, foreign aid, immigration, and trade practices are among the U.S. policies they target.[5]

The extraordinary number of interest groups in the United States does not mean that the nation's various interests are equally well organized. Groups develop when people with a shared interest have the opportunity and the incentive to join together. Some individuals or organizations have the skills, money, contacts, or time to participate in group politics; others do not. Moreover, some groups are inherently more attractive to potential members than others and thus find it easier to organize. Groups also differ in their financial resources and thus in their capacity for political action.

Therefore, a first consideration in regard to group politics in America is the issue of how thoroughly various interests are organized. Interests that are highly organized stand a good chance of having their views heard by policymakers. Those that are poorly organized run the risk of being ignored.

Economic Groups

No interests are more fully or effectively organized than those that have economic activity as their primary purpose. Corporations, labor unions, farm groups, and professional associations, among others, exist primarily for economic purposes—to make profits, provide jobs, improve pay, or protect an occupation. For the sake of discussion, we will call such organizations **economic groups.** Almost all such organizations engage in political activity as a means of promoting and protecting their economic interests. An indicator of this is the fact that Washington lobbyists who represent economic groups outnumber those of all other groups by more than two to one.

Among economic groups, the most numerous are *business groups.* Writing in 1929, political scientist E. Pendleton Herring noted, "Of the many organized groups maintaining offices in [Washington], there are no interests more fully, more comprehensively, and more efficiently represented than those of American industry."[6] Although corporations do not dominate lobbying as thoroughly as they once did, Herring's general conclusion still holds: more than half of all groups formally registered to lobby Congress are business organizations. Virtually all large corporations and many smaller ones are politically active.

Business firms are also represented through associations. Some of these "organizations of organizations" seek to advance the broad interests of business. One of the oldest associations is the National Association of Manufacturers, which was formed in 1894, and today represents fourteen thousand manufacturers. Another large business association is the U.S. Chamber of Commerce, which represents nearly three million businesses of all sizes. Other business associations, such as the American Petroleum Institute and the National Association of Home Builders, are confined to a single trade or industry.

Economic groups also include those associated with organized labor. *Labor groups* seek to promote policies that benefit workers in general and union members in particular. Although there are some major independent unions, such as the United Mine Workers and the Teamsters, the dominant labor group is the AFL-CIO, which has its national headquarters in Washington, D.C. The AFL-CIO has twelve million members in its nearly sixty affiliated unions, which include the International Brotherhood of Electrical Workers, the Sheet Metal Workers, and the American Federation of Teachers.

At an earlier time, about a third of the U.S. workforce was unionized. Today, only about one in eight workers is a union member. Historically, skilled and unskilled laborers constituted the bulk of organized labor, but their numbers have decreased as the economy has changed, while the number of professionals, technicians, and service workers has increased. Professionals have shown little interest in union organization, perhaps because they identify with management or consider themselves economically secure. A mere 2 percent of professionals are union members. Service workers and technicians can also be difficult for unions to organize because they work closely with managers and, often, in small offices. Nevertheless, unions have made inroads in their efforts to organize service and public employees. In fact, most union members today work in the public sector, despite the fact that it has only a fifth as many workers as does the private sector. The most heavily unionized employees are those who work for local government, such as teachers, police officers, and firefighters—roughly 40 percent of them are union members. State and federal employees are also heavily unionized. All told, more than a third of public-sector workers are union members, compared with less than a tenth of private-industry workers. Even the construction industry, which ranks high by comparison with most private-sector industries, has a unionization rate of less than 15 percent.[7]

Farm groups represent another large economic lobby. The American Farm Bureau Federation is the largest of the farm groups, with more than four million members. The National Farmers Union, the National Grange, and the National Farmers Organization are smaller farm lobbies. Agricultural groups do not always agree on policy issues. For instance, the Farm Bureau sides with agribusiness and owners of large farms, while the Farmers Union promotes the interests of smaller "family" farms. There are also numerous specialty farm associations, including the Association of Wheat Growers, the American Soybean Association, and the Associated Milk Producers. Each association acts as a separate lobby, seeking to obtain policies that will serve its members' particular interests.

Most professions also have lobbying associations. Among the most powerful of these *professional groups* is the American Medical Association (AMA), which includes more than 250,000 physicians. Other professional groups include the American Bar Association (ABA) and the American Association of University Professors (AAUP).

Citizens' Groups

Economic groups do not have a monopoly on lobbying. There is another category of interest groups—**citizens' groups** (or **noneconomic groups**). Group members in this category are joined together not by a *material incentive*—such as jobs, higher wages, or profits—but by a *purposive incentive*, the satisfaction of contributing to what they regard as a worthy goal or purpose.[8] Whether a group's purpose is to protect the environment, return prayer to the public schools, or feed the poor at home or abroad, there are citizens who are willing to participate simply because they believe the cause is a worthy one.

Nearly every conceivable issue or problem has its citizens' group, often several of them. Some citizens' groups work to advance the interests of a particular social grouping; examples are the National Association for the Advancement of Colored People (NAACP), the National Organization for Women (NOW), and La Raza, which is the largest Hispanic American lobbying group. Other citizens' groups have a broad agenda that derives from an ideological or moral position. The American Conservative Union (ACU) is the largest conservative organization and lobbies on issues like taxation and national defense. Americans for Democratic Action (ADA) is a liberal counterpart to the ACU. Another example is the Christian Coalition of America, which describes itself as "America's leading grassroots organization defending our godly heritage." The group addresses a wide range of issues, including school prayer, abortion, and television programming. Ideology is also a component of the state-level Public Interest Research Groups (PIRGs), such as NYPIRG (New York), CALPIRG (California), and TexPIRG (Texas). Almost every state has a PIRG, which usually has chapters on college campuses. Drawing on their network of researchers, students, and advocates, they approach issues from a public interest perspective. Ideological groups on both the left and the right have increased substantially in number since the 1960s.

P A R T Y
POLARIZATION

Political Thinking in Conflict

The Impact of Ideological Interest Groups

After the Watergate scandal in the early 1970s, Congress enacted campaign finance reforms that opened the door to a larger funding role for interest groups through provisions that relaxed legal restrictions on political action committees (PACs). Many of the citizen-based PACs that formed at that time were more ideological than were the parties or most of the voters. At first, these PACs concentrated on general election races, but then also became heavily involved in primary election contests, working to defeat moderate candidates within their party. Their efforts have contributed to the election of senators and representatives that hold uncompromising conservative or liberal views, which has contributed to the party polarization that has characterized Congress in recent years. Examples of such groups are Emily's List, which supports liberal candidates, and the Family Research Council, which supports conservative candidates. In recent elections, Emily's List has given virtually 100 percent of its PAC contributions to Democratic candidates, while Family Research Council has given virtually 100 percent of its PAC contributions to Republican candidates. The tendency of ideological groups to support one side of the partisan divide can also be seen in the figures below, which show how ideological PACs in a few selected categories divided their contributions between Republican and Democratic candidates during the 2012 election cycle.

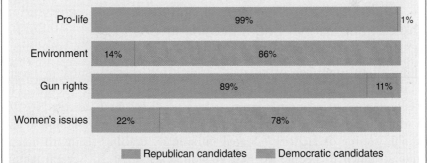

Source: Center for Responsive Politics, 2014.

Q. Why do you think politically active citizen groups are generally more ideological—whether conservative or liberal—than is the society as a whole? Are citizens with strong views somehow more attracted to organized political activity than those with more moderate opinions?

Most citizens' groups, however, have an issue-specific policy agenda. *Single-issue groups* have risen sharply in number in the past half century and now pressure government on almost every conceivable policy, from nuclear arms to drug abuse. Notable current examples are the National Rifle Association and the various right-to-life and pro-choice groups. Most environmental groups can also be seen as single-issue organizations in that they seek to influence public policy in a specific area, such as pollution reduction, wilderness preservation, or wildlife protection. The Sierra Club, one of the oldest environmental groups, was formed in the 1890s to promote the preservation of scenic areas. In contrast, the Environmental Defense Fund, established in 1967, concentrates on environmental problems, such as air and water pollution. Since 1960, membership in environmental groups has more than tripled in response to increased public concern about the environment.[9]

Citizens' groups are difficult to classify precisely because they differ so widely in their focus and goals. Some single-issue groups, for example, are ideological whereas others are pragmatic. A simple but precise way to describe citizens' groups is that they are "groups anyone can join." This does not mean that everyone would want to join a particular group. A conservative would not choose to join the ADA, just as a liberal would not join the ACU. But there is no barrier to joining a citizens' group if one is willing to contribute the required time or money. In this way, citizens' groups are distinct from business firms, which are closed to all but their employees, and distinct also from labor groups, farm groups, and professional associations, whose members have a particular type of training or vocation.[10]

The Organizational Edge: Economic Groups versus Citizens' Groups

Although the number of citizens' groups has mushroomed in recent decades, they are substantially outnumbered by economic groups. The predominance of economic interests was predicted in *Federalist* No. 10, in which James Madison declared that property is "the most common and durable source of factions." Stated differently, nothing seems to matter quite so much to people as their economic self-interest. Several factors (summarized in Table 9-1) give economic groups an organizational advantage, including their resources and their size.

Unequal Access to Resources   One reason for the abundance of economic groups is their access to financial resources. Political lobbying does not come cheap. If a group is to make its views known, it typically must have a headquarters, an expert staff, and communication facilities. Economic

table 9-1	ADVANTAGES AND DISADVANTAGES HELD BY ECONOMIC AND CITIZENS' GROUPS

Economic Groups	Citizens' Groups
Advantages	*Advantages*
Economic activity provides the organization with the resources necessary for political action.	Members are likely to support leaders' political efforts because they joined the group in order to influence policy.
Individuals are encouraged to join the group because of economic benefits they individually receive (such as wages).	*Disadvantages*
	The group has to raise funds, especially for its political activities.
In the case of firms within an industry, their small number encourages organization because the contribution of each firm can make a difference.	Potential members may choose not to join the group because they get collective benefits even if they do not join (the free-rider problem).
Disadvantages	Potential members may choose not to join the group because their individual contribution may be too small to affect the group's success one way or the other.
Persons within the group may not support leaders' political efforts because they did not join the group for political reasons.	

groups pay for these things with money generated by their economic activity. Corporations have the greatest built-in advantage. They do not have to charge membership dues or conduct fundraisers to support their lobbying. Their political money comes from their business profits.

Some economic groups rely on dues rather than profits to support their lobbying, but they have something of economic value to offer in exchange. Labor unions, for example, provide their members access to higher-paying jobs in return for the dues they pay. Such groups offer what is called a **private (individual) good**—a benefit, such as a job, that is given directly to a particular individual. An important feature of a private good is that it can be held back. If an individual is unwilling to pay organizational dues, the group can withhold the benefit.

Citizens' groups do not have these inherent advantages. They do not generate profits or fees as a result of economic activity. Moreover, the incentives they offer prospective members are not exclusive. As opposed to the private or individual goods provided by many economic groups, most noneconomic groups offer **collective (public) goods** as an incentive for membership. Collective goods are, by definition, goods that belong to all;

they cannot be granted or withheld on an individual basis. The air people breathe and the national forests people visit are examples of collective goods. They are available to one and all, those who do not pay dues to a clean-air group or a wilderness preservation group as well as those who do.

The shared characteristic of collective goods creates what is called the **free-rider problem:** individuals can obtain the good even if they do not contribute to the group's effort. Take the case of National Public Radio (NPR). Although NPR's programs are funded primarily through listeners' donations, those who do not contribute can listen to the programs. The noncontributors are free riders: they receive the benefit without paying for it. About 90 percent of regular NPR listeners are noncontributors.

In a purely economic sense, as economist Mancur Olson noted, it is not rational for an individual to contribute to a group when its benefit can be obtained for free.[11] Moreover, the dues paid by any single member are too small to affect the group's success one way or another. Why pay dues to an environmental group when any improvements in the air, water, or

This 1873 lithograph illustrates the benefits of membership in the National Grange, an agricultural interest group. Throughout their history, Americans have organized to influence government policy.

wildlife from its lobbying efforts are available to everyone and when one's individual contribution is too small to make a real difference? Although many people do join such groups anyway, the free-rider problem is one reason citizens' groups are organized less fully than economic groups.

In recent decades the free-rider problem has been lessened, but not eliminated, by advances in communication technology. Computer-assisted direct mail, e-mail, and social networks have greatly eased citizen groups' efforts to contact prospective donors. For some individuals, a contribution of $25 to $50 annually represents no great sacrifice and offers the satisfaction of supporting a cause in which they believe. "Checkbook membership" is how political scientist Theda Skocpol describes such contributions.[12]

The Internet has also been a boon to citizens' groups. Virtually every such group of any size has its own website and e-mail list. MoveOn illustrates the Internet's organizing capacity. MoveOn was started by a handful of liberal activists working out of a garage. It now has well over one million members. During the 2014 campaign, MoveOn prompted its members to contribute time and money to Democratic candidates, a strategy it has pursued in every election since its founding in 1998.

POLITICAL THINKING   **Does the "Big Bang Theory" Apply to Groups?**

The "big bang theory" holds that the universe has been expanding since its inception. Is there an analogous theory that could be applied to interest groups? Consider the environmental lobby, which now includes more than three times as many groups as it did in the 1960s. In response to demands from environmental scientists and activists, the federal government enacted major legislation, such as the Clean Water Act, that in turn spawned new environmental groups determined to see that the legislation was enforced. These specialized groups then pressed for additional policy programs, which in turn spawned ever more specialized groups. Is hyperpluralism— the runaway proliferation of specialized groups—an inevitable consequence of activist government?

The Advantages and Disadvantages of Size   Although citizens' groups have proliferated in recent decades, the organizational muscle in American politics rests primarily with economic groups. Business interests in particular have an advantage that economist Mancur Olson calls "the size factor."[13] Although it might be thought that groups with large memberships would typically prevail over smaller groups, the reverse is often true. Olson notes that small groups are ordinarily more united on policy issues and often have more resources, enabling them to win out against large groups. Business groups in a specific industry are usually few in number and have an incentive to work together to influence government on issues of joint interest. The U.S. automobile industry, for example, has its "Big Three"— General Motors, Ford, and Chrysler. Although they compete for car sales, they usually work together on policy issues. They have succeeded at times, for example, in persuading government to delay or reduce higher fuel efficiency and safety standards, which has meant billions in additional profits for them at an incalculable cost to car owners, who are many in number but are not an organized group.

Business associations testify to the advantage of small size. The business sector is divided into numerous industries, most of which include only a small number of major firms. Virtually every one of these industries, from oil to cereals to bow ties, has its own trade association. More than one thousand trade associations are represented in Washington, and they spend hundreds of millions of dollars annually on lobbying.

Their situation is far different from that of, say, taxpayers, who number in the tens of millions. Although taxpayers would be enormously powerful if they all joined together in a single cohesive group, most taxpayers have no real interest in paying dues to a taxpayers' group that would lobby on their behalf. In 2008, these differences came together in ways that conceivably hurt taxpayers while helping leading financial institutions. At issue was a government bailout aimed at protecting major investment banks from bankruptcy as a result of their purchase of mortgage-backed securities, which had declined sharply in value as the U.S. housing market weakened. With the backing of policymakers in the Federal Reserve, the Treasury Department, the White House, and Congress, troubled financial institutions received $700 billion in taxpayers' money to rescue them from bankruptcy, even though their risky investments had brought them to that point. Getting millions of taxpayers to work together to influence policy is infinitely more difficult than getting top financial firms to collaborate. "[T]he larger the group," Olson wrote, "the less it will further its common interests."[14]

Nevertheless, there can be strength in numbers. No group illustrates this better than AARP (formerly known as the American Association of Retired Persons). Although not every retired person belongs to AARP, its membership dues are so low (about $15 annually) that millions do. AARP has a staff of more than one thousand and is a formidable lobby on social security, Medicare, and other issues affecting retirees. A *Fortune* magazine survey of 2,200 Washington insiders, including members of Congress and their staffs, ranked AARP as the nation's most powerful lobbying group.[15]

INSIDE LOBBYING: SEEKING INFLUENCE THROUGH OFFICIAL CONTACTS

Modern government is involved in so many issues—business regulation, income maintenance, urban renewal, cancer research, and energy development, to name only a few—that hardly any interest in society could fail to benefit significantly from having influence over federal policies or programs. Moreover, officials are more inclined to solve problems than to ignore them. When a rash of tornadoes ripped through Illinois, Indiana, Kentucky, and Missouri in late 2013, the federal government rushed to provide funds to states and residents to meet the recovery costs.

Groups seek government's support through **lobbying,** a term that refers broadly to efforts by groups to influence public policy through contact with public officials.[16] Interest groups rely on two main lobbying strategies, which have been called *inside lobbying* and *outside lobbying*.[17] This section discusses **inside lobbying,** which is based on group efforts to develop and maintain close ("inside") contacts with policymakers. (Outside lobbying is described in the next section.)

Acquiring Access to Officials

Through inside lobbying, groups seek to gain direct access to officials in order to influence their decisions. Lobbying once depended significantly on tangible payoffs, including bribes. Such incidents are rare today. Bribery is illegal, and lobbying behavior is more closely regulated than in the past. Lobbyists are required by law to register and to file detailed reports on their lobbying expenditures.

Modern lobbying rests primarily on the skillful use of information. Lobbyists concentrate on providing lawmakers with arguments and evidence backing their position. Their goal is to persuade officials that what they want done is the proper course of action.[18] "If I don't explain what we do . . . Congress will make uninformed decisions without understanding the consequences to the industry," said one lobbyist.[19] For the most part, inside lobbying is directed at policymakers who are inclined to support the group rather than at those who have opposed it in the past. This tendency reflects both the difficulty of persuading opponents to change long-held views and the advantage of working through trusted officials. Thus, union lobbyists work mainly with pro-labor officeholders, just as corporate lobbyists work mainly with pro-business policymakers.

For lobbyists to be persuasive, they must understand the policy process as well as the issue under consideration. For this reason, a "revolving door" exists between lobbying firms and government. Many lobbyists worked previously in government, and some top officials were once lobbyists. Upon retirement, many members of Congress join lobbying firms. Although prohibited by law from lobbying Congress for a set period of time after leaving office, they are free to do so thereafter and usually lobby on policy issues they handled during their time in Congress.[20]

Money is a key element in inside-lobbying efforts. Many groups have a Washington office and a professional staff of lobbyists and public relations specialists. More than 20,000 lobbyists work in Washington, and the amount of money spent on lobbying is staggering—more than $3 billion a year. The Center for Responsive Politics divided the amount of money spent on lobbying in 2009 ($3.47 billion) by the number of hours Congress was in session (2,688) to dramatize the extent of lobbying. The figure turned out to be a whopping $1.3 million per hour.[21] Consistently among the top spenders is the U.S. Chamber of Congress with an annual lobbying budget of more than $40 million (see Figure 9-1). Other groups get by on much less, but it is hard to lobby effectively on a tiny budget. Given the costs of maintaining a Washington lobby, the domination by corporations and trade associations is understandable. These economic groups have the money to retain high-priced lobbyists, while many other interests do not.

Lobbying Congress   The targets of inside lobbying are officials of all three government branches—legislative, executive, and judicial. The benefits of a close relationship with members of Congress are the most obvious. With

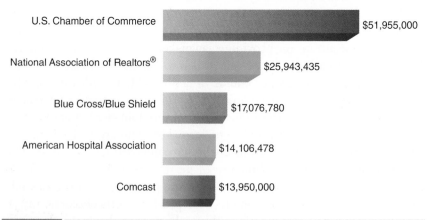

figure 9-1   THE FIVE TOP-SPENDING LOBBYING GROUPS

Lobbying is big business in two ways. First, huge sums of money are spent each year on lobbying; and, second, most of the money is spent by business firms and trade associations. *Source:* Center for Responsive Politics, 2014.

support in Congress, a group can obtain the legislative help it needs to achieve its policy goals. By the same token, members of Congress benefit from ties to lobbyists. The volume of legislation facing Congress is heavy, and members rely on trusted lobbyists to identify bills that deserve their attention. When Republican lawmakers took control of the House of Representatives in 2011, they consulted closely with corporate lobbyists on legislative issues affecting business. Congressional Democrats complained, but Republicans said they were merely getting advice from those who best understood business's needs and noted that Democrats had worked closely with organized labor when they were in power.

Lobbyists' effectiveness depends in part on their reputation for playing it straight. Said one congressman, "If any [lobbyist] gives me false or misleading information, that's it—I'll never see him again."[22] Bullying is also frowned upon. During the debate over the North American Free Trade Agreement in 1993, the AFL-CIO threatened to campaign against congressional Democrats who supported the legislation. The backlash from Democrats on both sides of the issue was so intense that the union withdrew its threat. The safe lobbying strategy is the aboveboard approach: provide information, rely on trusted allies in Congress, and push steadily but not too aggressively for favorable legislation.

Lobbying the Executive Branch   As the range of federal policy has expanded, lobbying of the executive branch has grown in importance. Some of this lobbying is directed at the president and presidential staff, but they are less accessible than top officials in the federal agencies, who are the chief targets.

Group influence is particularly strong in the regulatory agencies that oversee the nation's business sectors. Pharmaceutical companies, for example, provide much of the scientific evidence used by the Food and Drug Administration (FDA) in deciding whether a new drug is safe to market. The potential for influence is high, as are the stakes. After the FDA approved its marketing, the arthritis drug Vioxx generated $2.5 billion a year in sales for Merck, the pharmaceutical company that developed it. As it turned out, Vioxx was unsafe. Its users suffered an abnormally high number of strokes and heart attacks. A review panel concluded that the FDA had been lax in accepting Merck's assessments of the drug's safety.[23]

The FDA is sometimes cited as an example of "agency capture." The capture theory holds that regulatory agencies sometimes side with the industries they are supposed to regulate rather than with the public, which they are supposed to protect. Studies have found that capture theory explains some group-agency relationships, but not all of them. Agency officials are aware that they can lose support in Congress, which controls agency funding and program authorization, if they show too much favoritism toward an

HOW THE 50 STATES DIFFER

POLITICAL THINKING THROUGH COMPARISONS

Lobbyists

Although the largest concentration of registered lobbyists, by far, is in Washington, D.C., lobbyists are also found in significant numbers in state capitals, as the accompanying map indicates. In America's federal system of government, major policy decisions are made by state governments in areas such as education, health, social welfare, business, policing, and transportation. In addition, states are in charge of the licensing of everything from physicians to liquor stores. All these activities are subject to lobbying efforts.

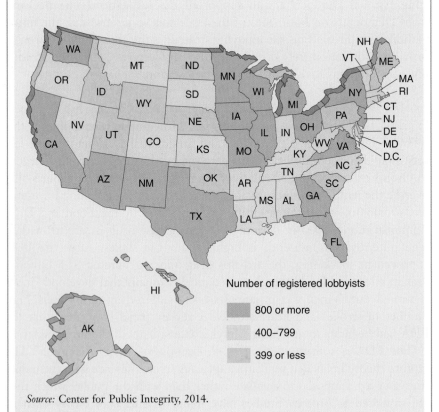

Source: Center for Public Integrity, 2014.

Q: What are characteristics of states that have the most registered lobbyists?

A: Most of these states have relatively large populations and diverse economies, each of which serves to increase a state's level of policy activity. As well, most of these states have relatively long legislative sessions, providing lobbyists with more opportunities to interact with lawmakers.

---

interest group.[24] In response to the Vioxx controversy, as well as problems with other new drugs, Congress passed legislation in 2007 that forced the FDA to toughen its pre- and post-marketing safety tests.

Lobbying the Courts   Judicial rulings in areas such as education and civil rights have made interest groups recognize that they can sometimes achieve their policy goals through the courts.[25] Interest groups have several judicial lobbying options, including efforts to influence the selection of federal judges. Right-to-life groups have pressured Republican administrations to make opposition to abortion a prerequisite for nomination to the federal bench. Democratic administrations have in turn faced pressure from pro-choice groups in their judicial nominations.[26] Judicial lobbying also includes lawsuits. For some organizations, such as the American Civil Liberties Union (ACLU), legal action is the primary means of lobbying. The ACLU often takes on unpopular causes, such as the free-speech rights of fringe groups. Such causes have little chance of success in legislative bodies but may prevail in a courtroom.

As interest groups have increasingly resorted to legal action, they have often found themselves facing one another in court. Environmental litigation groups such as the Environmental Defense Fund have fought numerous court battles with oil, timber, and mining corporations. Even when groups are not a direct party to a lawsuit, they sometimes get involved through amicus curiae ("friend of the court") briefs. An amicus brief is a written document in which a group explains to a court its position on a legal dispute the court is handling.

Webs of Influence: Groups in the Policy Process

To get a fuller picture of how inside lobbying works, it is helpful to consider two policy processes—iron triangles and issue networks—in which many groups are enmeshed.

Iron Triangles   An **iron triangle** consists of a small and informal but relatively stable set of bureaucrats, legislators, and lobbyists who seek to develop policies beneficial to a particular interest. The three "corners" of one such triangle are the Department of Agriculture (bureaucrats), the agriculture committees of Congress (legislators), and farm groups such as the Associated Milk Producers and the Association of Wheat Growers (lobbyists). Together they determine many of the policies affecting farmers. Although the support of the president and a majority in Congress is needed to enact new policies, they often defer to the judgment of the agricultural triangle, whose members are intimately familiar with farmers' needs.

Groups embedded in iron triangles have an inside track to well-positioned legislators and bureaucrats. They can count on getting a full hearing on issues affecting them. Moreover, because they have something to offer in return, the triangular relationship tends to be clad in "iron." The groups provide lobbying support for agency programs and campaign contributions to members of Congress. Agricultural groups, for instance, donate millions of dollars to congressional campaigns during each election cycle. Most of the money goes to the campaigns of House and Senate incumbents who sit on the agriculture committees. Figure 9-2 summarizes the benefits that flow to each member of an iron triangle.

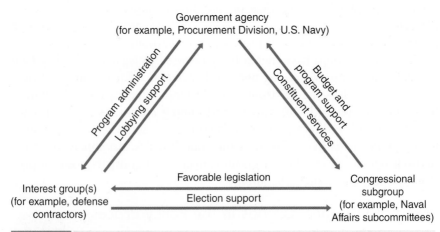

figure 9-2   HOW AN IRON TRIANGLE BENEFITS ITS PARTICIPANTS

An iron triangle works to the advantage of each of its participants—an interest group, a congressional subgroup, and a government agency.

Issue Networks   Iron triangles represent the pattern of influence in only certain policy areas and are less common now than in the past. A more frequent pattern of influence today is the **issue network**—an informal grouping of officials, lobbyists, and policy specialists (the "network") who come together *temporarily* around a policy problem (the "issue").

Issue networks are a result of the increasing complexity of policy problems. Participants must have a working knowledge of the issue at hand in order to address it effectively. Thus, unlike iron triangles, in which a participant's position is everything, an issue network is built around specialized interests and knowledge. On any given issue, the participants might come from a variety of executive agencies, congressional committees, interest groups, and institutions such as universities or think tanks. Compared to iron triangles, issue networks are less stable. As the issue develops, new participants may join the debate and old ones may drop out. Once the issue is resolved, the network disbands.[27]

An example of an issue network is the set of participants who would come together over the issue of whether a large tract of old forest should be opened to logging. A few decades ago, this issue would have been settled in an iron triangle consisting of the timber companies, the U.S. Forest Service, and relevant members of the House and Senate agriculture committees. But as forestlands have diminished and environmental concerns have grown, such issues can no longer be contained within the cozy confines of an iron triangle. Today, an issue network would form that included logging interests, the U.S. Forest Service, House and Senate agriculture committee members, research scientists, and representatives of environmental groups, the housing industry, and animal-rights groups. Unlike the old iron triangle, which was confined to like-minded interests, this issue network would include opposing interests (for example, the loggers and the environmentalists). And unlike an iron triangle, the issue network would dissolve once the issue that brought the parties together was resolved.

In sum, issue networks differ substantially from iron triangles. In an iron triangle, a common interest brings the participants together in a long-lasting and mutually beneficial relationship. In an issue network, an immediate issue brings together the participants in a temporary network that is based on their ability to knowledgeably address the issue and where they play out their separate interests before disbanding once the issue is settled. Despite these differences, iron triangles and issue networks do have one thing in common: they are arenas in which organized groups exercise influence. The interests of the general public may be taken into account in these webs of power, but the interests of the participating groups are foremost.

OUTSIDE LOBBYING: SEEKING INFLUENCE THROUGH PUBLIC PRESSURE

Although an interest group may rely solely on inside lobbying, this approach is more likely to be successful when the group can demonstrate that it represents an important constituency. Accordingly, groups also engage in **outside lobbying,** which involves bringing public ("outside") pressure to bear on policymakers (see Table 9-2).[28]

Constituency Advocacy: Grassroots Lobbying

Outside lobbying includes efforts, such as letter-writing campaigns or public demonstrations, aimed at convincing lawmakers that a group's policy position has popular support. A case in point is the 2000 legislation that resulted in the permanent normalization of trade relations with China. Most business lobbies supported the proposed legislation, and several of them launched grassroots lobbying efforts. Boeing Corporation, for example, asked its employees, subcontractors, and suppliers—more than 40,000 in all—to contact members of Congress. Motorola was among the other corporations that engaged in grassroots lobbying on the issue of trade with China. Motorola spent more than $1 million on media advertising that highlighted a toll-free number through which people could contact members of Congress.[29]

Few groups, however, are better at outside lobbying than AARP. When major legislation affecting retirees is pending, AARP swings into action,

table 9-2	TACTICS USED IN INSIDE AND OUTSIDE LOBBYING EFFORTS
Inside Lobbying	**Outside Lobbying**
Developing contacts with legislators and executives	Encouraging group members to write, phone, or e-mail their representatives in Congress
Providing information and policy proposals to key officials	Seeking favorable coverage by news media
Forming coalitions with other groups	Encouraging members to support particular candidates in elections
	Targeting group resources on key election races
	Making political action committee (PAC) contributions to candidates

encouraging its members to contact their congressional representatives. Congress receives more mail from members of AARP than it does from members of any other group.

Electoral Action: Votes and Money

An "outside" strategy can also include election activity. "Reward your friends and punish your enemies" is a political adage that loosely describes how interest groups approach elections. One lobbyist said it directly: "Talking to politicians is fine, but with a little money they hear you better."[30] The possibility of campaign opposition from a powerful group can restrain an officeholder. Opposition from the three-million-member National Rifle Association, for example, is a major reason the United States has lagged behind other Western societies in its handgun control laws, despite polls indicating that a majority of Americans favor such laws.

Political Action Committees (PACs)   A group's contributions to candidates are funneled through its **political action committee (PAC).** A group cannot give organizational funds (such as corporate profits or union dues) directly to candidates, but through its PAC, a group can solicit voluntary contributions from members or employees and then donate this money to candidates. A PAC can back as many candidates as it wants but is legally limited in the amount it can contribute to a single candidate. The ceiling is $10,000 per candidate—$5,000 in the primary campaign and $5,000 in the general election campaign. (These financial limits apply to candidates for federal office. State and local campaigns are regulated by state laws, and some states allow PACs to make unlimited contributions to individual candidates.)

There are more than four thousand PACs, and PAC contributions account for roughly one-fourth of total contributions to congressional campaigns. Their role is less significant in presidential campaigns, which are bigger in scale and depend largely on individual contributors.

More than 60 percent of all PACs are associated with businesses (see Figure 9-3). Most of these are corporate PACs, such as the Ford Motor Company Civic Action Fund, the Sun Oil Company Political Action Committee, and the Coca-Cola PAC. The others are tied to trade associations, such as RPAC (National Association of Realtors). The next-largest set of PACs consists of those linked to citizens' groups (that is, public-interest, single-issue, and ideological groups), such as the liberal People for the American Way and the conservative National Conservative Political Action Committee. Labor unions, once the major source of group contributions, constitute less than 10 percent of PACs.

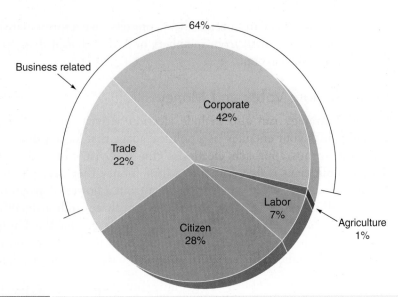

figure 9-3   PERCENTAGE OF PACs BY CATEGORY

Most PACs represent business. Corporate and trade association PACs make up roughly three out of every five PACs. *Source:* Federal Election Commission, 2014.

PACs contribute roughly eight times as much money to incumbents as to their challengers. PACs recognize that incumbents are likely to win and thus to remain in positions of power. One PAC director, expressing a common view, said, "We always stick with the incumbent when we agree with them both."[31]

Super PACs   A few short years ago, the term "super PAC" was not part of the political lexicon. That changed when the Supreme Court ruled in *Citizens United v. Federal Election Commission* (2010) that federal laws restricting campaign spending by corporations and unions violated their right of free expression. The Court held that corporations and unions can spend an unlimited amount of their funds on elections, as long as the spending is not coordinated directly with that of candidates and parties (see Chapters 1 and 8).[32] In a follow-up case, a lower federal court ruled that political activists can form independent campaign committees to solicit and spend corporate, union, and individual contributions.

These rulings spawned **super PACs** or, as they are officially called, *independent-expenditure-only-committees* (IEOCs). These campaign groups are not allowed to give money directly to candidates or parties, but they are otherwise more or less free to spend as much as they want. By 2012, more than 1,000 super PACs had been formed. They spent a combined total of $600 million to influence the outcome of the 2012 presidential and congressional races, helping to make it the most expensive election in the nation's history.

Super PACs have been a subject of hot debate. Critics have assailed the fact that super PACs can spend unlimited amounts of money and, unlike regular PACs, are not required to report their expenditures until nearly two years after they are formed, which can mean that their expenditures are not known until long after the votes are counted. One such critic is Vermont's Democratic senator Bernie Sanders. Election outcomes, says Sanders, should represent "all of the people, and not just those wealthy individuals and corporations who can put millions into political campaigns."[33] Proponents of super PACs say they bring voices and views into the campaign that voters have a right to hear. Says Bradley Smith, a Republican who served as chair of the Federal Election Commission: "While people like to complain about political spending, research shows that increased spending improves voter knowledge of candidates and issues."[34]

Super PACs have emerged as a major source of campaign spending. They can spend an unlimited amount as long as they do not coordinate their spending with the candidate or party they are supporting.

POLITICAL THINKING	Are Super PACs a Good Thing, or a Bad Thing?

The Supreme Court's 2010 Citizens' United *ruling paved the way for the creation of so-called super PACs—independent groups that are free to raise and spend as much money as they want on election campaigns as long as they don't coordinate their efforts with those of a candidate or political party. Critics say that super PACs give wealthy individuals and interests too much influence over elections. Proponents say that super PACs increase the amount of information available to voters. What's your view of super PACs?*

THE GROUP SYSTEM: INDISPENSABLE BUT BIASED IN FAVOR OF ECONOMIC GROUPS

As noted in the chapter's introduction, pluralist theory holds that organized groups are a source of sound governance. On one level, this claim is indisputable. Groups are a means of getting government to pay attention to people's needs and interests. Yet the issue of representation through groups is also a question of whether the various interests in society are fairly represented, and here the pluralist argument is less persuasive.

The Contribution of Groups to Self-Government: Pluralism

Government does not exist simply to serve majority interests. The fact that most people are not retirees or union members or farmers or college students is not an indication that the interests of such "minorities" are unworthy of government's attention. What better instrument exists for promoting their interests than lobbying groups working on their behalf?

Some pluralists even question the usefulness of terms such as the *public interest.* If people disagree on society's goals and priorities, as they always do, how can anyone claim that their goal or priority represents the public interest? As an alternative, pluralists say that society is best seen as a collection of separate interests and is best served by a process that serves a wide array of these interests. Thus, if manufacturing interests prevail on one issue, environmentalists on another, farmers on a third, minorities on a fourth, and so on until a great many interests are served, the "public interest" will have been served. Pluralists also note that the promotion of the special interest often benefits others as well. Tax incentives for corporations that encourage research and capital investment, for example, can result in job creation and improved goods and services.

Finally, interest groups expand the range of issues that come to lawmakers' attention. Political parties sometimes shy away from controversial issues and, in any case, concentrate on those that have broad impact, which leaves hundreds of issues unaddressed through the party system. Interest groups advocate for and against many of these issues.[35]

Flaws in Pluralism: Interest-Group Liberalism and Economic Bias

Pluralist theory has questionable aspects. Political scientist Theodore Lowi points out that there is no concept of the public interest in a system that gives special interests the ability to determine the policies affecting them.[36] Nor can it be assumed that what a lobbying group receives is what the majority would also want. Consider the case of the federal law that required auto dealers to list the known defects of used cars on window stickers. The law was repealed after the National Association of Automobile Dealers contributed more than $1 million to the reelection campaigns of members of Congress. Auto dealers won another victory when their loans to car buyers were exempted from regulation by the new consumer protection agency that was created as part of the Restoring American Financial Stability Act of 2010.

Republican and Democratic lawmakers alike are in the habit of using government to promote group interests. Each party has its favorites—for example, business groups usually do better when Republicans are in power, and labor groups usually do better when Democrats are in power. Neither party has shown a reluctance to use the power of government on behalf of the groups it favors.

Another flaw in the pluralist argument resides in its claim that the group system is representative. Although pluralists acknowledge that well-funded interests have more clout, they say that the group process is relatively open and few interests are entirely left out. This claim contains an element of truth, but it is not the full story. As this chapter has shown, economic interests, particularly corporations, are the most highly organized and the most advantaged when it comes to exerting influence on policy.[37] Of course, economic groups do not dominate everything, nor do they operate unchecked. Most environmental groups, for example, work to shield the environment from threats posed by business activity.

Sometimes the interests of a group are at odds with the interests of the majority, as when used car dealers were exempted from having to inform customers about defects in the autos they sell.

Activist government has also brought the group system into closer balance; the government's poverty programs have spawned groups that act to protect the programs. Nevertheless, the power of poverty-related groups is a pittance compared with the power of moneyed interests. Nearly two-thirds of all lobbying groups in Washington are business related, and their political clout is enormous.

A Madisonian Dilemma

James Madison recognized the dilemma inherent in group activity. Although he worried that interest groups would have too much political influence, he argued in *Federalist* No. 10 that a free society must allow the pursuit of self-interest. Unless people can promote the separate opinions that stem from differences in their needs, values, and possessions, they are not a free people.

Ironically, Madison's constitutional solution to the problem of factions is now part of the problem. Madison thought that the American system of checks and balances, with a separation of powers at its core, would prevent a majority faction from trampling on the interests of smaller groups. This same system, however, makes it relatively easy for minority factions—or, as they are called today, special-interest groups—to gain government support. Because of the system's division of power, they have numerous points at which to gain access and exert influence. Often, they

POLITICAL THINKING

Can Group Power Be Kept in Check?

"Liberty is to faction what air is to fire," wrote James Madison in Federalist No. 10. Madison was lamenting the self-interested behavior of factions or, as they are called today, interest groups. Yet Madison recognized that the only way to suppress this behavior was to destroy the liberty that allows people to organize. Numerous efforts have been made to restrict the power of groups without infringing on free expression rights. Laws have been enacted that restrict group contributions to candidates and that require lobbyists to register and report their expenditures. Yet nothing in the end seems to be all that effective in harnessing the self-interested actions of groups. Do you think there is an answer to Madison's concern? Or are the excesses of group politics simply one of the costs of living in a free society?

need only to find a single ally, whether it is a congressional committee or an executive agency or a federal court, to get at least some of what they seek. And once they obtain a government benefit, it is likely to last. Benefits are hard to eliminate because concerted action by the executive branch and both houses of Congress is usually required. If a group has strong support in even a single institution, it can usually fend off attempts to eliminate a policy or program that serves its interest. Such support ordinarily is easy to acquire, because the group has resources—information, money, and votes—that officeholders want. (Chapters 11 and 13 discuss further the issue of interest-group power.)

SUMMARY

A political interest group is composed of a set of individuals organized to promote a shared concern. Most interest groups owe their existence to factors other than politics. These groups form for economic reasons, such as the pursuit of profit, and maintain themselves by making profits (in the case of corporations) or by providing their members with private goods, such as jobs and wages. Economic groups include corporations, trade associations, labor unions, farm organizations, and professional associations. Collectively, economic groups are by far the largest set of organized interests. The group system tends to favor interests that are already economically and socially advantaged.

Citizens' groups do not have the same organizational advantages as economic groups. They depend on voluntary contributions from potential members, who may lack interest and resources or who recognize that they will get the collective good from a group's activity even if they do not participate (the free-rider problem). Citizens' groups include public-interest, single-issue, and ideological groups. Their numbers have increased dramatically since the 1960s despite their organizational problems.

Organized interests seek influence largely by lobbying public officials and contributing to election campaigns. Using an inside strategy, lobbyists develop direct contacts with legislators, government bureaucrats, and members of the judiciary in order to persuade them to accept the group's perspective on policy. Groups also use an outside strategy, seeking to mobilize public support for their goals. This strategy relies in part on grassroots lobbying—encouraging group members and the public to communicate their policy views to officials. Outside lobbying also includes efforts to elect officeholders who will support group aims. Through political action committees (PACs), organized groups now provide nearly a fourth of all contributions received by congressional candidates. A more recent development is the emergence of super PACs. They are independent campaign committees that can raise and spend nearly unrestricted amounts of money on elections as long as they do not coordinate their efforts with those of the candidate they are supporting.

The policies that emerge from the group system bring benefits to many of society's interests and often serve the collective interest as well. But when groups can essentially dictate policies, the common good is rarely served. The majority's interest is subordinated to group (minority) interests. In most instances, the minority consists of individuals who already enjoy a substantial share of society's benefits.

CRITICAL THINKING ZONE

KEY TERMS

citizens' (noneconomic) groups (*p. 274*)
collective (public) goods (*p. 277*)
economic groups (*p. 272*)
free-rider problem (*p. 278*)
inside lobbying (*p. 281*)
interest group (*p. 269*)
iron triangle (*p. 286*)

issue network (*p. 287*)
lobbying (*p. 281*)
outside lobbying (*p. 288*)
political action committee (PAC)
   (*p. 289*)
private (individual) goods (*p. 277*)
super PACs (*p. 290*)

APPLYING THE ELEMENTS OF CRITICAL THINKING

Conceptualizing: How do iron triangles and issue networks differ?

Synthesizing: Contrast the methods of inside lobbying with those of outside lobbying.

Analyzing: Why are there so many more organized interest groups in the United States than in other Western democracies? Why are so many of these groups organized around economic interests, particularly business?

EXTRA CREDIT

A Book Worth Reading: Lawrence Lessig, *Republic Lost: How Money Corrupts Congress—and a Plan to Stop It*. New York: Twelve Publishers, 2011. An insightful look at lobbying that includes a discussion of its positive contributions while concluding that it has grown out of control.

A Website Worth Visiting: **www.opensecrets.org.** The Center for Responsive Politics is a nonpartisan, nonprofit organization. Its website includes up-to-date analysis and data on lobbying, PAC spending, and other interest-group activity.

PARTICIPATE!

Consider contributing to a citizens' interest group. Such groups depend on members' donations for operating funds. Citizens' groups cover the political spectrum from right to left and touch on nearly every conceivable public issue. You will not have difficulty locating a group through the Internet that has policy goals consistent with your beliefs and values. If you are interested in contributing your time instead, some citizens' groups (for example, PIRG) have college chapters that might provide opportunities for you to work on issues of personal interest.

THE NEWS MEDIA: COMMUNICATING POLITICAL IMAGES

66 The press in America . . . determines what people will think and talk about, an authority that in other nations is reserved for tyrants, priests, parties, and mandarins. 99

THEODORE H. WHITE[1]

The news flashed across America. Mark Sanford, governor of South Carolina, was missing. Neither his wife nor the state troopers in charge of his security knew where he was. Repeated calls to his cell phone went unanswered. As concern mounted, Sanford's press secretary announced that the governor was hiking the Appalachian Trail and would be out of contact until his return. As it turned out, Sanford was in Argentina visiting a woman with whom he was having a relationship. At a press conference after his return, Sanford admitted to the extramarital affair, saying that it had begun years before as an innocent relationship, only to turn romantic a year earlier. He called her his "soul mate."

Sanford was elected after having first made a reputation as a tough-minded conservative in the U.S. House of Representatives. In early 2009, he had made headlines by announcing that he would reject the stimulus funds due to his state from the economic recovery bill that Congress had enacted. He was among a half-dozen Republicans whose name cropped up whenever discussion turned to possible 2012 GOP presidential nominees. Nevertheless, nothing that Sanford had done previously—not as a member of Congress, not as governor, and not as a potential presidential contender—generated anything like the headlines accompanying his extramarital affair. It was front-page news throughout the country, and provided plenty of grist for the late-night TV shows. David Letterman, after noting in his opening monologue that Sanford was having an affair with a woman from another country, quipped: "Once again, foreigners taking jobs that Americans won't do."

Although reporters sometimes compare the news to a mirror held up to reality, the news is described more accurately as a refracted version of reality. The **news** is mainly an account of obtruding events, particularly those that are *timely* (new or unfolding developments rather than old or static ones), *dramatic* (striking developments rather than commonplace ones), and *compelling* (developments that arouse people's emotions).[2] These tendencies have their origins in a number of factors, the most significant of which is that news organizations need to attract an audience in order to make a profit. Thus, compared with Sanford's sexual liaison, his work as a top public official was less newsworthy. It was part of the ongoing business of government and did not lend itself to the vivid storytelling of a sex scandal.

The news media are Americans' window into the world of politics. For most people politics is a secondhand experience, something they observe through the media rather than directly. People's mental images of politics stem largely from what they hear through the media. For example, whether people think the economy is performing well or poorly derives largely from what is reported in the news media on economic conditions.

Because reality itself is too complex to be described in its entirety, the media necessarily present a selective version of it. **Framing** is the process by which journalists select particular aspects of situations and craft their stories around these aspects.[3] In covering a congressional debate, for example, journalists could frame their stories in the context of the substance of the debate. Alternatively, they could frame their stories in the context of the partisan conflict over the proposed bill. As it happens, journalists typically frame their stories in the second way. They portray politics largely as a fight for partisan advantage, which affects how people perceive politics. Polls show that Americans overwhelmingly see politicians more as strategists who are intent on achieving partisan goals than as leaders who are intent on serving the public interest.[4]

This chapter examines the news media's role in American politics. The **news media** (or the **press,** as they are also called) are a key intermediary between Americans and their leaders, but they are a different kind of intermediary than political parties and interest groups. The latter seek influence in order to promote particular leaders or policies. Although some members

At a press conference, South Carolina governor Mark Sanford announces the real reason he had gone missing for several days. His office had claimed he was hiking the Appalachian Trail. As it turned out, Sanford was in Argentina to see a woman with whom he was having an affair. The news media, as their coverage of Sanford illustrates, presents a refracted version of reality, in which sensational developments typically get more attention than the day-to-day problems affecting Americans' lives.

of the press do the same, the media's basic goal is to inform the public about politics and government. Yet, because news organizations also seek to attract an audience in their pursuit of a profit, their news coverage provides a slanted version of politics. The main ideas presented in the chapter are:

- *The American press was initially tied to the nation's political party system (the partisan press) but gradually developed an independent position (the objective press).* In the process, the news shifted from a political orientation, which emphasizes political values and ideas, to a journalistic orientation, which stresses newsworthy information and events.

- *In recent years, traditional news organizations have faced increased competition for people's attention from cable and the Internet, which has contributed to audience fragmentation and an increase in opinionated and entertainment-laced journalism.*

- *The news media have several functions—signaling (the press brings relevant events and problems into public view), common-carrier (the press serves as a channel through which leaders and citizens can communicate), watchdog (the press scrutinizes official behavior for evidence of deceitful, careless, or corrupt acts), and partisan (the press promotes particular interests and values).* The traditional media (print and broadcast) contribute mainly to the first three functions whereas the "new" news media (cable and the Internet) contribute mainly to the last one.

- *The news audience has been shrinking and fragmenting, partly as a result of new technology and partly because young adults are less likely than older ones to pay attention to news.* One consequence has been a widening gap in the information levels of America's more-attentive and less-attentive citizens.

HISTORICAL DEVELOPMENT: FROM THE NATION'S FOUNDING TO TODAY

Democracy depends on a free flow of information,[5] a fact not lost on America's early leaders. Alexander Hamilton persuaded John Fenno to start a newspaper, the *Gazette of the United States*, as a means of publicizing the policies of George Washington's administration. To finance the paper, Hamilton, as secretary of the treasury, granted it the Treasury Department's printing contracts. Hamilton's political rival, Thomas Jefferson, dismissed the *Gazette's* reporting as "pure Toryism" and convinced Philip Freneau to start the *National Gazette* as an opposition paper. Jefferson, as secretary of state, gave Freneau the authority to print State Department documents.

Early newspapers were printed a page at a time on flat presses, a process that limited production and kept the cost of each copy beyond the reach of the ordinary citizen. Leading papers such as the *Gazette of the United States* had fewer than fifteen hundred readers and could not have survived without party support. Not surprisingly, the "news" they printed was laced with partisanship.[6] In this era of the **partisan press,** publishers openly backed one party or the other.

Technological innovation in the early 1800s helped bring about the gradual decline of partisan newspapers. With the invention of the telegraph, editors had access to breaking news about events outside the local area, which led them to substitute news reports for opinion commentary. The invention in the late nineteenth century of the power-driven printing press was equally important in that it enabled publishers to print the newspapers more cheaply and quickly. As circulations rose, so did advertising revenues, reducing newspapers' dependence on government patronage.

Yellow journalism was characterized by its sensationalism. William Randolph Hearst's *New York Journal* whipped up public support for a war in Cuba against Spain through inflammatory reporting on the sinking of the battleship *Maine* in Havana Harbor in 1898.

By 1900, some American newspapers had daily circulations in excess of a hundred thousand copies. The period marked the height of newspapers' power and the low point in their civic contribution. A new style of reporting—"yellow journalism"—had emerged as a way of selling papers. It was "a shrieking, gaudy, sensation-loving, devil-may-care kind of journalism which lured the reader by any possible means."[7] A circulation battle between William Randolph Hearst's *New York Journal* and Joseph Pulitzer's *New York World* may have contributed to the outbreak of the Spanish-American War through sensational (and largely inaccurate) reports on the cruelty of Spanish rule in Cuba. A young Frederic Remington (who later became a noted painter and sculptor), working as a news artist for Hearst, planned to return home because Cuba appeared calm and safe, but Hearst allegedly cabled back: "Please remain. You furnish the pictures and I'll furnish the war."[8]

POLITICAL THINKING	How Much Responsibility Comes with a Right?

Freedom of the press is guaranteed by the Constitution, making the news media the only private institution with a specific constitutional right designed for its benefit. How much of a public obligation does this bestow on the news media? Should news outlets that engage in sensationalism and infotainment—largely with an eye toward making a profit—be afforded the same First Amendment protections as those outlets that take their public responsibility more seriously?

The Objective-Journalism Era

The excesses of yellow journalism led some publishers to devise ways of reporting the news more responsibly. One step was to separate the newspaper's advertising department from its news department, thus reducing the influence of advertisers on news content. A second development was **objective journalism,** which is based on the reporting of "facts" rather than opinions and is "fair" in that it presents both sides of partisan debate. An architect of the new model of reporting was Adolph Ochs of the *New York Times.* Ochs bought the *Times* in 1896, when its daily circulation was nine thousand; four years later, its readership had grown to eighty-two thousand. Ochs told his reporters that he "wanted as little partisanship as possible . . . as few judgments as possible."[9] The *Times* gradually acquired a reputation as the country's best newspaper. Objective reporting was also promoted through newly formed journalism schools, such as those at Columbia University and the University of Missouri. Within a few decades, objective journalism had become the dominant reporting model.

Until the twentieth century, the print media were the only form of mass communication. By the 1920s, however, hundreds of radio stations were broadcasting throughout the nation. At first the government did not regulate radio broadcasting. The result was chaos. A common problem was that nearby stations often used the same or adjacent radio frequencies, interfering with each other's broadcasts. Finally, in 1934, Congress passed the Communications Act, which regulated broadcasting and created the Federal Communications Commission (FCC) to oversee the process. Broadcasters had to be licensed by the FCC, and because broadcasting frequencies are limited in number, licensees were required to be impartial in their political coverage and were prohibited from selling or giving airtime to a political candidate without offering to sell or give an equal amount of airtime to other candidates for the same office. (An exception was later made for election debates; broadcasters can televise them even if third-party candidates are excluded.)

Television followed radio, and by the late 1950s, more than 90 percent of American homes had a TV set. In this period, the FCC imposed a second restriction—the Fairness Doctrine—on broadcasters. The Fairness Doctrine required broadcasters to "afford reasonable opportunity for the discussion of conflicting views of public importance." Broadcasters were prohibited from using their news coverage to promote one party or issue position at the expense of another. In effect, the objective-reporting model practiced voluntarily by the newspapers was imposed by law on broadcasters.

The Rise of the "New" News

During the era of objective journalism, the news was not entirely devoid of partisanship. Although broadcasters were prohibited by law from editorializing, newspapers were not. Most of them backed one political party or the other on their editorial and opinion (op-ed) pages. Nevertheless, it was usually difficult to tell from their news pages which party they backed editorially. Nearly all of them highlighted the same national stories each day, and if a high-ranking public official got embroiled in a scandal or policy blunder, they played it up, whether the official was a Republican or a Democrat.

The 1980s marked a turning point. A major development occurred in 1987 when the FCC rescinded the Fairness Doctrine, claiming that the emergence of cable television and the expansion of FM radio had alleviated the problem of scarce frequencies. Radio stations quickly responded to the change in policy. They had previously been required to air a liberal or conservative talk show if they aired one of the opposite type. The elimination of the Fairness Doctrine freed broadcasters from this restriction, and hundreds of radio stations switched from playing music to airing partisan talk shows.

Cable television soon followed radio's lead. Because cable television was transmitted by privately owned wire rather than through broadcasting, it was not required to comply with the Fairness Doctrine. Nevertheless, when media mogul Ted Turner started CNN in 1980, he chose to abide by it, instructing his correspondents to pursue a path of partisan neutrality. Turner's policy was not, however, adopted by the cable news outlets that came later. Instead, as will be discussed later in this chapter, Fox News and MSNBC chose partisan approaches to the news.

These changes have transformed the news system into one that gives considerably more time than in the past to punditry and opinions. The transformation can be seen by comparing the formats of the traditional broadcast news outlets (ABC, NBC, and CBS) with those of the partisan cable news outlets (Fox and MSNBC). As Figure 10-1 shows, news reports take up a large majority of time on broadcast news but only a third of the time on cable news, which devotes the major share of its time to interviews with party leaders, pundits, and other political figures.

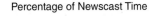

Percentage of Newscast Time

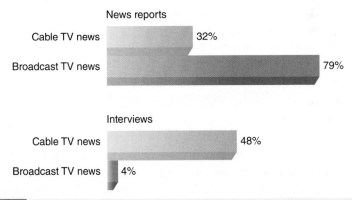

News reports

Cable TV news   32%

Broadcast TV news   79%

Interviews

Cable TV news   48%

Broadcast TV news   4%

figure 10-1 BROADCAST AND CABLE NEWS FORMATS

Partisan cable news outlets (Fox and MSNBC) rely most heavily on interviews with political figures while broadcast news outlets (ABC, CBS, and NBC) rely most heavily on the reporting of traditional news stories.

Source: Created by author from data of Pew Research Center's Project for Excellence in Journalism, 2013. Figures do not total to 100% because they exclude, for example, the time during newscast that anchor is talking.

JOURNALISM AND POLITICS

The news media operate as *gatekeepers*. Among the countless story possibilities each day, they determine which events will be covered and which ones will not. These selections, in turn, will influence what citizens are thinking and talking about. What determines these selections? What determines whether a story will make the news, and thus become known to the public, or will not make the news, and thus remain largely out of sight except to those affected directly?

For one thing, the news is shaped by the need of news organizations "to attract and hold a large audience for advertisers."[10] Without advertising or other revenue sources, news organizations would quickly go out of business. The very definition of news—what it is and what it is not—is built around the need to attract the audience's attention. This need leads journalists to cover what they call "hard events"—developments that have taken a clear and definable shape within the past twenty-four hours.[11] It is a reason, for example, that policy issues are not the main focus of political coverage. Issues don't change all that much from one day to the next, which reduces their news value. The first time that a political leader talks about a major policy issue, it is likely to be reported, and it may even make the front page. Thereafter, it's looked upon by journalists as "old news." Journalists are attentive primarily to the things that do change regularly, such as politicians' tactical moves and their level of political support. Almost daily in the last months of a presidential campaign, for example, journalists will report the latest poll results—a level of attention never accorded the campaign's issues.[12]

Yet journalists do not completely disregard their duty to inform the public. They perform four functions—the signaling, common-carrier, watchdog, and partisan functions—that contribute to the public's information needs. We'll look first at the signaling function.

The Signaling Function

The media's responsibilities include a **signaling (signaler) function**—alerting the public to important developments as soon as possible after they happen. The signaling function is performed largely by the traditional media—the wire services, the daily newspapers, and the television networks. Occasionally, an event enters the news stream through the Internet. For example, news of the mass killing of students and teachers at the Sandy Hook Elementary School in Newtown, Connecticut, in 2012 was first reported through social media. Nevertheless, hundreds of news stories enter the news stream daily, and the bulk of them are generated by traditional news outlets.

In their capacity as signalers, the media have the power to focus the public's attention. The term **agenda setting** is used to describe the media's ability to influence what is on people's minds.[13] By covering the same events, problems, issues, and leaders—simply by giving them space or time in the news—the media place them on the public agenda. The press, as Bernard Cohen notes, "may not be successful much of the time in telling people what to think, but it is stunningly successful in telling them what to think about."[14]

Even when media portrayals are out of synch with reality, they have an agenda-setting effect. A striking example occurred in the early 1990s when local television stations, in an attempt to bolster sagging news ratings, upped their crime coverage. "If it bleeds it leads" became the mantra of local TV news. Meanwhile, the national media were playing up several high-profile murder cases including the kidnap-murder of twelve-year-old Polly Klaas in California. Crime was the most heavily reported national issue, overshadowing even coverage of the nation's struggling economy. The effect on public opinion was dramatic. In the previous decade, no more than 5 percent of Americans had believed at any time that crime was the country's biggest problem. By 1994, however, more than 40 percent of Americans said that crime was the top issue facing the nation. Lawmakers got caught up in the public's anxiety by enacting tough new sentencing policies and building new prisons at the fastest rate in the nation's history. The irony was that the level of crime in America was actually *declining* during this period. According to U.S. Justice Department statistics, the rate of violent crime had dropped by 5 percent since 1990.[15]

The press is a powerful agenda setter in part because nearly all major news organizations focus on the same stories and interpret them in pretty much the same way. In view of the freedom and great number of news organizations—there are roughly fifteen hundred daily newspapers and a thousand local television outlets in the United States—it might be expected that Americans would be exposed to widely different versions of national news. With the exception of some cable and Internet outlets, such as Fox, MSNBC, and the Huffington Post, the opposite is true. Each day, newspapers and broadcast outlets from coast to coast tend to highlight the same national issues and events.

Objective journalism is one reason the national news is everywhere pretty much the same. Unlike some European news systems, in which journalism norms allow and even encourage reporters to present the news through a partisan lens, reporters at most U.S. news organizations are expected to treat the political parties and their leaders in a balanced way. They do not always do so, but in their quest for balance, American

The cramped space of the White House press room is where reporters gather to receive daily briefings on the president's activities. Much of the news conveyed by the media originates in the statements of top political leaders and their spokespersons.

reporters tend toward a common interpretation of political developments, as opposed to a Republican version or a Democratic version. In addition, most news outlets lack the resources to gather news outside their own location and rely for this coverage on the wire services, particularly the Associated Press (AP), which has three thousand reporters stationed throughout the country and the world to gather news stories and transmit them to subscribing news organizations. More than 90 percent of the nation's dailies (as well as most broadcast news stations) subscribe to the AP, which, because it serves the full range of American news outlets, studiously avoids partisanship in preparing its stories.

Local television stations also depend on outside sources for their national news coverage. Television production is hugely expensive, which limits the ability of local stations to produce anything except local news. For their national coverage, they rely on video feeds from the leading television networks—ABC, CBS, NBC, CNN, Fox, and MSNBC. Even the national networks have a similar lineup of stories. Most network newscasts are a half hour in length, with ten minutes devoted to advertising. With so little time for news, the day's top stories tend to dominate the newscasts of all networks. Moreover, network correspondents cover the same beats and rely on many of the same sources, which lead them to

HOW THE U.S. DIFFERS
POLITICAL THINKING THROUGH COMPARISONS

Public Broadcasting

Public broadcasting got off to a slow start in the United States. Unlike Europe, where public broadcasting networks (such as Britain's BBC) were created at the start of the radio age, the U.S. government in the 1930s handed control of broadcasting to commercial networks, such as NBC and CBS. By the time Congress decided in the 1960s that public broadcasting was needed, the commercial networks were powerful enough to convince Congress to assign it second-class status. Public broadcasting was poorly funded and was initially denied access to the most powerful broadcast frequencies.

Nevertheless, public broadcasting does have a success story—NPR (National Public Radio). Since the early 1990s, NPR's audience has more than tripled, while the audience for the commercial broadcast outlets has dropped by half. NPR has built its audience through a strategy opposite to that of the commercial networks. As the news audiences of these networks declined in the face of widening competition from cable television, they "softened" their newscasts—boosting entertainment content in the hope of luring viewers away from cable programs. In contrast, NPR held to the notion that news is news and not also entertainment. Studies indicate that NPR's audience is more politically interested and informed than other broadcast news audiences. Many of its listeners are refugees from the broadcast network news they used to watch but now find to lack substance.

Q: What effect on public information might have resulted from the U.S. government's decision in the 1930s to base the nation's broadcasting system on commercial stations rather than public stations?

A: In countries like Britain, where public broadcasting has been well funded from the start, it set a standard for high-quality news that conditioned the public to expect it from other news providers as well. In the United States, commercial broadcasting led the way and, with an interest in profits, developed a form of news aimed at holding the audience's attention. Accordingly, many Americans developed a preference for news that has an entertainment component.

report more or less the same things. After filming a congressional hearing, for example, network correspondents are likely to agree on what was most newsworthy about it—often a testy exchange between a witness and one of the committee members.

The Common-Carrier Function

The press also exercises a **common-carrier function,** serving as a conduit through which political leaders communicate with the public. The justification for this role is straightforward. Citizens cannot support or oppose a leader's plans and actions if they do not know about them, and leaders require news coverage if they are to get the public's attention and support.

Indeed, national news focuses largely on the words and actions of top political leaders, particularly the president (see Chapter 12). Presidents pursue what has come to be known as the "Rose Garden strategy"— so-called because many of their pronouncements are delivered in the flower garden just outside the Oval Office. More than two hundred reporters are assigned to cover the White House, where they receive daily briefings. In fact, the presidency gets substantially more coverage in the national press than does Congress and its members.[16]

Although officials sometimes succeed in getting favorable coverage, two things blunt their efforts to manage the news. One is journalists' norm of partisan neutrality. Although reporters depend heavily on official sources, they often present the positions of leaders of both parties—the "he said, she said" style of reporting. If the president, secretary of defense, Senate majority leader, or other high-ranking official says something newsworthy, the news report often includes a contrary statement by another individual, usually of the opposite party.

Second, although news typically originates in the words and actions of political leaders, they do not monopolize the news, particularly on television. TV news is now more journalist centered than it is newsmaker centered.[17] In an effort to keep their viewers tuned in, television newscasts use a fast-paced format in which each story has multiple pieces woven together in story form, with the journalist acting as the storyteller. One indicator of this format is the "shrinking sound bite" in presidential campaigns. In the 1960s, a candidate's sound bite (the length of time within a television story that a candidate speaks without interruption) was more than forty seconds on average.[18] In recent campaigns, the average sound bite has been less than ten seconds, barely enough time for the candidate to utter a long sentence (see Figure 10-2). It is the journalists, not the candidates, who do most of the talking. For every minute that presidential candidates

Average sound bite in seconds

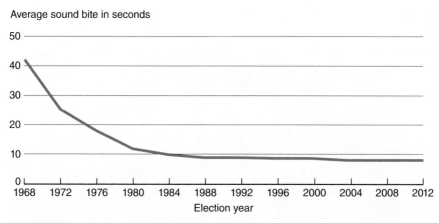

figure 10-2 THE SHRINKING SOUND BITE OF TELEVISION CAMPAIGN COVERAGE

The average length of time that presidential candidates are shown speaking without interruption on broadcast television newscasts has declined sharply in recent elections.
Source: Adapted from various sources.

spoke on the network evening newscasts during recent campaigns, the journalists who were covering them spoke for more than five minutes.[19]

The Watchdog Function

The American press has assumed responsibility for exposing incompetent, hypocritical, and corrupt officials. In this **watchdog function,** the press stands ready to expose officials who violate accepted legal, ethical, or performance standards. The American news media have rightfully been called a fourth branch of government—part of the political system's checks on abuses by those in power.

Journalists are typically skeptical of politicians' motives and actions. A turning point was the Watergate scandal. Led by investigative reporters at the *Washington Post,* the press uncovered evidence that high-ranking officials in the Nixon administration had lied about their role in the 1972 burglary of the Democratic National Committee's headquarters and the subsequent cover-up. President Richard Nixon was forced to resign, as was his attorney general, John Mitchell.

Ever since Watergate, the press has been quick to pounce on any sign of public wrongdoing. An example is the press coverage of the phone surveillance program of the National Security Agency (NSA). After Edward Snowden released classified documents in 2013 showing that the clandestine program was far more extensive than the Obama administration had indicated (see Chapter 4), the news media played up the story for weeks

Watchdog reporting traces to the Progressive Era of the early 1900s, when journalists aggressively uncovered and attacked political and corporate corruption. This colored illustration from the period portrays them as medieval crusaders, with gigantic ink pens instead of swords and lances as their weapons.

on end, helping fuel a national debate on the level of government surveillance that would keep the country safe while also respecting Americans' constitutional rights.

The Internet, with citizens acting in the role of journalists, has enlarged the media's watchdog capacity. Nearly any public event involving a major politician today is likely to be filmed or taped by someone in attendance, which can land a politician in trouble. At a private campaign fundraiser during the 2012 presidential election, for example, Mitt Romney was asked about his strategy for winning the election. "There are 47 percent of the people who will vote for [Obama] no matter what," Romney said. "[They] believe that they are entitled to health care, to food, to housing, to you-name-it." Dismissing them as people "who pay no taxes," Romney went on to say: "[M]y job is not to worry about those people. I'll never convince them they should take personal responsibility and care for their lives." Romney was unaware that someone at the fundraiser was recording his remarks on a cell phone, which ended up in the hands of the media. Pundits had a field day, asking whether the multimillionaire Romney was completely out of touch with ordinary people, that the nontaxpayers he was talking about included retirees on social security and members of the armed services.

The Partisan Function

Traditionally, the **partisan function**—acting as an advocate for a particular viewpoint or interest—has been the responsibility of political leaders, institutions, and organizations. Today, however, the news media—particularly the newer of these media—also function in that capacity.

Traditional Media: Mostly Neutral   During the era of the partisan press, newspapers sought to guide their readers' opinions. In the presidential election campaign of 1896, for example, the *San Francisco Call*, a Republican newspaper, devoted 1,075 column-inches of photographs to the Republican ticket of McKinley-Hobart and only 11 inches to their Democratic opponents, Bryan and Sewell.[20] The emergence of objective journalism brought an end to that style of reporting. Rather than slanting the news to favor the Republican or Democratic side, journalists sought to give their audience both sides, leaving it to them to decide which one was better.

The traditional media—the daily newspapers and broadcast networks—still operate largely in this way. Even their editorial pages, though slanted toward one party or the other, carry at least some opposing opinions so as not to alienate a portion of their readers. Most newspapers also make the safe choice in elections; they endorse incumbents of both parties with much greater frequency than they endorse their challengers.[21]

The traditional broadcast television networks—ABC, CBS, and NBC—do not endorse candidates and claim to be unbiased, although conservatives dispute the claim. In a best-selling book, a former network correspondent, Bernard Goldberg, accused the networks of having a liberal agenda.[22] Such allegations are not completely baseless. Until recently, for example, the concerns of evangelical Christians were rarely a subject of broadcast news except in the context of conflict-ridden issues like creationism and abortion. Also, most broadcast news journalists, as well as most journalists generally, lean Democratic in their personal beliefs.[23]

Nevertheless, scholarly research does not support the allegation that the traditional media have a substantial and systematic liberal bias. Communication scholars David D'Alessio and Mike Allen examined fifty-nine academic studies of media bias and found almost no pattern of bias in newspapers, a slight but insignificant bias in the Democratic direction on television news, and a slight but insignificant bias in the Republican direction in news magazines.[24] In fact, the television-age president with the worst press coverage was a Democrat, Bill Clinton. The Center for Media and Public Affairs found that Clinton's negative coverage exceeded his positive coverage in every quarter of every year of his two-term presidency—a dubious record that no president before or since has equaled.[25]

Instead of a strong partisan bias, scholars have highlighted a different kind of network bias—the networks' preference for the negative.[26] The news turned negative at the time of Watergate and has stayed that way. The networks' preference for "bad news" can be seen, for example, in their coverage of presidential candidates. Nearly all nominees since the 1980s have received mostly negative coverage during the course of the campaign. "Bad news" has characterized network coverage of Democratic and Republican nominees alike.[27] Congress has fared no better. Congressional coverage has been steadily negative since the 1970s, regardless of which party controlled Congress or how much or little was accomplished. "Over the years," concluded scholar Mark Rozell, "press coverage of Congress has moved from healthy skepticism to outright cynicism."[28] (Studies indicate that the press's negative bent is a prime reason why Americans have an unfavorable view of politicians and political institutions.[29])

The networks' negativity helps to explain why they are widely perceived as biased. Research indicates that negative news is perceived differently by those who support and those who oppose the politician being criticized. Opponents tend to see the criticism as valid whereas supporters tend to see it as unjustified and therefore biased.[30] It is not surprising, then, that Democrats during Bill Clinton's presidency thought that the networks favored the Republicans while Republicans during George W. Bush's presidency thought that the networks favored the Democrats. Such findings do not mean that the networks are completely unbiased, for they are not. The findings do indicate, however, that much of the perceived bias is in the eye of the beholder.[31]

Talk Shows: Mostly Conservative   The broadcast networks' partisan bias—real and perceived—has been an issue for conservatives at least since 1970 when Republican vice president Spiro Agnew called the networks "nattering nabobs of negativism." Nevertheless, Republicans could only pressure the networks to cover politics differently in that there was no ready alternative. Cable television and the rescinding of the Fairness Doctrine changed that situation by providing a host of new options, including partisan talk shows.

On both radio and television, most of the successful partisan talk shows have been hosted by conservatives. The host with the largest audience is radio's Rush Limbaugh. In the top twenty-five radio markets, Limbaugh's show has more listeners, in all age groups, than the listenership of all the top liberal talk shows combined. Limbaugh built his following in the early 1990s with attacks on Bill Clinton, whom Limbaugh variously characterized as a draft dodger, womanizer, and wimp. Limbaugh's success prompted billionaire media mogul Rupert Murdoch to start Fox News in 1996. Murdoch reasoned that hard-core conservatives, because of their distrust of the established networks, would embrace a conservative alternative. He hired Roger Ailes, a Republican political consultant, to run Fox News. Ailes in turn hired a number of conservative talk show hosts, including Bill O'Reilly. Within a few years, propelled by a largely Republican audience, Fox News was the most heavily watched cable news network.

The other two cable news outlets, CNN and MSNBC, responded by hiring talk show hosts of their own, although they chose different marketing strategies. CNN has had a diverse set of hosts while MSNBC has

Broadcast news dominated television until the advent of cable. Today, the ABC, CBS, and NBC newscasts compete for viewers with those of Fox News, CNN, and MSNBC. Cable news organizations have also developed new models of journalism. Fox News pursues a politically conservative news agenda while MSNBC pursues a liberal one. Pictured here is Bill O'Reilly of Fox News, who has the largest audience among TV talk show hosts.

cast itself as the liberal alternative to Fox. MSNBC's lineup features Rachel Maddow, a self-described "liberal policy wonk." The most heavily watched of the liberal talk shows, however, are on Comedy Central rather than a news channel. Jon Stewart's *The Daily Show* and Stephen Colbert's *The Colbert Report* are each seen by more than a million viewers a day.

The Internet: Mostly Liberal   Although the First Amendment protects each individual's right to press freedom, this right in practice was once reserved for a tiny few. Journalist A. J. Liebling wrote that freedom of the press belonged to those with enough money to own a news organization.[32]

Today, because of the Internet, freedom of the press is actively enjoyed by a larger number of Americans than ever before. Unlike a newspaper, broadcast station, or cable company, where the capital investment can run into the tens or even hundreds of millions of dollars, the Internet has a low cost of entry. Anyone with a computer and technical savvy can create a website or blog devoted to news and public affairs. The opportunities for citizen communication are at a level not seen since colonial days, when pamphleteers like Thomas Paine had a large voice in public affairs. Thomas Paine's pamphlet *Common Sense* sold over a hundred thousand copies and mobilized American opposition to British rule. "We have the power to begin the world over again," wrote Paine, who also penned the famous line "These are the times that try men's souls."

As was discussed in Chapter 7, the Internet has been a boon for political activists. It has allowed them to engage in unprecedented levels of organizing and fundraising. When it comes to news, however, the Internet's contribution is not as unique. Although there are literally hundreds upon hundreds of websites where news is regularly posted and examined, Internet news is characterized by what analysts call "the long tail." When news-based websites are arrayed by the number of visitors to each site, there are a few heavily visited sites on one end and thousands of lightly visited sites on the other end—the long tail. As it happens, most of the heavily visited sites are those of the traditional media, including CNN. com, and nytimes.com. In addition, most of the other heavily visited sites, such as Google News, carry news that was gathered and reported first by the established media. In other words, most Americans who go to the Internet for news are seeing news generated by the same sources they otherwise tap. A notable exception is the Huffington Post, which was started in 2005 by liberal activist Arianna Huffington and now has several hundred journalists on staff. The site has more than one hundred million visitors a month.

HOW THE 50 STATES DIFFER

POLITICAL THINKING THROUGH COMPARISONS

Internet Access

The Internet has greatly expanded Americans' access to news and information, and most Americans have regular access to the Internet in their home or through their work. However, the percentage varies considerably by state. Eight in every ten residents of Colorado, Minnesota, New Hampshire, and Washington—the states with the highest levels of Internet penetration—have regular access. In contrast, only six in every ten residents of Arkansas, Mississippi, New Mexico, and Tennessee—the states with the lowest levels of Internet penetration—have access.

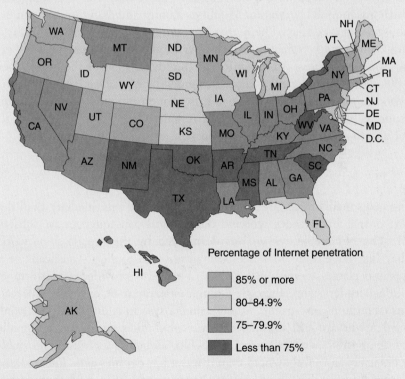

Source: U.S. Census Bureau, 2014.

Continued

> **Q:** What might account for state-to-state differences in Internet penetration?
>
> **A:** States that are poorer and more rural have lower rates of Internet penetration. Less-affluent citizens are less able to afford the Internet, and Internet companies are less likely to offer it in rural areas because of the higher installation costs.

Some political blogs also have substantial audiences, although nothing on the scale of the largest traditional outlets. The most successful ones— such as the Drudge Report and Daily Kos—are closer in form to talk shows than to news programs in that they freely mix opinion with information about current events. Unlike talk shows, however, most of the successful blogs have a liberal bias.[33] An example is the Daily Kos, which was founded by Markos Moulitsas Zúniga and draws several hundred thousand visitors a day. There, they encounter news reports that are mixed with commentary, sometimes including requests for donations to liberal causes or candidates. An exception to the liberal bent of the blogosphere is the conservative Drudge Report, founded by Matt Drudge, which ranks second among political blogs in terms of monthly visitors. The Drudge Report gained fame in 1998 when it revealed that President Bill Clinton had an affair with a White House intern, Monica Lewinsky.

THE NEWS AUDIENCE

The news media today are a far different political intermediary than they were only a few decades ago, and the political consequences are substantial. The old media system was dominated by the broadcast networks. They had huge daily audiences, enabling them to alert Americans of all ages and classes to the same events. They also provided a platform for political leaders who, through a single statement or event, could reach tens of millions of citizens. Today's media system is different. The traditional media are still the major players, but their audiences are smaller and their influence has diminished. The audience for news and public affairs is far more fragmented than it was a few decades ago. The audience is spread across dozens of outlets that vary widely in how they present politics, how they portray political leaders, and what aspects of politics they highlight. America today has a **high-choice media system,** one in which people have a great number of places to go for information. As a

The Internet has lowered the barriers to participation in news reporting to a level not seen since colonial days. Tens of thousands of citizens have created blog sites, and tens of thousands more have posted news-type pictures on YouTube and other outlets. On the other hand, the most heavily visited news sites are, for the most part, those hosted by traditional news outlets, such as *The New York Times* (nytimes.com).

result, people's media exposure—what they see and hear, as well as what they choose not to see and hear—is largely within their control. A consequence has been the widening of two divides, one relating to partisanship and one relating to public information.

The Partisan Divide

When cable and the Internet expanded people's options, some observers thought the change would result in a public exposed to a wider set of opinions. The opposite has happened.[34] The Pew Research Center for the People and the Press has been tracking Americans' media preferences for two decades and finds that Americans' news choices are narrowing. Traditional news outlets still have much larger audiences but outlets that convey a partisan point of view are gaining in popularity, particularly among younger adults. Americans increasingly rely on sources that communicate information supportive of what they already believe.[35] Conservatives tune to right-wing talk shows while liberals tune to those on the left.[36] Political blogs also have like-minded followings.[37] It is rare to find a political blog where people of opposing partisan views congregate.[38]

Research indicates that these tendencies contribute to party polarization.[39] Partisan outlets play up partisan differences, praising their side
while tearing down the other. In turn, exposure to these one-sided arguments tends to push people toward more extreme opinions, contributing
to the widening divide in the attitudes of liberals and conservatives (see
"Party Polarization").

P A R T Y POLARIZATION	Political Thinking in Conflict

Living in Different Media Worlds

Until the 1980s, Americans were immersed in what
political scientist Matthew Baum calls "an information
commons." The three television broadcast networks—ABC, CBS, and
NBC—had huge daily audiences and their newscasts varied only
slightly. Each headlined the same stories and interpreted them in much
the same way. Viewers were exposed equally to the views of leaders of
both political parties. The emergence of cable TV and the rescinding
of the Fairness Doctrine disrupted the pattern. Today, Americans have
a range of choices, including outlets that convey information through

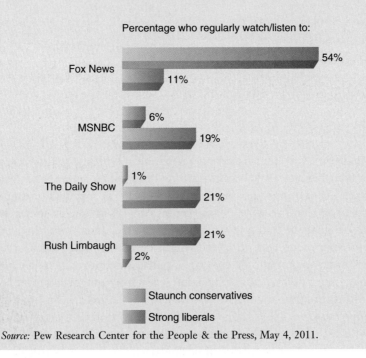

Percentage who regularly watch/listen to:

Fox News — 54% / 11%

MSNBC — 6% / 19%

The Daily Show — 1% / 21%

Rush Limbaugh — 21% / 2%

Staunch conservatives
Strong liberals

Source: Pew Research Center for the People & the Press, May 4, 2011.

a partisan lens, heaping praise on one party and criticizing the other. Research indicates that this form of communication contributes to partisan polarization. It reinforces citizens' preexisting views while at the same time convincing them that the other side's opinions lack merit.

In a recent Pew survey of news and political preferences, respondents were classified based on their answers to poll questions about policy issues. Two of the resulting classifications were "staunch conservatives" and "strong liberals." As can be seen from the accompanying graph, individuals in these two categories have markedly different media preferences, choosing like-minded outlets over those that play up the opposing party.

Q: Do you find it troubling that partisan media outlets contribute to party polarization or do you think they play an indispensable role in clarifying party differences? Do you personally rely mostly on the traditional news media or mostly on outlets of the type shown in the accompanying graph?

The Information Divide

The U.S. news system now has more outlets—including newspapers, television stations, talk shows, and bloggers—than at any time in its history. Although it might be assumed as a consequence that Americans are more informed about public affairs than ever before, it is not the case. The same media system that makes news available on demand at any time also makes it easy for people to avoid the news. The typical American is exposed to media for many hours each day, but only a small fraction of this time is devoted to news and current affairs (see Figure 10-3).

Through the 1970s, most Americans shared a common news experience. In most television markets at the dinner hour, the only choices available to viewers were the ABC newscast, the CBS newscast, and the NBC newscast. Viewers who were intent on watching television in this time period—and 85 percent of households had their TV sets turned on—had no alternative but to sit through the news. Many of them were "inadvertent news viewers"—brought to the news less by a strong preference for it than by an addiction to television.[40] This exposure rubbed off on the children. The evening news was a ritual in many families, and though the children might have preferred something else, they also watched it. By the time these children finished school, many of them had acquired a television news habit of their own.

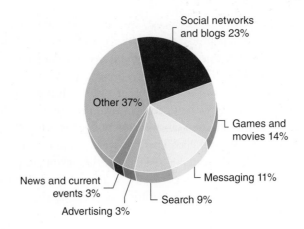

figure 10-3 NEWS AND TIME ON THE INTERNET

Americans spend great amounts of time on the Internet but only a tiny percentage of it is devoted to news and current events. *Source:* Derived from Nielsen data.

Television's capacity to generate an interest in news declined sharply in the 1980s with the rapid spread of cable. Viewers no longer had to sit through the news while waiting for entertainment programs to come on. And television's capacity to generate news interest in children was greatly diminished. Fewer of their parents were watching the dinner-hour news, and even if they were watching, the children, as a Kaiser Family Foundation study revealed, were often in another room watching entertainment shows.[41]

The effect has been to divide Americans in how much attention they pay to news and how much they know about politics. Some Americans get more news than was possible in earlier times. Round-the-clock news is available to anyone with cable TV or the Internet. Yet today's high-choice media system also makes it possible for people to avoid the news with ease. As a result, large numbers of Americans, mostly younger adults, have neglected news in favor of movies, sitcoms, comedy shows, computer games, and other content.[42]

A few decades ago, the news habits of younger and older adults were similar, as political scientist Martin Wattenberg has shown. In the late 1950s, for example, 53 percent of those in the 21–29 age group regularly read news coverage of national politics, compared with 61 percent in the 30–44 age group, 60 percent in the 45–60 age group, and 57 percent of those over 60. Wattenberg found a similar pattern for television news.

POLITICAL THINKING

Are the "New" Media to Blame?

Research indicates that the level of public "misinformation" is increasing. During the lead up to the U.S. invasion of Iraq in 2003, for example, a large portion of the American public falsely believed that the Iraqi regime was allied with the al Qaeda terrorist network. Do you think the slanted messaging of the "new" media—political talk shows, blogs, social networks, and the like—is largely to blame for the increase in misinformation? If not, what else might explain this development?

"There was little variation in news viewing habits by age," Wattenberg writes. "TV news producers could hardly write off young adults, given that two out of three said they had watched such broadcasts every night."[43] Today, younger adults are substantially less likely than older adults to follow the news regularly. Compared with adults over fifty years of age, those under thirty are only a third as likely to follow public affairs closely through a newspaper, only half as likely to watch television news regularly, and less likely even to consume news on the Internet.[44]

This widening attention gap has been accompanied by a widening "information gap." Wattenberg found that, until the early 1970s, young adults were nearly as knowledgeable about current events and leaders as older adults. Since the 1980s, and increasingly so, young adults have been less informed than older ones. In 2004, for example, adults sixty-five years of age and older could answer correctly 55 percent of factual questions about politics contained in the American National Election Studies (ANES) survey, while adults under thirty years of age could answer only 36 percent of the questions accurately. In fact, young adults scored lower than all other age groups on every ANES question, whether it was identification of current political leaders, information about the presidential candidates, knowledge of which party controlled Congress, or basic civic facts. The chapter of Wattenberg's book in which these findings are presented is titled pointedly, "Don't Ask Anyone Under 30."[45]

The widening attention and information gaps are most pronounced when comparing across age groups but cut across every age group. The high-choice media environment of today enables citizens of whatever age to pursue their interests, whether these are news, entertainment, or social networking. For citizens with an interest in news, there's a never-ending supply. For those who lack this interest, there are endless other selections. The choices that Americans make affect what they know and don't know about politics. Although the information gap is not new, the gap is widening because today's news system makes it easier for citizens without an interest in news to ignore it.

SUMMARY

In the nation's first century, the press was allied closely with the political parties and helped the parties mobilize public opinion. Gradually, the press freed itself from this partisan relationship and developed a form of reporting known as objective journalism, which emphasizes fair and accurate accounts of newsworthy developments. That model still governs the news reporting of the traditional media—daily newspapers and broadcasters—but does not hold for the newer media—radio talk shows, cable TV talk shows, and Internet blogs. Although some of them cover politics in the traditional way, many of them transmit news through a partisan lens.

The press performs four basic functions. First, in their signaling function, journalists communicate information to the public about breaking events and new developments. This information makes citizens aware of developments that affect their lives. However, because of the media's need to attract an audience, breaking news stories often focus on developments, such as celebrity scandals, that have little to do with issues of politics and government. Second, the press functions as a common carrier in that it provides political leaders with a channel for addressing the public. Increasingly, however, the news has centered nearly as much on the journalists themselves as on the newsmakers they cover. In a third function, that of watchdog, the press acts to protect the public by exposing deceitful, careless, or corrupt officials. Finally, the press functions as a partisan advocate. Although the traditional media perform this function to a degree, the newer media—the talk shows and blogs—specialize in it. Their influence has contributed to a rising level of political polarization in the United States.

The news audience has changed substantially in the past few decades. Daily newspapers and broadcast news have lost audiences to cable television and the Internet. At the same time, the emergence of cable television and the Internet has made it easier for citizens to avoid news when using the media. Although some citizens today consume more news than was possible at an earlier time, other citizens—young adults, in particular—consume less news than was previously typical. A consequence is that young adults are less informed politically relative to both older adults and to earlier generations of young adults.

CRITICAL THINKING ZONE

KEY TERMS

agenda setting (*p. 307*)
common-carrier function (*p. 310*)
framing (*p. 300*)
high-choice media system (*p. 318*)
news (*p. 299*)
objective journalism (*p. 303*)

partisan function (*p. 313*)
partisan press (*p. 302*)
news media (press) (*p. 300*)
signaling (signaler) function (*p. 306*)
watchdog function (*p. 311*)

APPLYING THE ELEMENTS OF CRITICAL THINKING

Conceptualizing: Define what is meant by a high-choice media system. How does it contribute to a less-informed public? To a more partisan public?

Synthesizing: Contrast the media's watchdog role with their common-carrier role. Is there a tension between these roles—does carrying out one of them work against carrying out the other?

Analyzing: What are the consequences of the fact that the press is charged with informing the public but at the same time needs to attract an audience in order to make a profit and fund its news-gathering operations?

EXTRA CREDIT

A Book Worth Reading: Jonathan M. Ladd, *Why Americans Hate the Media and How It Matters*. Princeton, NJ: Princeton University Press, 2012. Winner of the Goldsmith Book Prize, this book explores Americans' declining confidence in the media, attributing it largely to the rise of infotainment and to attacks on the media from the political right.

A Website Worth Visiting: **www.mediatenor.com.** Media Tenor is a nonpartisan organization that analyzes U.S. and overseas news coverage on a daily basis. The site has information of interest to anyone curious about tendencies in news coverage, such as how various news outlets portray the president.

PARTICIPATE!

Before the Internet opened new channels of communication, freedom of the press, which is granted by the First Amendment to all Americans, was enjoyed for the most part only by the very few who owned or worked in the news media. With the Internet, the opportunity for citizen communication, though not unlimited, is greater than at any time in the nation's history. Take advantage of the opportunity. Meetup.com is one of literally thousands of Internet sites where you can participate in discussion forums about politics and issues. A more ambitious alternative is to start your own Web log. Blogging is time consuming, but it allows you to create an agenda of news, information, and opinion—an activity previously reserved for newspaper editors and broadcast producers. Either of these options will enable you to make your voice heard and also help you to hone your citizenship skills—the ability to communicate, to defend your own views, and to learn the opinions of others.

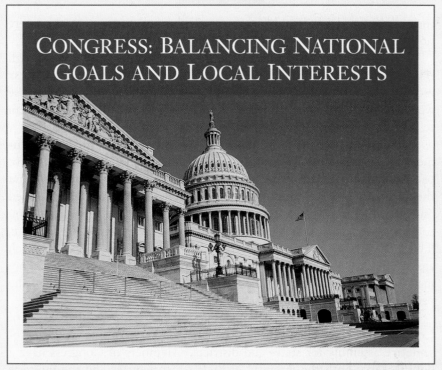

CONGRESS: BALANCING NATIONAL
GOALS AND LOCAL INTERESTS

❝ There are two Congresses. . . . The tight-knit complex world of Capitol Hill is a long
way from [the member's district], in perspective and outlook as well as in miles. ❞
ROGER DAVIDSON AND WALTER OLESZEK[1]

It was a fight the likes of which Washington had rarely seen. In the past, Congress had routinely raised the debt ceiling to give the federal government the authority to borrow the money necessary to pay its debt obligations. In 2011, however, House Republicans decided to use the ceiling limit to force Democrats into accepting steep cuts in federal spending. As other countries watched, worried that the U.S. government might default on its debt for the first time in history, Democratic and Republican lawmakers stubbornly refused to budge from their positions.

The House Republicans included five dozen newly elected members of Congress, nearly all of whom had campaigned on a pledge to cut government spending and oppose tax increases. Many of their senior colleagues had also received Tea Party backing in the campaign and had likewise pledged to hold the line on taxes and spending. Mindful of the backlash they might face from Republican voters in their next campaign, they were not about to go back on their promise.

The Democrats in Congress were also in a tough spot. Even though they were willing to accept some spending cuts, they insisted on a tax increase on wealthy Americans as part of the bargain. To do otherwise would be to put them at risk with Democratic voters, who expected them to protect the government programs upon which they depended.

In the end, Congress reached a compromise that prevented a government shutdown but otherwise left few members happy. The legislative package included modest spending cuts spread over a ten-year period and the formation of a joint bipartisan congressional committee (the so-called "super committee") that would negotiate a larger budget-deficit reduction package and submit it to the House and Senate for an up or down vote. Three months later, the committee disbanded, having failed to reach agreement. As with the earlier effort, Republican and Democratic lawmakers were deadlocked over whether tax increases would be part of the package.

The story of the debt ceiling negotiations illustrates the dual nature of Congress. It is both a lawmaking institution for the country and a representative assembly for states and districts.[2] Members of Congress have a duty to serve both the interests of their constituencies and the interests of the nation as a whole. The nation's needs sometimes come first, but not always, because the support of the voters back home is necessary to members' reelection.[3]

The framers of the Constitution regarded Congress as the preeminent branch of the federal government and granted it the greatest of all the powers of government, the power to make the laws: "All legislative powers herein granted shall be invested in a Congress, which shall consist of a Senate and House of Representatives." Congress is granted the authority even to decide the form and function of the executive departments and the lower courts. No executive agency or lower court can exist unless authorized by Congress.

The positioning of Congress as the first among equals in a system of divided powers reflected the framers' trust in representative institutions. The framers' vision of a preeminent Congress has not fully met the test of time, however. Over time, power has shifted from Congress to the presidency and, today, both institutions have a central role in lawmaking. The points emphasized in the chapter are:

- *Congressional elections usually result in the reelection of the incumbent.* Congressional office provides incumbents with substantial resources (free publicity, staff, and legislative influence) that give them (particularly House members) a major advantage in election campaigns.

- *Leadership in Congress is provided by party leaders, including the Speaker of the House and the Senate majority leader.* Party leaders are in a stronger position today than a few decades ago because the party caucuses in Congress are more ideologically cohesive than in the past.

- *Much of the work of Congress is done through its committees, each of which has its own leadership and its designated policy jurisdiction.*

- *Because of its fragmented structure, Congress is not well suited to take the lead on major national policies, which has allowed the president to assume this role. On the other hand, Congress is well organized to handle policies of narrower scope.*

- *In recent decades, congressional Republicans have become more uniformly conservative and congressional Democrats have become more uniformly liberal, which has made it easier for each party's members to band together but harder for them to reach agreement with the other party's members, which has increased the frequency of legislative deadlock.*

- *Congress's policymaking role is based on three major functions: lawmaking, representation, and oversight.*

CONGRESS AS A CAREER: ELECTION TO CONGRESS

In the nation's first century, service in Congress was not a career for most of its members. Before 1900, at least a third of the seats in Congress changed hands at each election. Most members left voluntarily. Because travel was slow and arduous, serving in the nation's capital meant spending months away from one's family. Moreover, the national government was not the center of power that it is today; many politicians preferred to serve in state capitals.

The modern Congress is a different kind of institution. Most of its members are professional politicians, and a seat in the U.S. Senate or House is as high as most of them can expect to rise in politics. The pay (about $175,000 a year) is substantial, as is the prestige of their office. Most members of Congress seek to make it a career, which requires them to keep the voters happy. Members of Congress, says political scientist David Mayhew, are "single-minded seekers of reelection."[4] Most of them succeed in getting reelected (see Figure 11-1). **Incumbents** (as officeholders

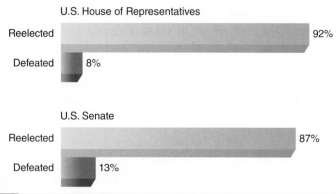

figure 11-1   RECENT REELECTION RATES OF HOUSE AND SENATE INCUMBENTS

Congressional incumbents have a very good chance of winning another term, as indicated by the reelection rates of U.S. representatives and senators who sought reelection during the last five congressional elections.

are called) have a roughly 90 percent probability of winning reelection. Even in congressional elections where an abnormally large number of incumbents lose, a much greater number win. In the 2010 congressional elections, for example, 54 House incumbents lost their reelection bids—more than twice the normal level. In the same election, 334 House incumbents were reelected—six times the number that lost.

Using Incumbency to Stay in Congress

The primary reason incumbents run so strongly is that many congressional districts and some states are so lopsidedly Democratic or Republican that candidates of the stronger party seldom lose. No more than 75 of the 435 House seats—about one in six—is competitive enough that the weaker party has a realistic chance of victory. In any case, whether their constituency is lopsided or competitive, incumbents have substantial advantages over their challengers, as will now be explained.

The Service Strategy: Taking Care of Constituents   An incumbent promotes his or her reelection prospects by catering to the **constituency:** the people residing in the incumbent's state or district. Members of Congress pay attention to constituency opinions when choosing positions on legislation, and they work hard to get their share of federal spending projects. Such projects are often derided as **pork** (or **pork-barrel spending**) by outsiders but are embraced by those who live in the state or district that gets a federally funded project, such as a new hospital, research center, or highway. Incumbents also respond to their constituents' individual requests, a practice known as the **service strategy.** Whether a constituent is seeking information about a government program or looking for help in obtaining a federal benefit, the representative's staff is ready to assist.

At times, constituency service has reached unbelievable heights. In September 2005, for example, Congress faced the question of how to come up with the billions of dollars that would be required to rebuild New Orleans and the other Gulf Coast communities devastated by Hurricane Katrina. One option was to trim the $286 billion transportation bill that Congress had enacted a little more than a month earlier. In it were hundreds of pork-barrel projects that members of Congress had secured for their home states and districts. One such project was a bridge that came to be known as "the bridge to nowhere." Nearly the length of the Golden Gate Bridge, it would link the town of Ketchikan, Alaska (population nine thousand), to Gravina Island (population fifty). Its inclusion in the transportation bill was due to the power of its sponsor, Representative Don Young (R-Alaska), who chaired the House Transportation and Infrastructure Committee that oversaw the legislation. When a reporter asked Representative Young whether he was willing to cancel the Ketchikan-Gravina bridge, he replied, "They can kiss my ear! That's the dumbest thing I've ever heard." Young later relented, but the money for the bridge, rather than being spent in the Gulf Coast area, was given to Alaska transportation officials to use on other projects in the state.

Congressional staffers spend most of their time not on legislative matters but on constituency service and public relations—efforts that can pay off on Election Day.[5] Each House member receives an annual office allowance of roughly $950,000 with which to hire up to eighteen permanent staff members.[6] Senators receive office allowances that range between $3 million and $5 million a year, depending on the population size of their state. Smaller-state senators have staffs in the range of thirty people whereas larger-state senators have staffs closer in number to fifty people.[7] Each member of Congress is also allowed free trips back to their home state and free mailings to constituent households (a privilege known as the "frank"). These trips and mailings, along with press releases and other public relations efforts, help incumbents build name recognition and constituent support—major advantages in their reelection campaigns.

It is noteworthy that European legislators do not have the large personal staffs or the travel and publicity budgets of members of Congress. Not surprisingly, European incumbents have much lower reelection rates than members of Congress. In the 2010 British elections, for example, nearly half of the candidates elected to the House of Commons were newcomers. No U.S. congressional election of the past eight decades has produced anywhere near this level of turnover.

Campaign Fundraising: Raking in the Money   Incumbents also have a decided advantage when it comes to raising campaign funds. Congressional elections are expensive because of the high cost of TV advertising, polling, and other modern campaign techniques (see Figure 11-2). Today a successful House campaign in a competitive district exceeds a million dollars. The price of victory in competitive Senate races is much higher, ranging from several million dollars in small states to $20 million or more in larger states. Rarely do incumbents have trouble raising enough money to conduct an effective campaign, whereas challengers usually fall far short of their fundraising goals.[8] In the most recent election cycle, House incumbents raised on average about $1.5 million in campaign funds—roughly six times the amount raised by their challengers.[9]

Incumbents' past campaigns and constituent service provide them a ready list of potential contributors. Individual contributions, most of which are $200 or less, account for about 60 percent of all funds received by congressional candidates and are obtained mainly through fundraising

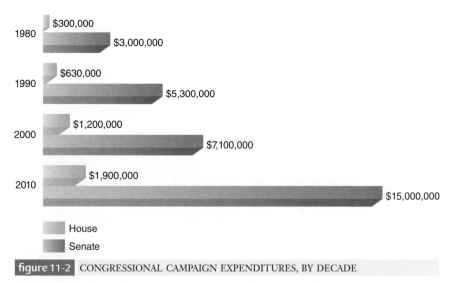

1980	$300,000
	$3,000,000
1990	$630,000
	$5,300,000
2000	$1,200,000
	$7,100,000
2010	$1,900,000
	$15,000,000

House
Senate

figure 11-2 CONGRESSIONAL CAMPAIGN EXPENDITURES, BY DECADE

Each decade, the cost of running for congressional office has risen sharply as campaign techniques—TV advertising, opinion polling, and so on—have become more elaborate and sophisticated. The increase in spending can be seen from a comparison of the approximate average spending by both candidates per House or Senate seat at ten-year intervals, beginning in 1980. Roughly speaking, the cost has doubled each decade.
Source: Federal Election Commission.

events, websites, and direct-mail solicitation. Incumbents also have an edge with political action committees (PACs), which are the fundraising arm of interest groups (see Chapter 9). Most PACs are reluctant to oppose an incumbent unless the candidate appears beatable. More than 85 percent of PAC contributions in recent elections have gone to incumbents (see Figure 11-3). "Anytime you go against an incumbent, you take a minute and think long and hard about what your rationale is," said Desiree Anderson, director of the Realtors PAC.[10] (A race without an incumbent—called an **open-seat election**—often brings out a strong candidate from each party and involves heavy spending, especially when the parties are rather evenly matched in the state or district.)

Redistricting: Favorable Boundaries for House Incumbents House members, but not senators, have a final electoral advantage. Because incumbents are hard to unseat, they are always a force to be reckoned with, a fact that is apparent during redistricting. Every ten years, after each population census, the 435 seats in the House of Representatives are reallocated among the states in proportion to their population. This process is called **reapportionment.** States that have gained population since the last census may acquire additional House seats, while those that have lost population may lose seats. After the 2010 census, for example, Texas and Florida

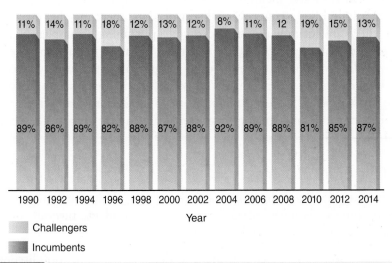

Challengers

Incumbents

figure 11-3 ALLOCATION OF PAC CONTRIBUTIONS BETWEEN CONGRESSIONAL INCUMBENTS AND CHALLENGERS IN RACES WITH AN INCUMBENT

In allocating campaign contributions, PACs favor incumbent members of Congress over their challengers by a wide margin.

Source: Federal Elections Commission. Figures for 2014 based on preliminary data.

were among the states that gained House seats and New York and Ohio were among those that lost seats.

States are required by law to have House districts that are as nearly equal in population as possible. As a result, they must redraw their district boundaries after each census to account for population shifts within the state during the previous ten years. (The Senate is not affected by population change, because each state has two senators regardless of its size.) The responsibility for redrawing House election districts—a process called **redistricting**—rests with the respective state legislatures. The party that controls the legislature typically redraws the boundaries in a way that favors candidates of its party—a process called **gerrymandering.** (Among the few exceptions to this practice are Arizona, California, and Iowa, which entrust redistricting to an independent commission.)

Incumbents typically benefit from gerrymandering. When redistricting, the majority party in the state legislature places enough of its party's voters in its incumbents' districts to ensure their reelection. Most of the minority party's incumbents are also given a safe district. Because they have a solid base of support, and are difficult to defeat, the optimal strategy is to pack their districts with as many voters of their party as possible, so that in effect the party "wastes" votes, reducing its competitiveness elsewhere in the state.

For a few House incumbents, redistricting is a threat to reelection. When a state loses a congressional seat or seats, there may be fewer seats than there are incumbents, who can end up running against each other. Moreover, the party in control of the state legislature might conclude that a particular incumbent of the opposite party is vulnerable and will redraw the boundaries of the incumbent's district to the incumbent's disadvantage. By and large, however, incumbents do not suffer greatly from redistricting, and the large majority of them wind up in districts that nearly guarantee their reelection.

Pitfalls of Incumbency

Incumbency is not without its risks. Senate and House incumbents can fall victim to disruptive issues, personal misconduct, turnout swings, strong challengers, and campaign money.

Disruptive Issues   Most elections are not waged in the context of disruptive issues, but when they are, incumbents are at greater risk. When voters are angry about existing political conditions, they are more likely to believe that those in power should be tossed out of office. The 2006 congressional election, which was waged in the context of Republican president George W. Bush's leadership of an unpopular war in Iraq, saw the defeat of more than twice the usual number of incumbents. Virtually all of them were Republicans, enabling the Democrats to seize control of both chambers. The parties' fortunes swung the other way in the 2010 congressional elections when public anger over economic conditions and the mushrooming federal deficit contributed to the defeat of an unusually high number of incumbents, nearly all of them Democrats.

POLITICAL THINKING	Should Partisan Gerrymandering Be Outlawed?

Most House districts are electorally uncompetitive, and partisan gerrymandering is a reason. In redrawing election district boundaries after the census, states tend to configure them in ways designed to create safe Democratic or Republican districts. It has been argued that partisan gerrymandering puts election of House members in the hands of the states rather than in the hands of the voters. Do you think there should be limits to partisan gerrymandering? Or do you think there is no fair way to restrict the practice even though the practice may weaken voters' influence?

Personal Misconduct   Life in Washington can be fast paced, glamorous, and expensive, and some members of Congress get caught up in influence peddling, sex scandals, and other forms of misconduct. "The first thing to being reelected is to stay away from scandal, even minor scandal," says political scientist John Hibbing.[11] Roughly a fourth of House incumbents who lost their bid for reelection in the past two decades were shadowed by ethical questions. In 2005, for example, Representative William Jefferson demanded $100,000 in cash from a firm in return for helping it obtain government contracts. The firm alerted authorities to Jefferson's acceptance of the money, and the FBI raided Jefferson's congressional office, finding $90,000 hidden in a small freezer. In the 2008 election, Jefferson lost to his Republican opponent, even though his Louisiana district was heavily Democratic.

Turnout Variation: The Midterm Election Problem   In twenty-one of the last twenty-five **midterm elections**—those that occur midway through a president's term—the president's party has lost House seats. The 2014 midterm elections, when the Democratic Party lost seats, fit the normal pattern. The pattern is partly attributable to the drop-off in turnout that accompanies a midterm election. The midterm electorate is substantially smaller than the presidential electorate. People who vote only in the presidential election tend to have weaker party ties and are more responsive to the issues of the moment. These issues typically favor one party, which contributes to the success not only of its presidential candidate but also of its congressional candidates. Two years later in the midterm elections, many of these voters stay home while those who do go the polls vote largely along party lines. Accordingly, the congressional candidates of the president's party do not get the boost they enjoyed in the previous election, and House seats are lost as a result.[12] Moreover, some voters treat the midterm elections as a referendum on the president's performance. Presidents usually lose popularity during the term of office as a result of their policy decisions. As the president's support declines, so does voters' support of congressional candidates of the president's party.[13] Polls indicated that voters' discontent with President Obama's performance contributed to the GOP's big gains in the 2014 midterms, including its takeover of the U.S. Senate.

Primary Election Challengers   Primary elections can also be a time of risk for incumbents, especially if they hold politically moderate views. If they are confronted with a strong challenger from the extreme wing of their party, they stand a chance of losing because strong partisans are more likely than party moderates to vote in primary elections.[14] In 2012, Richard Luger, a six-term incumbent and widely respected member of the Senate, was trounced in Indiana's GOP primary by conservative Richard Mourdock, who portrayed Lugar as too moderate and too much of a Washington insider.

General Election Challengers: A Problem for Senators   Incumbents, particularly those in the Senate, are also vulnerable to strong challengers. Senators often find themselves running against a high-ranking politician, such as the state's governor or attorney general. Such opponents have the voter base, campaign organization, fundraising ability, public recognition, and credentials to mount a strong campaign.

House incumbents are less likely to face strong challengers. A House seat is often not attractive enough to induce a prominent local politician, such as a mayor or state legislator, to risk losing to an incumbent.[15] As a result, most House incumbents face opponents who struggle to raise enough money to run a strong campaign.

A New Threat: Super PACs   Although incumbents ordinarily have a funding advantage over their challengers, the situation can change when they appear vulnerable. Contributors from outside the state or district may

Mike Lee exemplifies the type of primary election challenger that congressional incumbents increasingly fear. Lee, a lawyer and son of the founding dean of Brigham Young University's law school, challenged incumbent Bob Bennett in 2010 for Utah's Republican Senate nomination. Backed by staunch conservatives, Lee won the GOP nomination and then went on to win the general election.

target the race and donate money to the challenger. Although this threat has existed for years, it has increased with the emergence of super PACs, which have the capacity to pour millions of dollars into a race (see Chapters 8 and 9). This scenario played itself out in the 2010 Colorado Senate race, which pitted the Democratic incumbent Michael Bennett against Ken Buck, a Republican district attorney. Their race turned out to be one of the most expensive Senate campaigns in history. Although the Bennett and Buck campaigns spent a combined total of less than $15 million—about average for a contested Senate race in a midsized state—independent groups and super PACs spent an additional $22 million, mostly on behalf of Buck. Bennett narrowly survived the inflow of money, winning by less than two percentage points.

Who Are the Winners in Congressional Elections?

The Constitution places only a few restrictions on who can be elected to Congress. House members must be at least twenty-five years of age and have been a citizen for at least seven years. For senators, the age and citizenship requirements are thirty years and nine years, respectively. Senators and representatives alike must be residents of the state from which they are elected.

But if the formal restrictions are minimal, the informal limits are substantial. Congress is not a microcosm of the population. Although lawyers constitute less than 1 percent of the population, they make up a fourth of the House and more than half of the Senate. Attorneys enter politics in large numbers in part because knowledge of the law is an asset in Congress and also because campaign publicity—even if a candidate loses— is a good way to build up a law practice. Along with lawyers, professionals such as business executives, educators, bankers, and journalists account for roughly 90 percent of congressional membership.[16] Blue-collar workers, clerical employees, and homemakers are seldom elected to Congress. Farmers and ranchers fare better; a number of House members from rural districts have an agricultural background.

Finally, members of Congress are disproportionately white and male. Although the number of women in Congress is nine times that of four decades ago, they account for only about a fifth of the membership (see Chapter 5). Minorities account for a mere eighth of the membership. Women and minorities are also less likely than white men to attempt a run for Congress, even though the winning percentage of those who do is roughly the same as that of nonincumbent white males.[17] In local and state legislative elections, where running for office is less onerous, women and minority candidates have made greater inroads.[18]

PARTIES AND PARTY LEADERSHIP

The U.S. Congress is a **bicameral legislature,** meaning it has two chambers, the House and the Senate. Both chambers are organized largely along party lines. At the start of each two-year congressional term, party members in each chamber meet to elect their **party leaders**—the individuals who will lead their party's efforts in the chamber. Party members also meet periodically in closed session, which is called a **party caucus,** to plan strategy, develop issues, and resolve policy differences. (Table 11-1 shows the party composition in Congress during the past decade.)

Party Unity in Congress

Political parties are the strongest force within Congress. They are the greatest source of unity among members of Congress, as well as the greatest source of division.

table 11-1	THE NUMBER OF DEMOCRATS AND REPUBLICANS IN THE HOUSE OF REPRESENTATIVES AND THE SENATE, 2003–2016						
	2003–2004	2005–2006	2007–2008	2009–2010	2011–2012	2013–2014	2015–2016
House							
Democrats	208	203	235*	257	192	197	184
Republicans	227	232	200	178	243*	238*	251*
Senate							
Democrats	49	45	51*	60	53	55	46
Republicans	51	55	49	40	47	45	54*

*Chamber not controlled by the president's party. Senate and House members who are independents are included in the total for the party with which they caucused. Figures are based on party totals that result from the congressional elections as opposed to subsequent totals that result, for example, because of the death or resignation of seated members.

The partisan divide in Congress has steadily widened in the past three decades. Earlier, congressional Republicans were divided almost evenly between the party's conservative and progressive wings, and congressional Democrats consisted of a liberal northern wing and a conservative southern wing. Since then, the Republican Party's progressive wing and the Democratic Party's conservative southern wing have withered. In a recent study based on legislative votes, political scientists Keith Poole and Howard Rosenthal found that, in both the House and the Senate, the most liberal Republican was farther to the right than the most conservative Democrat.[19] As a result, each congressional party has attained a high level of **party unity**—in which members of a party band together on legislation and stand against the opposite party.[20]

The trend can be seen by looking at the party distribution on *roll-call votes* (these are votes on which each member's vote is officially recorded, as opposed to voice votes, where the members simply say "aye" or "nay" in unison and the presiding officer indicates which side prevails without tallying individual members' positions). Since the mid-1980s, party-line voting on roll calls has risen sharply (see "Party Polarization"). In the 1970s, roll-call votes generally did not pit most Republicans against most Democrats. More recently, most roll-call votes have divided along party lines. The ideological split in the congressional parties is most pronounced on major domestic issues. In a showdown on the budget in 2013, for example, House Republicans initially demanded a one-year delay in implementing the new health insurance program as a condition of passing

HOW THE 50 STATES DIFFER

POLITICAL THINKING THROUGH COMPARISONS

Women in the State Legislatures

Women have had more success in gaining election to state legislatures than to Congress, partly because there is more turnover and less incumbency advantage at the state level, which creates more opportunities for newcomers to run and to win. More than one in five state legislators are women, a fourfold increase since 1970. Colorado, with 41 percent, has the highest proportion of women legislators. Louisiana, with 12 percent, has the lowest.

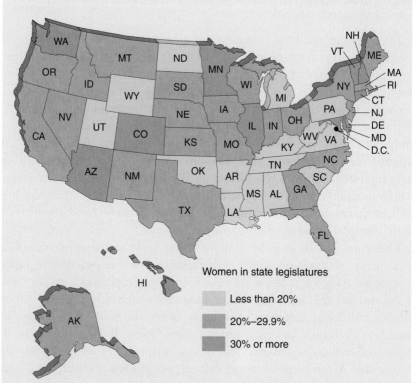

Women in state legislatures

☐ Less than 20%

☐ 20%–29.9%

☐ 30% or more

Sources: Created from data gathered by the Center for the American Woman and Politics (CAWP); National Information Bank on Women in Public Office; and Eagleton Institute of Politics, Rutgers University, 2014.

> **Q:** Why do the northeastern and western regions have the most women legislators?
>
> **A:** One reason is that northeastern and western regions have a higher proportion of college-educated women in the workforce than do other regions. College-educated working women are more likely to run for public office and to actively support those who do run.

a budget that would avert a government shutdown. The House vote on the one-year delay was 231-192, with all but two Republican members voting for the delay and all but two Democrats voting against it. (The effect of heightened partisanship on the congressional process is discussed later in the chapter.)

Party Leadership in Congress

Party leaders in Congress are usually chosen for their demonstrated leadership ability, as well as their ability to work effectively with other members. In European parliaments, party leaders can count on the backing of party members. The members depend on the party for nomination to office and can be denied nomination in the next election if they fail to support the party on key legislative votes. In contrast, members of the U.S. Congress depend on themselves for reelection, which gives them the freedom to selectively back or oppose the party's position on key votes. Accordingly, the effectiveness of party leaders in Congress depends to a considerable extent on their ability to gain the trust of party members and to forge positions in line with their policy preferences.

House Leaders   The Constitution specifies that the House of Representatives will be presided over by a Speaker, elected by the vote of its members. Since the majority party has the largest number of members, it also has the most votes, and the Speaker is invariably a member of the majority party. Thus, when the Republicans took control of the House after the 2010 election, John Boehner, the Republicans' leader in the chamber, replaced Democrat Nancy Pelosi as Speaker. Boehner, an Ohio representative, was first elected to the House in 1991.

Next to the president, the Speaker of the House is sometimes said to be the most powerful national official. The Speaker is active in developing the party's positions on issues and in persuading party members in

P A R T Y   **Political Thinking in Conflict**

POLARIZATION

Congress, the Keystone of Partisan Conflict?

To some observers, the partisan acrimony that has characterized American politics in recent years had its origins in Congress. In *The Broken Branch* (2008), congressional scholars Thomas Mann and Norman Ornstein argue that House Democrats started the partisan wars in the 1980s by employing rules that denied House Republicans a meaningful lawmaking role. The House Republicans then institutionalized the arrangement upon taking control of Congress in 1994. Underlying these developments was the eclipse of the Democratic Party's conservative wing and the Republican Party's progressive wing. As the congressional Democrats became more uniformly liberal and the congressional Republicans became more uniformly conservative, the overlap between the congressional parties diminished, making it harder to bridge party differences and easier for each side to attack the other. As the graph below indicates, party-line voting on roll-call votes has substantially increased since the 1970s. Before then, most roll-call votes did not pit a majority of Republicans against a majority of Democrats. Since then, roll-call votes have increasingly divided along party lines. When only major bills are considered (the graph is based on all roll-call votes), the

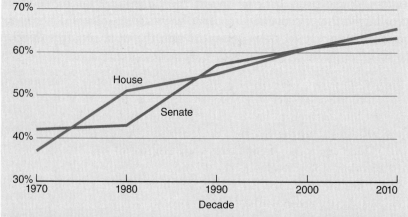

Percentage of roll-call votes in the House and Senate in which a majority of Democrats voted against a majority of Republicans

Source: Estimated by author from *Congressional Quarterly* figures. The 2010 figures are based on the 2010–2013 period.

---

partisan divide is even clearer. Voting on the 2009 stimulus bill, the 2010 health care reform bill, and the 2011 budget ceiling bill, for example, divided almost exactly along party lines.

Q: Some observers claim that partisanship in Congress has reached a level that is crippling the institution as an effective policymaking body. Party disputes on everything from health care to tax policy have produced legislative deadlock and delay. Do you share the view that excessive partisanship is warping the congressional process, or do you think members of Congress should stick to their partisan principles, whatever the consequences?

---

the House to support them. Although the Speaker cannot require party members to support the party's program, they look to the Speaker for leadership. The Speaker also has certain formal powers, including the right to speak first during House debate on legislation and the power to recognize members—that is, to grant them permission to speak from the floor. Because the House places a time limit on floor debate, not everyone has a chance to speak on a given bill, and the Speaker can sometimes influence legislation simply by exercising the power to decide who will speak and when. The Speaker also chooses the chairperson and the majority-party members of the powerful House Rules Committee, which controls the scheduling of bills. Those that the Speaker wants passed are likely to reach the floor under conditions favorable to their enactment; for example, the Speaker may ask the Rules Committee to delay sending a bill to the floor until there is sufficient support for its passage.

Although powerful, the Speaker is ultimately beholden to the party's membership. The Speaker cannot force them to vote for or against a particular bill. House members are separately elected and will normally not cast a vote that could jeopardize their reelection chances. In this sense, the Speaker must consider what party members will accept when taking positions on legislative issues. In 2013, John Boehner discovered the limits to the Speaker's power when he tried unsuccessfully to convince House Republicans to pass a budget measure that would avoid a temporary shutdown of some federal programs.

The Speaker is assisted by the House majority leader and the House majority whip, who are also chosen by the majority party's members. The majority leader acts as the party's floor leader, organizing the

The Speaker of the House is chosen by the majority party in the House of Representatives and has been called the second most powerful national official (after the president). The Speaker's power owes to the large size of the House and the restrictive rules under which it operates. Shown here are two recent Speakers, John Boehner (R-Ohio) and Nancy Pelosi (D-California).

debate on bills and lining up legislative support. The whip has the job of informing party members when critical votes are scheduled. As voting is getting under way on the House floor, the whip will sometimes stand at a location that is easily seen by party members and let them know where the leadership stands on the bill by giving them a thumbs-up or thumbs-down signal.

The minority party also has its House leaders. The House minority leader heads the party's caucus and its policy committee and plays the leading role in developing the party's legislative positions. The minority leader is assisted by a minority whip.

Senate Leaders   In the Senate, the most important party leadership position is that of the majority leader, who heads the majority-party caucus. The majority leader's role resembles that of the Speaker of the House in that the Senate majority leader formulates the majority party's legislative agenda and encourages party members to support it. Like the Speaker, the Senate majority leader chairs the party's policy committee and acts as the party's voice in the chamber. The majority leader is assisted by the majority whip, who sees to it that members know when important votes are scheduled. The minority party in the Senate also has its leaders.

The minority leader and minority whip have roles comparable to those of their House counterparts.

For several reasons, the Senate majority leader's position is less powerful than that of the Speaker of the House. Unlike the Speaker, the Senate majority leader is not the chamber's presiding officer. The Constitution assigns this position to the vice president of the United States. But because the vice president is allowed to vote only in case of a tie, the vice president rarely attends Senate sessions. In the absence of the vice president, the president pro tempore (temporary president) has the right to preside over the Senate. By tradition, the majority party's most senior member serves as president pro tempore. The position is largely honorary because the Senate's presiding officer has no real power. Unlike the House, where the Speaker directs the floor debate, the Senate has a tradition of unlimited debate. Ordinarily, any senator who wishes to speak on a bill can do so.

Compared with the House Speaker, the Senate majority leader's power is also limited by the fact that individual senators have more autonomy than do individual House members. The Senate is smaller in size—100 members versus 435 House members—which leads senators to see themselves as co-equals in a way that House members do not. As well, senators serve six-year terms and do not face the unrelenting reelection pressures on House members, who serve two-year terms. Bob Dole of Kansas, who served as Republican Senate leader, remarked: "There's a lot of free spirits in the Senate. About 100 of them."[21]

COMMITTEES AND COMMITTEE LEADERSHIP

Most of the work in Congress is conducted through **standing committees,** which are permanent committees with responsibility for particular areas of public policy. At present there are twenty standing committees in the House and sixteen in the Senate (see Table 11-2). Each chamber has, for example, a standing committee that handles foreign policy issues. Other important standing committees are those that deal with agriculture, commerce, the interior (natural resources and public lands), defense, government spending, labor, the judiciary, and taxation. House committees, which average about thirty-five to forty members each, are about twice the size of Senate committees. Each standing committee has legislative authority in that it can draft and rewrite proposed legislation and can recommend to the full chamber the passage or defeat of the bills it handles.

table 11-2	THE STANDING COMMITTEES OF CONGRESS
House of Representatives	**Senate**
Agriculture	Agriculture, Nutrition, and Forestry
Appropriations	Appropriations
Armed Services	Armed Services
Budget	Banking, Housing, and Urban Affairs
Education and the Workforce	Budget
Energy and Commerce	Commerce, Science, and Transportation
Ethics	Energy and Natural Resources
Financial Services	
Foreign Affairs	Environment and Public Works
Homeland Security	Finance
House Administration	Foreign Relations
Judiciary	Health, Education, Labor, and Pensions
Natural Resources	Homeland Security and Governmental Affairs
Oversight and Government Reform	Judiciary
Rules	Rules and Administration
Science, Space, and Technology	Small Business and Entrepreneurship
Small Business	Veterans' Affairs
Transportation and Infrastructure	
Veterans' Affairs	
Ways and Means	

Most of the standing committees have subcommittees, each of which has a defined jurisdiction. The Senate Committee on Health, Education, Labor, and Pensions, for instance, has three subcommittees: Primary Health and Aging, Children and Families, and Employment and Workplace Safety. Each House and Senate subcommittee has about a dozen members. These few individuals do most of the work and have a leading voice in the disposition of bills in their policy area.

Congress could not manage its workload without the help of its committee system. About ten thousand bills are introduced during each two-year session of Congress. Even though a large majority of these bills do not get serious consideration, Congress would grind to a halt if it was not divided among its standing committees, each of which has its own staff. Unlike the members' personal staffs, which concentrate on constituency relations, the committee staffs perform an almost entirely legislative function. They help draft legislation, gather information, and organize hearings.

In addition to its permanent standing committees, Congress also has a few *select committees* that have a designated responsibility but, unlike the standing committees, do not produce legislation. An example is the Senate Select Committee on Intelligence, which receives periodic classified briefings from the intelligence agencies. Congress also has *joint committees*, composed of members of both houses, which perform advisory functions. The Joint Committee on the Library, for example, oversees the Library of Congress, the largest library in the world. Finally, Congress has *conference committees*—joint committees formed temporarily to work out differences in House and Senate versions of a particular bill. The role of conference committees is discussed more fully later in the chapter.

Committee Jurisdiction

The 1946 Legislative Reorganization Act requires that each bill introduced in Congress be referred to the proper committee. An agricultural bill introduced in the Senate must be assigned to the Senate Agriculture Committee, a bill dealing with foreign affairs must be sent to the Senate Foreign Relations Committee, and so on. This requirement is a source of each committee's power. Even if a committee's members are known to oppose certain types of legislation, bills clearly within its **jurisdiction**—the policy area in which it is authorized to act—must be assigned to it.

Jurisdiction is not always clear-cut, however. Which House committee, for example, should handle a bill addressing the role of financial institutions in global trade? The Financial Services Committee? The Energy and Commerce Committee? The Foreign Affairs Committee? All committees seek legislative influence, and each is jealous of its jurisdiction, so a bill that overlaps committee boundaries can provoke a "turf war" over which committee will handle it.[22] Party leaders can take advantage of these situations by assigning the bill to the committee that is most likely to handle it in the way they would like. But because party leaders depend on the committees for support, they cannot regularly ignore a committee that has a strong claim to a bill. At times, party leaders have responded by dividing up a bill, handing over some of its provisions to one committee and other provisions to a second committee.

Committee Membership

Each committee has a fixed number of seats, with the majority party holding most of them. The ratio of Democrats to Republicans on each committee is approximately the same as the ratio in the full House or Senate, but there is no fixed rule on this matter, and the majority party determines the ratio (mindful that at the next election it could become the chamber's minority party). Members of the House typically serve on only two committees. Senators often serve on four, although they can sit on only two major committees, such as the Finance Committee or the Foreign Relations Committee. Once appointed to a committee, the member can usually chose to stay on it indefinitely.

Each committee has a fixed number of seats, and a committee must have a vacancy before a new member can be appointed. Most vacancies occur after an election as a result of the retirement or defeat of committee

Most of the work in Congress is done through its standing committees, each of which has a policy jurisdiction and the authority to rewrite legislation, and hold hearings. Typically, bills reach the floor of the House or Senate after first being shaped and voted upon in committee. Pictured here is a House Ways and Means Committee hearing.

members. Each party has a special committee in each chamber that decides who will fill the vacancies. A variety of factors influence these decisions, including members' preferences. Most newly elected members of Congress ask for and receive assignment to a committee on which they can serve their constituents' interests and at the same time enhance their reelection prospects. For example, when John Boozman was elected to the Senate in 2010 from Arkansas, a state that depends heavily on the farm sector, he asked for and received an appointment to the Senate Agriculture Committee.

Some members of Congress prefer a seat on the most prestigious committees, such as the Senate Foreign Relations Committee or the House Ways and Means (taxation) Committee. Although these committees do not align closely with constituency interests, they have responsibility for important policy issues. Factors such as party loyalty, level of knowledge, work ethic, and length of congressional service determine whether a member is granted a seat on a prestigious committe.[23]

Subcommittee assignments are handled differently. The members of each party on a committee decide who among them will serve on each of its subcommittees. The members' preferences and seniority, as well as the interests of their constituencies, are key factors in subcommittee assignments.

Committee Chairs

Each committee (as well as each subcommittee) is headed by a chairperson. The position of committee chair is a powerful one. The chair schedules committee meetings, determines the order in which committee bills are considered, presides over committee discussions, directs the committee's majority staff, and can choose to lead the debate when a committee bill goes to the floor of the chamber for a vote.

Committee chairs are always members of the majority party and usually are the party member with the most **seniority** (consecutive years of service) on the committee. Seniority is based strictly on time served on a committee, not on time spent in Congress. Thus, if a member switches committees, the years spent on the first committee do not count toward seniority on the new one. The seniority system has advantages: it reduces the number of power struggles that would occur if the chairs were decided each time by open competition, it places committee leadership in the hands of experienced members, and it enables members to look forward to the reward of a position as chair after years of service on the same committee. The seniority system is not absolute, however, and is applied less uniformly than in the past, as the next section will explain.

Committees and Parties: Which Is in Control?

In a sense, committees are an instrument of the majority party in that it controls most of each committee's seats and appoints its chair. In another sense, each committee is powerful in its own right. Committees have been described as "little legislatures," each secure in its jurisdiction and membership, and each wielding considerable influence over the legislation it handles.

Committees decentralize power in Congress and serve individual members' power and reelection needs. Less than a dozen members hold a party leadership position, but several hundred serve as committee or subcommittee chairs or are *ranking members*, the term for the minority party's committee and subcommittee leaders. In these positions, they can pursue local or personal policy agendas that may or may not coincide with the party leadership's goals.

When Republicans took control of Congress in 1995, they sought to reduce the power of committee chairs in an effort to strengthen the role of the party leaders. The seniority rule for selecting committee chairs was relaxed, giving party leaders more say in who would hold these positions. Some senior party members who would have become chairs under the old rules were passed over in favor of party members with policy views closer to those of the party leadership. In addition, term limits were placed on chairs. After six years a chair had to relinquish the post. When the Democrats took over Congress in 2007, they left the term limits in place.

Although the parties have more influence in Congress than they did a few decades ago, the balance between party power and committee power is a central issue. Congress is at once a place where the parties pursue their national policy agendas and where the members pursue the policy interests of their local constituencies by influencing the decisions of their particular committees. At times, the balance of power has tipped toward the committees and their members. At other times, it has tipped toward the parties and their members. At all times, there has been an effort to strike a workable balance between the two. The distinguishing feature of congressional power is its division among the membership, with provision for added power—sometimes more and sometimes less—in the hands of the top party leaders.

HOW A BILL BECOMES LAW

Parties, party leaders, and committees are critical actors in the legislative process. Their roles and influence, however, vary with the nature of the legislation under consideration. The formal process by which bills become law is shown in Figure 11-4. A **bill** is a proposed legislative act. Many

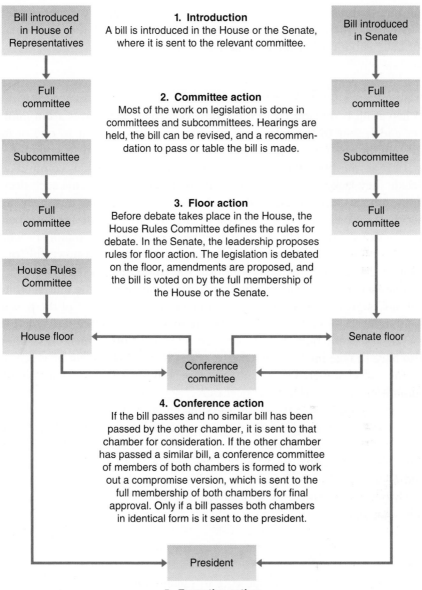

1. Introduction
A bill is introduced in the House or the Senate, where it is sent to the relevant committee.

Bill introduced in House of Representatives

Bill introduced in Senate

Full committee

2. Committee action
Most of the work on legislation is done in committees and subcommittees. Hearings are held, the bill can be revised, and a recommendation to pass or table the bill is made.

Full committee

Subcommittee

Subcommittee

3. Floor action
Before debate takes place in the House, the House Rules Committee defines the rules for debate. In the Senate, the leadership proposes rules for floor action. The legislation is debated on the floor, amendments are proposed, and the bill is voted on by the full membership of the House or the Senate.

Full committee

Full committee

House Rules Committee

House floor

Senate floor

Conference committee

4. Conference action
If the bill passes and no similar bill has been passed by the other chamber, it is sent to that chamber for consideration. If the other chamber has passed a similar bill, a conference committee of members of both chambers is formed to work out a compromise version, which is sent to the full membership of both chambers for final approval. Only if a bill passes both chambers in identical form is it sent to the president.

President

5. Executive action
If the president signs the bill, it becomes law. A presidential veto can be overridden by a two-thirds majority in each chamber.

figure 11-4 HOW A BILL BECOMES LAW

Although the legislative process can be short-circuited in many ways, this diagram describes a common way a bill becomes law.

bills are prepared by executive agencies, interest groups, or other outside parties, but members of Congress also draft bills, and they alone can formally submit a bill for consideration by their chamber.

Committee Hearings and Decisions

When a bill is introduced in the House or Senate, it receives a bill number and is sent to the relevant committee, which assigns it to one of its subcommittees. Less than 10 percent of the bills referred to committee will get to the floor for a vote; the others are "killed" when committees decide they lack merit. The full House or Senate can overrule such decisions, but this rarely occurs. Most bills die in committee because they are poorly conceived or of little interest to anyone other than a few members of Congress. Some bills are not even supported by the members who introduce them. A member may submit a bill to appease a powerful constituent group and then quietly inform the committee to ignore it.

The fact that committees kill more than 90 percent of the bills submitted in Congress does not mean that they exercise 90 percent of the power in Congress. Committees do not operate in a vacuum. They rarely decide the fate of major bills that are of keen interest to other members. They also have to take into account the fact that their decisions can be reversed by the full chamber, just as subcommittees must recognize that the full committee can override their decisions.[24]

If a bill appears to have merit, the subcommittee will schedule hearings on it. After the hearings, if the subcommittee still feels that the legislation is needed, members will recommend the bill to the full committee, which might hold additional hearings. In the House, both the full committee and a subcommittee can *mark up* a bill—that is, they have the authority to change its content. In the Senate, mark up usually is reserved for the full committee.

From Committee to the Floor

If a majority of the committee vote to recommend passage of the bill, it is referred to the full chamber for action. In the House, the Rules Committee has the power to determine when the bill will be voted on, and how long the debate on it will last. On most House bills, only a small number of legislators are granted the opportunity to speak on the floor; in most cases, the bill's chief sponsor and one of the bill's leading opponents will choose the speakers. The Rules Committee also decides whether a bill will receive a "closed rule" (no amendments will be permitted), an "open rule" (members can propose amendments relevant to any of the bill's sections), or something in between (for example, only certain sections of the bill will be subject to amendment). The rules are a means by which the majority party controls legislation. When they had a majority in the House in the period before 1995, Democrats employed closed rules to prevent Republicans from proposing amendments to major bills, a tactic House Republicans said they would forgo when they took control in 1995. Once in control, however, the Republicans applied closed rules to a number of major bills. The tactic was too effective to ignore.

The Senate also has a rules committee, but it is less important than its House counterpart because the Senate has less restrictive rules on debate and amendments. In the Senate, the majority leader, usually in consultation with the minority leader, schedules bills. All Senate bills are subject to unlimited debate unless a three-fifths majority (60 of the 100 senators) vote for **cloture,** which limits debate to thirty hours. Cloture is a way of defeating a Senate **filibuster,** which is a procedural tactic whereby a minority of senators can block a bill by talking until other senators give in and the bill is withdrawn from consideration or altered to fit opponents' demands. (In 2013, the filibuster was eliminated for Senate votes on presidential nominees, though retained for legislation and the confirmation of Supreme Court justices.)

POLITICAL THINKING	Eliminate the Filibuster?

Of all the impediments to congressional action, perhaps none is more imposing than a Senate filibuster, which can be ended only if three-fifths of the senators agree to end it. In effect, a minority of senators has the power to kill legislation, even if it is backed by the president and the House of Representatives. No other democratic legislature has a rule that allows the minority so much power. Should the filibuster be kept or eliminated? Why? In 2013, Senate Democrats used a parliamentary move to eliminate the filibuster in votes to confirm executive officials and federal judges, though retaining it for Supreme Court justices. If you favor the filibuster in general, would you make an exception for confirmation of executives and judges?

In the House, proposed amendments must directly relate to the bill's contents. In the Senate, however, members can propose any amendment to any bill. For example, a senator may propose an antiabortion amendment to a bill dealing with defense expenditures. Such amendments are called *riders.*

Leadership and Floor Action

A bill that emerges from committee with the support of all or nearly all of its members is usually passed by an overwhelming majority of the full chamber. On the other hand, when the committee vote is closely divided, other members may conclude that they need to give the bill a close look before deciding whether to support it. Other members are also less deferential to committee action on major bills and on those that affect their constituents.

On major bills, the majority party's leaders (particularly in the House) have increasingly assumed the lead.[25] They shape the bill's broad content and work closely with the relevant committee during the committee phase. Once the bill clears the committee, they often direct the floor debate. In these efforts, they depend on the ongoing support of their party's members. To obtain it, they consult their members informally and through the party caucus. (The role of parties in Congress is discussed further in the section on Congress's representation function.)

Conference Committees and the President

For a bill to pass, it must have the support of a simple majority (50 percent plus one) of the House or Senate members voting on it. To become law, however, a bill must be passed in identical form by both the House and the Senate. About 10 percent of the bills that pass both chambers differ in important respects in their House and Senate versions. These bills are referred to conference committees to resolve the differences. Each **conference committee** is formed temporarily for the sole purpose of handling a particular bill; its members are usually appointed from the House and Senate standing committees that drafted the bill. The conference committee's job is to develop a compromise version, which then goes back to the House and Senate floors for a final vote.

A bill passed in identical form by the House and the Senate is not yet a law. The president also has a say. If the president signs the bill, it becomes a **law.** If the president rejects the bill through use of the **veto,** the bill is sent back to Congress with the president's reasons for not signing it. Congress can override a veto by a two-thirds vote of each chamber; the bill then becomes law without the president's signature. A bill also becomes law if Congress is in session and the president fails to sign or veto the bill within ten days (Sundays excepted). However, if Congress has concluded its term and the president fails to sign a bill within ten days, the bill does not become law. This last situation, called a *pocket veto,* forces Congress in its next term to start over from the beginning: the bill again must pass both chambers and again is subject to presidential veto.

CONGRESS'S POLICYMAKING ROLE

The framers of the Constitution expected that Congress, as the embodiment of representative government, would be the institution to which the people looked for policy leadership. During most of the nineteenth century, Congress had that stature. Aside from a few strong leaders such as Andrew Jackson and Abraham Lincoln, presidents did not play a major legislative role (see Chapter 12). However, as national and international forces combined to place greater policy demands on the federal government, the president assumed a central role in the legislative process. Today Congress and the president share the legislative effort, although their roles differ.[26]

Congress's policymaking role revolves around its three major functions: lawmaking, representation, and oversight (see Table 11-3). In practice, the three functions overlap, but they are conceptually distinct.

The Lawmaking Function of Congress

Under the Constitution, Congress is granted the **lawmaking function:** the authority to make the laws necessary to carry out the powers granted to the national government. The constitutional powers of Congress are substantial; they include the power to tax, to spend, to regulate commerce, and to declare war. However, whether Congress takes the lead in the making of laws usually depends on the type of policy at issue.

table 11-3 THE MAJOR FUNCTIONS OF CONGRESS	
Function	**Basis and Activity**
Lawmaking	Through its constitutional grant to enact law, Congress makes the laws authorizing federal programs and appropriating the funds necessary to carry them out.
Representation	Through its elected constitutional officers— U.S. senators and representatives—Congress represents the interests of constituents and the nation in its deliberations and its lawmaking.
Oversight	Through its constitutional responsibility to see that the executive branch carries out the laws faithfully and spends appropriations properly, Congress oversees and sometimes investigates executive action.

Broad Issues: Fragmentation as a Limit on Congress's Role   Although Congress occasionally takes the lead on major national policy issues,[27] it does not ordinarily do so. One reason is that the structure of Congress is not well suited to tackling such issues. Congress is not one house but two, each with its own authority and constituency base. Neither the House nor the Senate can enact legislation without the other's approval, and the two chambers are hardly identical. California and North Dakota have exactly the same representation in the Senate (two senators each), but in the House, which is apportioned by population, California has fifty-three seats compared to North Dakota's one. Moreover, the House and Senate are sometimes controlled by opposite parties, making agreement between the two chambers even harder to attain.

Congress also includes a lot of lawmakers: 100 members of the Senate and 435 members of the House. They come from different constituencies and represent different and sometimes opposing interests, which leads to disagreements, even among members of the same party. Nearly every member of Congress, for example, supports the principle of global free trade. Yet when it comes to specific trade provisions, members often disagree. Foreign competition means different things to manufacturers who produce automobiles, computer chips, or underwear; and it means different things to farmers who produce corn, sugar, or grapes. Because it means different things to different people in different parts of the country, members of Congress who represent these different areas will often have conflicting views on when free trade is advantageous.

As an institution, the presidency is better suited to the task of providing leadership on major national issues. First, whereas Congress's authority is divided, executive power is vested constitutionally in the hands of a single individual—the president. Unlike congressional leaders, who must bargain with their party's members when taking a stand on legislation, the president has less need to negotiate with other executive officials in taking a position. Second, whereas members of Congress often see issues from the perspective of their state or constituency, presidents have a national constituency and tend to look at policy from that perspective.

The president has one other noteworthy advantage over Congress when it comes to major legislative initiatives, especially those involving complex problems. The president, as will be explained in the next chapter, is assisted by literally hundreds of policy specialists, both directly and through the executive agencies, such as the departments of Treasury and Defense. These specialists have the expertise required for crafting intricate legislative initiatives. Congress's bureaucracy, consisting of three agencies, is tiny by comparison. One of these agencies is the Congressional Budget Office (CBO), which has a staff of 250 employees and provides Congress with estimates of government expenditures and revenues, which Congress uses in determining fiscal policy. A second congressional agency is the Government Accountability Office (GAO), which has 3,000 employees. However, its focus is overseeing whether executive agencies are complying with laws passed by Congress rather than developing new legislation. The third agency is the Congressional Research Service (CRS) with 1,000 employees. The CRS functions as a research and information service for congressional members and committees. By law, it is required to act as a nonpartisan body and is prohibited from making policy recommendations.

Presidential leadership on major policy issues means that Congress will listen to White House proposals, not that it will act on them. It may reject a proposal outright, particularly when the president is from the opposing party. In 2013 and 2014, most of President Obama's major legislative initiatives were pronounced "dead on arrival" when they reached Congress. Republicans controlled the House of Representatives and were determined to block his agenda. On the other hand, if a presidential proposal has enough support, it becomes the starting point for congressional negotiations, saving Congress the time and trouble of developing the legislation from scratch. (The legislative roles of Congress and the president are discussed further in Chapter 12.)

Republican Susan Collins was first elected to the U.S. Senate from Maine in 1996. Collins is among the growing number of women who sit in the U.S. Congress. Collins won reelection to a fourth term in 2014.

Congress in the Lead: Fragmentation as a Policymaking Strength   Congress's strength as a legislative body is its ability to handle scores of small issues simultaneously. The great majority of the hundreds of bills that Congress considers each session deal with narrow issues, such as providing grants-in-aid to cities for their mass transit systems or authorizing a new weapons system for the navy. Such bills are handled largely through Congress's standing committees, each of which has policy expertise resulting from the fact that it concentrates on a particular policy area, such as taxation, agriculture, or military affairs. And because the standing committees operate somewhat independently of each other, the committee system as a whole can work simultaneously on a large number of bills. As political scientist James Sundquist noted, "Congress [is] organized to deal with narrow problems but not with broad ones."[28]

Most such policy issues also serve the reelection interests of members of Congress. The resulting legislation tends to be "distributive" in nature—that is, it confers a benefit on a particular group while spreading the cost across the taxpaying public. An example is the veterans' jobs bill that Congress enacted in late 2011. The bill extended tax credits to businesses that hire jobless veterans and provided funding for retraining older unemployed veterans. At the time, Congress was embroiled in a bitter partisan dispute over how to reduce the size of the federal deficit. Yet, when the veterans' bill was considered, despite the fact that it would add to the deficit, not a single member of Congress voted against it. The final vote was 95-0 in Senate and 422-0 in the House.

Distributive policies have a clear political advantage. The benefit is large enough that members of the recipient group will recognize and appreciate it, while the cost to each taxpayer is less noticeable. Such policies are also the type that Congress, through its committee system, is organizationally best suited to handle. Most committees parallel a major constituent interest, such as agriculture, commerce, labor, or veterans.

The Representation Function of Congress

In the process of making laws, the members of Congress represent various interests within American society, giving them a voice in the national legislature. The proper approach to the **representation function** has been debated since the nation's founding. A recurrent issue is whether the representative should respond primarily to the interests of the nation as a whole or those of the constituency. These interests overlap to some degree but do not coincide exactly. Policies that have broad benefits are not necessarily advantageous to particular localities. Free trade in steel is

HOW THE U.S. DIFFERS
POLITICAL THINKING THROUGH COMPARISONS

Legislative Structure

The U.S. House and Senate are equal in their legislative powers; without their joint agreement no law can be enacted. This arrangement is unusual. Although most democracies have a bicameral (two-chamber) legislature, one chamber is typically much more powerful than the other. The Canadian and German parliaments are examples. Moreover, some democracies, including Sweden and Israel, have unicameral (one-chamber) legislatures. If the United States had an equivalent legislature, it would consist only of the House of Representatives.

Power in the U.S. Congress is divided in other ways as well: it has elected leaders with limited formal powers, a network of committees, and members who are free to follow or ignore other members of their party. It is not uncommon for a legislator to vote against the party's position on legislative issues. In contrast, European legislatures have a centralized power structure. Top leaders have substantial authority, the committees are weak, and the parties are unified. European legislators are expected to support their party unless granted permission to vote otherwise on a particular bill.

Q: In terms of passing laws, what is the relative advantage and disadvantage of the way in which Congress is structured, compared with a national legislature with a single dominant chamber in which the majority party can count on its members to support its policy agenda?

A: Congress is structured in a way that slows the passage of legislation, which can be a safeguard against hastily prepared, ill-considered, or weakly supported laws. On the other hand, the structure of Congress can permit a determined minority to block legislation that has majority support within and outside Congress.

an example. Although U.S. manufacturers as a whole benefit from access to low-priced steel from abroad, domestic steel producers and the communities where they are located are hurt by it.

Representation of States and Districts   The choice between national and local interests is not a simple one, even for a legislator who is inclined toward one or the other orientation. To be fully effective, members of Congress must be reelected time and again, a necessity that compels them to pay attention to local demands. Yet, they serve in the nation's legislative body and cannot ignore national needs. In making the choice, most members of Congress, on narrow issues at least, vote in a way that will not antagonize local interests.[29] Opposition to gun control legislation, for example, is stronger among members of Congress representing rural areas where hunting is prevalent than it is among those from urban areas where guns are more likely to be perceived as a threat to public safety.

Local representation occurs in part through the committee system. Although studies indicate that the policy positions of most committees are not radically different from those of the full House or Senate,[30] committee memberships roughly coincide with constituency interests. For example, farm-state legislators dominate the membership of the House and Senate Agriculture Committees. Committees are also the site of most *logrolling*—the practice of trading one's vote with another member's so that both get what they want. For example, it is not uncommon in the agricultural committees for members from corn-producing states of the North to trade votes with members from cotton-producing states of the South.

Local representation also shapes how Congress distributes funds for federal programs. Members of Congress will often withhold their support unless their locality gets a share of the money, even if the effect is to make the program less efficient. An example is the State Homeland Security Program that helps states to buy security equipment and train security personnel. Even though the threat of a terrorist attack is much higher in cities like New York, Washington, and Los Angeles, the act specifies that 40 percent of the money is to be spread across all the states.

Nevertheless, representation of constituency interests has its limits. Constituents have little awareness of most issues that come before Congress. Whether Congress appropriates a few million dollars in foreign aid to Chad or Bolivia is not the sort of issue that local residents will hear about. Moreover, members of Congress often have no choice but to go against the wishes of a significant portion of their constituency. The interests of workers and employers in a district or state, for example, can differ considerably. In such cases, members of Congress typically side with the interest that aligns with their party. When local business and labor groups take opposing sides on issues before Congress, for example,

<table>
<tr><td>P O L I T I C A L
T H I N K I N G</td><td>Local or National?</td></tr>
</table>

> *Members of Congress represent both the nation and a particular state or district. These roles often complement each other but sometimes conflict. When should a representative place the interests of the nation ahead of those of the state or district? When should local interests come first? Try to place your answer in the context of a specific policy issue, such as energy, trade, or immigration.*

Republican members tend to back business's position, whereas Democratic members tend to line up with labor.

Representation of the Nation through Parties   When a vital national interest is at stake, members of Congress can be expected to respond to it. With the economy showing signs of a recession in early 2008, Congress enacted legislation that gave most taxpayers a rebate of several hundred dollars in the hope that they would spend it, thereby giving the economy a boost. The House voted 380-34 in favor of the tax rebate; the Senate vote was 81-16.

In most cases, however, members of Congress, though agreeing on a need for national action, disagree on the best course of action. Most Americans believe, for example, that the nation's education system requires strengthening. The test scores of American schoolchildren on standardized reading, math, and science examinations are substantially below those of children in many other industrial democracies. This situation creates pressure for political action. But what action is necessary and desirable? Does more money have to be funneled into public schools, and if so, which level of government—federal, state, or local—should provide it? Or does the problem rest with teachers? Should they be subject to higher performance standards? There is no general agreement on such issues.

In Congress, disagreements over national goals occur primarily along party lines. Republican and Democratic lawmakers have different perspectives on national issues because their parties differ philosophically and politically. Differences in the parties' approach to education policy, for example, played out in the legislative debate on No Child Left Behind (NCLB), which would tie federal education grants to public schools to their students' performance on standardized national tests. Republicans stressed a need for tough testing standards. Democrats stressed a need to provide schools, particularly those in poorer communities, with the financial support necessary for them to meet NCLB testing requirements.

Partisan divisions have increasingly defined congressional action. In the past, the diversity of the congressional parties—the presence of a large number of conservatives within Democratic ranks and a large number of progressives within Republican ranks—was a barrier to legislation rooted in party ideology. Neither party could muster the support of enough of its members to pursue such legislation on a regular basis. Democratic lawmakers from the South, for example, did not share the liberal outlook of Democratic lawmakers from the North. Today, as was discussed earlier, the large majority of congressional Democrats are liberal and the large majority of congressional Republicans are conservative, which has enabled each group to pursue a legislative agenda rooted in its ideology.

A nationalization of congressional politics has been the result. When Republican and Democratic lawmakers vote in the same way as their fellow partisans, regardless of constituency differences, what else but a shift of issues to the national level would accurately describe what's taken place? Of course, local influences still matter in Congress but less so than in the past. On small and large issues alike, Republican and Democratic lawmakers have been deeply divided, even when they come from the same state or region.

A positive aspect of this development is that party differences are increasingly apparent to voters. At times in the past, many voters believed that the parties did not offer a clear choice. In the view of some political scientists, this situation was a barrier to accountability. They argued that America's voters deserve to have the choice between "responsible parties"—parties that take clear-cut and opposing policy positions and seek to enact them when in office so that voters can more easily hold them to account for their actions.

Critics of this view say that it fails to account for the structure of U.S. institutions. In a European parliamentary system, the majority party has full control of legislative and executive power and can enact its agenda. At the next election, the voters can decide whether they approve or disapprove of what it has accomplished. In the American system, however, executive and legislative powers are divided, and legislative power is further divided between the House and the Senate. These divisions were put in place to foster compromise and cooperation. But when the two parties are strong and closely divided in strength, the division of powers enables each party to prevent the other from acting. The result can be policy deadlock and delay, even in the face of pressing policy needs.[31] In *Beyond*

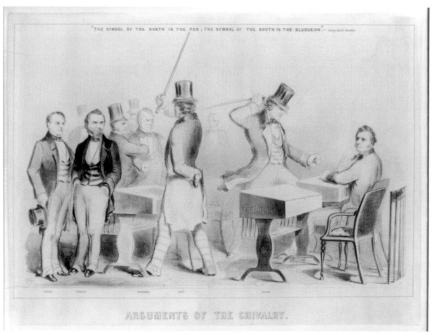

Although party polarization in Congress has reached a modern high, it pales alongside the partisan rancor of the period leading up to the Civil War. In 1856 on the Senate floor, Preston Brooks of South Carolina severely beat Charles Sumner of Massachusetts, causing brain injuries that kept Sumner out of the Senate for three years. Brooks was incensed by an abolitionist speech that Sumner had made. Brooks was greeted by cheering crowds when he returned to South Carolina after the assault.

Ideology, political scientist Frances Lee shows that, even on low-stake issues, lawmakers increasingly use congressional debate to attack opponents and activate their partisan base.[32]

As congressional partisanship has intensified, the public's image of Congress has plummeted. In a recent Pew Research Center poll, fewer than one in four Americans expressed approval of Congress—the lowest level ever recorded in a Pew survey (see Figure 11-5). In the 1980s, before partisan deadlock gripped Congress, two in three Americans approved of how Congress was doing its job.

The Oversight Function of Congress

Although Congress enacts the nation's laws, their administration is entrusted to the executive branch. Congress has the responsibility to see that the executive branch carries out the laws faithfully, a supervisory activity referred to as the **oversight function** of Congress.[33]

Percentage favorable view of Congress

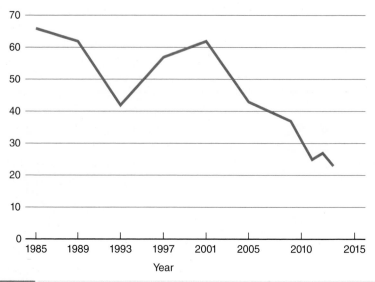

Percentage favorable view of Congress

figure 11-5 PUBLIC APPROVAL OF CONGRESS

Partisan polarization in Congress has been accompanied by declining public approval of Congress. *Source:* Pew Research Center for the People and the Press surveys.

Oversight is carried out largely through the committee system of Congress and is facilitated by the parallel structure of the committees and the executive bureaucracy: the House and Senate judiciary committees oversee the work of the Department of Justice, the House and Senate Agriculture Committees monitor the Department of Agriculture, and so on. The Legislative Reorganization Act of 1970 spells out each committee's responsibility for overseeing its parallel agency: "Each standing committee shall review and study, on a continuing basis, the application, administration, and execution of those laws, or parts of laws, the subject matter of which is within the jurisdiction of that committee."

Oversight is a demanding task. The bureaucracy has hundreds of agencies and thousands of programs. Congress gets some leverage from the fact that federal agencies have their funding renewed each year, which provides an opportunity for congressional committees to review agency activities.[34] Nevertheless, because the task is so large, oversight is not pursued vigorously unless members of Congress are annoyed with an agency, have discovered that a legislative authorization is being abused, or are intending to modify an agency program.

When an agency is alleged to have acted improperly, committee hearings into the allegations can occur. Congress's investigative power is not listed in the Constitution, but the Supreme Court has upheld this power as a reasonable extension of Congress's power to make the laws. Except in cases involving *executive privilege* (the right of the executive branch to withhold confidential information affecting national security), executive branch officials are required to testify when called by Congress to do so. If they refuse, they can be cited for contempt of Congress, a criminal offense.

Congressional interest in oversight increases substantially when the White House is the target, and the president is from the opposite party. When the computer system for the new health insurance program crashed at launch in 2013, House Republicans immediately scheduled hearings at which Obama administration officials were called to account for their role in the fiasco. The hearings had the effect of magnifying the political damage inflicted on the Democrats.

CONGRESS: AN INSTITUTION DIVIDED

Congress is not an institution where majorities rule easily. Agreement within each chamber, and between the two chambers, is required to pass legislation. That can normally be achieved only if lawmakers are willing to act in a spirit of compromise. Such was the intention of the framers of the Constitution. They designed the institution to foster compromise, for the purpose of having the resulting legislation reflect the interests of many rather than of a powerful faction.

What the writers of the Constitution did not anticipate was the degree to which members of Congress, because of their local base and determination to be reelected, would cater to the demands of special interests. The writers of the Constitution also did not anticipate how intense partisanship could disrupt the workings of Congress. Party unity is the clearest way for the majority to overcome the obstacles to action inherent in Congress's fragmented structure. At the same time, party unity is the most direct way for the minority to block action. And because Congress's structure makes it easier to block legislation than to enact it, a determined minority party can act in ways that deadlock the institution, even in the face of urgent national problems.

SUMMARY

Members of Congress, once elected, are likely to be reelected. Members of Congress can use their office to publicize themselves, pursue a service strategy of responding to the needs of individual constituents, and secure pork-barrel projects for their states or districts. House members gain a greater advantage from these activities than do senators, whose larger constituencies make it harder for them to build close personal relations with voters and whose office is more likely to attract strong challengers. Incumbency does have some disadvantages. Members of Congress must take positions on controversial issues, may blunder into political scandal or indiscretion, must deal with changes in the electorate, or may face strong challengers; any of these conditions can reduce members' reelection chances. By and large, however, the advantages of incumbency far outweigh the disadvantages. Incumbents' advantages extend into their reelection campaigns: their influential positions in Congress make it easier for them to raise campaign funds from PACs and individual contributors.

Congress is a fragmented institution. It has no single leader; rather, the House and Senate have separate leaders, neither of whom can presume to speak for the other chamber. The principal party leaders of Congress are the Speaker of the House and the Senate majority leader. They share leadership power with committee and subcommittee chairpersons, who have influence on the policy decisions of their committee or subcommittee.

It is in the committees that most of the day-to-day work of Congress is conducted. Each standing committee of the House or the Senate has jurisdiction over congressional policy in a particular area (such as agriculture or foreign relations), as does each of its subcommittees. In most cases, the full House and Senate accept committee recommendations about the passage of bills, although amendments to bills are quite common and committees are careful to take other members of Congress into account when making legislative decisions. Congress is a legislative system in which influence is widely dispersed, an arrangement that suits the power and reelection needs of its individual members. However, partisanship is a strong and binding force in Congress. It is the basis on which party leaders are able to build support for major legislative initiatives. On this type of legislation, party leaders and caucuses, rather than committees, are the central actors.

The major function of Congress is to enact legislation. Yet the role it plays in developing legislation depends on the type of policy involved. Because of its divided chambers and committee structure, as well as the concern of its members with state and district interests, Congress, through its party leaders and caucuses, only occasionally takes the lead on broad national issues. Congress instead typically looks to the president for this leadership. Nevertheless, presidential initiatives are passed by Congress only if they meet its members' expectations and usually only after a lengthy process of compromise and negotiation. Congress is more adept at handling legislation that deals with problems of narrow interest. Legislation of this sort is decided mainly in congressional committees, where interested legislators, bureaucrats, and groups concentrate their efforts on issues of mutual concern.

A second function of Congress is the representation of various interests. Members of Congress are highly sensitive to the state or district on which they depend for reelection. They do respond to overriding national interests, but for most of them local concerns generally come first. National or local representation often operates through party representation, particularly on issues that divide the Democratic and Republican parties and their constituent groups, which is increasingly the case.

Congress's third function is oversight—the supervision and investigation of the way the bureaucracy is implementing legislatively mandated programs. Although oversight is a difficult process, it is an important means of legislative control over the actions of the executive branch.

CRITICAL THINKING ZONE

KEY TERMS

bicameral legislature (*p.338*)
bill (*p. 350*)
cloture (*p. 353*)
conference committees (*p. 354*)
constituency (*p. 330*)
filibuster (*p. 353*)
gerrymandering (*p. 334*)
incumbent (*p. 329*)
jurisdiction (of a congressional
  committee) (*p. 347*)
law (as enacted by Congress) (*p. 354*)
lawmaking function (*p. 355*)
midterm election (*p. 335*)

open-seat election (*p. 333*)
oversight function (*p. 363*)
party caucus (*p. 338*)
party leaders (*p. 338*)
party unity (*p. 339*)
pork (pork-barrel spending) (*p. 330*)
reapportionment (*p. 333*)
redistricting (*p. 334*)
representation function (*p. 358*)
seniority (*p. 349*)
service strategy (*p. 331*)
standing committees (*p. 345*)
veto (*p. 354*)

APPLYING THE ELEMENTS OF CRITICAL THINKING

Conceptualizing: Define what is meant by the lawmaking, representation, and oversight functions of Congress.

Synthesizing: Contrast the advantages that incumbents have in seeking reelection with the disadvantages they have. Which of these advantages and disadvantages apply only to House members? Which apply only to senators?

Analyzing:

1. How does the structure of Congress—for example, its two chambers and its committee system—affect its role in the making of policy on broad national issues, as compared with its role on narrower group-centered issues?

2. Compared with past times, there are now fewer conservative Democrats and fewer progressive Republicans in Congress. How has this development increased the importance of party and party leaders in Congress? How has it increased the chances of partisan deadlock on key legislative issues?

EXTRA CREDIT

A Book Worth Reading: Thomas E. Mann and Norman J. Ornstein, *It's Even Worse Than It Looks: How the American Constitutional System Collided with the New Politics of Extremism*. New York: Basic Books, 2012. A best-selling book that identifies the problems that have led Congress into deadlock and dysfunction.

A Website Worth Visiting: **www.house.gov** or **www.senate.gov**. The websites of the U.S. House of Representatives and the U.S. Senate, respectively. Each site has information on the chamber's party leaders, pending legislation, and committee hearings, as well as links to each member's office and website.

PARTICIPATE!

Each year, thousands of college students serve as interns in Congress or a state legislature. Many internships are unpaid, but students can ordinarily receive college credit for the experience. Internships are not always a great adventure. Many legislative interns envision themselves contributing ideas and research that might influence public policy, only to find that they are answering letters, developing mailing lists, or duplicating materials. Nevertheless, few interns conclude that their experience has been a waste of time. Most find it rewarding and ultimately memorable. Information about internships can be obtained from the American Political Science Association (www.apsa.org). In addition, there are organizations in Washington that arrange internships in Congress and the executive agencies. These organizations frequently charge a fee for their services, so you might want to contact a legislative office or executive agency directly. It is important to make your request as early as possible in the college year, because some internship programs have deadlines and nearly all offices receive more requests than they can accommodate. You could also check with the student services office at your college or university. Some of these offices have information on internship programs and can be of assistance.

THE PRESIDENCY: LEADING THE NATION

> " [The president's] is the only voice in national affairs. Let him once win the admiration and confidence of the people, and no other single voice will easily overpower him. "
>
> WOODROW WILSON[1]

Barack Obama was sinking in the polls. The launch of his new health insurance program had gone badly as a result of a computer crash, and Americans were growing impatient with the slow speed of the economic recovery. The public was in a sour mood, and Obama's approval rating in early 2014 dropped to 40 percent—a new low. It was a far cry from the 70 percent approval rating he had enjoyed upon taking office five years earlier.

The Obama story is but one in the saga of the ups and downs of the modern presidency. Lyndon Johnson's and Richard Nixon's dogged pursuit of the Vietnam War led to talk of "the imperial presidency," an office so powerful that constitutional checks and balances were no longer an effective constraint on it. Within a few years, because of the Watergate scandal and intractable international problems during the Ford and Carter presidencies, the watchword became "the imperiled presidency," an office too weak to meet the nation's need for executive leadership. Ronald Reagan's policy successes prior to 1986 renewed talk heard in the Roosevelt and Kennedy years of "a heroic presidency," an office that is the inspirational center of American politics. After the Iran-Contra scandal in 1986, Reagan was more often called a lame duck. George H. W. Bush's handling of the Gulf crisis—leading the nation in 1991 into a major war and emerging from it with a stratospheric public approval rating—bolstered the heroic conception of the office. A year later, Bush was defeated in his campaign for a second term. Bill Clinton overcame a fitful start to his presidency to become the first Democrat since Franklin D. Roosevelt in the 1930s to win reelection. As Clinton was launching an aggressive second-term policy agenda, however, he got entangled in an affair with a White House

The presidency is the most visible of America's political institutions and also the one that varies the most in its power, not only from one president to the next but also during a particular president's term of office. Pictured here is the official seal of the President of the United States.

intern, Monica Lewinsky, which led to his impeachment by the House of Representatives and weakened his claim to national leadership. After the terrorist attacks of September 11, 2001, George W. Bush's job approval rating soared to a record high. By the time he left office, Americans had turned against his economic and war policies and only a third of the public had a positive view of his leadership.

No other political institution has been subject to such varying characterizations as the modern presidency. One reason is that the formal powers of the office are relatively modest and so presidential power changes with political conditions and the personal capacity of the office's occupant. The American presidency is always a central office in that its occupant is a focus of national attention. Yet the presidency operates in a system of divided powers, which means that presidential power is conditional. It depends on the president's own abilities but even more on circumstances—on whether the situation demands strong leadership and whether there is public and congressional support for that leadership. When circumstances are favorable, the president exercises considerable power. When circumstances are unfavorable, the president struggles to exercise power effectively.

This chapter examines the roots of presidential power, the presidential selection process, the staffing of the presidency, and the factors associated with the success and failure of presidential leadership. The main ideas of this chapter are:

- *Over time, the presidency has become a more powerful office.* This development owes largely to the legacy of strong presidents and to domestic and international developments that have increased the need for executive leadership.

- *The modern presidential campaign is a marathon affair in which self-selected candidates seek a strong start in the nominating contests and a well-run media campaign in the general election.*

- *The president could not control the executive branch without a large number of presidential appointees—advisors, experts, and skilled managers—but the sheer number of these appointees is itself a challenge to presidential control.*

- *The president's election by national vote and position as sole chief executive make the presidency the focal point of national politics.* Nevertheless, whether presidents are able to accomplish their goals depends on their personal capacity for leadership, national and international conditions, the stage of their presidency, the partisan composition of Congress, and whether the issue is foreign or domestic.

FOUNDATIONS OF THE MODERN PRESIDENCY

The framers of the Constitution knew what they wanted from the presidency— national leadership, statesmanship in foreign affairs, command in time of war, enforcement of the laws—but they did not have a precise sense of how the office would work in practice. Accordingly, they chose to describe the powers of the president in broad terms. By comparison with the precise listing in Article I of Congress's powers, the provisions in Article II that define the president's authority are broadly worded (see Table 12-1).[2] The clause that provides for the president's executive authority, for example, says simply, "He shall take care that the laws be faithfully executed, and shall commission all the officers of the United States."

Over the course of American history, each of the president's constitutional powers has been expanded in practice beyond the framers' expectation. For example, the Constitution grants the president command of the nation's military, but only Congress can declare war. In *Federalist* No. 69, Alexander Hamilton wrote that a surprise attack on the United States was the only justification for war by presidential decree. Nevertheless, presidents on their own authority have launched military attacks abroad on more than two hundred occasions. Of the roughly fifteen major wars included in that figure, only five were formally declared by Congress.[3] None of America's most recent major conflicts—the Korean, Vietnam, Persian Gulf, Balkans, Afghanistan, and Iraq wars—were waged on the basis of a congressional declaration of war.

The Constitution also empowers the president to act as diplomatic leader with the authority to appoint ambassadors and to negotiate treaties with other countries, subject to approval by a two-thirds vote of the Senate. The framers anticipated that Congress would define the nation's foreign policy objectives, while the president would oversee their implementation. However, presidents gradually took charge of U.S. foreign policy and have even acquired the power to make treaty-like arrangements with other nations. In 1937, the Supreme Court ruled that *executive agreements*— which are formal agreements that presidents make on their own with foreign nations—are legally binding as long as they do not conflict with the Constitution or a law enacted by Congress.[4] Since World War II, presidents have negotiated over fifteen thousand executive agreements— more than ten times the number of treaties ratified by the Senate during the same period.[5]

The Constitution also vests "executive power" in the president. This power includes the responsibility to execute the laws faithfully and to

table 12-1	THE CONSTITUTIONAL AUTHORITY FOR THE PRESIDENT'S ROLES

Commander in chief: Article II, Section 2: "The President shall be commander in chief of the Army and Navy of the United States, and of the militia of the several states."

Chief executive: Article II, Section 2: "He may require the opinion, in writing, of the principal officer in each of the executive departments, upon any subject relating to the duties of their respective offices, and he shall have power to grant reprieves and pardons for offences against the United States, except in cases of impeachment."

Article II, Section 2: "He shall have power, by and with the advice and consent of the Senate, to make treaties, provided two thirds of the senators present concur; and he shall nominate, and by and with the advice and consent of the Senate, shall appoint ambassadors, other public ministers and consuls, judges of the Supreme Court, and all other officers of the United States, whose appointments are not herein otherwise provided for, and which shall be established by law."

Article II, Section 2: "The President shall have power to fill up all vacancies that may happen during the recess of the Senate, by granting commissions which shall expire at the end of their next session."

Article II, Section 3: "He shall take care that the laws be faithfully executed, and shall commission all the officers of the United States."

Chief diplomat: Article II, Section 2: "He shall have power, and with the advice and consent of the Senate, to make treaties, provided two thirds of the senators present concur."

Article II, Section 3: "He shall receive ambassadors and other public ministers."

Legislative leader: Article II, Section 3: "He shall from time to time give to the Congress information of the state of the Union, and recommend to their consideration such measures as he shall judge necessary and expedient; he may, on extraordinary occasions, convene both houses, or either of them, and in case of disagreement between them, with respect to the time of adjournment, he may adjourn them to such time as he shall think proper." (Article I, Section 7, which defines the president's veto power, is also part of his legislative authority.)

appoint major administrators, such as the heads of federal agencies. In *Federalist* No. 76, Hamilton indicated that the president's real authority as chief executive was to be found in this appointive capacity. Presidents have indeed exercised power through their appointments, but they have also found their administrative authority—the power to execute the laws—to be significant, because it enables them to decide how laws will be implemented. President George W. Bush used his executive power to *prohibit* the use of federal funds by family-planning clinics that offered abortion counseling. President Barack Obama exerted the same power to *permit* the use of federal funds for this purpose. The same act of Congress was the basis for each of these decisions. The act authorizes the use of federal funds for family-planning services, but it neither requires nor prohibits their use for abortion counseling, enabling the president to decide the issue.

Finally, the Constitution provides the president with legislative authority, including use of the veto and the ability to propose legislation to Congress. The framers expected this authority to be used in a limited way. George Washington acted as the framers anticipated: he proposed only three legislative measures and vetoed only two acts of Congress. Modern presidents have assumed a more active legislative role. They regularly submit proposals to Congress and do not hesitate to veto legislation they dislike.

The Changing Conception of the Presidency

The presidency, for many reasons, is a more powerful office than the framers envisioned. But two features of the office in particular—*national election* and *singular authority*—have enabled presidents to make use of changing demands on government to claim national policy leadership. It is a claim that no other elected official can routinely make. Unlike the president, who is elected by nationwide vote and is the sole chief executive, members of Congress are elected from separate states or districts and operate in an institution where they share power with the other members. Unlike the president, no member of Congress can fully claim to be the nation's leader.

The first president to forcefully assert a broad claim to national policy leadership was Andrew Jackson, who was elected in 1828 on a tide of popular support that broke the upper class's hold on the presidency (see Chapter 2). Jackson used his popular backing to challenge Congress's claim to national policy leadership, contending that he represented "the people's voice." Jackson's view, however, was not shared by his immediate successors. The nation's major issues were of a sectional nature (especially the North-South split over slavery) and were suited to action by Congress, which represented state interests. In fact, throughout most of the nineteenth century (the Civil War presidency of Abraham Lincoln was an exception), Congress jealously guarded its constitutional authority over national policy. James Bryce wrote in the 1880s that Congress paid no more attention to the president's policy pronunciations than it did to the editorial stands of newspaper publishers.[6]

The nineteenth-century conception of the presidency was expressed in the **Whig theory,** which holds that the presidency is a limited office. According to this "weak presidency" theory, the president is primarily an administrator, charged with carrying out the will of Congress. "My duty," said President James Buchanan, a Whig adherent, "is to execute the laws . . . and not my individual opinions."[7]

Upon taking office in 1901, Theodore Roosevelt cast aside the Whig tradition.[8] He embraced what he called the **stewardship theory,** which calls for a "strong presidency" that is limited, not by what the Constitution

Theodore Roosevelt is regarded by many historians and political scientists as the first of the "modern" presidents. Operating from an activist view of the presidency, Roosevelt ignored the nation's isolationist tradition and extended America's influence into Latin America and the Pacific. On the domestic front, he battled the business trusts, believing that unfettered capitalism was incompatible with social justice. Roosevelt held the presidency as a Republican from 1901 to 1908 and was defeated when he tried to recapture it as a third-party candidate in 1912.

allows, but by what it prohibits. The stewardship theory holds that presidents are free to act as they choose, as long as they do not violate the law. In his autobiography, Roosevelt wrote: "My belief was that it was not only [the president's] right but his duty to do anything that the needs of the nation demanded unless such action was forbidden by the Constitution or by the laws."[9] Acting on his belief, Roosevelt challenged the power of business monopolies. When coal mine owners refused to bargain with miners, he threatened to seize the mines, forcing owners to improve mine safety and increase miners' wages. He also opened world markets to American goods, using the navy and marines to project U.S. influence southward into the Caribbean and Latin America and westward toward Hawaii, the Philippines, and China (the "Open Door" policy). When congressional leaders objected, he forced a showdown, knowing that the American people would support the troops. Roosevelt said: "I have the money to send [the navy's ships] halfway around the world—let Congress bring them back."

Theodore Roosevelt's conception of a strong presidency was not shared by most of his immediate successors.[10] Herbert Hoover was slow to respond to the human misery caused by the Great Depression, saying that he did not have the constitutional authority to take strong action. His successor, Franklin D. Roosevelt (a distant cousin of Theodore Roosevelt), felt no such constraint. His New Deal policies included unprecedented public works projects, social welfare programs, and economic regulatory actions (see Chapter 3). The New Deal effectively marked the end of the limited (Whig) presidency. FDR's successor, Harry S Truman, wrote in his memoirs: "The power of the President should be used in the interest of the people and in order to do that the President must use whatever power the Constitution does not expressly deny him."[11]

The Need for a Strong Presidency

Today the presidency is an inherently strong office, made so by the federal government's increased policy responsibilities. Although individual presidents differ in their capacity for leadership, the office they hold is one that requires active involvement in a broad range of policy areas.

Modern government consists of thousands of programs and hundreds of agencies. Congress is ill suited to directing and coordinating them. Congress is a fragmented institution that acts through negotiation, bargaining, and compromise. It is simply not structured in a way that would enable it to easily and regularly oversee government activity and develop comprehensive approaches to policy. The presidency is structured in a way that enables it to do so. Final authority rests with a single individual, the president, who is thereby able to direct the actions of others and to undertake large-scale planning.[12] As a result, major domestic policy initiatives since the New Deal era have usually come from the White House, as exemplified by Lyndon Johnson's Great Society and Ronald Reagan's New Federalism (see Chapter 3). In fact, as the size of government has increased, all democracies have seen a shift in power from their legislature to their executive. In Britain, for example, the prime minister has taken on policy responsibilities that once belonged to the cabinet or the Parliament.

The presidency has also been strengthened by the expanded scope of foreign policy. World War II fundamentally changed the nation's international role and the president's role in foreign policy. The United States emerged from the war as a global superpower, a giant in world trade, and the recognized leader of the noncommunist world—a development that had a one-sided effect on America's institutions.[13] Because of the president's constitutional authority as chief diplomat and military commander and the special demands of foreign policy leadership, the president, not Congress, assumed the dominant role.[14] Foreign policy requires singleness of purpose and, at times, fast action. Congress—a large, divided, and often unwieldy institution—is poorly suited to such a response. In contrast, the president, as sole head of the executive branch, can act quickly and speak authoritatively for the nation as a whole in its relations with other nations. After the terrorist attacks of September 11, 2001, for example, President Bush took the lead in obtaining international support for U.S. military, intelligence, and diplomatic initiatives. Although Congress backed these actions, it had little choice but to support Bush's decision. Americans wanted decisive action and looked to the president, not to Congress, for leadership in combating terrorism. (The changing shape of the world and its implications for presidential power and leadership are discussed more fully later in the chapter.)

CHOOSING THE PRESIDENT

As the president's policy and leadership responsibilities changed during the nation's history, so did the process of electing presidents. The public's role in selecting the president has grown ever more direct.[15] The United States in its history has had four systems of presidential selection, each more "democratic" than the previous one in the sense that it gave ordinary citizens a larger role in the president's election (see Table 12-2).

table 12-2	THE FOUR SYSTEMS OF PRESIDENTIAL SELECTION	
Selection System	**Period**	**Features**
1. Original	1788–1828	Party nominees are chosen in congressional caucuses. Electoral College members act somewhat independently in their presidential voting.
2. Party convention	1832–1900	Party nominees are chosen in national party conventions by delegates selected by state and local party organizations. Electoral College members cast their ballots for the popular-vote winner in their respective states.
3. Party convention, primary	1904–1968	As in system 2, except that a *minority* of national convention delegates are chosen through primary elections (the majority still being chosen by party organizations).
4. Party primary, open caucus	1972–present	As in system 2, except that a *majority* of national convention delegates are chosen through primary elections.

The delegates to the constitutional convention of 1787 feared that popular election of the president would make the office too powerful and accordingly devised an electoral vote system (the so-called Electoral College). The president was to be chosen by electors picked by the states, with each state entitled to one elector for each of its members of Congress (House and Senate combined). This system was modified after the election in 1828 of Andrew Jackson, who believed that the people's will had been denied four years earlier when he got the most popular votes but failed to receive an electoral majority. Although Jackson failed to persuade Congress to support a constitutional amendment to eliminate the Electoral College, he achieved the next-best alternative. Under Jackson's reform, which is still in effect today, the candidate who wins a state's popular vote is awarded its electoral votes (see Chapter 2). Thus, the popular vote for the candidates directly affects their electoral vote, and one candidate is likely to win both forms of the presidential vote. Since Jackson's time, only Rutherford B. Hayes (in 1876), Benjamin Harrison (in 1888), and George W. Bush (in 2000) have won the presidency after having lost the popular vote.

Jackson also championed the national party convention as a means of nominating the party's presidential candidate (before this time, nominations were made by party caucuses in Congress and in state legislatures). Jackson saw the national convention—where each state is represented by delegates who select the party nominee—as a means of strengthening the link between the presidency and the people. Since Jackson's time, all presidential nominees have been formally chosen at national party conventions.

Jackson's system of presidential nomination remained intact until the early twentieth century, when the Progressives devised the primary election as a means of curbing the power of the party bosses (see Chapter 2). State party leaders had taken control of the nominating process by handpicking their states' convention delegates. The Progressives sought to give voters the power to select the delegates. Such a process is called an *indirect primary* because the voters are not choosing the nominees directly (as they do in House and Senate races) but rather are choosing delegates who in turn select the nominees. However, the Progressives were unable to persuade most states to adopt presidential primaries, which meant that party leaders continued to control a majority of the convention delegates.

That arrangement held until 1968 when Democratic Party leaders ignored the strength of anti–Vietnam War sentiment in the primaries and nominated Vice President Hubert Humphrey, who had not entered a single primary and was closely identified with the Johnson administration's Vietnam policy. After Humphrey narrowly lost the 1968 general election to Richard Nixon, reform-minded Democrats forced changes in the nominating process. The new rules gave the party's voters more control by requiring states to select their delegates through either primary elections or **open party caucuses** (meetings open to any registered party voter who wants to attend). Although the Democrats initiated the change, the Republicans also adopted it. Today it is the voters in state primaries and open caucuses who choose the Democratic and Republican presidential nominees.[16] (About forty states choose their delegates through a primary election; the others use the caucus system.)

In sum, the presidential election system has changed from an elite-dominated process to one based on voter support. This arrangement has strengthened the presidency by providing the office with the added authority that the vote of the people confers. By virtue of having been chosen in a national election, the president has a claim to national leadership that no other U.S. official is in a position to make.

The Nominating Campaign: Primaries and Caucuses

The fact that voters pick the party nominees has opened the nominating races to nearly any prominent politician with the energy, resources, and desire to run. The competition is intense, except in the case of an incumbent president seeking renomination. The list of candidates is always long. Two years in advance of the 2016 presidential election, more than a dozen politicians had signaled that they might enter the race.

Candidates for nomination have no choice but to start early and run hard. The year before the first contest in Iowa is a critical period, one that has been called the **invisible primary.** Although no votes are cast in this period, it is the time when candidates demonstrate through their fundraising ability, poll standing, and debate performance that they are serious contenders for the nomination. A candidate who fails to show strength in these areas is quickly dismissed as an also-ran. In fact, in nearly every nominating race of the past three decades, the winner has been the candidate who, before a single vote was cast, had raised the most money or ranked first in the opinion polls.[17] The 2012 Republican race was no exception. On the eve of the Iowa caucuses, Mitt Romney was ahead in the national polls and had easily outpaced his Republican rivals in fundraising.

Once the state caucuses and primaries get under way, a key to success is **momentum**—a strong showing in the early contests that contributes to voter support in subsequent ones. Nobody—not the press, not donors, not the voters—has an interest in candidates who are at the back of the pack. No candidate in recent decades has got off to a lousy start in the first few contests and then picked up enough steam to win nomination. The advantage rests with the fast starters. They get more attention from the press, more money from contributors, and more consideration by the voters. It's not surprising that presidential contenders strive to do well in the early contests, particularly the first caucus in Iowa and the first primary in New Hampshire.

Until the 2000 election, primary-election candidates relied upon federal funding to underwrite their campaigns. Under the Federal Election Campaign Act of 1974 (as amended in 1979), a candidate qualifies for this funding by raising at least $5,000 in individual contributions in twenty or more states. In such cases, the government matches up to $250 per contributor, provided that the candidate agrees to limit campaign spending to a set amount in each state and overall (the overall limit for the 2016 election is roughly $50 million).

In 2000, George W. Bush declined matching funds so that he could spend an unrestricted amount of money on his nominating campaign.

Unlike the era when the political party organizations picked the presidential nominees, the choice today rests with the voters in primaries and caucuses. An effect has been to open the nominating process to nearly any prominent political figure who wants to run, which results in widespread speculation by the news media about who will actually run. No potential candidate for 2016 was the source of more speculation than Hillary Clinton, who had run unsuccessfully in 2008 and had served as secretary of state, U.S. senator, and First Lady.

He spent more than $100 million in winning the Republican nomination. Since then, with the exception of John McCain in 2008, all of the winning candidates, and some of the losers, have declined public funds. Barack Obama's successful run for the 2008 Democratic nomination was easily the most expensive. He raised and spent more than $300 million to defeat his main challenger, Hillary Clinton.

The National Party Conventions

The summertime national party conventions mark the end of the nominating campaign. In an earlier era, the delegates from the various states actually bargained and negotiated over the choice of a presidential nominee. However, after the delegate selection process was changed in 1972, the strongest candidate in every case has acquired enough delegates through the primaries and caucuses to secure nomination in advance of the convention. Despite the lack of suspense, the convention is an important event. It brings together the delegates elected in the state caucuses

Although the national party conventions are not the tumultuous and decisive events they once were, they offer the parties a showcase for their candidates and platforms. Shown here is a scene from the 2012 Republican convention, which nominated Mitt Romney for president and Paul Ryan for vice president.

and primaries, who approve a party platform and formally nominate the party's presidential and vice presidential candidates. It also serves as a time for the party to heal any divisions created by the nominating race and to persuade the party faithful to rally behind its presidential candidate. Studies indicate that the conventions are a point in the campaign when large numbers of voters settle on their choice of a candidate, usually the one nominated by their preferred party.[18]

The convention is also the time when the parties choose their vice presidential nominees. By tradition, this choice rests with the presidential nominee. In 2012, Romney selected Wisconsin representative Paul Ryan, a rising star in the Republican Party and also someone who could shore up Romney's support among fiscal conservatives. Ryan was a strong proponent in the House for deep cuts in government spending.

The General Election Campaign

The winner in the November general election is certain to be the Republican or the Democratic candidate. Two-thirds of the nation's voters identify with the Republican or Democratic Party, and most independents lean toward one or the other party. As a result, the major-party presidential nominees have a reservoir of votes. Even Democrat George McGovern, whose level of party support was the lowest in the past half century, was backed in 1972 by 60 percent of his party's identifiers. Because the Democratic and Republican nominees have this built-in advantage, a third-party candidate has no realistic hope of victory. Even Ross Perot, who in 1992 ran the most successful third-party campaign in nearly a century, attracted only a fifth of the vote.

Election Strategy   The candidates' strategies in the general election are shaped by several considerations, none more so than the Electoral College (see Chapter 2). Each state has two electoral votes for its Senate representation and a varying number of electoral votes depending on its House representation. Altogether, there are 538 electoral votes, including 3 for the District of Columbia, even though it has no voting representatives in Congress. To win the presidency, a candidate must receive at least 270 votes, an electoral majority. (If no candidate receives a majority, the election is decided in the House of Representatives. No president since John Quincy Adams in 1824 has been elected in this way.)

The importance of electoral votes is magnified by the **unit rule:** all states except Maine and Nebraska grant all their electoral votes as a unit to the candidate who wins the state's popular vote. For this reason, candidates are concerned with winning the most populous states, such as California, Florida, Illinois, Michigan, New York, Ohio, Pennsylvania, and Texas. California's winner, for example, gets all of its 55 electoral votes, which is roughly a fifth of the votes necessary to win the presidency.

POLITICAL THINKING	Should the Electoral College Be Retained?

The president is chosen by an indirect system of election. Voters cast ballots for their preferred candidate, but their votes choose only their state's electors, whose subsequent vote determines the actual winner of the election. Electoral votes are apportioned to the states based on their representation in Congress, which creates the possibility, as happened in the 2000 election, that the popular vote winner will lose the electoral vote. What argument would you make for keeping the Electoral College system? What argument would you make for abolishing it? Which argument do you find more persuasive?

Nevertheless, a larger strategic factor than a state's size is its competitiveness. Because of the unit rule, candidates have no incentive to campaign in a lopsidedly Republican or Democratic state because its electoral votes are not in doubt. As a result, the fall campaign becomes a fight to win the toss-up states (see "How the 50 States Differ"). Other states might as well be located in Canada for the amount of attention they receive.

Media and Money   At an earlier time, candidates based their campaigns on the party organizations. Today, they rely on the media, particularly the Internet and television. The Internet is used mostly for fundraising and organizing. Television is used mostly as a way to persuade undecided voters. Through appearances on news and interview programs, as well as through their televised advertising (which accounts for most of their spending), the nominees try to win over those voters who are undecided or wavering in their choice (see Chapter 8).[19] The televised presidential debates are part of this effort, although the debates normally do not have a large impact on the candidates' support, largely because most voters have already picked their candidate by this point in the campaign. The first debate in 2012 did not follow the typical pattern. Before that debate, Romney had been dropping in the polls. However, he won the opening debate decisively, which energized Republican voters and helped him gain support among undecided and wavering voters.

The Republican and Democratic nominees are eligible for federal funding of their general election campaigns even if they do not accept it during the primaries. The amount was set at $20 million when the policy was instituted in 1976 and has been adjusted for inflation in succeeding elections—the figure for the 2016 election is roughly $95 million. The only string attached to this money is that a nominee who accepts it cannot spend additional funds on the general election campaign. In 2008, Barack Obama declined public funding, becoming the first major-party nominee to do so. He had promised to run on public funds but reneged upon discovering that he could raise a much larger sum on his own. Obama outspent by three to one his opponent, John McCain, who did accept public funding. In 2012, neither Obama nor Romney accepted public funding. (Minor-party and independent presidential candidates can qualify for federal funding if they receive at least 5 percent of the vote. Their funding is proportional to the votes they attract. If, for example, a third-party candidate receives half the number of votes as the average for the major-party nominees, that candidate would get half the federal funding that each of them was eligible to receive.)

HOW THE 50 STATES DIFFER

POLITICAL THINKING THROUGH COMPARISONS

Electoral Vote Strategy in the 2016 Election

The Constitution of the United States specifies that the president is to be chosen by electoral votes. The candidate receiving a majority of the electoral vote, even if receiving fewer popular votes than the opponent, becomes president. The Constitution further specifies that states have authority to determine how their electors will be chosen. Today, all states except two (Maine and Nebraska, which give one electoral vote to the winner of each congressional district and two electoral votes to the statewide winner), give all their electoral votes to the popular-vote winner in the state—the so-called unit rule. This winner-take-all feature of the electoral vote system leads presidential

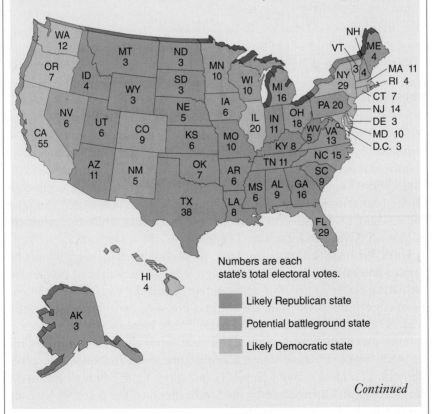

Numbers are each state's total electoral votes.

Likely Republican state

Potential battleground state

Likely Democratic state

Continued

candidates to focus on toss-up states—those that conceivably could be won by either party. These battleground states are the only ones where the candidates spend appreciable amounts of time and money during the general election. One-sided states—those that are solidly Republican or Democratic—are more or less ignored during the fall campaign. The accompanying map identifies the potential battleground states in the 2016 presidential race, based on an analysis of states' voting patterns in recent elections.

Q: The unit rule is only one of the possible ways of allocating electoral votes. As indicated on the previous page, Maine and Nebraska use a different method. Some state legislatures are considering yet a third method: allocating their state's electoral votes among the candidates in proportion to the popular votes they each receive. What's your view? Do you think the unit rule is a fair way for states to distribute their electoral votes, or do you prefer one of the alternatives?

The Winners   The Constitution specifies that the president must be at least thirty-five years old, be a natural-born U.S. citizen, and have been a U.S. resident for at least fourteen years. Except for four army generals, all presidents to date have served previously as vice presidents, members of Congress, state governors, or top federal executives (see Table 12-3). Historians have devised rankings of the presidents, and their rankings reveal that there is no template for a successful presidency. The strong presidents have differed considerably in their backgrounds, as have the weak ones. Of the four army generals, for example, two of them (George Washington and Dwight D. Eisenhower) are in the upper ranks while the other two (Ulysses S. Grant and Zachary Taylor) are in the lower ranks.

Until Obama's election in 2008, all presidents had been white. No woman has won the presidency, though it is only a matter of time before the nation elects its first woman president. Until the early 1950s, a majority of Americans polled said they would not vote for a woman for president. Today, fewer than 5 percent hold this view. A similar change of opinion preceded John F. Kennedy's election to the presidency in 1960. Kennedy was the nation's first Catholic president and only the second Catholic to receive a major party's nomination. By the time of Kennedy's candidacy, anti-Catholic sentiment had declined to the point where it did not block his election.

table 12-3	THE PATH TO THE WHITE HOUSE		
President	**Years in Office**	**Highest Previous Office**	**Second Highest Office**
Theodore Roosevelt	1901–1908	Vice president*	Governor
William Howard Taft	1909–1912	Secretary of war	Federal judge
Woodrow Wilson	1913–1920	Governor	None
Warren G. Harding	1921–1924	U.S. senator	Lieutenant governor
Calvin Coolidge	1925–1928	Vice president*	Governor
Herbert Hoover	1929–1932	Secretary of commerce	War relief administrator
Franklin D. Roosevelt	1933–1945	Governor	Assistant secretary of Navy
Harry S Truman	1945–1952	Vice president*	U.S. senator
Dwight D. Eisenhower	1953–1960	None (Army general)	None
John F. Kennedy	1961–1963	U.S. senator	U.S. representative
Lyndon Johnson	1963–1968	Vice president*	U.S. senator
Richard Nixon	1969–1974	Vice president	U.S. senator
Gerald Ford	1974–1976	Vice president*	U.S. representative
Jimmy Carter	1977–1980	Governor	State senator
Ronald Reagan	1981–1988	Governor	None
George H. W. Bush	1989–1992	Vice president	Director, CIA
Bill Clinton	1993–2000	Governor	State attorney general
George W. Bush	2001–2008	Governor	None
Barack Obama	2009–	U.S. senator	State senator

*Became president on death or resignation of incumbent.

STAFFING THE PRESIDENCY

When Americans go to the polls on Election Day, they are electing more than a president. They are also picking a secretary of state, the director of the FBI, and hundreds of other federal executives. Each of these is a presidential appointee, and each of these is an extension of the president's authority. Although the president cannot be in a hundred places at once, the president's appointees collectively can be. Not surprisingly, presidents typically appoint party loyalists who are committed to the administration's policy goals.

The Vice President

The vice president holds a separate elective office from the president but, in practice, is part of the presidential team. Because the Constitution assigns no executive authority to the office, the vice president's duties within the administration are determined by the president. At an earlier time, presidents largely ignored their vice presidents, who did not even have an office in the White House. Nomination to the vice presidency was declined by several leading politicians, including Daniel Webster and Henry Clay. Said Webster, "I do not propose to be buried until I am really dead."[20] When Jimmy Carter assumed the presidency in 1977,

The vice presidency is a separately elected office. However, because the Constitution assigns it no authority other than to serve as president of the Senate and to cast a vote there in case of a tie, the duties of the vice president are determined by the president. Recent presidents have assigned significant policy responsibilities to their vice presidents. Pictured here is the official seal of the Vice President of the United States.

he redefined the office by assigning important policy duties to his vice president and relocating him to an office in the White House. The vice president is now entrenched in the White House and is supported by a staff of policy advisors (the Office of the Vice President).

The Executive Office of the President (EOP)

The key staff organization is the Executive Office of the President (EOP), created by Congress in 1939 to provide the president with the staff necessary to coordinate the activities of the executive branch.[21] The EOP has since become the command center of the presidency. Its exact configuration is determined by the president, but some of its organizational units have carried over from one president to the next. These include the White House Office (WHO), which consists of the president's closest personal advisors; the Office of Management and Budget (OMB), which consists of experts who formulate and administer the federal budget; and the National Security Council (NSC), which advises the president on foreign and military affairs.

Of the EOP's organizational units, the **White House Office (WHO)** serves the president most directly. The WHO includes the Communications Office, the Office of the Press Secretary, the Office of the Counsel to the President, and the Office of Legislative Affairs. As these labels suggest, the WHO consists of the president's personal assistants, including top advisors, press agents, legislative and group liaison aides, and special assistants for domestic and international policy. These individuals tend to be skilled at developing political strategy and communicating with the public, the media, and other officials. They are among the most powerful individuals in Washington because of their proximity to the president.

Most of the EOP's other organizational units are staffed by policy experts. These include economists, legal analysts, national security specialists, and others. The president is advised on economic issues, for example, by the National Economic Council (NEC).

The Cabinet and Agency Appointees

The heads of the fifteen executive departments, such as the Department of Defense and the Department of Agriculture, constitute the president's **cabinet**. They are appointed by the president, subject to confirmation by the Senate. Although the cabinet once served as the president's main advisory group, it has not played this role in nearly a century. As issues have increased in complexity, presidents have relied for advice on presidential advisors rather than on the cabinet as a whole. Nevertheless, cabinet members, as individuals who head major departments, are important figures in any administration. The president selects them for their prominence in politics, business, government, or the professions.[22] In every administration, a few of them, usually the attorney general or the secretary of state, defense, or treasury, become trusted advisors.

In addition to cabinet secretaries, the president appoints the heads and top deputies of federal agencies and commissions, as well as the nearly two hundred ambassadors. There are more than two thousand full-time presidential appointees, a much larger number than are appointed by the chief executive of any other democracy.[23] About half of these appointees (including ambassadors and agency heads, but not the president's personal advisors) are subject to Senate confirmation. Reflecting the increased level of party polarization in Washington, presidential nominees in recent years were increasingly blocked or slowed down by Senate filibusters. In 2013 the Senate Democratic majority used a parliamentary move to eliminate use of the filibuster in the case of confirmations.

The Problem of Control

Although the president's appointees are a major asset, their large number poses a control problem for the president. President Truman kept a wall chart in the Oval Office that listed the more than one hundred officials who reported directly to him. He often told visitors, "I cannot even see all of these men, let alone actually study what they are doing."[24] Since Truman's time, the number of bureaucratic agencies has more than doubled, compounding the problem of presidential control over subordinates.[25]

The president's problem is most severe in the case of appointees who work in the departments and agencies. Their offices are located outside the White House, and their loyalty is sometimes split between a desire to promote the president's goals and an interest in promoting their own agenda. During Obama's first term, Steven Chu, his secretary of energy, accompanied the president on a visit to the island nation of Trinidad and Tobago for a Summit of the Americas meeting. Chu was not scheduled to speak at the summit but pleaded for the opportunity to do so. Given the chance, he spoke about his own issue, which was climate change, rather than about Obama's issue, which was economic development. He upset the host nation by saying: "The island states . . . some of them will disappear." Afterward, White House chief of staff Rahm Emanuel told a staff member, "If you don't kill [Chu], I'm going to." It was one of several

Presidents rely on trusted advisors in making critical policy decisions. During the Cuban missile crisis in 1962, this group of advisors to President John F. Kennedy helped him decide on a naval blockade as a means of forcing the Soviet Union to withdraw its missiles from Cuba.

missteps by Chu, who, at the start of Obama's second term, was replaced as energy secretary.[26]

Lower-level appointees within the departments and agencies pose a different type of problem. The president rarely, if ever, sees them, and many of them are political novices (most have less than two years of government or policy experience). They are sometimes "captured" by the agency in which they work because they depend on the agency's career bureaucrats for advice and information.

In short, the modern presidential office is a mixed benefit. Although presidential appointees enable presidents to extend their influence into every executive agency, these appointees do not always act in ways that serve the president's interest. (The subject of presidential control of the executive branch is discussed further in Chapter 13.)

FACTORS IN PRESIDENTIAL LEADERSHIP

All presidents are expected to provide national leadership, but not all presidents are equally adept at it.[27] Strong presidents have typically had a clear sense of where they want to lead the country and an ability to communicate that vision effectively.[28] Ronald Reagan had this capacity, which helped him to alter the direction of domestic and foreign policy. Jimmy Carter lacked it. In what was arguably the most important speech of his presidency, Carter said that Americans were having "a crisis of confidence" and needed to adopt a more positive attitude. At a time when Americans were struggling with rising inflation and unemployment and were seeking strong leadership, Carter criticized them for worrying about their future.

Although effective leadership is a key to presidential success, it is only one component. The president operates within a system of separate institutions that share power (see "How the U.S. Differs"). Significant presidential action typically depends on the approval of Congress, the cooperation of the bureaucracy, and sometimes the acceptance of the judiciary. Because other officials have their own priorities, presidents do not always get their way. Congress in particular—more than the courts or the bureaucracy—holds the key to presidential success. Without congressional authorization and funding, most presidential proposals are nothing but ideas, empty of action. Dwight D. Eisenhower, whose personal integrity made him perhaps the most trusted president of the twentieth century, had a keen awareness of the need to win over Congress. "I'll tell you what leadership is," he said. "It's persuasion, and conciliation, and education, and patience. It's long, slow, tough work."[29]

Whether a president's initiatives succeed depends substantially on several factors, including the force of circumstance, the stage of the president's term, the nature of the particular issue, the president's support in Congress, and the president's standing with the American people. The remainder of this chapter discusses the importance of these factors.

The Force of Circumstance

During his first months in office and in the midst of the Great Depression, Franklin D. Roosevelt accomplished the most sweeping changes in domestic policy in the nation's history. Congress moved quickly to pass nearly every New Deal initiative he proposed. In 1964 and 1965, Lyndon Johnson pushed landmark civil rights and social welfare legislation through Congress on the strength of the civil rights movement, the legacy of the assassinated President Kennedy, and large Democratic majorities in the House and Senate. When Ronald Reagan assumed the presidency in 1981, inflation and high unemployment had greatly weakened the national economy and created a mood for change, enabling Reagan to persuade Congress to enact some of the most substantial taxing and spending changes in history.

HOW THE U.S. DIFFERS
POLITICAL THINKING THROUGH COMPARISONS

Systems of Executive Leadership

The United States instituted a presidential system in 1789 as part of its constitutional checks and balances. This form of executive leadership was not copied in Europe. European democracies adopted parliamentary systems, in which executive leadership rests with a prime minister, who is a member of the legislature.

The policy leadership of a president differs from that of a prime minister. As the head of a separate branch of government, a president does not share executive authority but is dependent on the legislative branch for support. In contrast, a prime minister shares executive leadership with a cabinet, but once agreement within the cabinet is reached, he or she is usually guaranteed the legislative support necessary to carry out policy initiatives.

On the other hand, the American president has the advantage of being both the head of state and the head of government. Most democracies divide the executive office between a head of state, who is the ceremonial leader, and the head of government, who is the policy leader. In Great Britain, these positions are filled by the queen and the prime minister, respectively. In Germany, the head of state is the president, chosen by a special commission, while the head of government is the chancellor, chosen by the legislature. A disadvantage of the American system is that the president must devote considerable time to ceremonial functions, such as hosting visiting heads of state. An offsetting advantage is that the president alone is the center of national attention.

Q: Which executive leadership do you think is preferable—a presidential system, in which the chief executive heads only the executive branch, or a parliamentary system, in which the chief executive heads both the executive and the legislative branches? Why?

From presidencies such as these has come the popular impression that presidents single-handedly decide national policy. However, each of these presidencies was marked by a special set of circumstances—a decisive election victory that gave added force to the president's leadership, a compelling national problem that convinced Congress and the public that bold presidential action was needed, and a president who was mindful of what was expected and championed policies consistent with expectations.

When conditions are favorable, the power of the presidency is remarkable. The problem for most presidents is that they serve at a time when conditions are not conducive to ambitious goals. Political scientist Erwin Hargrove suggests that presidential influence depends largely on circumstance.[30] Some presidents serve in periods when resources are scarce or when important problems are surfacing in American society but have not yet reached a critical stage. Such situations, Hargrove notes, work against the president's efforts to accomplish significant policy changes. In 1994, reflecting on the constraints of budget deficits and other factors beyond his control, President Clinton said he had no choice but "to play the hand that history had dealt" him. Even Abraham Lincoln admitted as much: "I claim not to have controlled events, but confess plainly that events controlled me."[31]

The Stage of the President's Term

If conditions conducive to great accomplishments occur irregularly, it is nonetheless the case that nearly every president has favorable moments. Such moments often come during the first months in office. Most newly elected presidents enjoy a **honeymoon period** during which Congress, the press, and the public anticipate initiatives from the Oval Office and are more predisposed than usual to support them. Most presidents propose more new programs in their first year in office than in any subsequent year.[32] Later in their terms, presidents may have run out of good ideas or depleted their political resources; meanwhile, the momentum of their election is gone, and sources of opposition have emerged. Even successful presidents like Johnson and Reagan had weak records in their final years. Franklin D. Roosevelt began his presidency with a remarkable period of achievement—the celebrated "Hundred Days"—that he was unable to duplicate later in his presidency.

An irony of the presidency, then, is that presidents are often most powerful when they are least experienced—during their first months in office. These months can, as a result, be times of risk as well as times of opportunity. An example is the Bay of Pigs fiasco during the first year of John F. Kennedy's presidency, in which a U.S.-backed invasion force of anticommunist Cubans was easily defeated by Fidel Castro's army.

The Nature of the Issue: Foreign or Domestic

In the 1960s, political scientist Aaron Wildavsky wrote that the nation has only one president but two presidencies: one domestic and one foreign.[33] Wildavsky was referring to Congress's greater deference to presidential leadership on foreign policy than on domestic policy. He had in mind the broad leeway Congress had granted Truman, Eisenhower, Kennedy, and Johnson in their foreign policies. Wildavsky's thesis is now regarded as a somewhat time-bound conception of presidential influence. Today, many of the same factors that affect a president's domestic policy success, such as the partisan composition of Congress, also affect foreign policy success.

Nevertheless, presidents still have an edge when the issue is foreign policy, because they have more authority to act on their own and are more likely to have congressional support.[34] The president is recognized by other nations as America's voice in world affairs, and members of Congress will sometimes defer to the president in order to maintain America's credibility abroad. In some cases, presidents can literally dictate the terms of foreign policy. In 2014, acting on his own authority, Obama imposed economic sanctions on close acquaintances of Russian president Vladimir Putin for Russia's takeover of the Crimean peninsula and its support for Russian separatists in eastern Ukraine. In the same year, acting again on his own authority, he ordered air strikes on Islamic State militants operating in Syria and Iraq.

Presidents also acquire leverage in foreign and defense policy because of their special relationship with the defense, diplomatic, and intelligence agencies. Other agencies are sometimes more responsive to Congress than to the president. The Department of Agriculture, for example, relies more heavily on the support of farm-state senators and representatives than on the president's backing. The defense, diplomatic, and intelligence agencies are a different matter. Their missions closely parallel the president's constitutional authority as commander in chief and chief diplomat. In the period before the Iraq invasion in 2003, for example, U.S. intelligence agencies provided assessments that bolstered President Bush's assertion that Iraq's weapons systems threatened American interests. Only later did Congress discover that some of the assessments were tailored to fit Bush's claims about Iraq's capabilities.

A president's domestic policy initiatives usually encounter stiffer opposition than their foreign policy efforts. The Republican and Democratic parties differ sharply in their domestic policy philosophies, and there are strong interest groups on each side of nearly every important

Presidents typically have had more influence over foreign policy than domestic policy. Few presidencies illustrate the point more clearly than that of George W. Bush, who persuaded Congress and a majority of the public to back his plan to invade Iraq, even though U.S. troops were already fighting in Afghanistan.

domestic issue. Attempts at significant action in the domestic policy realm invariably activate contending forces. A case in point is President Obama's effort to overhaul the nation's agricultural policy. Obama promised it would be done in 2013 but the legislative battle dragged on into 2014, as members of Congress and lobbying groups with competing interests fought over the bill's particulars. When the bill finally emerged from Congress, it contained provisions that nearly led Obama to veto it. In the end, he signed the farm bill, recognizing that he had virtually no chance at getting Congress to pass a bill that was more to his liking.

Relations with Congress

Although the power of the presidency is not nearly as substantial as some Americans assume, the president's ability to set the national agenda is unrivaled. Whenever the president directs attention to a particular issue, members of Congress take notice. But will they take action? The answer is sometimes yes and sometimes no, depending in part on whether the president takes their interests into account.

Seeking Cooperation from Congress   As the center of national attention, presidents can start to believe that their ideas should prevail over those of Congress. This reasoning invariably gets the president into trouble. Jimmy Carter had not held national office before he was elected president in 1976 and lacked a sense of how Washington operates.[35] Soon after taking office, Carter cut from his budget nineteen public works projects that he regarded as a waste of taxpayers' money, ignoring the determination of members of Congress to obtain federally funded projects for their constituents. Carter's action set the tone for a conflict-ridden relationship with Congress.

To get the help of members of Congress, the president must respond to their interests.[36] The most basic fact about presidential leadership is that it takes place in the context of a system of divided powers. Although the president gets most of the attention, Congress has lawmaking authority, and presidents need its cooperation to achieve their legislative goals. In 2011, after the so-called "super committee"—a bipartisan committee of House and Senate members—failed to reach agreement on a plan to reduce the federal budget deficit, President Obama was criticized for not forcing the committee into a decision. This criticism ignored the fact that members of Congress are separately elected and serve in a different branch of government. Presidents can cajole them but cannot require them to act. President Truman expressed the situation in blunt terms: "The people can never understand why the President does not use his supposedly great power to make 'em behave. Well, all the President is, is a glorified public relations man who spends his time flattering, kissing and kicking people to do what they are supposed to do anyway."[37]

Even the president's most direct legislative tool, the veto, has limits. Congress can seldom muster the two-thirds majority in each chamber required to override a presidential veto, so the threat of a veto can make Congress bend to the president's demands. Yet, as presidential scholar Richard Neustadt argued, the veto is as much a sign of presidential weakness as it is a sign of strength, because it arises when Congress refuses to accept the president's ideas.[38]

Congress is a constituency that all presidents must serve if they expect to have its support. Neustadt concluded that presidential power, at base, is "the power to persuade."[39] Like any singular notion of presidential power, Neustadt's has limitations. Presidents at times have the power to command and to threaten. They can also appeal directly to the American people as a means of pressuring Congress. But Congress can never be taken for granted. Theodore Roosevelt expressed the wish that he could "be the president and Congress too for just ten minutes." Roosevelt would then have had the power to enact as well as to propose legislation.

Benefiting from Partisan Support in Congress   For most presidents, the next best thing to being "Congress, too" is to have a Congress loaded with members of their own party. The sources of division within Congress are many. Legislators from urban and rural areas, wealthier and poorer constituencies, and different regions of the country often have conflicting policy views. To obtain majority support in Congress, the president must find ways to overcome these divisions.

No source of unity is more important to presidential success than partisanship. Presidents are far more likely to succeed when their own party controls Congress (see Figure 12-1). Between 1954 and 1992, each Republican president—Eisenhower, Nixon, Ford, Reagan, and Bush—had to contend with a Democratic majority in one or both houses of Congress. Congress passed a smaller percentage of the initiatives backed by each of these presidents than those supported by any Democratic president of the period: Kennedy, Johnson, or Carter. In Clinton's first two

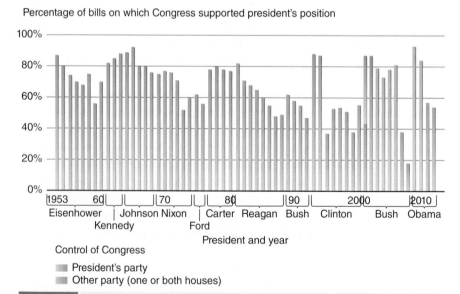

figure 12-1   PERCENTAGE OF BILLS PASSED BY CONGRESS ON WHICH THE PRESIDENT ANNOUNCED A POSITION

In most years, presidents have been supported by Congress on a majority of policy issues on which they have taken a stand. Nevertheless, presidents fare much better when their party controls Congress than when the other party has a majority in one or both chambers.
Source: Congressional Quarterly Weekly Report, various dates.

years in office, backed by Democratic majorities in the House and Senate, more than 80 percent of the bills that he supported were enacted into law. After Republicans took control of Congress in 1995, Clinton's legislative success rate sank below 40 percent. Obama's success rate followed a similar downward trajectory after Republicans took control of House in the 2011. In his first two years in office, when Democrats controlled both the House and the Senate, Obama's success rate exceeded 85 percent. In 2011, with Republicans holding the House, it dropped to 32 percent and then fell to 20 percent in 2012, one of the lowest rates on record. Without doubt, presidential power depends significantly on which party controls Congress. As the historian Arthur Schlesinger put it: "In the end, arithmetic is decisive."[40] (*Unified government* is the term used to describe the situation where one party controls the presidency and both houses of Congress, whereas *divided government* is used to describe the situation where control is split between the parties.)

Colliding with Congress   On rare occasions, presidents have pursued their goals so zealously that Congress has taken steps to curb their use of power. Congress's ultimate sanction is its constitutional authority to impeach and remove the president from office. The House of Representatives decides by majority vote whether the president should be impeached (placed on trial), and the Senate conducts the trial and then votes on the president's case, with a two-thirds vote required for removal from office. In 1868, Andrew Johnson came within one Senate vote of being removed from office for his opposition to Congress's harsh Reconstruction policies after the Civil War. In 1974, Richard Nixon's resignation halted congressional proceedings on the Watergate affair that almost certainly would have ended in his impeachment and removal from office. In 1998, the House of Representatives impeached President Clinton on grounds he had lied under oath about a sexual relationship with intern Monica Lewinsky. The Senate acquitted Clinton, partly because polls indicated that most Americans did not think Clinton's behavior constituted "treason, bribery, or other high crimes and misdemeanors," which is what the Constitution defines as the grounds for removing a president from office.

The gravity of impeachment action makes it an unsuitable basis for curbing presidential action except in rare instances. More often, Congress has responded legislatively to what it sees as unwarranted assertions of executive power. An example is the Budget Impoundment and Control Act of 1974, which prohibits a president from indefinitely withholding funds that have been appropriated by Congress. The legislation grew out of President Nixon's practice of withholding funds from programs he disliked.

Congress's most ambitious effort to curb presidential power is the War Powers Act. During the Vietnam War, Presidents Johnson and Nixon misled Congress, supplying it with intelligence estimates that painted a falsely optimistic picture of the military situation. Having been told the war was being won, Congress regularly voted to provide the money to keep it going. However, congressional support changed abruptly in 1971 with publication in the *New York Times* of classified documents (the so-called Pentagon Papers) that revealed the Vietnam situation to be more perilous than Johnson and Nixon had said.

In an effort to prevent future presidential wars, Congress in 1973 passed the War Powers Act. Nixon vetoed the measure, but Congress overrode his veto. The act does not prohibit the president from sending troops into combat, but it does require the president to consult with Congress whenever feasible before doing so and requires the president to inform Congress within forty-eight hours of the reason for the military action. The War Powers Act also requires hostilities to end within sixty days unless Congress extends the period. The act gives the president an additional thirty days to withdraw the troops from hostile territory, although Congress can shorten the thirty-day period. Presidents have claimed that the War Powers Act infringes on their constitutional power as commander in chief, but the Supreme Court has not ruled on the issue, leaving open the question of whether it constrains the president's war-making powers.

| POLITICAL THINKING | Can the President's War Power Be Checked? |

The U.S. government is based on a system of checks and balances. In practice, there is an area where the system is deficient— the president's power to wage war. As commander in chief of the armed forces, the president has the authority to order troops into combat. Once this action occurs, Congress is almost powerless to reverse it. Congress could withhold funding for the conflict but in doing so might risk the lives of the troops. The War Powers Act of 1973 is an attempt by Congress to assert more control over America's wars. Do you think Congress should have more say in this area? How do you think the Supreme Court would rule if Congress invoked the War Powers Act and the president defied it, citing as the basis the constitutional provision that establishes the president as commander in chief of the armed forces?

In sum, the effect of presidential efforts to circumvent congressional authority has been to heighten congressional opposition. Even if presidents gain in the short run by acting on their own, they undermine their capacity to lead in the long run if they fail to keep in mind that Congress is a coequal branch of the American governing system.

Public Support

Presidential power rests in part on a claim to national leadership, and the strength of that claim is roughly proportional to the president's public support. **Presidential approval ratings** are predictably high at the start of the president's time in office. When asked in polls whether they "approve or disapprove of how the president is doing his job," most Americans express approval during a president's first months in office. The honeymoon rarely lasts long, however. Difficult issues and adverse developments inevitably cut away at the president's public support, and more than half of post–World War II presidents have left office with an approval rating of less than 50 percent (see Table 12-4).

table 12-4	PERCENTAGE OF PUBLIC EXPRESSING APPROVAL OF PRESIDENT'S PERFORMANCE			
President	Years in Office	Average during Presidency (%)	First-Year Average (%)	Final-Year Average (%)
Harry S Truman	1945–1952	41	63	35
Dwight D. Eisenhower	1953–1960	64	74	62
John F. Kennedy	1961–1963	70	76	62
Lyndon Johnson	1963–1968	55	78	40
Richard Nixon	1969–1974	49	63	24
Gerald Ford	1974–1976	46	75	48
Jimmy Carter	1977–1980	47	68	46
Ronald Reagan	1981–1988	53	58	57
George H. W. Bush	1989–1992	61	65	40
Bill Clinton	1993–2000	57	50	60
George W. Bush	2001–2008	51	68	33
Barack Obama	2009–	—	58	—

Source: Averages compiled from Gallup polls.

With public backing, the president's leadership cannot easily be dismissed by other Washington officials. When the president's public support sinks, however, officials are less inclined to accept that leadership. During his first two years in office, President George W. Bush was bolstered by public backing resulting from his handling of the terrorist attacks of September 11, 2001. In this period, Congress enacted seventeen of his major initiatives, the second highest in such a short period among postwar presidents.[41] However, congressional opposition mounted as Bush's popularity fell in response to a deteriorating economy and a worsening of the Iraq conflict. Among the Bush initiatives rejected by Congress were his social security and immigration reform proposals.

Events and Issues   Public support for the president is conditioned by developments at home and abroad. International crises can result in a patriotic "rally around the flag" response that gives the president wider latitude in deciding policy. For example, when Islamic State militants in 2014 made territorial gains in Syria and Iraq, massacring Christians and moderate Muslims and beheading captives, including Americans, U.S. public opinion on military action in the region shifted. Until then, Americans in large majority had opposed renewed military action in the Middle East, fearing the United States would be drawn back into an Iraq-type war. With public opinion now behind a military response, President Obama ordered a prolonged series of air strikes on the militants.

Economic conditions also play a part in a president's public support. Economic downturns invariably reduce public confidence in the president.[42] Ford, Carter, and the first President Bush lost their reelection bids when their popularity plummeted after the economy dipped. In contrast, Clinton's popularity rose in 1995 and 1996 as the economy strengthened, contributing to his 1996 reelection. In 2012, Obama was helped by an improving economy, though a continuing high rate of unemployment held down his popularity. He won by 3 percentage points, the third smallest reelection margin in the nation's history. The irony, of course, is that presidents do not have all that much control over the economy. If they did, the economy would always be strong.

The Televised Presidency   An advantage that presidents have in their efforts to nurture public support is their access to the media, particularly television. Only the president can expect the networks to provide free airtime to address the nation, and in terms of the amount of news coverage, the presidency receives twice as much news coverage as Congress.

PARTY POLARIZATION 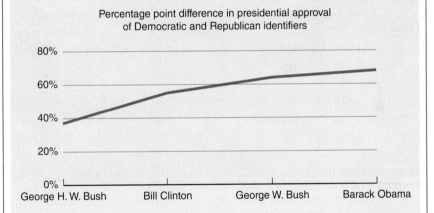	Political Thinking in Conflict

President of All the People, or Just Those of the Same Party?

Increasingly, Americans have diverged sharply in their opinions about the president's performance. As would be expected, Democrats are more likely to approve of the performance of a Democratic president and disapprove of that of a Republican president, while the reverse is true of Republicans. However, the gap in Democrats and Republicans' opinions has widened significantly in recent years. During the three-decade period from Harry Truman's presidency in the late 1940s to Jimmy Carter's presidency in the late 1970s, the difference in the presidential approval level of Republicans and Democrats averaged roughly 35 percent. The difference now exceeds 60 percent, as can be seen in the figure below. As two *Washington Post* reporters said: "We are simply living in an era in which Democrats dislike a Republican president (and Republicans dislike a Democratic one) even before [he] has taken a single official action."

Percentage point difference in presidential approval
of Democratic and Republican identifiers

80%

60%

40%

20%

0%

George H. W. Bush   Bill Clinton   George W. Bush   Barack Obama

Q: Why has the partisan approval gap widened?

A: The reasons are many but one of them is that Democrats and Republicans are now further apart in their opinions on controversial policy issues. When it comes to these issues, presidents usually take positions that are in line with prevailing opinion within their party. As a result, their positions please most of their party's followers while displeasing, even angering, most of the other party's followers.

President Barack Obama speaks at a news conference. Although the presidency offers "a bully pulpit," presidents' rhetorical efforts tend to succeed only when conditions are favorable. When things are going badly, presidents' news coverage is invariably negative.

Political scientist Samuel Kernell calls it "going public" when the president bypasses bargaining with Congress and promotes "his policies by appealing to the American public for support."[43] Such appeals are at least as old as Theodore Roosevelt's use of the presidency as a "bully pulpit," but they have increased substantially in recent decades. Television has made it easier for presidents to go public with their programs, though the public's response depends partly on the president's rhetorical skill. President Reagan was so adept at the use of television that he was labeled the "Great Communicator." Nevertheless, presidents are unable to control everything that reporters say about them.[44] Journalists are adept at putting their own spin on what political leaders say and generally place a lot more emphasis on adverse developments than on positive ones.

THE ILLUSION OF PRESIDENTIAL GOVERNMENT

Presidents have no choice but to try to counter negative press portrayals by putting their own spin on developments. Such efforts can carry a president only so far, however. No president can fully control his communicated image, and national conditions ultimately have the largest impact on a president's public support. No amount of public relations can disguise adverse developments at home or abroad. Indeed, presidents run a risk by building up their images through public relations. By thrusting themselves into the limelight, presidents contribute to the public's belief that the president is in charge of the national government, a perception political scientist Hugh Heclo calls "the illusion of presidential government."[45] If they are as powerful as they project themselves to be, they will be held responsible for policy failures as well as policy successes.

Because the public's expectations are high, presidents get too much credit when things go well and too much blame when things go badly. Therein rests an irony of the presidential office. More than from any constitutional grant, more than from any statute, and more than from any crisis, presidential power derives from the president's position as the sole official who can claim to represent the entire American public. Yet because presidential power rests on a popular base, it erodes when public support declines. The irony is that the presidential office typically grows weaker as problems mount, which is the time when strong presidential leadership is needed most.[46]

SUMMARY

The presidency has become a much stronger office than the framers envisioned. The Constitution grants the president substantial military, diplomatic, legislative, and executive powers, and in each case the president's authority has increased measurably over the nation's history. Underlying this change is the president's position as the one leader chosen by the whole nation and as the sole head of the executive branch. These features of the office have enabled presidents to claim broad authority in response to the increased demands placed on the federal government by changing global and national conditions.

During the course of American history, the presidential selection process has been altered in ways intended to make it more responsive to the preferences of ordinary people. Today, the electorate has a vote not only in the general election but also in the selection of party nominees. To gain nomination, a presidential hopeful must win the support of the electorate in state primaries and open caucuses. Once nominated, the candidates are eligible to receive federal funds for their general election campaigns, which today are based on Internet and televised appeals.

Although the campaign tends to personalize the presidency, the responsibilities of the modern presidency far exceed any president's personal capacities. To meet their obligations, presidents have surrounded themselves with large staffs of advisors, policy experts, and managers. These staff members enable the president to extend control over the executive branch while at the same time providing the information necessary for policymaking. All recent presidents have discovered, however, that their control of staff resources is incomplete and that some things that others do on their behalf can work against what they are trying to accomplish.

As sole chief executive and the nation's top elected leader, presidents can always expect that their policy and leadership efforts will receive attention. However, other institutions, particularly Congress, have the authority to make presidential leadership effective. No president has come close to winning approval of all the programs he has placed before Congress, and presidents' records of success have varied considerably. The factors in a president's success include whether national conditions that require strong leadership from the White House are present and whether the president's party has a majority in Congress.

Presidential success stems from the backing of the American people. Recent presidents have made extensive use of the media to build public support for their programs, yet they have had difficulty maintaining that support throughout their terms of office. A major reason is that the public expects far more from its presidents than they can deliver.

CRITICAL THINKING ZONE

KEY TERMS

cabinet (*p. 389*)
honeymoon period (*p. 394*)
invisible primary (*p. 380*)
momentum (in campaigns) (*p. 380*)
open party caucuses (*p. 379*)

presidential approval ratings (*p. 401*)
stewardship theory (*p. 375*)
unit rule (*p. 383*)
Whig theory (*p. 375*)
White House Office (WHO) (*p. 389*)

APPLYING THE ELEMENTS OF CRITICAL THINKING

Conceptualizing: Define the Whig theory of the presidency and the stewardship theory. How did the increase in the federal government's policy responsibilities and the expanded role of the United States in world affairs contribute to the emergence of the powerful presidency suggested by the stewardship theory?

Synthesizing: Contrast the pre-1972 methods of selecting presidential nominees with the post-1972 method, noting particularly the public's increased role in the selection process.

Analyzing: Why is presidential power "conditional"—that is, why is it affected so substantially by circumstance, the nature of the issue, the makeup of Congress, and popular support? (The separation of powers should be part of your answer.)

EXTRA CREDIT

A Book Worth Reading: Richard E. Neustadt, *Presidential Power and the Modern Presidents*. New York: Free Press, 1990. A winner of multiple awards, this book is the classic analysis of the nature of presidential power. Although now somewhat dated in its arguments, it has had, as one leading political scientist put it, "a greater effect than any other book about a political institution."

A Website Worth Visiting: www.ipl.org/div/potus. A site that profiles the nation's presidents, their cabinet officers, and key events during their time in office.

PARTICIPATE!

Consider writing a letter or sending an e-mail to the president or a top presidential appointee that expresses your opinion on an issue that is currently the object of executive action. You can inform yourself about the administration's policy or stance on the issue through the website of the White House (www.whitehouse.gov) or of the agency in question (for example, the State Department's site, www.state.gov).

13
CHAPTER

THE FEDERAL BUREAUCRACY: ADMINISTERING THE GOVERNMENT

> " From a purely technical point of view, a bureaucracy is capable of attaining the highest degree of efficiency, and is in this sense formally the most rational known means of exercising authority over human beings. "
>
> MAX WEBER[1]

On April 20, 2010, as the *Deepwater Horizon* was drilling an exploratory oil well nearly a mile deep in the Gulf of Mexico, methane gas shot out from the drilling pipe and exploded, engulfing the oil platform in flames, killing eleven workers and forcing the rest to jump into the rig's lifeboats. Two days later, still aflame, the *Deepwater Horizon* sank, collapsing the drilling pipe, which sent oil from the well gushing into the Gulf. Nearly three months elapsed before the oil well could be capped, resulting in the worst environmental disaster in the nation's history. The resulting oil spill forced closure of much of the Gulf to fishing, damaged hundreds of miles of beaches and wetlands, and killed unknown quantities of marine life.

The U.S. government blamed the disaster on the oil firm BP, which owned the drilling rights and was supervising the ill-fated drilling operation. But the government itself had a hand in the disaster. Oversight of offshore drilling was the responsibility of the Minerals Management Service (MMS), a bureau within the Department of the Interior. MMS had been lax, or worse, in its responsibilities. Rather than closely regulating offshore drilling, top MMS managers had given oil companies wide latitude in meeting safety and environmental standards. When this information became known in the days following the sinking of the *Deepwater Horizon*, MMS's top officials were forced to resign and a reorganization of MMS was undertaken. In announcing this action, President Barack Obama said: "For a decade or more, the cozy relationship between the oil companies and the federal agency was allowed to go unchecked. That allowed drilling permits to be issued in exchange not for safety plans, but assurances of safety from oil companies. That cannot and will not happen anymore."

Government agencies are seldom in the headlines unless something goes wrong, as in the case of MMS. Nor do federal agencies rank high in public esteem. Even though most Americans respond favorably to personal encounters with the federal bureaucracy (as, for example, when a senior citizen applies for social security), they have a low opinion of the bureaucracy as a whole. A recent Pew Research Center poll found, for example, that roughly two-thirds of Americans see the bureaucracy as "inefficient and wasteful."

Yet, ambitious programs like space exploration, social security, interstate highways, and universal postal service would be impossible without the federal bureaucracy. In fact, the bureaucratic form of organization is found wherever there is a need to manage large numbers of people and tasks. Its usefulness is clear from the fact that virtually every large private organization is also a bureaucracy, although such organizations typically operate by a different standard than do most public organizations. Efficiency is the chief goal of private organizations but is only sometimes the goal of public organizations. The most efficient way to administer government loans to college students, for instance, would be to give money to the first students who apply and then shut down the program when the money runs out. College loan programs, like many other government programs, operate on the principles of fairness and need, which require that each application be judged on its merit.

In formal terms, **bureaucracy** is a system of organization and control that is based on three principles: hierarchical authority, job specialization, and formalized rules. These features are the reason bureaucracy, as a form

As one of thousands of services provided by the federal bureaucracy, the National Park Service operates the national parks, which host millions of visitors annually.

of organization, is the most efficient means of getting people to work together on tasks of large magnitude. **Hierarchical authority** refers to a chain of command whereby the officials and units at the top of a bureaucracy have authority over those in the middle, who in turn control those at the bottom. Hierarchy speeds action by reducing conflict over the power to make decisions: those higher in the organization have authority over those below them. **Job specialization** refers to explicitly defined duties for each job position and to a precise division of labor within the organization. Specialization yields efficiency because each individual concentrates on a particular job and becomes proficient at the tasks it involves. **Formalized rules** are the established procedures and regulations by which a bureaucracy conducts its operations. Formalized rules enable workers to make quick and consistent judgments because decisions are based on preset rules rather than on a case-by-case basis.

The noted German sociologist Max Weber (1864–1920) was the first scholar to systematically analyze the bureaucratic form of organization. Although Weber admired the bureaucratic form of organization for its efficiency, he recognized that its advantages carried a price. Bureaucrats' actions are dictated by position, specialty, and rule. In the process, they can become insensitive to circumstance. They often stick to the rules even when it's clear that bending them would produce a better result. "Specialists without spirit," was Weber's unflattering description of the bureaucratic mindset.[2]

This chapter examines both the need for bureaucracy and the problems associated with it. The chapter describes the bureaucracy's responsibilities, organizational structure, and management practices. The chapter also explains the "politics" of the bureaucracy. Although the three constitutional branches of government impose a degree of accountability on the bureaucracy, its sheer size confounds their efforts to control it fully. The main points discussed in this chapter are:

- *Bureaucracy is an inevitable consequence of complexity and scale.* Modern government could not function without a large bureaucracy. Through authority, specialization, and rules, bureaucracy provides a means of managing thousands of tasks and employees.

- *Bureaucrats naturally take an "agency point of view," seeking to promote their agency's programs and power.* They do this through their expert knowledge, support from clientele groups (those that benefit from the agency's programs), and backing by Congress or the president.

- *Although agencies are subject to oversight by the president, Congress, and the judiciary, bureaucrats exercise considerable power in their own right.*

ORIGIN AND STRUCTURE OF THE FEDERAL BUREAUCRACY

The federal bureaucracy was initially small (three thousand employees in 1800, for instance). The federal government's role was confined largely to defense and foreign affairs, currency and interstate commerce, and the delivery of the mail. In the latter part of the 1800s, the bureaucracy began to grow rapidly in size (see Figure 13-1), largely because economic growth was generating new demands on government. Farmers were among the groups clamoring for help, and Congress in 1889 created the Department of Agriculture. Business and labor interests also pressed their claims, and Congress in 1903 established the Department of Commerce and Labor. (A decade later, the department was split into separate commerce and labor departments.) The biggest spurt in the bureaucracy's growth, however, took place in the 1930s. Franklin D. Roosevelt's New Deal included creation of the Securities and Exchange Commission (SEC), the Social Security Administration (SSA), the Federal Deposit Insurance Corporation (FDIC), the Tennessee Valley Authority (TVA), and numerous other federal agencies. Three decades later, Lyndon Johnson's Great Society initiatives, which thrust the federal government into policy areas traditionally dominated by the states, resulted in the creation of additional

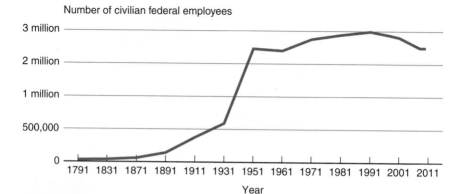

figure 13-1 NUMBER OF FULL-TIME FEDERAL EMPLOYEES

The federal bureaucracy grew slowly until the 1930s, when an explosive growth began in the number of programs that required ongoing administration by the federal government.
Sources: Historical Statistics of the United States and *Statistical Abstract of the United States, 1986,* 322; recent figures from U.S. Office of Personnel Management. Figure excludes military personnel.

federal agencies, including the Department of Transportation and the Department of Housing and Urban Development.

Although the federal bureaucracy is sometimes portrayed as an entity that grows larger by the year, the facts say otherwise. Federal employment today is at roughly the same level as it was fifty years ago, despite the fact that the U.S. population has nearly doubled in size since then.

Types of Federal Agencies

At present, the U.S. federal bureaucracy has roughly 2.5 million full-time employees, who have responsibility for administering thousands of programs. The president and Congress get far more attention in the news, but the federal bureaucracy has a more direct impact on Americans' daily lives. It performs a wide range of functions; for example, it delivers the mail, oversees the national forests, administers social security, enforces environmental protection laws, maintains the country's defense systems, provides foodstuffs for school lunch programs, and regulates the stock markets.

The U.S. federal bureaucracy is organized along policy lines. One agency handles veterans' affairs, another specializes in education, a third is responsible for agriculture, and so on. No two units are exactly alike. Nevertheless, most of them take one of five forms: cabinet department, independent agency, regulatory agency, government corporation, or presidential commission.

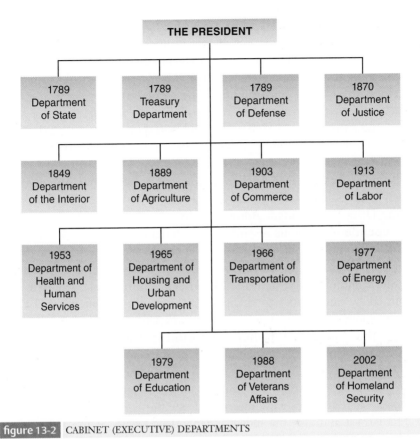

THE PRESIDENT

| 1789 Department of State | 1789 Treasury Department | 1789 Department of Defense | 1870 Department of Justice |

| 1849 Department of the Interior | 1889 Department of Agriculture | 1903 Department of Commerce | 1913 Department of Labor |

| 1953 Department of Health and Human Services | 1965 Department of Housing and Urban Development | 1966 Department of Transportation | 1977 Department of Energy |

| 1979 Department of Education | 1988 Department of Veterans Affairs | 2002 Department of Homeland Security |

figure 13-2 CABINET (EXECUTIVE) DEPARTMENTS

Each executive department is responsible for a general policy area and is headed by a secretary or, in the case of Justice, the attorney general, who serves as a member of the president's cabinet. Shown is each department's year of origin. (The Office of the Attorney General was created in 1789 and was reorganized as the Justice Department in 1870.)

The leading administrative units are the fifteen **cabinet (executive) departments** (see Figure 13-2). Except for the Department of Justice, which is led by the attorney general, the head of each department is its secretary (for example, the secretary of defense), who also serves as a member of the president's cabinet. Cabinet departments vary greatly in their visibility, size, and importance. The Department of State, one of the oldest and most prestigious departments, is also one of the smallest, with approximately 30,000 employees. The smallest with a mere 4,500 employees is the Department of Education. The Department of Defense has the largest budget and workforce, with more than 600,000 civilian employees (apart from the roughly 1.4 million uniformed active service members).

The Department of Health and Human Services has the second largest budget, most of which goes for Medicaid and Medicare payments (but not social security payments, which are handled by the Social Security Administration, an independent agency). The Department of Homeland Security is the newest department, dating from 2002.

Each cabinet department has responsibility for a general policy area, such as defense or law enforcement. This responsibility is carried out within each department by operating units that typically carry the label "bureau," "agency," "division," or "service." The Department of Justice, for example, has thirteen such operating units, including the Federal Bureau of Investigation (FBI), the Civil Rights Division, the Tax Division, and the Drug Enforcement Administration (DEA).

Independent agencies resemble the cabinet departments but typically have a narrower area of responsibility. They include organizations such as the Central Intelligence Agency (CIA) and the National Aeronautics and Space Administration (NASA). The heads of these agencies are appointed by and report to the president but are not members of the cabinet. Some independent agencies exist apart from cabinet departments because their placement within a department would pose symbolic or practical problems. NASA, for example, could conceivably be located in the Department of Defense, but such positioning would suggest that the space program exists solely for military purposes and not also for civilian purposes, such as space exploration and satellite communication.

The largest and also the oldest independent agency is the U.S. Postal Service, with more than half a million career employees. Established at the nation's founding, the postal service delivers a first-class letter for the same low price to any postal address in the United States, a policy made possible by its status as a government agency. If the postal service were a private firm, the price of a first-class stamp would vary by location, with remote areas of states like Wyoming and the Dakotas paying extremely high rates.

Regulatory agencies are created when Congress recognizes the need for ongoing regulation of a particular economic activity. Examples of such agencies are the Securities and Exchange Commission (SEC), which oversees the stock and bond markets, and the Environmental Protection Agency (EPA), which regulates industrial pollution. In addition to their administrative function, regulatory agencies have a legislative function and a judicial function. They develop lawlike regulations and then judge whether individuals or organizations are complying with them. The EPA, for example, can impose fines and other penalties on business firms that violate environmental regulations.

HOW THE 50 STATES DIFFER

POLITICAL THINKING THROUGH COMPARISONS

The Size of State Bureaucracies

Although the federal bureaucracy is criticized as being "too big," it is smaller on a per-capita basis than all the state bureaucracies. There are 83 federal employees for every 1,000 Americans. The Illinois bureaucracy, with 103 state employees per 1,000 residents, is the smallest. Hawaii has the largest—428 state employees per 1,000 residents.

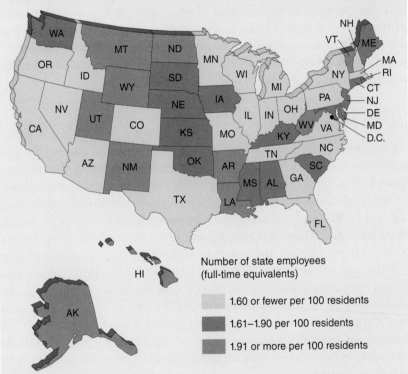

Number of state employees (full-time equivalents)

◻ 1.60 or fewer per 100 residents

◼ 1.61–1.90 per 100 residents

◼ 1.91 or more per 100 residents

Source: U.S. Census Bureau, 2014.

Q: What typifies the states with larger per-capita bureaucracies?

A: In general, the less populous states, especially those that cover a large geographical area, have larger bureaucracies on a per-capita basis. This pattern reflects the fact that a state, whatever its population or area, must provide basic services (such as highway maintenance and policing).

Government corporations are similar to private corporations in that they charge for their services and are governed by a board of directors. However, government corporations receive federal funding to pay for some of their operating expenses, and their directors are appointed by the president with Senate approval. Government corporations include the Federal Deposit Insurance Corporation (FDIC), which insures personal savings accounts against bank failures, and the National Railroad Passenger Corporation (Amtrak), which provides passenger rail service.

Presidential commissions provide advice to the president. Some of them are permanent bodies; examples include the Commission on Civil Rights and the Commission on Fine Arts. Other presidential commissions are temporary and disband after making recommendations on specific issues. An example is the National Commission on Fiscal Responsibility and Reform (popularly known as the Simpson-Bowles Commission from the names of its co-chairs, Alan Simpson and Erskine Bowles), which was created by President Obama in 2010 to propose policies that would reduce the nation's budget deficit.

Federal Employment

The roughly 2.5 million full-time civilian employees of the federal government include professionals who bring their expertise to the problems involved in governing a large and complex society, service workers who perform such tasks as the typing of correspondence and the delivery of mail, and middle and top managers who supervise the work of the various federal agencies. Most civil servants are hired through the government's **merit system,** whereby they have to score high on a competitive exam (as in the case of postal service, civil service, and foreign service employees) or have specialized training (as in the case of lawyers, engineers, and scientists). The merit system is overseen by two independent agencies. The Office of Personnel Management supervises the hiring and job classification of federal employees. The Merit Service Protection Board hears appeals from career civil servants who have been fired or face other disciplinary action.

The merit system is an alternative to the **patronage system** that governed federal employment during much of the nineteenth century. Patronage was the postelection practice of filling administrative offices with people who had supported the winning party. In the view of President Andrew Jackson, its chief advocate, the patronage system was a way to tie the administration of government to the people it served. Later presidents extended patronage to all levels of administration without much regard for its impact on the quality of administration, which led critics to label it a **spoils system**—a device for the awarding of government jobs to friends and party hacks. In any case, as the federal government grew in size and complexity, the need for a more skilled workforce emerged. In 1883, Congress passed the Pendleton Act, which established a merit system for certain positions. By 1885, roughly 10 percent of federal positions were filled on a merit basis. The proportion increased sharply when the Progressives championed the merit system as a way of eliminating partisan corruption (see Chapter 2). By 1920, as the Progressive Era was concluding, more than 70 percent of federal employees were merit appointees. Today, they make up more than 90 percent of the federal workforce.[3] (Among the nonmerit employees are patronage appointees, who include those holding presidential and congressional staff positions—see Chapters 11 and 12.)

The administrative objective of the merit system is **neutral competence**.[4] A merit-based bureaucracy is "competent" in the sense that employees are hired and retained on the basis of their skills, and it is "neutral" in the sense that employees are not partisan appointees and are expected to be of service to everyone, not just those who support the incumbent president. Although the merit system contributes to impartial and proficient administration, it has its own biases and inefficiencies. Career bureaucrats tend to place their agency's interests ahead of those of other agencies and typically oppose efforts to trim their agency's programs. They are not partisans in a Democratic or Republican sense, but they are partisans in terms of protecting their own agencies, as will be explained more fully later in the chapter.

The large majority of federal employees have a GS (Graded Service) job ranking. The regular civil service rankings range from GS-1 (the lowest rank) to GS-15 (the highest). College graduates who enter the federal service usually start at the GS-5 level, which provides an annual salary of roughly $28,000 for a beginning employee. With a master's degree, employees begin at level GS-9 with a salary of roughly $42,000 a year. Federal employees' salaries increase with rank and length of service. Although higher-level federal employees are underpaid in comparison with their counterparts in the private sector, while those in some lower-level jobs are comparatively overpaid, federal workers receive better fringe benefits—including full health insurance, secure retirement plans, and substantial vacation time and sick leave—than do most private-sector employees.

Federal employees can form labor unions, but their unions by law have limited scope; the government has full control of job assignments, compensation, and promotion. Moreover, the Taft-Hartley Act of 1947 prohibits strikes by federal employees and permits the firing of striking workers. When federal air traffic controllers went on strike anyway in 1981, President Reagan fired them. There are also limits on the partisan activities of civil servants. The Hatch Act of 1939 prohibited them from holding key jobs in election campaigns. Congress relaxed this prohibition in 1993, although some high-ranking administrators are still barred from taking such positions.

THE BUDGETARY PROCESS

The Constitution mentions executive agencies but does not grant them authority. Their authority derives from grants of power to the three constitutional branches: Congress, the president, and the courts. Of special importance to executive agencies is the **budgetary process**—the process through which annual federal spending and revenue decisions are made. It is no exaggeration to say that agencies live and die by their budgets. No agency or program can exist without funding.

Agencies play an active role in the budgetary process, but the elected branches have final authority. The Constitution assigns Congress the power to tax and spend, but the president, as chief executive, also has a major role in determining the budget (see Chapter 12). The budgetary process involves give-and-take between Congress and the president as each tries to influence how federal funding will be distributed among various agencies and programs.[5] From beginning to end, the budgetary process lasts a year and a half (see Figure 13-3).

The President and Agency Budgets

The budgetary process begins in the executive branch when the president, in consultation with the Office of Management and Budget (OMB), establishes general budget guidelines. OMB is part of the Executive Office of the President (see Chapter 12) and takes its directives from the president. Hundreds of agencies are covered by the budget, and OMB uses the president's directives to issue guidelines for each agency's budget preparations. Each agency, for example, is assigned a budget ceiling that it cannot exceed in developing its budget proposal.

The agencies receive their guidelines in the spring and then work through the summer to create a detailed agency budget, taking into account their existing programs and new proposals. Agency budgets are then submitted to OMB in September for a full review that invariably

Executive Action

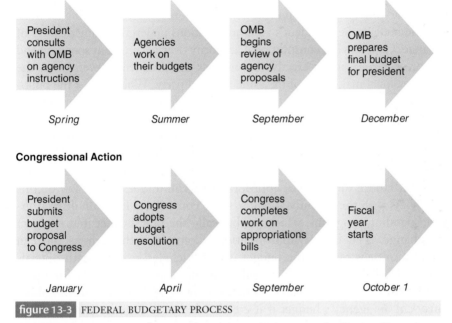

President consults with OMB on agency instructions	Agencies work on their budgets	OMB begins review of agency proposals	OMB prepares final budget for president
Spring	*Summer*	*September*	*December*

Congressional Action

President submits budget proposal to Congress	Congress adopts budget resolution	Congress completes work on appropriations bills	Fiscal year starts
January	*April*	*September*	*October 1*

figure 13-3 FEDERAL BUDGETARY PROCESS

The budget begins with the president's instructions to the agencies and ends when Congress enacts the budget. The entire process spans about eighteen months.

includes further consultation with each agency and the White House. OMB then finalizes the agency budgets and combines them into the president's budget proposal.

The agencies naturally seek additional funding for their programs, whereas OMB has the job of matching the budget to the president's priorities. However, the president does not have any real say over most of the budget, about two-thirds of which involves mandatory spending. This spending is required by law, as in the case of social security payments to retirees. The president has no authority to suspend or reduce such payments. Accordingly, OMB focuses on the one-third of the budget that involves discretionary spending, which includes spending on defense, foreign aid, education, national parks, space exploration, and highways. In reality, even a large part of this spending is not truly discretionary. No president would slash defense spending to almost nothing or cut off funding for the national parks. The president, then, works on the margins of the budget. In most policy areas, the president will propose a modest spending increase or decrease over the previous year.

Congress and the Agency Budgets

In January, the president's budget is submitted to Congress. During its work on the budget, the president's recommendations undergo varying degrees of change. Congress has constitutional authority over government spending and its priorities are never exactly the same as the president's, even when the congressional majority is of the same political party. When it is of the opposite party, its priorities will differ substantially from those of the president.

Upon reaching Congress, the president's budget proposal goes to the House and Senate budget committees. Their job is to recommend overall spending and revenue levels. Once approved by the full House and Senate, the levels are a constraint on the rest of Congress's work on the budget.

The House and Senate appropriations committees take over at this point. As with the executive branch, these committees focus on discretionary spending programs, which are basically the only budget items subject to change. The House Appropriations Committee through its thirteen subcommittees reviews the budget, which includes hearings with officials from each federal agency. Each subcommittee has responsibility for a particular substantive area, such as defense or agriculture. A subcommittee may cut an agency's budget if it concludes that the agency is overfunded or may increase the budget if it concludes that the agency is underfunded. The subcommittees' recommendations are then reviewed by the House Appropriations Committee as a whole. The budget is also reviewed by the Senate Appropriations Committee and its subcommittees. However, the Senate is a smaller body, and its review of agency requests is less exacting than that of the House. To a degree, the Senate Appropriations Committee serves as a "court of last resort" for agencies that have had their funding requests cut by OMB or by the House Appropriations Committee.

Throughout this process, members of the House and Senate rely on the Congressional Budget Office (CBO), which is the congressional equivalent of OMB. If CBO believes that OMB or an agency has miscalculated the amount of money needed to carry out its mandated programs, it will alert Congress to the discrepancy.

After the House and Senate appropriations committees have completed their work, they submit their recommendations to the full chambers for a vote. If approved by a majority in the House and in the Senate, differences in the Senate and House versions are then reconciled in conference committee (see Chapter 11). The reconciled version of the budget is then voted upon in the House and Senate and, if approved, is sent to the president to sign or veto. The threat of a presidential veto can be enough to persuade Congress to accept many of the president's recommendations.

POLITICAL THINKING	Balanced Budget, Good Idea or Bad Idea?

A constitutional amendment to require a balanced federal budget has been proposed from time to time. The amendment would force lawmakers to bring spending and revenues into line each year. Do you think a balanced budget amendment is a good idea? Would you make an exception in time of war or economic recession? If such an amendment were enacted, what combination of spending cuts and tax increases would you suggest in order to balance the budget? (Even if some politicians say otherwise, every serious analyst who's looked at the issue has concluded that the budget cannot be balanced only by cutting spending or by raising taxes.)

In the end, the budget inevitably reflects both presidential and congressional priorities. Neither branch gets everything it wants, but each branch always gets some of what it seeks.

After the budget has been signed by the president, it takes effect on October 1, the starting date of the federal government's fiscal year. If agreement on the budget has not been reached by October 1, temporary funding legislation is required in order to maintain government operations. In 2013, Democratic and Republican lawmakers could not agree on a budget and missed the October 1 deadline, resulting in a temporary shutdown of nonessential government programs, including the national parks.

POLICY AND POWER IN THE BUREAUCRACY

Administrative agencies' main task is **policy implementation**—that is, the carrying out of decisions made by Congress, the president, and the courts. When a directive is issued by Congress, the president, or the courts, the bureaucracy is charged with executing it. In implementing these decisions, the bureaucracy is constrained by the budget. It cannot spend money on an activity unless Congress has appropriated the necessary funds.

Some of what the bureaucracy does is fairly straightforward, as in the case of delivering the mail, processing government loan applications, and imprisoning those convicted of crime. Yet the bureaucracy sometimes has considerable discretion in implementing policy. Consider the example of the Consumer Financial Protection Bureau (CFPB) that Congress created in 2010 to protect consumers from financial institutions that exploit consumers in the granting of home mortgages, credit cards, and the like. The legislation that created the CFPB instructed the agency to:

- Conduct rulemaking, supervision, and enforcement for federal consumer financial protection laws
- Restrict unfair, deceptive, or abusive acts or practices
- Take consumer complaints
- Promote financial education
- Research consumer behavior
- Monitor financial markets for new risks to consumers

However, the legislation did not spell out in detail how the CFPB was to implement these tasks. What type of enforcement would it conduct? Which unfair practices would it restrict, and how would this be done? What action would be taken on consumer complaints? How would financial education occur? What consumer behaviors would be studied? How would financial markets be monitored and new risks identified? It was left to CFPB bureaucrats to devise the answers to these questions. Such *rulemaking*—determining how a law will work in practice—is the chief way administrative agencies exercise control over policy.[6]

As the CFPB example illustrates, the bureaucracy is far more than an administrative extension of the three branches. Administrative agencies make policy in the process of determining how to implement congressional, presidential, and judicial decisions. FBI agents, for example, pursue organized crime more vigorously than they pursue white-collar crime, even though the law does not say that white-collar crime should be pursued less aggressively.[7] Or consider the U.S. Forest Service, which is required by law to employ a "multiple use" policy of forest land—preserving the forests as an environmental heritage while also opening up the forests for harvesting by lumber companies. The Forest Service's decisions have sometimes favored environmental interests and at other times have favored logging interests.

In the course of their work, administrators also develop policy ideas that they then propose to the White House or Congress. The origin of the Occupational Safety and Health Act is an example. A bureaucrat believed that worker safety was not receiving enough attention and encouraged his brother, a presidential speechwriter, to bring it to the attention of the White House. Department of Labor officials then picked up the issue, as did some labor unions and members of Congress. When the legislation was under consideration by congressional committees,

U.S. Postal Service is regarded by many as the best entity of its kind anywhere. It delivers more mail to more addresses than any other postal service in the world, and it does so inexpensively and without undue delay. Yet, like many other government agencies, it is often criticized as inefficient and inept.

bureaucrats who had pressed for the creation of an occupational safety and health program were among those invited to testify.[8]

In sum, administrators initiate policy, develop it, evaluate it, apply it, and decide whether others are complying with it. The bureaucracy does not simply administer policy. It also *makes* policy.

The Agency Point of View

A key issue about bureaucratic policymaking is the perspective that bureaucrats bring to their decisions. Do they operate from the perspective of the president or do they operate from the perspective of Congress? The answer is that, although bureaucrats are responsive to both of them, they are even more responsive to the needs of the agency in which they work, a perspective called the **agency point of view.** This outlook comes naturally to most high-ranking civil servants. More than 80 percent of top bureaucrats reach their high-level positions by rising through the ranks of the same agency.[9] As one top administrator said when testifying before the House Appropriations Committee, "Mr. Chairman, you would not think it proper for me to be in charge of this work and not be enthusiastic about it . . . would you? I have been in it for thirty years, and I believe in it."[10] One study found, for example, that social welfare administrators are three times as likely as other civil servants to believe that social welfare programs should be a top spending priority.[11]

Professionalism also cements agency loyalties. High-level administrative positions have increasingly been filled by scientists, engineers, lawyers, educators, physicians, and other professionals. Most of them take a job in an agency whose mission they support, as in the case of the aeronautical engineers who work for NASA or the doctors who work for the National Institutes of Health (NIH).

Although the agency point of view distorts government priorities, bureaucrats have little choice but to look out for their agency's interests. The president and members of Congress differ in their constituencies and thus in the agencies to which they are most responsive. Republican and Democratic officials also differ in their priorities, a reality that is never more apparent than when party control of the presidency or Congress changes. Some agencies rise or fall in their level of political support for that reason alone. In sum, if an agency is to operate successfully in America's partisan system of divided power, it must seek support wherever it can find it. If the agency is a low priority for the president, it needs to find backing in Congress. If Republican lawmakers want to cut the agency's programs, it must turn to Democratic lawmakers for help. In other words, agencies are forced to play politics if they want to protect their programs.[12] An agency that sits on the sidelines while other agencies seek support from the White House and Congress is likely to lose out in budget negotiations.

Sources of Bureaucratic Power

In promoting their agency's interests, bureaucrats rely on their specialized knowledge, the support of interests that benefit from their programs, and the backing of the president and Congress.

The Power of Expertise   Most of the policy problems confronting the federal government are extraordinarily complex. Whether the problem relates to space travel or hunger in America, a solution requires deep knowledge of the problem. Much of this expertise is provided by bureaucrats. They spend their careers working in a particular policy area, and many of them have had scientific, technical, or other specialized training (see "How the U.S. Differs").[13] Elected officials, on the other hand, are generalists, none more so than the president, who must deal with dozens of issues. Members of Congress acquire some expertise through their committee work, but most of them lack the time, training, or inclination to become deeply knowledgeable of the issues they handle. It's not surprising that Congress and the president rely heavily on career administrators for policy advice.

All agencies acquire some influence over policy through their careerists' expertise. No matter how simple a policy issue may appear at first, it nearly always has layers of complexity. The recognition that the United States has a trade deficit with China, for example, can be the premise for policy change, but this recognition does not begin to address basic issues such as the form the new policy might take, its probable cost and effectiveness, and its links to other issues, such as America's standing in Asia. Among the officials most likely to understand these issues are the career bureaucrats in the Treasury Department, the Department of State, the Commerce Department, and the Federal Trade Commission.

The Power of Clientele Groups   Most federal agencies were created for the purpose of promoting, protecting, or regulating a particular interest. Indeed, nearly every major interest in society—commerce, labor, agriculture, banking, and so on—has a corresponding federal agency. In most cases, these interests are **clientele groups** in the sense that they benefit directly from the agency's programs. As a result, clientele groups can be counted on to lobby Congress and the president on behalf of the agency when its programs and funding are being reviewed.[14] Even a relatively weak or loosely organized clientele group can be of help to an agency if its programs—and therefore, the group's benefits—are threatened with cuts or elimination. When House Speaker Newt Gingrich threatened in 1995 to "zero out" funding for the Corporation for Public Broadcasting, Congress was inundated by complaints from listeners of National Public Radio (NPR) and viewers of the Public Broadcasting System (PBS) who worried that programs like *Sesame Street* and *All Things Considered* might be canceled. Many of the complaints came from Republicans in rural areas where the local NPR station is a leading source of local news and information. Within a few weeks, Gingrich had retreated from his position, saying that a total funding cut was not what he had in mind.

The relationship between an agency and its clientele group is a reciprocal one. Just as a clientele group can be expected to protect its agency, the agency will work to protect the group.[15] The Department of Agriculture,

HOW THE U.S. DIFFERS
POLITICAL THINKING THROUGH COMPARISONS

Educational Backgrounds of Bureaucrats

To staff its bureaucracy, the U.S. government tends to hire persons with specialized educations to hold specialized jobs. By comparison, Great Britain tends to recruit its bureaucrats from the arts and humanities, on the assumption that general aptitude is the best qualification for detached professionalism. The continental European democracies also emphasize detached professionalism, but in the context of the supposedly impartial application of rules. As a consequence, high-ranking civil servants in Europe tend to have legal educations. The college majors of senior civil servants in the United States and other democracies reflect these tendencies.

College major of senior civil servants

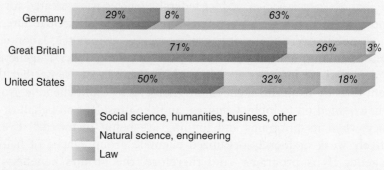

	Social science, humanities, business, other
	Natural science, engineering
	Law

Q: Why might the hiring pattern for the U.S. bureaucracy make it more likely that civil servants in the United States will take an agency point of view than will civil servants in some other democracies?

A: Compared with other western bureaucracies, the U.S. bureaucracy has a higher proportion of employees with a specialized education. They tend to take jobs in agencies where their specialty is particularly desirable, as in the case of the aeronautical engineers who work at NASA. Accordingly, their training would incline them to support their agency's mission—the agency point of view. European civil servants are more likely to have a type of education, as in the case of law or the humanities, that is less specific to the work of a particular agency, which presumably makes them less likely to deeply embrace their agency's mission.

The popular children's program *Sesame Street* is produced through the Corporation for Public Broadcasting, a government agency that gains leverage in budgetary deliberations from its public support. Shown here in a photo of a display at the Smithsonian National Museum of American History is Oscar the Grouch, a *Sesame Street* puppet whose home is a garbage can.

for instance, is a dependable ally of farm interests year after year. The same cannot be said of the president or Congress as a whole, which must balance farmers' demands against those of other groups.

The Power of Friends in High Places   Although the goals of the president or Congress can conflict with those of the bureaucracy, they need it as much as it needs them. An agency's resources—its programs, expertise, and group support—can help elected officials achieve their policy goals. When President Obama early in his presidency announced the goal of making the United States less dependent on foreign oil, he needed the help of the Department of Energy's experts to develop programs that would further that objective. At a time when other agencies were feeling the pinch of a tight federal budget, the Department of Energy's budget nearly doubled.

Agencies also have allies in Congress. Agencies with programs that benefit important key voting blocs are particularly likely to have congressional support. A prime example is the Department of Agriculture. Although the agricultural sector is just one of the president's many concerns, it is a primary concern of farm-state senators and representatives. They can normally be counted on to support Department of Agriculture funding and programs.

DEMOCRACY AND BUREAUCRATIC ACCOUNTABILITY

Studies have found that the U.S. federal bureaucracy compares favorably to government bureaucracies elsewhere. "Some international bureaucracies," Charles Goodsell writes, "may be roughly the same [as the U.S. bureaucracy] in quality of performance, but they are few in number."[16] The U.S. Postal Service, for example, has an on-time and low-cost record that few national postal services can match.

Nevertheless, the federal bureaucracy's policy influence is at odds with democratic principles. The bureaucratic form of governing is the antithesis of the democratic form. Bureaucracy entails hierarchy, command, permanence of office, appointment to office, and fixed rules, whereas self-government involves equality, consent, rotation of office, election to office, and open decision making. The president and members of Congress are accountable to the people through elections. Bureaucrats are not elected and yet exercise a significant degree of independent power.

Their influence raises the question of **bureaucratic accountability**— the degree to which bureaucrats are held accountable for the power they exercise. To a small degree, they are accountable directly to the public. In some instances, for example, agencies are required to hold public hearings before issuing new regulations. For the most part, however, bureaucratic accountability occurs largely through the president, Congress, and the courts.[17]

Accountability through the Presidency

Periodically, presidents have launched broad initiatives aimed at making the bureaucracy more responsive. The most recent was the National Performance Review, which Bill Clinton began when he assumed the presidency in 1993. He had campaigned on the issue of "reinventing government" and assembled "reinventing teams" that produced 384 specific recommendations grouped into four broad imperatives: reducing red tape, putting customers first, empowering administrators, and eliminating wasteful spending.[18] Although different in its particulars, the National

Performance Review was like earlier reform panels, including the Brownlow, Hoover, and Volcker commissions,[19] which sought with some success to improve the bureaucracy's efficiency, responsiveness, and accountability.

Presidents can also intervene more directly through *executive orders* to force agencies to pursue particular administrative actions. In the closing days of his presidency, for example, Bill Clinton ordered federal agencies to take the steps necessary to ensure that eligible individuals with limited English proficiency obtained full access to federal assistance programs.

Nevertheless, presidents do not have the time or knowledge to exercise personal oversight of the federal bureaucracy. It is far too big and diverse. Presidents rely instead on management tools that include reorganization, presidential appointees, and the executive budget.[20]

Reorganization   The bureaucracy's size—its hundreds of separate agencies— makes it difficult for presidents to coordinate its activities. Agencies pursue independent and even conflicting paths. For example, the United States spends more than $50 billion annually to gather intelligence on threats to the nation's security and does so through several agencies. Each of them has its own priorities and a desire to retain control of the intelligence information it has gathered. A lack of communication between the CIA and the FBI contributed to the failure to prevent the terrorist attacks on the World Trade Center and the Pentagon on September 11, 2001. Each agency had information that might have disrupted the attack if the information had been shared.

Presidents have sought to streamline the bureaucracy in an attempt to make it more accountable. After the intelligence breakdown in 2001, for example, President Bush commissioned a study of the intelligence agencies that resulted in the creation of the Office of the Director of National Intelligence in 2004. Fifteen intelligence agencies, including the CIA and the FBI, now report directly to the director of national intelligence, who has responsibility for coordinating their activities. Like most reorganizations, this one improved agency performance, but not dramatically.[21] Although the various intelligence agencies now share more information than previously, they have continued to operate somewhat independently of each other—an indication of the tendency of agencies to protect their spheres of operation.

Presidents have had more success in controlling the bureaucracy by moving activities out of the agencies and into the Executive Office of the Presidency (EOP). As explained in Chapter 12, EOP is directly under White House control and functions to a degree as the president's personal bureaucracy. The EOP now makes some policy decisions that at an earlier

The annual federal budget is at the heart of many of the efforts to hold the bureaucracy accountable, The budget defines what each agency can spend and on what programs and activities, giving the president and Congress a basis for determining whether agencies are acting within the law.

time would have been made in the agencies. For example, the office of the United States Trade Representative, which is part of the EOP, has assumed some of the policy authority that once belonged to the Department of Commerce.

Presidential Appointments   For day-to-day oversight of the bureaucracy, presidents rely on their political appointees. The president has roughly two thousand full-time partisan appointees, twenty times the number appointed, for example, by the British prime minister.

The top positions in every agency are held by presidential appointees. Their influence is greatest in agencies that have substantial discretionary authority. Some agencies, like the Social Security Administration (SSA), operate within guidelines that limit what agency heads can do. Although the SSA has a huge budget and makes monthly payments to more than 40 million Americans, recipient eligibility is determined by fixed rules. The head of the SSA does not have the option, say, of granting a retiree an extra $100 a month because the retiree is facing financial hardship. At the other extreme are the regulatory agencies, which have considerable latitude in their decisions. For example, in the first eighteen months of the Obama administration, the Environmental Protection Agency (EPA) instigated 50 percent more waste management cases than did the Bush administration in its first eighteenth months and achieved settlements in nearly all of them, compared with a 78 percent rate under Bush.[22]

Nevertheless there are limits to what presidents can accomplish through their appointees. Many appointees lack detailed knowledge of the agencies they head, making them dependent on agency careerists. By the time they come to understand the agency's programs, they often leave. The typical presidential appointee stays on the job for only two years before moving on to other employment.[23]

P A R T Y
POLARIZATION

Political Thinking in Conflict

The Politicization of the Bureaucracy

The top-level positions in the federal bureaucracy—the positions occupied by presidential appointees—have become increasingly partisan. Although presidents seek to appoint well-qualified individuals, they also want them to be loyal to the president's policy agenda. Accordingly, as the division between the parties has widened in the past few decades, presidential appointees have increasingly had policy views that are sharply at odds with those of the other party. Moreover, when the presidency changes hands from one party to the other, the new appointees at the head of an agency can have policy agendas that are radically different from those of the appointees they replaced, disrupting the agency's operations.

These developments are significant enough to lead some observers to conclude that the federal bureaucracy has been weakened by them. They would prefer a bureaucracy in which neutral competence—impartial and expert administration—is the overriding principle. Other observers dismiss this claim, arguing that the bureaucracy needs to be responsive to partisan politics—that the will of the voters should be reflected in administrative staffing and policymaking. They do not deny the need for competent administrators but argue that strong political leadership at the top—even if highly partisan—is the key to a more accountable and responsive bureaucracy.

Q: What's your view of the increased politicization of the bureaucracy? On balance, do you regard it as a favorable development? Would you have the same opinion if control of the presidency were to change to the other party?

OMB: Budgets, Regulations, and Legislative Proposals Of the management tools available to the president, few are more direct than the Office of Management and Budget. Funding is the foundation of every agency, and OMB has substantial control over agency budgets. Moreover, no agency can issue a major regulation without OMB's verification that the benefits of the regulation outweigh its costs. Nor can an agency propose legislation to Congress without OMB's approval. A proposed regulation or bill that conflicts with the president's goals is unlikely to get OMB's approval.

Accountability through Congress

A common misperception is that the president, as the chief executive, has sole authority over executive agencies. In fact, Congress also claims ownership because it is the source of each agency's programs and funding. One presidential appointee asked a congressional committee whether it had a problem with his plans to reduce an agency's programs. The committee chair replied, "No, you have the problem, because if you touch that bureau I'll cut your job out of the budget."[24]

The most substantial control that Congress exerts over the bureaucracy is through its "power of the purse." Congress has constitutional authority over spending; it decides how much money will be appropriated for agency programs. Without funding, a program simply does not exist, regardless of how important the agency believes it is. Congress can also void an administrative decision through legislation that instructs the agency to follow a different course of action. Congress can also exert control by taking authority away from the bureaucracy. In 1978, as a first step in what would become a decades-long wave of deregulation, Congress passed the Airline Deregulation Act, which took away the Civil Aeronautics Board's authority to set airfares and gave it to the airlines.

Congress also has control through its oversight function, which involves monitoring the bureaucracy's work to ensure its compliance with legislative intent.[25] If any agency steps out of line, Congress can call hearings to ask tough questions and, if necessary, take legislative action to correct the problem. Bureaucrats are required by law to appear before Congress when asked to do so, and the mere possibility of being grilled by a congressional panel can lead administrators to stay in line. The effect is not altogether positive. Bureaucrats are sometimes reluctant to try innovative approaches out of a fear that particular members of Congress will disapprove.[26]

Nevertheless, Congress lacks the time and expertise to define in detail how programs should be run.[27] Accordingly, Congress has delegated much of its oversight responsibility to the Government Accountability Office (GAO). At an earlier time, the GAO's role was limited largely to keeping track of agency spending. The GAO now also monitors whether agencies are implementing policies in the way that Congress intended. When the GAO finds a problem with an agency's handling of a program, it notifies the appropriate congressional committees, which can then take corrective action.

Oversight cannot correct mistakes or abuses that have already occurred. Recognizing this limit, Congress has devised ways to constrain the bureaucracy *before* it acts. The simplest method is to draft laws that contain specific instructions on how they are to be implemented by the bureaucracy. In doing so, Congress limits administrators' options. *Sunset provisions* are another restrictive device. These provisions establish specific dates when all or part of a law will expire unless extended by Congress. Sunset provisions are a method of countering the bureaucracy's reluctance to give up outdated programs. However, because members of Congress usually want the programs they create to last, most bills do not include a sunset provision.

Accountability through the Courts

The bureaucracy is also overseen by the judiciary. Legally, the bureaucracy derives its authority from acts of Congress, and an injured party can bring suit against an agency on the grounds that it has failed to carry out a law properly. If the court agrees, the agency must change its policy.[28] In 1999, for example, a federal court approved a settlement in favor of African American farmers who demonstrated that the Department of Agriculture had systematically favored white farmers in granting federal farm loans.[29]

Nevertheless, the courts tend to support administrators if their actions are at least somewhat consistent with the law they are administering. The Supreme Court has held that agencies can apply any reasonable interpretation of statutes unless Congress has stipulated something to the contrary.[30] This position reflects the Court's recognition that administrators must have flexibility if they are to operate effectively and that the federal courts would be overloaded with cases if petitioners could challenge almost any administrative decision they disliked.

Accountability within the Bureaucracy Itself

The recognition of the difficulty of ensuring adequate accountability of the bureaucracy through the presidency, Congress, and the courts has led to the development of mechanisms of accountability within the bureaucracy itself. Four of these mechanisms—the Senior Executive Service, administrative law judges, whistleblowing, and demographic representativeness—are particularly noteworthy.

Senior Executive Service   The agency point of view within the bureaucracy is partly a result of career patterns. Most civil servants work in the same agency throughout their time in government service. As they acquire the skills and knowledge associated with a particular agency, they rise through its ranks and derive job satisfaction and security from supporting its mission.

Recognizing that the bureaucracy's employment system encourages an agency point of view, Congress in 1978 established the **Senior Executive Service (SES)**. Enacted at the urging of President Jimmy Carter, the SES represents a compromise between a president-led bureaucracy and an expert one.[31] The SES consists of roughly seven thousand top-level career civil servants who qualify through a competitive process to receive a higher salary than their peers but, in return, can be assigned by the president to any position within the bureaucracy. Unlike the president's regular appointees, SES bureaucrats cannot be fired; if the president relieves them of their job, they have "fallback rights" to their former rank in the regular civil service.

The SES has been less successful in practice than its proponents anticipated. A 2009 study found that most senior executives are assigned to work within their original agency. The study found that most SES employees are assigned to agencies that mesh with their policy expertise, which is typically the same agency in which they have spent their career. Their value rests in significant part on their knowledge of their particular agency's programs and to move them elsewhere diminishes that value. Of course, some SES employees are exceptions to this pattern and all SES employees benefit from the extra leadership training they receive. But the idea that they can move fluidly between agencies and quickly strengthen the leadership of a new agency has not been borne out. Said one former senior executive: "I got promoted because I became an expert in the policies in that area, not because I'm such a great executive who can go anywhere and do anything."[32]

Administrative Law Judges   Every day, bureaucrats make tens of thousands of decisions affecting individuals. Occasionally, an individual will believe that he or she was unfairly disadvantaged by a bureaucrat's decision and will contest it. Such disputes are usually handled by an **administrative law judge.** These judges are empowered to administer oaths, seek evidence, take testimony, make factual and legal determinations, and render decisions. However, they operate through a less formal process than do regular federal judges. Administrative law hearings usually take place in an office or meeting room rather than a courtroom, and administrative law judges do not wear a robe or sit on a high bench. The system is designed to provide a less formal, less expensive, and faster method of resolving administrative disputes than would be the case if they were handled through the regular federal courts. Under some circumstances, the decision of an administrative law judge can be appealed to such a court, although this seldom occurs.

Administrative law judges typically work within the confines of a particular agency and specialize in the laws and regulations governing its activities. Although they are employees of their agency, they are charged with protecting individuals from arbitrary, prejudicial, or incorrect decisions by the agency. Accordingly, their positions are insulated from agency pressure. Administrative law judges are not subject to performance or salary review by agency heads, and their superiors are prohibited from interfering with their hearings or undermining their rulings.

Whistleblowing   Although the bureaucratic corruption that is commonplace in some countries is rare in the United States, a certain amount of fraud and abuse is inevitable in any large bureaucracy. One way to stop these prohibited practices is **whistleblowing**—the act of reporting instances of official mismanagement. To encourage whistleblowers to come forward with their information, Congress enacted the Whistleblower Protection Act. It protects whistleblowers from retaliation by their superiors and gives them a financial reward in cases where their information results in a savings to government.

Nevertheless, whistleblowing is not for the fainthearted. Many federal employees are reluctant to report instances of mismanagement because they fear retaliation. Their superiors might claim that they are malcontents or liars and find ways to ruin their careers. A case in point is Bunnatine Greenhouse who filed a complaint alleging that the U.S. Army Corps of Engineers was greatly overpaying a contractor because it had accepted the contractor's multiyear no-bid cost estimates rather than conducting its own assessment. Her complaint was ignored by the Corps of Engineers and she was demoted, stripped of her top-secret security clearance, and subjected to on-the-job harassment after she took her complaint to Congress. In 2011, more than six years after her initial

The best-known whistleblower of recent times is Edward Snowden, who released through the news media documents indicating that the National Security Agency's surveillance of American citizens was far more extensive than the government had said, prompting widespread criticism of the NSA's surveillance policy.

complaint, she was vindicated when a U.S. district court ruled in her favor. In responding to the ruling, Greenhouse said she hoped that her experience would prompt lawmakers to give whistleblowers "the legal rights that they need."[33]

Demographic Representativeness   Although the bureaucracy is an unrepresentative institution in the sense that its officials are unelected, it can be representative in the demographic sense. The concept of a demographically representative civil service was endorsed in 1961 by the President's Commission on Equal Employment Opportunity, which was created by President John F. Kennedy. The commission concluded that if civil servants were a demographic microcosm of the general public, they would treat the various groups and interests in society more fairly.[34]

The federal government has made progress in improving the employment status of women and, to a lesser extent, minorities. If all employees are taken into account, the federal bureaucracy comes reasonably close to being representative of the nation's population (see Table 13-1).

table 13-1	FEDERAL JOB RANKINGS (GS) OF VARIOUS DEMOGRAPHIC GROUPS					
	Women (%)		Blacks (%)		Hispanics (%)	
Grade level*	1982	2011	1982	2011	1982	2011
GS 13–15 (highest ranks)	5	37	5	13	2	6
GS 9–12	20	46	10	17	4	8
GS 5–8	60	61	19	26	4	9
GS 1–4 (lowest ranks)	78	66	23	25	5	9

*In general, the higher-numbered grades are managerial and professional positions, and the lower-numbered grades are clerical and manual labor positions.
Source: Office of Personnel Management, 2012.

Moreover, women and minorities are better represented among the top ranks of administrators than they are in Congress or the judiciary. Nevertheless, the bureaucracy is not demographically representative at the top levels. About three in every five managerial and professional positions are held by white males, a marked improvement over earlier periods but less than fully representative.

In any case, **demographic representativeness** is only a partial answer to the problem of bureaucratic accountability. The careerists in the defense and welfare agencies, for example, have similar demographic backgrounds, but they differ markedly in their opinions about policy. Each group believes that the goals of its agency should be a top priority. In this sense, agency loyalty trumps demographics. Once in an agency, civil servants—whatever their demographic background—become advocates for its programs.

SUMMARY

Bureaucracy is a method of organizing people and work, based on the principles of hierarchical authority, job specialization, and formalized rules. As a form of organization, bureaucracy is the most efficient means of getting people to work together on tasks of great magnitude and complexity. It is also a form of organization that is prone to waste and rigidity, which is why efforts are always being made to reform it.

The United States could not be governed without a large federal bureaucracy. The day-to-day work of the federal government, from mail delivery to provision of social security to international diplomacy, is done by federal agencies. Federal employees work in roughly four hundred major agencies, including cabinet departments, independent agencies, regulatory agencies, government corporations, and presidential commissions. Yet the bureaucracy is more than simply an administrative giant. Administrators have discretion when making policy decisions. In the process of implementing policy, they make important policy and political choices.

Administrative agencies operate within budgets established by the president and Congress, and they participate in the budgetary process. The process begins with the president's budget instructions, conveyed through OMB, to the agencies. They then develop their budgets, which are consolidated and sent by the president to Congress, where the House and Senate budget and appropriations committees do the bulk of the work, including holding hearings involving agency heads. Throughout, Congress, the president, and the agencies seek to promote their respective budgetary goals. Once the annual budget has been passed by the House and Senate and signed by the president, it takes effect on October 1, the starting date of the federal government's fiscal year.

Administrators are actively engaged in politics and policymaking. The fragmentation of power and the pluralism of the American political system result in a contentious policy process, which leads government agencies to compete for power and resources. Accordingly, civil servants tend to have an agency point of view: they seek to advance their agency's programs and to repel attempts by others to weaken them. In promoting their agencies, civil servants rely on their policy expertise, the backing of their clientele groups, and the support of the president and Congress.

Administrators are not elected by the people they serve, yet they wield substantial independent power. Because of this, the bureaucracy's accountability is a central issue. The major checks on the bureaucracy occur through the president, Congress, and the courts. The president has some power to reorganize the bureaucracy and the authority to appoint the political head of each agency. The president also has management tools (such as the executive budget) that can be used to limit administrators' discretion. Congress has influence on bureaucratic agencies through its authorization and funding powers and through various devices (including enabling provisions, sunset provisions, and oversight hearings) that can increase administrators' accountability. The judiciary's role in ensuring the bureaucracy's accountability is smaller than that of the elected branches, but the courts have the authority to force agencies to act in accordance with legislative intent, established procedures, and constitutionally guaranteed rights. Internal checks on the bureaucracy—the Senior Executive Service, administrative law judges, whistleblowing, and demographic representativeness—are also mechanisms for holding the bureaucracy accountable.

CRITICAL THINKING ZONE

KEY TERMS

administrative law judge *(p. 434)*

agency point of view *(p. 423)*

budgetary process *(p. 418)*

bureaucracy *(p. 409)*

bureaucratic accountability *(p. 428)*

cabinet (executive) departments *(p. 413)*

clientele groups *(p. 425)*

demographic representativeness
(p. 437)

formalized rules *(p. 410)*

government corporations *(p. 416)*

hierarchical authority *(p. 410)*

independent agencies *(p. 414)*

job specialization *(p. 410)*

merit system *(p. 416)*

neutral competence *(p. 417)*

patronage system *(p. 416)*

policy implementation *(p. 421)*

presidential commissions *(p. 416)*

regulatory agencies *(p. 414)*

Senior Executive Service (SES)
(p. 434)

spoils system *(p. 417)*

whistleblowing *(p. 435)*

APPLYING THE ELEMENTS OF CRITICAL THINKING

Conceptualizing: Define what is meant by "agency point of view." Why do bureaucrats tend to have an agency point of view?

Synthesizing: Contrast the patronage system and the merit system as methods of hiring government employees.

Analyzing: What are the major sources of bureaucrats' power? What mechanisms for controlling that power are available to the president and Congress?

EXTRA CREDIT

A Book Worth Reading: David Osborne and Ted Gaebler, *Reinventing Government: How the Entrepreneurial Spirit Is Transforming the Public Sector.* New York: Addison-Wesley, 1992. The award-winning book that Washington officials in the 1990s regarded as the guide to reforming the bureaucracy.

A Website Worth Visiting: **www.whistleblower.org.** The Government Accountability Project is a nonpartisan organization devoted to protecting and encouraging whistleblowers, in the private sector as well as the public sector.

PARTICIPATE!

If you are considering a semester or summer internship, you might want to look into working for a federal, state, or local agency. Compared with legislative interns, executive interns are more likely to get paid and to be given significant duties. (Many legislative interns spend the bulk of their time answering phones or responding to mail.) Internship information can often be obtained through an agency's website. You should apply as early as possible; some agencies have application deadlines.

You might consider a career in government. President John F. Kennedy said that government is "the highest calling." A study by Harvard's Kennedy School of Government found that public-sector managers get more intrinsic satisfaction from their work, which focuses on improving public life, than do private-sector managers. For people who want to pursue a government career, a first step is often a master's degree program in public administration or public policy. Many of these programs require only a year of study after the bachelor's degree. For an entry-level employee with a master's degree rather than a bachelor's degree, the initial salary is 40 percent higher. Appointees with master's degrees enter the civil service at a higher rank (GS-9 rather than GS-5) and are placed in positions that entail greater responsibility than those assigned to newly hired appointees with bachelor's degrees. Those who enter the civil service at the higher rank also are more likely to advance to top positions as their careers develop.

THE FEDERAL JUDICIAL SYSTEM: APPLYING THE LAW

❝It is emphatically the province and duty of the judicial department to say what the law is. Those who apply the rule to particular cases, must of necessity expound and interpret that rule. If two laws conflict with each other, the courts must decide on the operation of each.❞

JOHN MARSHALL[1]

Through its ruling in *Citizens United v. Federal Election Commission* (2010), the Supreme Court opened the door to unrestricted corporate and union spending in federal election campaigns. At issue was a provision of the 2002 Bipartisan Campaign Reform Act that banned corporations and unions from using organization funds to pay for broadcasts or other advertisements that were designed to promote a political candidate. The ban applied thirty days before a primary and sixty days before the general election and extended a century-old policy of limiting election contributions by economic organizations on grounds that such spending would give them undue influence with lawmakers.

The Supreme Court concluded that Congress had overstepped its constitutional boundaries, holding that that spending restrictions infringed on the free speech rights of corporations and unions. Writing for the five justices in the majority, Justice Anthony Kennedy said: "If the First Amendment has any force, it prohibits Congress from fining or jailing citizens, or associations of citizens, for simply engaging in political speech." Kennedy went on to say: "When government seeks to use its full power . . . to command where a person may get his or her information or what distrusted source he or she may not hear, it uses censorship to control thought. This is unlawful." The four justices in the minority took issue with this argument, saying that allowing powerful organizations to spend freely on elections could corrupt the political process. "While American democracy is imperfect," Justice John Paul Stevens wrote, "few outside the majority of this court would have thought its flaws included a dearth of corporate money in politics." Stevens added that the First Amendment was intended to protect the free speech rights of individuals and not of corporations or unions.[2]

The Court's campaign finance ruling illustrates three key points about court decisions. First, the judiciary is an important policymaking body. Some of its rulings are as consequential as a law of Congress or an executive order of the president. Second, the judiciary has considerable discretion in its rulings. The *Citizens United* decision was not based on any literal reading of the law or else the justices would have been in full agreement on the proper ruling. Third, the judiciary is a political

---

POLITICAL THINKING | **Is the Issue Political or Judicial?**

The Supreme Court has made a distinction between political issues (which are to be decided by elected officials) and judicial issues (which can be ruled on by the judiciary). At times, however, the Supreme Court has ruled on issues that it had previously left in the hands of elected officials. An example is the 2010 campaign finance ruling in which the Court held that Congress could not prevent corporations and unions from spending freely on elections. The Court had previously held that Congress had the power to regulate such spending. Is the line between political questions and judicial questions therefore an artificial one? Is it a line the Court can cross whenever it chooses, and therefore a line without inherent meaning?

as well as legal institution. The campaign finance ruling was a product of contending political forces, had political content, and was decided by political appointees. All five justices who voted to allow unlimited corporate spending were appointed to the Court by a Republican president. Of the four justices who voted to ban such spending, three were Democratic appointees.

This chapter describes the federal judiciary. Like the executive and legislative branches, the judiciary is an independent branch of the U.S. government, but unlike the other two branches, its top officials are not elected by the people. The judiciary is not a democratic institution, and its role is different from and, in some ways, more controversial than the roles of the executive and legislative branches. This chapter explores this issue in the process of discussing the following main points:

- *The federal judiciary includes the Supreme Court of the United States, which functions mainly as an appellate court; courts of appeals, which hear appeals; and the district courts, which hold trials.* Each state has a court system of its own, which for the most part is independent of supervision by the federal courts.

- *Judicial decisions are constrained by applicable constitutional law, statutory and administrative law, and precedent.* Nevertheless, political factors have a major influence on judicial appointments and decisions; judges are political officials as well as legal ones.

- *The judiciary has become an increasingly powerful policymaking body in recent decades, raising the question of the judiciary's proper role in a democracy.* The philosophies of judicial restraint and judicial activism provide different answers to this question.

THE FEDERAL JUDICIAL SYSTEM

The Constitution establishes the judiciary as a separate and independent branch of the federal government. The Constitution provides for the Supreme Court of the United States but gives Congress the power to determine the number and types of lower federal courts.

All federal judges are nominated and appointed to office by the president, subject to confirmation by majority vote in the Senate. Unlike the office of president, senator, or representative, the Constitution places no age, residency, or citizenship requirements on the office of federal judge. Nor does the Constitution require judges to have legal training, though by tradition they do. Once seated on the bench, as specified in the

Constitution, they "hold their offices during good behavior." This has meant, in effect, that federal judges serve until they die or retire voluntarily. No Supreme Court justice and only a handful of lower-court judges have been removed through impeachment and conviction by Congress, the method of early removal specified by the Constitution.

Alexander Hamilton argued forcefully for life tenure for federal judges in *Federalist* No. 78. Responding to arguments by anti-Federalists that unelected, life-appointed judges would be a threat to the republic, Hamilton argued that the judicial branch would be the weakest of the three branches. Whereas congressional power rests on spending authority ("the power of the purse") and presidential power rests on control of military force ("the power of the sword"), judicial power rests on what Hamilton called "judgment"—the reasonableness and fairness of its decisions. The best way to ensure that judicial decisions meet this standard, Hamilton claimed, is to grant life tenure to federal judges so that they are free of all allegiances except to the rule of law.

The Supreme Court of the United States

The Supreme Court of the United States is the nation's highest court. It has nine members—the chief justice and eight associate justices. The chief justice presides over the Court but has the same voting power as each of the other justices.

The Supreme Court's *Citizens United* decision in 2010, which declared corporations to be people and therefore entitled to the protection of the First Amendment, illustrates that the judiciary is a political institution as well as a legal one. Not surprisingly, many of its decisions, including *Citizens United*, are controversial.

Article III of the Constitution grants the Supreme Court both original and appellate jurisdiction. A court's **jurisdiction** is its authority to hear cases of a particular type. **Original jurisdiction** is the authority to be the first court to hear a case. The Supreme Court's original jurisdiction includes legal disputes involving foreign diplomats and cases in which the opposing parties are state governments. The Court has convened as a court of original jurisdiction only a few hundred times in its history and has seldom done so in recent decades. One of the rarities was *South Carolina v. North Carolina* (2010), which involved a dispute between the two states over the distribution of water in the Catawba River, which flows through both states.[3]

The Supreme Court does its most important work as an appellate court. **Appellate jurisdiction** is the authority to review cases that have already been heard in lower courts and are appealed to a higher court by the losing party. These higher courts are called *appeals courts* or *appellate courts*. Appellate courts do not retry cases; rather, they determine whether a trial court in hearing a case has acted in accord with applicable law. The Supreme Court's appellate jurisdiction extends to cases arising under the Constitution, federal law and regulations, and treaties. The Court also hears appeals involving legal controversies that cross state or national boundaries. Article III of the Constitution gives Congress the power to create "exceptions" to the Supreme Court's appellate jurisdiction, whereas its original jurisdiction is unalterable by Congress.

Selecting and Deciding Cases

Nearly all cases that reach the Supreme Court do so after the losing party in a lower court asks the Court to hear its case. If at least four of the justices agree to do so, the Court issues a **writ of certiorari,** which is a request to the lower court to submit to the Supreme Court a record of the case. Each year roughly eight thousand parties apply for certiorari, but the Court grants certiorari to fewer than a hundred cases (see Figure 14-1).

The Supreme Court is most likely to grant certiorari when the U.S. government through the solicitor general (the high-ranking Justice Department official who serves as the government's lawyer in Supreme Court cases) requests it.[4] When the government loses a lower-court case, the solicitor general decides whether to appeal it. Such cases sometimes make up half or more of the cases the Supreme Court hears in a term.

The Supreme Court seldom accepts a routine case, even if the justices believe that a lower court made a mistake. The Court's job is not to correct the errors of other courts but to resolve substantial legal issues.

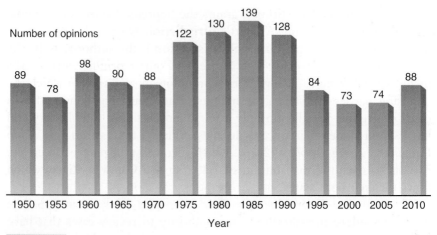

figure 14-1   SUPREME COURT OPINIONS, 1950–2010

The number of signed Supreme Court opinions each term is relatively small. The Court has considerable control over the cases it selects. The cases that are heard by the Supreme Court tend to be ones that have legal significance beyond the particular case itself. The Courts term runs from October 1 to June 30; the year indicated is the closing year of the term.
Source: Supreme Court of the United States.

The Court's own guidelines say that there must be "compelling reasons" for accepting a case, which include resolving issues that are being decided inconsistently by the lower courts, correcting serious departures from accepted standards of justice, settling key questions of federal law, and reviewing lower-court rulings that conflict with a previous Supreme Court decision. When the Court does accept a case, chances are that most of the justices disagree with the lower court's ruling. About three-fourths of Supreme Court decisions reverse the lower court's judgment.[5]

During a Supreme Court hearing, the attorney for each side presents its oral argument, which typically is limited to thirty minutes.[6] Each side also provides the Court a written *brief,* which contains its fuller argument. The oral session is followed by the *judicial conference*, which is attended only by the nine justices and in which they discuss and vote on the case. The conference's proceedings are secret, which allows the justices to speak freely about a case and to change their mind as the discussion progresses.[7]

Issuing Decisions and Opinions

After a case has been decided, the Court issues its ruling, which consists of a decision and one or more opinions. The **decision** indicates which party won the case. The most important part of the ruling, however, is the **opinion,** which explains the legal basis for the decision. In the land-mark *Brown v. Board of Education* opinion, for instance, the Court held that government-sponsored school segregation was unconstitutional because it violated the Fourteenth Amendment provision that guarantees equal protection under the law to all citizens (see discussion in Chapter 5). This opinion became the legal basis by which public schools throughout the South were ordered by lower courts to end their policy of racial segregation.

When a majority of the justices agree on the legal basis of a decision, the result is a **majority opinion.** In some cases there is no majority opin-ion because, although a majority of the justices agree on the decision, they disagree on the legal basis for it. The result in such cases is a **plurality opinion,** which presents the view held by most of the justices who vote with the winning side. Another type of opinion is a **concurring opinion,** a separate view written by a justice who votes with the majority but dis-agrees with all or part of its reasoning. The final type is a **dissenting opinion;** in it, a justice (or justices) on the losing side explains the reasons for disagreeing with the majority position.

When part of the majority, the chief justice decides which justice will write the majority opinion. Otherwise, the senior justice in the majority picks the author. The justice who writes the Court's majority opinion has the responsibility to express accurately the majority's reasoning. The vote on a case is not considered final until the opinion is written and agreed upon, so give-and-take can occur during the writing stage. In rare instances, the writing stage has produced a change in the Court's decision. In *Lee v. Weisman* (1992), a case involving prayer at a public school grad-uation, Justice Anthony Kennedy originally sided with the four justices who said the prayer was permissible. While writing the 5-4 majority opinion, Kennedy found that he could not make a persuasive case for allowing it. He switched sides, resulting in a 5-4 majority the other way.

Other Federal Courts

The Supreme Court's position at the top of the judicial system gives it unrivaled importance. Nevertheless, the Supreme Court is not the only court that matters. Judge Jerome Frank once wrote of the "upper-court myth," which is the view that lower courts dutifully follow the rulings handed down by the courts above them.[8] The reality is different, as the following discussion explains.

U.S. District Courts   The lowest federal courts are the district courts (see Figure 14-2). There are ninety-four federal district courts altogether—at

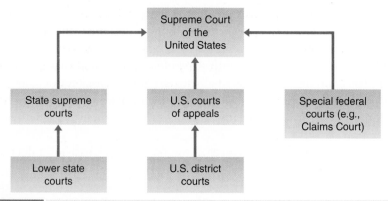

figure 14-2 THE FEDERAL JUDICIAL SYSTEM

The simplified diagram shows the relationships among the various levels of federal courts and between state and federal courts. The losing party in a case can appeal a lower-court decision to the court at the next-highest level, as the arrows indicate. Decisions normally can be moved from state courts to federal courts only if they raise a constitutional question.

least one in every state and as many as four in the most populous states. Each district includes several judges, who number roughly eight hundred in all. The federal district courts are the chief trial courts of the federal system. Virtually all criminal and civil cases arising under federal law are argued first in the district courts. They are the only courts in the federal system where the two sides present their case to a jury for a verdict. Cases at this level are usually presided over by a single judge.

Lower federal courts rely on and follow Supreme Court decisions in their own rulings. The Supreme Court reiterated this requirement in a 1982 case, *Hutto v. Davis:* "Unless we wish anarchy to prevail within the federal judicial system, a precedent of this Court must be followed by the lower federal courts no matter how misguided the judges of those courts may think it to be."[9] However, the idea that lower courts are rigidly bound to Supreme Court rulings is part of the upper-court myth. The facts of a case before a district court are seldom identical to those of a case settled by the Supreme Court. The lower-court judge must decide whether a different legal judgment is appropriate. As well, ambiguities or unaddressed issues in Supreme Court rulings give lower courts some flexibility in deciding cases.

Another indication of the significant role of district court judges is that most federal cases end with the district court's decision. Typically, the losing party decides not to appeal the decision to a higher court.

U.S. Courts of Appeals   Cases appealed from district courts go to federal courts of appeals, which are the second level of the federal court system. Courts of appeals do not use juries. Ordinarily, no new evidence is submitted in an appealed case; rather, appellate courts base their decision on a review of the lower court's records. Appellate judges act as overseers, reviewing trial court decisions and correcting what they consider to be legal errors.

The United States has thirteen courts of appeals. Eleven of them have jurisdiction over a "circuit" made up of the district courts in anywhere from three to nine states (see Figure 14-3). Of the remaining two, one has jurisdiction over the District of Columbia (the D.C. "circuit") and the other (the U.S. Court of Appeals for the Federal Circuit) has jurisdiction over appeals involving patents and international trade, regardless of the circuit in which they arise. Between four and twenty-six judges sit on each court of appeals, but each case usually is heard by a panel of three judges.

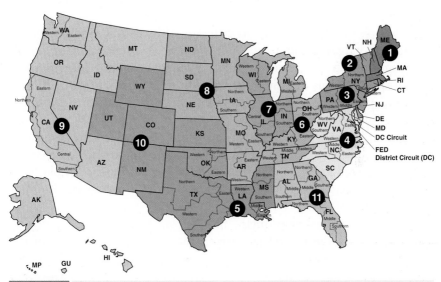

figure 14-3 GEOGRAPHIC BOUNDARIES OF U.S. COURTS OF APPEALS

The United States has thirteen courts of appeals, each of which serves a "circuit." Eleven of these circuit courts serve anywhere from three to nine states, as the map shows. The other two are located in the District of Columbia: the Court of Appeals for the District of Columbia and the Court of Appeals for the Federal Circuit, which specializes in appeals involving patents and international trade. Within each circuit are federal trial courts, most of which are district courts. Each state has at least one district court within its boundaries. Larger states, such as California (which has four district courts, as can be seen on the map), have more than one. *Source:* Administrative Office of the U.S. Courts.

On rare occasions, all the judges of a court of appeals sit as a body (*en banc*) in order to resolve difficult controversies, typically ones that have resulted in conflicting decisions within the same circuit. Each circuit is monitored by a Supreme Court justice, who typically takes the lead in reviewing appeals originating in that circuit. Conflict or inconsistency in how the different circuits are applying a law can lead the Supreme Court to review such cases.

Courts of appeals offer the only real hope of reversal for most appellants, because the Supreme Court hears so few cases. The Supreme Court reviews less than 1 percent of the cases heard by federal appeals courts.*

The State Courts

The American states are separate governments within the U.S. political system. The Tenth Amendment protects each state in its sovereignty, and each state has its own court system. Like the federal courts, state court systems have trial courts at the bottom level and appellate courts at the top.

Each state decides for itself the structure of its courts and the method of selecting judges. In some states the governor appoints judges, but in most states judges are elected to office. The most common form involves competitive elections of either a partisan or a nonpartisan nature. Other states use a mixed system called the *merit plan* (also called the "Missouri Plan" because Missouri was the first state to use it), under which the governor appoints a judge from a short list of acceptable candidates provided by a judicial selection commission. At the first scheduled election after the selected judge has served for a year, the voters by a simple "yes" or "no" vote decide whether the judge should be allowed to stay in office (see "How the 50 States Differ").

Besides the upper-court myth, there exists a "federal court myth," which holds that the federal judiciary is the most significant part of the judicial system and that state courts play a subordinate role. This view is also inaccurate. More than 95 percent of the nation's legal cases are decided by state or local courts. Most cases arising under *criminal law*

---

*In addition to the Supreme Court, the courts of appeals, and the district courts, the federal judiciary includes a few specialty courts. Among them are the U.S. Claims Court, which hears cases in which the U.S. government is being sued for damages; the U.S. Court of International Trade, which handles cases involving appeals of U.S. Customs Office rulings; and the U.S. Court of Military Appeals, which hears appeals of military courts-martial. Some federal agencies and commissions also have judicial powers (for example, the issuing of fines), and their decisions can be appealed to a federal court of appeals.

HOW THE 50 STATES DIFFER

POLITICAL THINKING THROUGH COMPARISONS

Principal Methods of Selecting State Judges

The states use a variety of methods for selecting the judges on their highest court, including the merit plan, election, and political appointment. The states that appoint judges grant this power to the governor, except in Virginia, Connecticut, and South Carolina, where the legislature makes the choice.

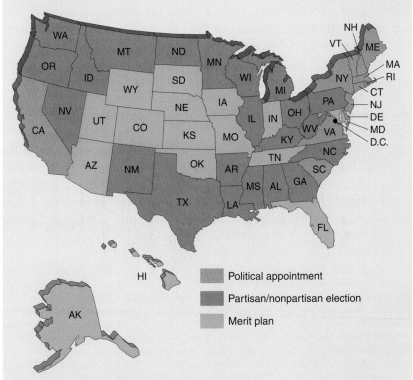

- Political appointment
- Partisan/nonpartisan election
- Merit plan

Source: The Council of State Governments. Reprinted with permission.

Q: What might explain why several states in the middle of the nation use the merit plan for selecting judges?

A: The merit plan originated in the state of Missouri. Innovations in one state sometimes spread to adjacent states with similar political cultures.

(from shoplifting to murder) and most cases arising under *civil law* (such as divorces and business disputes) are defined by state laws or by local ordinances, which are derived from state laws.*

Moreover, nearly all cases that originate in state or local courts also end there. The federal courts do not come into the picture because the case does not involve a federal issue. The losing party in a divorce suit, for example, cannot appeal the decision to federal court because no federal law is involved. In most state criminal cases, there is also no federal issue, unless state authorities are alleged to have violated a right protected by the U.S. Constitution, such as the right of the accused to remain silent (see Chapter 4). In such instances, an individual convicted in a state court, after exhausting the avenues of appeal in the state system, can appeal to a federal court. If the federal court accepts the appeal, it ordinarily confines itself to the federal aspects of the case, such as whether the defendant's constitutional rights were violated.

However, issues traditionally within the jurisdiction of the states can become federal issues through the rulings of federal courts. In its *Lawrence v. Texas* decision in 2003, for example, the Supreme Court invalidated state laws that had made it illegal for consenting adults of the same sex to engage in private sexual relations.[10] John Lawrence had been convicted under a Texas sodomy law and appealed his conviction on grounds that it violated his Fourteenth Amendment due process rights. By grounding his appeal in federal law, Lawrence was able to have his case heard in federal court. When the Supreme Court then decided in his favor, federal law became the governing authority in such cases. Until its *Lawrence*

---

*Laws fall into three broad categories—procedural, civil, and criminal. Procedural law refers to rules that govern the legal process. In some cases, these rules apply to government, as in the example of the obligation of police to inform suspects of their right to an attorney. In other cases, the rules apply to private parties. For example, in some states, a homeowner cannot take an insurance company to court over a policy claim without first having that claim heard, and possibly resolved, by an arbitration board. *Civil law* governs relations with and between private parties as when a person injured in an accident sues the other party for monetary damages. Marriage, divorce, business contracts, and property ownership are examples of relations covered by civil law. The losing party in a civil suit might be ordered to pay or otherwise compensate the other party but would not face jail unless he or she refuses to comply with a court order, which can be a punishable offense. Government can also be a party to a civil suit, as when the IRS sues a taxpayer in a dispute over how much the taxpayer owes the government. *Criminal law* deals with acts that government defines as illegal, which can result in a fine, imprisonment, or other punishment. Murder, assault, and drunk driving are examples of acts covered by criminal law. The government is always a party to a criminal law case; the other party is the individual alleged to have broken the law. (Legal relationships between government and private parties, whether criminal or civil, are defined as *public law*. The term *private law* is used to refer to the legal rights and relationships between private parties.)

decision, the Court held that states had the authority to decide whether sexual relations among same-sex partners were unlawful.[11]

FEDERAL COURT APPOINTEES

Appointments to the federal courts are controlled by the president, who selects the nominees, and by the Senate, which confirms or rejects them. The quiet dignity of the courtroom gives the impression that the judiciary is as far removed from the world of politics as a governmental institution can possibly be. In reality, federal judges and justices bring their political views with them to the courtroom and have opportunities to promote their beliefs through the cases they decide. Not surprisingly, the process by which federal judges are appointed is a partisan one.

Supreme Court Nominees

A Supreme Court appointment is a significant opportunity for a president.[12] Most justices retain their positions for many years, enabling presidents to influence judicial policy through their appointments long after they have left office. The careers of some Supreme Court justices provide dramatic testimony to the enduring nature of judicial appointments. For example, Franklin D. Roosevelt appointed William O. Douglas to the Supreme Court in 1939, and for thirty years after Roosevelt's death in 1945, Douglas remained a strong liberal influence on the Court.

Presidents usually appoint jurists who have a compatible political philosophy. Although Supreme Court justices are free to make their own decisions, their legal positions can usually be predicted from their background. A study by judicial scholar Robert Scigliano found that about three of every four appointees have behaved on the Supreme Court approximately as presidents could have expected.[13] Of course, a president has no guarantee that a nominee will actually do so. Justices Earl Warren and William Brennan, for example, proved to be more liberal than President Dwight D. Eisenhower had anticipated. Asked whether he had made any mistakes as president, Eisenhower replied, "Yes, two, and they are both sitting on the Supreme Court."[14]

Although presidents seek nominees who share their political philosophy, they also must take into account a nominee's acceptability to others. Every nominee is scrutinized closely by the legal community, interested groups, and the media; must undergo an extensive background check by the FBI; and then must gain the approval of a Senate majority. Within the Senate, the key body is the Judiciary Committee, whose members

<table>
<tr><td>

POLITICAL THINKING

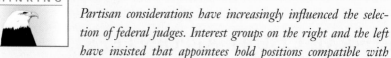

</td><td>

Partisanship or Merit?

</td></tr>
</table>

Partisan considerations have increasingly influenced the selection of federal judges. Interest groups on the right and the left have insisted that appointees hold positions compatible with their stands. Presidents and members of Congress have also increasingly sought appointees who will decide issues in a certain way. What is your view? Should politics play such a large role in judicial appointments? Or should merit—an appointee's legal credentials—be given greater weight?

have responsibility for conducting hearings on judicial nominees and recommending their confirmation or rejection by the full Senate.

Nearly 20 percent of presidential nominees to the Supreme Court have been rejected by the Senate on grounds of judicial qualification, political views, personal ethics, or partisanship. Most of these rejections occurred before 1900, and partisan politics was the usual reason. Today a nominee with strong professional and ethical credentials is less likely to be blocked

John Roberts is the seventeenth chief justice of the Supreme Court. Appointed to the position when he was forty-seven years of age by President George W. Bush, Roberts could serve on the Court for several decades, perhaps surpassing even the tenure of Chief Justice John Marshall, who served the longest in the position. Marshall led the Court for thirty-four years, a period that spanned six presidencies.

for partisan reasons alone. An exception was Robert Bork, whose 1987 nomination by President Reagan was rejected primarily because of Senate Democrats' opposition to his conservative judicial philosophy. On the other hand, nominees can expect confirmation if they have a clean personal record and a strong professional record, and are able to demonstrate during Senate confirmation hearings that they have the temperament and intellect expected of a Supreme Court justice. President Bush's nomination of John Roberts in 2005 to be chief justice is a case in point. Roberts faced tough questioning during Senate hearings, but nothing startlingly new or disturbing came out, and he was confirmed by a 78-22 vote. The Senate vote in 2010 on Elena Kagan, who was nominated by President Obama, was closer, even though the Senate hearings went smoothly. Although Kagan was confirmed by a 63-37 vote, most GOP senators voted against her. Expressing a view held by many Senate Republicans, Orrin Hatch of Utah said she lacked an "appropriate judicial philosophy," which was his way of saying that her legal views were at odds with his own.

Lower-Court Nominees

The president typically delegates to the deputy attorney general the task of identifying nominees for lower-court judgeships, a process that includes seeking recommendations from U.S. senators of the president's party, and sometimes House members as well. *Senatorial courtesy*, a tradition that dates back to the 1840s, holds that a senator from the state in which a vacancy has arisen should be consulted on the choice of a district court nominee if the senator is of the same party as the president.[15] If not consulted, the senator can request that confirmation be denied. Other senators usually grant the request as a "courtesy" to their colleague.

Although presidents are not as personally involved in selecting lower-court nominees as in naming potential Supreme Court justices, lower-court appointments are collectively significant. A president who serves two terms can shape the federal judiciary for years to come. By the time he left office, George W. Bush had appointed more than a third of the seated federal judges. Bill Clinton appointed a similar number during his two terms.

Presidents typically nominate members of their own political party. More than 90 percent of recent district and appeals court nominees have come from the president's party.[16] This fact does not mean that federal judges engage in blatant partisanship while on the bench. They are officers of a separate branch of government and prize their judicial independence.

Nevertheless, partisanship influences judicial decisions. A study of the voting records of appellate court judges, for example, found that Democratic appointees were more likely than Republican appointees to side with defendants who claim the government violated their civil liberties.[17]

Personal Backgrounds of Judicial Appointees

White males are overrepresented on the federal bench, just as they dominate in Congress and at the top levels of the executive branch. However, women and minority-group members have made substantial gains in recent decades, largely through appointment by Democratic presidents. Women and minority-group members are key Democratic constituencies, and Democratic presidents have responded accordingly when filling vacancies on the federal bench (see Figure 14-4). In his first term, more than two-thirds of Barack Obama's appointees were women or minorities, an all-time high.[18] Of Democratic President Bill Clinton's appointees, half were women or minority-group members, compared with a third for his Republican successor George W. Bush.

Of the nine current Supreme Court justices, three are women (Ruth Bader Ginsburg, Sonia Sotomayor, and Elena Kagan) and two are minority-group members (Clarence Thomas and Sotomayor). The historical pattern is more uneven. Until 1916, when Louis D. Brandeis was appointed to the Court, no Jewish justice had ever served. Prior to the twentieth century, only one Catholic, Roger Taney, had served on the Court. Six of the current

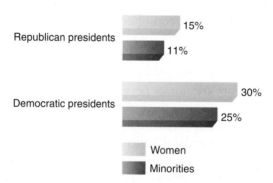

figure 14-4 POLITICAL PARTIES, PRESIDENTS, AND WOMEN AND MINORITY JUDICIAL APPOINTEES

Reflecting differences in their parties' coalitions, recent Republican and Democratic presidents have quite different records in terms of the percentage of their judicial appointees who have been women or minority-group members.

Sources: Various sources. Data based on appointees of Presidents Carter, Reagan, G. H. W. Bush, Clinton, G. W. Bush, and Obama (first term).

justices are Catholic and three are Jewish, marking the first time the Court has been without a Protestant member. Thurgood Marshall in 1967 was the first black justice, and Sandra Day O'Connor in 1981 was the first woman justice. Antonin Scalia in 1986 was the Court's first justice of Italian descent. Sotomayor, who was appointed in 2009, is the first Hispanic justice. No person of Asian descent has been appointed to the Supreme Court.

In one respect, however, the Supreme Court is less diverse than in the past. Elective office (particularly a seat in the U.S. Senate) was once a common route to the Supreme Court, but recent appointees have come overwhelmingly from the appellate courts (see Table 14-1). The assumption is that such individuals have the type of experience best suited to the duties of a Supreme Court justice. Not all observers agree. They note that many of the leading justices of the past, including John Marshall and Earl Warren, had political rather than legal backgrounds. They contend that, because Supreme Court decisions have political as well as legal implications, the Court would be better served if some of its justices had high-level political experience.

table 14-1 JUSTICES OF THE SUPREME COURT

Justice	Year of Appointment	Nominating President	Position before Appointment
Antonin Scalia	1986	Reagan	Judge, D.C. Circuit Court of Appeals
Anthony Kennedy	1988	Reagan	Judge, 9th Circuit Court of Appeals
Clarence Thomas	1991	G. H. W. Bush	Judge, D.C. Circuit Court of Appeals
Ruth Bader Ginsburg	1993	Clinton	Judge, D.C. Circuit. Court of Appeals
Stephen Breyer	1994	Clinton	Judge, 1st Circuit Court of Appeals
John Roberts Jr.*	2005	G. W. Bush	Judge, D.C. Circuit Court of Appeals
Samuel Alito Jr.	2006	G. W. Bush	Judge, 3rd Circuit Court of Appeals
Sonia Sotomayor	2009	Obama	Judge, 2nd Circuit Court of Appeals
Elena Kagan	2010	Obama	Solicitor general of the United States

*Chief justice.

THE NATURE OF JUDICIAL DECISION MAKING

Unlike the president or members of Congress, federal judges make their decisions within the context of a legal system. Yet, they are also political officials: they constitute one of three coequal branches of the national government. As a result, their decisions are both legal and political in nature.

Legal Influences on Judicial Decisions

Article III of the Constitution bars a federal court from issuing a decision except in response to a case presented to it. This restriction is a substantial one. For one thing, it limits judges to issues that arise from actual legal disputes. As federal judge David Bazelon noted, a judge "can't wake up one morning and simply decide to give a helpful little push to a school system, a mental hospital, or the local housing agency."[19]

The facts of a particular case also limit judicial action. The **facts** of a case are the relevant circumstances of a legal dispute or offense. In the case of a person accused of murder, for example, key facts would include evidence about the crime and whether the rights of the accused had been upheld by police. A judge must handle a murder case as a murder case, applying to it the laws that define murder and the penalties for it. A murder case cannot be used as an occasion for a judge to pronounce judgment on free speech rights or campaign finance laws.

The major constraint on the courts is the law itself. Although a president or Congress can make almost any decision that is politically acceptable, the judiciary must work within the confines of the law. When asked by a friend to "do justice," Justice Oliver Wendell Holmes Jr. said that he was bound to follow the law rather than his personal sense of right and wrong.[20]

The judiciary works within the context of three main sources of law: the Constitution, legislative statutes, and legal precedents (see Table 14-2). The Constitution of the United States is the nation's highest law, and judges and justices are sworn to uphold it. When a case raises a constitutional issue, a court has the duty to apply the Constitution to it. For example, the Constitution prohibits the states from printing their own currency. If a state decided that it would do so anyway, a federal judge would be obligated to rule against the practice.

The large majority of cases that arise in courts involve issues of statutory and administrative law rather than constitutional law. *Statutory law*

table 14-2	SOURCES OF LAW THAT CONSTRAIN THE DECISIONS OF THE FEDERAL JUDICIARY

U.S. Constitution: The federal courts are bound by the provisions of the U.S. Constitution. The sparseness of its wording, however, requires the Constitution to be applied in the light of present circumstances. Thus, judges are accorded some degree of discretion in their constitutional judgments.

Statutory law: The federal courts are constrained by statutes and by administrative regulations derived from the provisions of statutes. Many laws, however, are somewhat vague in their provisions and often have unanticipated applications. As a result, judges have some freedom in deciding cases based on statutes.

Precedent: Federal courts tend to follow precedent (or stare decisis), which is a legal principle developed through earlier court decisions. Because times change and not all cases have a clear precedent, judges have some discretion in their evaluation of the way earlier cases apply to a current case.

is legislative (statute) law. *Administrative law* is based on statutory law but is set by government agencies rather than by legislatures. Administrative law consists of the rules, regulations, and judgments that agencies make in the process of implementing and enforcing statutory law. All federal courts are bound by federal statutory and administrative laws, as well as by treaties, and judges must work within the confines of these laws. A company that is charged with violating an air pollution law, for example, will be judged within the context of that law—what it permits and what it prohibits, and what penalties apply if the company is found to have broken the law. When hearing such a case, a judge will typically try to determine whether the meaning of the statute or regulation can be determined by common sense (the "plain meaning rule"). The question for the judge is what the law or regulation was intended to safeguard (such as clean air). In most cases, the law or regulation is clear enough that when the facts of the case are determined, the decision is fairly straightforward.

The U.S. legal system developed from the English common-law tradition, which includes the principle that a court's decision on a case should be consistent with **precedent,** a term that refers to previous court rulings on similar cases. Deference to precedent gives predictability to the application of law. Government has an obligation to make clear what its laws are and how they are being applied. If courts routinely ignored how similar cases had been decided in the past, they would create confusion and uncertainty about what is lawful and what is not. A business firm that is seeking to comply with environmental protection laws, for example, can develop company policies that will keep the company safely within the law if court decisions in this area are consistent. If courts routinely ignored precedent, a firm could unintentionally engage in an activity that a court might conclude was unlawful.

Although judges are required to follow the Constitution, statutes, and precedent, the law is not always a precise guide, with the result that judges often have leeway in their rulings.[21] The Constitution, for example, is a sparsely worded document and must be adapted to new and changing situations. The judiciary also has no choice at times but to impose meaning on statutory law. Statutes are typically more detailed in their provisions than is the Constitution, but Congress cannot always anticipate the specific applications of a legislative act and often defines statutory provisions in general terms. The judiciary is then required to determine what the language means in the context of a specific case. Precedent is even less precise as a guide to decisions in that it is specific to particular cases. A new case may differ in important ways from its closest precedent or rest at the intersection of competing precedents. In such instances, a judge must determine which precedent, if any, applies to the case at hand.

The Supreme Court's ruling in *Faragher v. City of Boca Raton* (1998), involving sexual harassment in the workplace, illustrates the ambiguity that can exist in the law. The Court developed its ruling in the context of the antidiscrimination provisions of the Civil Rights Act of 1964. However, the act itself contains no description of, or even reference to, job-related sexual harassment. Yet the act does prohibit workplace discrimination, and the Court was unwilling to dismiss sexual harassment as an irrelevant form of job-related discrimination. In this sense, the Court was "making" law; it was deciding how legislation enacted by Congress applied to behavior that Congress had not specifically addressed when it wrote the legislation. In the end, the Court decided that sexual harassment on the job is among the types of job-related discrimination prohibited by the Civil Rights Act.[22]

Political Influences on Judicial Decisions

When judges have leeway in deciding a case, political influences can affect their decisions. These influences come from both inside and outside the judicial system.

The Supreme Court's power is never more evident than when its strikes down a law passed by Congress or a state legislature on grounds that it violates the Constitution. Over the years, the Court has invalidated a number of state laws that have sought to promote religion in public schools. The Court considers the issue of religion in the schools to be an issue of individual rights rather than of majority rule.

Inside the Court: Judges' Political Beliefs   Although the judiciary symbolizes John Adams's description of the U.S. political system as "a government of laws, and not of men," court rulings are not simply an extension of the laws. They are also influenced by the political beliefs of the men and women who sit on the federal bench.[23] Changes in the Supreme Court's membership, for example, can bring about a change in its position (see "Party Polarization"). Samuel Alito's appointment to the Court in 2006 produced that kind of change. Although the justice he replaced, Sandra Day O'Connor, usually voted with the Court's four most conservative justices, she sometimes switched sides. Voting with the Court's four most liberal justices, she cast the deciding vote, for example, in the 2000 Nebraska case that upheld the use of partial-birth abortion when the mother's life is endangered. In contrast, Alito cast the deciding vote in the 2007 decision to uphold a congressional ban on the use of partial-birth abortion. Alito's decision in this case and others prompted observers to say that the Supreme Court had swung to the right. Even one of the Supreme Court justices admitted as much. "It is not often in the law," wrote Justice Stephen Breyer, "that so few have so quickly changed so much."[24]

P A R T Y
POLARIZATION

Political Thinking in Conflict

Has Polarization Reached into the Supreme Court?

University of Chicago law professor William Landes and federal appellate judge Richard Posner, who was appointed to the bench in the 1980s by President Reagan, examined the voting records of the forty-three Supreme Court justices who have sat on the Court since 1937. For each case heard by the Court during this seventy-five year period, Landes and Rosner assessed whether a vote could be said to favor the liberal or the conservative side. For example, in cases alleging that the government had violated a criminal defendant's constitutional rights, a vote in favor of the government would be considered conservative and a vote in favor of the defendant would be considered liberal. Then, using all the votes cast by each justice, Landes and Posner ranked the forty-three justices from the justice who voted most consistently in the conservative direction to the justice that voted most consistently in the liberal direction. According to their analysis, here is the rank ordering of the ten most conservative and ten most liberal Supreme Court justices since 1937 (with the president who appointed the justice in parentheses):

Ten Most Conservative	Ten Most Liberal
1. Clarence Thomas (G. H. W. Bush)	1. Thurgood Marshall (Johnson)
2. William Rehnquist (Nixon)	2. William O. Douglas (Roosevelt)
3. Antonin Scalia (Reagan)	3. Frank Murphy (Roosevelt)
4. John Roberts (G. W. Bush)	4. Wiley Blount Rutledge (Roosevelt)
5. Samuel Alito (G. W. Bush)	5. Arthur Goldberg (Johnson)
6. Warren Burger (Nixon)	6. William Brennan (Eisenhower)
7. Sandra Day O'Connor (Reagan)	7. Hugo Black (Roosevelt)
8. Lewis Powell (Nixon)	8. Earl Warren (Eisenhower)
9. Charles Whittaker (Eisenhower)	9. Ruth Bader Ginsburg (Clinton)
10. Anthony Kennedy (Reagan)	10. Benjamin Cardozo (Hoover)

> **Q:** Is there anything in the rankings that would suggest today's party polarization has reached into the Supreme Court?
>
> **A:** Five of the most conservative justices of the past seventy-five years are currently on the Court (Thomas, Scalia, Roberts, Alito, and Kennedy). They tend to vote together on cases, forming what Court observers have labeled the institution's "conservative bloc." It might be noted that all five were appointed by a Republican president, as were the other five most conservative justices. Three of the most liberal justices (Brennan, Warren, and Cardozo) were appointed by a Republican president. Given the current level of partisanship, the likelihood is near zero today that a Republican president would appoint a justice who turned out to vote on the liberal side or that a Democratic president would appoint a justice who turned out to vote on the conservative side.

Studies by political scientists Jeffrey Segal and Harold Spaeth show that justices tend to vote in line with their political attitudes. Segal and Spaeth examined thousands of non-unanimous Court decisions, looking at the extent to which each justice voted on the same side or the opposite side from each of the other justices. Clear patterns emerged, such as the tendency of Antonin Scalia and Clarence Thomas, who are Republican appointees, to vote the same way and opposite that of Stephen Breyer and Ruth Bader Ginsburg, who are Democratic appointees. Compared with Democratic appointees to the Court, Republican appointees were found to be more likely to side with employers rather than with employees, with law enforcement officials rather than with the criminally accused, with corporations rather than with unions, and with government rather than with those claiming discrimination. Segal and Spaeth conclude that the "[policy] preferences of the justices go a long way toward explaining their decisions."[25]

It is true, of course, that disputes that reach the Supreme Court are anything but clear-cut. If they were, they would have been settled in the lower federal courts. It is also true that Supreme Court justices have less leeway in making their decisions than elected officials have in making their choices. Justices operate within the confines of established laws and legal principles, which constrain their choices. The fact that Republican appointees to the Supreme Court are more likely than Democratic appointees to side with law enforcement officials than with the criminally accused does not mean that they invariably do so or that they are unmind-ful of legal restraints on law enforcement officials. In *United States v. Jones* (2012), for example, the Supreme Court held that law enforcement offi-cials had exceeded their authority under the law by placing a GPS track-ing device on a suspect's car without first obtaining a search warrant from a judge (see Chapter 4). The ruling was unanimous, meaning that the Court's Republican appointees sided with its Democratic appointees in concluding that police had violated the suspect's constitutional rights. Nevertheless, when viewed as a whole, Supreme Court decisions are unquestionably a mix of law and politics.

Outside the Court: The Public, Groups, and Elected Officials   The courts can and do make unpopular decisions. In the long run, however, judicial decisions must be seen as fair if they are to be obeyed. In other words, the judiciary cannot routinely ignore the expectations of the general public, interest groups, and elected officials.

Even though the Supreme Court tried to temper the public response to its 1954 *Brown v. Board of Education* decision by ruling that desegregation of public schools should proceed with "all deliberate speed" rather than immediately or on a fixed timetable, the delay in implementation did little to quell the anger of many white southerners. Shown here is one of the many billboards in the South that called for the impeachment of Chief Justice Earl Warren.

Judges are less responsive to public opinion than are elected officials. Nevertheless, the Supreme Court in some instances has tempered its rulings in an effort to get public support or reduce public resistance. The Supreme Court usually stays close enough to public opinion to reduce the likelihood of outright defiance of its decisions.[26] In the 1954 *Brown* case, for example, the justices, recognizing that school desegregation would be an explosive issue in the South, required only that desegregation take place "with all deliberate speed" rather than immediately or on a fixed timetable.

Interest groups also have an influence on the judiciary. Groups petition the White House and Congress to appoint judges and justices who share their outlook on legal disputes. More directly, they submit amicus curiae ("friend of the court") briefs to make their positions known on court cases (see Chapters 5 and 9) and file lawsuits to advance their policy goals. Groups that rely on a judicial strategy pick their cases carefully, choosing those that offer the greatest chance of success. They also carefully pick the courts in which they file their lawsuits, knowing that some judges will be more sympathetic than others to their argument. In fact, some groups rely almost entirely on legal action, knowing they have a better chance of success in the courts than in Congress or the White House. The American Civil Liberties Union (ACLU), for example, has filed hundreds of lawsuits over the years on issues of individual rights, including a recent suit aimed at forcing federal agents to meet constitutional requirements for search and seizure before they are allowed to examine documents stored on travelers' laptop computers.

Elected officials also have ways of influencing the courts. Congress can rewrite legislation that it feels the judiciary has misinterpreted. Meanwhile, the president is responsible for enforcing court decisions and has some influence over the cases that come before the courts. Under President Reagan, for example, the Justice Department vigorously pursued lawsuits that challenged the legality of affirmative action programs, a strategy consistent with Reagan's determination to limit their use.

Judicial appointments offer the president and Congress their biggest opportunity to influence the courts. In 2008, when it became clear that their party was likely to win the presidency, Senate Democrats slowed action on the confirmation of President Bush's judicial nominees. When Barack Obama took office in 2009, scores of judgeships were vacant, which he filled with loyal Democrats. It was a tactic Senate Republicans had employed in 2000. They had delayed action on President Clinton's nominees, enabling Bush to appoint Republicans to existing vacancies when he took office in 2001. In 2013 in response to Senate Republicans' delaying tactics on President Obama's nominees, Senate Democrats eliminated the filibuster on lower-court appointments, which has sped up somewhat the filling of judicial vacancies.

As a result of the party polarization that has worked its way into the nation's politics, the judicial appointment process has become increasingly contentious. Democratic and Republican lawmakers alike recognize the power of the courts to determine policy in areas such as affirmative action and environmental protection, and each party's lawmakers have been determined to confirm judicial appointees whose policy views align with their own. They have been joined in these efforts by interest groups on both sides of the partisan divide. In the case of Supreme Court appointments, there have even been televised advertising campaigns in support of or opposition to the nominees. In *Electing Justices*, political scientist Richard Davis shows that the Supreme Court appointments are now conducted more like political campaigns than like the dignified process the writers of the Constitution had envisioned.[27]

JUDICIAL POWER AND DEMOCRATIC GOVERNMENT

Federal judges are unelected officials with lifetime appointments, which places them beyond the reach of the voters. Because the United States has a constitutional system that places limits on the power of the majority, the judiciary has a legitimate role in the system. Yet court decisions reflect in part the personal political beliefs of the judges. A basic question is how far judges should go in substituting their judgments for those of elected officials.

This power is most dramatically evident when courts declare a law to be unconstitutional. This power, called **judicial review,** was first asserted by the Supreme Court in *Marbury v. Madison* (1803), when the Court rebuked both Congress and the president (see Chapter 2). In such instances, unelected judges substitute their judgment for that of the people's elected representatives. In almost every case, their judgment is the final word. The difficulty of amending the Constitution (approval by two-thirds majorities in the House and Senate and by three-fourths of the states) makes it an impracticable means of reversing Supreme Court decisions. The Sixteenth Amendment, which grants the federal government the power to levy income taxes, is one of the few times that a Supreme Court decision has been reversed through constitutional amendment.

The judiciary's power has been a source of controversy throughout the nation's history, but the debate has seldom been livelier than during recent decades. The sheer number of legal disputes is among the reasons. Federal cases have increased threefold (and federal appeals have increased tenfold) over the past half century as Americans have increasingly turned to the courts to settle their disputes. The judiciary at times has acted almost

HOW THE U.S. DIFFERS
POLITICAL THINKING THROUGH COMPARISONS

Judicial Review

The power of U.S. courts is nowhere more evident than in the exercise of judicial review—the voiding of a legislative or executive action on the grounds that it violates the Constitution. Judicial review had its origins in European experience and thought, but it was first formally applied in the United States at the federal level when, in *Marbury v. Madison* (1803), the Supreme Court declared an act of Congress unconstitutional. Some democracies, including Great Britain, still do not allow broad-scale judicial review, but most democracies now provide for it.

In the so-called American system of judicial review (which is used in Canada, Australia, Sweden, and some other countries, as well as the United States), all judges can declare ordinary law invalid when it conflicts with constitutional law. By comparison, the so-called Austrian system (used in Austria and several other European countries) restricts judicial review to a special constitutional court. Judges in other courts cannot declare a law void on the grounds that it is unconstitutional. In the Austrian system, moreover, constitutional decisions can be made in response to requests for judicial review by elected officials when they are considering legislation. In the American case, judges can act only within the framework of actual legal cases; thus, their rulings are made only after laws have been enacted.

Q: Do you think it would be advantageous if the U.S. Supreme Court, in response to queries by Congress or the president, could issue advisory opinions on the constitutionality of policies under consideration? Or do you prefer the current American system, whereby the Supreme Court can issue opinions only in the context of an actual court case, which means that legislative or executive action must take place in advance of any court ruling?

legislatively by addressing broad social issues, such as abortion, busing, affirmative action, church-state relations, campaign finance, and prison reform. During the 1990s, for example, the prison systems in forty-two states were operating under federal court orders that mandated improvements in health care or reductions in overcrowding. Through such actions the judiciary has restricted the policymaking authority of the states, has narrowed legislative discretion, and has made judicial action an effective political strategy for some groups.[28]

The judiciary has become more extensively involved in policymaking for many of the same reasons that Congress and the president have been thrust into new policy areas and become more deeply involved in old ones. Social and economic changes have required government to play a larger role in society, and this development has generated a seemingly endless series of new legal controversies. Environmental pollution, for example, was not a major issue until the 1960s; since then, it has been the subject of numerous court cases.

How far should judges go in asserting their interpretations of the law, as opposed to those put into effect by the people's elected representatives? What is the proper role of an unelected judiciary in a system rooted in the principle of majority rule? There are competing schools of thought on this issue, none of which is definitive. The Constitution is silent on the question of how it should be interpreted, which has left the judiciary's proper role open to dispute. Nevertheless, a brief review of some of the major competing theories is instructive.

Originalism Theory versus Living Constitution Theory

Originalism theory, a prominent philosophy of conservatives, holds that the Constitution should be interpreted in the way that a reasonable person would have interpreted it at the time it was written.[29] Originalists emphasize the wording of the law, arguing that the words of the framers are the only reliable indicator of how the law should be interpreted. As Supreme Court justice Antonin Scalia, an avowed originalist, has said: "You figure out what [the Constitution] was understood to mean when it was adopted and that's the end of it." The difficult part, Scalia claims, is trying to figure out what the words meant to those who wrote and ratified them. "It requires immersing oneself in the political and intellectual atmosphere of the time—somehow placing out of mind knowledge that we have which an earlier age did not."[30]

An opposing theory, embraced more often by liberals, holds that the Constitution is a living document that should be interpreted in light of

POLITICAL THINKING	Originalism or Living Constitution?

Where do you stand in the debate between proponents of originalism theory (which holds that the Constitution should be interpreted in the way it was meant when written) and proponents of living constitution theory (which holds that the Constitution should be adapted to present-day realities by interpreting it in terms of the kind of government it was meant to create)? Why? What are the weaknesses in the argument for the theory you favor?

changing circumstances. Proponents of the **living constitution theory** claim that the framers, through the use of broad language and basic principles, intended the Constitution to be an adaptable instrument. They cite the preamble of the 1787 Constitutional Convention's Committee of Detail, which says the Constitution "ought to be accommodated to times and events." Supreme Court justice Stephen Breyer embraces this view, saying that the judiciary should promote in today's world the kind of government the Constitution was meant to establish. "The Constitution," Breyer argues, "provides a framework for the creation of democratically determined solutions, which protect each individual's basic liberties . . . while securing a democratic form of government."[31]

Critics of the living constitution theory argue that, in practice, it allows judges to promote their personal views by enabling them to devise arguments that support the rulings they prefer. Such judges are said to turn the law into what they want it to say, rather than what it actually says. On the other hand, critics of originalism theory say that the framers in using broad terms such as "search and seizure" could not possibly have had the practices of their time solely in mind. If that was their intention, they would have provided detailed information on how such terms were to be interpreted.

Judicial Restraint versus Judicial Activism

A longer-standing debate over the judiciary's proper role has pitted the advocates of judicial restraint against the advocates of judicial activism. This debate centers on the degree to which judges should defer to precedent and elected officials.

The doctrine of **judicial restraint** holds that judges should generally defer to precedent and to decisions made by legislatures. The restraint doctrine holds that in nearly every instance policy issues should be decided by elected lawmakers and not by appointed judges. The role of the judge is to apply the law rather than determine it. Advocates of judicial restraint say that when judges substitute their views for those of elected representatives, they undermine the fundamental principle of self-government—the right of the majority, through its elected representatives, to determine how they will be governed.[32] Underlying this argument is the idea that policy is the result of conflicts between contending interests and that elected representatives, because they have to deal directly with these interests, are better positioned than judges to determine how these conflicts should be resolved.[33]

In contrast, the doctrine of **judicial activism** holds that judges should actively interpret the Constitution, statutes, and precedents in light of fundamental principles and should intervene when elected representatives fail to act in accord with these principles. Although advocates of judicial activism acknowledge the importance of deference to majority rule, they claim that the courts should not blindly uphold the decisions of elected officials when core principles—such as liberty, equality, and self-government—are threatened. They also contend that precedent should be respected only if based on legal reasoning that is as sound today as it was when the precedent was established.

Over its history, the Supreme Court has had strong proponents of each doctrine. Chief Justice John Marshall was an avowed activist who used the Court to enlarge the judiciary's power and to promote the national government (see Chapters 2 and 3). Judicial review—the most substantial form of judicial power—is not granted explicitly by the Constitution but was claimed through Marshall's opinion in *Marbury v. Madison.*

Associate Justice Oliver Wendell Holmes Jr. was Marshall's philosophical opposite. One of the nation's most influential jurists, Holmes argued that the judiciary should defer to the elected branches unless they blatantly overstep their authority.[34] An example of judicial restraint is the Supreme Court's 2012 ruling upholding the individual mandate provision of the health care reform bill enacted by Congress in 2010. The Court's majority creatively invoked Congress's taxing power in order to uphold the provision (see Chapter 3). "Because the Constitution permits such a tax, it is not our role to forbid it, or to pass upon its wisdom or fairness," said the Court's majority.[35]

Although judicial activism is sometimes associated with liberal justices, history indicates it has also been practiced by conservative justices. During the period between the Civil War and the Great Depression, the

John Marshall was an ardent nationalist who saw himself as a guardian of federal authority, Marshall led the Court to a series of activist rulings that established it as a powerful institution and helped lay the foundation for a strong Union. Marshall saw himself as a framer of the Constitution, acting as the ongoing architect of the work begun in Philadelphia during the summer of 1787.

Supreme Court was dominated by conservatives and had an activist agenda, striking down most state and congressional legislation aimed at economic regulation (see Chapter 3). In the period after World War II, the Court was again in an activist mode, but this time in a different direction. Dominated by liberal justices, the Court struck down numerous state statutes in the course of expanding fair-trial rights and civil rights (see Chapters 4 and 5).

In recent years, the conservative-dominated Supreme Court has also been an activist court. In the past fifteen years or so, the Supreme Court has struck down more acts of Congress than were invalidated during the previous half century.[36] A case in point is the Court's 2010 ruling on campaign spending. In deciding that corporations and unions could spend freely on election campaigns, the Court overturned congressional action, thus substituting its judgment for that of elected officials. The ruling also overturned precedent—in earlier cases, the Court had held that Congress could regulate election spending by corporations and unions.

What Is the Judiciary's Proper Role?

Like the debate between originalism and living Constitution theorists, the debate between advocates of judicial restraint and activism is a normative one. There is no conclusive way of settling the issue because the Constitution does not specify the method by which judges should arrive at their decisions.

Nevertheless, the debates are important because they address the fundamental question of the role of judges in a governing system based on the often-conflicting concepts of majority rule and individual rights. The United States is a constitutional democracy that recognizes both the power of the majority to rule and the claim of the minority to protection of its rights and interests. The judiciary was not established as the nation's final authority on all things relating to the use of political power. Yet the judiciary was established as a coequal branch of government charged with responsibility for protecting individual rights and constraining political authority. The question of how far the courts should go in asserting their authority is one that every student of government should ponder.

SUMMARY

At the lowest level of the federal judicial system are the district courts, where most federal cases begin. Above them are the federal courts of appeals, which review cases appealed from the lower courts. The U.S. Supreme Court is the nation's highest court. Each state has its own court system, consisting of trial courts at the bottom and one or two appellate levels at the top. Cases originating in state courts ordinarily cannot be appealed to the federal courts unless a federal issue is involved, and then the federal courts can choose to rule only on the federal aspects of the case. Federal judges at all levels are nominated by the president, and if confirmed by the Senate, they are appointed by the president to the office. Once on the federal bench, they serve until they die, retire, or are removed by impeachment and conviction.

The Supreme Court is unquestionably the most important court in the country. The legal principles it establishes are binding on lower courts, and its capacity to define the law is enhanced by the control it exercises over the cases it hears. However, it is inaccurate to assume that lower courts are inconsequential (the upper-court myth). Lower courts have considerable discretion, and the great majority of their decisions are not reviewed by a higher court. It is also inaccurate to assume that federal courts are far more significant than state courts (the federal court myth).

The courts have less discretionary authority than elected institutions do. The judiciary's positions are constrained by the facts of a case and by the laws as defined through the Constitution, legal precedent, and statutes (and government regulations derived from statutes). Yet existing legal guidelines are seldom so precise that judges have no choice in their decisions. As a result, political influences have a strong impact on the judiciary. It responds to national conditions, public opinion, interest groups, and elected officials, particularly the president and members of Congress. Another political influence on the judiciary is the personal beliefs of judges, who have individual preferences that affect how they decide issues that come before the courts. It's not surprising that partisan politics plays a significant role in judicial appointments.

In recent decades, as the Supreme Court has crossed into areas traditionally left to lawmaking majorities, the issue of judicial power has become more pressing, which has prompted claims and counterclaims about the judiciary's proper role. Advocates of originalism theory argue that judges should apply the law in terms of the words of the law as they were understood at the time of enactment. Advocates of the living constitution theory hold that the law should be interpreted in light of changing circumstances. Judicial restraint and activism are two additional theories of the judiciary's proper role. Advocates of judicial restraint claim that the justices' personal values are inadequate justification for exceeding the proper judicial role; they argue that the Constitution entrusts broad issues of the public good to elective institutions and that the courts should ordinarily defer to the judgment of elected officials. Judicial activists counter that the courts were established as an independent branch and should not hesitate to promote general principles when necessary, even if this action brings them into conflict with elected officials.

CRITICAL THINKING ZONE

KEY TERMS

appellate jurisdiction (*p. 445*)
concurring opinion (*p. 447*)
decision (*p. 446*)
dissenting opinion (*p. 447*)
facts (of a court case) (*p. 458*)
judicial activism (*p. 470*)
judicial restraint (*p. 470*)
judicial review (*p. 466*)
jurisdiction (of a court) (*p. 445*)

living constitution theory (*p. 469*)
majority opinion (*p. 447*)
opinion (of a court) (*p. 447*)
original jurisdiction (*p. 445*)
originalism theory (*p. 468*)
plurality opinion (*p. 447*)
precedent (*p. 459*)
writ of certiorari (*p. 445*)

APPLYING THE ELEMENTS OF CRITICAL THINKING

Conceptualizing: Define majority opinion, concurring opinion, and dissenting opinion in the context of Supreme Court decision making. What role is the majority opinion expected to play in decisions made by lower-court judges?

Synthesizing: Contrast the doctrines of judicial restraint and judicial activism.

Analyzing: Explain the influence of politics on the selection of Supreme Court justices and on the decisions the justices make. In comparison with lower-court judges, why would Supreme Court justices be expected to let their political beliefs play a greater role in their decisions? (Consider here the nature of the cases heard by the Supreme Court.)

EXTRA CREDIT

A Book Worth Reading: Jeffrey Toobin, *The Nine: Inside the Secret World of the Supreme Court*. New York: Anchor, 2008. Winner of the J. Anthony Lewis Book Prize, this book by a noted journalist provides a riveting look at the inside workings of the Supreme Court.

A Website Worth Visiting: **www.law.cornell.edu.** The Cornell University Legal Information Institute's website includes the full versions of historic and recent Supreme Court decisions, updates on cases before the Court, and links to state constitutions and other material.

PARTICIPATE!

The right to a jury trial is one of the oldest features—dating to the colonial period—of the American political experience. Jury trials also offer the average citizen a rare opportunity to be part of the governing structure. Yet Americans increasingly shirk jury duty. When summoned, many of them find all sorts of reasons why they should be excused from jury duty. In some areas of the country, the avoidance rate exceeds 50 percent. Some citizens even give up their right to vote because they know that jurors in their area are selected from names on voter registration lists. There are reasons, however, to look upon jury duty as an opportunity as well as a responsibility. Studies indicate that citizens come away from the jury experience with a fuller appreciation of the justice system. Jurors acquire an understanding of the serious responsibility handed to them when asked to decide upon someone's guilt or innocence. The legal standard in American courts—"guilty beyond a reasonable doubt"—is a solemn one. The fairness of the jury system also requires full participation by the community. Studies show that jurors' life experiences can affect the decisions they reach. If everyone on a jury is from the same background and one that is different from the defendant's, the odds of a wrongful verdict increase. "A jury of one's peers" should mean just that—a jury of individuals who, collectively, represent the range of groups in the community. If you are called to serve on a jury, you should answer the call. You would want nothing less from others than if you, a family member, or a friend were the person on trial.

15

CHAPTER

ECONOMIC AND ENVIRONMENTAL
POLICY: CONTRIBUTING TO
PROSPERITY

66We the People of the United States, in Order to . . . insure domestic Tranquility.99

PREAMBLE, U.S. CONSTITUTION

The economy was in turmoil. The housing market was collapsing from the inability of homeowners with subprime adjustable-rate mortgages to make their monthly payments. Then, on September 15, 2008, after its stock had dropped precipitously, Lehman Brothers, one of the nation's oldest and largest commercial banks, went out of business. Its bankruptcy sent shock waves through Wall Street—the Dow Jones Industrial Average plunged 500 points, followed soon thereafter by an even larger one-day drop. Was the United States headed for an economic meltdown that would rival the Great Depression of the 1930s?

Although some pundits suggested another Great Depression might be in the offing, few economists predicted as much, and for good reason.

When the Great Depression began in 1929, there were no government programs in place to stabilize and stimulate the economy. Back then, panic had swept through society, accelerating the downturn. Businesses cut back on production, investors fled the stock market, depositors withdrew their bank savings, and consumers slowed their spending—all of which fueled the downward spiral. In 2008, by contrast, government programs were in place to protect depositors' savings, slow the drop in home and stock prices, and steady the economy through adjustments in interest rates and government spending. Among the government initiatives was the Troubled Asset Relief Program (TARP) of 2008 that made $700 billion available to bolster shaky financial institutions. By 2010, job loss had lessened, the financial markets were beginning to stabilize, and businesses were starting to recover. The turnaround was slower and more fitful than many economists had predicted, but government intervention had helped prevent a repeat of the 1930s, when unemployment rose as high as 25 percent and never dropped below 10 percent.

This chapter examines economic and environmental policy. As was discussed in Chapter 1, public policy is a decision by government to follow a course of action designed to produce a particular result. In this vein, economic policy aims to promote and regulate economic interests and, through fiscal and monetary actions, to foster economic growth and stability. The main ideas presented in this chapter are:

- *Through regulation, the U.S. government imposes restraints on business activity for the purpose of promoting economic efficiency and equity.*
- *Through regulatory and conservation policies, the U.S. government seeks to protect and preserve the environment from the actions of business firms and consumers.*
- *Through promotion, the U.S. government helps private interests achieve their economic goals.* Business in particular benefits from the government's promotional efforts, including, for example, tax breaks and loans.
- *Through its taxing and spending decisions (fiscal policy), the U.S. government seeks to generate a level of economic supply and demand that will maintain economic prosperity.*
- *Through its money supply decisions (monetary policy), the U.S. government— through the Federal Reserve System (the "Fed")—seeks to maintain a level of inflation consistent with sustained, controllable economic growth.*

GOVERNMENT AS REGULATOR OF THE ECONOMY

An **economy** is a system of production and consumption of goods and services that are allocated through exchange. When a shopper selects an item at a store, and pays for it with cash or credit card, the transaction is one of the millions of exchanges that make up the economy.

In *The Wealth of Nations* (1776), Adam Smith advanced the doctrine of **laissez-faire economics,** which holds that private firms should be free to make their own production decisions. Smith reasoned that firms will produce a good when there is a demand for it (that is, when people are willing and able to buy it). Smith argued that the profit motive is the "invisible hand" that guides supply decisions in a capitalist system. He acknowledged that laissez-faire capitalism had limits. Certain areas of the economy, such as roadways, are natural monopolies and are better handled by government than by private firms. Government is also needed to impose order on private transactions by regulating banking, currency, and contracts. Otherwise, Smith argued, the economy should be left largely in private hands.

Although laissez-faire economics prevailed in the United States during the nineteenth century, government was not sidelined completely. Through

The federal government's bailout of troubled financial institutions was politically unpopular, but economists claim it prevented the economic downturn that began in 2008 from becoming much worse.

table 15-1	THE MAIN OBJECTIVES OF REGULATORY POLICY	
Objective	Definition	Representative Actions by Government
Efficiency	Fulfillment of as many of society's needs as possible at the cost of as few of its resources as possible. The greater the output for a given input, the more efficient the process.	Preventing restraint of trade; requiring producers to pay the costs of damage to the environment; reducing restrictions on business that cannot be justified on a cost-benefit basis.
Equity	When the outcome of an economic transaction is fair to each party.	Requiring firms to bargain in good faith with labor; protecting consumers in their purchases; protecting workers' safety and health.

the Pacific Railways Act of 1862, for example, Congress authorized the issuance of government bonds and the use of public lands to build the transcontinental railroad, which, though operated by private firms, was subject to government regulation. Nevertheless, it was not until the Great Depression of the 1930s that government assumed a broad economic role. Today, the United States has what is called a *mixed economy*. Although the economy operates mainly through private transactions, government plays a substantial role. The stock market, for example, is regulated by the Securities and Exchange Commission (SEC), which requires publicly traded companies to disclose their assets to investors. The U.S. government even owns some industry (for example, the Tennessee Valley Authority, which produces electricity). Nevertheless, in comparison, say, with the Scandinavian countries, where government provides health care to all citizens and controls several major industries, including the airlines, the United States relies more heavily on free-market mechanisms.

One way the U.S. government participates in the economy is through the **regulation** of privately owned businesses.[1] U.S. firms are not free to act as they please but instead operate within the limit of government regulation, which is designed to promote economic *efficiency* and *equity* (see Table 15-1).

Efficiency through Government Intervention

Economic efficiency results when the output of goods and services is the highest possible given the amount of input (such as labor and material) that is used to produce it.[2] Efficiency is an important goal. It means that society is getting as many goods and services as possible from the resources used in producing them.

Promoting Competition   Adam Smith and other classical economists argued that the free market is the optimal means of achieving efficiency. In producing goods and services, firms will try to use as few resources as possible in order to keep their prices low, which will make their products more attractive to consumers. To compete, less-efficient producers will have to cut their production costs or face the loss of customers to lower-priced competitors.

Markets are not always competitive, however. If a producer can acquire a monopoly on a particular product or conspires with other producers to fix the price of the product at an artificially high level, the producer does not have to be concerned with efficiency. Consumers who need a good will have no choice but to pay the seller's price. Price fixing was prevalent in the United States in the late nineteenth century when large trusts came to dominate many areas of the economy, including the oil, railroad, and sugar industries. Railroad companies, for example, had no competition on short routes and charged such high rates that many farmers went broke because they could not afford to ship their crops to markets. In 1887, Congress enacted the Interstate Commerce Act, which created the Interstate Commerce Commission (ICC) and assigned it responsibility for regulating railroad practices, including shipping rates.

The goal of such regulatory activity is to improve efficiency by restoring market competition or by placing a limit on what monopolies can charge for goods and services. Business competition today is overseen by a wide range of federal agencies, including, for example, the Federal Trade Commission and the Antitrust Division of the Justice Department. These agencies blocked the attempted merger of Office Depot and Staples, on grounds that it would undermine competition in the sale of office supplies. On the other hand, the government allows concentrated ownership in industries, such as oil and automobiles, where the capital costs are so high that small firms cannot hope to compete.[3] Government acceptance of corporate giants also reflects the fact that market competition is no longer simply an issue of domestic firms. For example, the major U.S. automakers—Chrysler, Ford, and General Motors—compete for customers not only with each other but also with Asian and European auto manufacturers, such as Honda and BMW.

Making Business Pay for Indirect Costs   Economic inefficiencies also result when businesses or consumers fail to pay the full costs of resources used in production. Take, for example, companies whose industrial wastes seep

P A R T Y
POLARIZATION

Political Thinking in Conflict

Business Regulation

There is barely an economic issue on which Republican and Democratic lawmakers now agree. It was not always that way. When Republican President Richard Nixon took the United States off the gold standard in 1971 he said, "I am now a Keynesian in economics," embracing an economic theory that had been associated with the Democratic Party. Nixon also issued the executive order that created the Environmental Protection Agency (EPA)—an action that was applauded by lawmakers from both parties. This bipartisan spirit began to unravel in the 1980s when Republican President Ronald Reagan, despite Democratic opposition, got Congress to cut taxes on upper incomes and deregulate key industries, including banking. Reagan argued that the policies would unleash the private sector as a source of jobs and profits. Democrats said the policies would impose costs on consumers and the less wealthy. The divide has persisted, with Republicans advocating policies that would reduce government regulation of business activity and Democrats advocating policies that would allow for close oversight of business. The differences surfaced, for example, in the passage of the 2010 Dodd-Frank Wall Street Reform and Consumer Protection Act, which broadened government oversight of financial institutions and created a new consumer agency to protect borrowers against abuses by credit card companies, mortgage companies, and other lenders. The bill was enacted along party lines, with Democrats overwhelmingly voting for it and Republicans overwhelmingly voting against it—positions that meshed with the parties' ideologies and constituencies. President Obama said the legislation would "protect consumers and lay the foundation for a stronger and safer financial system." Senate Republican leader Mitch McConnell took an opposing view. "The White House will call this a victory," he said. "But as credit tightens, regulations multiply and job creation slows even further as a result of this bill, they'll have a hard time convincing the American people that this is a victory for them."

Q: What's your view on business regulation? Would you prefer less regulation, even though it could subject consumers to unfair business practices, or would you prefer more regulation, even though it could slow economic growth?

into nearby rivers. The price of these companies' products does not reflect the cost to society of the resulting water pollution. Economists label these unpaid costs **externalities.**

Until the 1960s, the federal government did not require firms to pay such costs. The impetus to begin doing so came from the scientific community and environmental groups. The Clean Air Act of 1963 and the Water Quality Act of 1965 required firms to install antipollution devices in order to reduce air and water pollution. In 1970, Congress created the Environmental Protection Agency to monitor firms and ensure their compliance with federal regulations governing air and water quality and the disposal of toxic wastes. (Environmental policy is discussed more fully later in the chapter.)

Deregulation and Underregulation   Although government regulation is intended to increase economic efficiency, it can have the opposite effect if it unnecessarily increases the cost of doing business.[4] Firms have to devote work hours to monitor and implement government regulations, which in some instances (for example, pollution control) also require companies to buy and install expensive equipment. These costs are efficient to the degree that they produce corresponding benefits. Yet if government places excessive regulatory burdens on firms, they waste resources in the process of complying. The result of overregulation is higher-priced goods that are more expensive for consumers and less competitive in the domestic and global markets.

To curb overregulation, Congress in 1995 enacted legislation that prohibits administrators in some instances from issuing a regulation unless they can show that its benefits outweigh its costs. A more concerted response is **deregulation**—the rescinding of regulations already in force for the purpose of improving efficiency. This process began in 1977 with passage of the Airlines Deregulation Act, which eliminated the requirement that airlines provide service to smaller-sized cities and gave them the authority to set ticket prices (before then, the prices were set by a government agency). The change had its intended effect. Competition between airlines increased on routes between larger-sized cities, resulting in cheaper airfares on these routes. Congress followed airline deregulation with partial deregulation of, among others, the trucking, banking, energy, and communications industries.

Deregulation can be carried too far.[5] Freed of regulatory restrictions, firms can engage in reckless or unethical practices. Such was the case with the recent subprime mortgage crisis. Mortgage firms lured marginally qualified homebuyers by offering low interest rates and small down

A meltdown in the subprime mortgage sector in 2008 contributed to falling home prices and a rise in foreclosures, triggering a steep downturn in the economy. Mortgage firms were largely to blame; they had given mortgages to hundreds of thousands of unqualified and marginally qualified homebuyers.

payments. After pocketing the up-front profit, they sold the mortgages to unsuspecting investors in order to reduce their risk. When the economy weakened, many homeowners defaulted on their mortgages, precipitating the 2008 financial crisis. Expressing a view held by political leaders of both parties, Barack Obama said that "the free market was never meant to be a free license to take whatever you can get." In 2010, Congress enacted the most substantial regulation of financial institutions since the New Deal. Designed to curb the abuses that contributed to the financial crisis, the Dodd-Frank Wall Street Reform and Consumer Protection Act empowers government to more closely oversee financial activities. It also created a new federal agency (the Consumer Financial Protection Bureau) to protect consumers from exploitation by credit card companies, lending institutions, and other creditors.

The crisis in America's financial system demonstrates that the issue of business regulation is not a simple question of whether or not to regulate. Too much regulation can burden firms with excessive implementation costs, whereas too little regulation can give firms the leeway to engage in risky or unethical practices. Either too little or too much regulation can result in economic inefficiency.

Equity through Government Intervention

The government intervenes in the economy to bring equity as well as efficiency to the marketplace. **Economic equity** occurs when an economic transaction is fair to each party.[6] A transaction can be considered fair if each party enters into it freely and ethically. For example, if a seller knows that a product is defective, equity requires that the buyer also know of the defect.

Equity regulation has come in response to changing economic conditions. The first wave of regulation came during the Progressive Era, when reformers sought to stop abusive business practices. An example of a Progressive reform was the creation in 1907 of the Food and Drug Administration (FDA). Unsafe food and drugs were being widely marketed, and the FDA was charged with keeping them off the market.

The second wave of equity regulation came during the Great Depression, when New Deal reformers sought to restrict destructive business practices. The Securities and Exchange Act of 1934, for example, was designed in part to protect investors from dishonest or imprudent stock and bond brokers. The New Deal also provided greater equity for organized labor, which had been in a weak position in dealing with management. The Fair Labor Standards Act of 1938, for example, required employers to pay workers a minimum wage.

The third wave of regulatory reforms came in the 1960s and 1970s and sought to promote environmental protection, consumer protection, and worker safety. Ten federal agencies, including the Consumer Product Safety Commission and the Environmental Protection Agency, were established to curtail harmful business activity. Among the products declared to be unsafe in the 1960s and 1970s were cigarettes, leaded paint, and gasoline. This regulatory activity has had remarkable effects. Brain damage in children from lead poisoning, for example, has declined sharply in the past few decades.[7]

POLITICAL THINKING

Thank You for Smoking?

Jason Reitman's Thank You for Smoking *is a satirical film about the efforts of big tobacco companies to hook young people on smoking. A leading cause of death, cigarettes were a target of the wave of regulatory reform that began in the late 1960s. After a tough new tobacco law was passed in 2009, the FDA ordered tobacco makers to place graphic warnings, such as a photo of diseased lungs, on cigarette packages, but a federal appellate court ruled in 2012 that the mandate violated tobacco companies' free-speech rights. What's your view on this issue? Should the government have the regulatory authority to require firms to warn consumers of dangerous products, even to the extent of requiring these firms to display graphic images?*

The Politics of Regulatory Policy

Although business firms fought the Progressive Era and New Deal reforms, their opposition diminished gradually as they came to realize that the new regulatory agencies could be influenced. Because these agencies were charged with overseeing particular industries, such as banking or pharmaceuticals, a regulated industry could develop a close relationship with its associated agency. Pharmaceutical firms, for example, have cultivated a relationship with the FDA that at times has served their interest. In the 1990s, for instance, drug companies convinced the FDA to streamline its drug-safety reviews in order to speed the marketing of new drugs.[8] In some cases, the FDA's fast-track reviews were harmful to consumers. One fast-tracked drug, Vioxx, had to be taken off the market in 2004 after it was found to cause strokes and heart attacks.

The third wave of regulatory reforms of the 1960s and 1970s differed from the Progressive and New Deal reforms in their structure. Most of the regulatory agencies established in the third wave were granted a broader mandate than those created earlier. They have responsibility not for a single industry but for firms of all types, and their policy scope covers a wide range of activities. The Environmental Protection Agency (EPA), for example, is charged with regulating environmental pollution of almost any kind by almost any firm. Because newer agencies such as the EPA deal with so many industries, no single industry can easily influence agency decisions.

Most of the older agencies, including the Federal Communications Commission (FCC) and the Securities and Exchange Commission (SEC), are run by a commission whose members are nominated by the president and serve fixed terms but cannot be removed by the president during their term of office, which is a reason they sometimes get too friendly with the industry they regulate. Most of the newer agencies, including the EPA, are headed by a single director who can be removed from office at the president's discretion. As a result, the newer agencies tend to be more responsive to the president than to the firms they oversee.

GOVERNMENT AS PROTECTOR OF THE ENVIRONMENT

Few changes in public opinion and policy during recent decades have been as dramatic as those relating to the environment. Most Americans today recycle some of their garbage, and roughly two-thirds say they are either an active environmentalist or sympathetic to environmental concerns.

Silent Spring brought lasting fame to Rachel Carson. Even before the book was published in 1962, chemical companies were threatening lawsuits and portraying her as mentally unstable and scientifically untrained. Despite the attacks, *Silent Spring* became a huge best-seller and contributed to passage of the first federal safe air and water legislation.

In the 1960s, few Americans sorted their trash, and few could have answered a polling question that asked them whether they were an "environmentalist." The term was not widely used, and most people would not have understood its meaning.

The publication in 1962 of Rachel Carson's *Silent Spring* helped launch the environmental movement.[9] Written at a time when the author was dying of breast cancer, *Silent Spring* revealed the threat to birds and animals of pesticides such as DDT. Carson's appearance at a Senate hearing contributed to legislative action that produced the 1963 Clean Air Act and the 1965 Water Quality Act—the first major federal laws aimed at protecting the environment from man-made pollution. Today, environmental protection extends to nearly two hundred harmful forms of emission.

Conservationism: The Older Wave

Although antipollution policy is relatively new, the government has been involved in land conservation for more than a century.[10] The first national park was created at Yellowstone in 1872 and, like the later ones, was established to preserve the nation's natural heritage for generations to come. Today, the national park system serves more than one hundred million visitors each year and includes a total of eighty million acres, an area larger than every state except Alaska, Texas, California, and Montana. The national parks are run by the National Park Service, an agency within the Department of the Interior. Another agency, the U.S. Forest Service, located within the Department of Agriculture, manages the national forests, which cover an area more than twice the size of the national parks. They too have been established in order to protect America's natural heritage.

The nation's parks and forests are subject to a "multiple use" policy. They are nature preserves and recreation areas, but they are also rich in natural resources—minerals, timber, and grazing lands. The federal government sells permits to ranchers, logging companies, and mining firms that authorize them to take some of these resources, which can bring them into conflict with conservationists. A case in point is Alaska's Arctic National Wildlife Refuge (ANWR). The refuge is home to numerous species, including caribou and moose, but it also contains substantial oil and natural gas reserves. Oil companies have long wanted to drill in ANWR, whereas environmental groups have sought to block drilling.

Some of the nation's untapped oil reserves are on public lands. Oil companies and conservationists often clash when the question arises as to whether a particular site should be opened for drilling.

Over the past few decades, ANWR has periodically been the focus of intense political debate and lobbying. President George W. Bush sought to open ANWR to drilling while President Obama acted to oppose it.

Conservation is more than an issue of protecting nature's unspoiled beauty. Also involved is the protection of species that cannot survive outside their natural habitat. Some species, such as the deer and the raccoon, adapt easily to human encroachment. Other species are harmed by it. These species are covered by the Endangered Species Act (ESA) of 1973, which requires federal agencies to protect threatened and endangered species. Hundreds of mammals, birds, fishes, insects, and plants are currently on the ESA's protection list.

Environmentalism: The Newer Wave

The 1960s were pivotal to the federal government's realization of the harmful effects of air, water, and ground pollutants. The period was capped by the first Earth Day. Held in the spring of 1970, it was the brainchild of Senator Gaylord Nelson (D-Wis.), who had devoted nearly ten years to finding ways to create public interest in environmental issues. With Earth Day, Nelson succeeded to a degree not even he might have imagined: ten thousand grade and high schools, two thousand colleges, and one thousand communities participated in the event, which included public rallies and environmental cleanup efforts. Earth Day has been held every year since 1970 and is now a worldwide event.

Environmental Protection   The year 1970 also marked the creation of the Environmental Protection Agency. Within a few months, the EPA was issuing new regulations at such a rapid pace that business firms had difficulty implementing them. Corporations eventually found an ally in President Gerald Ford, who in a 1975 speech claimed that business regulation was costing $150 billion annually, or $2,000 for every American family.[11] Although Ford's estimate was disputed by economic analysts, his point was not lost on policymakers or the public. The economy was in a slump, and the costs of complying with the new regulations were slowing the recovery. Polls indicated declining public support for regulatory action. Since then, environmental protection policy has not greatly expanded, nor has it greatly contracted. The emphasis has been on carrying out the laws put into effect in the 1960s and 1970s.

Environmental regulation has led to dramatic improvements in air and water quality. Pollution levels today are far below their levels of the 1960s, when yellowish-gray fog ("smog") hung over cities like Los Angeles and New York and when bodies of water like the Potomac River and Lake

Erie were open sewers. In the past four decades, toxic waste emissions have been halved, hundreds of polluted lakes and rivers have been revitalized, energy efficiency has increased, food supplies have been made safer, and urban air pollution has declined by 60 percent.[12]

Badly contaminated toxic waste sites are also a problem. These sites pollute local water supplies, resulting in increased rates of cancer and other illnesses. Although Congress in the 1980s established the so-called Superfund program to rid these sites of their contaminants, the cleanup process has been slow and contentious. Firms that caused the pollution are liable for some of the cleanup costs, but many of them are no longer in business, have since been sold to another company, or lack the necessary funds. Firms that could pay the costs have often chosen to fight the issue in court, further delaying the cleanup. According to EPA figures, more than a third of the most dangerous sites are still contaminated.

Global Warming and Energy Policy   No environmental issue receives more attention than global warming. The earth's temperature level has been rising and the rate of increase has accelerated (see Figure 15-1). Most scientists theorize that the temperature rise is attributable to emissions from carbon-based fuels, such as oil and coal. They hypothesize that the emissions produce a "greenhouse effect"—heat gets trapped in the

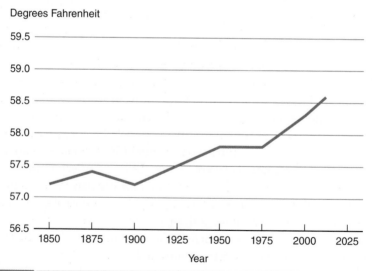

figure 15-1   AVERAGE TEMPERATURE OF THE EARTH'S SURFACE

The average surface temperature of the earth has risen substantially in the past century and has done so at an accelerating pace in the past three decades.
Source: National Weather Service, Great Britain, 2014.

atmosphere rather than escaping into space, resulting in rising temperature levels. This theory has not gone unchallenged. Although virtually all credible scientists accept as fact the increase in temperature, some of them think much of it is due to the earth's natural cycle of warming and cooling.

As would be expected, there is greater disagreement on climate change among U.S. lawmakers. Some hold to the view that climate change is a problem that needs to be addressed urgently and in a substantial way. Others say that a substantial response should be delayed until the consequences of global warming are more clearly understood. Still others say that the remedies for global warming, such as requiring companies to reduce their carbon emissions, would slow economic growth to an unacceptable level.

This lack of consensus has led U.S. lawmakers to prefer clean energy sources and energy conservation as answers to global warming. In 2007, a bipartisan majority in Congress enacted the Energy Independence and Security Act, which established higher fuel-efficiency standards for vehicles and set a goal of eliminating incandescent light lightbulbs within a decade. President Bush said the legislation was a "major step . . . toward confronting global climate change."

Nevertheless, the United States lags behind most Western countries, including Germany, France, and Great Britain, in reducing its greenhouse gas emissions. The reasons are several, including the structure of the U.S. political system. The division of power between the president, the House, and the Senate makes it difficult to garner the support necessary to implement policies that impose economic costs. In 1997, after helping to negotiate an international agreement on carbon emissions (the Kyoto Protocol), President Clinton was unable to persuade the Senate to ratify it. When George W. Bush assumed office in 2001, he rejected the agreement, saying that it would blunt economic growth. A congressional effort in 2010 to reduce greenhouse gases also failed to gain the necessary support. Although Democrats in the House of Representatives passed a bill that capped carbon emissions, the legislation died when Senate Republicans and Democrats were unable to reach agreement on key provisions.

The issue of climate change is confounded by the fact that no single nation can solve the problem on its own. When carbon emissions get into the atmosphere, they affect conditions elsewhere. The problem is also confounded by the rapid expansion of the economies of China, India, and other developing nations, which has increased the level of carbon emissions. These countries say they should not bear the burden of curbing global warming, arguing that the problem stems from decades-long carbon emissions by the industrialized nations, including the United States (see "How the U.S. Differs").

HOW THE U.S. DIFFERS
POLITICAL THINKING THROUGH COMPARISONS

Carbon-Fuel Emissions and Global Warming

The United States, as the chart indicates, is the world's single largest source of carbon-fuel emissions on a per-capita basis. The United States emits about 20 percent of the world total. Carbon-fuel emissions have been linked to global warming and have increasingly drawn the attention of the international community. Most scientists believe global warming can be retarded only by curbing greenhouse gas emissions. Politics stands in the way of such action. Curbs on emissions would slow a country's economic growth, and no country by itself has the capacity to reduce global warming significantly. These realities have blocked a binding, comprehensive international agreement to address the problem. However, the United Nations

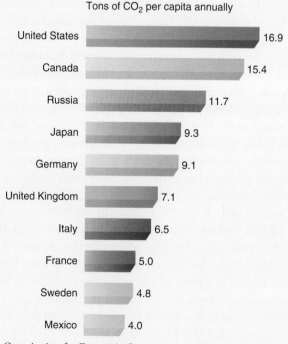

Tons of CO_2 per capita annually

United States	16.9
Canada	15.4
Russia	11.7
Japan	9.3
Germany	9.1
United Kingdom	7.1
Italy	6.5
France	5.0
Sweden	4.8
Mexico	4.0

Source: Organization for Economic Cooperation and Development, 2014.

Climate Change Conference, which met in Poland in 2013, did make progress when the advanced industrialized countries renewed their commitment to help developing countries meet the costs of reducing their carbon emissions.

Q: Why might it make sense to place most of the burden for reducing carbon-fuel emissions on nations with developing economies such as China and India? How might advanced industrialized nations such as the United States and Germany contribute to this effort?

A: An argument for placing the burden on developing economies is that their carbon emissions are increasing at the fastest rate. Advanced industrialized nations such as the United States and Germany could then provide developing countries with clean-energy technology that can be used, for example, when they install new power plants, which are a major source of carbon emissions. Developed countries could also provide monetary assistance to ease the economic burden that would fall on developing countries as a result of implementing costly carbon-reduction measures.

GOVERNMENT AS PROMOTER OF ECONOMIC INTERESTS

Congress in 1789 gave a boost to the nation's shipping industry by imposing a tariff on goods brought into the United States on foreign ships, which prompted importers to make greater use of American ships. Since that first favor, the U.S. government has provided thousands of direct and indirect benefits to economic interests. The following sections describe some of these benefits.

Promoting Business

Business firms are not opposed to government regulation as such. They object only to regulatory policies that harm their interests. At various times and in different ways, as in the case of the FDA and pharmaceutical firms, some regulatory agencies have sided with the very industries they are supposed to regulate in the public interest.

Loans and tax breaks are other ways that government promotes business interests. Firms receive loan guarantees, direct loans, tax credits for capital investments, and tax deductions for capital depreciation. However, the most significant contribution that government makes to business is in the traditional services it provides, such as education, transportation, and defense. Colleges and universities, which are funded primarily by government, furnish business with most of its professional and technical workforce and with much of the basic research that goes into product development. The nation's roadways, waterways, and airports are other public-sector contributions without which business could not function. In short, America's business has no bigger booster than government.

Promoting Labor

Laissez-faire thinking dominated government's approach to labor well into the twentieth century. Union activity was held by the courts to be illegal because it interfered with the rights of business. Government hostility toward labor included the use of police and soldiers to break up strikes. In 1914 in Ludlow, Colorado, state militia attacked a tent colony of striking miners and their families, killing nineteen, including eleven children.

The 1930s Great Depression brought about a change in labor's position. The National Labor Relations Act of 1935, for example, gave workers the right to bargain collectively and prohibited business from disrupting union activities or discriminating against union employees. Government support for labor now also includes minimum-wage and maximum-work-hour guarantees, unemployment benefits, safer and more healthful working conditions, and nondiscriminatory hiring practices. Although the federal government's support of labor extends beyond these examples, its support is much less extensive than its support of business.

Promoting Agriculture

Government support for agriculture has a long history. The Homestead Act of 1862, for example, opened government-owned lands to settlement. The federal government provided 160 acres of land free to any family that staked a claim, built a house, and farmed the land for five years.

Government programs today provide billions of dollars of assistance annually to farmers, small and large. Federal payments account for more than a fifth of net agricultural income, making America's farmers among the most heavily subsidized in the world. This assistance is intended in part to reduce the market risks associated with farming. Weather, global conditions, and other factors can radically affect crop and livestock prices, and federal subsidies lend stability to farm incomes.

A major contribution that government makes to economic interests—particularly business, but also labor and agriculture—is through public colleges and universities. Supported in significant part by taxpayer dollars, they provide research and workforce training of benefit to economic interests, which otherwise would have to pay these costs themselves. Shown here is a campus scene at the University of Texas at San Antonio.

Farm subsidies traditionally have had strong support in Congress, particularly from rural-state senators and representatives. In 2008, Congress passed a five-year, $300 billion farm bill that would put farmers in line for hefty government assistance in future years. President Bush vetoed it, but Congress overrode his veto. In 2014, driven by the desire of lawmakers to reduce the budget deficit, Congress passed a new five-year farm bill that tightened the conditions under which farmers get federal support. Although its provisions are less generous, the new program does not leave farmers out in the cold. Farmers remain one of the nation's most heavily subsidized groups.

FISCAL POLICY AS AN ECONOMIC TOOL

Before the 1930s, prevailing economic theory held that the economy was self-regulating, that it would correct itself after a downturn. The greatest economic collapse in the nation's history—the Great Depression of the 1930s—shattered that idea. The economy did not recover on its own, but instead continued to decline. President Franklin D. Roosevelt's spending and job programs, which stimulated the economy and put Americans back to work, ushered in the modern era.[13] Today, government is expected to intervene when the economy dips.

The government's efforts to maintain a thriving economy occur in part through its taxing and spending decisions, which together are referred to as its **fiscal policy**. Through changes in its level of spending and taxation, government can stimulate or slow the economy (see Table 15-2).

table 15-2	FISCAL POLICY: A SUMMARY OF THE GOVERNMENT'S ROLE
Economic Problem	**Fiscal Policy Actions**
Recession	Demand side: increase spending Supply side: cut business taxes
Inflation	Demand side: decrease spending Supply side: increase business taxes

Demand-Side Policy

Fiscal policy has its origins in the early twentieth-century economic theories of John Maynard Keynes. Noting that employers tend to cut their production and workforce when the economy begins to weaken, Keynes challenged the traditional idea that government should also cut back on its spending. Keynes claimed that a downturn could be shortened only if government compensates for the slowdown in private spending by increasing its spending level. In doing so, the government pumps money into the economy, which stimulates consumer spending, which in turn stimulates business production and creates jobs, thereby hastening the economic recovery.[14]

Keynesian theory holds that the level of the government's response should be commensurate with the severity of the downturn. During an **economic depression**—an exceptionally steep and sustained decline in the economy—the government should engage in massive new spending programs to speed the recovery. During an **economic recession,** which is a more common but less-severe downturn, government spending should also be increased but by a lesser amount.

Keynes's theory is based on **demand-side economics.** It emphasizes the consumer "demand" component of the supply-demand equation. When the economy is sluggish, the government, by increasing its spending, places additional money in consumers' hands. With more money in their pockets, consumers spend more, which boosts economic activity. The theory is that if more goods and services are being purchased, whether for groceries or for new construction projects, firms will have to retain or hire workers to produce the goods and services, which will lessen the severity of the downturn. This line of reasoning was behind the $787 billion economic stimulus bill that Congress passed in 2009 as a means of combating the steep economic slide precipitated by the near collapse

HOW THE 50 STATES DIFFER

POLITICAL THINKING THROUGH COMPARISONS

Federal Taxes and Benefits: Winners and Losers

Fiscal policy (the federal government's taxing and spending policies) varies in its effect on the states. The residents of some states pay a lot more in federal taxes than they receive in benefits. The biggest loser is New Jersey, whose taxpayers get back in federal spending in their state only $0.61 for every dollar they pay in federal taxes. Nevada taxpayers ($0.65 for every dollar) are the next-biggest losers. In contrast, the residents of some states get back more from federal spending programs than they contribute in taxes. The biggest winners are

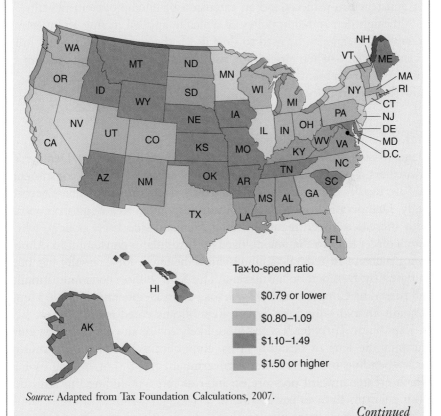

Tax-to-spend ratio

$0.79 or lower

$0.80–1.09

$1.10–1.49

$1.50 or higher

Source: Adapted from Tax Foundation Calculations, 2007.

Continued

New Mexico and Mississippi, whose taxpayers get back $2.03 and $2.02, respectively, in federal spending in their states for every dollar they pay in federal taxes.

Q: Why are many of the "losers" in the Northeast?

A: The federal taxes that originate in a state reflect its wealth, and states in the Northeast are generally wealthier than most other states. Because of this, they also get less federal assistance for programs designed to help lower-income people and areas. Finally, most federal lands and military installations—sources of federal money—lie outside the Northeast.

of the financial markets. The legislation included, for example, funding for construction projects and an extension of unemployment benefits.

Although demand-side policy is typically applied during an economic downturn, it can also be used to slow down the economy during an inflationary period—when prices are rising rapidly. By cutting back on its spending, government places less money in consumers' hands, helping to slow the rise in prices.

Supply-Side Policy

Demand-side stimulation has been the preferred policy of Democratic lawmakers. Lower-income Americans are a core Democratic constituency and are usually the most deeply affected by rising unemployment. Accordingly, Democratic leaders have typically responded to a sluggish economy with increased government spending (demand-side fiscal policy), which offers direct help to the unemployed and stimulates consumption. Almost every increase in federal unemployment benefits, for example, has been initiated by Democratic lawmakers. The $787 billion economic stimulus bill passed by Congress in 2009 was basically a Democratic bill. No House Republican and only three Senate Republicans voted for it.

Republican Party leaders are more likely to see an economic downturn through the lens of business firms. Republicans have typically resisted large spending increases because government has to borrow the money, which creates upward pressure on interest rates, including the rates that business firms have to pay for loans.

A fiscal policy alternative to demand-side stimulation is **supply-side economics,** which emphasizes the business (supply) component of the supply-demand equation. Supply-side theory was a cornerstone of President Ronald Reagan's response to the economic downturn that began before he took office in 1981. Rather than relying on government spending programs to boost consumer spending, Reagan turned to tax cuts as a means of stimulating business activity. "Reaganomics" included large tax breaks for firms and upper-income individuals.[15] These supply-side measures were intended to encourage business investment with resulting increases in employment and income. As jobs and wages increased, consumer spending was also expected to increase, fostering economic growth.

Supply-side theory was also the basis of President George W. Bush's economic initiatives, which included reductions in the personal income tax and in the **capital-gains tax** (the tax that individuals pay on gains in capital investments such as property and stocks). Claiming that taxes on the wealthy were stunting economic growth, Bush persuaded Congress to reduce the capital-gains tax rate from 28 percent to 15 percent and to cut the highest marginal tax rate on personal income from 39 percent to 35 percent. The savings to Americans in the top 1 percent of income was $54,493 per year, compared with an average of $67 for those in the bottom 20 percent and $611 for those in the middle 20 percent.[16]

Bush's supply-side tax cuts had the support of 90 percent of congressional Republicans and only 20 percent of congressional Democrats.[17] In contrast to the philosophy behind the Bush tax cuts, Democratic

The unemployment office is an all-too-familiar scene for jobless Americans during an economic downturn. Through demand-side or supply-side policies, U.S. policymakers seek to stimulate the economy in order to reduce the unemployment rate.

POLITICAL THINKING

Who Should Get the Tax Cuts?

Few issues spark more controversy than taxes. When a tax cut is being debated, the argument usually centers on how the cut should be divided. Supply-side economists have one answer to the question: the taxpayers who are personally least in need of tax relief are the ones who should get the biggest share of the cut. Supply-side theory holds that high-income taxpayers will invest the extra income, which gives the economy a boost and thereby helps others. Warren Buffett, one of America's richest individuals, has a different answer to the question. He argues that tax cuts should be targeted for the less well off, because they have less income, which means they spend nearly every dollar they receive through a tax cut, thereby giving the economy a boost. Which of the two views is closer to your own?

policymakers have pursued tax policies that favor working-class and lower-middle-class Americans. Democrats typically advocate a progressive, or **graduated, personal income tax,** in which the tax rate increases significantly as income rises, thus shifting more of the tax burden to wealthier individuals. (A progressive tax differs from a *regressive tax*, where lower-income individuals pay a higher rate. An example is the social security tax. After a worker's income reaches roughly $110,000, it is no longer subject to the social security tax. Accordingly, those with incomes above this level have a lower social security tax rate on their total income than do those with incomes below the level.)

Fiscal Policy: Practical and Political Limits

Demand-side stimulation as an economic tool emerged in the era when the federal government had a relatively small and mostly balanced budget. As a result, it was feasible for government to boost spending or cut taxes during an economic downturn without going so deeply in debt as to jeopardize long-term economic growth. Today, however, the use of either a supply-side or a demand-side approach carries greater risk.

Excessive spending or overly deep tax cuts result in a **budget deficit**—in which the federal government spends more in a year than it receives in tax and other revenues. The shortfall increases the **national debt,** which is the total cumulative amount the federal government owes to its creditors. Many observers believe the United States faces a looming fiscal crisis because of a combination of high spending and low taxation.

In recent years the government has spent far more than it has received in taxes. In 2014, for example, the federal government's budget deficit was roughly $500 billion, meaning that it borrowed more than a fourth of what it spent. The U.S. government has not had a **balanced budget** (in which revenues are equal to government expenditures) in roughly fifteen years (see Figure 15-2). Projections indicate that high deficits will continue far into the future, adding to the national debt, which already exceeds $18 trillion. The U.S. government spends an enormous amount each year just to pay the interest on the debt. The interest accounts for nearly 15 percent of the federal budget—roughly the total of all federal income taxes paid by Americans living west of the Mississippi.

Leaders of each political party blame the other party for the fiscal problem. In truth, both parties have contributed to it. In combination with the costs of the Iraq war, President Bush's supply-side tax cuts led to a ballooning of the budget deficit and the national debt. The Bush administration had overestimated the stimulus effect of the tax cuts; they gave the economy a boost, but the resulting extra tax revenue was insufficient to offset the revenue lost from the tax cuts. When Bush took office, the budget was balanced and the national debt stood at $5.7 trillion. By the time he left office, the budget deficit had reached nearly $500 billion and the national debt had risen to more than $10 trillion. Under President

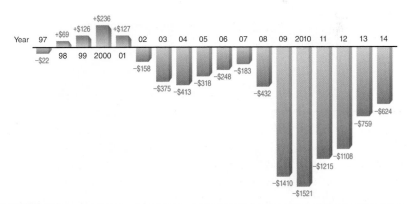

Annual federal budget deficit/surplus
(in billions of dollars)

figure 15-2 THE FEDERAL BUDGET DEFICIT/SURPLUS

The federal government ran a budget deficit until 1998, when a surplus emerged that was expected to last. In 2001, however, the surplus disappeared as a result of an economic downturn, the war on terrorism, and the Bush tax cuts. The deficit ballooned further because of the declining tax revenues and stimulus spending accompanying the economic recession that began in 2008. *Source:* Office of Management and Budget, 2014.

Obama, the debt also jumped sharply, largely because of the economic recession but also because of his demand-side policies, including the $787 billion stimulus package passed by Congress in 2009.

In the case of both the Bush and Obama years, there is no question that the government needed to act to help the economy. The point here, however, is that the application of fiscal policy tools came at a price— large budget deficits and a rising level of national debt—as well as an increase in the odds that, if a large stimulus is needed again anytime soon, America's fiscal problem would worsen dramatically.

MONETARY POLICY AS AN ECONOMIC TOOL

Fiscal policy is not the only instrument of economic management available to government. A second is **monetary policy,** which is based on adjustments in the amount of money in circulation. Monetarists, as economists who emphasize monetary policy are called, contend that the money supply is the key to sustaining a healthy economy. Their leading theorist, the American economist Milton Friedman, held that supply and demand are best controlled by manipulating the money supply.[18] Too much money in circulation contributes to inflation because too many dollars are chasing too few goods, which drives up prices. Too little money in circulation results in a slowing economy and rising unemployment, because consumers

The economist Milton Friedman helped devise the theory of monetary policy, arguing that control of the money supply is the key to sustaining a healthy economy. *Time* magazine named Friedman "the economist of the century," ranking him ahead of John Maynard Keynes, who devised fiscal policy theory.

lack the ready cash and easy credit required to maintain spending levels. Monetarists believe in increasing the money supply when the economy needs a boost and decreasing the supply when it needs to be slowed down.

The Fed

Control over the money supply rests not with the president or Congress but with the Federal Reserve System ("the Fed"). Created by the Federal Reserve Act of 1913, the Fed was designed to be the "lender of last resort" for banks that did not have enough cash on hand to pay their depositors during a bank panic. Lawmakers had the Panic of 1907 in mind when creating it. The panic had begun after a sudden drop in the stock market spooked depositors, who rushed to withdraw their bank savings. A banking catastrophe was averted when a group of wealthy financiers pooled their capital to provide temporary loans to banks that did not have enough cash on hand to pay their depositors. Congress decided that the United States needed a permanent central bank—the Federal Reserve—to serve that purpose.

Headquartered in Washington, D.C., the Fed is directed by a board of governors whose seven members serve for fourteen years, except for the chair and vice chair, who serve for four years. All members are appointed by the president with the approval of the Senate. The Fed regulates the activities of all national banks and those state banks that chose to become members of the Federal Reserve System—about six thousand banks in all. The policies of the Fed's board are carried out through twelve regional Federal Reserve banks, each of which has responsibility for the member banks in its district (see Figure 15-3). Most of the checks and electronic financial transactions that take place in the U.S. banking system are coordinated through the regional banks, which also conduct research that informs the Fed's board of governors. The federal reserve bank for the Ninth District, for example, is located in Minneapolis and serves member banks in Montana, North and South Dakota, Minnesota, and northern areas of Wisconsin and Michigan.

Over time, the Fed has become became the instrument through which monetary policy is applied. The Fed decides how much money to add to or subtract from the economy, seeking a balance that will permit steady growth without causing an unacceptable level of inflation (see Table 15-3). One method the Fed uses is to raise or lower the percent of funds that member banks are required to hold in reserve—meaning they cannot loan or invest these funds. When the Fed raises the reserve rate, member banks are required to keep more of their money out of circulation, thereby

figure 15-3 THE FEDERAL RESERVE SYSTEM

The Federal Reserve is the central bank of the United States. It is directed by a board of governors and its day-to-day operations are conducted through twelve regional Federal Reserve banks, each of which services and oversees the member banks in its district.

table 15-3 MONETARY POLICY: A SUMMARY OF THE FED'S POLICY TOOLS

Problem: Low productivity and high unemployment (requires increase in money supply)

Fed Actions: Decrease interest rate on loans to member banks
Lower percentage (reserve rate) of funds banks must hold in reserve
Buy securities

Problem: Excess productivity and high inflation (requires decrease in money supply)

Fed Actions: Increase interest rate on loans to member banks
Raise percentage (reserve rate) of funds banks must hold in reserve
Sell securities

reducing the money supply. When it lowers the reserve rate, the Fed allows banks to use more of their money for loans to consumers and firms. During the 2008 subprime mortgage crisis, the Fed reduced the reserve rate several times so that member banks would have more money available to deal with the shortfall resulting from failed mortgages.

A second and more publicly visible way in which the Fed affects the money supply is by lowering or raising the interest rate that member banks pay when they borrow money from the Federal Reserve. When the Fed raises the interest rate for banks, they in turn raise the rate they charge their customers for new loans, which discourages borrowing, thereby reducing the amount of money entering the economy. Conversely, when the Fed lowers the interest rate on its loans to member banks, they are able to lower the rate they charge for their loans, which leads to additional borrowing by firms and consumers, resulting in an increase in the money supply. As the economy slowed in 2008, for example, the Fed dropped the interest rate by several percentage points, enabling member banks to lower their rates, making loans more affordable for firms and consumers.

There is also a third mechanism that the Fed uses—the buying and selling of government securities. When it sells government securities in exchange for cash, the Fed is taking that money out of circulation, thereby reducing the amount of money available for consumption and investment. On the other hand, when it buys government securities, the Fed is putting the money used to purchase the securities into private hands to be spent or invested, thus stimulating the economy.

The Fed and Control of Inflation

Although the meltdown of financial markets in 2008 placed the Fed in the role of trying to stimulate the economy, a sluggish economy is not the only problem the Fed is expected to address. Another is **inflation**—an increase in the average level of prices of goods and services. Before the late 1960s, inflation was a minor problem, rising by less than 4 percent annually. However, inflation jumped during the last years of the Vietnam War and remained high throughout the 1970s, reaching a postwar high of 13 percent in 1979. The impact was substantial. Prices were rising but personal income was stagnant. Many Americans were forced to cut back on basics, such as food purchases and medical care. Personal and business bankruptcies increased as a result of rising costs and skyrocketing borrowing rates. The interest rate on business loans and home mortgages topped 15 percent—up from 5 percent a few years earlier.

To fight inflation, the Fed applies policies exactly the opposite of those used to fight an economic downturn. By increasing interest and reserve rates and by selling government securities, the Fed takes money out of the economy, which has the effect of reducing economic demand. As demand weakens, the price of goods and services drop, thereby easing inflationary pressures. During the inflationary period of the late 1970s and early 1980s,

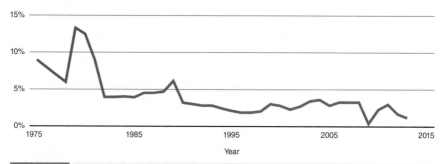

figure 15-4 THE ANNUAL RATE OF INFLATION

Price increases have been low in recent years compared with those of the late 1970s and early 1980s. In 2009, because of declining consumer demand associated with the economic recession, the inflation rate fell to 0 percent for the first time in the postwar era.
Source: U.S. Department of Labor, 2014.

the Fed kept the prime interest rate above 10 percent for seven years, an action that is widely credited with bringing inflation under control. (In 1980, the interest rate hit an all-time high—21.5 percent.) Since the 1980s, inflation has been kept largely in check. The inflation rate has not topped 5 percent in any year during the past two decades (see Figure 15-4).

Ironically, through its recent stimulus policies, the Fed may have set the stage for another inflationary period. Its actions included a controversial device. Known as quantitative easing (QE), it involves the buying of financial assets strictly for the purpose of injecting more money into the economy and paying for them through the simple act of printing more money. This device came into use after the Fed had lowered interest rates almost to the point of zero and therefore could not lower them further as a means of injecting money into the economy. So it turned to quantitative easing, buying assets that were paid for by printing more money, taking advantage of the fact that the government can print as much money as it wants. The Fed used this approach, for example, to buy billions of dollars in problematic mortgages from financial institutions. The purchases had the effect of strengthening these institutions by relieving them of questionable assets while putting cash in their hands that they could then lend out, thereby increasing the money supply.

If the Fed were to pursue this policy endlessly, there would be so many dollars in circulation that runaway inflation would result. For this reason, quantitative easing is considered the tool of "last resort," to be used only when other devices have reached the point where they are no longer effective.[19] Some analysts think the Fed went too far with it—roughly

Janet Yellen was appointed to chair the Federal Reserve in 2014, becoming the first woman to hold the position. Like other recent Fed chairs, she is a trained economist, having received a Ph.D. in economics from Yale before starting her career. The Fed's chair has been called the second most powerful official in Washington.

$3 trillion were dispersed. Even Ben Bernanke, chair of the Federal Reserve at the time, conceded that the policy was risky. Testifying at a Senate Banking Committee hearing in 2012, Bernanke said: "The United States is on an unsustainable fiscal path looking out over the next couple of decades. If we continue along that path, eventually we will face a fiscal and financial crisis."

The Politics of the Fed

Compared with fiscal policy, monetary policy can be implemented more quickly. The Fed can adjust interest and reserve rates on short notice, thus providing the economy with a psychological boost to go along with the actual effect of a change in the money supply. In contrast, changes in fiscal policy usually take months to implement. Congressional action is relatively slow, and new taxing and spending programs ordinarily require a preparation period before they can be put into effect. In early 2010, a full year after Congress passed the $787 billion economic stimulus bill, half of the money had not yet been spent. The greater flexibility of monetary policy is a reason the Fed has emerged as the institution that has primary responsibility for keeping the U.S. economy on a steady course.[20]

When the Fed was created in 1913, no one imagined that it would have such a prominent role. Economists had not yet "invented" the theory of monetary policy. All that has changed, which has raised questions about the power the Fed wields. One concern is the issue of representation: whose interest should the Fed serve—that of the public as a whole or that of the banking sector? The Fed is not a wholly impartial body. Although it makes decisions in the context of economic theories and projections, it is "the bankers' bank" and as such tends to be protective of financial institutions. In 2008, the Fed provided emergency loans to keep banking institutions, including Citibank and JPMorgan Chase, from bankruptcy. The Fed justified its intervention by saying that the financial markets might otherwise have collapsed, adversely affecting every American. Many taxpayers saw it differently. A Pew Research Center national poll found that 87 percent of Americans opposed the use of taxpayer money to bail out banks.

Another question about the Fed is the issue of its accountability. Should the Fed, an unelected body, have so much power? Though appointed by the president, members of the Federal Reserve Board are not subject to removal. They serve for fixed terms and are relatively insulated from political pressure. The Fed's policies are not always popular with elected officials. Some members of Congress, for example, were sharply critical of the Fed's bank bailout.

POLITICAL THINKING

Bail Them Out, or Let Them Fail?

When the subprime mortgage crisis hit in 2008, a number of large financial institutions, including Bank of America and AIG, were in danger of collapsing. They didn't have the cash to meet the shortfall from failed investments. At this point, Congress and the Fed stepped in with huge loans to keep them afloat, arguing that the alternative—a further downward spiral in the economy—was too dangerous to risk. However, some lawmakers, including Senator Richard Shelby (R-Alabama), argued that financial institutions should live or die in the marketplace rather than by government action. What's your view? Should government help big financial firms with loans during severe economic downturns in order to prevent their failure from spreading to other firms and deepening the problem? Or should big firms be left to fail, sending the message that they bear responsibility for risky practices that jeopardize their existence?

Regardless, the Fed is part of the new way of thinking about the federal government and the economy that emerged during the Great Depression of the 1930s. Roosevelt's New Deal permanently changed how policy-makers thought about the government and the economy. Through its economic management and regulatory activities, the government has assumed an ongoing role in managing the economy. The overall result is impressive. Although the American economy has suffered from economic downturns during the roughly three-quarters of a century in which the U.S. government has played a significant policy role, none of them has matched the severity of the depressions of earlier times. (The economic policies of the federal government in the areas of social welfare and national security are discussed in Chapters 16 and 17.)

SUMMARY

Although private enterprise is the main force in the American economic system, the federal government plays a significant role through its policies to regulate, promote, and stimulate the economy.

Regulatory policy is designed to achieve efficiency and equity, which require the government to intervene, for example, to maintain competitive trade practices (an efficiency goal) and to protect vulnerable parties in economic transactions (an equity goal). Many of the regulatory decisions of the federal government, par-ticularly those of older agencies (such as the Food and Drug Administration), are made largely in the context of group politics. Business lobbies have an especially strong influence on the regulatory policies that affect them. In general, newer regulatory agencies (such as the Environmental Protection Agency) have policy responsibilities that are broader in scope and apply to a larger number of firms than those of the older agencies. As a result, the policy decisions of the newer agencies are more often made in the context of party politics. Republican admin-istrations are less vigorous in their regulation of business than are Democratic administrations.

Business is the major beneficiary of the federal government's efforts to pro-mote economic interests. A large number of these programs, including those that provide loans and research grants, are designed to assist business firms, which are also protected from failure through measures such as tariffs and favorable tax laws. Labor, for its part, obtains government assistance through laws covering areas such as worker safety, the minimum wage, and collective bargaining. Yet America's individualistic culture tends to put labor at a disadvantage, keeping it less power-ful than business in its dealings with the government. Agriculture is another economic sector that depends substantially on government's help, particularly in the form of income stabilization programs such as crop insurance subsidies.

The U.S. government pursues policies that are designed to protect and con-serve the environment. A few decades ago, the environment was not a policy priority. Today, there are many programs in this area, and the public has become an active participant in efforts to conserve resources and prevent exploitation of the environment. The continuing challenge is to find a proper balance between the nation's natural environment, its economic growth, and its energy needs.

Through its fiscal and monetary policies, Washington attempts to maintain a strong and stable economy—one characterized by high productivity, high employment, and low inflation. Fiscal policy is based on government decisions in regard to spending and taxing, which are aimed at either stimulating a weak economy or dampening an overheated (inflationary) economy. Fiscal policy is worked out through Congress and the president and consequently is responsive to political pressures. However, because it is difficult to raise taxes or cut programs, the government's ability to apply fiscal policy as an economic remedy is somewhat limited. Monetary policy is based on the money supply and works through the Federal Reserve System, which is headed by a board whose members hold office for fixed terms and operates through the work of its twelve regional Federal Reserve banks. The Fed, as the Federal Reserve is commonly called, has become the primary instrument from managing the economy. It can affect the amount of money circulating in the economy by raising or lowering the interest rate that banks are charged for borrowing from the Fed, by raising or lowering the percentage of their funds (reserve rate) that member banks are required to keep on hand, and by buying and selling securities.

CRITICAL THINKING ZONE

KEY TERMS

balanced budget (*p.499*)

budget deficit (*p.498*)

capital-gains tax (*p.497*)

demand-side economics (*p.494*)

deregulation (*p.481*)

economic depression (*p.494*)

economic efficiency (*p.478*)

economic equity (*p.482*)

economic recession (*p.494*)

economy (*p.477*)

externalities (*p.481*)

fiscal policy (*p.493*)

graduated personal income tax (*p.498*)

inflation (*p.503*)

laissez-faire economics (*p.477*)

monetary policy (*p.500*)

national debt (*p.498*)

regulation (*p.478*)

supply-side economics (*p.496*)

APPLYING THE ELEMENTS OF CRITICAL THINKING

Conceptualizing: Define *economic efficiency* and *economic equity*. Provide an example of a regulatory policy aimed at achieving economic efficiency. Also provide one that has economic equity as its goal.

Synthesizing: Contrast demand-side economics and supply-side economics in terms of theory, government policy, and partisan politics.

Analyzing: What are the tools of monetary policy? How are they applied to deal with an economic recession? How are they applied to deal with high inflation?

EXTRA CREDIT

A Book Worth Reading: Milton Friedman, *Capitalism and Freedom*. Chicago: University of Chicago Press, 2002. First published in 1962, this classic by the Nobel Prize–winning economist provides a defense of free markets that argues against Keynesian economics, which at the time was the prevailing approach to managing the economy.

A Website Worth Visiting: **www.ftc.gov** The website of the Federal Trade Commission, one of the older regulatory agencies, has information on pending disputes. The site gives the reader a sense of how the regulatory process works in practice.

PARTICIPATE!

The environment is a policy area in which individual citizens can make a difference by reducing waste and pollution. If you have a car, you will burn significantly less fuel if you drive and accelerate more slowly. Choosing a fuel-efficient car, keeping your car properly tuned, walking rather than driving short distances to stores, and living closer to work or school are other ways to cut gas consumption. In your residence, the simplest steps are to use lights sparingly and keep the thermostat lower during cold periods and higher during hot periods. Smaller but meaningful savings can be achieved through simple things such as using low-flow shower heads and replacing incandescent bulbs with fluorescent lights, which require less energy and last longer. Even a change in eating habits can make a difference. Frozen convenience foods are wasteful of energy. They are cooked, frozen, and then cooked again—not to mention the resources used up in packaging. Fresh foods are more nutritious and less wasteful. And if you prefer bottled water to tap water, consider using a water filter system instead. Nearly all of the cost of bottled water is due to the plastic container, which is a nonbiodegradable petroleum product. The recycling of paper, plastics, and bottles also conserves natural resources. However, the recycling process uses energy. By cutting back on the use of recyclables and by recycling those you do use, you will contribute twice to a cleaner environment.

WELFARE AND EDUCATION POLICY: PROVIDING FOR PERSONAL SECURITY AND NEED

"We the People of the United States, in order to . . . promote the general Welfare.**"**

PREAMBLE, U.S. CONSTITUTION

The first day of 2014 marked the start of the federal requirement for Americans to have health insurance or face a tax penalty. It also marked the time when some people who were ineligible to enroll in Medicaid—the federal health care assistance program for those with low incomes—would become eligible. But there was a catch: eligibility for the extended Medicaid program depended on the state in which a person lived.

The Medicaid program had been limited to those with incomes below the federally defined poverty line. The new program expanded eligibility to a higher income level—an additional five million individuals and families now met the income threshold. However, the Supreme Court in a 2012 ruling said that states could not be compelled to expand their Medicaid program to include the newly eligible. Twenty-five states chose to participate. Twenty-five states declined.

510

Most of the states that opted in were controlled by Democratic law-makers. Neil Abercrombie, Hawaii's Democratic governor, said the program provides "a healthcare system that ensures high quality, safety, and sustainable costs."[1] On the other hand, all of the states that declined to participate were headed by Republican governors. They argued that, even though the federal government would initially pay the full cost of the Medicaid expansion, there would come a day when some of the burden would be shifted to them. Said Mississippi governor Phil Bryant: "For us to enter into an expansion program would be a fool's errand. I mean, here we would be saying to 300,000 Mississippians, 'We're going to provide Medicaid coverage to you,' and then the federal government through Congress or through the Senate, would do away with or alter the Afford-able Care Act, and then we have no way to pay that."[2]

Health policy issues, like other social welfare policy issues, are highly partisan. Some Americans hold that government should intervene in the marketplace to assist disadvantaged individuals. Others hold that government assistance discourages personal effort and creates dependency. America's federal system of government also fuels conflict over welfare policies. Welfare was traditionally a responsibility of state governments. Only since the 1930s has the federal government also played a major role, which has sometimes brought it into conflict with the states over the best course of action.

This chapter describes federal social welfare and education policies and explains why disagreements in these areas are so substantial. The issues involve hard choices that inevitably require trade-offs between federal and state power and between the values of individual self-reliance and egalitarian compassion. The main points of the chapter are:

- *Poverty is a large and persistent problem in America, affecting about one in eight Americans, including many of the country's most vulnerable—children, female-headed families, and minority-group members.*

- *Welfare policy has been a partisan issue, with Democrats taking the lead on government programs to alleviate economic insecurity and Republicans acting to slow down or restrict these initiatives.*

- *Social welfare programs are designed to reward and foster self-reliance or, when this is not possible, to provide benefits only to those individuals who are truly in need.* U.S. welfare policy is not based on the assumption that every citizen has a right to material security.

- *Americans favor social insurance programs (such as social security) over public assistance programs (such as food stamps).* As a result, most social welfare expenditures are not targeted toward the nation's neediest citizens.

The health care reform legislation that was passed by Congress in 2010 was bitterly contested. No Senate or House Republican voted for the bill. The dispute was not confined to the halls of Congress. Shown here is a rally held to protest the bill.

- *A prevailing principle in the United States is equality of opportunity, which in terms of policy is most evident in the area of public education.* America invests heavily in its public schools and colleges.

POVERTY IN AMERICA: THE NATURE OF THE PROBLEM

In the broadest sense, social welfare policy includes any effort by government to improve social conditions. In a narrower sense, which is the way the term is used in this chapter, social welfare policy refers to government programs that help individuals meet basic needs, including food, clothing, and shelter. Social welfare policy can differ markedly even among countries that are similar in many other respects. As this chapter shows, U.S. social welfare policy is distinctive, even by comparison with Canada and other Western industrialized nations.

The Poor: Who and How Many?

Although Americans are far better off economically than most of the world's peoples, poverty is a significant and persistent problem in the United States. The government defines the **poverty line** as the annual cost of a thrifty food budget for an urban family of four, multiplied by three to include the cost of housing, clothes, and other necessities. Families whose incomes fall below that line are officially considered poor. In 2014, the poverty line was set at an annual income of roughly $24,000 for a family of four. One in seven Americans—roughly 45 million people—live below the poverty line. If they could all join hands, they would form a line stretching from New York to Los Angeles and back again.

America's poor include individuals of all ages, races, religions, and regions (see "How the 50 States Differ"), but poverty is concentrated among certain groups. Children are one of the largest groups of poor Americans. One in every five children—more than ten million in total—live in poverty. Most poor children live in families with a single parent, usually the mother. Single-parent, female-headed families are roughly five times as likely as two-income families to fall below the poverty line, a situation referred to as "the feminization of poverty."[3]

Poverty is widespread among minority-group members. Compared with whites, African Americans and Hispanics are more than twice as likely to live below the poverty line. Poverty is also geographically concentrated. Although poverty is often portrayed as an urban problem, it is somewhat more prevalent in rural areas. About one in seven rural residents—compared with one in nine urban residents—lives in a family with income below the poverty line. The urban figure is misleading, however, in that the level of poverty is very high in some inner-city areas. Suburbs are the safe haven from poverty. Because suburbanites are far removed from it, many of them have no sense of the impoverished condition of what Michael Harrington called "the other America."[4]

The "invisibility" of poverty is evident in polls showing that most Americans greatly underestimate the level of poverty in the United States. Nothing in the daily lives of many Americans or in what they see on television would lead them to think that poverty rates are

HOW THE 50 STATES DIFFER

POLITICAL THINKING THROUGH COMPARISONS

Poverty Rates

Based on the government-defined poverty line, about one in eight Americans lives in poverty. However, poverty is spread unevenly among the states. At one extreme are Louisiana, Mississippi, and New Mexico, each of which has a poverty rate above 18 percent. New Mexico has the highest rate. At the other extreme are New Hampshire and Utah, which have poverty rates that are less than half that of the highest states.

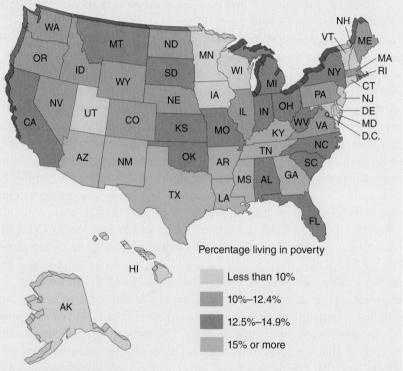

Percentage living in poverty

- Less than 10%
- 10%–12.4%
- 12.5%–14.9%
- 15% or more

Source: U.S. Census Bureau, 2014.

Q: What might explain the difference in poverty levels between the states?

A: States differ considerably in their natural wealth, level and type of economic activity, level of education, number of newer immigrants, and percentage of minority-group members. Each of these factors is correlated with level of poverty.

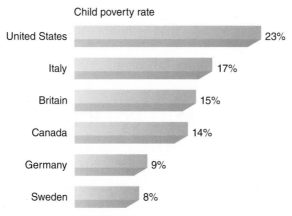

Child poverty rate

United States	23%
Italy	17%
Britain	15%
Canada	14%
Germany	9%
Sweden	8%

figure 16-1   CHILD POVERTY RATES

The United States has the highest child poverty rate among Western democracies. One in five American children lives in poverty; in most other Western democracies, the number is fewer than one in seven. Households with incomes less than half that of the median household are classified as living in poverty.
Source: United Nations Childrens Fund, 2014.

uncommonly high. Yet the United States has the highest level of poverty among the advanced industrialized nations. Moreover, its rate of child poverty is twice the average rate of these other nations (see Figure 16-1).

Living in Poverty: By Choice or Chance?

Many Americans hold to the idea that poverty is largely a matter of choice—that most low-income Americans are unwilling to make the effort to hold a responsible job and get ahead in life. In his book *Losing Ground*, Charles Murray argues that America has a permanent underclass of unproductive citizens who prefer to live on welfare and whose children receive little educational encouragement at home and grow up to be copies of their parents.[5] There are, indeed, many such people in America. They number in the millions. They are the toughest challenge for policymakers because almost nothing about their lives equips them to escape from poverty and its attendant ills.

Yet most poor Americans are in their situation as a result of circumstance rather than choice. In their exhaustive poverty study, economists Signe-Mary McKernan and Caroline Ratcliffe found that most of the poor are poor only for a while, and then for reasons largely beyond their control—such as a job layoff or desertion by the father—rather than because they prefer not to work.[6] When the U.S. economy goes into a tailspin, the impact devastates many families. According to U.S. Department of Labor figures, more than seven million Americans lost their jobs during the economic downturn that began in 2008.

THE POLITICS AND POLICIES OF SOCIAL WELFARE

At one time in the nation's history, the federal government was not involved in social welfare policy. Poverty and other welfare problems were deemed to fall within the powers reserved to the states by the Tenth Amendment and to be adequately addressed by them, even though they offered few welfare services. Individuals were expected to fend for themselves, and those unable to do so were usually supported by relatives and friends.

The Great Depression changed that outlook. The unemployment level reached 25 percent, and many of those with jobs were working for pennies an hour. Americans looked to the federal government for help. Franklin D. Roosevelt's New Deal brought economic relief in the form of public jobs and assistance programs and altered public attitudes.[7] The federal government was seen as having a responsibility to assist individuals whose economic problems were due to circumstances beyond their control.

Not all Americans embraced the new philosophy. Many Republican leaders clung to traditional ideas about self-reliance and free markets. A key vote in the House of Representatives on the Social Security Act of 1935, for example, had 85 percent of Democrats voting in favor of it and 99 percent of Republicans voting against it.[8] Republicans gradually accepted the idea that the federal government has a social welfare role but argued that it should be kept as small as practicable. Thus, in the 1960s, Republican opposition to President Lyndon Johnson's Great Society was substantial. His programs included federal initiatives in health care, education, public housing, nutrition, and other areas traditionally dominated by state and local governments. More than 70 percent of congressional Republicans voted against the 1965 Medicare and Medicaid programs, which provide government-paid medical assistance for the elderly and the poor, respectively. In contrast, the 1996 Welfare Reform Act, which was designed to cut welfare rolls and costs, had the overwhelming support of congressional Republicans, whereas a majority of congressional Democrats voted against it.

P A R T Y	**Political Thinking in Conflict**

POLARIZATION

Government's Social Welfare Role

The two major ways that economic benefits are distributed in America is through the economic marketplace in the form of jobs, wages, dividends, and the like and through the government in the form of programs such as social security, Medicaid, and food stamps. In few areas have the differences between the Republican and Democratic parties been more consistent over the years than their positions on the use of government as an instrument of economic security. Although both parties see a need for some sort of safety net for the economically vulnerable, the Democratic Party has taken the lead on extending it. Nearly every major U.S. social insurance and public assistance program was put into place by Democratic lawmakers, usually in the face of opposition from their Republican counterparts. The policy conflicts among lawmakers are aligned with how the parties' identifiers see the issue of government's role in providing assistance to the economically disadvantaged, as the figure below indicates.

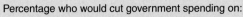

Percentage who would cut government spending on:

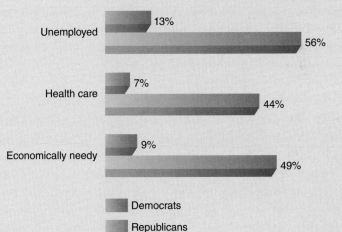

Unemployed — 13%, 56%

Health care — 7%, 44%

Economically needy — 9%, 49%

■ Democrats
■ Republicans

Source: Pew Research Center for the People & the Press survey, February 22, 2013.

Q: What's your opinion on how far government should go in providing economic assistance to the less-well-off?

The health care reform bill that Congress passed in 2010 also brought out partisan divisions. No Senate or House Republican voted for the bill, and Republican lawmakers have promised to repeal it if they gain control of Congress and the presidency.

Although the Republican and Democratic parties have been at odds on social welfare issues, they have also had reason to work together. Millions of Americans depend on the federal government to provide benefits to ease the loss of income caused by retirement, disability, unemployment, and the like. Some social welfare programs, such as federal grants for health research, benefit all of society. Other spending is aimed at helping particular individuals. Most of this spending occurs through **entitlement programs,** meaning that any individual who meets the eligibility criteria is entitled to the benefit. For example, upon reaching the legal retirement age, any senior citizen who has paid social security taxes for the required amount of time is entitled to receive social security benefits. In this sense, entitlement programs have the same force of law as taxes. Just as individuals are required by law to pay taxes on the income they earn, they are entitled by law to receive government benefits for which they qualify.

Individual-benefit programs fall into two broad groups: social insurance programs and public assistance programs. Social insurance programs enjoy broader public support, are more heavily funded, and provide benefits to individuals of all income levels. Public assistance programs have less public support, receive less funding, and are restricted to people of low income. The next sections discuss these two types of programs.

Social Insurance Programs

More than fifty million Americans receive monthly benefits from social insurance programs—including social security, Medicare, unemployment insurance, and workers' compensation. The cost of the two major programs, social security and Medicare, exceeds one trillion dollars a year. Such programs are labeled **social insurance** because eligibility is restricted to individuals who paid special payroll taxes during their working years. Those who paid the taxes get the benefit, no matter how rich they are. Those who did not pay them are ineligible for the benefit, no matter how poor they are.

Social Security   The main social insurance program is social security for retirees. Social security is one of the few welfare programs run entirely by the federal government. Washington collects the payroll taxes that fund the program and sends monthly checks directly to social security recipients, who receive on average about $1,300 a month.

The program began with passage of the Social Security Act of 1935 and is funded through payroll taxes on employees and employers (currently set at 6.2 percent). Franklin D. Roosevelt emphasized that retiring workers would receive an insurance benefit they had earned through their payroll taxes, not a handout from the government. This method of financing the program has given it strong public support.[9] Polls indicate that a large majority of Americans favor current or higher levels of social security benefits for the elderly.

Although people qualify for social security by paying payroll taxes during their working years, the money they receive upon retirement is funded by the payroll taxes paid by those currently working. This arrangement poses a threat to the long-term viability of the social

With the possible exception of Franklin D. Roosevelt, no American president had a greater impact on social welfare policy than Lyndon B. Johnson. Johnson's Great Society programs included Medicare and Medicaid, as well as increased federal spending in areas such as education, childhood nutrition, and poverty alleviation. Johnson was also instrumental in passage of the 1964 Civil Rights Act and the 1965 Voting Rights Act.

security program. People are living longer than they once did, with the result that there are fewer workers relative to the number of retirees. At some future time, the payroll tax dollars from workers will not pay the cost of retirees' social security checks unless adjustments are made to the program.

Unemployment Insurance The 1935 Social Security Act provides for unemployment benefits for workers who lose their jobs involuntarily. Unemployment insurance is a joint federal-state program. The federal government collects the payroll taxes that fund unemployment benefits, but states have the option of deciding whether the taxes will be paid by both employees and employers or by employers only (most states use the latter option). Although unemployment benefits vary widely among states, they average about $300 a week, roughly a fourth of the pay of the average worker. Unemployment benefits are usually terminated after twenty-six weeks, but Congress, as it did in the recent economic downturn, sometimes extends the eligibility period.

The unemployment program lacks the broad public support that social security enjoys. This situation reflects the widespread assumption that the loss of a job, or the failure to find a new one right away, is often a personal failing. Unemployment statistics indicate otherwise. A U.S. Bureau of Labor study found that only one in seven workers who lost their jobs were fired or quit voluntarily. The rest became unemployed because of either the temporary or permanent elimination of their job.

Medicare After World War II, most European democracies created government-paid health care systems, and Democratic president Harry S Truman proposed a similar program for Americans. The American Medical Association (AMA) called Truman's plan "un-American" and vowed to mobilize local physicians to campaign against members of Congress who supported "socialized medicine." Truman's proposal never came to a vote in Congress.

The 1964 elections swept a tide of liberal Democrats into Congress, and the result was Medicare. Enacted in 1965, the program provides medical assistance to retirees and is funded primarily through payroll taxes. Medicare is based on the insurance principle, and because of this, it has gained as much public support as social security. Like social security, Medicare faces an insolvency problem in the long term because it is funded through payroll taxes on the current workforce, which is shrinking relative to the number of retirees.

Public Assistance Programs

Unlike social insurance programs, **public assistance** programs are funded through general tax revenues and are available only to the financially needy. Eligibility for these programs is established by a **means test;** that is, applicants must prove that they are poor enough to qualify for the benefit. Once they have done so, they are entitled to the benefit, unless their personal situation changes or government changes the eligibility criteria. These programs often are referred to as "welfare" and the recipients as "welfare cases."

Americans are far less supportive of public assistance programs than they are of social insurance programs. Americans look upon social insurance benefits as having been earned by the recipient, whereas some people see public assistance benefits as handouts. Support for public assistance programs is also weakened by Americans' belief that government is already spending vast amounts on welfare. A poll found that Americans believe public assistance programs to be the second costliest item in the federal budget. In fact, the federal government spends hundreds of billions more on its two major social insurance programs—social security and Medicare—than it does on all public assistance programs combined.

Supplemental Security Income (SSI)   Supplemental Security Income (SSI) originated as federal assistance to the blind and elderly poor as part of the Social Security Act of 1935. Although SSI is primarily a federal program, the states have retained some control over benefits and eligibility and provide some of the funding. Because SSI recipients (who now include disabled individuals in addition to the blind and elderly poor) have physical limitations on their ability to provide fully for themselves, SSI is not widely criticized.

Temporary Assistance for Needy Families (TANF)   Before passage of the 1996 Welfare Reform Act, needy American families with children had an open-ended guarantee of cash assistance. As long as their income was below a certain level, they were assured of government support. The program (Aid for Families with Dependent Children, or AFDC for short) was created in the 1930s to assist children whose fathers had died prematurely. Relatively small at the outset, the program became controversial as Americans increasingly linked it to welfare dependency. AFDC was an entitlement program, which meant that any single parent (and in some states two parents) living in poverty could claim the benefit. Some AFDC recipients were content to live on this assistance, and in some cases their

Supplemental Security Income (SSI) is a combined federal-state program that provides public assistance to individuals with disabilities.

children also grew up to become AFDC recipients, creating what was called "a vicious cycle of poverty." By 1995, AFDC was supporting 14 million Americans.

The 1996 Welfare Reform Act abolished AFDC, replacing it with the program titled Temporary Assistance for Needy Families (TANF). TANF's goal is to reduce long-term welfare dependency by limiting to five years the length of time recipients can normally receive assistance and by giving the states an incentive to place welfare recipients into jobs. Each state is given an annual federal block grant that it uses to help poor families meet their subsistence needs and to develop programs that will help the parents find employment. The biggest challenge facing the states has been the creation of welfare-to-work programs that are effective enough to qualify people for secure jobs. Most welfare recipients who have found employment since 1996 had enough skills that they required little or no job training from the state. In contrast, most of those who have been unable to find stable long-term employment have limited education and few job-related skills.[10]

TANF has dramatically reduced the size of the welfare rolls (see Figure 16-2). Within five years of its enactment, the number of people on welfare had dropped by 50 percent. In only three states—Hawaii,

POLITICAL
THINKING

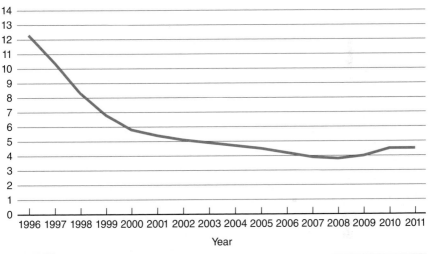

Childhood Poverty in America

Among Western societies, America has one of the highest rates of child poverty. About a fifth of American children live in families with incomes below the poverty line, and about half of these live in very poor families. Whatever your view of society's responsibility to poor adults, do you think it has an added responsibility to poor children? If so, what steps would you take to reduce childhood poverty in America?

Number of welfare recipients (in millions)

figure 16-2 NUMBER OF WELFARE RECIPIENTS, 1996–2011

The number of welfare recipients dropped sharply after the Temporary Assistance for Needy Families (TANF) program was instituted. The last year of the Aid for Families with Dependent Children (AFDC) program was 1996; it was replaced by TANF.
Source: U.S. Department of Health and Human Services, 2014.

Rhode Island, and New Mexico—was the drop less than 20 percent. However, the decline was not simply the result of TANF. The American economy expanded at a rapid rate in the late 1990s, which created millions of new jobs. Nevertheless, even as the economy weakened in 2000, the number of welfare recipients continued to decline. Although the downward trend was reversed during the recent economic recession, the number of American families receiving TANF payments is only about a third of the number that were getting assistance under the old program.

Head Start   Education programs for the poor are not limited to job training. In the 1960s, as part of Lyndon Johnson's Great Society, the federal government started an education program, Head Start, aimed at helping poor children at an early age. Head Start provides free preschool education to low-income children in order to help them succeed when they begin kindergarten. Roughly a million children are currently enrolled in Head Start, at an average annual cost of about $7,500 per child. However, Head Start has never been funded at a level that would allow all eligible to participate. Today, somewhat less than half of eligible children are enrolled.

Earned Income Tax Credit (EITC)   A full-time job does not guarantee that a family will rise above the poverty line. A family of four with one employed adult who works forty hours a week at $8 an hour (slightly higher than the federal minimum wage) has an annual income of about $16,000, which is $8,000 below the poverty line. Millions of Americans—mostly household workers, service workers, unskilled laborers, and farmworkers—are in this position. The U.S. Bureau of Labor Statistics estimates that roughly 10 percent of full-time workers, the so-called working poor, do not earn enough to lift their family above the poverty line.[11]

Some of these workers are eligible to receive the Earned Income Tax Credit (EITC). Enacted in 1975 under President Gerald Ford and expanded during the presidencies of Ronald Reagan and Bill Clinton, EITC now covers about 10 million low-income American families. The maximum yearly payment for a family with two children is $5,400, and eligibility is limited to wage-earning families. EITC payments occur when the worker files a personal income tax return. Those whose incomes are sufficiently low receive an EITC payment, the amount of which depends on their income level and number of dependents. The EITC program is now the federal government's largest means-tested cash assistance program. According to U.S. Census Bureau calculations, the EITC lifts about a third of low-income Americans above the poverty line.

EITC has more public support than most assistance programs. The reason is simple: EITC is tied to employment. Only those who work are eligible for the payment. Polls that span more than a half century reveal that Americans have consistently favored work-based assistance to welfare payments. Work is widely believed to foster initiative and accountability; welfare is widely held to breed dependency and irresponsibility.

In-Kind Benefits: Food Stamps and Housing Vouchers   The Food Stamps program, which took its present form in 1961, is fully funded by the federal government. The program provides an **in-kind benefit**—not cash, but food stamps that can be spent only on grocery items. Food stamps are available only to people who qualify on the basis of low income. The program is intended to improve the nutrition of poor families by enabling them to purchase qualified items—mainly foodstuffs—with food stamps. Recipients receive, on average, about $110 a month. Some critics say that food stamps stigmatize their users by making it obvious to onlookers in the checkout line that they are "welfare cases." More prevalent criticisms are that the program is too costly and that too many undeserving people receive food stamps.

Low-income persons are also eligible for subsidized housing. Most of the federal spending in this area is on rent vouchers, an in-kind benefit. The government gives the individual a monthly rent payment voucher, which the individual gives in lieu of cash to the landlord, who then hands the voucher over to the government in exchange for cash. About five million households annually receive a federal housing subsidy.

Like other public assistance programs, housing subsidies are criticized as being too costly. Nevertheless, the federal government spends less on public housing for the poor than it gives in tax breaks to homeowners, most of whom are middle- and upper-income Americans. Homeowners are allowed tax deductions for their mortgage interest payments and their local property tax payments. The total of these tax concessions is three times as much as is spent by the federal government on low-income housing. In many European democracies, there is no tax deduction for home mortgage payments.

Medicaid When Medicare was created for retirees in 1965, Congress also established Medicaid, which provides health care for the poor. It is a public assistance program, rather than a social insurance program like Medicare, because it is based on need and funded by general tax revenues. More than 60 percent of Medicaid funding is provided by the federal government with the rest coming from the states. Over 40 million Americans receive Medicaid assistance. This number that will increase as a result of expanded Medicaid eligibility under the new federal health care system.

As health care costs have spiraled far ahead of the inflation rate, so have the costs of Medicaid. It absorbs roughly half of all public assistance dollars spent by the U.S. government and has forced state and local governments to cut other services to meet their share of the costs. Medicare is now the first or second biggest budget item for most states. "It's killing us" is how one official described the impact of Medicaid on the annual budget.[12] As is true of other public assistance programs, Medicaid has been criticized for supposedly helping too many people who could take care of themselves.

The SCHIP Program Enacted in 1997 at the urging of President Bill Clinton, the State Children's Health Insurance Program (commonly called CHIP) provides health insurance for uninsured children of lower-income families that do not qualify for Medicaid insurance. CHIP is a matching

One of the many ironies of U.S. social welfare policy is that tax deductions for home mortgages for the middle and upper class are a form of government subsidy, just as are rent vouchers for the poor, but only the latter are stigmatized as a government "handout."

program with the federal government providing some of the funds and the states providing the rest.

The 2010 Health Care Reform Act   Although the health care reform bill (the Patient Protection and Affordable Care Act) passed by Congress in 2010 expanded the Medicaid program, it aims to increase health insurance coverage primarily through mandates on individuals and companies. Starting in 2014, individual Americans face a tax penalty if they don't have health insurance. At the same time, most companies with more than two hundred employees are now required to provide their employees with health insurance and most companies with fifty to two hundred employees must provide insurance or pay a tax penalty.

The bill includes mechanisms designed to hold down insurance costs in order to ease the burden on individuals and firms. One mechanism is state-based insurance exchanges that will negotiate with insurance companies to obtain the lowest insurance rates possible. The legislation also prohibits a number of practices that insurance companies had formerly employed, such as placing lifetime limits on insurance payments and canceling policies when people became sick.

The Congressional Budget Office (CBO) estimates that the new health care system will cost about $100 billion a year, which will be

POLITICAL THINKING	Buy Health Insurance, or Take the Tax Penalty?

Under the new health insurance system, Americans must either obtain health insurance or pay a tax penalty. Young adults are a key to making the system work. In the state insurance exchanges that have been established, young adults—because they are generally healthier and use fewer medical services—help through their insurance payments to lower the cost of insurance for others in their state's exchange. But if not enough young adults join the exchange, the insurance rate for those who do join could skyrocket, because the exchanges must accept individuals with chronic or medically costly conditions. If the latter became too large a share of the people in the exchange, the costs for everyone will go up, leading additional people to drop out, creating an ever upward spiral in the cost of insurance. Do you think healthy young adults have a public responsibility to join an exchange if they don't otherwise have health insurance?

financed by new taxes and fees and by cost savings in other federal health care programs. The CBO estimates that these payment mechanisms will come close to covering the program's cost. Critics have challenged the CBO's estimate as being far too low. In truth, no one knows yet what the actual cost will be. It will depend on a number of factors, including how many Americans enroll in the expanded Medicaid program and how many healthy young adults choose to take the tax penalty rather than buy insurance.

Culture and Social Welfare

Surveys repeatedly show that most Americans are convinced that people on welfare could get along without it if they tried. As a consequence, there is constant political pressure to reduce welfare expenditures and to weed out undeserving recipients. The unwritten principle of social welfare in America, reflecting the country's individualistic culture, is that the individual must somehow earn a social welfare benefit or, barring that, demonstrate a convincing need for it. The result is a welfare system that is both inefficient, in that much of the money spent on welfare never reaches the intended recipients, and inequitable, in that less than half of social welfare spending goes to the people most in need.[13]

Inefficiency   The United States has the most inefficient welfare system in the Western world. The unwritten principle that the individual must somehow earn or be in absolute need of assistance makes the U.S. welfare system heavily bureaucratic. For example, the 1996 Welfare Reform Act—which limits eligibility to families with incomes below a certain level and, in most instances, to families with a single parent living in the home—requires that the eligibility of each applicant be checked periodically by a caseworker. This procedure makes such programs doubly expensive; in addition to making payments to recipients, the programs must pay local caseworkers, supervisors, and support staffs (see Figure 16-3). These costs do not include the administrative costs of the state and federal agencies that oversee the programs.

The bureaucratic costs of welfare are substantially lower in Europe because most European countries have unitary rather than federal systems, which eliminates a layer of government, and also because eligibility is often universal, as in the case of government-paid health care. Caseworkers do not have to pore over records to determine who is and who is not eligible for government-provided medical treatment—everyone is.[14]

Inequity   European welfare programs are also more equitable in the sense that the major beneficiaries are those individuals most in need. In contrast, the United States spends as much, or more, on assistance programs for the nonpoor than it does for the poor.

Social security and Medicare are examples. Spending on these programs, which assist rich and poor alike, exceeds the total of all spending on public assistance programs, which help only the needy (see Figure 16-4). Many social security recipients are in the higher-income categories, and thus have no absolute economic need for the benefit. In fact, their monthly social security income is substantially higher than that of those in the lower-income categories as a result of the formula for determining social

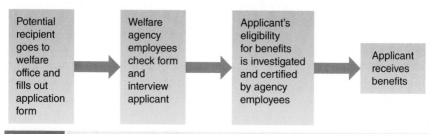

figure 16-3   THE WELFARE BUREAUCRACY

Because U.S. social welfare benefits are distributed on the basis of demonstrated need, a large bureaucracy is required to ascertain applicants' eligibility and to monitor whether changes in recipients' circumstances render them ineligible for further assistance.

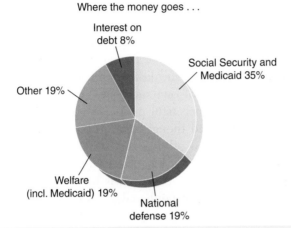

Where the money goes . . .

figure 16-4 FEDERAL BUDGET, BY CATEGORY

Although many Americans believe that welfare assistance programs, such as food stamps and Medicaid, account for a huge share of federal spending, they actually account for a much smaller share than do the Social Security and Medicare programs.
Source: Office of Management and Budget, 2014.

security payouts—the higher your income while working, the larger your social security benefit upon retirement. Moreover, most retirees receive more in social security benefits than they contributed in payroll taxes while working. The excess payment could be regarded as public assistance and has been increasing as a result of lengthening life spans. The prime beneficiaries are the more affluent. Poverty takes a toll on people's health and cuts short their retirement years. The poorest 10 percent of Americans live five fewer years on average than the wealthiest 10 percent.

Of course, social insurance programs help many who are needy. Monthly social security checks keep millions of Americans, mostly widows, out of poverty. About one-fourth of America's elderly have no significant monthly income aside from what they receive from social security. Nevertheless, families in the top fifth of the income population receive more in social security and Medicare benefits than the government spends in total on TANF, SSI, food stamps, and housing subsidies for the poor.

EDUCATION AS EQUALITY OF OPPORTUNITY

Although few Americans would support economic equality for all, most Americans endorse the principle of **equality of opportunity**—the idea that people should have a reasonable chance to succeed if they make the effort. It is a form of equality shaped by personal freedom because the outcome—personal success or personal failure—depends on what individuals do with their opportunity. It is sometimes said that equality of opportunity gives individuals an equal chance to become unequal.

Equality of opportunity is an ideal. Americans do not start life on an equal footing. It was said of one successful American politician, whose father before him was a successful politician and a millionaire, that "he was born on third base and thought he hit a triple."[15] Some Americans are born into privilege, and others start life in such abject poverty that few of them escape it. Nonetheless, equality of opportunity is more than a catchphrase. It is the philosophical basis for a number of government programs, none more so than public education.

Public Education: Leveling through the Schools

During the nation's first century, the question of a free education for all children was a contentious issue. Wealthy interests feared that an educated public would challenge their power. Egalitarians, on the other hand, saw education as a means of enabling ordinary people to get ahead. The egalitarians won out. Public schools sprang up in nearly every community and were free of charge.[16]

Equality continues to be a guiding principle of American public education. Unlike the situation in countries that divide children even at the grade school level into different tracks that lead ultimately to different occupations, the curriculum in U.S. schools is relatively standardized. Of course, public education has never been a uniform experience for American children. During the first half of the twentieth century, southern public schools for black children were designed to keep them down, not lift them up. Today, many children in poorer neighborhoods attend overcrowded, understaffed, and underfunded public schools. The quality of education depends significantly on the wealth of the community in which a child resides. The Supreme Court has upheld this arrangement, saying that the states are obliged to give all children an "adequate" education as opposed to one that is "equal" across communities.

The uneven quality of America's public schools is a reason its students rank below students in Canada and most European countries on standardized reading, math, and science tests (see "How the U.S. Differs"). The United States is more segregated residentially by income than are European countries. As a result, America's poor children are more likely to go to schools where most of the other students are also poor.

HOW THE U.S. DIFFERS

POLITICAL THINKING THROUGH COMPARISONS

Education Performance

Although the United States spends more heavily on its public schools than do nearly all other countries, its students perform poorly on standardized tests. Consider the results of the periodic surveys conducted by the Organization for Economic Cooperation and Development (OECD), which are administered to a sample of fifteen-year-old students. The surveys cover literacy in reading, mathematics, and science. Only questions that are approved unanimously by the participating countries are included in the testing. In the most recent survey, the United States ranked 36 out of the 65 countries studied, trailing nearly every Asian and Western European country. Most of the countries below the United States are in Eastern Europe and Latin America. The accompanying chart shows the average test score in selected countries.

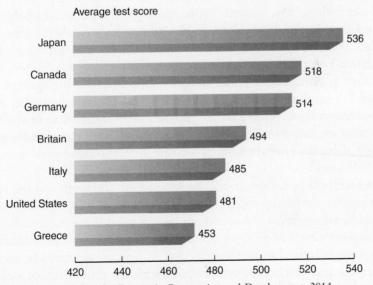

Average test score

Japan	536
Canada	518
Germany	514
Britain	494
Italy	485
United States	481
Greece	453

Source: Organization for Economic Cooperation and Development, 2014.

Continued

Q: Why might the United States lag behind other advanced industrialized democracies in student performance, even though it spends more heavily on public education?

A: Although the blame for the relatively poor performance of U.S. students on standardized tests is often directed at teachers, other factors have been found to be more important. Compared with most Western democracies, the United States has a relatively high proportion of non-native-speaking children, who on average do less well in school than other students. In addition, the United States has more residential segregation by income and more poor children than do other Western democracies. Poor children, particularly those residing in poor neighborhoods or communities, tend to perform less well in school than do their peers.

Moreover, because the wealth of a community affects the level of school funding, schools with a high proportion of poor students tend to have fewer resources, even though in those schools the need is greater. In fact, the best predictor of students' performance on standardized tests is the wealth of the community in which their school is located.[17]

Nevertheless, the United States through its public schools seeks to broadly educate its children. Public education was labeled "the great leveler" when it began in the early nineteenth century, and the tradition continues. Few countries make an equivalent effort to give children, whatever their parents' background, an equal opportunity in life through education. Per-pupil spending on public schools is substantially higher in the United States than it is in Europe. America's commitment to broad-based education extends to college. The United States has the world's largest system of higher education—it has nearly four thousand two- and four-year colleges.[18]

The nation's education system preserves both the myth and the reality of an equal-opportunity society. The belief that success is within the reach of anyone who works for it could not be sustained if the public education system were designed to serve the privileged few. Moreover, educational attainment is related to personal success, at least as measured by income. In fact, the gap in income between those with and those without a college degree is greater now than at any time in the country's history. On average during their lifetime, college graduates will earn about 65 percent more than those without a college degree.

The Federal Government's Role in Education Policy

Education is largely the responsibility of state and local governments, and they continue to provide more than 90 percent of school funding and to determine the bulk of school policies, from the length of the academic year to teachers' qualifications. Differences in the wealth of states and localities are a reason America's schools vary substantially in quality.

Historically the federal government played little part in education policy. The situation began to change after World War II when economic and social change made the public more aware of deficiencies in its education system. Since the 1960s the federal government has played a larger, though still secondary, role in education policy.

Federal Grants-in-Aid for Education   As part of President Johnson's War on Poverty, the federal government began in the 1960s to provide financial assistance in the education area. The 1965 Elementary and Secondary Education Act became the cornerstone of the federal government's efforts to assist public schools. The legislation authorizes funds for items such as school construction, textbooks, special education, and teacher training. Although Johnson's goal was to help schools in poorer areas, members of Congress insisted that all states and districts be eligible for some funding. As a result, the formulas for allocating the grants favor poorer school districts but not completely.

The 1965 Higher Education Act, which President Johnson signed into law at his alma mater, Texas State University, is the basis for federal assistance to institutions of higher education. Among its components are Pell Grants, federal loans to college students, and federally subsidized college work-study programs. Of these, Pell Grants account for the largest share of federal spending. Millions of college students over the years have received Pell Grants, which are directed at students from modest- and low-income families. The federal student loan program has also helped millions of students, although it is a relatively small spending item in that most of the money is returned through loan repayment. In 2010, as a cost-saving measure, the federal government took full control of the loan program. Before then, some student loans were issued by banks, which had the safety of a government-insured loan while receiving a fee for handling the loan.

Federal education grants are administered through the Department of Education, a cabinet-level agency that was created in 1979 to handle Washington's increased role in the education area. Nevertheless, the size of the Department of Education is an indicator of the degree to which education remains largely a state and local policy responsibility.

The Supreme Court has held that American children are entitled to an "adequate" education but do not have a right to an "equal" education. America's public schools differ greatly in quality primarily as a result of differences in the wealth of the communities they serve. Some public schools are overcrowded and have few facilities and little equipment. Others are very well equipped, have spacious facilities, and offer small class sizes.

The education department is by far the smallest of the executive departments, with only 4,400 employees. The next smallest is the Department of Labor, which has four times the staff.

The creation of the Department of Education was an object of partisan conflict, as was the 1960s legislation that authorized federal education grants. Some Republican lawmakers opposed these initiatives on grounds that the federal government had no business involving itself in education policy. In his 1980 presidential campaign, Ronald Reagan said he would abolish the Department of Education, although he changed his mind once in office. Since then, congressional Republicans and Democrats have fought numerous budget battles over federal assistance to education, with Democrats seeking higher levels of spending and Republicans pushing for lower levels.

Mandatory High-Stakes Testing   In 2001, responding to growing public concern about underperforming schools, President George W. Bush persuaded Congress to pass the No Child Left Behind Act (NCLB). The legislation requires national testing in reading, math, and science and ties federal funding to the test results. Schools that show no improvement in students' test scores after two years receive an increased amount of federal aid. If these schools show no improvement by the end of the third year, however, their students become eligible to transfer elsewhere, and their school's federal assistance is reduced.

POLITICAL THINKING

Does High-Stakes Testing Improve Learning?

Few education issues have provoked such sharply different reactions as mandatory high-stakes testing of public school students. Advocates say that it is the best way to hold schools and teachers accountable. If they repeatedly fail to perform, they, rather than their students, will suffer the consequences, as in the case of a school that loses funding because its students fail to improve on standardized tests. Opponents argue that mandatory high-stakes testing distorts what happens in the classroom. Teachers devote their time to "teaching to the test"—preparing their students to do well on the test, at whatever the cost to other forms of learning. What's your view on mandatory high-stakes testing? Is your opinion the result of being required to take such tests while you were in primary or secondary school?

NCLB has been a source of controversy since its inception.[19] Whereas the federal government had previously used financial aid as a means of influencing education policy, NCLB thrust the federal government directly into the classroom. The national testing process has nearly forced public schools to concentrate on tested subjects, such as math and science. The National Education Association (NEA) has argued that the law forces teachers to teach to the national tests, undermining true learning. Congressional Democrats have claimed that the program has failed to provide struggling schools with enough funds to improve the quality of classroom education. For their part, congressional Republicans have generally supported the law, saying that it holds teachers and schools accountable for student performance. House Republican leader John Boehner said: "Money alone is not the answer to the problems facing our children's schools. High standards and accountability for results—not just spending—are the key to erasing the achievement gap in education."[20]

In 2009, at President Obama's urging, the Democratic-controlled Congress enacted the Race to the Top program, which rewards states for school performance and innovation. States that score high by the program's criteria are eligible to receive federal funds that can be used to further strengthen their schools. A distinguishing feature of the program is that it requires the states to compete for funding. In the first round of competition, only Delaware and Tennessee were awarded funds. Seventeen additional states received funds in the second and third rounds. Although most states have chosen to compete for the funds, which has required them to align their education systems with the program's criteria, some states have opted not to do so. Texas governor Rick Perry, who was a candidate for the 2012 Republican presidential nomination, said: "We would be foolish and irresponsible to place our children's future in the hands of unelected bureaucrats and special interest groups thousands of miles away in Washington."[21]

Partisan Conflict over Education Policy   Many of the partisan and philosophical differences that affect federal welfare policy also affect federal education policy. Democrats are more inclined to find the answer to how to improve schools in increased federal spending on education, particularly in less-affluent communities, whereas Republicans are more inclined to look to market-like mechanisms such as achievement tests.

Partisan conflict has spilled even into policy areas outside the scope of federal authority. School choice is an example. Parents of students at poorly performing schools have increasingly pressured state and local officials to allow students to transfer to better schools. The charter school movement is one of the results of this pressure. Although charter schools are publicly funded, they have greater latitude in designing their curricula and picking their students. In order to remain open, they must meet performance standards set by state and local officials. Charter schools have been aggressively championed by Republican lawmakers. "Charters schools," said President Bush, "are helping foster a culture of educational innovation, accountability, and excellence." On the other hand, some Democratic lawmakers have criticized charter schools on grounds they weaken the regular public schools by siphoning away funding and top students. The California Democratic Party came out strongly against a wholesale move toward charter schools, saying many of the backers of such schools are seeking to "dismantle a free public education for every student . . . and replace it with company run charter schools."[22]

THE AMERICAN WAY OF PROMOTING THE GENERAL WELFARE

All democratic societies promote economic security, but they do so in different ways and to different degrees. Economic security has a higher priority in European democracies than in the United States. European democracies have instituted programs such as government-paid health care for all citizens, compensation for all unemployed workers, and retirement benefits for all elderly citizens. As this chapter shows, the United States provides these benefits only to some citizens in each category. On the other hand, the American system of higher education dwarfs those in Europe.

The differences between the European and American approaches to welfare stem from historical and cultural differences. Democracy in Europe developed in reaction to centuries of aristocratic rule, which brought the issue of economic privilege to the forefront. European democracies initiated sweeping social welfare programs designed to bring about greater economic equality. Social inequality was harder to root out because it was thoroughly embedded in European society, shaping everything from social manners to education. Private schools and university training were the preserve of the elite, a tradition that, though now in the past, continues to affect how Europeans think about educational opportunity.

The American experience was a different one. Democracy in America grew out of a tradition of limited government that emphasized personal liberty, which included a belief in self-reliance. This belief contributed to Americans' strong support for public education, their weak support for public assistance, and their persistent preference for low tax rates. Unlike political equality, the idea of economic equality has never captured Americans' imagination. Political scientists Stanley Feldman and John Zaller found that Americans' support for public assistance programs rests more on feelings of compassion for the poor than on an ideological belief in economic sharing.[23] Or, as the political scientist Robert Lane expressed it, Americans have a preference for market justice, meaning that they prefer that society's material benefits be allocated through the economic marketplace rather than through government policies.[24] It's thus not surprising that the United States has a high level of income inequality (see Figure 16-5).

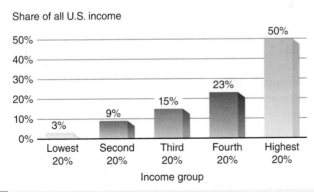

figure 16-5   INCOME INEQUALITY IN THE UNITED STATES

The United States has the highest degree of income inequality of any industrialized democracy. Citizens in the top fifth by income get half of all income; those in the bottom fifth get less than a twentieth of all income.

Source: U.S. Census Bureau, 2014.

Americans in the top fifth by income receive roughly 50 percent of total U.S. income, whereas those in the bottom fifth get about 3 percent. This 17-to-1 income difference between the top and bottom earners is easily the highest among Western democracies.

SUMMARY

The United States has a complex social welfare system of multiple programs addressing specific welfare needs. Each program applies only to those individuals who qualify for benefits by meeting the specific eligibility criteria. In general, these criteria are designed to encourage self-reliance or, when help is necessary, to ensure that laziness is not rewarded or fostered. This approach to social welfare reflects Americans' traditional belief in individualism.

Poverty is a large and persistent problem in the United States. About one in nine Americans falls below the government-defined poverty line, including a disproportionate number of children, female-headed families, minority-group members, and rural and inner-city dwellers. The ranks of the poor are increased by economic recessions and are reduced through government assistance programs.

Welfare policy has been a partisan issue, with Democrats taking the lead on government programs to alleviate economic insecurity and Republicans acting to slow down or decentralize these initiatives. Changes in social welfare have usually resulted from presidential leadership in the context of public support for the change. Welfare policy traditionally has involved programs to provide jobs and job training, education programs, income measures, and especially individual-benefit programs.

Individual-benefit programs fall into two broad categories: social insurance and public assistance. The former includes programs such as social security for retired workers and Medicare for the elderly. Social insurance programs are funded by payroll taxes paid by potential recipients, who, in this sense, earn the benefits they later receive. Because of this arrangement, social insurance programs have broad public support. Public assistance programs, in contrast, are funded by general tax revenues and are targeted toward needy individuals and families. These programs are not controversial in principle; most Americans believe that government should assist the truly needy. However, because of a widespread belief that most welfare recipients could get along without assistance if they tried, these programs do not have universal public support, receive only modest funding, and are politically divisive.

Social welfare is a contentious issue. In one view, social welfare is too costly and assists too many people who could help themselves; another view holds that social welfare is not broad enough and that too many disadvantaged Americans live in poverty. Because of these irreconcilable beliefs and because of federalism and the widely shared view that welfare programs should target specific problems, the existing system of multiple programs, despite its administrative complexity and inefficiency, has been the only politically feasible solution.

The balance between economic equality and individualism tilts more heavily toward individualism in the United States than in other advanced industrialized democracies. Other democracies, for example, have government-paid health care for all citizens. The United States does not, although the recently enacted health care reform bill provides coverage to many of the previously uninsured.

Compared to other democracies, the United States attempts to more equally educate its children, a policy consistent with its cultural emphasis on equality of opportunity. Like social welfare, however, education is a partisan issue involving disputes over the federal government's role, school choice, spending levels, and mandatory high-stakes testing.

CRITICAL THINKING ZONE

KEY TERMS

entitlement programs (*p. 518*)
equality of opportunity (*p. 529*)
in-kind benefit (*p. 524*)
means test (*p. 521*)

poverty line (*p. 513*)
public assistance (*p. 521*)
social insurance (*p. 518*)

APPLYING THE ELEMENTS OF CRITICAL THINKING

Conceptualizing: The Supreme Court has held that American children are entitled to an "adequate education" but not an "equal education." Explain the difference.

Synthesizing: Contrast social insurance benefits and public assistance benefits. How do they differ in terms of how individuals qualify to get a benefit? How do they differ in terms of the level of public support they have?

Analyzing: How has U.S. social welfare policy been influenced by America's federal system of government and by Americans' belief in individualism?

EXTRA CREDIT

A Book Worth Reading: David Shipler, *The Working Poor: Invisible in America*. New York: Vintage, 2004. Written by a Pulitzer Prize–winning journalist, this book looks at the people who work, largely unnoticed, on the lowest rung of the American economy.

A Website Worth Visiting: **www.journalistsresource.org** Journalists' Resource, located at Harvard University's Kennedy School of Government, is dedicated to identifying the top policy-relevant research and connecting it to current issues. Many of its postings are in the area of social welfare policy.

PARTICIPATE!

When it comes to partisan politics, poverty is a contentious issue. Republicans and Democrats disagree mightily on the question of how far government should go in helping the poor. On the other hand, virtually all Americans—on the right and on the left—support private efforts to help the poor. Numerous local religious, civic, social, and economic groups run programs for the poor, such as food kitchens and clothing drives. Also, many national organizations work locally to assist the poor. An example is Habitat for Humanity, which builds modest houses with volunteer labor and then makes them available to low-income families, which assist in the construction and receive low-interest or no-interest mortgages to pay for the cost of construction materials. Consider volunteering some of your time to a group that gives a helping hand to those in need—whether a church or a community group or a nonprofit organization like Habitat for Humanity. Habitat for Humanity has a website that makes it easy for you to volunteer.

17
CHAPTER

FOREIGN POLICY: PROTECTING THE AMERICAN WAY

"We the People of the United States, in Order to . . . provide for the common defence."

PREAMBLE, U.S. CONSTITUTION

The leaders of top economic nations were scheduled to meet in 2014 in Sochi, Russia, for the annual G-8 summit, with Russian president Vladimir Putin as the host. Economic growth and stability were to be at the top of the agenda. The global economy had not fully recovered from the steep downturn of six years earlier and new initiatives were to be adopted. The policy planning was disrupted in March after Russia forcefully annexed the Crimean Peninsula, which had been part of the Ukraine. The United States and Western European countries responded with sanctions against Russia, which were expanded when Putin gave military assistance to Russian separatists on Ukraine's eastern border.

When the national leaders finally met, it was in Brussels rather than Sochi, and the group was the G-7 rather than the G-8. Putin's invitation had been withdrawn, and the group now included only the leaders of Canada, France, Germany, Italy, Japan, Great Britain, and the United States. Said one of the participants: "Ever since the start of the crisis in

Ukraine, members of the G7 . . . have stood united in their response. To acts of aggression, we have reacted not only politically but also economically with sanctions."

Although Russian aggression dominated the first day of the two-day summit, the second day was devoted to economic issues. The national leaders discussed speeding up global economic growth, fostering closer trade relations, and addressing the high level of unemployment that had persisted since the 2008 economic downturn. In assessing the day's deliberations, U.S. President Barack Obama could not resist taking a potshot at Russia. Said Obama: "Today, in contrast to a growing global economy, a sluggish Russian economy is even weaker because of the choices made by Russia's leadership."

As the G-7 summit illustrates, foreign policy is an issue of economic vitality as well as one of military strength. The motivation behind every nation's foreign policy is its *national interest*—what's best for the nation in terms of protecting its physical security and advancing its economic prosperity. People do not always agree on the best way to promote the national interest, but it is the central issue of foreign policy.

Unlike other policy areas, foreign policy rests on relations with actors outside rather than within the country. As a result, the chief instruments of national security policy differ from those of domestic policy. One of these instruments is diplomacy—the process of negotiation between countries. The lead agency in U.S. diplomatic efforts is the Department of State, which is headed by the secretary of state and coordinates the efforts of U.S. embassies abroad, each of which is directed by a U.S. ambassador. American diplomacy also takes place through international organizations—such as the United Nations—to which the United States belongs. A second instrument of foreign policy is military power. The lead agency in military affairs is the Department of Defense, which is headed by the secretary of defense and oversees the military services—the army, air force, navy, and marine corps. Here, too, the United States sometimes works through alliances, the most important of which is the North Atlantic Treaty Organization (NATO). NATO has nearly thirty member nations, including the United States, Canada, and most Western and Eastern European countries. A third instrument of world politics is intelligence gathering, or the process of monitoring other countries' activities. For many reasons, but primarily because all countries pursue their self-interest, each nation keeps a watchful eye on other nations. In the United States, the task of intelligence gathering falls to specialized federal agencies including the Central Intelligence Agency (CIA) and the National Security Agency (NSA). Economic exchange, the fourth instrument of foreign affairs, involves both international trade and foreign aid. U.S. interests in this area are promoted by a range of U.S. agencies, such as the Agriculture, Commerce, Labor, and Treasury Departments, as well as specialty agencies such as the Federal Trade Commission. The United States also pursues its economic goals through international organizations of which it is a member, including the World Trade Organization, the World Bank, and the International Monetary Fund.

The national security policies of the United States include an extraordinary array of activities—so many, in fact, that they could not possibly be addressed adequately in an entire book, much less a single chapter. There are roughly two hundred countries in the world, and the United States has relations of one kind or another—military, diplomatic, economic—with all of them. This chapter narrows the subject by concentrating on a few main ideas:

- *Since World War II, the United States has acted in the role of world leader, which has substantially affected its military, diplomatic, and economic policies.*
- *The United States maintains a high degree of defense preparedness, which requires a substantial level of defense spending and a worldwide deployment of U.S. conventional and strategic forces.*
- *Changes in the international marketplace have led to increased economic interdependence among nations, which has had a marked influence on the U.S. economy and on America's security planning.*

THE ROOTS OF U.S. FOREIGN AND DEFENSE POLICY

Before World War II, except within its own hemisphere, the United States was a mostly **isolationist** country. It was preoccupied with its internal development and intent on avoiding European entanglements. A different America emerged after World War II. It had more land, sea, and air power than any other country and more than a hundred overseas military installations. The United States had become a fully **internationalist** country—a nation deeply involved in world affairs.[1]

The United States was also a nation not fully at peace. It was locked in a wide-reaching conflict with the Soviet Union, which, after World War II, had engineered the communist takeover of Poland, Hungary, Czechoslovakia, and other Eastern European nations. President Harry S Truman and other American leaders regarded communist Russia as an implacable foe, a view that led to adoption of the doctrine of **containment**—the notion that Soviet aggression could be stopped only by the determined use of American power.[2] This doctrine had roots in the failed efforts to appease Germany's Adolf Hitler in the years leading up to World War II. At the 1938 Munich conference, Germany was allowed to annex Czechoslovakia's Sudetenland, which had a substantial German population. The annexation whetted Hitler's expansionist goals. The "Lesson of Munich" was that totalitarian leaders could not be appeased; they had to be confronted.

The Cold War Era and Its Lessons

Developments in the late 1940s embroiled the United States in a **cold war** with the Soviet Union.[3] The term refers to the fact that the two countries were not directly engaged in actual combat (a "hot war") but were locked in deep-seated hostilities that lasted forty-five years. The structure of international power was **bipolar**—the United States versus the Soviet Union. Each side was supreme in its sphere and was blocked by the power of the other from expanding its influence. A first application of containment policy was a massive aid program for Greece, where communists were gaining headway. President Truman believed that if Greece went communist, Turkey would be the next "domino" to fall, which would give control of the eastern Mediterranean to the Soviets. Then, in June 1950, when the Soviet-backed North Koreans invaded South Korea, Truman sent U.S. forces into the conflict in an attempt to stop the spread of communism in Northeast Asia. Nearly thirty-five thousand U.S. troops lost their lives in the Korean War, which ended in stalemate.

The turning point in U.S. foreign policy was the Vietnam War. Responding to the threat of a communist takeover in Vietnam, the United States became ever more deeply involved. Washington policymakers were driven by the "domino theory"—the claim that if Vietnam fell to the communists, so too would Laos, Cambodia, and the rest of Southeast Asia. By the late 1960s, 550,000 Americans were fighting in South Vietnam. Although U.S. forces had military superiority, Vietnam was a guerrilla war, with no front lines and few set battles.[4] U.S. public opinion, most visibly among the young, gradually turned against the war. U.S. combat troops left Vietnam in 1973, and two years later North Vietnamese forces completed their takeover of the country. Vietnam was the most painful and costlier application of the containment doctrine: fifty-eight thousand Americans lost their lives in the fighting.

Cold war propaganda, like this poster warning of the danger of communism, contributed to a climate of opinion in the United States that led to public support for efforts to contain Soviet power.

America's failure in Vietnam led U.S. policymakers to reconsider the country's international role. The "Lesson of Vietnam" was that there were limits to the country's ability to assert its will in the world. President Richard Nixon proclaimed that the United States could no longer act as the free world's "Lone Ranger" and sought to reduce tensions with communist countries. In 1972, Nixon visited the People's Republic of China, the first official contact with that country since the communists seized power in 1949. Nixon also initiated the Strategic Arms Limitation Talks (SALT), which resulted in reductions in the nuclear arsenals of the United States and the Soviet Union. This spirit of cooperation lasted until the Soviet invasion of Afghanistan in 1979, which convinced U.S. leaders that the Soviet Union had not changed its ways. Ronald Reagan, elected president in 1980, called for a renewed hard line toward the Soviet Union, which he described as the "evil empire."

Although U.S. policymakers did not realize it, the Soviet Union was collapsing under the weight of its heavy defense expenditures, its isolation from Western technology, and its inefficient centralized economy. In 1985, Soviet leader Mikhail Gorbachev undertook a restructuring of

Soviet society, an initiative known as *perestroika*. Gorbachev's reforms came too late to prevent the Soviet Union's collapse. In 1988, the Soviet Union withdrew its troops from Afghanistan, followed a year later by a withdrawal from Eastern Europe. Shortly thereafter, nearly all of the Soviet republics declared their independence, marking the end of the Soviet Union as a governing entity. The bipolar power structure of the cold war era was finished. The new structure was **unipolar**—the United States was now the world's unrivaled superpower.

The Post–Cold War Era and Its Lessons

The end of the cold war prompted the first President Bush in 1990 to call for a "new world order." George H. W. Bush advocated **multilateralism**— the idea that major nations should act together in response to problems and crises. Included in Bush's plan was a stronger role for multinational organizations such as the United Nations and NATO.

The Air Wars of the 1990s   Multilateralism defined America's response to the Iraqi invasion of Kuwait in August 1990. President Bush secured UN resolutions ordering Iraq to withdraw from Kuwait. When it failed to do so, a half-million troops, mostly American but including contingents from nearly two dozen nations, attacked Iraq. The fighting ended in four days.

The Gulf operation was a military triumph, prompting President Bush to declare that the United States had "kicked the Vietnam syndrome [the legacy of America's defeat in Vietnam] once and for all." The Gulf War, however, was otherwise less successful. Believing that an overthrow of Saddam Hussein's regime would destabilize Iraq, Bush halted the hostilities after Iraqi forces retreated. Hussein remained in power but was ordered by a UN resolution to dismantle his weapons program. However, Hussein repeatedly interfered with UN inspectors' attempts to verify the status of his weapons programs, raising suspicions about his intentions.

Multilateralism carried over into the Clinton administration. Confronting Serb atrocities in Bosnia—where tens of thousands of Muslims and Croats were murdered, raped, or driven from their homes—the United States and its NATO allies attacked Serb forces with air power in 1995, which culminated in a U.S.-negotiated peace agreement (the Dayton Accords) that included the deployment to Bosnia of nearly sixty thousand peacekeeping troops, including twenty thousand Americans. War in the Balkans flared again in 1999 when the Serbs undertook a campaign of "ethnic cleansing" in the Serbian province of Kosovo, whose population was 90 percent Albanian. When attempts at a negotiated settlement failed, NATO planes, including U.S. aircraft, attacked Serbia.[5] After nearly three months of intensive bombing, Serb president Slobodan Milosevic (who died in 2006 while on trial for war crimes) pulled his troops out of Kosovo. Ethnic Albanians moved back in and launched revenge attacks on Serbs who remained. (In 2008, Kosovo became an independent state.)

As these examples indicate, multilateralism was not a wholly successful strategy for resolving international conflicts. With the deployment of enough resources, the world's major powers showed that they could act together with some success. However, these interventions offered no guarantee of long-term success. Regional and internal conflicts typically stem from enduring ethnic, religious, factional, or national hatreds or from chronic problems such as famine, overcrowding, or government corruption. Even if these hatreds or problems can be eased momentarily, they are often too deep-seated to be settled permanently.

The War on Terrorism and the Afghanistan War   Upon assuming the presidency in 2001, George W. Bush rejected his father's multilateral approach to foreign policy. He announced plans to reduce America's military presence abroad. His position changed when terrorists attacked the World Trade Center and the Pentagon on September 11, 2001. In a televised address, Bush urged other nations to join the United States in a multilateral "war on terrorism."

The war on terrorism resulted in the first major reorganization of the U.S. national security bureaucracy since the Department of Defense was formed from the War and Navy Departments after World War II. This time, the new agency was the Department of Homeland Security (DHS), which was created in 2002 to coordinate domestic antiterrorism efforts. The DHS's responsibilities include securing the nation's borders, enhancing defenses against biological attacks, preparing emergency personnel (police, firefighters, and rescue workers) for their roles in responding to terrorist attacks, and coordinating efforts to stop domestic terrorism.[6]

The first U.S. military action in the war on terrorism was an attack on Afghanistan, which commenced barely a month after the September 11 attacks. Afghanistan's Taliban-led government had granted sanctuary and training sites to the al Qaeda terrorists who carried out the attacks. Supported by troops from other NATO countries, U.S. forces quickly toppled the Taliban government, but failed to capture al Qaeda leader Osama bin Laden and his top lieutenants.

The Afghan invasion marked the start of what was to become the longest war in U.S. history. The Taliban regrouped, slowly reasserting control over parts of the country. In 2009, with Barack Obama now in the presidency, 50,000 additional U.S. troops were dispatched to Afghanistan for the purpose of disrupting the Taliban insurgence and speeding the training of Afghan army and police. In 2011, U.S. forces succeeded in locating and killing bin Laden (he was hiding in neighboring Pakistan), but the Afghan conflict otherwise dragged on. Obama had initially called for the withdrawal of all U.S. combat troops by 2014 with only "a support mission" to remain behind to help the Afghan army cope with the Taliban. That timetable was later pushed back to 2016 because of continued fighting with Taliban forces and the slower-than-expected development of the Afghan army as an effective fighting force.

The Iraq War In 2002, President Bush labeled Iraq, Iran, and North Korea "the axis of evil." A few months later, he announced a new national security doctrine: the **preemptive war doctrine**.[7] Speaking at West Point, Bush asserted that the United States would not wait until it was attacked by hostile nations. Instead, America would take "preemptive action."[8] The concept was not entirely new—U.S. officials had long maintained a right to strike first if faced with an imminent attack. What was new in the Bush Doctrine was its embrace of a first-strike option before a threat became imminent.

In the summer of 2002, Bush targeted the regime of Iraq's Saddam Hussein, claiming that it was stockpiling weapons of mass destruction (WMDs)—chemical and biological weapons, and possibly nuclear weapons— for use against U.S. interests. That October, Congress authorized the use of military force against Iraq if it did not disarm voluntarily.

Despite the UN's refusal to authorize a military attack and in the face of strenuous opposition from France, Germany, and Russia, President Bush in March 2003 ordered U.S. forces to invade Iraq. British troops were also involved, but the attack was essentially an act of **unilateralism**—the situation in which one nation takes action against another state or states.[9] The Iraqi regime collapsed quickly, but the post-invasion phase was far more difficult than the Bush administration had anticipated. Age-old animosities between Sunni, Shiite, and Kurdish groups within Iraq blocked political compromise and fueled internal violence. Moreover, weapons inspectors did not find the WMDs that the Bush administration had claimed were in Iraq's possession, which undermined public support for the war. At the beginning, Americans by three-to-one had expressed support for the invasion. Two years later, the public was evenly split on the question of whether the invasion was smart decision.[10]

In 2007, President Bush authorized a "surge" to give the struggling Iraqi government an opportunity to govern more effectively. Some 30,000

U.S. combat troops were added to the 130,000 military personnel already there. The surge contributed to a significant reduction in the violence, leading Bush to announce a phased withdrawal of U.S. combat forces from Iraq. President Obama stayed with the plan when he came into office and the last of America's combat units left Iraq in late 2011. Nearly nine years of war there had resulted in the deaths of more than 4,500 American troops and had cost nearly a trillion dollars—all with no assurance that the new Iraqi government would be on friendly terms with the United States over the long run.

Thus, as is true of multilateralism, unilateralism has limits. Even with the world's most powerful military, the United States found it difficult to bear the brunt of the Iraq conflict, just as it struggled for success in Afghanistan. Wars of this type do not lend themselves to quick and tidy battlefield solutions. It is one thing to defeat a conventional army in open warfare and quite another to prevail in a conflict in which the fight is not so much a battle for territory as it is a struggle for people's loyalties, especially when they harbor age-old distrust of each other, as in the case of Iraq's and Afghanistan's ethnic groups.

America's Most Challenging Regions   Even though the United States has withdrawn most of its troops from these regions, the Middle East and South Asia (where Afghanistan is located) remain the most challenging regions militarily. They are unsettled, driven by historical animosities, revolutionary demands, and Islamic terrorist groups.

In late 2010, the United States was caught off guard when demonstrators flooded the streets of Tunisia's capital to protest government corruption and oppression. Within a month, Tunisia's authoritarian president

---

POLITICAL THINKING	**Was It Worth It?**

After more than a dozen years of war in Iraq and Afghanistan, the United States has cut back on its combat mission in that troubled region of the world. Observers agree that much has been accomplished in this period but also that the costs have been high—over a trillion dollars spent and seven thousand U.S. troops killed. Based on your understanding of these wars, do you think they were worth the cost, or do you think the United States would have been better off if it had chosen not to go to war? Do you have the same opinion of both wars, or do you feel differently about the Iraq war than about the Afghan war?

In late 2011, the last U.S. combat troops left Iraq, crossing the border into neighboring Kuwait.

had been forced from office. Egypt and Libya were next. In Egypt, demonstrators overthrew Hosni Mubarak, who had been the country's authoritarian president for three decades. In Libya, the United States and its NATO allies intervened with an aerial bombardment that helped overthrow the regime of the country's long-time ruler, Muammar Gaddafi. Unrest then spread into Syria, sparking a bloody civil war. Initially seen as an "Arab Spring"—a demand of Arab populations for a larger say in their governing—these uprisings were far more complicated, challenging American leaders' efforts to respond effectively. In Egypt, for example, elections led to a victory by an Islamist party that then tried to govern by fiat, only to be overthrown in turn by a military coup. In Syria, the United States threatened military action after the Syrian government used chemical weapons on its opponents; the U.S. stopped short of intervening when the Assad regime agreed to the destruction of the weapons.

In 2014, the United States found itself caught off guard again. Syria's tumultuous three-year civil war had spawned a radical Islamic group—the Islamic State—that had swept across the border into Iraq, seizing a large swath of territory that included Iraq's second-largest city, Mosul. Comprised of Sunni Muslims, ISIS brutally murdered as heretics the Shiite

Muslim and Christian men it captured and declared its intention to establish a Caliphate—an Islamic state headed by a supreme religious and political leader. As the threat mounted, President Obama ordered targeted air strikes on Islamic State forces in an effort to bolster Iraq's government, which had proven too weak and divided to counter it on its own. At the same time, Obama made it clear that the airstrikes did not mark a fundamental shift in American policy. Obama declared that the United States would not be "dragged into fighting another war in Iraq."

Nuclear weapons are also at issue in the Middle East and South Asia regions. Iran's nuclear program had led the United States to freeze Iranian financial assets in U.S. banks and their overseas branches and, along with its European allies, to impose an embargo on Iranian oil. Iran's 2013 election, in which a more moderate president was elected, led to talks aimed at resolving the impasse peacefully. The nuclear issue extends also to Pakistan, which shares a porous border with Afghanistan. Afghan rebels hide out in Pakistan and stage cross-border raids from there, supported covertly by factions within the Pakistani military and government. Pakistan is a Muslim nation and has a large nuclear arsenal. If radical Islamists should come to power in Pakistan, the threat to U.S. interests would increase exponentially.

There is little question but that the Middle East and South Asia will occupy the attention of U.S. policymakers for years to come. Ambassador Nicholas Burns, one of America's most respected diplomats, has called the situation "the most challenging . . . for the United States since World War II."[11]

THE MILITARY DIMENSION OF NATIONAL SECURITY POLICY

Defense spending by the United States is far higher than that of any other nation. In fact, the United States accounts for more than 40 percent of all military spending worldwide (see "How the U.S. Differs"). The U.S. defense budget is six times that of China and ten times that of Russia.

Military Power, Uses, and Capabilities

U.S. military forces are trained for different types of military action, ranging from nuclear conflict to terrorism.

Nuclear War   Although the possibility of all-out nuclear war declined dramatically with the collapse of the Soviet Union, the United States retains a nuclear arsenal designed to prevent such a war. Deterrence policy is

HOW THE U.S. DIFFERS

POLITICAL THINKING THROUGH COMPARISONS

Worldwide Military Spending

With an annual defense budget in excess of $500 billion, the United States spends more than 40 percent of all the money spent worldwide on the military. China is second in military spending, but its expenditures are only a sixth of those of the United States. Russia spends about a tenth as much.

U.S. efforts to get their European allies to bear more of the defense burden have been largely unsuccessful, although Britain, France, and Germany spend more per capita on defense than any country except the United States.

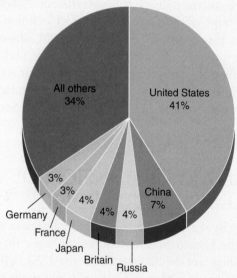

Source: From Center for Arms Control and Non-Proliferation, 2014.

Q: What do you make of the disparity in military spending between the United States and its military allies? Do you think they spend too little on defense, relying too heavily on the United States for their security? Or do you think the United States spends too much on defense, placing too much emphasis on military force as an instrument of foreign policy?

based on the concept of **mutually assured destruction (MAD).** The assumption is that any nation will be deterred from launching a full-scale nuclear attack by the knowledge that, even if it destroyed the United States, it too would be obliterated.

America's nuclear weapons are deployed in what is called the "nuclear triad." This term refers to the three ways—by land-based missiles, submarine-based missiles, and bombers—that nuclear weapons can be launched. The triad provides a second-strike capability—that is, the ability to absorb a first-strike nuclear attack and survive with enough nuclear capacity for a massive retaliation (second strike). Since the end of the cold war, the United States and Russia have negotiated substantial reductions in their nuclear arsenals and have established monitoring systems designed to reduce the possibility that either side could launch an effective surprise attack.

A greater fear today than nuclear war with Russia is the possibility that a terrorist group or rogue nation will smuggle a nuclear device into the United States and detonate it. The technology and materials necessary to build a nuclear weapon (or to buy one clandestinely) are more readily available than ever before. Accordingly, the United States, Russia, and other nations are cooperating to halt the spread of nuclear weapons, although, as the nuclear weapons program of North Korea illustrates, the effort has not been completely successful.

Conventional War   Not since World War II has the United States fought an all-out conventional war, nor at present does it have the capacity to do so. Such a war would require the reinstatement of the military draft and the full mobilization of the nation's industrial capacity. Instead, the U.S. armed forces are structured to be capable of fighting two medium-sized wars simultaneously, although they are currently undergoing a restructuring in response to budget pressures and changing military tactics. Conventional forces—soldiers and marines—are to be reduced by one hundred thousand while the military's special forces units and quick-strike capacity will be increased. The United States, said defense secretary Leon Panetta in 2012, is aiming for "a smaller, leaner force" while "retaining the ability to defeat any enemy on land."[12]

The United States today relies on an all-volunteer military force (see "How the 50 States Differ") that is second to none in its destructive power. The U.S. Navy has a dozen aircraft carriers, scores of attack submarines, and hundreds of fighting and supply ships. The U.S. Air Force has thousands of high-performance aircraft, ranging from fighter jets to jumbo transport planes. The U.S. Army has roughly five hundred

HOW THE 50 STATES DIFFER

POLITICAL THINKING THROUGH COMPARISONS

The All-Volunteer Military's Recruits

Until 1973, the United States had an active military draft. Upon reaching age eighteen, males were required to register for the draft. Local draft boards would then pick the draftees based on quotas that varied with the size of the local population. Accordingly, each state contributed equally to the military's manpower needs relative to its population size. Today's military is an all-volunteer force, and the states' contributions

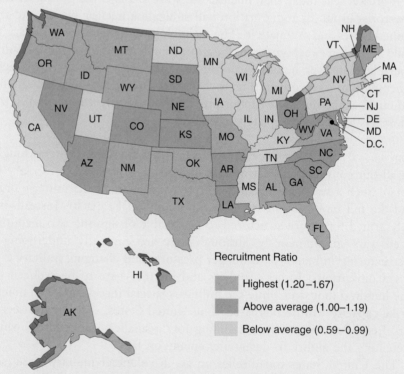

Recruitment Ratio

- Highest (1.20–1.67)
- Above average (1.00–1.19)
- Below average (0.59–0.99)

Source: Adapted from Tim Kane, "Who Bears the Burden? Demographic Characteristics of U.S. Military Recruits before and after 9/11," Heritage Foundation, Center for Data Analysis Report #05-08, November 7, 2005. Used by permission of The Heritage Foundation.

vary significantly. The accompanying map indicates the degree to which each state is over- and underrepresented in the military, as indicated by the ratio of military recruits from a state to the number of males aged eighteen to thirty-four in that state's population. Montana has the largest number of recruits relative to its population, followed in order by Alaska, Wyoming, and Maine. Utah, Rhode Island, and Massachusetts rank lowest, in that order.

Q: What might explain why military recruits come disproportionately from states like Montana, Alaska, Wyoming, and Maine, as well as from the southern states?

A: According to Department of Defense data, recruits are more likely to come from rural areas, particularly areas where few well-paying jobs are available to young adults. The four states with the highest recruitment ratios have these characteristics. As for the South, higher recruitment levels have been explained in terms of its stronger military tradition and its numerous military installations. Individuals from areas near these installations, as well as the sons and daughters of military personnel, are more likely to enlist in the military. (Mississippi and Tennessee, with the South's lowest recruitment rates, have relatively few military installations.)

thousand regular troops and more than three hundred thousand Reserve and National Guard soldiers, who are supplied with tanks, artillery pieces, armored personnel carriers, and attack helicopters. This armament is doubly lethal because it is linked to sophisticated surveillance, targeting, and communication systems. No other nation has anywhere near the advanced weapons systems that the United States possesses.

Unconventional (Guerrilla) War   America's military firepower is not a large advantage in so-called unconventional wars of the type in Afghanistan. The insurgents employed guerrilla tactics including hit-and-run attacks, roadside explosive devices, and suicide bombings, as well as the killing and intimidation of civilians who sided with the Afghan government. Such tactics are extremely difficult to defend against and virtually impossible to stop by conventional means.

Unlike a conventional war, in which the measures of success are territory gained and casualties inflicted, an unconventional war requires winning the support of the people or, as it is described, "winning their hearts

---

<table>
<tr><td>POLITICAL THINKING</td><td>What Level of Military Spending Is Necessary?</td></tr>
</table>

In 2012, President Obama announced cuts in military spending, partly because Congress was seeking ways to reduce federal spending and partly because his national security advisors had concluded that the U.S. military should be slimmed down to meet emerging threats. Conventional forces would be reduced and greater emphasis would be placed on special forces operations, drone capability, and the like. This plan was attacked during the 2012 presidential campaign by Republican nominee Mitt Romney. He argued that the Obama administration failed to understand America's special role in the world, which requires that it maintain a large conventional force. "The United States," said Romney, "should always retain military supremacy to deter would-be aggressors." What is your view of this issue? What military structure and spending levels do you think are appropriate for the challenges the United States will face in the coming years?

---

and minds." Insurgents depend on the local population for recruits, intelligence, hiding places, and food. If they can be denied access to these resources, their military capability falls dramatically. Tactically, an unconventional war is fought with small and highly mobile combat units that can seek out insurgents and provide security to local populations, while also training indigenous military and police forces to gradually assume responsibility for their nation's security.[13]

Although the U.S. military has special operations units (such as the U.S. Army's Special Forces), and provides its regular units with some training in counterinsurgency warfare, the U.S. military for the most part is not structured to fight unconventional wars. As a consequence, it had difficulty adapting to the wars in Iraq and Afghanistan, just as it struggled to adapt to the war in Vietnam four decades earlier. The restructuring of the armed services that is now under way is intended to correct this imbalance.

Transnational Terrorism   The terrorist attacks of September 11, 2001, thrust the U.S. military into a new kind of war—a war on terrorism. The United States was not prepared for a terrorist war when it was attacked in 2001. Its intelligence agencies had not focused their efforts on terrorist activity, and its military units had few linguists who spoke the terrorists' languages.

Terrorism is not by itself a new form of warfare. It has been employed in many places over the centuries, but it has become a broader threat in recent years. Historically, terrorism was a domestic problem, employed by disgruntled groups against their own government. Terrorism today has an international dimension. **Transnational terrorism** is terrorism that transcends national borders and includes attacks on nonmilitary targets.[14] When terrorists attacked the United States in 2001, or bombed the Madrid commuter system in 2004, they were not seeking to take over the United States or Spain. They were seeking to alter the balance of power in the Middle East by forcing Western nations to rethink their presence in the region.

America's war on terrorism is aimed at groups, such as al Qaeda, rather than nations. Al Qaeda is a nonstate actor without clearly defined borders,

FBI TEN MOST WANTED FUGITIVE

MURDER OF U.S. NATIONALS OUTSIDE THE UNITED STATES; CONSPIRACY TO MURDER U.S. NATIONALS OUTSIDE THE UNITED STATES; ATTACK ON A FEDERAL FACILITY RESULTING IN DEATH

USAMA BIN LADEN

Date of Photograph Unknown

Aliases: Usama Bin Muhammad Bin Ladin, Shaykh Usama Bin Ladin, the Prince, the Emir, Abu Abdallah, Mujahid Shaykh, Hajj, the Director

Shown here is one of the many wanted posters that the U.S. government circulated in its hunt for Osama bin Laden, who planned the deadly attacks of September 11, 2001. He was killed in a clandestine U.S. operation in Pakistan in 2011.

which complicates the task of locating and destroying it. Moreover, transnational terrorists have become adept at waging "asymmetric war," so called because they lack the strength to directly engage opposing military forces. In fighting their wars, terrorists resort to improvised weapons, including suicide bombers.

The war on terrorism lacks sharply defined battlefronts and is being waged through a variety of instruments, including military force, intelligence gathering, law enforcement, foreign aid, international cooperation, and immigration control. In reality, much of the responsibility for rooting out terrorist cells rests with law enforcement and intelligence agencies in the United States and abroad rather than with military units. Recent arrests of suspected terrorists in the United States, Europe, Africa, Asia, and South America have usually been the result of the work of nonmilitary agencies.

The Politics of National Defense

Policy elites, public opinion, and special interests all play significant roles in national defense policy. The American public usually backs the judgment of its political leaders on the use of military force. In nearly all military initiatives of the past half century, Americans have supported the action at the outset. When President Bush ordered U.S. forces to invade Iraq in 2003,[15] two-thirds of Americans supported his decision. The rest were split between those who opposed the war and those who were unsure about the proper course of action.

On the other hand, if a war begins to seem endless, public support inevitably erodes.[16] A swing in public opinion against the Vietnam War forced U.S. policymakers to withdraw American troops in 1973. Public opinion on the Iraq war soured more quickly, partly because the stated reason for the war—the threat of Iraq's WMDs—proved faulty.

Although the public has an influence on war policy, it is not informed or interested enough to affect most national security policies, which are decided largely by the president and Congress in consultation with top experts and military officers. Of these various actors, the president has the most say, as indicated by President Obama's decision in 2014 to commit U.S. airpower to repel Islamic State forces in Iraq and Syria.

The defense industry also has a say in national security policy. In his 1961 farewell address, President Dwight D. Eisenhower, who had commanded U.S. forces in Europe during World War II, warned Americans against "the unwarranted influence" and "misplaced power" of what he termed "the military-industrial complex." Eisenhower was referring to the fact that national defense is big business, involving the annual expenditure of hundreds of billions of dollars.[17] As Eisenhower described it, the **military-industrial complex** has three main components: the military establishment, the arms industry, and the members of Congress from states and districts that depend heavily on the arms industry. All three benefit from a high level of defense spending, whether needed or not.

The defense industry suffered a rare defeat in 2009 when Congress, backed by President Obama and Defense Secretary Robert Gates, refused to appropriate funds for building additional F-22 fighter jets. The F-22 is the world's most sophisticated fighter jet, but it is hugely expensive and excels at air-to-air combat, a type of warfare that the United States has not fought on any scale since the Korean War. Secretary Gates said the military would be better served by less-expensive aircraft suited to wars of the type fought in Iraq and Afghanistan. Nevertheless, forty-two senators voted to continue production of the F-22. Some of them were less concerned with the F-22's cost and capabilities than with the fact that thousands of jobs in their state would be lost if production stopped.

THE ECONOMIC DIMENSION OF NATIONAL SECURITY POLICY

National security is more than an issue of military might. It is also a question of maintaining a strong position in the global economy. Geographically, the world has three major economic centers. One is the United States, which produces roughly a fifth of the world's goods and services. Another center, responsible for about a fourth of the world's economy, is the European Union (EU), which includes most European countries. The EU is dominated by Germany, Britain, and France, which together account for roughly half its economy. The third center is the Pacific Rim, anchored by the economies of Japan and China, which together account for more than a fifth of the world's economy.

By some indicators, the United States is the weakest of the three economic centers. Its trade deficit is easily the world's largest. The United States imports substantially more goods and services than it exports. In fact, the United States has not had a trade surplus since 1975 and over the past decade its deficit has exceeded $300 billion annually (see Figure 17-1).

In other ways, however, the United States is the strongest of the three centers. According to the Switzerland-based World Economic Forum, the United States is economically more competitive than its major rivals. The United States owes this position to several factors,

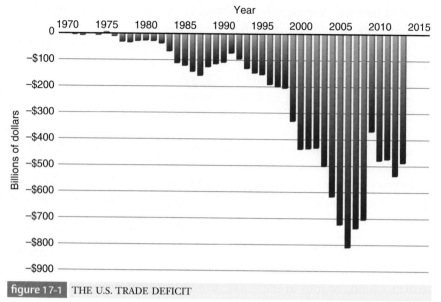

figure 17-1   THE U.S. TRADE DEFICIT
Not since 1975 has the United States had a trade surplus; the annual deficit has not dropped
below $300 billion at any time during the past decade.
Source: U.S. Bureau of Economic Analysis, 2012.

including its technological innovation, financial institutions, and extensive higher education system.[18] The U.S. economy is also the most
diversified of the three. In addition to its industrial base, the United
States has a strong agricultural sector and abundant natural resources.
Its vast fertile plains and advanced farming methods have made it the
world's leading agricultural producer. The United States ranks among
the top three countries worldwide in production of wheat, corn, soy-
beans, peanuts, cotton, eggs, cattle, and pigs. As for natural resources,
the United States ranks among the top five nations in deposits of copper,
uranium, lead, sulfur, zinc, coal, gold, iron ore, natural gas, silver, and
magnesium.[19]

Nevertheless, the United States does not have the option of "going it
alone" economically. To meet Americans' production and consumption
needs, the country depends on other countries' raw materials, finished
goods, markets, and capital. This imperative requires the United States
to exert global economic influence. The broad goals of the United States in
the world economy include the following:[20]

- Sustaining a stable and open system of trade that will promote
prosperity at home

- Maintaining access to oil and other natural resources vital to the strength of the U.S. economy
- Preventing the widening gap between rich and poor countries from disrupting the world economy
- Contributing to the stability of the global economy

Promoting Global Trade

After World War II, the United States helped enact a global trading system with itself at the center. The U.S. dollar had become the leading currency of international trade, replacing the English pound, which held that position for more than a century. World War II had weakened Britain's global economic position and elevated that of the United States, which quickly asserted its dominance. A key initiative was the European Recovery Plan, better known as the Marshall Plan. It included an unprecedented amount of aid (more than $100 billion in today's dollars) for the postwar rebuilding of Europe. Apart from enabling the countries of Western Europe to better confront the perceived Soviet threat, the Marshall Plan served America's economic needs. Wartime production had lifted the United States out of the Great Depression, but the immediate postwar period was marked by a recession and renewed fears of hard times. A rebuilt Western Europe would become a much-needed market for American products.

Since then, major shifts have taken place in the world economy. Germany is now a trading rival of the United States, as is Japan, which also received substantial postwar reconstruction aid from the United States. More recently, China and the European Union have taken their place as trading giants, and Russia, propelled by its huge oil and gas reserves, has the potential to become one.

Today, the American economy depends more heavily on international commerce than in any period in history. The domestic manufacturing sector that at one time was the source of most jobs has shrunk. Most of the nonagricultural goods that Americans now buy, from television sets to automobiles, are produced by foreign firms. Indeed, nearly all large U.S. firms are themselves *multinational corporations* (or *transnational corporations*), with operations in more than one country. From a headquarters in New York City, a firm has no difficulty managing a production facility in Thailand that is filling orders for markets in Europe and South America. Money, goods, and services today flow freely and rapidly across national borders, and large U.S. firms increasingly think about markets in global terms. As a result, they sometimes engage in activities that conflict with

America's foreign policy goals. In Africa, for example, U.S. oil companies have sometimes supported dictatorial regimes in order to maintain access to oil fields.

Economic globalization is a term that describes the increased inter-dependence of nations' economies. This development is both an opportunity for and a threat to U.S. economic interests. The opportunity rests with the possibility of increased demand abroad for U.S. products and lower prices to U.S. consumers as a result of inexpensive imports. The threat lies in the fact that foreign firms also compete in the global marketplace and may use their competitive advantages, such as cheaper labor, to outposition U.S. firms.

In general, international commerce works best when countries trade freely with one another. This situation keeps the price of traded items, whether finished goods or raw materials, at their lowest level, resulting in economic efficiency (see Chapter 15). However, global trade is a political issue as well as an economic one, and there are conflicting views on international trade. **Free trade** holds that barriers to international trade should be kept to a minimum. Proponents of free trade claim that the long-term economic interests of all countries are advanced when **tariffs** (taxes on imported goods) and other trade barriers are kept to a minimum. Most free-trade advocates couple their advocacy with fair-trade demands, but they are committed, philosophically and practically, to the idea that free trade results in a net gain for firms and consumers. The 1993 North American Free Trade Agreement (NAFTA) was a product of this thinking. It created a largely free market between the United States, Canada, and Mexico.

Since then, the United States has negotiated free-trade agreements with several countries. The most recent are bilateral agreements with Panama, Columbia, and Korea, which were negotiated during the Bush administration and ratified under the Obama administration. In 2011, President Obama proposed yet another such agreement, perhaps the most ambitious yet. If approved by Congress, the Trans Pacific Partnership (also called the Pacific Rim Trade Agreement) would include Australia, Brunei, Chile, Malaysia, New Zealand, Peru, Singapore, Vietnam, and the United States and could eventually include other Pacific nations. A free trade agreement with the European Union is also being negotiated.

The United States has been deeply involved in the World Trade Organization (WTO). Created in 1995, the WTO is the formal international institution through which most nations negotiate general rules of trade.[21] The WTO's mission is to promote global free trade through reductions

If successfully negotiated and approved by Congress, the Trans Pacific Partnership (TPP) would be the most ambitious free-trade agreement to which the United States has been a party. The TPP would literally rim the Pacific Ocean. Among the countries involved in the proposed trade agreement are Vietnam, Australia, and Chile.

in tariffs, protections for intellectual property (copyrights and patents), and other policies. Trade disputes among WTO members are settled by arbitration panels, which consist of representatives from the member nations. Under WTO rules, an arbitration panel's ruling, once approved by the WTO's full membership, is binding on the countries involved in the dispute.

Although the United States has clearly been a leader in promoting free trade, some Americans advocate **protectionism,** which holds that domestic producers should be protected from foreign competitors. The classic protectionist measure is a tariff on a particular import, which raises the market price of the foreign-made product, thereby giving domestic producers of the same product a competitive advantage. For some protectionists, the issue is simply a matter of defending domestic firms against their foreign competitors. For others, the issue is one of fair trade. They are protectionists in those instances where foreign firms have an unfair competitive advantage as a result, for example, of a subsidy from their government that enables them to market their goods at an artificially low price.

Protectionist sentiment is usually stronger in Congress than in the White House. Although most members of Congress say they support free trade, many of them respond differently when a key economic interest in their state or district is threatened by foreign competition. In such cases, they seek protective measures, such as a tariff on the competitor's products. Often, they find public support for their position. Although many Americans regard free trade as a net benefit for the United States in terms of less-expensive products and export opportunities, many others think that free trade harms American firms and workers by opening the U.S. market to goods from countries that have cheap labor and poor environmental standards (see Figure 17-2).

Economists argue that economic disruption is an inevitable result of market change and that firms should try to adapt to the change rather than turn to government for protection. Elected officials, however, cannot take the long-range view so easily because they face immediate pressures from constituents who have lost jobs and from communities that have lost firms. In response to such pressures, U.S. officials have insisted that foreign governments halt practices that put American firms at an unfair disadvantage. In 2009, for example, President Obama placed a 35 percent tariff on the import of Chinese tires on the grounds that the Chinese government was subsidizing their production. However, other countries are not convinced that the United States itself always plays fair. In 2006, international trade talks collapsed in part because the United States refused to reduce its hefty farm subsidies, which enable U.S. agricultural producers to sell their products at a low price in world markets, thereby giving them a competitive advantage.

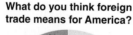

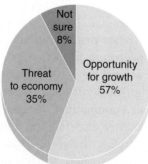

figure 17-2   AMERICANS' OPINIONS ON FREE TRADE

Americans are divided in their opinions on free trade, with some thinking that it helps the country and others thinking that it harms American firms and workers.
Source: Gallup poll, February 26, 2013.

Trade with China is a particularly vexing issue.[22] In the past decade, America's trade deficit with China has increased more than thirtyfold, surpassing $250 billion annually. The United States has provided China with a marketplace for its goods, which has helped fuel China's economic growth. In turn, China has provided the United States with inexpensive goods, which has satisfied the demands of America's consumers and kept inflation in check. Nevertheless, the trade deficit with China is a growing concern. The United States has pressured China to increase the value of its currency (the yuan), which would increase the price of the goods it exports for sale, thereby making American goods more competitive with those produced in China.

China is also a key to the future of the U.S. dollar as the world's preferred reserve currency. Because of its trade advantage with the United States, China holds more than $1 trillion in U.S. treasury bonds—the largest such holding in the world. The value of China's holding declines as the dollar declines in value, which is a realistic prospect given America's huge national debt (see Chapter 15). China and other countries, including Russia and Japan, have threatened to reduce their holdings in dollars, which would put additional pressure on the value of the dollar. "We have lent a huge amount of money to the U.S.," Chinese premier Wen Jiabao said in 2009. "Of course we are concerned about the safety of our assets." If the dollar should decline sharply in value, the United States would be forced to pay a higher rate of interest to get other countries to buy its bonds, which would raise the cost of borrowing and add to America's debt problem.

China's growing economy has enabled it to enlarge its navy, which had been structured to protect China's territorial waters but is now being configured to operate throughout the Pacific. China launched its first aircraft carrier in 2012 and is in the process of building attack submarines and missile ships. China has also tried to flex its military power by laying claim to islands off the coasts of Vietnam and the Philippines in the South China Sea. In response to China's naval buildup, the United States has enlarged its Pacific fleet and has increased the number of joint naval exercises with Asian countries, including in 2012 a naval exercise with its onetime adversary, Vietnam.

Concern with China's military buildup is magnified by Russia's increasingly aggressive foreign policies. Although China and Russia have had a contentious relationship at times, China is Russia's biggest trading partner outside of the European Union. When the issue of censuring Russia over its takeover of the Crimean Peninsula was raised in the UN Security Council, China was the only country to side with Russia. Subsequently,

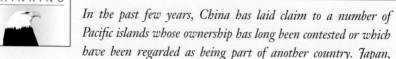

POLITICAL THINKING	**A Flash Point in the Making?**

In the past few years, China has laid claim to a number of Pacific islands whose ownership has long been contested or which have been regarded as being part of another country. Japan, Vietnam, and the Philippines are among the countries involved in these disputes. If China were to use force to take any of these islands, as it has threatened it might, how do you think the United States should respond?

the two countries reached a $400 billion deal that involves building a natural gas pipeline from Russia to China. In signing the agreement, Russian president Vladimir Putin said: "Our relations with China are developing quite successfully and are at an unprecedentedly high level of trust and cooperation. China will be the world's No. 1 power eventually. That can be considered a hard fact." More recently, China and Russia conducted joint naval exercises in the vicinity of disputed islands currently controlled by Japan. "We have powerful enemies but we don't have powerful friends, that's why we need the support of such a giant as China," said a top Russian official.

Maintaining Access to Oil and Other Natural Resources

For decades, America has used its economic and military power to protect its access to natural resources, particularly oil. Although the United States produces a significant amount of oil domestically, it provides only about half of what the nation consumes. The United States gets most of its oil imports from Canada and Latin America, but the price of oil is determined by worldwide production and demand. The demand for oil has risen as a result of rapid economic growth in China, India, Brazil, and other developing countries, which has created upward pressure on oil prices and has intensified efforts to increase oil production.[23]

The key oil-producing region is the Middle East, which has substantially larger oil reserves than elsewhere in the world. After World War II, the United States acquired a foothold in the region when its oil companies, with their technical capacity and huge amounts of capital, acquired a stake in Middle Eastern oil fields. Since then, U.S. firms have been leaders in worldwide oil exploration and production. Underpinning their activities is the military might of the United States. The U.S. Navy patrols the world's shipping routes to ensure that oil tankers reach their destinations safely.

Although the Chinese yuan (also called the renminbi) will not rival the American dollar as the dominant international currency anytime soon, it has become a symbol of China's rise to global economic prominence.

Assisting Developing Nations

Industrialized nations have a stake in helping developing nations to grow. With growth comes greater political stability as well as markets for the goods and services that industrialized nations produce. For such reasons, the United States provides developmental assistance to poorer countries. Contributions include direct foreign aid and also indirect assistance through international organizations, such as the International Monetary Fund (IMF) and the World Bank, which were created by the United States and Great Britain at the Bretton Woods Conference near the end of World War II. The IMF makes short-term loans to keep countries experiencing temporary problems from collapsing economically or resorting to destructive practices such as the unrestricted printing of paper money. For its part, the World Bank makes long-term development loans to poor countries for capital investment projects such as dams, highways, and factories.

Since World War II, the United States has been the top source of aid to developing countries. Although the United States still contributes the

PARTY POLARIZATION

Political Thinking in Conflict

Hard Power or Soft Power?

Until the Vietnam War, there was little partisan difference in Americans' views on national security. A bipartisan consensus prevailed with Republicans and Democrats alike convinced of the need to contain Soviet communism, by force if necessary. America's defeat in Vietnam disrupted the consensus. Since then, nearly every American conflict has been less strongly supported by Democrats, who have placed more emphasis on diplomacy, economic sanctions, and foreign aid as the means of protecting U.S. interests. Joseph Nye, who served in national security positions in the Carter and Clinton administrations, coined the term **soft power** to describe this approach, contrasting it with the use of military force, which he characterized as hard power.

It must be noted that the difference between Republicans and Democrats is one of degree rather than of kind. Democrats and Republicans alike recognize that military action, diplomacy, sanctions, and foreign aid all have a part to play in protecting the United States. Nevertheless, there are clear partisan differences when it comes to the instruments of national security policy, as indicated by the response of Republicans and Democrats in recent polls that have asked Americans which programs they would prefer to cut as a means of reducing the federal budget deficit.

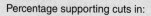

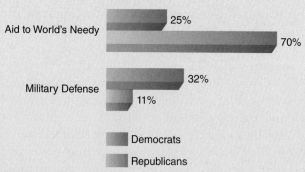

Percentage supporting cuts in:

Aid to World's Needy — 25% / 70%

Military Defense — 32% / 11%

Democrats

Republicans

Source: Pew Research Center survey, February 22, 2013.

Q: Where do you stand on the question of the relative use of "hard power" and "soft power" as instruments of national security policy? Why do you think Republicans and Democrats differ in their opinions on foreign aid and military spending?

most in terms of total dollars, Canada and European countries now spend more on a per capita basis than does the United States (see Figure 17-3). America's fiscal problems, and its costly wars in Iraq and Afghanistan, have weakened it ability to strengthen its position in the world through the use of foreign aid. Public opinion is also an obstacle to increased foreign aid spending. Most Americans believe the United States is already spending too much on foreign aid. In a poll that asked Americans to name the largest federal programs, foreign aid topped the list, with 27 percent identifying it as the most expensive program.[24] In reality, foreign aid is far down the list, accounting for only about 1 percent of federal spending.

As the United States has cut back on foreign aid spending, China has stepped up its spending. Through loans and grants, China is spending heavily on infrastructure and commercial projects in scores of countries in Africa, South America, and Asia. It is also pursuing mining and drilling projects in many of these countries, seeking to secure the raw materials needed to sustain its economic growth. In a sense, China is following the path laid out by the United States after World War II, when it pursued a similar strategy as a means of extending its influence to other parts of the globe.

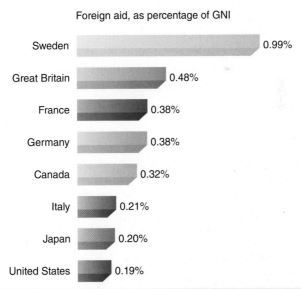

Foreign aid, as percentage of GNI

Sweden	0.99%
Great Britain	0.48%
France	0.38%
Germany	0.38%
Canada	0.32%
Italy	0.21%
Japan	0.20%
United States	0.19%

figure 17-3 ASSISTANCE TO DEVELOPING COUNTRIES, AS A PERCENTAGE OF GROSS NATIONAL INCOME

The United States ranks highest in terms of total amount spent on foreign aid to developing countries but ranks lower in terms of percentage of gross national income (GNI).
Source: Organization for Economic Cooperation and Development, 2014.

Stabilizing the Global Economy

When U.S. financial markets teetered on the edge in 2008, the impact was felt around the globe. Stock markets tumbled and governments rushed to institute policies that could stem the fall. The crisis taught policymakers a key lesson: economic turbulence in one part of today's global economy spreads quickly to other parts as a result of increased economic interdependency.[25]

The United States has led other efforts to stabilize the global economy. In 2009, for example, America's leading banks were subjected to a "stress test" to determine their ability to withstand defaults on the debt they are owed. Banks that failed the test were provided government loans to protect them from such defaults. U.S. policymakers urged other nations to do the same, recognizing that major financial institutions operate around the globe and that the collapse of even one of them can send a shock through the world economy.

As the example illustrates, the new global economy poses risks as well as benefits to the United States. At the end of World War II, the U.S. economy accounted for half of the world's economic output, and the United States was in a position to nearly define the terms of its economic relations with other countries. Today, it operates in a global economy marked by mutual dependence. The United States depends on the economic health of other nations, just as they are dependent on the health of the American economy. Thus, just as the United States faces a set of nearly unprecedented military challenges around the globe, it is confronting a set of nearly unprecedented economic ones. In the end, its national security will rest on its ability to respond effectively to both sets of challenges.

SUMMARY

The chief instruments of national security policy are diplomacy, military force, economic exchange, and intelligence gathering. These are exercised through specialized agencies of the U.S. government, such as the Departments of State and Defense that are largely responsive to presidential leadership. National security policy has also relied on international organizations, such as the United Nations and the World Trade Organization, that are responsive to the global concerns of major nations.

From 1945 to 1990, U.S. foreign and defense policies were dominated by a concern with the Soviet Union. During most of this period, the United States pursued a policy of containment based on the premise that the Soviet Union was an aggressor nation bent on global conquest. Containment policy led the United States to enter into wars in Korea and Vietnam and to maintain a large defense establishment.

A first response to the end of the cold war period was multilateralism—the idea that major nations could achieve common goals by working together, including the use of force to restrain regional conflicts. The interventions in the Persian Gulf and the Balkans during the 1990s are examples. They demonstrated that major nations can intervene with some success in global hot spots but also showed that the ethnic, religious, and national conflicts that fuel these conflicts are not easily resolved.

The terrorist attacks on the World Trade Center and the Pentagon in 2001 led to broad changes in national security organization and strategy. Increased defense and homeland security spending has been coupled with a partial reorganization of U.S. intelligence, law enforcement, and immigration agencies, as well as new laws affecting the scope of their activities. However, the defining moment of the post–September 11 period was America's invasion of Iraq in 2003, which was rooted in President George W. Bush's preemptive war doctrine and his willingness to commit the United States to unilateral action.

In recent decades, the United States has increasingly taken economic factors into account in its national security considerations, which has meant, for example, that trade has played a larger part in defining its relationships with other countries. The trading system that the United States helped erect after World War II has given way to one that is global in scale and more competitive. Changes in communication, transportation, and computing have altered the way large corporations operate, and as businesses have changed their practices, nations have had to adapt. The changes include the emergence of regional and international economic structures, such as the European Union, NAFTA, and the WTO. Nevertheless, nations naturally compete for economic advantage, including access to natural resources; accordingly, trade is a source of conflict as well as a source of cooperation.

CRITICAL THINKING ZONE

KEY TERMS

bipolar (power structure) (*p. 544*)
cold war (*p. 544*)
containment (*p. 544*)
economic globalization (*p. 562*)
free trade (*p. 562*)
internationalist (*p. 543*)
isolationist (*p. 543*)
military-industrial complex (*p. 559*)
multilateralism (*p. 546*)

mutually assured destruction (MAD) (*p. 553*)
preemptive war doctrine (*p. 548*)
protectionism (*p. 563*)
soft power (*p. 568*)
transnational terrorism (*p. 557*)
tariffs (*p. 562*)
unilateralism (*p. 548*)
unipolar (power structure) (*p. 546*)

APPLYING THE ELEMENTS OF CRITICAL THINKING

Conceptualizing: Explain the difference between a bipolar international power structure and a unipolar one. Which one is containment doctrine associated with?

Synthesizing: Contrast free trade and protectionism as approaches to global trade and competition. Identify policies associated with each one.

Analyzing: What are the two major objectives of U.S. foreign policy? What are the mechanisms for pursuing each of these objectives?

EXTRA CREDIT

A Book Worth Reading: Joseph Nye, *Presidential Leadership and the Creation of the American Era*. Princeton, NJ: Princeton University Press, 2013. An insightful look at the role various U.S. presidents have played in shaping the nation's place in the world. The author's earlier award-winning book, *Soft Power*, helped change the way policymakers think about foreign policy.

A Website Worth Visiting: www.cfr.org The Council on Foreign Relations brings together foreign policy leaders, analysts, scholars, and others in order to promote a better understanding of international issues. Its website includes foreign policy reports, assessments, speeches, and other information.

PARTICIPATE!

In his 1961 inaugural address, President John F. Kennedy said, "Ask not what your country can do for you. Ask what you can do for your country." Kennedy called America's young people to service on behalf of their country. His call was not just a call to military service. One of Kennedy's early initiatives, the Peace Corps, offered Americans the opportunity to apply their skills to development projects in other countries. Under Kennedy's successor, President Lyndon Johnson, a domestic version of the Peace Corps—Volunteers in Service to America (VISTA)—was established. Before the military draft ended in 1973, male Americans were expected to serve their country. Not all did so, but millions served in the army, navy, air force, or marine corps. Since the end of the draft, Congress has from time to time considered establishing a national service that would require every young American man and woman to serve the country in one way or another for a set period of time. However, you do not need an act of Congress if you want to serve your country. A range of alternatives are available, including the all-volunteer military, the Peace Corps, and AmeriCorps (a network of local, state, and national service programs).

APPENDIXES

The Declaration of Independence
IN CONGRESS, JULY 4, 1776

The Unanimous Declaration of the Thirteen United States of America

When, in the course of human events, it becomes necessary for one people to dissolve the political bands which have connected them with another, and to assume, among the powers of the earth, the separate and equal station to which the laws of nature and of nature's God entitle them, a decent respect to the opinions of mankind requires that they should declare the causes which impel them to the separation.

We hold these truths to be self-evident, that all men are created equal; that they are endowed by their Creator with certain unalienable rights; that among these, are life, liberty, and the pursuit of happiness. That, to secure these rights, governments are instituted among men, deriving their just powers from the consent of the governed; that, whenever any form of government becomes destructive of these ends, it is the right of the people to alter or to abolish it, and to institute a new government, laying its foundation on such principles, and organizing its powers in such form, as to them shall seem most likely to effect their safety and happiness. Prudence, indeed, will dictate that governments long established, should not be changed for light and transient causes; and, accordingly, all experience hath shown, that mankind are more disposed to suffer, while evils are sufferable, than to right themselves by abolishing the forms to which they are accustomed. But, when a long train of abuses and usurpations, pursuing invariably the same object, evinces a design to reduce them under absolute despotism, it is their right, it is their duty, to throw off such government and to provide new guards for their future security. Such has been the patient sufferance of these colonies, and such is now the necessity which constrains them to alter their former systems of government. The history of the present King of Great Britain is a history of repeated injuries and usurpations, all having, in direct object, the establishment of an absolute tyranny over these States. To prove this, let facts be submitted to a candid world:

He has refused his assent to laws the most wholesome and necessary for the public good.

He has forbidden his governors to pass laws of immediate and pressing importance, unless suspended in their operation till his assent should be obtained; and, when so suspended, he has utterly neglected to attend to them.

He has refused to pass other laws for the accommodation of large districts of people, unless those people would relinquish the right of representation in the legislature; a right inestimable to them, and formidable to tyrants only.

He has called together legislative bodies at places unusual, uncomfortable, and distant from the depository of their public records, for the sole purpose of fatiguing them into compliance with his measures.

He has dissolved representative houses repeatedly for opposing, with manly firmness, his invasions on the rights of the people.

He has refused, for a long time after such dissolutions, to cause others to be elected; whereby the legislative powers, incapable of annihilation, have returned to the people at large for their exercise; the state remaining, in the meantime, exposed to all the danger of invasion from without, and convulsions within.

He has endeavored to prevent the population of these States; for that purpose, obstructing the laws for naturalization of foreigners, refusing to pass others to encourage their migration hither, and raising the conditions of new appropriations of lands.

He has obstructed the administration of justice, by refusing his assent to laws for establishing judiciary powers.

He has made judges dependent on his will alone, for the tenure of their offices, and the amount and payment of their salaries.

He has erected a multitude of new offices, and sent hither swarms of officers to harass our people, and eat out their substance.

He has kept among us, in time of peace, standing armies, without the consent of our legislatures.

He has affected to render the military independent of, and superior to, the civil power.

He has combined, with others, to subject us to a jurisdiction foreign to our Constitution, and unacknowledged by our laws; giving his assent to their acts of pretended legislation:

For quartering large bodies of armed troops among us:

For protecting them by a mock trial, from punishment, for any murders which they should commit on the inhabitants of these States:

For cutting off our trade with all parts of the world:

For imposing taxes on us without our consent:

For depriving us, in many cases, of the benefit of trial by jury:

For transporting us beyond seas to be tried for pretended offences:

For abolishing the free system of English laws in a neighboring province, establishing therein an arbitrary government, and enlarging its boundaries, so as to render it at once an example and fit instrument for introducing the same absolute rule into these colonies:

For taking away our charters, abolishing our most valuable laws, and altering, fundamentally, the powers of our governments:

For suspending our own legislatures, and declaring themselves invested with power to legislate for us in all cases whatsoever.

He has abdicated government here, by declaring us out of his protection, and waging war against us.

He has plundered our seas, ravaged our coasts, burnt our towns, and destroyed the lives of our people.

He is, at this time, transporting large armies of foreign mercenaries to complete the works of death, desolation, and tyranny, already begun, with circumstances of cruelty and perfidy scarcely paralleled in the most barbarous ages, and totally unworthy of the head of a civilized nation.

He has constrained our fellow citizens, taken captive on the high seas, to bear arms against their country, to become the executioners of their friends, and brethren, or to fall themselves by their hands.

He has excited domestic insurrections amongst us, and has endeavored to bring on the inhabitants of our frontiers, the merciless Indian savages, whose known rule of warfare is an undistinguished destruction of all ages, sexes, and conditions.

In every stage of these oppressions, we have petitioned for redress, in the most humble terms; our repeated petitions have been answered only by repeated injury. A prince, whose character is thus marked by every act which may define a tyrant, is unfit to be the ruler of a free people.

Nor have we been wanting in attention to our British brethren. We have warned them, from time to time, of attempts made by their legislature to extend an unwarrantable jurisdiction over us. We have reminded them of the circumstances of our emigration and settlement here. We have appealed to their native justice and magnanimity, and we have conjured them, by the ties of our common kindred, to disavow these usurpations, which would inevitably interrupt our connections and correspondence. They, too, have been deaf to the voice of justice and of consanguinity. We must, therefore, acquiesce in the necessity which denounces our separation, and hold them as we hold the rest of mankind, enemies in war, in peace, friends.

We, therefore, the representatives of the United States of America, in general Congress assembled, appealing to the Supreme Judge of the world for the rectitude of our intentions, do, in the name, and by the authority of the good people of these colonies, solemnly publish and declare, that these united colonies are, and of right ought to be, free and independent states: that they are absolved from all allegiance to the British Crown, and that all political connection between them and the state of Great Britain is, and ought to be, totally dissolved; and that, as free and independent states, they have full power to levy war, conclude peace, contract alliances, establish commerce, and to do all other acts and things which independent states may of right do. And, for the support of this declaration, with a firm reliance on the protection of Divine Providence, we mutually pledge to each other our lives, our fortunes, and our sacred honor.

The foregoing Declaration was, by order of Congress, engrossed, and signed by the following members:

JOHN HANCOCK

New Hampshire
Josiah Bartlett
William Whipple
Matthew Thornton

Massachusetts Bay
Samuel Adams
John Adams
Robert Treat Paine
Elbridge Gerry

Rhode Island
Stephen Hopkins
William Ellery

Connecticut
Roger Sherman
Samuel Huntington
William Williams
Oliver Wolcott

New York
William Floyd
Philip Livingston
Francis Lewis
Lewis Morris

New Jersey
Richard Stockton
John Witherspoon
Francis Hopkinson

John Hart

Abraham Clark

Pennsylvania

Robert Morris

Benjamin Rush

Benjamin Franklin

John Morton

George Clymer

James Smith

George Taylor

James Wilson

George Ross

Delaware

Caesar Rodney

George Reed

Thomas M'Kean

Maryland

Samuel Chase

William Paca

Thomas Stone

Charles Carroll, of
    Carrollton

Virginia

George Wythe

Richard Henry Lee

Thomas Jefferson

Benjamin Harrison

Thomas Nelson, Jr.

Francis Lightfoot Lee

Carter Braxton

North Carolina

William Hooper

Joseph Hewes

John Penn

South Carolina

Edward Rutledge

Thomas Heyward, Jr.

Thomas Lynch, Jr.

Arthur Middleton

Georgia

Button Gwinnett

Lyman Hall

George Walton

Resolved, That copies of the Declaration be sent to the several assemblies, conventions, and committees, or councils of safety, and to the several commanding officers of the continental troops; that it be proclaimed in each of the United States, at the head of the army.

The Constitution of the United States of America[1]

We the People of the United States, in Order to form a more perfect Union, establish Justice, insure domestic Tranquility, provide for the common defence, promote the general Welfare, and secure the Blessings of Liberty to ourselves and our Posterity, do ordain and establish this CONSTITUTION for the United States of America.

ARTICLE I

Section 1

All legislative Powers herein granted shall be vested in a Congress of the United States, which shall consist of a Senate and House of Representatives.

Section 2

The House of Representatives shall be composed of Members chosen every second Year by the People of the several States, and the Electors in each State shall have the Qualifications requisite for Electors of the most numerous Branch of the State Legislature.

No Person shall be a Representative who shall not have attained to the Age of twenty-five Years, and been seven Years a Citizen of the United States, and who shall not, when elected, be an Inhabitant of that State in which he shall be chosen.

[Representatives and direct Taxes[2] shall be apportioned among the several States which may be included within this Union, according to their respective Numbers, which shall be determined by adding to the whole Number of free Persons, including those bound to Service for a Term of Years, and excluding Indians not taxed, three fifths of all other Persons.][3] The actual Enumeration shall be made within three Years after the first Meeting of the Congress of the United States, and within every subsequent Term of ten Years, in such Manner as they shall by Law direct. The Number of Representatives shall not exceed one for every thirty Thousand, but each State shall have at Least one Representative; and until such enumeration shall be made, the State of New Hampshire shall be entitled to chuse three, Massachusetts eight, Rhode-Island and Providence Plantations one, Connecticut five, New York six, New Jersey four, Pennsylvania eight, Delaware one, Maryland six, Virginia ten, North Carolina five, South Carolina five, and Georgia three.

When vacancies happen in the Representation from any State, the Executive Authority thereof shall issue Writs of Election to fill such Vacancies.

---

[1]This version, which follows the original Constitution in capitalization and spelling, was published by the United States Department of the Interior, Office of Education, in 1935.
[2]Altered by the Sixteenth Amendment.
[3]Negated by the Fourteenth Amendment.

The House of Representatives shall chuse their Speaker and other Officers; and shall have the sole Power of Impeachment.

Section 3

The Senate of the United States shall be composed of two Senators from each State, chosen by the Legislature thereof, for six Years; and each Senator shall have one Vote.

Immediately after they shall be assembled in Consequence of the first Election, they shall be divided as equally as may be into three Classes. The Seats of the Senators of the first Class shall be vacated at the Expiration of the second Year, of the second Class at the Expiration of the fourth Year, and of the third Class at the Expiration of the sixth Year, so that one-third may be chosen every second Year; and if Vacancies happen by Resignation, or otherwise, during the Recess of the Legislature of any State, the Executive thereof may make temporary Appointments until the next Meeting of the Legislature, which shall then fill such Vacancies.

No Person shall be a Senator who shall not have attained to the Age of thirty Years, and been nine Years a Citizen of the United States, and who shall not, when elected, be an Inhabitant of that State for which he shall be chosen.

The Vice President of the United States shall be President of the Senate, but shall have no vote, unless they be equally divided.

The Senate shall chuse their other Officers, and also a President pro tempore, in the absence of the Vice President, or when he shall exercise the Office of President of the United States.

The Senate shall have the sole Power to try all Impeachments. When sitting for that purpose they shall be on Oath or Affirmation. When the President of the United States is tried, the Chief Justice shall preside: And no person shall be convicted without the Concurrence of two thirds of the Members present.

Judgment in Cases of Impeachment shall not extend further than to removal from Office, and disqualification to hold and enjoy any Office of honor, Trust, or Profit under the United States: but the Party convicted shall nevertheless be liable and subject to Indictment, Trial, Judgment and Punishment, according to Law.

Section 4

The Times, Place and Manner of holding Elections for Senators and Represent-atives, shall be prescribed in each State by the Legislature thereof; but the Con-gress may at any time by Law make or alter such Regulations, except as to the Places of Chusing Senators.

The Congress shall assemble at least once in every Year, and such Meeting shall be on the first Monday in December, unless they shall by Law appoint a different Day.

Section 5

Each House shall be the Judge of the Elections, Returns and Qualifications of its own Members, and a Majority of each shall constitute a Quorum to do Business; but a smaller number may adjourn from day to day, and may be authorized to compel the Attendance of absent Members, in such Manner, and under such Penalties, as each House may provide.

Each House may determine the Rules of its Proceedings, punish its Members for disorderly Behaviour, and, with the Concurrence of two thirds, expel a Member.

Each House shall keep a Journal of its Proceedings, and from time to time publish the same, excepting such Parts as may in their Judgment require Secrecy; and the Yeas and Nays of the Members of either House on any question shall, at the Desire of one fifth of those Present, be entered on the Journal.

Neither House, during the Session of Congress, shall, without the Consent of the other, adjourn for more than three days, nor to any other Place than that in which the two Houses shall be sitting.

Section 6

The Senators and Representatives shall receive a Compensation for their Services, to be ascertained by Law, and paid out of the Treasury of the United States. They shall in all Cases, except Treason, Felony, and Breach of the Peace, be privileged from Arrest during their Attendance at the Session of their respective Houses, and in going to and returning from the same; and for any Speech or Debate in either House, they shall not be questioned in any other Place.

No Senator or Representative shall, during the Time for which he was elected, be appointed to any civil Office under the Authority of the United States, which shall have been created, or the Emoluments whereof shall have been increased, during such time; and no Person holding any Office under the United States shall be a Member of either House during his continuance in Office.

Section 7

All Bills for raising Revenue shall originate in the House of Representatives; but the Senate may propose or concur with Amendments as on other bills.

Every Bill which shall have passed the House of Representatives and the Senate, shall, before it becomes a Law, be presented to the President of the United States; if he approve he shall sign it, but if not he shall return it, with his Objections, to that House in which it shall have originated, who shall enter the Objections at large on their Journal, and proceed to reconsider it. If after such Reconsideration two thirds of that House shall agree to pass the bill, it shall be sent, together with the objections, to the other House, by which it shall likewise be reconsidered, and if approved by two thirds of that House, it shall become a Law. But in all such Cases the Votes of both Houses shall be determined by Yeas and Nays, and the Names of the Persons voting for and against the Bill shall be entered on the Journal of each House respectively. If any Bill shall not be returned by the President within ten Days (Sundays excepted) after it shall have been presented to him, the Same shall be a Law, in like Manner as if he had signed it, unless the Congress by their Adjournment prevent its Return, in which Case it shall not be a Law.

Every Order, Resolution, or Vote to which the Concurrence of the Senate and House of Representatives may be necessary (except on a question of Adjournment) shall be presented to the President of the United States; and before the Same shall take Effect, shall be approved by him, or being disapproved by him, shall be repassed by two thirds of the Senate and House of Representatives, according to the Rules and Limitations prescribed in the Case of a Bill.

Section 8

The Congress shall have Power To lay and collect Taxes, Duties, Imposts and Excises, to pay the Debts and provide for the common Defence and general Welfare of the United States; but all Duties, Imposts and Excises shall be uniform throughout the United States;

To borrow money on the credit of the United States;

To regulate Commerce with foreign Nations, and among the several States, and with the Indian Tribes;

To establish a uniform rule of Naturalization, and uniform Laws on the subject of Bankruptcies throughout the United States;

To coin Money, regulate the Value thereof, and of foreign Coin, and fix the Standard of Weights and Measures;

To provide for the Punishment of counterfeiting the Securities and current Coin of the United States;

To establish Post Offices and post Roads;

To promote the Progress of Science and useful Arts, by securing for limited Times to Authors and Inventors the exclusive Right to their respective Writings and Discoveries;

To constitute Tribunals inferior to the Supreme Court;

To define and punish Piracies and Felonies committed on the high Seas, and Offenses against the Law of Nations;

To declare War, grant Letters of Marque and Reprisal, and make Rules concerning Captures on Land and Water;

To raise and support Armies, but no Appropriation of Money to that Use shall be for a longer Term than two Years;

To provide and maintain a Navy;

To make Rules for the Government and Regulation of the land and naval forces;

To provide for calling forth the Militia to execute the Laws of the Union, suppress Insurrections and repel Invasions;

To provide for organizing, arming, and disciplining the Militia, and for governing such Part of them as may be employed in the Service of the United States, reserving to the States respectively, the Appointment of the Officers, and the Authority of training the Militia according to the discipline prescribed by Congress;

To exercise exclusive Legislation in all Cases whatsoever, over such District (not exceeding ten Miles square) as may, by Cession of particular States, and the acceptance of Congress, become the Seat of the Government of the United States, and to exercise like Authority over all Places purchased by the Consent of the Legislature of the State in which the Same shall be, for the Erection of Forts, Magazines, Arsenals, Dock-yards, and other needful Buildings;—And

To make all Laws which shall be necessary and proper for carrying into Execution the foregoing Powers, and all other Powers vested by this Constitution in the Government of the United States, or in any Department or Officer thereof.

Section 9

The Migration or Importation of such Persons as any of the States now existing shall think proper to admit, shall not be prohibited by the Congress prior to the

Year one thousand eight hundred and eight, but a tax or duty may be imposed on such Importation, not exceeding ten dollars for each Person.

The privilege of the Writ of Habeas Corpus shall not be suspended, unless when in Cases of Rebellion or Invasion the public Safety may require it.

No bill of Attainder or ex post facto Law shall be passed.

No capitation, or other direct, Tax shall be laid unless in Proportion to the Census or Enumeration herein before directed to be taken.

No Tax or Duty shall be laid on Articles exported from any State.

No Preference shall be given by any Regulation of Commerce or Revenue to the Ports of one State over those of another: nor shall Vessels bound to, or from, one State, be obliged to enter, clear, or pay Duties in another.

No Money shall be drawn from the Treasury, but in Consequence of Appropriations made by Law; and a regular Statement and Account of the Receipts and Expenditures of all public Money shall be published from time to time.

No Title of Nobility shall be granted by the United States: And no Person holding any Office of Profit or Trust under them, shall, without the Consent of the Congress, accept of any present, Emolument, Office, or Title, of any kind whatever, from any King, Prince, or foreign State.

Section 10

No State shall enter into any Treaty, Alliance, or Confederation; grant Letters of Marque and Reprisal; coin Money; emit Bills of Credit; make any Thing but gold and silver Coin a Tender in Payment of Debts; pass any Bill of Attainder, ex post facto Law, or Law impairing the Obligation of Contracts, or grant any Title of Nobility.

No State shall, without the Consent of the Congress, lay any Imposts or Duties on Imports or Exports, except what may be absolutely necessary for executing its inspection Laws; and the net Produce of all Duties and Imposts, laid by any State on Imports or Exports, shall be for the use of the Treasury of the United States; and all such Laws shall be subject to the Revision and Control of the Congress.

No state shall, without the Consent of Congress, lay any duty of Tonnage, keep Troops, or Ships of War in time of Peace, enter into any Agreement or Compact with another State, or with a foreign Power, or engage in War, unless actually invaded, or in such imminent Danger as will not admit of delay.

ARTICLE II

Section 1

The executive Power shall be vested in a President of the United States of America. He shall hold his Office during the Term of four years, and, together with the Vice President, chosen for the same Term, be elected, as follows:

Each State shall appoint, in such Manner as the Legislature thereof may direct, a Number of Electors, equal to the whole Number of Senators and Representatives to which the State may be entitled in the Congress: but no Senator or Representative, or Person holding an Office of Trust or Profit under the United States, shall be appointed an Elector.

[The Electors shall meet in their respective States, and vote by Ballot for two persons, of whom one at least shall not be an Inhabitant of the same State with themselves. And they shall make a List of all the Persons voted for, and of the Number of Votes for each; which List they shall sign and certify, and transmit sealed to the Seat of the Government of the United States, directed to the President of the Senate. The President of the Senate shall, in the Presence of the Senate and House of Representatives, open all the Certificates, and the Votes shall then be counted. The Person having the greatest Number of Votes shall be the President, if such Number be a Majority of the whole Number of Electors appointed; and if there be more than one who have such Majority, and have an equal Number of Votes, then the House of Representatives shall immediately chuse by Ballot one of them for President; and if no Person have a Majority, then from the five highest on the List the said House shall in like Manner chuse the President. But in chusing the President, the Votes shall be taken by States, the Representation from each State having one Vote; a quorum for this Purpose shall consist of a Member or Members from two-thirds of the States, and a Majority of all the States shall be necessary to a Choice. In every Case, after the Choice of the President, the Person having the greatest Number of Votes of the Electors shall be the Vice President. But if there should remain two or more who have equal votes, the Senate shall chuse from them by Ballot the Vice President.][4]

The Congress may determine the Time of chusing the Electors, and the Day on which they shall give their Votes; which Day shall be the same throughout the United States.

No person except a natural-born Citizen, or a Citizen of the United States, at the time of the Adoption of this Constitution, shall be eligible to the Office of President; neither shall any Person be eligible to that Office who shall not have attained to the Age of thirty-five years, and been fourteen Years a Resident within the United States.

In Case of the Removal of the President from Office, or of his Death, Resignation, or Inability to discharge the Powers and Duties of the said Office, the same shall devolve on the Vice President, and the Congress may by Law provide for the Case of Removal, Death, Resignation, or Inability, both of the President and Vice President, declaring what Officer shall then act as President, and such Officer shall act accordingly, until the disability be removed, or a President shall be elected.

The President shall, at stated Times, receive for his Services a Compensation, which shall neither be increased nor diminished during the Period for which he shall have been elected, and he shall not receive within that Period any other Emolument from the United States, or any of them.

Before he enter on the execution of his Office, he shall take the following Oath or Affirmation:—"I do solemnly swear (or affirm) that I will faithfully execute the Office of President of the United States, and will, to the best of my Ability, preserve, protect, and defend the Constitution of the United States."

Section 2

The President shall be Commander in Chief of the Army and Navy of the United States, and of the Militia of the several States, when called into the actual Service

---

[4]Revised by the Twelfth Amendment.

of the United States; he may require the Opinion, in writing, of the principal Officer in each of the executive Departments, upon any subject relating to the Duties of their respective Offices, and he shall have Power to Grant Reprieves and Pardons for Offenses against the United States, except in Cases of Impeachment.

He shall have Power, by and with the Advice and Consent of the Senate, to make Treaties, provided two-thirds of the Senators present concur; and he shall nominate, and by and with the Advice and Consent of the Senate, shall appoint Ambassadors, other public Ministers and Consuls, Judges of the supreme Court, and all other Officers of the United States, whose Appointments are not herein otherwise provided for, and which shall be established by Law: but the Congress may by Law vest the Appointment of such inferior Officers, as they think proper, in the President alone, in the Courts of Law, or in the Heads of Departments.

The President shall have Power to fill up all Vacancies that may happen during the Recess of the Senate, by granting Commissions which shall expire at the End of their next Session.

Section 3

He shall from time to time give to the Congress Information of the State of the Union, and recommend to their Consideration such Measures as he shall judge necessary and expedient; he may, on extraordinary occasions, convene both Houses, or either of them, and in Case of Disagreement between them, with respect to the Time of Adjournment, he may adjourn them to such Time as he shall think proper; he shall receive Ambassadors and other public Ministers; he shall take care that the Laws be faithfully executed, and shall Commission all the Officers of the United States.

Section 4

The President, Vice President and all civil Officers of the United States, shall be removed from Office on Impeachment for, and Conviction of, Treason, Bribery, or other high Crimes and Misdemeanors.

ARTICLE III

Section 1

The judicial Power of the United States, shall be vested in one supreme Court, and in such inferior Courts as the Congress may from time to time ordain and establish. The Judges, both of the supreme and inferior Courts, shall hold their Offices during good Behaviour, and shall, at stated Times, receive for their Services, a Compensation, which shall not be diminished during their Continuance in Office.

Section 2

The judicial Power shall extend to all Cases, in Law and Equity, arising under this Constitution, the Laws of the United States, and Treaties made, or which shall be made, under their Authority;—to all Cases affecting ambassadors, other public ministers and consuls;—to all cases of admiralty and maritime Jurisdiction;—to Controversies to which the United States shall be a Party;—to Controversies between two or more states;—between a State and Citizens of another State;[5]—between Citizens of different States—between Citizens of the same State claiming Lands under Grants of different States, and between a State, or the Citizens thereof, and foreign States, Citizens, or Subjects.

In all Cases affecting Ambassadors, other public Ministers and Consuls, and those in which a State shall be Party, the supreme Court shall have original Jurisdiction. In all the other Cases before mentioned, the supreme Court shall have appellate Jurisdiction, both as to Law and Fact, with such Exceptions, and under such Regulations as the Congress shall make.

The trial of all Crimes, except in Cases of Impeachment, shall be by Jury; and such Trial shall be held in the State where the said Crimes shall have been committed; but when not committed within any State, the Trial shall be at such Place or Places as the Congress may by Law have directed.

Section 3

Treason against the United States, shall consist only in levying War against them, or in adhering to their Enemies, giving them Aid and Comfort. No Person shall be convicted of Treason unless on the Testimony of two Witnesses to the same overt Act, or on Confession in open Court.

The Congress shall have power to declare the Punishment of Treason, but no Attainder of Treason shall work Corruption of Blood, or Forfeiture except during the Life of the Person attainted.

ARTICLE IV

Section 1

Full Faith and Credit shall be given in each State to the public Acts, Records, and judicial Proceedings of every other State. And the Congress may by general Laws prescribe the Manner in which such Acts, Records and Proceedings shall be proved, and the Effect thereof.

Section 2

The Citizens of each State shall be entitled to all Privileges and Immunities of Citizens in the several States.

A Person charged in any State with Treason, Felony, or other Crime, who shall flee from Justice, and be found in another State, shall on demand of the executive Authority of the State from which he fled, be delivered up, to be removed to the State having Jurisdiction of the crime.

No Person held to Service or Labour in one State, under the Laws thereof, escaping into another, shall, in Consequence of any Law or Regulation therein, be discharged from such Service or Labour, but shall be delivered up on Claim of the Party to whom such Service or Labour may be due.

---

[5]Qualified by the Eleventh Amendment.

Section 3

New States may be admitted by the Congress into this Union; but no new State shall be formed or erected within the Jurisdiction of any other State; nor any State be formed by the Junction of two or more States, or parts of States, without the Consent of the Legislatures of the States concerned as well as of the Congress.

The Congress shall have Power to dispose of and make all needful Rules and Regulations respecting the Territory or other Property belonging to the United States; and nothing in this Constitution shall be so construed as to Prejudice any Claims of the United States, or of any particular State.

Section 4

The United States shall guarantee to every State in this Union a Republican Form of Government, and shall protect each of them against Invasion; and on Application of the Legislature, or of the Executive (when the Legislature cannot be convened) against domestic Violence.

ARTICLE V

The Congress, whenever two-thirds of both Houses shall deem it necessary, shall propose Amendments to this Constitution, or, on the Application of the Legislatures of two-thirds of the several States, shall call a Convention for proposing Amendments, which, in either Case, shall be valid to all Intents and Purposes, as part of this Constitution, when ratified by the Legislatures of three-fourths of the several States, or by Conventions in three-fourths thereof, as the one or the other Mode of Ratification may be proposed by the Congress; Provided that no Amendment which may be made prior to the Year One thousand eight hundred and eight shall in any Manner affect the first and fourth Clauses in the Ninth Section of the first Article; and that no State, without its Consent, shall be deprived of its equal Suffrage in the Senate.

ARTICLE VI

All Debts contracted and Engagements entered into, before the Adoption of this Constitution, shall be as valid against the United States under this Constitution, as under the Confederation.

This Constitution, and the Laws of the United States which shall be made in Pursuance thereof; and all Treaties made, or which shall be made, under the Authority of the United States, shall be the supreme Law of the Land; and the Judges in every State shall be bound thereby, any Thing in the Constitution or Laws of any State to the Contrary notwithstanding.

The Senators and Representatives before mentioned, and the Members of the several State Legislatures, and all executive and judicial Officers, both of the United States and of the several States, shall be bound by Oath or Affirmation to support this Constitution; but no religious Tests shall ever be required as a qualification to any Office or public Trust under the United States.

ARTICLE VII

The Ratification of the Conventions of nine States shall be sufficient for the Establishment of this Constitution between the States so ratifying the same.

Done in Convention by the Unanimous Consent of the States present the Seventeenth Day of September in the Year of our Lord one thousand seven hundred and Eighty seven, and of the Independence of the United States of America the Twelfth. In Witness whereof We have hereunto subscribed our Names.[6]

George Washington
President and deputy
from Virginia

New Hampshire
John Langdon
Nicholas Gilman

Massachusetts
Nathaniel Gorham
Rufus King

Connecticut
William Samuel Johnson
Roger Sherman

New York
Alexander Hamilton

New Jersey
William Livingston
David Brearley
William Paterson
Jonathan Dayton

Pennsylvania
Benjamin Franklin
Thomas Mifflin
Robert Morris
George Clymer
Thomas FitzSimmons
Jared Ingersoll
James Wilson
Gouverneur Morris

Delaware
George Read
Gunning Bedford, Jr.
John Dickinson
Richard Bassett
Jacob Broom

Maryland
James McHenry
Daniel of St. Thomas
  Jenifer
Daniel Carroll

Virginia
John Blair
James Madison, Jr.

North Carolina
William Blount
Richard Dobbs Spaight
Hugh Williamson

South Carolina
John Rutledge
Charles Cotesworth
  Pinckney
Charles Pinckney
Pierce Butler

Georgia
William Few
Abraham Baldwin

Articles in Addition to, and Amendment of, the Constitution of the United States of America, Proposed by Congress, and Ratified by the Legislatures of the Several States, Pursuant to the Fifth Article of the Original Constitution[7]

AMENDMENT I

Congress shall make no law respecting an establishment of religion, or prohibiting the free exercise thereof; or abridging the freedom of speech, or of the press;

---

[6]These are the full names of the signers, which in some cases are not the signatures on the document.

[7]This heading appears only in the joint resolution submitting the first ten amendments, which are collectively known as the Bill of Rights. They were ratified on December 15, 1791.

or the right of the people peaceably to assemble, and to petition the Government for a redress of grievances.

AMENDMENT II

A well regulated Militia, being necessary to the security of a free State, the right of the people to keep and bear Arms shall not be infringed.

AMENDMENT III

No Soldier shall, in time of peace, be quartered in any house, without the consent of the Owner, nor in time of war, but in a manner to be prescribed by law.

AMENDMENT IV

The right of the people to be secure in their persons, houses, papers, and effects, against unreasonable searches and seizures, shall not be violated, and no Warrants shall issue, but upon probable cause, supported by Oath or affirmation, and particularly describing the place to be searched, and the persons or things to be seized.

AMENDMENT V

No person shall be held to answer for a capital or otherwise infamous crime, unless on a presentment or indictment of a Grand Jury, except in cases arising in the land or naval forces, or in the Militia, when in actual service in time of War or public danger; nor shall any person be subject for the same offence to be twice put in jeopardy of life or limb; nor shall be compelled in any criminal case to be a witness against himself, nor be deprived of life, liberty, or property, without due process of law; nor shall private property be taken for public use, without just compensation.

AMENDMENT VI

In all criminal prosecutions, the accused shall enjoy the right to a speedy and public trial, by an impartial jury of the State and district wherein the crime shall have been committed, which district shall have been previously ascertained by law, and to be informed of the nature and cause of the accusation; to be confronted with the witnesses against him; to have compulsory process for obtaining witnesses in his favour, and to have the Assistance of Counsel for his defence.

AMENDMENT VII

In suits at common law, where the value in controversy shall exceed twenty dollars, the right of trial by jury shall be preserved, and no fact tried by a jury, shall be otherwise reexamined in any Court of the United States, than according to the rules of the common law.

AMENDMENT VIII

Excessive bail shall not be required, nor excessive fines imposed, nor cruel and unusual punishments inflicted.

AMENDMENT IX

The enumeration of the Constitution, of certain rights, shall not be construed to deny or disparage others retained by the people.

AMENDMENT X

The powers not delegated to the United States by the Constitution, nor prohibited by it to the States, are reserved to the States respectively, or to the people.

AMENDMENT XI [1795]

The Judicial power of the United States shall not be construed to extend to any suit in law or equity, commenced or prosecuted against one of the United States by Citizens of another State, or by Citizens or Subjects of any Foreign State.

AMENDMENT XII [1804]

The Electors shall meet in their respective States and vote by ballot for President and Vice-President, one of whom, at least, shall not be an inhabitant of the same State with themselves; they shall name in their ballots the person voted for as President, and in distinct ballots the person voted for as Vice-President, and they shall make distinct lists of all persons voted for as President, and of all persons voted for as Vice-President, and of the number of votes for each, which lists they shall sign and certify, and transmit sealed to the seat of the government of the United States, directed to the President of the Senate;—The President of the Senate shall, in the presence of the Senate and House of Representatives, open all the certificates and the votes shall then be counted;—The person having the greatest number of votes for President, shall be the President, if such number be a majority of the whole number of Electors appointed; and if no person have such majority, then from the persons having the highest numbers not exceeding three on the list of those voted for as President, the House of Representatives shall choose immediately, by ballot, the President. But in choosing the President, the votes shall be taken by states, the representation from each state having one vote; a quorum for this purpose shall consist of a member or members from two-thirds of the states, and a majority of all the states shall be necessary to a choice. And if the House of Representatives shall not choose a President whenever the right of choice shall devolve upon them, before the fourth day of March next following, then the Vice-President shall act as President, as in the case of the death or other constitutional disability of the President.—The person having the greatest number of votes as Vice-President, shall be the Vice-President, if such number be a majority of the whole number of Electors appointed, and if no person have a majority, then from the two highest numbers on the list, the Senate shall choose the Vice-President; a quorum for the purpose shall consist of two-thirds of the whole number of Senators, and majority of the whole number shall be necessary to a choice. But no person constitutionally ineligible to the office of President shall be eligible to that of Vice-President of the United States.

AMENDMENT XIII [1865]

Section 1

Neither slavery nor involuntary servitude, except as a punishment for crime whereof the party shall have been duly convicted, shall exist within the United States, or any place subject to their jurisdiction.

Section 2

Congress shall have power to enforce this article by appropriate legislation.

AMENDMENT XIV [1868]

Section 1

All persons born or naturalized in the United States, and subject to the jurisdiction thereof, are citizens of the United States and of the State wherein they reside. No State shall abridge the privileges or immunities of citizens of the United States; nor shall any State deprive any person of life, liberty, or property, without due process of law; nor deny to any person within its jurisdiction the equal protection of the laws.

Section 2

Representatives shall be apportioned among the several States according to their respective numbers, counting the whole number of persons in each State, excluding Indians not taxed. But when the right to vote at any election for the choice of electors for President and Vice-President of the United States, Representatives in Congress, the Executive and Judicial officers of a State, or the members of the Legislature thereof, is denied to any of the male inhabitants of such State, being twenty-one years of age, and citizens of the United States, or in any way abridged, except for participation in rebellion, or other crime, the basis of representation therein shall be reduced in the proportion which the number of such male citizens shall bear to the whole number of male citizens twenty-one years of age in such State.

Section 3

No person shall be a Senator or Representative in Congress, or elector of President and Vice-President, or hold any office, civil or military, under the United States, or under any State, who, having previously taken an oath, as a member of Congress, or as an officer of the United States, or as a member of any State legislature, or as an executive or judicial officer of any State, to support the Constitution of the

United States, shall have engaged in insurrection or rebellion against the same, or given aid or comfort to the enemies thereof. But Congress may by a vote of two-thirds of each House, remove such disability.

Section 4

The validity of the public debt of the United States, authorized by law, including debts incurred for payment of pensions and bounties for services in suppressing insurrection or rebellion, shall not be questioned. But neither the United States nor any State shall assume or pay any debts or obligation incurred in aid of insurrection or rebellion against the United States, or any claim for the loss or emancipation of any slave; but all such debts, obligations, and claims shall be held illegal and void.

Section 5

The Congress shall have the power to enforce, by appropriate legislation, the provisions of this article.

AMENDMENT XV [1870]

Section 1

The right of citizens of the United States to vote shall not be denied or abridged by the United States or by any State on account of race, color, or previous condition of servitude.

Section 2

The Congress shall have power to enforce this article by appropriate legislation.

AMENDMENT XVI [1913]

The Congress shall have power to lay and collect taxes on incomes, from whatever source derived, without apportionment among the several States, and without regard to any census or enumeration.

AMENDMENT XVII [1913]

The Senate of the United States shall be composed of two Senators from each State, elected by the people thereof, for six years; and each Senator shall have one vote. The electors in each State shall have the qualifications requisite for electors of the most numerous branch of the State legislatures.

When vacancies happen in the representation of any State in the Senate, the executive authority of such State shall issue writs of election to fill such vacancies: Provided, That the legislature of any State may empower the executive thereof to make temporary appointments until the people fill the vacancies by election as the legislature may direct.

This Amendment shall not be so construed as to affect the election or term of any Senator chosen before it becomes valid as part of the Constitution.

AMENDMENT XVIII [1919]

Section 1

After one year from the ratification of this article the manufacture, sale, or transportation of intoxicating liquors within, the importation thereof into, or the exportation thereof from the United States and all territory subject to the jurisdiction thereof for beverage purposes is hereby prohibited.

Section 2

The Congress and the several States shall have concurrent power to enforce this article by appropriate legislation.

Section 3

This article shall be inoperative unless it shall have been ratified as an Amendment to the Constitution by the legislatures of the several States, as provided in the Constitution, within seven years from the date of the submission hereof to the States by the Congress.

AMENDMENT XIX [1920]

The right of citizens of the United States to vote shall not be denied or abridged by the United States or by any State on account of sex.

Congress shall have power to enforce this article by appropriate legislation.

AMENDMENT XX [1933]

Section 1

The terms of the President and Vice-President shall end at noon on the 20th day of January, and the terms of Senators and Representatives at noon on the 3d day of January, of the years in which such terms would have ended if this article had not been ratified; and the terms of their successors shall then begin.

Section 2

The Congress shall assemble at least once in every year, and such meeting shall begin at noon on the 3d day of January, unless they shall by law appoint a different day.

Section 3

If, at the time fixed for the beginning of the term of the President, the President elect shall have died, the Vice-President elect shall become President. If a President shall not have been chosen before the time fixed for the beginning of his term or if the President elect shall have failed to qualify, then the Vice-President elect shall act as President until a President shall have qualified; and the Congress may by law provide for the case wherein neither a President elect nor a Vice-President elect shall have qualified, declaring who shall then act as President, or the manner in which one who is to act shall be selected, and such person shall act accordingly until a President or Vice-President shall have qualified.

Section 4

The Congress may by law provide for the case of the death of any of the persons from whom the House of Representatives may choose a President whenever the right of choice shall have devolved upon them, and for the case of the death of any of the persons from whom the Senate may choose a Vice-President whenever the right of choice shall have devolved upon them.

Section 5

Sections 1 and 2 shall take effect on the 15th day of October following the ratification of this article.

Section 6

This article shall be inoperative unless it shall have been ratified as an amendment to the Constitution by the legislatures of three-fourths of the several States within seven years from the date of its submission.

AMENDMENT XXI [1933]

Section 1

The eighteenth article of amendment to the Constitution of the United States is hereby repealed.

Section 2

The transportation or importation into any State, Territory, or possession of the United States for delivery or use therein of intoxicating liquors, in violation of the laws thereof, is hereby prohibited.

Section 3

This article shall be inoperative unless it shall have been ratified as an amendment to the Constitution by conventions in the several States, as provided in the Constitution, within seven years from the date of the submission hereof to the States by the Congress.

AMENDMENT XXII [1951]

No person shall be elected to the office of the President more than twice, and no person who has held the office of President, or acted as President, for more than two years of a term to which some other person was elected President shall be elected to the office of the President more than once.

But this Article shall not apply to any person holding the office of President when this Article was proposed by the Congress, and shall not prevent any person who may be holding the office of President, or acting as President, during the term within which this Article becomes operative from holding the office of President or acting as President during the remainder of such term.

This article shall be inoperative unless it shall have been ratified as an amendment to the Constitution by the legislatures of three-fourths of the several states within seven years from the date of its submission to the states by the Congress.

AMENDMENT XXIII [1961]

Section 1

The District constituting the seat of Government of the United States shall appoint in such manner as the Congress may direct:

A number of electors of President and Vice-President equal to the whole number of Senators and Representatives in Congress to which the District would be entitled if it were a State, but in no event more than the least populous State; they shall be in addition to those appointed by the States, but they shall be considered, for the purposes of the election of President and Vice-President, to be electors appointed by a State; and they shall meet in the District and perform such duties as provided by the twelfth article of Amendment.

Section 2

The Congress shall have power to enforce this article by appropriate legislation.

AMENDMENT XXIV [1964]

Section 1

The right of citizens of the United States to vote in any primary or other election for President or Vice President, for electors for President or Vice President, or for Senator or Representative in Congress, shall not be denied or abridged by the United States or any state by reason of failure to pay any poll tax or other tax.

Section 2

The Congress shall have the power to enforce this article by appropriate legislation.

AMENDMENT XXV [1967]

Section 1

In case of the removal of the President from office or of his death or resignation, the Vice President shall become President.

Section 2

Whenever there is a vacancy in the office of the Vice President, the President shall nominate a Vice President who shall take office upon confirmation by a majority vote of both Houses of Congress.

Section 3

Whenever the President transmits to the President Pro Tempore of the Senate and the Speaker of the House of Representatives his written declaration that he is unable to discharge the powers and duties of his office, and until he transmits to them a written declaration to the contrary, such powers and duties shall be discharged by the Vice President as Acting President.

Section 4

Whenever the Vice President and a majority of either the principal officers of the executive departments or of such other body as Congress may by law provide, transmit to the President Pro Tempore of the Senate and the Speaker of the House of Representatives their written declaration that the President is unable to discharge the powers and duties of his office, the Vice President shall immediately assume the powers and duties of the office as Acting President.

Thereafter, when the President transmits to the President Pro Tempore of the Senate and the Speaker of the House of Representatives his written declaration that no inability exists, he shall resume the powers and duties of his office unless the Vice President and a majority of either the principal officers of the executive departments or of such other body as Congress may by law provide, transmit within four days to the President Pro Tempore of the Senate and the Speaker of the House of Representatives their written declaration that the President is unable to discharge the powers and duties of his office. Thereupon Congress shall decide the issue, assembling within forty-eight hours for that purpose if not in session. If the Congress, within twenty-one days after receipt of the latter written declaration, or, if Congress is not in session, within twenty-one days after Congress is required to assemble, determines by two-thirds vote of both Houses that the President is unable to discharge the powers and duties of his office, the Vice President shall continue to discharge the same as Acting President; otherwise, the President shall resume the powers and duties of his office.

AMENDMENT XXVI [1971]

Section 1

The right of citizens of the United States, who are eighteen years of age or older, to vote shall not be denied or abridged by the United States or by any State on account of age.

Section 2

The Congress shall have the power to enforce this article by appropriate legislation.

AMENDMENT XXVII [1992]

No law varying the compensation for the service of Senators and Representatives shall take effect until an election of Representatives shall have intervened.

Federalist No. 10
(JAMES MADISON)

Among the numerous advantages promised by a well-constructed union, none deserves to be more accurately developed than its tendency to break and control the violence of faction. The friend of popular governments never finds himself so much alarmed for their character and fate as when he contemplates their propensity to this dangerous vice. He will not fail, therefore, to set a due value on any plan which, without violating the principles to which he is attached, provides a proper cure for it. The instability, injustice, and confusion introduced into the public councils have, in truth, been the mortal diseases under which popular governments have everywhere perished, as they continue to be the favorite and fruitful topics from which the adversaries to liberty derive their most specious declamations. The valuable improvements made by the American constitutions on the popular models, both ancient and modern, cannot certainly be too much admired; but it would be an unwarrantable partiality to contend that they have as effectually obviated the danger on this side, as was wished and expected. Complaints are everywhere heard from our most considerate and virtuous citizens, equally the friends of public and private faith and of public and personal liberty, that our governments are too unstable, that the public good is disregarded in the conflicts of rival parties, and that measures are too often decided, not according to the rules of justice and the rights of the minor party, but by the superior force of an interested and overbearing majority. However anxiously we may wish that these complaints had no foundation, the evidence of known facts will not permit us to deny that they are in some degree true. It will be found, indeed, on a candid review of our situation, that some of the distresses under which we labor have been erroneously charged on the operation of our governments; but it will be found, at the same time, that other causes will not alone account for many of our heaviest misfortunes; and, particularly, for that prevailing and increasing distrust of public engagements and alarm for private rights which are echoed from one end of the continent to the other. These must be chiefly, if not wholly, effects of the unsteadiness and injustice with which a factious spirit has tainted our public administration.

By a faction I understand a number of citizens, whether amounting to a majority or minority of the whole, who are united and actuated by some common impulse of passion, or of interest, adverse to the rights of other citizens, or to the permanent and aggregate interests of the community.

There are two methods of curing the mischiefs of faction: the one, by removing its causes; the other, by controlling its effects.

There are again two methods of removing the causes of faction: the one, by destroying the liberty which is essential to its existence; the other, by giving to every citizen the same opinions, the same passions, and the same interests.

It could never be more truly said than of the first remedy that it was worse than the disease. Liberty is to faction what air is to fire, an aliment without which it instantly expires. But it could not be a less folly to abolish liberty, which is essential to political life, because it nourishes faction than it would be to wish the annihilation of air, which is essential to animal life, because it imparts to fire its destructive agency.

The second expedient is as impracticable as the first would be unwise. As long as the reason of man continues fallible, and he is at liberty to exercise it, different opinions will be formed. As long as the connection subsists between his reason and his self-love, his opinions and his passions will have a reciprocal influence on each other; and the former will be objects to which the latter will attach themselves. The diversity in the faculties of men, from which the rights of property originate, is not less an insuperable obstacle to a uniformity of interest. The protection of these faculties is the first object of government. From the protection of different and unequal faculties of acquiring property, the possession of different degrees and kinds of property immediately results; and from the influence of these on the sentiments and views of the respective proprietors ensues a division of the society into different interests and parties.

The latent causes of faction are thus sown in the nature of man; and we see them everywhere brought into different degrees of activity, according to the different circumstances of civil society. A zeal for different opinions concerning religion, concerning government, and many other points, as well of speculation as of practice; an attachment to different leaders ambitiously contending for pre-eminence and power; or to persons of other descriptions whose fortunes have been interesting to the human passions, have, in turn, divided mankind into parties, inflamed them with mutual animosity, and rendered them much more disposed to vex and oppress each other than to co-operate for their common good. So strong is this propensity of mankind to fall into mutual animosities that where no substantial occasion presents itself the most frivolous and fanciful distinctions have been sufficient to kindle their unfriendly passions and excite their most violent conflicts. But the most common and durable source of factions has been the various and unequal distribution of property. Those who hold and those who are without property have ever formed distinct interests in society. Those who are creditors, and those who are debtors, fall under a like discrimination. A landed interest, a manufacturing interest, a mercantile interest, a moneyed interest, with many lesser interests, grow up of necessity in civilized nations, and divide them into different classes, actuated by different sentiments and views. The regulation of these various and interfering interests forms the principal task of modern legislation and involves the spirit of party and faction in the necessary and ordinary operations of government.

No man is allowed to be a judge in his own cause, because his interest would certainly bias his judgment, and, not improbably, corrupt his integrity. With equal, nay with greater reason, a body of men are unfit to be both judges and parties at the same time; yet what are many of the most important acts of legislation but so many judicial determinations, not indeed concerning the rights of single persons, but concerning the rights of large bodies of citizens? And what are the different classes of legislators but advocates and parties to the causes which they determine? Is a law proposed concerning private debts? It is a question to which the creditors are parties on one side and the debtors on the other. Justice ought to hold the balance between them. Yet the parties are, and must be, themselves the judges; and the most numerous party, or in other words, the most powerful faction must be expected to prevail. Shall domestic manufacturers be encouraged, and in what degree, by restrictions on foreign manufacturers? [These] are questions which would be differently decided by the landed and the manufacturing classes, and probably by neither with a sole regard to justice and the public good.

The apportionment of taxes on the various descriptions of property is an act which seems to require the most exact impartiality; yet there is, perhaps, no legislative act in which greater opportunity and temptation are given to a predominant party to trample on the rules of justice. Every shilling with which they overburden the inferior number is a shilling saved to their own pockets.

It is in vain to say that enlightened statesmen will be able to adjust these clashing interests and render them all subservient to the public good. Enlightened statesmen will not always be at the helm. Nor, in many cases, can such an adjustment be made at all without taking into view indirect and remote considerations, which will rarely prevail over the immediate interest which one party may find in disregarding the rights of another or the good of the whole.

The inference to which we are brought is that the *causes* of faction cannot be removed and that relief is only to be sought in the means of controlling its *effects*.

If a faction consists of less than a majority, relief is supplied by the republican principle, which enables the majority to defeat its sinister views by regular vote. It may clog the administration, it may convulse the society; but it will be unable to execute and mask its violence under the forms of the Constitution. When a majority is included in a faction, the form of popular government, on the other hand, enables it to sacrifice to its ruling passion or interest both the public good and the rights of other citizens. To secure the public good and private rights against the danger of such a faction, and at the same time to preserve the spirit and the form of popular government, is then the great object to which our inquiries are directed. Let me add that it is the great desideratum by which alone this form of government can be rescued from the opprobrium under which it has so long labored and be recommended to the esteem and adoption of mankind.

By what means is this object attainable? Evidently by one of two only. Either the existence of the same passion or interest in a majority at the same time must be prevented, or the majority, having such coexistent passion or interest, must be rendered, by their number and local situation, unable to concert and carry into effect schemes of oppression. If the impulse and the opportunity be suffered to coincide, we well know that neither moral nor religious motives can be relied on as an adequate control. They are not found to be such on the injustice and violence of individuals, and lose their efficacy in proportion to the number combined together, that is, in proportion as their efficacy becomes needful.

From this view of the subject it may be concluded that a pure democracy, by which I mean a society consisting of a small number of citizens, who assemble and administer the government in person, can admit of no cure for the mischiefs of faction. A common passion or interest will, in almost every case, be felt by a majority of the whole, a communication and concert result from the form of government itself; and there is nothing to check the inducements to sacrifice the weaker party or an obnoxious individual. Hence it is that such democracies have ever been spectacles of turbulence and contention; have ever been found incompatible with personal security or the rights of property; and have in general been as short in their lives as they have been violent in their deaths. Theoretic politicians, who have patronized this species of government, have erroneously supposed that by reducing mankind to a perfect equality in their political rights, they would at the same time be perfectly equalized and assimilated in their possessions, their opinions, and their passions.

A republic, by which I mean a government in which the scheme of representation takes place, opens a different prospect and promises the cure for which we are seeking. Let us examine the points in which it varies from pure democracy, and we shall comprehend both the nature of the cure and the efficacy which it must derive from the Union.

The two great points of difference between a democracy and a republic are: first, the delegation of the government, in the latter, to a small number of citizens elected by the rest; secondly, the greater number of citizens and greater sphere of country over which the latter may be extended.

The effect of the first difference is, on the one hand, to refine and enlarge the public views by passing them through the medium of a chosen body of citizens, whose wisdom may best discern the true interest of their country and whose patriotism and love of justice will be least likely to sacrifice it to temporary or partial considerations. Under such a regulation it may well happen that the public voice, pronounced by the representatives of the people, will be more consonant to the public good than if pronounced by the people themselves, convened for the purpose. On the other hand, the effect may be inverted. Men of factious tempers, of local prejudices, or of sinister designs, may, by intrigue, by corruption, or by other means, first obtain the suffrages, and then betray the interests of the people. The question resulting is, whether small or extensive republics are most favorable to the election of proper guardians of the public weal; and it is clearly decided in favor of the latter by two obvious considerations.

In the first place it is to be remarked that however small the republic may be the representatives must be raised to a certain number in order to guard against the cabals of a few; and that however large it may be they must be limited to a certain number in order to guard against the confusion of a multitude. Hence, the number of representatives in the two cases not being in proportion to that of the constituents, and being proportionally greatest in the small republic, it follows that if the proportion of fit characters be not less in the large than in the small republic, the former will present a greater option, and consequently a greater probability of a fit choice.

In the next place, as each representative will be chosen by a greater number of citizens in the large than in the small republic, it will be more difficult for unworthy candidates to practice with success the vicious arts by which elections are too often carried; and the suffrages of the people being more free, will be more likely to center on men who possess the most attractive merit and the most diffusive and established characters.

It must be confessed that in this, as in most other cases, there is a mean, on both sides of which inconveniencies will be found to lie. By enlarging too much the number of electors, you render the representative too little acquainted with all their local circumstances and lesser interests; as by reducing it too much, you render him unduly attached to these, and too little fit to comprehend and pursue great and national objects. The federal Constitution forms a happy combination in this respect; the great and aggregate interests being referred to the national, the local and particular to the State legislatures.

The other point of difference is the greater number of citizens and extent of territory which may be brought within the compass of republican than of democratic government; and it is this circumstance principally which renders factious combinations less to be dreaded in the former than in the latter. The smaller the society, the fewer probably will be the distinct parties and interests composing it; the fewer the distinct parties and interests, the more frequently will a majority be found of the same party; and the smaller the number of individuals composing a majority, and the smaller the compass within which they are placed, the more easily will they concert and execute their plans of oppression. Extend the sphere and you take in a greater variety of parties and interests; you make it less probable that a majority of the whole will have a common motive to invade the rights of other citizens; or if such a common motive exists, it will be more difficult for all who feel it to discover their own strength and to act in unison with each other. Besides other impediments, it may be remarked that, where there is a consciousness of unjust or dishonorable purposes, communication is always checked by distrust in proportion to the number whose concurrence is necessary.

Hence, it clearly appears that the same advantage which a republic has over a democracy in controlling the effects of faction is enjoyed by a large over a small republic—is enjoyed by the Union over the States composing it. Does this advantage consist in the substitution of representatives whose enlightened views and virtuous sentiments render them superior to local prejudices and to schemes of injustice? It will not be denied that the representation of the Union will be most likely to possess these requisite endowments. Does it consist in the greater security afforded by a greater variety of parties, against the event of any one party being able to outnumber and oppress the rest? In an equal degree does the increased variety of parties comprised within the Union increase this security. Does it, in fine, consist in the greater obstacles opposed to the concert and accomplishment of the secret wishes of an unjust and interested majority? Here again the extent of the Union gives it the most palpable advantage.

The influence of factious leaders may kindle a flame within their particular States but will be unable to spread a general conflagration through the other States. A religious sect may degenerate into a political faction in a part of the Confederacy; but the variety of sects dispersed over the entire face of it must secure the national councils against any danger from that source. A rage for paper money, for an abolition of debts, for an equal division of property, or for any other improper or wicked project, will be less apt to pervade the whole body of the Union than a particular member of it, in the same proportion as such a malady is more likely to taint a particular county or district than an entire State.

In the extent and proper structure of the Union, therefore, we behold a republican remedy for the diseases most incident to republican government. And according to the degree of pleasure and pride we feel in being republicans ought to be our zeal in cherishing the spirit and supporting the character of Federalists.

Federalist No. 51
(JAMES MADISON)

To what expedient, then, shall we finally resort, for maintaining in practice the necessary partition of power among the several departments as laid down in the Constitution? The only answer that can be given is that as all these exterior provisions are found to be inadequate, the defect must be supplied, by so contriving the interior structure of the government as that its several constituent parts may, by their mutual relations, be the means of keeping each other in their proper places. Without presuming to undertake a full development of this important idea I will hazard a few general observations which may perhaps place it in a clearer light, and enable us to form a more correct judgment of the principles and structure of the government planned by the convention.

In order to lay a due foundation for that separate and distinct exercise of the different powers of government, which to a certain extent is admitted on all hands to be essential to the preservation of liberty, it is evident that each department should have a will of its own; and consequently should be so constituted that the members of each should have as little agency as possible in the appointment of the members of the others. Were this principle rigorously adhered to, it would require that all the appointments for the supreme executive, legislative, and judiciary magistracies should be drawn from the same fountain of authority, the people, through channels having no communication whatever with one another. Perhaps such a plan of constructing the several departments would be less difficult in practice than it may be in contemplation appear. Some difficulties, however, and some additional expense would attend the execution of it. Some deviations, therefore, from the principle must be admitted. In the constitution of the judiciary department in particular, it might be inexpedient to insist rigorously on the principle; first, because peculiar qualifications being essential in the members, the primary consideration ought to be to select that mode of choice which best secures these qualifications; second, because the permanent tenure by which the appointments are held in that department must soon destroy all sense of dependence on the authority conferring them.

It is equally evident that the members of each department should be as little dependent as possible on those of the others for the emoluments annexed to their offices. Were the executive magistrate, or the judges, not independent of the legislature in this particular, their independence in every other would be merely nominal.

But the great security against a gradual concentration of the several powers in the same department consists in giving to those who administer each department the necessary constitutional means and personal motives to resist encroachments of the others. The provision for defense must in this, as in all other cases, be made commensurate to the danger of attack. Ambition must be made to counteract ambition. The interest of the man must be connected with the constitutional rights of the place. It may be a reflection on human nature that such devices should be necessary to control the abuses of government. But what is government itself but the greatest of all reflections on human nature? If men were angels no government would be necessary. If angels were to govern men, neither external nor internal controls on government would be necessary. In framing a government which is to be administered by men over men, the great difficulty lies in this: you must first enable the government to control the governed; and in the next place oblige it to control itself. A dependence on the people is, no doubt, the primary control on the government; but experience has taught mankind the necessity of auxiliary precautions.

This policy of supplying, by opposite and rival interests, the defect of better motives, might be traced through the whole system of human affairs, private as well as public. We see it particularly displayed in all the subordinate distributions of power, where the constant aim is to divide and arrange the several offices in such a manner as that each may be a check on the other—that the private interest of every individual may be a sentinel over the public rights. These inventions of prudence cannot be less requisite in the distribution of the supreme powers of the State.

But it is not possible to give to each department an equal power of self-defense. In republican government, the legislative authority necessarily predominates. The remedy for this inconveniency is to divide the legislature into different branches; and to render them, by different modes of election and different principles of action, as little connected with each other as the nature of their common functions and their common dependence on the society will admit. It may even be necessary to guard against dangerous encroachments by still further precautions. As the weight of the legislative authority requires that it should be thus divided, the weakness of the executive may require, on the other hand, that it should be fortified. An absolute negative on the legislature appears, at first view, to be the natural defense with which the executive magistrate should be armed. But perhaps it would be neither altogether safe nor alone sufficient. On ordinary occasions it might not be exerted with the requisite firmness, and on extraordinary occasions it might be perfidiously abused. May not this defect of an absolute negative be supplied by some qualified connection between this weaker department and the weaker branch of the stronger department, by which the latter may be led to support the constitutional rights of the former, without being too much detached from the rights of its own department?

If the principles on which these observations are founded be just, as I persuade myself they are, and they be applied as a criterion to the several State constitutions, and to the federal Constitution, it will be found that if the latter does not perfectly correspond with them, the former are infinitely less able to bear such a test.

There are, moreover, two considerations particularly applicable to the federal system of America, which place that system in a very interesting point of view.

First. In a single republic, all the power surrendered by the people is submitted to the administration of a single government; and the usurpations are guarded against by a division of the government into distinct and separate departments. In the compound republic of America, the power surrendered by the people is first divided between two distinct governments, and then the portion allotted to each subdivided among distinct and separate departments. Hence a double security arises to the rights of the people. The different governments will control each other, at the same time that each will be controlled by itself.

Second. It is of great importance in a republic not only to guard the society against the oppression of its rulers, but to guard one part of the society against the injustice of the other part. Different interests necessarily exist in different classes of citizens. If a majority be united by a common interest, the rights of the minority will be insecure. There are but two methods of providing against this evil: the one by creating a will in the community independent of the majority—that is, of the society itself;

the other, by comprehending in the society so many separate descriptions of citizens as will render an unjust combination of a majority of the whole very improbable, if not impracticable. The first method prevails in all governments possessing an hereditary or self-appointed authority. This, at best, is but a precarious security; because a power independent of the society may as well espouse the unjust views of the major as the rightful interests of the minor party, and may possibly be turned against both parties. The second method will be exemplified in the federal republic of the United States. Whilst all authority in it will be derived from and dependent on the society, the society itself will be broken into so many parts, interests and classes of citizens, that the rights of individuals, or of the minority, will be in little danger from interested combinations of the majority. In a free government the security for civil rights must be the same as that for religious rights. It consists in the one case in the multiplicity of interests, and in the other in the multiplicity of sects. The degree of security in both cases will depend on the number of interests and sects; and this may be presumed to depend on the extent of country and number of people comprehended under the same government. This view of the subject must particularly recommend a proper federal system to all the sincere and considerate friends of republican government, since it shows that in exact proportion as the territory of the Union may be formed into more circumscribed Confederacies, or States, oppressive combinations of a majority will be facilitated; the best security, under the republican forms, for the rights of every class of citizen, will be diminished; and consequently the stability and independence of some member of the government, the only other security, must be proportionately increased. Justice is the end of government. It is the end of civil society. It ever has been and ever will be pursued until it be obtained, or until liberty be lost in the pursuit. In a society under the forms of which the stronger faction can readily unite and oppress the weaker, anarchy may as truly be said to reign as in a state of nature, where the weaker individual is not secured against the violence of the stronger; and as, in the latter state, even the stronger individuals are prompted, by the uncertainty of their condition, to submit to a government which may protect the weak as well as themselves; so, in the former state, will the more powerful factions or parties be gradually induced, by a like motive, to wish for a government which will protect all parties, the weaker as well as the more powerful. It can be little doubted that if the State of Rhode Island was separated from the Confederacy and left to itself, the insecurity of rights under the popular form of government within such narrow limits would be displayed by such reiterated oppressions of factious majorities that some power altogether independent of the people would soon be called for by the voice of the very factions whose misrule had proved the necessity of it. In the extended republic of the United States, and among the great variety of interests, parties, and sects which it embraces, a coalition of a majority of the whole society could seldom take place on any other principles than those of justice and the general good; whilst there being thus less danger to a minor from the will of a major party, there must be less pretext, also, to provide for the security of the former, by introducing into the government a will not dependent on the latter, or, in other words, a will independent of the society itself. It is no less certain than it is important, notwithstanding the contrary opinions which have been entertained, that the larger the society, provided it lie within a practicable sphere, the more duly capable it will be of self-government. And happily for the republican cause, the practicable sphere may be carried to a very great extent by a judicious modification and mixture of the federal principle.

GLOSSARY

administrative law judge An official who presides at a trial-like administrative hearing to settle a dispute between an agency and someone adversely affected by a decision of that agency.

affirmative action Refers to programs designed to ensure that women, minorities, and other traditionally disadvantaged groups have full and equal opportunities in employment, education, and other areas of life.

agency point of view The tendency of bureaucrats to place the interests of their agency ahead of other interests and ahead of the priorities sought by the president or Congress.

agenda setting The power of the media through news coverage to focus the public's attention and concern on particular events, problems, issues, personalities, and so on.

agents of socialization Those agents, such as the family and the media, that have significant impact on citizens' political socialization.

alienation A feeling of personal powerlessness that includes the notion that government does not care about the opinions of people like oneself.

Anti-Federalists A term used to describe opponents of the Constitution during the debate over ratification.

apathy A feeling of personal disinterest in or lack of concern with politics.

appellate jurisdiction The authority of a given court to review cases that have already been tried in lower courts and are appealed to it by the losing party; such a court is called an appeals court or appellate court. (See also **original jurisdiction.**)

authoritarian government A form of government in which those in power openly repress their opponents in order to stay in power.

authority The recognized right of officials to exercise power as a result of the positions they hold. (See also **power.**)

balanced budget The situation in which the government's tax and other revenues for the year are roughly equal to its expenditures.

bicameral legislatures A legislature that has two chambers (the House and the Senate, in the case of the United States)

bill A proposed law (legislative act) within Congress or another legislature. (See also **law.**)

Bill of Rights The first ten amendments to the Constitution. They include rights such as freedom of speech and religion and due process protections (such as the right to a jury trial) for persons accused of crimes.

bipolar (power structure) A power structure dominated by two powers only, as in the case of the United States and the Soviet Union during the cold war.

block grants Federal grants-in-aid that permit state and local officials to decide how the money will be spent within a general area, such as education or health. (See also **categorical grants.**)

budgetary process The process through which annual federal spending and revenue determinations are made.

budget deficit The situation in which the government's expenditures exceed its tax and other revenues.

bureaucracy A system of organization and control based on the principles of hierarchical authority, job specialization, and formalized rules. (See also **formalized rules; hierarchical authority; job specialization.**)

bureaucratic accountability The degree to which bureaucrats are held accountable for the power they exercise.

cabinet A group consisting of the heads of the (cabinet) executive departments, who are appointed by the president, subject to confirmation by the Senate. The cabinet was once the main advisory body to the president but no longer plays this role. (See also **cabinet (executive) departments.**)

cabinet (executive) departments The major administrative organizations within the federal executive bureaucracy, each of which is headed by a secretary or, in the case of Justice, the attorney general. Each department has responsibility for a major function of the federal government, such as defense, agriculture, or justice. (See also **cabinet; independent agencies.**)

candidate-centered campaigns Election campaigns and other political processes in which candidates, not political parties, have most of the initiative and influence. (See also **party-centered campaigns.**)

capital-gains tax The tax that individuals pay on money gained from the sale of a capital asset, such as property or stocks.

categorical grants Federal grants-in-aid to states and localities that can be used only for designated projects. (See also **block grants.**)

checks and balances The elaborate system of divided spheres of authority provided by the U.S. Constitution as a means of controlling the power of government. The separation of powers among the branches of the national government, federalism, and the different methods of selecting national officers are all part of this system.

citizens' (noneconomic) groups Organized interests formed by individuals drawn together by opportunities to promote a cause in which they believe but that does not provide them significant individual economic benefits. (See also **economic groups; interest group.**)

civic duty The belief of an individual that civic and political participation is a responsibility of citizenship.

civil liberties The fundamental individual rights of a free society, such as freedom of speech and the right to a jury trial, which in the United States are protected by the Bill of Rights.

civil rights (equal rights) The right of every person to equal protection under the laws and equal access to society's opportunities and public facilities.

civil service system See **merit system.**

clear-and-present-danger test A test devised by the Supreme Court in 1919 to define the limits of free speech in the context of national security. According to the test, government cannot abridge political expression unless it presents a clear and present danger to the nation's security.

clientele groups Special interest groups that benefit directly from the activities of a particular bureaucratic agency and therefore are strong advocates of the agency.

cloture A parliamentary maneuver that, if a three-fifths majority votes for it, limits Senate debate to thirty hours and has the effect of defeating a filibuster. (See also **filibuster.**)

cold war The lengthy period after World War II when the United States and the USSR were not engaged in actual combat (a "hot war") but were nonetheless locked in a state of deep-seated hostility.

collective (public) goods Benefits that are offered by groups (usually citizens' groups) as an incentive for membership but that are nondivisible (such as a clean environment) and therefore are available to nonmembers as well as members of the particular group. (See also **free-rider problem; private (individual) goods.**)

commerce clause The authority granted Congress in Article I, Section 8 of the Constitution "to regulate commerce" among the states.

common-carrier function The media's function as an open channel through which political leaders can communicate with the public. (See also **partisan function; signaling (signaler) function; watchdog function.**)

concurring opinion A separate opinion written by a Supreme Court justice who votes with the majority in the decision on a case but who disagrees with their reasoning. (See also **dissenting opinion; majority opinion; plurality opinion.**)

confederacy A governmental system in which sovereignty is vested entirely in subnational (state) governments. (See also **federalism; unitary system.**)

conference committees A temporary committee that is formed to bargain over the differences in the House and Senate versions of a bill. A conference committee's members are usually appointed from the House and Senate standing committees that originally worked on the bill.

constituency The people residing within the geographical area represented by an elected official.

constitution The fundamental law that defines how a government will legitimately operate.

constitutional democratic republic A government that is constitutional in its provisions for minority rights and rule by law; democratic in its provisions for majority influence through elections; and a republic in its mix of deliberative institutions, which check and balance each other.

constitutionalism The idea that there are lawful limits on the power of government.

containment A doctrine, developed after World War II, based on the assumptions that the Soviet Union was an aggressor nation and that only a determined United States could block Soviet territorial ambitions.

cooperative federalism The situation in which the national, state, and local levels work together to solve problems.

corporate power The power that corporations exercise in their effort to influence government and maintain control of the workplace.

cultural (social) conservatives Those who believe government power should be used to uphold traditional values.

cultural (social) liberals Those who believe it is not government's role to buttress traditional values at the expense of unconventional or new values.

decision A vote of the Supreme Court in a particular case that indicates which party the justices side with and by how large a margin.

de facto discrimination Discrimination on the basis of race, sex, religion, ethnicity, and the like that results from social, economic, and cultural biases and conditions. (See also **de jure discrimination.**)

de jure discrimination Discrimination on the basis of race, sex, religion, ethnicity, and the like that results from a law. (See also **de facto discrimination.**)

delegates Elected representatives whose obligation is to act in accordance with the expressed wishes of the people they represent. (See also **trustees.**)

demand-side economics A form of fiscal policy that emphasizes "demand" (consumer spending). Government can use increased spending or tax cuts to place more money in consumers' hands and thereby increase demand. (See also **fiscal policy; supply-side economics.**)

democracy A form of government in which the people govern, either directly or through elected representatives.

democracy (according to the framers) A form of government in which the power of the majority is unlimited, whether exercised directly or through a representative body.

demographic representativeness The idea that the bureaucracy will be more responsive to the public if its employees at all levels are demographically representative of the population as a whole.

denials of power A constitutional means of limiting governmental action by listing those powers that government is expressly prohibited from using.

deregulation The rescinding of excessive government regulations for the purpose of improving economic efficiency.

devolution The passing down of authority from the national government to the state and local governments.

direct primary See **primary election.**

dissenting opinion The opinion of a justice in a Supreme Court case that explains his or her reasons for disagreeing with the majority's decision. (See also **concurring opinion; majority opinion; plurality opinion.**)

dual federalism A doctrine based on the idea that a precise separation of national power and state power is both possible and desirable.

due process clause (of the Fourteenth Amendment) The clause of the Constitution that has been used by the judiciary to apply Bill of Rights protections to the actions of state governments.

economic conservatives Those who believe government tries to do too many things that should be left to private interests and economic markets. (See also **cultural (social) conservatives; cultural (social) liberals; economic liberals; libertarians; populists.**)

economic depression A very severe and sustained economic downturn. Depressions are rare in the United States: the last one was in the 1930s.

economic efficiency An economic principle holding that firms should fulfill as many of society's needs as possible while using as few of its resources as possible. The greater the output (production) for a given input (for example, an hour of labor), the more efficient the process.

economic equity The situation in which the outcome of an economic transaction is fair to each party. An outcome can usually be considered fair if each party enters into a transaction freely and is not unknowingly at a disadvantage.

economic globalization The increased interdependence of nations' economies. The change is a result of technological, transportation, and communication advances that have enabled firms to deploy their resources across the globe.

economic groups Interest groups that are organized primarily for economic reasons but that engage in political activity in order to seek favorable policies from government. (See also **citizens' (noneconomic) groups; interest group.**)

economic liberals Those who believe government should do more to assist people who have difficulty meeting their economic needs on their own. (See also **cultural (social) conservatives; cultural (social) liberals; economic liberals; libertarians; populists.**)

economic recession A moderate but sustained downturn in the economy. Recessions are part of the economy's normal cycle of ups and downs.

economy A system for the exchange of goods and services between the producers of those goods and services and the consumers of them.

elastic clause See **"necessary and proper" clause.**

Electoral College An unofficial term that refers to the electors who cast the states' electoral votes.

electoral votes The method of voting used to choose the U.S. president. Each state has the same number of electoral votes as it has members in Congress (House and Senate combined). By tradition, electoral voting is tied to a state's popular voting. The candidate with the most popular votes in a state (or, in a few states, the most votes in a congressional district) receives its electoral votes.

elitism The notion that wealthy and well-connected individuals exercise power over certain areas of public policy.

entitlement program Any of a number of individual benefit programs, such as social security, that require government to provide a designated benefit to any person who meets the legally defined criteria for eligibility.

enumerated (expressed) powers The seventeen powers granted to the national government under Article I, Section 8 of the Constitution. These powers include taxation and the regulation of commerce as well as the authority to provide for the national defense.

equality The notion that all individuals are equal in their moral worth and are thereby entitled to equal treatment under the law.

equality of opportunity The idea that all individuals should be given an equal chance to succeed on their own.

equal-protection clause A clause of the Fourteenth Amendment that forbids any state to deny equal protection of the laws to any individual within its jurisdiction.

equal rights See **civil rights.**

establishment clause The First Amendment provision stating that government may not favor one religion over another or favor religion over no religion, and prohibiting Congress from passing laws respecting the establishment of religion.

exclusionary rule The legal principle that government is prohibited from using in trials evidence that was obtained by unconstitutional means (for example, illegal search and seizure).

executive departments See **cabinet (executive) departments.**

externalities Burdens that society incurs when firms fail to pay the full costs of production. An example of an externality is the pollution that results when corporations dump industrial wastes into lakes and rivers.

facts (of a court case) The relevant circumstances of a legal dispute or offense as determined by a trial court. The facts of a case are crucial because they help determine which law or laws are applicable in the case.

federalism A governmental system in which authority is divided between two sovereign levels of government: national and regional. (See also **confederacy; unitary system.**)

Federalists A term used to describe supporters of the Constitution during the debate over ratification.

filibuster A procedural tactic in the U.S. Senate whereby a minority of legislators prevents a bill from coming to a vote by holding the floor and talking until the majority gives in and the bill is withdrawn from consideration. (See also **cloture.**)

fiscal federalism A term that refers to the expenditure of federal funds on programs run in part through states and localities.

fiscal policy A tool of economic management by which government can attempt to maintain a stable economy through its taxing and spending policies. (See also **demand-side economics; monetary policy; supply-side economics.**)

formalized rules A basic principle of bureaucracy that refers to the standardized procedures and established regulations by which a bureaucracy conducts its operations. (See also **bureaucracy.**)

framing The process by which the media play up certain aspects of a situation while downplaying other aspects, thereby providing a particular interpretation of the situation.

freedom of expression Americans' freedom to communicate their views, the foundation of which is the First Amendment rights of freedom of conscience, speech, press, assembly, and petition.

free-exercise clause A First Amendment provision that prohibits the government from interfering with the practice of religion.

free-market system An economic system based on the idea that government should interfere with economic transactions as little as possible. Free enterprise and self-reliance are the collective and individual principles that underpin free markets.

free-rider problem The situation in which the benefits offered by a group to its members are also available to nonmembers. The incentive to join the group and to promote its cause is reduced because nonmembers (free riders) receive the benefits (for example, a cleaner environment) without having to pay any of the group's costs. (See also **collective (public) goods.**)

free trade The condition in which tariffs and other barriers to trade between nations are kept to a minimum.

gender gap The tendency of white women and men to differ in their political attitudes and voting preferences.

gerrymandering The process by which the party in power draws election district boundaries in a way that enhances the reelection prospects of its candidates.

good faith exception The legal principle that otherwise excludable evidence can be admitted in trial if police believed they were following proper procedures.

government corporations Government bodies, such as the U.S. Postal Service and Amtrak, that are similar to private corporations in that they charge for their services but differ in that they receive federal funding to help defray expenses. Their directors are appointed by the president with Senate approval.

graduated personal income tax A tax on personal income in which the tax rate increases as income increases; in other words, the tax rate is higher for higher income levels.

grants-in-aid Federal cash payments to states and localities for programs they administer.

grants of power The method of limiting the U.S. government by confining its scope of authority to those powers expressly granted in the Constitution.

grassroots party A political party organized at the level of the voters and dependent on their support for its strength.

Great Compromise The agreement of the constitutional convention to create a two-chamber Congress with the House apportioned by population and the Senate apportioned equally by state.

hard money Campaign funds given directly to candidates to spend as they choose.

hierarchical authority A basic principle of bureaucracy that refers to the chain of command within an organization whereby officials and units have control over those below them. (See also **bureaucracy**.)

high-choice media system A media system in which audiences have such a wide range of choices that they can largely control the type of information to which they are exposed.

honeymoon period The president's first months in office, a time when Congress, the press, and the public are more inclined than usual to support presidential initiatives.

ideology A general belief about the role and purpose of government.

imminent lawless action test A legal test that says government cannot lawfully suppress advocacy that promotes lawless action unless such advocacy is aimed at producing, and is likely to produce, imminent lawless action.

implied powers The federal government's constitutional authority (through the "necessary and proper" clause) to take action that is not expressly authorized by the Constitution but that supports actions that are so authorized. (See also **"necessary and proper" clause**.)

inalienable (natural) rights Those rights that persons theoretically possessed in the state of nature, prior to the formation of governments. These rights, including those of life, liberty, and property, are considered inherent and as such are inalienable. Since government is established by people, government has the responsibility to preserve these rights.

incumbent The current holder of a particular public office.

independent agencies Bureaucratic agencies that are similar to cabinet departments but usually have a narrower area of responsibility. Each such agency is headed by a presidential appointee who is not a cabinet member. An example is the National Aeronautics and Space Administration.

individual goods See **private (individual) goods**.

individualism The idea that people should take the initiative, be self-sufficient, and accumulate the material advantages necessary for their well-being.

inevitable discovery exception The legal principle that otherwise excludable evidence can be admitted in trial if police would eventually have discovered the evidence by other means.

inflation A general increase in the average level of prices of goods and services.

in-kind benefit A government benefit that is a cash equivalent, such as food stamps or rent vouchers. This form of benefit ensures that recipients will use public assistance in a specified way.

inside lobbying Direct communication between organized interests and policymakers, which is based on the assumed value of close ("inside") contacts with policymakers.

interest group Any organization that actively seeks to influence public policy. (See also **citizens' (noneconomic) groups; economic groups.**)

internationalist The view that the country should involve itself deeply in world affairs (See also **isolationist.**)

invisible primary The critical period before the first presidential primaries and caucuses when the candidates compete for the public support, media attention, and financial contributions that can spell the difference between winning and losing once the voting begins.

iron triangle A small and informal but relatively stable group of well-positioned legislators, executives, and lobbyists who seek to promote policies beneficial to a particular interest. (See also **issue network.**)

isolationist The view that the country should deliberately avoid a large role in world affairs and instead concentrate on domestic concerns (See also **internationalist.**)

issue network An informal and relatively open network of public officials and lobbyists who come together in response to a proposed policy in an area of interest to each of them. Unlike an iron triangle, an issue network disbands after the issue is resolved. (See also **iron triangle.**)

job specialization A basic principle of bureaucracy holding that the responsibilities of each job position should be defined explicitly and that a precise division of labor within the organization should be maintained. (See also **bureaucracy.**)

judicial activism The doctrine that the courts should develop new legal principles when judges see a compelling need, even if this action places them in conflict with precedent or the policy decisions of elected officials. (See also **judicial restraint.**)

judicial restraint The doctrine that the judiciary should broadly defer to precedent and the judgment of legislatures. The doctrine claims that the job of judges is to work within the confines of laws set down by tradition and lawmaking majorities. (See also **judicial activism.**)

judicial review The power of courts to decide whether a governmental institution has acted within its constitutional powers and, if not, to declare its action null and void.

jurisdiction (of a congressional committee) The policy area in which a particular congressional committee is authorized to act.

jurisdiction (of a court) A given court's authority to hear cases of a particular kind. Jurisdiction may be original or appellate.

laissez-faire economics A classic economic philosophy holding that owners of business should be allowed to make their own production and distribution decisions without government regulation or control.

large-state plan See **Virginia (large-state) Plan.**

law (as enacted by Congress) A legislative proposal, or bill, that is passed by both the House and the Senate and is not vetoed by the president. (See also **bill.**)

lawmaking function The authority (of a legislature) to make the laws necessary to carry out the government's powers. (See also **oversight function; representation function.**)

legal action The use of courts of law as a means by which individuals protect their rights and settle their conflicts.

Lemon test A three-part test to determine whether a law relating to religion is valid under the religious establishment clause. To be valid, a law must have a secure purpose, serve neither to advance nor inhibit religion, and avoid excessive government entanglement with religion.

libel Publication of false material that damages a person's reputation.

libertarians Those who believe government tries to do too many things that should be left to firms and markets, and who oppose government as an instrument for upholding traditional values. (See also **cultural (social) conservatives;**

cultural (social) liberals; economic
liberals; libertarians; populists.)

liberty The principle that individuals
should be free to act and think as they
choose, provided they do not infringe
unreasonably on the rights and freedoms
of others.

limited government A government that is
subject to strict limits on its lawful uses
of power and, hence, on its ability to
deprive people of their liberty.

linkage institution An institution that
serves to connect citizens with government. Linkage institutions include
elections, political parties, interest
groups, and the media.

living constitution theory A method of
interpreting the Constitution that
emphasizes the principles it embodies
and their application to changing
circumstances and needs.

lobbying The process by which interest
group members or lobbyists attempt to
influence public policy through contacts
with public officials.

majoritarianism The idea that the majority prevails not only in elections but also
in determining policy.

majority opinion A court opinion that
results when a majority of the justices is
in agreement on the legal basis of
the decision. (See also **concurring
opinion; dissenting opinion; plurality
opinion.**)

means test The requirement that
applicants for public assistance must
demonstrate they are poor in order to be
eligible for the assistance. (See also
public assistance.)

median voter theorem The theory that
parties in a two-party system can
maximize their vote by locating themselves at the position of the median
voter—the voter whose preferences are
exactly in the middle.

merit system An approach to managing
the bureaucracy whereby people are
appointed to government positions on
the basis of either competitive examinations or special qualifications, such as
professional training. (See also
patronage system.)

midterm election The congressional
election that occurs midway through the
president's term of office.

military-industrial complex The three
components (the military establishment,
the industries that manufacture weapons,
and the members of Congress from
states and districts that depend heavily
on the arms industry) that mutually
benefit from a high level of defense
spending.

momentum (in campaigns) A strong
showing by a candidate in early presidential nominating contests, which leads
to a buildup of public support for the
candidate.

monetary policy A tool of economic
management based on manipulation of
the amount of money in circulation.
(See also **fiscal policy.**)

money chase A term used to describe
the fact that U.S. campaigns are
very expensive and candidates must
spend a great amount of time raising funds in order to compete
successfully.

multilateralism The situation in which
nations act together in response to
problems and crises.

multiparty system A system in which
three or more political parties have the
capacity to gain control of government
separately or in coalition.

national debt The total cumulative
amount that the U.S. government owes
to creditors.

nationalization The process by which
national authority has increased over the
course of U.S. history as a result primarily of economic change but also of
political action.

natural rights See **inalienable (natural)
rights.**

"necessary and proper" clause (elastic
clause) The authority granted Congress
in Article I, Section 8 of the Constitution "to make all laws which shall be
necessary and proper" for the implementation of its enumerated powers. (See
also **implied powers.**)

neutral competence The administrative
objective of a merit-based bureaucracy.

Such a bureaucracy should be "competent" in the sense that its employees are hired and retained on the basis of their expertise and "neutral" in the sense that it operates by objective standards rather than partisan ones.

New Jersey (small-state) Plan A constitutional proposal for a strengthened Congress but one in which each state would have a single vote, thus granting a small state the same legislative power as a larger state.

news The news media's version of reality, usually with an emphasis on timely, dramatic, and compelling events and developments.

news media See **press (news media).**

nomination The designation of a particular individual to run as a political party's candidate (its "nominee") in the general election.

noneconomic groups See **citizens' (noneconomic) groups.**

objective journalism A model of news reporting that is based on the communication of "facts" rather than opinions and that is "fair" in that it presents all sides of partisan debate. (See also **partisan press.**)

open party caucuses Meetings at which a party's candidates for nomination are voted on and that are open to all the party's rank-and-file voters who want to attend.

open-seat election An election in which there is no incumbent in the race.

opinion (of a court) A court's written explanation of its decision, which serves to inform others of the legal basis for the decision. Supreme Court opinions are expected to guide the decisions of lower courts. (See also **concurring opinion; dissenting opinion; majority opinion; plurality opinion.**)

original jurisdiction The authority of a given court to be the first court to hear a case. (See also **appellate jurisdiction.**)

originalism theory A method of interpreting the Constitution that emphasizes the meaning of its words at the time they were written.

outside lobbying A form of lobbying in which an interest group seeks to use public pressure as a means of influencing officials.

oversight function A supervisory activity of Congress that centers on its constitutional responsibility to see that the executive carries out the laws faithfully. (See also **lawmaking function; representation function.**)

packaging A term of modern campaigning that refers to the process of recasting a candidate's record into an appealing image.

partisan function Efforts by media actors to influence public response to a particular party, leader, issue, or viewpoint.

partisan press Newspapers and other communication media that openly support a political party and whose news tends to follow the party line. (See also **objective journalism.**)

party caucus A group that consists of a party's members in the House or Senate and that serves to elect the party's leadership, set policy goals, and plan party strategy.

party-centered campaigns Election campaigns and other political processes in which political parties, not individual candidates, hold most of the initiative and influence. (See also **candidate-centered campaigns.**)

party coalition The groups and interests that support a political party.

party competition A process in which conflict over society's goals is transformed by political parties into electoral competition in which the winner gains the power to govern.

party identification The personal sense of loyalty that an individual may feel toward a particular political party. (See also **party realignment.**)

party leaders Members of the House and Senate who are chosen by the Democratic or Republican caucus in each chamber to represent the party's interests in that chamber and who give some central direction to the chamber's work.

party organizations The party organizational units at national, state, and local levels; their influence has decreased over time because of many factors. (See also **candidate-centered campaigns; party-centered campaigns; primary election.**)

party (partisan) polarization The condition in which opinions and actions in response to political issues and situations divides substantially along political party lines.

party realignment An election or set of elections in which the electorate responds strongly to an extraordinarily powerful issue that has disrupted the established political order. A realignment has a lasting impact on public policy, popular support for the parties, and the composition of the party coalitions. (See also **party identification.**)

party unity The degree to which a party's House or Senate members act as a unified group to exert collective control over legislative action. 11

patronage system An approach to managing the bureaucracy whereby people are appointed to important government positions as a reward for political services they have rendered and because of their partisan loyalty. (See also **merit system; spoils system.**)

plain view exception The legal principle that otherwise excludable evidence can be admitted in trial if discovered in plain sight in the process of arresting a suspect for another infraction.

pluralism A theory of American politics that holds that society's interests are substantially represented through the activities of groups.

plurality (winner-take-all) system An electoral system in which the candidate who gets the most votes (the plurality) is an election district is elected to office from that district.

plurality opinion A court opinion that results when a majority of justices agrees on a decision in a case but do not agree on the legal basis for the decision. In this instance, the legal position held by most of the justices on the winning side is called a plurality opinion. (See also **concurring opinion; dissenting opinion; majority opinion.**)

policy implementation The primary function of the bureaucracy; it refers to the process of carrying out the authoritative decisions of Congress, the president, and the courts.

political action committee (PAC) The organization through which an interest group raises and distributes funds for election purposes. By law, the funds must be raised through voluntary contributions.

political culture The characteristic and deep-seated beliefs of a particular people.

political movements See **social (political) movements.**

political participation Involvement in activities intended to influence public policy and leadership, such as voting, joining political groups, contacting elected officials, demonstrating for political causes, and giving money to political candidates.

political party An ongoing coalition of interests joined together to try to get their candidates for public office elected under a common label.

political science The systematic study of government and politics.

political socialization The learning process by which people acquire their political opinions, beliefs, and values.

political thinking Reflective thinking focused on deciding what can reasonably be believed and then using this information to make political judgments.

politics The process through which a society settles its conflicts.

population In a public opinion poll, the people (for example, the citizens of a nation) whose opinions are being estimated through interviews with a sample of these people.

populists Those who believe government should do more to assist people who have difficulty meeting their economic needs and who look to government to uphold traditional values. (See also **cultural (social) conservatives; cultural (social) liberals; economic liberals; libertarians; populists.**)

pork (pork-barrel spending) Spending whose tangible benefits are targeted at a particular legislator's constituency.

poverty line As defined by the federal government, the annual cost of a thrifty food budget for an urban family of four, multiplied by three to allow also for the cost of housing, clothes, and other expenses. Families below the poverty line are considered poor and are eligible for certain forms of public assistance.

power The ability of persons or institutions to control policy. (See also **authority.**)

precedent A judicial decision that serves as a rule for settling subsequent cases of a similar nature.

preemptive war doctrine The idea, espoused by President George W. Bush, that the United States could attack a potentially threatening nation even if the threat had not yet reached a serious and immediate level.

presidential approval ratings A measure of the degree to which the public approves or disapproves of the president's performance in office.

presidential commissions Organizations within the bureaucracy that are headed by commissioners appointed by the president. An example is the Commission on Civil Rights.

press (news media) Print, broadcast, cable, and Internet organizations that are in the news-reporting business.

primary election (direct primary) A form of election in which voters choose a party's nominees for public office. In most states, eligibility to vote in a primary election is limited to voters who designated themselves as party members when they registered to vote.

prior restraint Government prohibition of speech or publication before the fact, which is presumed by the courts to be unconstitutional unless the justification for it is overwhelming.

private (individual) goods Benefits that a group (most often an economic group) can grant directly and exclusively to individual members of the group. (See also **collective goods.**)

procedural due process The constitutional requirement that government must follow proper legal procedures before a person can be legitimately punished for an alleged offense.

proportional representation system A form of representation in which seats in the legislature are allocated proportionally according to each political party's share of the popular vote. This system enables smaller parties to compete successfully for seats. (See also **single-member districts.**)

protectionism The placing of the immediate interests of domestic producers (through, for example, protective tariffs) above that of free trade between nations.

public assistance A term that refers to social welfare programs funded through general tax revenues and available only to the financially needy. Eligibility for such a program is established by a means test. (See also **means test; social insurance.**)

public goods See **collective (public) goods.**

public opinion The politically relevant opinions held by ordinary citizens that they express openly.

public opinion poll A device for measuring public opinion whereby a relatively small number of individuals (the sample) is interviewed for the purpose of estimating the opinions of a whole community (the population).

public policies Decisions by government to pursue particular courses of action.

realignment See **party realignment.**

reapportionment The reallocation of House seats among states after each census as a result of population changes.

reasonable-basis test A test applied by courts to laws that treat individuals unequally. Such a law may be deemed constitutional if its purpose is held to be "reasonably" related to a legitimate government interest.

redistricting The process of altering election districts in order to make them as nearly equal in population as possible. Redistricting takes place every ten years, after each population census.

registration The practice of placing citizens' names on an official list of voters before they are eligible to exercise their right to vote.

regulation A term that refers to government restrictions on the economic practices of private firms.

regulatory agencies Administrative units, such as the Federal Communications Commission and the Environmental Protection Agency, that have responsibility for the monitoring and regulation of ongoing economic activities.

representation function The responsibility of a legislature to represent various interests in society. (See also **lawmaking function; oversight function.**)

representative government A government in which the people govern through the selection of their representatives.

republic A form of government in which the people's representatives decide policy through institutions structured in ways that foster deliberation, slow the progress of decision making, and operate within restraints that protect individual liberty. To the framers, the Constitution's separation of powers and other limits on power were defining features of a republican form of government, as opposed to a democratic form, which places no limits on the majority.

reserved powers The powers granted to the states under the Tenth Amendment to the Constitution.

right of privacy A right implied by the freedoms in the Bill of Rights that grants individuals a degree of personal privacy upon which government cannot lawfully intrude. The right gives individuals a level of free choice in areas such as reproduction and intimate relations.

sample In a public opinion poll, the relatively small number of individuals who are interviewed for the purpose of estimating the opinions of an entire population. (See also **public opinion poll.**)

sampling error A measure of the accuracy of a public opinion poll; mainly a function of sample size and usually expressed in percentage terms.

selective incorporation The process by which certain of the rights (for example, freedom of speech) contained in the Bill of Rights become applicable through the Fourteenth Amendment to actions by the state governments.

self-government The principle that the people are the ultimate source and proper beneficiary of governing authority; in practice, a government based on majority rule.

Senior Executive Service (SES) Top-level career civil servants who qualify through a competitive process to receive higher salaries than their peers but who can be assigned or transferred by order of the president.

seniority A member of Congress's consecutive years of service on a particular committee.

separated institutions sharing power The principle that, as a way to limit government, its powers should be divided among separate branches, each of which also shares in the power of the others as a means of checking and balancing them. The result is that no one branch can exercise power decisively without the support or acquiescence of the others.

separation of powers The division of the powers of government among separate institutions or branches.

service strategy Use of personal staff by members of Congress to perform services for constituents in order to gain their support in future elections.

signaling (signaler) function The responsibility of the media to alert the public to important developments as soon as possible after they happen or are discovered. (See also **common-carrier function; partisan function; watchdog function.**)

single-member districts The form of representation in which only the candidate who gets the most votes in a district wins office. (See also **proportional representation system.**)

slander Spoken falsehoods that damage a person's reputation.

small-state plan See **New Jersey (small-state) Plan.**

social capital The sum of the face-to-face interactions among citizens in a society.

social contract A voluntary agreement by individuals to form a government that is then obligated to work within the confines of that agreement.

social insurance Social welfare programs are based on the "insurance" concept, requiring that individuals pay into the program in order to be eligible to receive funds from it. An example is social security for retired people. (See also **public assistance.**)

social (political) movements Active and sustained efforts to achieve social and political change by groups of people who feel that government has not been properly responsive to their concerns.

sovereignty The supreme (or ultimate) authority to govern within a certain geographical area.

spoils system The practice of granting public office to individuals in return for political favors they have rendered. (See also **patronage system.**)

standing committees Permanent congressional committees with responsibility for a particular area of public policy. An example is the Senate Foreign Relations Committee.

stewardship theory A theory that argues for a strong, assertive presidential role, with presidential authority limited only at points specifically prohibited by law. (See also **Whig theory.**)

strict-scrutiny test A test applied by courts to laws that attempt a racial or an ethnic classification. In effect, the strict-scrutiny test eliminates race or ethnicity as legal classification when it places minority-group members at a disadvantage. (See also **suspect classifications.**)

suffrage The right to vote.

super PACs Election committees that are unrestricted in their fund raising and spending as long as they do not coordinate their campaign efforts with that of a candidate.

supply-side economics A form of fiscal policy that emphasizes "supply" (production). An example of supply-side economics would be a tax cut for business. (See also **demand-side economics; fiscal policy.**)

supremacy clause Article VI of the Constitution, which makes national law supreme over state law when the national government is acting within its constitutional limits.

suspect classifications Legal classifications, such as race and national origin, that have invidious discrimination as their purpose and therefore are unconstitutional. (See also **strict-scrutiny test.**)

symbolic speech Action (for example, the waving or burning of a flag) for the purpose of expressing a political opinion.

tariffs The taxes that a country levies on goods shipped into it from other countries.

Three-Fifths Compromise A compromise worked out at the 1787 convention between northern states and southern states. Each slave was to be counted as three-fifths of a person for purposes of federal taxation and congressional apportionment (number of seats in the House of Representative).

transnational terrorism Terrorism that transcends national borders and often targets people and locations other than the ones directly at issue.

trustees Elected representatives whose obligation is to act in accordance with their own consciences as to what policies are in the best interests of the public. (See also **delegates.**)

two-party system A system in which only two political parties have a real chance of acquiring control of the government.

tyranny of the majority The potential of a majority to monopolize power for its own gain and to the detriment of minority rights and interests.

unilateralism The situation in which one nation takes action against another state or states.

unipolar (power structure) A power structure dominated by a single powerful actor, as in the case of the United States after the collapse of the Soviet Union.

unitary system A governmental system in which the national government alone has sovereign (ultimate) authority. (See also **confederacy; federalism.**)

unit rule The rule that grants all of a state's electoral votes to the candidate who receives most of the popular votes in the state.

veto The president's rejection of a bill, thereby keeping it from becoming law unless Congress overrides the veto.

Virginia (large-state) Plan A constitutional proposal for a strong Congress with two chambers, both of which would be based on numerical representation, thus granting more power to the larger states.

voter turnout The proportion of persons of voting age who actually vote in a given election.

watchdog function The accepted responsibility of the media to protect the public from incompetent or corrupt officials by standing ready to expose any official who violates accepted legal, ethical, or performance standards. (See also **common-carrier function; partisan function; signaling (signaler) function.**)

Whig theory A theory that prevailed in the nineteenth century and held that the presidency was a limited or restrained office whose occupant was confined to expressly granted constitutional authority. (See also **stewardship theory.**)

whistleblowing An internal check on the bureaucracy whereby employees report instances of mismanagement that they observe.

White House Office (WHO) A subunit of the Executive Office of the President, the White House Office is the core of the presidential staff system in that it includes the president's closest and most trusted personal advisors.

writ of certiorari Permission granted by a higher court to allow a losing party in a legal case to bring the case before it for a ruling; when such a writ is requested of the U.S. Supreme Court, four of the Court's nine justices must agree to accept the case before it is granted certiorari.

NOTES

CHAPTER ONE

[1]John Stuart Mill, *On Liberty*, eds. Michael B. Mathias and Daniel Kolak (New York: Longman, 2006), 43.

[2]PIPA/Knowledge Networks Poll, "Misperceptions, the Media, and the Iraq War," Center on Policy Attitudes and the Center for International Security Studies, University of Maryland, October 2, 2003.

[3]This misperception persisted even into 2004 as an October 2004 Harris poll discovered.

[4]Ibid.

[5]Walter Lippmann, *Public Opinion* (New York: Free Press, 1997), 82.

[6]Bruce Ackerman and James Fishkin, *Deliberation Day* (New Haven, Conn.: Yale University Press, 2004), 5.

[7]"Take the Quiz: What We Don't Know," *Newsweek*, March 20, 2011.

[8]Clay Ramsey, Steven Kull, Evan Lewis, and Stefan Subias, "Misinformation and the 2010 Election: A Study of the US Electorate," The Program on International Policy Attitudes, University of Maryland, College Park, Maryland, December 10, 2010, pp. 20–23.

[9]Mark Bauerlein, *The Dumbest Generation* (New York: Penguin, 2008), 28.

[10]Mill, *On Liberty*, 224.

[11]James David Barber, "Characters in the Campaign," in James David Barber, ed. *Race for the Presidency* (Englewood Cliffs, N.J.: Prentice-Hall, 1978), 181.

[12]See, for example, Doris A. Graber, *Processing the News: How People Tame the Information Tide*, 2d ed. (New York: Longman, 1988), 107–15.

[13]Pew Internet and American Life survey, March 1, 2010.

[14]Ellen Hume, "Talk Show Culture," Web posting, 2009.

[15]Ramsey et al., "Misinformation and the 2010 Election," 13.

[16]See Bryant Welch, *State of Confusion: Political Manipulation and the Assault on the American Mind* (New York: Thomas Dunne Books, 2008).

[17]Martha Joynt Kumar, *Managing the President's Message* (Baltimore, Md.: Johns Hopkins University Press, 2007).

[18]Thomas E. Patterson, *News and Democracy; The Need for Knowledge-Based Journalism* (New York: Vintage, 2013).

[19]Marvin Kalb, "The Rise of the 'New News,'" Discussion Paper D-34, Joan Shorenstein Center on the Press, Politics, and Public Policy, John F. Kennedy School of Government, Harvard University, October 1998.

[20]Todd K. Hartman and Christopher R. Weber, "Who Said What? The Effects of Source Cues in Issue Frames." *Political Behavior* 31 (2009): 537–58.

[21]Diana Mutz, *Hearing the Other Side: Deliberative versus Participatory Democracy* (New York: Cambridge University Press, 2006).

[22]Mill, *On Liberty*, 35.

[23]Intercollegiate Studies Association, "Greater Civic Knowledge Trumps a College Degree as the Leading Factor in Encouraging Active Civic Engagement," online report, 2011.

[24]See Michael Foley, *American Credo: The Place of Ideas in American Politics* (New York: Oxford University Press, 2007).

[25]James Bryce, *The American Commonwealth*, vol. 2 (New York: Macmillan, 1960), 247–54. First published in 1900.

[26]Bryce, *The American Commonwealth*, 132.

[27]Louis Hartz, *The Liberal Tradition in America* (New York: Harcourt, Brace, 1952), 12.

[28]Raymond T. Bond, ed., *The Man Who Was Chesterton* (Garden City, N.Y.: Image Books, 1960), 125.

[29]Alexis de Tocqueville, *Democracy in America, Volume 2* (New York: Vintage Classics), 89.

[30]William Watts and Lloyd A. Free, eds., *The State of the Nation* (New York: University Books, Potomac Associates, 1967), 97.

[31]Bryce, *The American Commonwealth*, 182.

[32]U.S. Census Bureau figures, 2012.

[33]Quoted in Ralph Volney Harlow, *The Growth of the United States*, vol. 2 (New York: Henry Holt, 1943), 497.

[34]*Tinker v. Colwell*, 193 U.S. 473 (1904).

[35]David Herbert Donald, *Lincoln* (New York: Simon & Schuster, 1996), 406.

[36]Martin Luther King Jr., Speech at Civil Rights March on Washington, August 28, 1963.

[37]Theodore H. White, "The American Idea," *The New York Times*, August 3, 1986.

[38]Harold D. Lasswell, *Politics: Who Gets What, When, How* (New York: McGraw-Hill, 1936).

[39]Russell Hardin, *Liberalism, Constitutionalism, and Democracy* (New York: Oxford University Press, 1999).

[40]Foucault's phrasing was a deliberate inversion of von Clausewitz's famous line, "War is politics by other means." Foucault is not the only writer who has applied this inversion.

[41]Bin Liang and Hong Lu, "Internet Development, Censorship, and Cyber Crimes in China," *Journal of Contemporary Criminal Justice* (26) 2010: 103–120.

[42]Adam Przworski and José María Maravall, eds., *Democracy and the Rule of Law* (New York: Cambridge University Press, 2003).

[43]See Robert Dahl, *On Democracy* (New Haven, Conn.: Yale University Press, 2000).

[44]See Paul Steinhauser, "Poll: U.S. Split over Afghan Troop Buildup," CNN online, November 24, 2009.

[45]Seymour Martin Lipset, *American Exceptionalism: A Double-Edged Sword* (New York: W. W. Norton: 1996), 37.

[46]*Gideon v. Wainwright*, 372 U.S. 335 (1963).

[47]Figures based on American Bar Association and Council of European Lawyers data as of 2007.

[48]James Q. Wilson, "American Exceptionalism," AEI Online, August 29, 2006, 9.

[49]Figures are for 2008.

[50]See William G. Domhoff, *Who Rules America? Challenges to Corporate and Class Dominance*, 6th ed. (New York: McGraw-Hill, 2009).

[51]C. Wright Mills, *The Power Elite* (New York: Oxford University Press, 1965).

[52]See Joseph A. Schumpeter, *Capitalism, Socialism and Democracy* (New York: Harper, 1975).

[53]E. E. Schattschneider, *Two Hundred Million Americans in Search of a Government* (New York: Holt, Reinhart and Winston, 1969), 42.

CHAPTER TWO

[1]Quoted in Charles S. Hyneman, "Republican Government in America," in George J. Graham Jr. and Scarlett G. Graham, eds., *Founding Principles of American Government*, rev. ed. (Chatham, N.J.: Chatham House, 1984), 19.

[2]See John Harmon McElroy, *American Beliefs: What Keeps a Big Country and a Diverse People United* (Chicago: I. R. Dee, 1999).

[3]See Russell Hardin, *Liberalism, Constitutionalism, and Democracy* (New York: Oxford University Press, 1999); A. John Simmons, *The Lockean Theory of Rights* (Princeton, N.J.: Princeton University Press, 1994).

[4]Thomas Hobbes, *Leviathan* (1651).

[5]John Locke, *Second Treatise on Civil Government* (1690).

[6]Quoted in "The Constitution and Slavery," Digital History website, December 1, 2003.

[7]Gaillard Hunt, ed., *The Writings of James Madison* (New York: Putnam, 1904), 274; see also Garret Ward Sheldon, *The Political Philosophy of James Madison* (Baltimore, Md.: Johns Hopkins University Press, 2000).

[8]See Vincent Ostrom, *The Political Theory of a Compound Republic: Designing the American Experiment* (Lanham, Md.: Lexington Books, 2007).

[9]See *Federalist* Nos. 47 and 48.

[10]Richard Neustadt, *Presidential Power* (New York: Macmillan, 1986), 33.

[11]Henry J. Abraham, *The Judicial Process*, 6th ed. (New York: Oxford University Press, 1993), 320–22.

[12]*Marbury v. Madison*, 1 Cranch 137 (1803).

[13]Martin Diamond, *The Founding of the Democratic Republic* (Itasca, Ill.: Peacock, 1981), 62–71.

[14]*Federalist* No. 10.

[15]Leslie F. Goldstein, "Judicial Review and Democratic Theory: Guardian Democracy vs. Representative Democracy," *Western Political Quarterly* 40 (1987): 391–412.

[16]See Douglas Bradburn, *The Citizenship Revolution: Politics and the Creation of the American Union 1774–1804* (Charlottesville: University of Virginia Press, 2009).

[17]Benjamin Ginsberg, *The Consequences of Consent* (New York: Random House, 1982), 22.

[18]Robert Dahl, *Pluralist Democracy in the United States* (Chicago: Rand McNally, 1967), 92.

[19]This interpretation is taken from Walter Lippmann, *Public Opinion* (New York: Free Press, 1965), 178–79.

[20]Michael McGeer, *A Fierce Discontent: The Rise and Fall of the Progressive Movement in*

America, 1870–1920 (New York: Free Press, 2005).

²¹Charles S. Beard, *An Economic Interpretation of the Constitution* (New York: Macmillan, 1941). First published in 1913.

²²John M. Scheb and John M. Scheb II, *Introduction to the American Legal System* (Clifton Park, N.Y.: Delmar Cengage Learning System, 2001), 6.

²³See Randall G. Holcombe, *From Liberty to Democracy* (Ann Arbor: University of Michigan Press, 2002).

CHAPTER THREE

¹Woodrow Wilson, *Constitutional Government in the United States* (New York: Columbia University Press, 1908), 173.

²*National Federation of Independent Business v. Sebelius*, No. 11-393 (2012).

³See Samuel Beer, *To Make a Nation: The Rediscovery of American Federalism* (Cambridge, Mass.: The Belknap Press of Harvard University, 1993).

⁴*Antifederalist* No. 9. This essay appeared in the *Independent Gazetteer* on October 17, 1787, under the pen name "Montezuma."

⁵Alison L. LaCroix, *The Ideological Origins of American Federalism* (Cambridge, Mass.: Harvard University Press, 2010).

⁶*McCulloch v. Maryland*, 4 Wheaton 316 (1819).

⁷*Gibbons v. Ogden*, 22 Wheaton 1 (1824). [22 U.S. 1 (1824)].

⁸Oliver Wendell Holmes Jr., *Collected Legal Papers* (New York: Harcourt, Brace, 1920), 295–96.

⁹See John C. Calhoun, *The Works of John C. Calhoun* (New York: Russell & Russell, 1968).

¹⁰*Dred Scott v. Sanford*, 19 Howard 393 (1857).

¹¹*U.S. v. Cruikshank*, 92 U.S. 452 (1876).

¹²*Slaughter-House Cases*, 16 Wallace 36 (1873); *Civil Rights Cases*, 109 U.S. 3 (1883).

¹³*Plessy v. Ferguson*, 163 U.S. 537 (1896).

¹⁴See, for example, Douglas A. Blackmon, *Slavery by Another Name: The Re-Enslavement of Black America from the Civil War to World War II* (New York: Anchor Books, 2009).

¹⁵*Santa Clara County v. Southern Pacific Railroad Co.*, 118 U.S. 394 (1886).

¹⁶*U.S. v. E. C. Knight Co.*, 156 U.S. 1 (1895).

¹⁷*Hammer v. Dagenhart*, 247 U.S. 251 (1918).

¹⁸*Lochner v. New York*, 198 U.S. 25 (1905).

¹⁹Alfred H. Kelly, Winifred A. Harbison, and Herman Belz, *The American Constitution*, 7th ed. (New York: Norton, 1991), 529; but also see Kimberley Johnson, *Governing the American State: Congress and the New Federalism, 1877–1929* (Princeton, N.J.: Princeton University Press, 2006).

²⁰James E. Anderson, *The Emergence of the Modern Regulatory State* (Washington, D.C.: Public Affairs Press, 1962), 2–3.

²¹*Schechter Poultry Corp. v. United States*, 295 U.S. 495 (1935).

²²*NLRB v. Jones and Laughlin Steel*, 301 U.S. 1 (1937).

²³*American Power and Light v. Securities and Exchange Commission*, 329 U.S. 90 (1946).

²⁴Louis Fisher, *American Constitutional Law*, 6th ed. (Durham, N.C.: Carolina Academic Press, 2005), 390.

²⁵*North American Company v. Securities and Exchange Commission*, 327 U.S. 686 (1946).

²⁶*Brown v. Board of Education*, 347 U.S. 483 (1954).

²⁷See Thomas Anton, *American Federalism and Public Policy* (Philadelphia: Temple University Press, 1989).

²⁸Morton Grodzins, *The American System: A New View of Government in the United States* (Chicago: Rand McNally, 1966).

²⁹John D. Nugent, *Safeguarding Federalism: How States Protect Their Interests in National Policymaking* (Norman: University of Oklahoma Press, 2009).

³⁰Rosella Levaggi, *Fiscal Federalism and Grants-in-Aid* (Brookfield, Vt.: Avebury, 1991).

³¹Beth Fouhy, "GOP Governors Press Congress to Pass Stimulus Bill," Associated Press wire story, January 31, 2009.

³²Timothy J. Conlan, *From New Federalism to Devolution* (Washington, D.C.: Brookings Institution, 1998).

³³*Garcia v. San Antonio Authority*, 469 U.S. 528 (1985).

³⁴See Tinsley E. Yarbrough, *The Rehnquist Court and the Constitution* (New York: Oxford University Press, 2000); David L. Hudson, *The Rehnquist Court: Understanding Its Impact and Legacy* (Westport, Conn.: Praeger, 2006).

³⁵*United States v. Lopez*, 514 U.S. 549 (1995).

³⁶*Kimel v. Florida Board of Regents*, 528 U.S. 62 (2000).

[37]Andrew W. Dobelstein, *Politics, Economics, and Public Welfare* (Englewood Cliffs, N.J.: Prentice-Hall, 1980), 5.

[38]Lloyd A. Free and Hadley Cantril, *The Political Beliefs of Americans* (New York: Simon & Schuster, 1968), 21.

[39]Survey for the Times Mirror Center for the People and the Press by Princeton Survey Research Associates, July 12–27, 1994.

CHAPTER FOUR

[1]Julian P. Boyd, ed., *The Papers of Thomas Jefferson*, vol. 12 (Princeton, N.J.: Princeton University Press, 1955), 440.

[2]*United States v. Jones*, No. 10-1250 (2012).

[3]*Barron v. Baltimore*, 32 U.S. (7 Pet.) 243 (1833).

[4]*Gitlow v. New York*, 268 U.S. 652 (1925).

[5]*Fiske v. Kansas*, 274 U.S. 30 (1927); *Near v. Minnesota*, 283 U.S. 697 (1931); *Hamilton v. Regents, U. of California*, 293 U.S. 245 (1934); *DeJonge v. Oregon*, 299 U.S. 253 (1937).

[6]*Near v. Minnesota*, 283 U.S. 697 (1931).

[7]*Mapp v. Ohio*, 367 U.S. 643 (1961).

[8]*Gideon v. Wainright*, 372 U.S. 335 (1963)

[9]*Malloy v. Hogan*, 378 U.S. 1 (1964).

[10]*Miranda v. Arizona*, 384 U.S. 436 (1966); see also *Escobedo v. Illinois*, 378 U.S. 478 (1964).

[11]*Pointer v. Texas*, 380 U.S. 400 (1965).

[12]*Klopfer v. North Carolina*, 386 U.S. 213 (1967).

[13]*Duncan v. Louisiana*, 391 U.S. 145 (1968).

[14]*Benton v. Maryland*, 395 U.S. 784 (1969).

[15]*Schenck v. United States*, 249 U.S. 47 (1919).

[16]*Dennis v. United States*, 341 U.S. 494 (1951); for a broad look at the relationship between issues of national security and liberty, see Geoffrey Stone, *War and Liberty: An American Dilemma: 1790 to the Present* (New York: W. W. Norton, 2007).

[17]See, for example, *Yates v. United States*, 354 U.S. 298 (1957); *Noto v. United States*, 367 U.S. 290 (1961); *Scales v. United States*, 367 U.S. 203 (1961).

[18]*Brandenburg v. Ohio*, 395 U.S. 444 (1969).

[19]*R.A.V. v. St. Paul*, No. 90-7675 (1992).

[20]*Wisconsin v. Mitchell*, No. 92-515 (1993).

[21]*Snyder v. Phelps*, No. 09-7571 (2011)

[22] *McCullen v. Coakley*, No. 12-1168 (2014).

[23]*Texas v. Johnson*, 109 S. Ct. 2544 (1989).

[24]*National Socialist Party v. Skokie*, 432 U.S. 43 (1977).

[25]*Forsyth County v. Nationalist Movement*, No. 91-538 (1992).

[26]*New York Times Co. v. United States*, 403 U.S. 713 (1971).

[27]*Nebraska Press Assn. v. Stuart*, 427 U.S. 539 (1976).

[28]*Milkovich v. Lorain Journal*, 497 U.S. 1 (1990); see also *Masson v. The New Yorker*, No. 89-1799 (1991).

[29]*New York Times Co. v. Sullivan*, 376 U.S. 254 (1964).

[30]*Engel v. Vitale*, 370 U.S. 421 (1962).

[31]*Abington School District v. Schempp*, 374 U.S. 203 (1963).

[32]*Wallace v. Jaffree*, 472 U.S. 38 (1985).

[33]*Town of Greece v. Galloway*, No. 12-698 (2014).

[34]*Van Orden v. Perry*, No. 03-1500 (2005).

[35]*McCreary County v. American Civil Liberties Union*, No. 03-1693 (2005).

[36]*Lemon v. Kurtzman*, 403 U.S. 602 (1971).

[37]*Board of Regents v. Allen*, 392 U.S. 236 (1968).

[38]*Zelman v. Simmons-Harris*, No. 00-1751 (2002); see also *Locke v. Davey*, No. 02-1315 (2004).

[39]*Burwell v. Hobby Lobby Stores*, No. 13-354 (2014).

[40]*Edwards v. Aguillard*, 487 U.S. 578 (1987).

[41]*District of Columbia v. Heller*, 554 U.S. 570 (2008).

[42]*McDonald v. Chicago*, 561 U.S. 3025 (2010).

[43]*Griswold v. Connecticut*, 381 U.S. 479 (1965); for an assessment of the Ninth Amendment, see Daniel A. Farber, *Retained by the People: The "Silent" Ninth Amendment and the Constitutional Rights Americans Don't Know They Have* (New York: Basic Books, 2007).

[44]*Roe v. Wade*, 401 U.S. 113 (1973).

[45]*Webster v. Reproductive Health Services*, 492 U.S. 490 (1989); see also *Rust v. Sullivan*, No. 89-1391 (1991).

[46]*Planned Parenthood v. Casey*, No. 91-744 (1992).

[47]*Gonzalez v. Carhart*, No. 05-380 (2007).

[48]*Bowers v. Hardwick*, 478 U.S. 186 (1986).

[49]*Lawrence v. Texas*, 539 U.S. 558 (2003).

[50]*McNabb v. United States*, 318 U.S. 332 (1943).

[51]The structure and content of the discussion that follows on arrest, search, interrogation,

formal charge, trial, appeal, and punishment is informed by Walter F. Murphy and Michael N. Danielson, *Robert K. Carr and Marver H. Bernstein's American Democracy* (Hinsdale, Ill.: Dryden Press, 1977), 465–74.

[52]David Fellman, *The Defendant's Rights Today* (Madison: University of Wisconsin Press, 1979), 256.

[53]*Kyllo v. United States*, No. 99-8508 (2001). 533 U.S. 27 (2010).

[54]*Riley v. California*, No. 13-132 (2014); *United States v. Wurie*, 13-132 (2014).

[55]*Maryland v. King*, 12-207 (2013).

[56]*Board of Education of Independent School District No. 92 of Pottawatomie County v. Earls*, No. 01-332 (2002).

[57]*Michigan v. Sitz*, No. 88-1897 (1990).

[58]*Indianapolis v. Edmund*, No. 99-1030 (2001).

[59]*Dickerson v. United States*, No. 99-5525 (2000), reaffirming *Miranda v. Arizona*, 384 U.S. 436 (1966).

[60]*Missouri v. Siebert*, 542 U.S. 600 (2004).

[61]*Berghuis v. Thompkins*, No. 08-1470 (2010).

[62]*Johnson v. Zerbst*, 304 U.S. 458 (1938).

[63]*Gideon v. Wainwright*, 372 U.S. 335 (1963).

[64]*Batson v. Kentucky*, 476 U.S. 79 (1986).

[65]*Witherspoon v. Illinois*, 391 U.S. 510 (1968).

[66]*Weeks v. United States*, 232 U.S. 383 (1914).

[67]*United States v. Leon*, 468 U.S. 897 (1984).

[68]*Nix v. Williams*, 467 U.S. 431 (1984).

[69]*Whren v. United States*, 517 U.S. 806 (1996).

[70]*Horton v. California*, 496 U.S. 128 (1990).

[71]*Lockyer v. Andrade*, No. 01-1127 (2003); see also *Ewing v. California*, No. 01-6978 (2003).

[72]*Atkins v. Virginia*, No. 01-8452 (2002).

[73]*Hall v. Florida*, No 12-10882 (2014).

[74]*Roper v. Simmons*, No. 03-633 (2005).

[75]*Graham v. Florida*, No. 08-7412 (2010).

[76]*Townsend v. Sain*, 372 U.S. 293 (1963).

[77]*Felker v. Turpin*, No. 95-8836 (1996); but see *Stewart v. Martinez-Villareal*, No. 97-300 (1998).

[78]*Williams v. Taylor*, No. 99-6615 (2000).

[79]ACLU study, 1999. A 1999 report by the New Jersey Attorney General's Office revealed a similar pattern in that state.

[80]See Heather MacDonald, "Fighting Crime Where the Criminals Are," *The New York Times*, June 25, 2010.

[81]*Korematsu v. United States*, 323 U.S. 214 (1944).

[82]Case cited in Charles Lane, "In Terror War, 2nd Track for Suspects," *The Washington Post*, December 1, 2001, A1.

[83]*Rasul v. Bush*, No. 03-334 (2004); *al-Odah v. United States*, No. 03-343 (2004).

[84]*Hamdi v. Rumsfeld*, No. 03-6696 (2004); see also *Rumsfeld v. Padilla*, No. 03-1027 (2004).

[85]*Hamdan v. Rumsfeld*, No. 05-184 (2006).

[86]See Alpheus T. Mason, *The Supreme Court: Palladium of Freedom* (Ann Arbor: University of Michigan Press, 1962); see also Jeffrey Rosen, *The Most Democratic Branch: How the Courts Serve America* (New York: Oxford University Press, 2006).

CHAPTER FIVE

[1]Abraham Lincoln, "Speech on the Dred Scott Decision," Springfield, Illinois, June 26, 1857.

[2]*The Washington Post* wire story, May 14, 1991.

[3]Robert Nisbet, "Public Opinion versus Popular Opinion," *Public Interest* 41 (1975): 171.

[4]See, for example, Gloria J. Browne-Marshall, *Race, Law, and American Society: 1607 to Present* (New York: Routledge, 2007).

[5]*Plessy v. Ferguson*, 163 U.S. 537 (1896).

[6]Ada Lois Sipuel Fisher, Danney Gable, and Robert Henry, *A Matter of Black and White: The Autobiography of Ada Lois Sipuel Fisher* (Norman: University of Oklahoma Press, 1996).

[7]*Brown v. Board of Education of Topeka*, 347 U.S. 483 (1954).

[8]*Swann v. Charlotte-Mecklenburg County Board of Education*, 402 U.S. 1 (1971).

[9]Christopher Jencks and Meredith Phillips, eds., *The Black-White Test Score Gap* (Washington, D.C.: Brookings Institution, 1998).

[10]*Milliken v. Bradley*, 418 U.S. 717 (1974).

[11]*Board of Education of Oklahoma City v. Dowell*, 498 U.S. 237 (1991).

[12]*Parents Involved in Community Schools v. Seattle*, No. 05-908551 U.S. 701 (2007); *Meredith, Custodial Parent and Next Friend of McDonald v. Jefferson County Board of Education*, No. 05-915548 U.S. 938 (2007).

[13]U.S. Department of Education statistics, 2010.

[14]*Loving v. Virginia*, 388 U.S. 1 (1967).

[15] *Craig v. Boren*, 429 U.S. 190 (1976).

[16]*Rostker v. Goldberg*, 453 U.S. 57 (1980).

[17]*United States v. Virginia*, 518 U.S. 515 (1996), No. 94-1941 (1996).

[18]Blackmon, *Slavery by Another Name*.

[19]Eric J. Sundquist, *King's Dream: The Legacy of Martin Luther King's "I Have a Dream" Speech* (New Haven, Conn.: Yale University Press, 2009).

[20]See Kathleen S. Sullivan, *Women and Rights Discourse in Nineteenth-Century America* (Baltimore, Md.: Johns Hopkins University Press, 2007).

[21]*Tinker v. Colwell*, 193 U.S. 473 (1904).

[22]See Jane Mansbridge, *Why We Lost the ERA* (Chicago: University of Chicago Press, 1986).

[23]Marshall Gazn, *Why David Sometimes Wins: Leadership, Organization and Strategy in the California Farm Worker Movement* (New York: Oxford University Press, 2009).

[24]*Lau v. Nichols*, 414 U.S. 563 (1974).

[25]Michael J. Klarman, *From Jim Crow to Civil Rights: The Supreme Court and the Struggle for Racial Equality* (New York: Oxford University Press, 2004), 236.

[26]*Smith v. Allwright*, 321 U.S. 649 (1944).

[27]*League of United Latin American Voters v. Perry*, 548 U. S. 399 (2006), No. 05-204 (2006).

[28]*28 Shelby County v. Holder*, No. 12-96 (2013).

[29]See Manny Fernandez, "Study Finds Disparities in Mortgages by Race," *The New York Times*, October 15, 2007; see also U.S. Conference of Mayors report, 1998; Survey by Federal Financial Institutions Examination Council, 1998.

[30]"Public Backs Affirmative Action, But Not Minority Preferences," Pew Research Center report, June 2, 2009, Web release.

[31]*University of California Regents v. Bakke*, 438 U.S. 265 (1978).

[32]*Fullilove v. Klutnick*, 448 U.S. 448 (1980).

[33]*Adarand v. Pena*, 515 U.S. 200 (1995).

[34]*Ricci v. DeStefano*, 557 U.S. 687 (2009).

[35]*Gratz v. Bollinger*, 539 U.S. 244 (2003).

[36]*Grutter v. Bollinger*, 539 U.S. 306 (2003).

[37]*Fisher v. University of Texas at Austin*, No. 11-345 (2012).

[38]*Schuette v. Coalition to Defend Affirmative Action*, No. 12-682 (2014).

[39]See, for example, Alejandro Del Carmen, *Racial Profiling in America* (Upper Saddle River, N.J.: Prentice-Hall, 2007).

[40]Data from U.S. Census Bureau and Centers for Disease Control and Prevention, 2010.

[41]Data from National Office of Drug Control Policy, 1997.

[42]Data from U.S. Department of Justice, 2010.

[43]See Keith Reeves, *Voting Hopes or Fears?* (New York: Oxford University Press, 1997); Tali Mendelberg, *The Race Card* (Princeton, N.J.: Princeton University Press, 2001).

[44]Jennifer L. Lawless and Richard L. Fox, *It Takes a Candidate: Why Women Don't Run for Office* (New York: Cambridge University Press, 2005).

[45]U.S. Department of Education, 2006.

[46]See Sara M. Evans and Barbara Nelson, *Wage Justice* (Chicago: University of Chicago Press, 1989).

[47]Eric C. Henson et al., *The State of the Native Nations: Conditions under U.S. Policies of Self-Determination* (New York: Oxford University Press, 2007).

[48]See David E. Wilkins, *American Indian Politics and the American Political System* (Lanham, Md.: Rowman & Littlefield, 2006).

[49]William Evans and Julie Topoleski, "The Social and Economic Impact of Native American Casinos," National Bureau of Economic Research, Working Paper No. 9198, September 2002, Cambridge, Massachusetts.

[50]W. Dale Mason, "Tribes and States: A New Era in Intergovernmental Affairs," *Publius* 28 (1998): 129.

[51]Data from U.S. Census Bureau, 2008; see also Daniel McCool, Susan M. Olson, and Jennifer L. Robinson, *Native Vote: American Indians, the Voting Rights Act, and the Right to Vote* (New York: Cambridge University Press, 2007).

[52]See Timothy P. Fong, *Contemporary Asian American Experience: Beyond the Model Minority* (Upper Saddle River, N.J.: Prentice-Hall, 2009).

[53]See Gordon Chang, ed., *Asian Americans and Politics* (Stanford, Calif.: Stanford University Press, 2001).

[54]See William N. Eskridge Jr., *Dishonorable Passions: Sodomy Laws in America, 1861–2003* (New York: Viking, 2008); Nancy D. Polikoff, *Beyond (Straight and Gay) Marriage: Valuing All Families under the Law* (Boston: Beacon Press, 2009); Craig A. Rimmerman and Clyde Wilcox, *The Politics of Same-Sex Marriage* (Chicago: University of Chicago Press, 2007).

[55]*Lawrence v. Texas*, 539 U.S. 558 (2003).

[56]The estimate was compiled by author in 2012 from multiple sources.

[57]*United States v. Windsor*, No. 12-307 (2013).

[58]*Kimel v. Florida Board of Regents*, No. 98-791528 U.S. 62 (2000); but see *CBOCS West, Inc. v. Humphries*, No. 06-1431553 U.S. 442 (2008).

[59]*Board of Trustees of the University of Alabama v. Garrett*, No. 99-1240 (2002); *Tennessee v. Lane*, No. 02-1667541 U.S. 509 (2004).

[60]Gunnar Myrdal, *An American Dilemma: The Negro Problem and Modern Democracy* (New York: Harper, 1944).

[61]See Joe R. Feagin, *The White Racial Frame: Centuries of Racial Framing and Counter-Framing* (New York: Routledge, 2009).

CHAPTER SIX

[1]James Bryce, *The American Commonwealth*, vol. 2 (Indianapolis, Ind.: Liberty Fund, 1995), 225. Frst published in 1888.

[2]Elisabeth Noelle-Neumann, *The Spiral of Silence*, 2d ed. (Chicago: University of Chicago Press, 1993), ch. 1.

[3]Herbert Hyman, *Political Socialization* (Glencoe, Ill.: Free Press, 1959), 51.

[4]M. Kent Jennings and Richard G. Niemi, *Generations and Politics* (Princeton, N.J.: Princeton University Press, 1981).

[5]See Orit Ichilov, *Political Socialization, Citizenship Education, and Democracy* (New York: Teachers College Press, 1990).

[6]See, however, Dietram A. Scheufele, Matthew C. Nisbet, and Dominique Brossard, "Pathways to Political Participation: Religion, Communication Contexts, and Mass Media," *International Journal of Public Opinion Research* 15 (Autumn 2003): 300–324.

[7]Noelle-Neumann, *Spiral of Silence*.

[8]Walter Lippmann, *Public Opinion* (New York: Free Press, 1965), ch. 1.

[9]Thomas E. Patterson, *The Vanishing Voter* (New York: Knopf, 2003), 89–90.

[10]Jon Western, *Selling Intervention and War: The Presidency, the Media, and the American Public* (Baltimore, Md.: Johns Hopkins University Press, 2005); see also Wojtek Mackiewicz Wolfe, *Winning the War of Words: Selling the War on Terror from Afghanistan to Iraq* (Westport, Conn.: Praeger, 2008).

[11]See Angus Campbell, Philip Converse, Warren Miller, and Donald Stokes, *The American Voter* (New York: Wiley, 1960), chs. 3 and 4.

[12]Martin P. Wattenberg, *Where Have All the Voters Gone?* (Cambridge, Mass.: Harvard University Press, 2002).

[13]See, Sidney Kraus *Televised Presidential Debates and Public Policy* (New York: Routledge, 2000).

[14]Donald Green, Bradley Palmquist, and Eric Schickler, *Partisan Hearts and Minds* (New Haven, Conn.: Yale University Press, 2002).

[15]Daniel Bell, *The End of Ideology* (New York: Collier, 1961), 67.

[16]Daniel Boorstin, *The Genius of American Politics* (Chicago: University of Chicago Press, 1953).

[17]Kenneth D. Wald, *Religion and Politics in the United States* (Lanham, Md.: Rowman & Littlefield, 2003).

[18]Lois Duke Whitaker, ed., *Voting the Gender Gap* (Urbana: University of Illinois Press, 2008).

[19]Los Angeles Times poll, November 2011.

[20]Cass Sunstein, *Republic.com 2.0* (Princeton, N.J.: Princeton University Press, 2007).

[21]See, for example, Dean R. Hoge and Teresa L. Ankney, "Occupations and Attitudes of Student Activists Ten Years Later," *Journal of Youth and Adolescence* 11 (1982): 365.

[22]See Herbert Asher, *Polling and the Public*, 7th ed. (Washington, D.C.: CQ Press, 2007).

[23]Political Arithmetic, May 31, 2007; see at http://politicalarithmetik.blogspot.com/2007/05/support-for-death-penalty-and-question.html.

[24]Robert J. Samuelson, "What If We're to Blame? Public Opinion and Muddled Policies," *The Washington Post*, November 1, 2006.

[25]"Study Finds Widespread Misperceptions on Iraq Highly Related to Support for War,"

Program on International Policy Attitudes, School of Public Affairs, University of Maryland, October 2, 2003; see at www.pipa.org/OnlineReports/Iraq/IraqMedia_Oct03/IraqMedia_Oct03_pr.pdf.

[26]Joshua Buntin III, "Start with Civics 101," *Miami Herald*, January 21, 2008, 25A.

[27]Survey of students of the eight Ivy League schools by Luntz & Weber Research and Strategic Services, for the University of Pennsylvania's Ivy League Study, November 13–December 1, 1992.

[28]See R. Michael Alvarez and John Brehm, *Hard Choices, Easy Answers* (Princeton, N.J.: Princeton University Press, 2002); see also Samuel L. Popkin, *The Reasoning Voter* (Chicago: University of Chicago Press, 1991).

[29]Robert S. Erikson, Michael B. MacKuen, and James A. Stimson, *The Macro Polity* (New York: Cambridge University Press, 2008), xxi.

[30]V. O. Key Jr., *Public Opinion and American Democracy* (New York: Alfred A. Knopf, 1964).

[31]Benjamin I. Page and Robert Y. Shapiro, "Effects of Public Opinion on Policy," *American Political Science Review* 77 (March 1983): 178; see also Richard Sobel, *The Impact of Public Opinion on U.S. Foreign Policy* (New York: Oxford University Press, 2001); James Stimson, *Tides of Consent: How Public Opinion Shapes American Politics* (New York: Cambridge University Press, 2004).

[32]John W. Kingdon, *Agendas, Alternatives, and Public Policies*, 2d ed. (New York: Longman, 2003), 148–49.

[33]Jeff Manza and Fay Lomax Cook, "A Democratic Polity: Three Views of Policy Responsiveness to Public Opinion in the United States," *American Politics Research* 30 (2002): 630–67.

[34]Vincent Hutchings, *Public Opinion and Democratic Accountability: How Citizens Learn about Politics* (Princeton, N.J.: Princeton University Press, 2005).

[35]See, for example, Sidney Verba and Norman H. Nie, *Participation in America: Political Democracy and Social Equality* (New York: Harper & Row, 1972), 332.

[36]Robert D. Benford and David A. Snow, "Framing Processes and Social Movements," *Annual Review of Sociology* 40 (2000): 611–39.

[37]Scott McClellan, *What Happened: Inside the Bush White House and Washington's Culture of Deception* (New York: Public Affairs, 2008).

[38]See William Domhoff, *Who Rules America?* 5th ed. (New York: McGraw-Hill, 2005).

[39]Noam Chomsky and Edward S. Herman, *Manufacturing Consent: The Political Economy of the Mass Media* (New York: Pantheon, 2002).

[40]Page and Shapiro, "Effects of Public Opinion on Policy," 189.

[41]Erikson et al., *The Macro Polity*, 314; James A. Stimson and Robert S. Erickson, "Dynamic Representation," *The American Political Science Review* 89 (1995): 543–65.

CHAPTER SEVEN

[1]Walter Lippmann, *Public Opinion* (New York: Free Press, 1965), 36.

[2]Quoted in Ralph Volney Harlow, *The Growth of the United States* (New York: Henry Holt, 1943), 312.

[3]Mark N. Franklin, *Voter Turnout and the Dynamics of Electoral Competition in Established Democracies since 1945* (New York: Cambridge University Press, 2004).

[4]Thomas E. Patterson, *The Vanishing Voter* (New York: Knopf, 2002), 134.

[5]Ibid.

[6]Russell Dalton, "The Myth of the Disengaged American," Web publication of the Comparative Study of Electoral Systems, October 2005, 2.

[7]Patterson, *Vanishing Voter*, 179–80.

[8]*Crawford et al. v. Marion County Election Board et al.*, No. 07-21 (2008).

[9]Ivor Crewe, "Electoral Participation," in David Butler, Howard R. Penniman, and Austin Ranney, eds., *Democracy at the Polls* (Washington, D.C.: American Enterprise Institute, 1981), 251–53.

[10]Richard Boyd, "Decline of U.S. Voter Turnout," *American Politics Quarterly* 9 (April 1981): 142.

[11]Larry Bartels, *Unequal Democracy: The Political Economy of the Gilded Age* (Princeton, N.J.: Princeton University Press, 2008).

[12]Patterson, *Vanishing Voter*, 135.

[13]David C. Leege, Kenneth D. Wald, Brian S. Krueger, and Paul D. Mueller, *The Politics of Cultural Differences* (Princeton, N.J.: Princeton University Press, 2002).

[14]Jose Antonio Vargas, "Obama Raised Half a Billion Online," http://washingtonpost.com, November 20, 2008, p. 1.

[15]Dalton, "Myth of the Disengaged American," 2.

[16]Robert Putnam, *Bowling Alone* (New York: Simon & Schuster, 2000); but see Cliff Zukin et al., *A New Engagement: Political Participation, Civic Life, and the Changing American Citizen* (New York: Oxford University Press, 2006).

[17]Russell J. Dalton, *The Good Citizen: How a Younger Generation Is Reshaping American Politics*, rev. ed. (Washington, D.C.: CQ Press, 2008).

[18]Mark Hugo Lopez, "Volunteering among Young People," Web-released report of The Center for Information & Research on Civic Learning and Engagement, School of Public Affairs, University of Maryland, College Park, Maryland. February 2004.

[19]See Benjamin Ginsberg, *The Consequences of Consent* (New York: Random House, 1982), ch. 2.

[20]See, for example, Charles J. Stewart, Craig Allen Smith, and Robert E. Denton Jr., *Persuasion and Social Movements*, 5th ed. (Long Grove, Ill.: Waveland Press, 2007).

[21]Dalton, *Citizen Politics*, 38.

[22]Pew Research Center poll, November 29, 2011.

[23]CBS News/New York Times poll, October 25, 2011.

[24]Public Policy Polling, November 16, 2011.

[25]William Watts and Lloyd A. Free, eds., *The State of the Nation* (New York: University Books, Potomac Associates, 1967), 97.

[26]Sidney Verba and Norman Nie, *Participation in America* (New York: Harper & Row, 1972), 131.

[27]Bartels, *Unequal Democracy*.

CHAPTER EIGHT

[1]E. E. Schattschneider, *Party Government* (New York: Rinehart, 1942), 1.

[2]See John Aldrich, *Why Parties? The Origin and Transformation of Political Parties in America* (Chicago: University of Chicago Press, 1995); L. Sandy Maisel, *American Political Parties and Elections* (New York: Oxford University Press, 2007).

[3]E. E. Schattschneider, *The Semisovereign People: A Realist's View of Democracy in America* (New York: Holt, Rinehart & Winston, 1961), 140.

[4]Thomas E. Patterson, *The Vanishing Voter* (New York: Knopf, 2002), ch. 2.

[5]See Richard P. McCormick, *The Second American Party System: Party Formation in the Jacksonian Era* (Chapel Hill: University of North Carolina Press, 1966).

[6]Alexis de Tocqueville, *Democracy in America (1835–1840)*, eds. J. P. Mayer and A. P. Kerr (Garden City, N.Y.: Doubleday/Anchor, 1969), 60.

[7]Aldrich, *Why Parties?* 151.

[8]Kristi Andersen, *The Creation of a Democratic Majority, 1928–1936* (Chicago: University of Chicago Press, 1979).

[9]See Kevin Phillips, *The Emerging Republican Majority* (New Rochelle, N.Y.: Arlington House, 1969).

[10]See Arthur C. Paulson, *Electoral Realignment and the Outlook for American Democracy* (Boston: Northeastern University Press, 2006).

[11]Lewis L. Gould, *Grand Old Party* (New York: Random House, 2003); but also see Jacob S. Hacker and Paul Pierson, *Off Center: The Republican Revolution and the Erosion of American Democracy* (New Haven, Conn.: Yale University Press, 2006).

[12]See John B. Judis and Ruy Teixeira, *The Emerging Democratic Majority* (New York: Scribner, 2002).

[13]See Duncan Black, "On the Rationale of Group Decision-Making," *Journal of Political Economy* 56 (1948): 23–24; Anthony Downs, *An Economic Theory of Democracy* (New York: HarperCollins, 1957).

[14]Mark Brewer, *Party Images in the Electorate* (New York: Routledge, 2008).

[15]Jeffrey M. Stonecash, *Political Parties Matter: Realignment and the Return of Partisan Voting* (Boulder, Colo.: Lynne Rienner Publishers, 2005).

[16]See Lois Duke Whitaker, ed., *Voting the Gender Gap* (Urbana: University of Illinois Press, 2008); Karen M. Kaufmann, "The Gender Gap," *PS: Political Science & Politics*, July 2006, pp. 447–53.

[17]John Green, Mark Rozell, and William Clyde Wilcox, eds., *The Christian Right in American Politics* (Washington, D.C.: Georgetown University Press, 2003).

[18]James G. Gimpel, "Latinos and the 2002 Election: Republicans Do Well When Latinos Stay Home," Center for Immigration Studies, University of Maryland, January 2003, Web download; see also Jorge Ramos,

The Latino Wave: How Hispanics Are Transforming Politics in America (New York: Harper Paperbacks, 2005); F. Chris Garcia and Gabriel Sanchez, *Hispanics and the U.S. Political System: Moving into the Mainstream* (Upper Saddle River, N.J.: Prentice-Hall, 2007).

[19]Micah L. Sifrey, *Spoiling for a Fight: Third-Party Politics in America* (New York: Routledge, 2003).

[20]Daniel A. Mazmanian, *Third Parties in Presidential Elections* (Washington, D.C.: Brookings Institution, 1984), 143–44.

[21]Lewis L. Gould, *Four Hats in the Ring: The 1912 Election and the Birth of Modern American Politics* (Lawrence: University Press of Kansas, 2008).

[22]See Lawrence Goodwyn, *The Populist Movement* (New York: Oxford University Press, 1978).

[23]See Anthony King, *Running Scared* (New York: Free Press, 1997); but see James E. Campbell, *The American Campaign: U.S. Presidential Campaigns and the National Vote* (College Station: Texas A&M Press, 2008).

[24]See Paul S. Herrnson and John C. Green, eds., *Responsible Partisanship* (Lawrence: University Press of Kansas, 2003).

[25]See Marjorie Randon Hershey, *Party Politics in America*, 13th ed. (New York: Longman, 2009).

[26]Joseph Napolitan, *The Election Game and How to Win It* (New York: Doubleday, 1972); for a contemporary look at the campaigning process, see D. Sunshine Hillygus and Todd G. Shields, *The Persuadable Voter: Wedge Issues in Presidential Campaigns* (Princeton, N.J.: Princeton University Press, 2008).

[27]Center for Responsive Politics data, 2012.

[28]David B. Magleby, J. Quin Monson, and Kelly D. Patterson, eds., *Dancing Without Partners: How Candidates, Parties and Interest Groups Interact in the New Campaign Finance Environment* (Provo, Utah: Brigham Young University Press, 2005).

[29]Lawrence R. Jacobs and Robert Y. Shapiro, *Politicians Don't Pander: Political Manipulation and the Loss of Democratic Responsiveness* (Chicago: University of Chicago Press, 2000).

[30]Emmett H. Buell Jr. and Lee Sigelman, *Attack Politics: Negativity in Presidential Campaigns since 1960* (Lawrence: University Press of Kansas, 2008). For opposing views on the effect of negative advertising, see Stephen Ansolabehere and Shanto Iyengar,

Going Negative (New York: Free Press, 1995); and John Geer, *In Defense of Negativity* (Chicago: University of Chicago Press, 2006).

[31]Darrell M. West, *Air Wars: Television Advertising in Election Campaigns, 1952–2004*, 4th ed. (Washington, D.C.: CQ Press, 2005), 140–46.

[32]See, for example, http://factcheck.org/2012/06/romneys-solar-flareout/.

[33]West, *Air Wars*, 12.

[34]Brad Lockerbie, *Do Voters Look to the Future?* (Albany: State University of New York Press, 2009).

CHAPTER NINE

[1]E. E. Schattschneider, *The Semisovereign People: A Realist's View of Democracy in America* (New York: Holt, Rinehart & Winston, 1960), 35.

[2]Anthony J. Nownes, *Total Lobbying: What Lobbyists Want (and How They Try to Get It)* (New York: Cambridge University Press, 2006).

[3]See Matthew J. Burbank, Ronald J. Hrebenar, and Robert C. Benedict, *Parties, Interest Groups, and Political Campaigns* (Boulder, Colo.: Paradigm Publishers, 2008).

[4]Alexis de Tocqueville, *Democracy in America (1835–1840)*, eds. J. P. Mayer and A. P. Kerr (Garden City, N.Y.: Doubleday/Anchor, 1969), bk. 2, ch. 4.

[5]Kay Lehman Schlozman and John T. Tierney, *Organized Interests and American Democracy* (New York: Harper & Row, 1986), 54; see also Jeffrey M. Berry and Clyde Wilcox, *The Interest Group Society*, 5th ed. (New York: Longman, 2008).

[6]E. Pendleton Herring, *Group Representation before Congress* (Washington, D.C.: Brookings Institution, 1929), 78.

[7]U.S. Bureau of Labor Statistics, 2011.

[8]See Jack L. Walker, *Mobilizing Interest Groups in America* (Ann Arbor: University of Michigan Press, 1991).

[9]Christopher J. Bosso, "The Color of Money: Environmental Groups and the Pathologies of Fund Raising," in Allan J. Cigler and Burdett Loomis, eds., *Interest Group Politics*, 4th ed. (Washington, D.C.: CQ Press, 1995), 101–3.

[10]See Nownes, *Total Lobbying*. The author is indebted to Professor Anthony Nownes of the University of Tennessee for the observations contained in this paragraph.

[11]Mancur Olson, *The Logic of Collective Action*, rev. ed. (Cambridge, Mass.: Harvard University Press, 1971), 64.

[12]Theda Skocpol, *Diminished Democracy* (Norman: University of Oklahoma Press, 2003).

[13]Olson, *Logic of Collective Action*, 147.

[14]Ibid.

[15]Jeffrey N. Birnbaum, "Washington's Power 25: Which Pressure Groups Are Best at Manipulating the Laws We Live By?" *Fortune*, December 8, 1997, Web copy.

[16]Frank R. Baumgartner, Jeffrey M. Berry, Marie Hojnacki, David C. Kimball, and Beth L. Leech, *Lobbying and Policy Change: Who Wins, Who Loses, and Why* (Chicago: University of Chicago Press, 2009).

[17]Norman J. Ornstein and Shirley Elder, *Interest Groups, Lobbying, and Policymaking* (Washington, D.C.: CQ Press, 1978), 82–86.

[18]See Paul S. Herrnson, Ronald G. Shaiko, and Clyde Wilcox, *The Interest Group Connection: Electioneering, Lobbying, and Policymaking in Washington*, 2d ed. (Washington, D.C.: CQ Press, 2004).

[19]Quoted in a *National Journal* excerpt in Thomas E. Patterson, *The American Democracy*, 9th ed. (New York: McGraw-Hill, 2009), 245b.

[20]See John Mark Hansen, *Gaining Access* (Chicago: Chicago University Press, 1991); Bruce Wolpe and Bertram Levine, *Lobbying Congress* (Washington, D.C.: CQ Press, 1996).

[21]Bara Vaida, "K-Street Paradox: $1.3 Million Per Hour," *The National Journal*, March 13, 2010.

[22]Quoted in Ornstein and Elder, *Interest Groups, Lobbying, and Policymaking*, 77.

[23]Steve Reinberg, "Debate Builds over Drug Companies' Fees to FDA," *The Washington Post*, April 13, 2007; see at www.washingtonpost.com/wp-dyn/content/article/2007/04/13/AR2007041301449.html.

[24]Paul J. Quirk, *Industry Influence in Federal Regulatory Agencies* (Princeton, N.J.: Princeton University Press, 1981); John E. Chubb, *Interest Groups and the Bureaucracy: The Politics of Energy* (Stanford, Calif.: Stanford University Press, 1983), 200–201.

[25]Lee Epstein and C. K. Rowland, "Interest Groups in the Courts," *American Political Science Review* 85 (1991): 205–17.

[26]Richard Davis, *Electing Justice: Fixing the Supreme Court Nomination Process* (New York: Oxford University Press, 2005).

[27]Hugh Heclo, "Issue Networks and the Executive Establishment," in Anthony King, ed., *The New American Political System* (Washington, D.C.: American Enterprise Institute, 1978), 87–124.

[28]Ornstein and Elder, *Interest Groups, Lobbying, and Policymaking*, 88–93.

[29]"Why the Lobbying Disclosure Act Needs to Be Broadened to Include Grass-Roots Lobbying," Posting on Congress Watch, a website of Public Citizen; see at www.cleanupwashington.org/policy/page.cfm?id=7861&SectionID=108&SubSecID=1009&SecID=1407.

[30]Quoted in Mark Green, "Political PAC-Man," *The New Republic*, December 13, 1982, 20; see also Richard Skinner, *More Than Money: Interest Group Action in Congressional Elections* (Lanham, Md.: Rowman & Littlefield, 2006); Mark J. Rozell, Clyde Wilcox, and David Madland, *Interest Groups in American Campaigns*, 2d ed. (Washington, D.C.: CQ Press, 2005).

[31]Quoted in Larry Sabato, *PAC Power: Inside the World of Political Action Committees* (New York: Norton, 1984), 72.

[32]*Citizens United v. Federal Election Commission*, 558 U.S. 50 (2010).

[33]Bernie Sanders, "Overturn Citizens United," *US News & World Report*, January 13, 2012; see at www.usnews.com/debate-club/are-super-pacs-harming-us-politics/overturn-citizens-united.

[34]Bradley Smith, "Super PACs Level the Playing Field," *US News & World Report*, January 13, 2012; see at www.usnews.com/debate-club/are-super-pacs-harming-us-politics/super-pacs-level-the-playing-field.

[35]Walker, *Mobilizing Interest Groups in America*, 112.

[36]Theodore J. Lowi, *The End of Liberalism: The Second Republic of the United States* (New York: Norton, 1979).

[37]Larry Bartels, *Unequal Democracy: The Political Economy of the New Gilded Age* (Princeton, N.J.: Princeton University Press, 2008).

CHAPTER TEN

[1]Theodore H. White, *The Making of the President, 1972* (New York: Bantam Books, 1973), 327.

[2]See Bill Kovach and Tom Rosenstiel, *The Elements of Journalism* (New York: Three Rivers Press, 2001).

[3]Robert Entman, "Framing: Towards Clarification of a Fractured Paradigm," in Denis McQuail, ed., *McQuail's Reader in Mass Communication Theory* (London: Sage Publications, 2002), 391–92.

[4]Thomas E. Patterson, *The Vanishing Voter* (New York: Knopf, 2002), 59.

[5]See Rodger Streitmatter, *Mightier Than the Sword: How the News Media Have Shaped American History* (Westport, Conn.: Praeger Publishers, 2008).

[6]Frank Luther Mott, *American Journalism, a History: 1690–1960* (New York: Macmillan, 1962), 114–15; see also Si Sheppard, *The Partisan Press: A History of Media Bias in the United States* (Jefferson, N.C.: McFarland, 2007).

[7]Edwin Emery, *The Press and America: An Interpretive History of the Mass Media* (Englewood Cliffs, N.J.: Prentice-Hall, 1977), 350.

[8]Quoted in Mott, *American Journalism*, 529.

[9]Quoted in David Halberstam, *The Powers That Be* (New York: Knopf, 1979), 208–9.

[10]Kathleen Hall Jamieson and Karlyn Kohrs Campbell, *The Interplay of Influence*, rev. ed. (Boston: Wadsworth, 2005), 4.

[11]Michael Schudson, "What Time Means in a News Story," Occasional Paper No. 4 (New York: Gannett Center for Media Studies, 1986), 8.

[12]Thomas E. Patterson, "Of Polls, Mountains: U.S. Journalists and Their Use of Election Surveys," *Public Opinion Quarterly* 69 (Special Issue 2005): 716–24.

[13]Donald Shaw and Maxwell McCombs, *The Emergence of American Political Issues: The Agenda-Setting Function of the Press* (St. Paul, Minn.: West Publishing, 1977).

[14]Bernard C. Cohen, *The Press and Foreign Policy* (Princeton, N.J.: Princeton University Press, 1963), 13.

[15]Thomas E. Patterson, *The American Democracy*, 5th ed. (New York: McGraw-Hill, 2001), 309–10.

[16]See Kathleen Hall Jamieson, *Eloquence in an Electronic Age* (New York: Oxford University Press, 1988), 42.

[17]Stephen J. Farnsworth and S. Robert Lichter, *The Mediated Presidency: Television News and Presidential Governance* (Lanham, Md.: Rowman & Littlefield, 2006).

[18]Kiku Adatto, "Sound Bite Democracy," Joan Shorenstein Center on the Press, Politics, and Public Policy, Research Paper R-2, Harvard University, June 1990.

[19]Center for Media and Public Affairs studies, available at: //www.cmpa.com/studies.

[20]Walter Lippmann, *Public Opinion* (New York: Free Press, 1965), 214. First published in 1922.

[21]See Mark Harmon, "Non-Presidential U.S. Newspaper Endorsements, 2002, 2004, 2006," paper presented at the annual meeting of the Midwest Political Science Association, Chicago, April 12, 2007.

[22]Bernard Goldberg, *Bias: A CBS Insider Exposes How the Media Distort News* (New York: Harper Paperbacks, 2003).

[23]David H. Weaver, Randal A. Beam, Bonnie J. Brownlee, Paul S. Voakes, and G. Cleveland Wilhoit, *The American Journalist in the 21st Century* (Mahwah, N.J.: LEA, 2006).

[24]David D'Alessio and Mike Allen, "Media Bias in Presidential Elections: A Meta-Analysis," *Journal of Communication* 50 (2000): 133–56.

[25]Center for Media and Public Affairs, Media Monitor, various dates.

[26]Michael Robinson, "Public Affairs Television and the Growth of Political Malaise," *American Political Science Review* 70 (1976): 409–32.

[27]Center for Media and Public Affairs, Media Monitor, various dates.

[28]Mark Rozell, "Press Coverage of Congress," in Thomas Mann and Norman Ornstein, eds., *Congress, the Press, and the Public* (Washington, D.C.: American Enterprise Institute and Brookings Institution, 1994), 109.

[29]Joseph N. Cappella and Kathleen Hall Jamieson, *Spiral of Cynicism* (New York: Oxford University Press, 1997), 159.

[30]Robinson, "Public Affairs Television and the Growth of Political Malaise."

[31]The press's negativity and sensationalism have had another effect as well; they have damaged the press's credibility. According to a 2007 survey conducted by the Center for Public Leadership at Harvard University's John F. Kennedy School of Government, the press has the lowest public confidence rating of any major U.S. institution.

[32]William Cole, ed., *The Most of A. J. Liebling* (New York: Simon, 1963), 7.

[33]See Kerbel, *Netroots;* Eric Boehlert, *Bloggers on the Bus* (New York: Free Press, 2010).
[34]Natalie Jomini Stroud, "Media Use and Political Predispositions: Revisiting the Concept of Selective Exposure," *Political Behavior* 30 (2008): 341–66.
[35]Jonathan S. Morris, "Slanted Objectivity? Perceived Media Bias, Cable News Exposure, and Political Attitudes," *Social Science Quarterly* 88 (2007): 725.
[36]Kathleen Hall Jamieson and Joseph N. Cappella, *Echo Chamber* (New York: Oxford University Press, 2008), 232.
[37]Richard Davis, *Politics Online* (New York: Routledge, 2005), 43.
[38]Ibid.
[39]Marcus Prior, *Post-Broadcast Democracy* (New York: Cambridge University Press, 2007).
[40]Robinson, "Public Affairs Television and the Growth of Political Malaise."
[41]Donald F. Roberts, Uila G. Foehr, Victoria J. Rideout, and Mollyann Brodie, "Kids and Media at the New Millennium," A Kaiser Family Foundation Report, November 1999, p. 19.
[42]See David T. Z. Mindich, *Tuned Out: Why Americans under 40 Don't Follow the News* (New York: Oxford University Press, 2005).
[43]Martin P. Wattenberg, *Is Voting for Young People?* (New York: Pearson Longman, 2008), 32.

CHAPTER ELEVEN

[1]Roger H. Davidson and Walter J. Oleszek, *Congress and Its Members*, 10th ed. (Washington, D.C.: CQ Press, 2008), 4.
[2]See Paul S. Herrnson, *Congressional Elections: Campaigning at Home and in Washington*, 5th ed. (Washington, D.C.: CQ Press, 2008).
[3]See Gary C. Jacobson, *The Politics of Congressional Elections*, 5th ed. (New York: Longman, 2001).
[4]David Mayhew, *Congress: The Electoral Connection* (New Haven, Conn.: Yale University Press, 2004), 5.
[5]Bruce Cain, John Ferejohn, and Morris P. Fiorina, *The Personal Vote* (Cambridge, Mass.: Harvard University Press, 1987).
[6]Information provided by Clerk of the House.
[7]"Congressional Staff: Duties and Functions," CRS Report for Congress, April 21, 2003, 1; see at www.llsdc.org/attachments/wysiwyg/544/CRS-98-340.pdf.
[8]Edward Sidlow, *Challenging the Incumbent: An Underdog's Undertaking* (Washington, D.C.: CQ Press, 2003); David C. W. Parker, *The Power of Money in Congressional Campaigns, 1880–2006* (Norman: University of Oklahoma Press, 2008). See also Marian Currinder, *Money in the House: Campaign Funds and Congressional Party Politics* (Boulder, Colo.: Westview Press, 2008).
[9]Federal Elections Commission data, 2012.
[10]Quoted in Jennifer Babson and Kelly St. John, "Momentum Helps GOP Collect Record Amounts from PACs," *Congressional Quarterly Weekly Report*, December 3, 1994, 3456.
[11]Quoted in "A Tale of Myths and Measures: Who Is Truly Vulnerable?" *Congressional Quarterly Weekly Report*, December 4, 1993, 7; see also Dennis F. Thompson, *Ethics in Congress* (Washington, D.C.: Brookings Institution, 1995).
[12]James E. Campbell, *The Presidential Pulse of Congressional Elections* (Lexington: University Press of Kentucky, 1993).
[13]Robert Erikson, "The Puzzle of Midterm Losses," *Journal of Politics* 50 (November 1988): 1011–29.
[14]See Eric D. Lawrence, Forrest Maltzman, and Steven S. Smith, "Who Wins? Party Effects in Legislative Voting," *Legislative Studies Quarterly* 31 (2006): 33–69.
[15]Linda L. Fowler and Robert D. McClure, *Political Ambition* (New Haven, Conn.: Yale University Press, 1989).
[16]*Congressional Quarterly Weekly Report*, various dates.
[17]Linda Witt, Karen M. Paget, and Glenna Matthews, *Running as a Woman: Gender and Power in American Politics* (New York: Free Press, 1993); Sue Thomas, *How Women Legislate* (New York: Oxford University Press, 1994); Tali Mendelberg, *The Race Card* (Princeton, N.J.: Princeton University Press, 2001).
[18]Beth Reingold, ed., *Legislative Women: Getting Elected, Getting Ahead* (Boulder, Colo.: Lynne Rienner Publishers, 2008).
[19]Cited in Ryan Lizza, "The Obama Memos," *The New Yorker*, January 30, 2012, 36.

[20]Steven Smith, *Party Influence in Congress* (New York: Cambridge University Press, 2007); Barbara Sinclair, *Party Wars: Polarization and the Politics of National Policy Making* (Norman: University of Oklahoma Press, 2006).

[21]Quoted in Stephen E. Frantzich and Claude Berube, *Congress: Games and Strategies* (Lanham, MD: Rowman and Littlefield, 2009), 159.

[22]Randall Strahan, *Leading Representatives: The Agency of Leaders in the Politics of the U.S. House* (Baltimore, Md.: Johns Hopkins University Press, 2007); David King, *Turf Wars* (Chicago: University of Chicago Press, 1997).

[23]See Stephen E. Frantzich and Steven E. Schier, *Congress: Games and Strategies* (Dubuque, Iowa: Brown & Benchmark, 1995), 127.

[24]See Gerald S. Strom, *The Logic of Lawmaking* (Baltimore, Md.: Johns Hopkins University Press, 1990).

[25]See Barbara Sinclair, *Unorthodox Lawmaking: New Legislative Processes in the U.S. Congress*, 3d ed. (Washington, D.C.: CQ Press, 2007).

[26]See Jon R. Bond and Richard Fleisher, eds., *Polarized Politics: Congress and the President in a Partisan Era* (Washington, D.C.: CQ Press, 2000).

[27]See Gary Orfield, *Congressional Power: Congress and Social Change* (New York: Harcourt Brace Jovanovich, 1975).

[28]James L. Sundquist, "Congress and the President: Enemies or Partners?" in Lawrence C. Dodd and Bruce I. Oppenheimer, eds., *Congress Reconsidered* (New York: Praeger, 1977), 240.

[29]Barry C. Burden, *Personal Roots of Representation* (Princeton, N.J.: Princeton University Press, 2007).

[30]Keith Krehbiel, "Are Congressional Committees Composed of Preference Outliers?" *American Political Science Review* 84 (1990): 149–64; Richard L. Hall and Bernard Grofman, "The Committee Assignment Process and the Conditional Nature of Committee Bias," *American Political Science Review* 84 (1990): 1149–66.

[31]Fareed Zakaria, "Why Political Polarization Has Gone Wild in America (and What to Do About It)," *CNN World*, July 24, 2011.

[32]Frances E. Lee, *Beyond Ideology: Politics, Principles, and Partisanship in the U.S. Senate* (Chicago: University of Chicago Press, 2009).

[33]Joel A. Aberbach and Mark A. Peterson, eds., *The Executive Branch* (New York: Oxford University Press, 2005), 534–535.

[34]Joel Aberback, *Keeping a Watchful Eye* (Washington, D.C.: Brookings Institution, 1990); David Rosenbloom, *Building a Congress Centered Public Administration* (Tuscaloosa: University of Alabama Press, 2001).

CHAPTER TWELVE

[1]Woodrow Wilson, *Constitutional Government in the United States* (New York: Columbia University Press, 1908), 67.

[2]James W. Davis, *The American Presidency* (New York: Harper & Row, 1987), 13; Sidney Milkis and Michael Nelson, *The American Presidency: Origins and Development, 1790–2007*, 5th ed. (Washington, D.C.: CQ Press, 2007); see also Bruce Ackerman, *The Failure of the Founding Fathers* (Cambridge, Mass.: Belknap Press of Harvard University Press, 2005)

[3]See Barry M. Blechman and Stephen S. Kaplan, *Force without War* (Washington, D.C.: Brookings Institution, 1978); Arthur M. Schlesinger Jr., *War and the American Presidency* (New York: W. W. Norton, 2004).

[4]*United States v. Belmont*, 57 U.S. 758 (1937).

[5]Robert DiClerico, *The American President*, 6th ed. (Englewood Cliffs, N.J.: Prentice-Hall, 1999), 47.

[6]James Bryce, *The American Commonwealth* (New York: Commonwealth Edition, 1908), 230.

[7]Quoted in Wilfred E. Binkley, *President and Congress*, 3d ed. (New York: Vintage, 1962), 142.

[8]Peri E. Arnold, *Remaking the Presidency* (Lawrence: University Press of Kansas, 2009).

[9]Theodore Roosevelt, *An Autobiography* (New York: Scribner, 1931), 383.

[10]See Richard M. Pious, *The American Presidency* (New York: Basic Books, 1979), 83.

[11]Harry S Truman, *Years of Trial and Hope* (New York: Signet, 1956), 535.

[12]Erwin C. Hargrove, *The Effective Presidency: Lessons on Leadership from John F. Kennedy to*

George W. Bush (Boulder, Colo.: Paradigm, 2007).

[13]See Thomas S. Langston, The Cold War Presidency: A Documentary History (Washington, D.C.: CQ Press, 2006).

[14]See Garry Willis, Bomb Power: The Modern Presidency and the National Security State (New York: Penguin Press, 2010).

[15]James W. Ceaser, Presidential Selection: Theory and Development (Princeton, N.J.: Princeton University Press, 1979).

[16]John S. Jackson and William J. Crotty, The Politics of Presidential Selection (New York: Longman, 2001).

[17]William Mayer, The Front-Loading Problem in Presidential Nominations (Washington, D.C.: Brookings Institution Press, 2004).

[18]See Thomas E. Patterson, The Vanishing Voter (New York: Knopf, 2003), 120.

[19]See Roderick P. Hart, Seducing America: How Television Charms the Modern Voter (Thousand Oaks, Calif.: Sage, 1998).

[20]Quoted in Stephen J. Wayne, Road to the White House, 1992 (New York: St. Martin's Press, 1992), 143; but see Jody C. Baumgartner, The American Vice Presidency Reconsidered (Westport, Conn.: Praeger, 2006).

[21]John P. Burke, The Institutionalized Presidency (Baltimore, Md.: Johns Hopkins University Press, 1992); Charles E. Walcott and Karen M. Hult, Governing the White House (Lawrence: University Press of Kansas, 1995).

[22]See Jeffrey E. Cohen, The Politics of the United States Cabinet (Pittsburgh: University of Pittsburgh Press, 1988); Shirley Anne Warshaw, Powersharing: White House–Cabinet Relations in the Modern Presidency (Albany: State University of New York Press, 1995).

[23]James Pfiffner, The Modern Presidency (New York: St. Martin's Press, 1994), 123; James Pfiffner, "Recruiting Executive Branch Leaders: The Office of Presidential Personnel," Brookings Institution, Spring 2001; see at www.brookings.edu/research/articles/2001/03/spring-governance-pfiffner Web article.

[24]Quoted in James MacGregor Burns, "Our Super-Government—Can We Control It?" The New York Times, April 24, 1949, 32.

[25]See Paul C. Light, Thickening Government: Federal Hierarchy and the Diffusion of Accountability (Washington, D.C.: Brookings Institution, 1995).

[26]Glenn Thrush, "Locked in the Cabinet," Politico Magazine, November 2013. www.politico.com/magazine/story/2013/11/locked-in-the-cabinet-99374.html#.VE7Txlfsp-0.

[27]David Goetsch, Effective Leadership (Upper Saddle River, N.J.: Prentice-Hall, 2004).

[28]Stephen Skowronek, Presidential Leadership in Political Time (Lawrence: University of Kansas Press, 2008).

[29]Quoted in Emmet John Hughes, The Ordeal of Power: A Political Memoir of the Eisenhower Years (New York: Athenaeum 1963), 124.

[30]Erwin Hargrove, The Power of the Modern Presidency (New York: Knopf, 1974); see also John H. Kessel, Presidents, the Presidency, and the Political Environment (Washington, D.C.: CQ Press, 2001); Stephen Skowronek, Presidential Leadership in Political Time: Reprise and Reappraisal (Lawrence: University Press of Kansas, 2008).

[31]Quoted in Ryan Lizza, "The Obama Memos," The New Yorker, January 30, 2012, 49.

[32]James P. Pfiffner, The Strategic Presidency: Hitting the Ground Running, 2d ed. (Chicago: Dorsey Press, 1996).

[33]Aaron Wildavsky, "The Two Presidencies," Trans-Action, December 1966, 7.

[34]Pfiffner, Modern Presidency, ch. 6.

[35]Thomas P. (Tip) O'Neill, with William Novak, Man of the House: The Life and Political Memoirs of Speaker Tip O'Neill (New York: Random House, 1987), 297.

[36]Charles O. Jones, The Presidency in a Separated System (Washington, D.C.: Brookings Institution, 2005).

[37]Quoted in Lizza, "The Obama Memos," 44.

[38]Richard E. Neustadt, Presidential Power and the Modern Presidents (New York: Free Press, 1990), 71–72.

[39]Ibid., 33.

[40]Quoted in Lizza, "The Obama Memos," 49.

[41]Charles O. Jones, The President in a Separated System (Washington, D.C.: Brookings Institution, 2005), 173.

[42]John E. Mueller, "Presidential Popularity from Truman to Johnson," American Political Science Review 64 (March 1970): 18–34; Kathleen Frankovic, "Public Opinion in the 1992 Campaign," in Gerald M. Pomper, ed., The Election of 1992 (Chatham, N.J.: Chatham House, 1993); Chris J. Dolan, The Presidency

and Economic Policy (Lanham, Md.: Rowman & Littlefield, 2007).

[43]Samuel Kernell, Going Public: New Strategies of Presidential Leadership, 3d ed. (Washington, D.C.: CQ Press, 1997), 1; see also Robert M. Eisinger, The Evolution of Presidential Polling (New York: Cambridge University Press, 2003); Stephen J. Farnsworth and S. Robert Lichter, Mediated Presidency: Television News & Presidential Governance (Lanham, Md.: Rowman & Littlefield, 2005).

[44]Jeffrey E. Cohen, The Presidency in the Era of 24-Hour News (Princeton, N.J.: Princeton University Press, 2008).

[45]Hugh Heclo, "Introduction: The Presidential Illusion," in Hugh Heclo and Lester M. Salamon, eds., The Illusion of Presidential Government (Boulder, Colo.: Westview Press, 1981), 2.

[46]Theodore J. Lowi, The "Personal" Presidency: Power Invested, Promise Unfulfilled (Ithaca, N.Y.: Cornell University Press, 1985).

CHAPTER THIRTEEN

[1]Max Weber, Economy and Society (New York: Bedminster Press, 1968), 223. Translated and edited by Guenther Roth and Claus Wittich. Originally published in 1921.

[2]Ibid., 23.

[3]Office of Personnel Management data, 2010.

[4]Gregory A. Huber, The Craft of Bureaucratic Neutrality: Interests and Influence in Governmental Regulation of Occupational Safety (New York: Cambridge University Press, 2007); Herbert Kaufman, "Emerging Conflicts in the Doctrine of Public Administration," American Political Science Review 50 (December 1956): 1060.

[5]See Allen Schick, The Federal Budget: Politics, Policy, Process, 3rd ed. (Washington, D.C.: Brookings Institution, 2007).

[6]See Cornelius M. Kerwin, Rulemaking, 3d ed. (Washington, D.C.: CQ Press, 2003); Daniel E. Hall, Administrative Law: Bureaucracy in a Democracy (Upper Saddle River, N.J.: Prentice-Hall, 2005).

[7]Michael Lipsky, Street-Level Bureaucracy (New York: Russell Sage Foundation, 1980).

[8]Steven Kelman, "Occupational Safety and Health Administration," in James Q. Wilson, ed., The Politics of Regulation (New York: Basic Books, 1980), 239–40.

[9]See Hugh Heclo, A Government of Strangers (Washington, D.C.: Brookings Institution, 1977), 117–18.

[10]Quoted in Aaron Wildavsky, The Politics of the Budgetary Process, 4th ed. (Boston: Little, Brown, 1984), 19; see also Dennis D. Riley, Bureaucracy and the Policy Process: Keeping the Promises (Lanham, Md.: Rowman & Littlefield, 2005).

[11]Joel D. Aberbach and Bert A. Rockman, "Clashing Beliefs within the Executive Branch," American Political Science Review 70 (June 1976): 461.

[12]Norton E. Long, "Power and Administration," Public Administration Review 10 (Autumn 1949): 269; Joel D. Aberbach and Bert A. Rockman, In the Web of Politics (Washington, D.C.: Brookings Institution, 2000).

[13]See B. Guy Peters, The Politics of Bureaucracy, 5th ed. (New York: Routledge, 2001).

[14]See B. Dan Wood and Richard W. Waterman, Bureaucratic Dynamics (Boulder, Colo.: Westview Press, 1994); Edward C. Page and Bill Jenkins, Policy Bureaucracy: Government with a Cast of Thousands (New York: Oxford University Press, 2005).

[15]Long, "Power and Administration," 269; see also John Mark Hansen, Gaining Access (Chicago: University of Chicago Press, 1991).

[16]Charles T. Goodsell, The Case for Bureaucracy, 2d ed. (Chatham, N.J.: Chatham House, 1985), 55–60.

[17]William T. Gormley Jr. and Steven J. Balla, Bureaucracy and Democracy (Washington, D.C.: CQ Press, 2003); Kevin B. Smith, Public Administration: Power and Politics in the Fourth Branch of Government (New York: Oxford University Press, 2006).

[18]James P. Pfiffner, "The National Performance Review in Perspective," working paper 94-4, Institute of Public Policy, George Mason University, 1994, 2.

[19]Ibid., 12.

[20]Kaufman, "Emerging Conflicts," 1062.

[21]Charles Perrow, "Disaster after 9/11: The Department of Homeland Security and the Intelligence Reorganization," Homeland Security Affairs 2 (2006). http://calhoun.nps.edu/handle/10945/25072.

[22]Deanne L. Miller and Roger K. Smith, "The Obama Administration and EPA Enforcement: A Look Back, A Look Forward,"

Agriculture Management Committee Newsletter, American Bar Association, 17 (2013): 11.

[23]Heclo, *Government of Strangers,* 104.

[24]Ibid., 225.

[25]See Joel D. Aberbach, *Keeping a Watchful Eye* (Washington, D.C.: Brookings Institution, 1990).

[26]Douglas A. Van Belle and Kenneth M. Mash, *A Novel Approach to Politics* (Washington, D.C.: CQ Press, 2006).

[27]See Donald Kettl, *Deficit Politics* (New York: Macmillan, 1992).

[28]David Rosenbloom, "The Evolution of the Administrative State, and Transformations of Administrative Law," in David Rosenbloom and Richard Schwartz, eds., *Handbook of Regulation and Administrative Law* (New York: Marcel Dekker, 1994), 3–36.

[29]*Pigeford v. Veneman,* U.S. District Court for the District of Columbia, Civil Action No. 97-1978 (1999).

[30]See *Vermont Yankee Nuclear Power Corp. v. National Resources Defense Council,* Inc., 435 U.S. 519 (1978); *Chevron v. National Resources Defense Council,* 467 U.S. 837 (1984); *Heckler v. Chaney,* 470 U.S. 821 (1985); but see *FDA v. Brown & Williamson Tobacco Co.,* 529 U.S. 120 (2000).

[31]See Mark W. Huddleston, "The Carter Civil Service Reforms," *Political Science Quarterly* (Winter 1981–82): 607–22.

[32]Ed O'Keefe, "Senior Executive Service Needs Overhaul, Outside Study Finds," *The Washington Post,* August 20, 2009.

[33]Joe Davidson, "Whistleblower 'Bunny' Davidson Wins Settlement Near $1 Million," *The Washington Post,* July 26, 2011, Web release. www.washingtonpost.com/blogs/federal-eye/post/whistleblower-bunny-greenhouse-wins-settlement-near-1-million/2011/04/15/gIQANfFAbI_blog.html.

[34]See Brian J. Cook, *Bureaucracy and Self-Government* (Baltimore, Md.: Johns Hopkins University Press, 1996).

CHAPTER FOURTEEN

[1]*Marbury v. Madison,* 5 U.S. 137 (1803).

[2]*Citizens United v. Federal Election Commission,* 558 U.S. 50 (2010).

[3]Org. 138, *South Carolina v. North Carolina* (2010).

[4]Rebecca Mae Salokar, *The Solicitor General: The Politics of Law* (Philadelphia: Temple University Press, 1992); see also Cornell W. Clayton, *The Politics of Justice: The Attorney General and the Making of Legal Policy* (Armonk, N.Y.: Sharpe, 1992).

[5]Henry Glick, *Courts, Politics, and Justice,* 3d ed. (New York: McGraw-Hill, 1993), 120.

[6]Timothy R. Johnson, Paul Wahlbeck, and James Spriggs, "The Influence of Oral Arguments on the U.S. Supreme Court," *American Political Science Review,* 100 (2006): 99–113.

[7]Lawrence Baum, *The Supreme Court,* 8th ed. (Washington, D.C.: CQ Press, 2003), 120.

[8]From a letter to the author by Frank Schwartz of Beaver College; this section reflects substantially Professor Schwartz's recommendations to the author, as does the later section that addresses the federal court myth.

[9]*Hutto v. Davis,* 370 U.S. 256 (1982).

[10]*Lawrence v. Texas,* No. 02-102 (2003).

[11]*Bowers v. Hardwick,* 478 U.S. 186 (1986).

[12]See Richard Davis, *Electing Justices* (New York: Oxford University Press, 2005).

[13]Robert Scigliano, *The Supreme Court and the Presidency* (New York: Free Press, 1971), 146; see also Lee Epstein and Jack Knight, *The Choices Justices Make* (Washington, D.C.: CQ Press, 1998); Stefanie A. Lundquist, David A. Yalof, and John A. Clark, "The Impact of Presidential Appointments to the Supreme Court: Cohesive and Divisive Voting within Presidential Blocs," *Political Research Quarterly* 53 (2000): 795–814.

[14]Quoted in Baum, *Supreme Court,* 37.

[15]See Lee Epstein and Jeffrey Segal, *Advice and Consent: The Politics of Judicial Appointments* (New York: Oxford University Press, 2005).

[16]See Virginia A. Hettinger et al., *Judging on a Collegial Court: Influences on Federal Appellate Decision Making* (Charlottesville: University of Virginia Press, 2006).

[17]John Gottschall, "Reagan's Appointments to the U.S. Courts of Appeals," *Judicature* 48 (1986): 54.

[18]Jesse J. Holland, "Obama Increases Number of Female, Minority Judges," Associated Press wire story, September 14, 2011.

[19]Quoted in Louis Fisher, *American Constitutional Law* (New York: McGraw-Hill, 1990), 5.

[20]Quoted in Charles P. Curtis, *Law and Large as Life* (New York: Simon & Schuster, 1959), 156–57.

[21]See Lee Epstein and Jack Knight, *The Choices Justices Make* (New York: Longman, 1995); Thomas G. Hansford and James F. Spriggs II, *The Politics of Precedent on the Supreme Court* (Princeton, N.J.: Princeton University Press, 2006).

[22]*Faragher v. City of Boca Raton*, No. 97-282 (1998).

[23]John Schmidhauser, *The Supreme Court* (New York: Holt, Rinehart & Winston, 1964), 6.

[24]Linda Greenhouse, "In Steps Big and Small, Supreme Court Moved Right," *The New York Times*, July 1, 2007, Web copy.

[25]Jeffrey A. Segal and Harold J. Spaeth, *The Supreme Court and the Attitudinal Model Revisited* (New York: Cambridge University Press, 2002), 404.

[26]Stephen L. Wasby, *The Supreme Court in the Federal Judicial System*, 4th ed. (Chicago: Nelson-Hall, 1993), 53.

[27]Davis, *Electing Justices*.

[28]Ross Sandler and David Schoenbrod, *Democracy by Decree* (New Haven, Conn.: Yale University Press, 2003).

[29]See Antonin Scalia, *A Matter of Interpretation: Federal Courts and the Law* (Princeton, N.J.: Princeton University Press, 1997).

[30]Remarks by Antonin Scalia at the University of Delaware, April 30, 2007. Reported on the Web by *University of Delaware Daily*.

[31]Stephen Breyer, "Our Democratic Constitution," James Madison Lecture, New York University Law School, New York, October 22, 2001.

[32]Henry J. Abraham, "The Judicial Function under the Constitution," *News for Teachers of Political Science* 41 (Spring 1984): 14.

[33]Alexander M. Bickel, *The Supreme Court and the Idea of Progress* (New Haven, Conn.: Yale University Press, 1978), 173–81.

[34]Frederic R. Kellogg and Oliver Wendell Holmes Jr., *Legal Theory and Judicial Restraint* (New York: Cambridge University Press, 2006).

[35]*National Federation of Independent Business v. Sebelius*, No. 11-393 (2012).

[36]Frank H. Easterbrook, "Do Liberals and Conservatives Differ in Judicial Activism?" *University of Colorado Law Review* 73 (2002): 1401.

CHAPTER FIFTEEN

[1]Marc Allen Eisner, Jeffrey Worsham, and Evan J. Rinquist, *Contemporary Regulatory Policy* (Boulder, Colo.: Lynne Rienner, 2006).

[2]The section titled "Efficiency through Government Intervention" relies substantially on Alan Stone, *Regulation and Its Alternatives* (Washington, D.C.: CQ Press, 1982).

[3]See Marc Allen Eisner, *Regulatory Politics in Transition*, 2d ed. (Baltimore, Md.: Johns Hopkins University Press, 1999).

[4]See Richard A. Harris and Sidney M. Milkis, *The Politics of Regulatory Change* (New York: Oxford University Press, 1996).

[5]Lawrence E. Mitchell, *Corporate Irresponsibility* (New Haven, Conn.: Yale University Press, 2003).

[6]H. Peyton Young, *Equity: In Theory and Practice* (Princeton, N.J.: Princeton University Press, 1995).

[7]American Academy of Pediatrics, "Blood Lead Levels Declining, but Children Still at Risk for Lead Poisoning," March 2, 2009; see at www.aap.org/en-us/about-the-aap/aap-press-room/pages/Blood-lead-levels-declining.

[8]Board on Population Health and Public Health Practice, *The Future of Drug Safety: Promoting and Protecting the Health of the Public* (Washington, D.C.: National Academies Press, 2007).

[9]Rachel Carson, *Silent Spring* (Boston: Houghton Mifflin, 1962); see also Lester R. Brown, *Plan B2.0: Rescuing a Planet under Stress and a Civilization in Trouble* (New York: W. W. Norton, 2006).

[10]Robert B. Keiter, *Keeping Faith with Nature* (New Haven, Conn.: Yale University Press, 2003).

[11]*U.S. News & World Report*, June 30, 1975, 25.

[12]See Walter A. Rosenbaum, *Environmental Politics and Policy*, 6th ed. (Washington, D.C.: CQ Press, 2004); Norman J. Vig and Michael E. Kraft, eds., *Environmental Policy: New Directions for the Twenty-First Century* (Washington, D.C.: CQ Press, 2003).

[13]Elliot A. Rosen, *Roosevelt, the Great Depression, and the Economics of Recovery* (Charlottesville: University of Virginia Press, 2007).

[14]See Robert Lekachman, *The Age of Keynes* (New York: Random House, 1966); see also Richard Kopke, Geoffrey M. B. Tootell, and Robert K. Trist, eds., *The Macroeconomics of Fiscal Policy* (Cambridge, Mass.: MIT Press, 2006).

[15]See Bruce Bartlett, *Reaganomics: Supply-Side Economics* (Westport, Conn.: Arlington House, 1981).

[16]Paul Krugman, "Hey, Lucky Duckies," *The New York Times*, December 3, 2002, A31.

[17]Mona Lewandoski, "The Bush Tax Cuts of 2001 and 2003: A Brief Legislative History," Harvard Law School Briefing Paper, No. 37, May 6, 2008. www.law.harvard.edu/faculty/hjackson/2001-2003TaxCuts_37.pdf.

[18]Alan O. Ebenstein, *Milton Friedman: A Biography* (New York: Palgrave Macmillan, 2007).

[19]Edward Hadas and Hugh Dixon, "Quantitative Easing: A Therapy of Last Resort," *The New York Times*, January 1, 2009; see at www.nytimes.com/2009/01/11/business/worldbusiness/11iht-views12.1.19248009.html.

[20]Martin Mayer, *FED: The Inside Story of How the World's Most Powerful Financial Institution Drives the Markets* (New York: Free Press, 2001).

CHAPTER SIXTEEN

[1]Quoted in National Reach Coalition, "Medicaid Expansion in Hawaii," undated. http://reachcoalition.org/wp-content/uploads/Medicaid-Expansion-Hawaii1.pdf.

[2]Quoted in Sahil Kapur, "Mississippi Gov. Phil Bryant Opposes Medicaid Expansion in Case Obamacare Is Repealed," *TPM*, January 2, 2014. http://talkingpointsmemo.com/livewire/phil-bryant-medicaid-expansion.

[3]See Felicia Ann Kornbluh, *The Battle for Welfare Rights: Politics and Poverty in Modern America* (Philadelphia: University of Pennsylvania Press, 2007).

[4]Michael Harrington, *The Other America: Poverty in the United States* (New York: Macmillan, 1962); see also James T. Patterson, *America's Struggle against Poverty in the Twentieth Century* (Cambridge, Mass.: Harvard University Press, 2000).

[5]Charles Murray, *Losing Ground: American Social Policy, 1950–1980* (New York: Basic Books, 1984).

[6]Signe-Mary McKernan and Caroline Ratcliffe, "Events That Trigger Poverty Entries and Exits," *Social Science Quarterly* 86 (2005): 1146–69.

[7]V. O. Key Jr., *The Responsible Electorate* (Cambridge, Mass.: Belknap Press of Harvard University, 1966), 43.

[8]Everett Carll Ladd, *American Political Parties* (New York: Norton, 1970), 205.

[9]Institute on Taxation and Economic Policy poll, 2002.

[10]See Jason DeParle, *American Dream: Three Women, Ten Kids, and a Nation's Drive to End Welfare* (New York: Penguin, 2005).

[11]See Katherine S. Newman, *No Shame in My Game* (New York: Alfred A. Knopf and Russell Sage Foundation, 1999), 41.

[12]Quoted in Malcolm Gladwell, "The Medicaid Muddle," *The Washington Post National Weekly Edition*, January 16–22, 1995, 31.

[13]See Christopher Howard, *The Welfare State Nobody Knows* (Princeton, N.J.: Princeton University Press, 2006).

[14]Alberto Alesina and Edward Glaeser, *Fighting Poverty in the U.S. and Europe* (New York: Oxford University Press, 2006).

[15]Said of George H. W. Bush at the 1988 Democratic Convention. The quote is variously attributed to Ann Richards or Jim Hightower.

[16]For a history of public education, see Joel H. Spring, *The American School 1642–2004* (New York: McGraw-Hill, 2008).

[17]"The 2012 Kids Count Data Book: State Trends in Child Well-Being," a report of the Annie E. Casey Foundation, July 25, 2012. www.aecf.org/resources/the-2012-kids-count-data-book/.

[18]Based on Organization for Economic Cooperation and Development (OECD) data, 2006; see Douglas S. Reed, *On Equal Terms: The Constitutional Politics of Educational Opportunity* (Princeton, N.J.: Princeton University Press, 2003).

[19]See, for example, David Hursh, *High Stakes Testing and the Decline of Teaching and Learning* (Lanham, Md.: Rowman & Littlefield, 2008.)

[20]Press release, Representative John Boehner, January 4, 2003.

[21]Rick Perry, "Texas Knows Best How to Educate Our Students: Texas Will Not Apply

for Federal Race to the Top Funding," Office of the Governor press release, 2010.

[22]Resolution 13-04.47 of the California Democratic Party, "Supporting California's Public Schools and Dispelling the Corporate 'Reform' Agenda," undated. www.cadem.org/admin/miscdocs/files/Resolutions-Report-FINAL-2.pdf.

[23]Stanley Feldman and John Zaller, "The Political Culture of Ambivalence: Ideological Responses to the Welfare State," *American Journal of Political Science* 36 (1992): 268–307.

[24]Robert E. Lane, "Market Justice, Political Justice," *American Political Science Review* 80 (June 1986): 383–402.

CHAPTER SEVENTEEN

[1]See Douglas T. Stuart, *Creating the National Security State* (Princeton, N.J.: Princeton University Press, 2008).

[2]See Mr. X. (George Kennan), "The Sources of Soviet Conduct," *Foreign Affairs* 25 (July 1947): 566–82.

[3]See Wilson Miscamble, *From Roosevelt to Truman: Potsdam, Hiroshima, and the Cold War* (New York: Cambridge University Press, 2008).

[4]David M. Barrett, *Uncertain Warriors: Lyndon Johnson and His Vietnam Advisors* (Lawrence: University Press of Kansas, 1993); see also Stanley Karnow, *Vietnam: A History* (New York: Penguin, 1983).

[5]See Dag Henriksen, *NATO's Gamble* (Annapolis, Md.: Naval Institute Press, 2007).

[6]See Mark Sauter and James Carafano, *Homeland Security* (New York: McGraw-Hill, 2005).

[7]See Ron Susskind, *The One-Percent Solution* (New York: Simon & Schuster, 2007).

[8]West Point speech, June 1, 2002; for an opposing view, see Gary Hart, *The Shield and the Cloak: The Security of the Commons* (New York: Oxford University Press, 2006).

[9]Nick Ritchie, *The Political Road to War with Iraq: Bush, 9/11 and the Drive to Overthrow Saddam* (New York: Routledge, 2007).

[10]Pew Research Center for the People and the Press, "Public Attitudes Toward the War in Iraq: 2003–2008," March 19, 2008; see at http://pewresearch.org/pubs/770/iraq-war-five-year-anniversary.

[11]Remarks of Nicholas Burns, World Affairs Council, Washington, D.C., June 23, 2011.

[12]Statement of the U.S. Secretary of Defense Leon Panetta, January 26, 2012.

[13]Thomas Rid and Thomas A. Keaney, eds., *Understanding Counterinsurgency Warfare* (New York: Routledge, 2010).

[14]See Richard Pearlstein, *Fatal Torture? Transnational Terrorism and the New Global Disorder* (Austin: University of Texas Press, 2004), 15–23.

[15]See Ofira Seliktar, *The Politics of Intelligence and American Wars with Iraq* (New York: Palgrave Macmillan, 2008).

[16]John Mueller, "Trends in Popular Support for the Wars in Korea and Vietnam," *American Political Science Review* 65 (June 1971): 358–75; see also John Mueller, "The Iraq Syndrome," *Foreign Affairs* (November/December 2005).

[17]George C. Wilson, *This War Really Matters: Inside the Fight for Defense Dollars* (Washington, D.C.: CQ Press, 2000).

[18]*The World Competitiveness Yearbook* (Lausanne, Switzerland: International Institute for Management Development, 2008).

[19]U.S. government data, various agencies, 2008.

[20]American Assembly Report (cosponsored by the Council on Foreign Relations), *Rethinking America's Security* (New York: Harriman, 1991), 9.

[21]Robert Z. Lawrence, *The United States and the WTO Dispute Settlement System* (New York: Council on Foreign Relations, 2007).

[22]Ted C. Fishman, *China, Inc.: How the Rise of the Next Superpower Challenges America and the World* (New York: Scribner, 2005).

[23]Michael T. Klare, *Rising Powers, Shrinking Plant: The New Geopolitics of Energy* (New York: Holt, 2009).

[24]Hobart Rowen, "The Budget: Fact and Fiction," *The Washington Post National Weekly Edition*, January 16–22, 1995, p. 5.

[25]Paola Subacchi and Stephen Pickford, "Legitimacy vs. Effectiveness for the G20: A Dynamic Approach to Global Economic Governance," Chatham House Briefing Paper, Royal Institute of International Affairs, London, England, October 2011, p. 2.

637

TEXT CREDITS

Chapter 1 Page 11: Organization for Economic Cooperation and Development, 2014.

Chapter 2 Figure 2.1: U.S. Bureau of the Census.

Chapter 3 Page 84: Bartholomew, "The Sherman Anti-Trust Law Returns from the Dead," *Minneapolis Journal*, 1904; fig 3.2: U.S. Department of Commerce, 2014; 3.3: Office of Management and Budget (OMB), FY2015; p. 90: U.S. Census Bureau, 2014.

Chapter 4 Page 120: Pew Research Center for the People and the Press, 2011; p. 130: U.S. Department of Justice, 2010; fig 4.1: International Centre for Prison Studies, 2014.

Chapter 5 Page 150: Pew Research Center for the People & the Press, July 22, 2011; p. 153: U.S. Immigration and Naturalization Service, 2014; fig 5.2: U.S. Census Bureau, 2012-2014; p. 163: Inter-Parliamentary Union, "Women in National Parliaments (2012-2014)"; 5.3: U.S. Census Bureau, 2012; 5.4: Gallup poll, 2011-2013.

Chapter 6 Figure 6.1: American National Election Studies; 6.2: Pew Research Center for the People and the Press, 2011.

Chapter 7 Figure 7.1: U.S. Census Bureau; 7.2: U.S. Census Bureau, 2014; 7.3: Russell J. Dalton, "The Myth of the Disengaged American," *CSES Report*, October 25, 2005; p. 222: Corporation for National and Community Service, 2010.

Chapter 8 Figure 8.2: American National Election Study; p. 243: American National Election Studies, 1972–2012; 8.4: The Pew Research Center, "Surveys of the Pew Hispanic Center, 2000-2012"; p. 254: National Council of State Legislatures, 2014; p. 256: Brian Fray, "So, can I put you down as undecided?" *Cartoon Stock*. All rights reserved. Used with permission; 8.5–8.6: Center for Responsive Politics, 2014.

Chapter 9 Page 271: World Values Survey Association, 2012; p. 275: Center for Responsive Politics, 2012; fig 9.1: Center for Responsive Politics, 2014; p. 284: Center for Public Integrity, 2014; 9.3: Federal Election Commission, 2014.

Chapter 10 Page 317: U.S. Census Bureau, 2014; p. 320: Pew Research Center for the People & the Press, May 4, 2011; fig 10.3: News and Time on the Internet.

Chapter 11 Figures 11.2–11.3: Federal Election Commission; p. 340: Center for American Woman and Politics (CAWP), National Information Bank on Women in Public Office, and Eagleton Institute of Politics, Rutgers University, 2010; 11.5: Pew Research Center for the People and the Press surveys.

Chapter 12 Figure 12.1: Congressional Quarterly Weekly Reports, various dates; Table 12.4: Averages compiled from Gallup Polls 1945–2013.

Chapter 13 Figure 13.1: Historical Statistics of the United States and Statistical Abstract of the United States, 1986; p. 322 and recent figures from U.S. Office of Personnel Management; p. 415: U.S. Census Bureau, 2014; Table 13.1: Office of Personnel Management, 2012.

Chapter 14 Figure 14.3: Administrative Office of the U.S. Courts; p. 475: The Council of State Governments.

Chapter 15 Figure 15.1: National Weather Service, Great Britain, 2014; p. 490: Organization for Economic Cooperation and Development, 2010; p. 495: Adapted from Tax Foundation Calculations, 2007; 15.2: Office of Management and Budget, 2014; 15.4: U.S. Department of Labor, 2014.

Chapter 16 Page 514: U.S. Census Bureau, 2014; fig 16.1: United Nations Children's Fund, 2014; p. 517: Pew Research Center for the People & the Press survey, February 22, 2013; 16.2: U.S. Department of Health and Human Services, 2014; 16.4: Office of Management and Budget, 2014; p. 531: Organization for Economic Cooperation and Development, 2014; 16.5: U.S. Census Bureau, 2014.

Chapter 17 Page 552: Center for Arms Control and Non-Proliferation, 2014; p. 554: Adapted from Tim Kane, "Who Bears the Burden? Demographic Characteristics of U.S. Military Recruits Before and After 9/11," *Center for Data Analysis Report #05-08*. Washington, DC: Heritage Foundation, November 7, 2005. All rights reserved. Used with permission; fig 17.1: U.S. Bureau of Economic Analysis, 2012; 17.2: Gallup Poll, February 26, 2013; p. 568: Pew Research Center Survey, February 22, 2013; 17.3: Organization for Economic Cooperation and Development, 2014.

INDEX